ONE MIGHTY TORRENT

By Edgar Johnson

FICTION

UNWEAVE A RAINBOW: A SENTIMENTAL FANTASY
THE PRAYING MANTIS

BIOGRAPHY

CHARLES DICKENS: HIS TRAGEDY AND TRIUMPH
THE HEART OF CHARLES DICKENS: HIS LETTERS TO ANGELA BURDETT COUTTS

ANTHOLOGIES

A TREASURY OF BIOGRAPHY
A TREASURY OF SATIRE

ONE MIGHTY TORRENT

THE DRAMA OF BIOGRAPHY

by

EDGAR JOHNSON

NEW YORK
THE MACMILLAN COMPANY
1955

PRINTED IN THE UNITED STATES OF AMERICA

. . . a great stream
Of people there was hurrying to and fro,
Numerous as gnats upon the evening gleam . . .
Old age and youth, manhood and infancy,
Mixed in one mighty torrent . . .

SHELLEY

To Eleanor

PREFACE TO THE NEW EDITION

ALTHOUGH it bears my name, this book is not mine—or perhaps I might more accurately say that I am no longer its. It was originally published eighteen years ago and had taken six years to write. Physiologists claim, I am told, that in the course of seven years every single cell in our bodies dies and is replaced by another. Thus I am in a way the grandson, almost the great-grandson, of the younger man who wrote the book. I can now look on it, as Henry Adams did on the writings of John Adams or John Quincy Adams, no doubt with a certain grandfilial sentiment, but with no sense of personal responsibility beyond that of an editor. To suggest otherwise would be a kind of scientific heresy.

More seriously, I do indeed disapprove of making radical changes in what we have once printed, even if we no longer agree with every detail. A man in his thirties has the right to speak for himself without being subjected to the insolence of censorship by a later self. If our styles, standards of literary merit, and other judgments have altered drastically, we should write a new book, not chop up an older one. Thus, I believe that Henry James was wrong, when he was preparing the New York edition of his works, in remolding everything to that strangely coagulated and intricately qualified style of which he became the master and victim. Not merely did he destroy some of the values of his earlier writing, he made it seem as if he had undergone no development whatever throughout his life, but had always been a sort of literary milk-white elephant, immortal and unchanged.

Whether the younger Henry James would have resented these interferences I cannot know; I do know that my younger self would have rejected such pretensions in a man he had not even met. Furthermore, what modifications I might now be inclined to make are no more than matters of emphasis, not of essence. I am not sure that my former self would agree with them even now; and I am sure that he has the right to speak for himself. With the literary judgments expressed in this book I am still fundamentally in accord. Its presentation of the principles and standards of biography, and its analyses of technique, I think are sound. Therefore in this new edition I have confined myself to rectifying such typographical errors as survived earlier proofreadings and correcting occasional mistakes of fact. Both these types of improvement I should have welcomed from the start.

If I were writing this book today, however, I should be much less hopeful than I was then that Russia might work harmoniously with the West, and much more hopeful of the potentialities of liberalism. But the moral atmosphere of the 1930's was vastly different from that of the present. We were still struggling painfully out of the depression that followed the crash of 1929. We had just recognized Russia, with whom we were to be drawn into a united front against Fascism, and who was to be our ally in World War II, warmly supported by lend-lease and glowingly hailed for the gallant defense of Moscow. From the intervening years of the cold war we have learned that totalitarianism can have more than one face. And we have also learned from the development of American society since the War that liberalism can transcend the limitations that made it seem moribund to Lincoln Steffens, and seen it confront the future with enlarged sympathies and renewed fruitfulness.

But even eighteen years ago the author of this book was no zealot of faction. (Please to remember that I am writing, not of myself but a spiritual ancestor.) If he revolted against Henry Adams as the forerunner of a wasteland distemper and shared some of the hopes of John Stuart Mill, he could see hysteria in the radicalism of John Ruskin and sympathize with both the traditionalism of Walter Scott and the reasoned toryism of Samuel Johnson. He perceived both the dangerous proto-Fascism and the gentle-hearted humanitarianism in

Thomas Carlyle. Though he admired the enthusiast Shelley, he thought still more highly of Keats, who was almost entirely cold to Shelley's political goals and repudiated his propagandist zeal. His real interest was no partisan doctrine, but the color and variety and richness of human life.

A vivid sense of that fullness was the principle aim of this book. It tries to portray four centuries of modern history—not political, economic, sociological, or even ideological history, though all these are implied in it—but *human* history, in terms of the thronging lives and personalities who lived it and what the experience of living was like to them. That story it endeavors to see, moreover, as a connected narrative which is really an interpretation of the changing consciousness of western civilization. With these are interwoven the threads of the development of biography and the clarification of its principles as a literary form. It is not for me to say how well these things were done. But out of the mingling of all three arises the pattern of the book.

EDGAR JOHNSON

FOREWORD TO THE ORIGINAL EDITION

When John Foxe quoted Cicero's words, 'the witnesse of truth, the glasse of times,' it was of history that he was writing. But they are equally appropriate, in a way even more true, of biography. History is important only because it happens to human beings; a Genghis Khan of the groundhogs would move us hardly at all, or a Rhodes among the rhododendrons. Fabre can fascinate us with the social life and engineering skill of ants, spiders, and bees (humanizing them a little in so doing); but he would strain our attention if he tried to tell their history for even a hundred years. Without a living sense of personality suffusing its framework, the abstractions of history are only half-truths. Biography never lets us forget that the processes of history clothe themselves in human lives; it is indeed 'personal history.'

That is why in recent years biography has been so enormously popular. Biographers portray their living fellows even before these have reached their middle years; they turn a backward exploring telescope on all of time from the Pharaohs to Henry Ford. More men write the stories of their own lives than ever before, trying to see and understand themselves in relation to their times. The *Journals* of Arnold Bennett, the *Letters* of D. H. Lawrence, the reminiscences of William Butler Yeats, are read eagerly; parts of them may even appear in magazines. Biography steadily expands on publishers' lists, almost rivaling the novel, and a tremendous public responds to its lure. Biography is no longer the possession of the hackwriter and the journeyman of letters: it has become a serious and dignified realm of literary art.

Very little has been done, however, to clarify the principles of biographical art or to reveal its function in reflecting and deepening our understanding of our human heritage. The few volumes that have been published, some of them excellent in their own realm, are mainly historical surveys of various periods in English or American biography or else studies of formal biography excluding all the variety of other forms. No critical work in biography has taken all this wealth for its province; tried to reveal the intensity and vividness with which biography can light present and past, and how it does so. These I have attempted in the present volume.

With such a range, encyclopaedic inclusiveness would be self-defeating. Bold emphasis and omission must be our principles, not reduction to scale. And so, although we range far afield, drawing from all the forms of biographical writing, in each period we focus on only a selected few. It was tempting to consider including the *Confessions* of St Augustine, the *Vita Nuova* of Dante, Cellini, Casanova, and Rousseau, Benjamin Franklin, Goethe's *Dichtung und Wahrheit*, Thoreau, Emerson, and Hawthorne as revealed in their respective notebooks, Amiel, Gide, and many another. But ultimately I decided to confine myself to English biography, although in a few places I have violated my own rule. It would be almost heresy, it seemed, to discuss letter-writing without even mentioning Madame de Sévigné; and in modern times I could find no satisfactory English rendering of tendencies represented in *The Education of Henry Adams*, some of the works of Van Wyck Brooks and André Maurois, and *The Autobiography of Lincoln Steffens.*

Even so, there were many inclusions in my original plan that had in the end to be discarded. Hervey's *Memoirs of the Reign of George II* almost persuaded me to a chapter on court memoirs that would have included the Duc de Saint-Simon, Horace Walpole, Fanny Burney's *Diaries and Letters*, and the entire body of the *Greville Diaries.* It would have been fascinating to compare Newman's *Apologia* with Bunyan's *Grace Abounding* (which I have included) and Pascal's *Pensées* (which I have not). And there are *The Autobiography of Leigh Hunt*, and the charming *Letters* of Edward Fitzgerald, and the waspishly witty ones of Jane Welsh Carlyle—any scholar, should he do me the honor of glancing at this book, could point out many other glaring omissions.

It would have been easy, of course, on another plan, to mention more names. Like the historians of literature I might have summarized writer after writer in three or four pages of exposition, starred here and there with graceful allusion or gossip, and dismissed scores more in a marble Roman aphorism. But writing thus, we convey information only to those who already have it. To those acquainted with our subject we may point or illumine their experience, and if we are lucky shoot a new gleam on their familiar landscape. Otherwise, no matter how felicitous our phrases, we will tell facts but not reveal essences.

My hope for this book is something more ambitious. I wish, first, to convey the flavor of each life and personality; to re-create a vignette of the original subject, by narrative in miniature, by rich and flavorous quotation, by sample as it were, by re-evoking and realizing the character. If my second aim of critical and historical interpretation *is* to be attained, only so can it be done. Lacking the vital foundation of such a re-creation, discussions of the literary qualities of books, their success in rendering personality, their revelations of historical color and living currents in their time, are hardly more than barren obiter dicta. I have tried to remember that history and biography are about human beings—and I have tried to fill this book full of them, and never forget them as human beings.

E. J.

New York City,
December, 1936.

THE CONTENTS

CONTENTS

CONTENTS

BIOGRAPHY

and the

VITALIZING OF HISTORY

INTRODUCTION

BIOGRAPHY AND THE VITALIZING OF HISTORY

THE deadness of Queen Anne is a special and deeply mortuary kind of deadness because, poor lady, for most of us she was never alive. Perhaps we faintly recall some portrait with a glitter of diamonds on a slab chest and a heavy face with unsparkling eyes. But what was she like, this Queen who gave her name to the age of Swift and Addison? She was alive enough for Samuel Johnson, remembering the stout lady richly dressed who leaned over him when he was a child and touched him for scrofula. She is probably alive for Winston Churchill, recreating the life and times of his soldier-ancestor, the Duke of Marlborough. She is alive for historians like Macaulay and Trevelyan, living in imagination the events and personalities of her age. But for those with no special interest in her personality or her day she is only a forgotten face and a name for the proverbially dead. But she need not remain entirely so, for the art of biography has the magic to reanimate this dead Queen. Guided by biography we can explore the box mazes and topiary work of Hampton Court and its rose-flushed brick parterres, and wander through rooms adorned with marquetry cabinets acquired under Dutch William. We can repeople the drawing rooms and terraces with Marlborough and Bolingbroke in their steep periwigs, and the crowds of statesmen, soldiers, beaux, fops, ladies-in-waiting, belles, in conclave or at play. In biography's mirror we may observe the royal jaw drop in displeasure at the irreverent humors of Swift's *Tale of a Tub*, see her being forced by Sarah, Marlborough's indomitable Duchess, into sharing even the privacy of her bedroom, and behold her at last substituting for her bullying favorite the less arbitrary Mrs Masham. Gradually, by many such touches, this plain, malleable, obstinate, and not too intelligent lady may be given solidity, and become a living if not a vivacious creature.

Her deadness, however, is only a part of the deadness of history. For history is almost necessarily abstract in design, and in subduing everything to its intellectual structure the historian sometimes loses sight of the fact that he is dealing in the end with human beings. All the warm drama of men passionately believing and struggling, men toiling and starving or idling and luxuriating, he is too prone to bury beneath an avalanche of generalization. History sorely needs the humanizing voice of biography to remind us of the flesh and blood behind its abstractions. To realize that this is true we need only remember what history is and how historians operate.

History is whatever we know about the past. In our less thoughtful moments we are apt to associate it exclusively with great and striking events: Marathon, the signing of Magna Carta at Runnymede, Socrates drinking the hemlock, the retreat from Moscow, Marco Polo returning to Venice and telling the golden wonders of Cathay, Descartes' *Discours sur la méthode*, the growth of industrialism, the discovery of gold at Sutter's Mill. But history is really much more queer and inclusive than this. History is the erection of the Parthenon and the tearing-down of Madison Square Garden; it is clay pots dug up from the site of Nineveh, and oily waste and tar belched out of modern steamers polluting ocean beaches; it is Louis XIV teetering on red heels through Versailles and the soft moccasin-tread of Indians; it is the magnificent banquets served by Vatel and it is canned soups and potted meats.

The plays Samuel Pepys tells us he enjoyed in seventeenth century London are no more a part of history than the glorification of the American Girl by Florenz Ziegfeld. Benjamin Franklin's declaration, 'Where liberty is, there is my country,' is part of history, and so is Jimmie Durante's 'There's a traitor in our midst.' The materials of history may be found in yellowing laundry lists like those Catherine Morland drew from the old chest at Northanger Abbey as well as in brown Greek manuscripts revealing three lost and surpassingly beautiful words by Sappho. Everything rememberable or findable, everything not lost or totally forgotten, is a part of history. History is the entire recoverable past.

In such huge heaps of the most incongruous things, rubbish and jewels, delusions and blinding flashes of truth, lyric poems and advertising folders, the historian delves for the significant. He must find within himself some principle of organization other than one of mere chronology. Historians have tried to solve this problem in many ways. The simplest solution has seen the important events of history as the results of personal forces—the interplay of ambitions or loyalties in the leaders of mankind, the deeds of great soldiers, the emotions swayed by great orators, the policies of kings and emperors, the dreams of poets, the machinations of scoundrels, the revelations of philosopher and scientist and sage. It sees the eighteenth century in France as Louis XV and a luscious parade of Pompadours and Du Barrys; and the Middle Ages as Frederick Hohenstaufen kneeling down to let the Pope place the ecclesiastical foot on his neck, but muttering 'Non tibi, sed Petro,' while the Pope grinds his heel down a little harder and grunts back '*Et* mihi, *et* Petro.'

It is easy to ridicule this naive mode of interpreting history, but it has its illuminating qualities. Not only is a single person or a trivial event sometimes at the fulcrum of circumstances. Sometimes a man may seem to concentrate within himself one of those great forces of his time, to be the voice of the human spirit giving form to the deep convictions or the strong passions of his age. It may be hard to tell whether Voltaire molded in certain ways the temper of his age and fired its scornful anger or whether that temper charged him with its energy until he broke out in the electric discharges of the *Dictionnaire Philosophique* and the pamphlet on Jean Calas. But whether instrument or explosive force, the grinning skull of Voltaire is a violent center of eighteenth century activity; without the fierce turmoil surrounding him our picture of the century would be changed.

Such men seem to be powers shocking the world into directions it might never have entered without their startling appearance at certain times—or floods of light illuminating paths that without their aid might never have been seen. Sometimes they fall wholly and harmoniously, as Newton did, within the pattern of their age; sometimes they run afoul of its currents and have to struggle against hatred or persecution, like Shelley or William Lloyd Garrison or Tom Paine. The genius of Newton epitomized the most passionate faith of his age: the faith in Reason as a guide surveying the labyrinth of the universe and plotting the clockwork movements of the world-machine. Others who have been buffeted in the currents of their time may appear like the Emperor Julian to be trying vainly to turn back a flood—to reverse time's arrow and bring back an irrecoverable past—or they may be, as Socrates said of himself, midwives of the truth that struggles to be born.

The truth is that any time is really a mixture of times, with many people living culturally in different ages. We all live physically in a world of telephones and tractors, wireless and linotype machines. Emotionally some of us are still blue-daubed Britons with clubs, or seventeenth century witch-hunters, or prehistoric devil-worshipers. Only an adventurous few nose ahead into what may prove either blind alleys or the road the rest of the world is laggingly to follow.

For these reasons it seems hopeless to deal with the essence of history in the characters of its great men. To remedy these defects historians in modern times have tried to interpret their material in terms of abstract forces. They have tried to achieve a philosophy of history. In so doing they gave us a wider view of the events included within history. Trying to discover the functioning of its laws, they expanded its view, raising their eyes from the amours of monarchs and the bloodsoaked battlefields, to take in the panorama of fields of corn and manufacturies and counting-houses, trying to see between them and the battlefield deeper connections than the mere dynastic ambitions of princes. They made us aware of the existence of masses of peasants and Chinese coolies and negro slaves and urban proletariat. History thrust out a rich network of interpretation connecting the dominant forms of society —economic, social, political—and their cultural flowerings in art, morals, philosophy, science. Everywhere it scooped things into associations that had not been felt before; worked the mediaeval cathedral into a synthesis with the moated castle, the feudal system, villeins, chivalry, the Courts of Love, the worship of the Blessed Virgin, morality plays, and the craft guilds.

This was a great and serious achievement in interpretation of human behavior. But in widening the scope of history, it made history dryer and less concrete. Manipulating their figures, statistics, and graphs, historians sometimes came to forget the sweat and the laughter and the toil and the eating or starving that were buried deep in the significance of their tables and charts. Even a gifted historian, when he tries to teach his knowledge, may forget that its structure was derived from the experiences of living beings and that its significance will be lost for others unless it is shown in relationship to those lives. To that human past biography is a significant key.

Reanimating Queen Anne and a thousand others among the great or obscure dead, with them it can reflesh the skeletal structure of history. In real experience the struggle of abstract forces is always embodied in the behavior and feelings of living men. Only if we try to glimpse the colors of human lives will the great empty abstractions round into fullness and begin to move; only when we can see the wide panorama and at the same time the individual hearthstone. The little backwaters of self-absorbed lives may seem to themselves to be entirely independent, but they are part of the moving stream of events in which all unknown to themselves they are participating, quite as much as those few lives that are consciously at the focal points of action and change.

Biography is thus almost a vital necessity to history. It includes not only formal biography, but all the kinds of autobiography—letters, journals, reminiscences—for all biography is ultimately founded in a kind of autobiography. They contain within them history in the concrete, its meanings made tangible, its struggles brought near. Personality everywhere permeates living experience and is the very breath of biography. It enables biography to rectify the deadness of abstract history by flooding it with breathing life.

This is perhaps why the Soviet Union decided in 1935 that teachers should lay more stress upon the subject-matter–the people and events–and less upon an 'exclusively Marxist'–that is, 'economically materialist'–interpretation.[1] The seventeenth century struggle in England between royal prerogative and the insistence of a rising bourgeoisie on parliamentary control of taxation has little meaning if we are unable to clothe it in an awareness of what it was like to be alive when John Hampden refused to pay twenty shillings for ship-money. Interpretation to which we can supply no living content is merely an empty shell of pretended knowledge, all the more dangerous because we may be deceived by our scientific terminology into believing that we have the substance as well. History without a philosophy is only a tale of wonder, but a philosophy of history without life–a history accepted on faith in a conceptual world void of the color and shape and breath and movement of living things–is an impoverishment of the very meaning of experience.

As readers, then, we need to try doing what the historians do not often enough do for us: we need to bring the awareness of individual life and personality back into history. Not by forgetting or turning our backs on the struggle of abstract forces, not by denying their reality or significance, but by realizing that in living experience they are always embodied in the behavior and feelings of individuals. There is no contradiction or antagonism between this and sociological history or economic history, or any of the other ways of realizing the past.

Nowhere is this sense of personality in history more amply rewarded than in biography. It enables us to avoid being blind dwellers in a parochial present; it enables us to see a living past, errors and triumphs, in all the mist of contention, hope, debate, indifference, or despair it wore at the time it was taking place. It puts us in no sort of competition with the scientific historian. What it does do is to fill in the vast framework of the historian with some knowledge of what it has been like for individuals to be alive in all ages.

They themselves have voiced for us their sense of their lives. We may find Sir Walter Raleigh on the night when he believed he was to be put to death, penning a letter to his wife, and saying

[1] Has this salutary emphasis been swept away since then?

'Written with the dying hand of sometime thy Husband, but now (alas) overthrown

Wa: Raleigh.
Yours that was, But now not my own.'

There is Henry Adams telling how as a little boy rebelling against going to school, he was taken in hand by his grandfather, the President, an old man of almost eighty, and led all the way over a long dusty road on a hot summer day until he found himself much to his surprise seated in the school. Then we have men recording their sense of the lives of others: John Aubrey telling us that Hobbes in his old age would sit bare-headed and never take cold, but complained of the flies walking over his baldness; and Hazlitt describing how Jeremy Bentham made such a fetich of reason that if he could discern no error in the projects of inventors he felt himself bound *in reason* to stake his money on their ventures.

In letters, in diaries, in table-talk, memoirs, and autobiographies, men have recorded how the passing current of their lives and feelings seemed to them, what they thought of their friends and enemies, and all the things that colored the passing current of their days. Therein, sometimes with no thought of being a witness to future generations, they have exclaimed over the trivia of their existences, aired their quarrels, jotted down a comment on their pleasures. What a rich fragrance of the life and personality of the past arises out of these personal records! As we read them, the dust that has sifted down over the far-away is blown from its surface by a wind of life; and the dried yellow pages that have been so hard and shriveled gradually open, expand, and take on bright colorings, like those tight little pellets of paper that placed in water unfold into flowers and trees and fountains and tiny castles.

Such a stirring of the life of the past is both like and different from that which we find in its novels and poems. They too reflect what life has meant for people in the days when they were written, and sometimes in ways of far deeper significance than the merely factual report. But the responses men have had to their actual fellows, the cravings they have had for their actual possessions—whether shoe-buckles or spiritual integrity—their laughter over personal joys and their tears over personal despairs, will always have a kind of meaning for us, a special character of reality, which is not more meaningful in the end, but differently meaningful from their works of imagination. We need their works of art if we are to recover some of the deepest manifestations of what past times were like, but we also need their personal and intimate revelations of their individual lives, their lives of everyday fact and material surrounding.

Not only has biographical literature this profound importance to the realization of history. It has another value as well: it is exciting and moving in itself. The lives that men have really led, the characters they have really displayed, the adventures they have really had, and the fates that have overtaken them, are as strange and fascinating as those they have imagined. Although sometimes men's accounts of themselves and their fellows have become entangled in falsehood or imagination, there is an intimacy of revelation in the biographical realm that their ideal creations do not entirely parallel. Achilles and Don Quixote stir us in unequaled ways, but Wellington and Faraday have a meaning for us that even the grandest heroes of epic and tragedy do not. If there are ways in which real life cannot compete with poetry there are also ways in which poetry cannot compete with life.

The biographical muse presides over a hybrid realm. She is inspired by the power of imagination, but ever held, too, within the limits of what has actually been attained among all the range of the possible. Her Pegasus is hobbled and cannot soar. It is the hard earth, no insubstantial field of asphodel, that rings beneath his hooves. He leaves that earth only briefly by spurning it with sharp blows, not in winged flights. But the realms to which he gallops are as exciting and even as real as Valhalla and Olympus.

Let us try to follow on some of these journeys. The whole world is before us, but that would be too unending an adventure. We might write a library of comment alone and never get to biography itself. Let us stay within the realm of the biographical literature of our own language. There we may find statesmen, men of letters, merchants, ecclesiastics, tinkers, kings, queens, actors, dilettantes, soldiers, bricklayers, explorers—'God's plenty'! Their stories range through grandeur, pathos, laughter, meanness, triumph, despair. And these personal lives will enable us to see also, in tangible form, something of the history of the western world, intimate and warm: the profile of time.

Biography written in the English language makes its first formal appearance in the reign of Henry VIII, and from then on the stream grows ever fuller and richer. And almost from the same time Englishmen, who had been insignificant islanders on the edge of Europe, despised for their uncouthness by the polished Italians, elbowed and bullied by the swaggering grandeur of Spain, and troublesome mainly to their neighbor France, began to be a power in the western world. By the eighteenth century England's political and cultural stars were ascendant; during the nineteenth they were dominant. Her arts and letters grew international, borrowing sometimes polish and lustre from France, and exchanging in philosophy and science the influence of Newton and Darwin for that of Descartes and Pasteur. And during all this time, in English biographical writing, we may see the personal threads running through the widespread destinies of peoples. If I can give some sense of the lighting and vitalization the experience of such literature brings to our understanding of the human adventure, even in only a part and over only a few centuries, then this book will have accomplished its purpose.

And because biographical writing is literature as well—a realm of art—I have tried also to suggest some principles by which we may evaluate its merits. Sometimes the technician—including the literary technician and craftsman—may be carried too far, and in his enthusiastic preoccupation with analysis lose sight of the life for which analysis exists. But all true analysis rightly used can only deepen our sense of the meaning and value of experience. We never understand all the life in a work of art unless we also understand why it is as it is and not otherwise.

Partly, then, in the following chapters we shall be concerned with the aims and standards of the different forms of biographical art. Knowing what the biographer and autobiographer are trying to achieve, or what they should be trying to achieve, cannot fail to enhance our realization of the personality they mirror. Understanding by what means they have achieved the ends of biographical literature, or why they have failed, must clarify and enrich our perception of their nature. To do so is no barren aestheticism but a vital necessity to the experiencing of all the life they may contain.

Only by coming to them so shall we be able to see it when they are most truly themselves, when they attain in the highest degree the life that is theirs.

When they do, there stirs before us an intimate revelation of personality, moving among the surroundings in which it found significance. With a multiplied sense of personalities crowding within those surroundings, a part of the past awakes for us, and we flash into awareness of the breathing existence of its society. And then we begin to have an understanding of history; it is alive for us; and the quest for a philosophy of history is not a juggling of grey and dusty abstractions but an exciting adventure in the life of the understanding. We find a living, glowing, and organic past.

TOWARDS AN UNDERSTANDING OF BIOGRAPHY

1

TOWARDS AN UNDERSTANDING OF BIOGRAPHY

Chiaroscurists of Souls

Men have always been fascinated by the lives of those who have appealed to their imagination, from Euripides, a sad old man with a long beard, meditating on something great and high as he gazed seaward from his cave on Salamis, to Napoleon marooned on his bare rock at St Helena or Gordon madly dying pierced with lances at Khartoum. The motives of such interest are usually of the simplest: curiosity, admiration, the action and excitement of a true story. More complex and various, though, are the motives of the biographer; and so inter-related that they often quarrel with each other and destroy the effectiveness of the biography.

In *The Development of English Biography* Mr Harold Nicolson divides the reasons for biography-writing into two, which he identifies as a commemorative instinct and a didactic instinct. Only if we take these terms loosely and stretch them to their utmost capacity is the statement true. The commemorative impulse may proceed from personal affection for a man, from admiration for his character or achievements, from the glamour of a particular historical background or series of events, from dislike for his opponents or the principles they represent (leading to glorifying their antagonist simply because he is in the other camp from them), from an indignant desire to defend him from slander and calumny —from hosts of other reasons as tangled and obscure. And the didactic impulse may run all the way from sheer crankism through various kinds of religious, ethical, or political affiliations, to the desire to find and communicate some key to the involutions of human character and destiny.

On the level of the crank and partisan biography is vulgar, and sometimes vicious; but when it reaches the height of an honest and intelligent effort to understand those elements of the universal in the life of an individual it achieves its finest justification as a literary art. Any telling of the story of a human life involves having some criterion of choice, some standards of judgment. The difference between the meretricious and the valuable is a matter of integrity and intelligence. The artist in biography must inevitably have a philosophy, but he must refrain from doctrinaire systematizing. Many degrees of sincerity and thoughtfulness separate the conscious liar from the ideal biographer, but not one involves having no point of view. And put in its crudest terms, the demonstration or illustration of a point of view is didactic.

Certain kinds of motive for writing biographies we could not include under Mr Nicolson's classification without distending the meanings until they cracked. Large numbers of memoirs have proceeded from the very opposites of the mood of pious commemoration: and could accurately be characterized as biographies of hate. Rufus Griswold's life of Poe is an infamous example of biographical rancor. And we can often find a vicious reverse-didacticism in the stories told by the devout of those whose lives they disapprove, such as the pious legends of the deathbed terrors of notorious infidels like Voltaire and Ingersoll.

Like in subject matter but different in intent are various popular lives of criminals. Pearson and Roughead in our day have retold the stories of many gory murders. They gratify an old human fascination, mingling delight with nausea and blood-horror. In the eighteenth century the publishers were forever busy with the lives of highwaymen, footpads, housebreakers, and shoplifters. Jack

Sheppard and Jonathan Wilde each inspired several books; and, a century later, one of De Quincey's most horribly effective pieces of writing was a veracious account of the Ratcliffe murders. The expression of loathing for their subjects that such writers often let fall was but a sop to conventional morality; they really regarded their criminal heroes with no more hatred than one does the ogres in the fairy tales.

But hatred may play a part in biography, and a very useful part—providing it is kept in hand. I do not believe any first-rate biography could ever be dominated by hate, but with a certain amount of dislike as a seasoning much may be done. Strong antagonism falsifies just as strong affection does. But who can doubt that much of the flavor of Mr Strachey's *Eminent Victorians* comes from a certain dash of the *malign* that pervades his attitude? At its best such a quality makes for a kind of detachment, a judicial irony. At its worst it may lead to the dullness of some of Mr Strachey's cheaper imitators, who will allow their subjects no virtues, no abilities, no merits whatever, until the reader wonders why they ever chose to chronicle so futile a clown.

The motives of the autobiographer resemble in many ways those of the biographer, but they differ to the extent that men's attitudes toward themselves differ in kind and degree from their attitude toward other people. The man who writes his own life may be fond of himself, and he may despise himself; he may wish to blow up and exhibit still farther his self-esteem, and he may want to abase and humiliate himself. The well-nourished ego, even after a lifetime of feeding, may still find a few tidbits previously overlooked by spreading its feast between the pages of a book; and the man who has been hurt, defeated, laughed at, or overwhelmed with abuse may seek there to defend himself against attack, to justify himself, and demonstrate that if he failed it was not his fault: it was the world that was cruel and wrong. Such lives, whether they are a tortured confession or a boast, a triumphant crow or an apologia, are emanations of the personal ego.

Not all autobiographers, however, find so sweet the meat that clings to their own bones. There are abstract enthusiasms, devotions to principles and causes here as well as among the biographers. The man who has participated in great events may desire that their memory be perpetuated with truth and fervor, just as they were: deeds of war, achievements of art, triumphs of science. The man who has served an ideal may want to record struggles that, in his mind, are less his than its. A man may believe his life is important for what he has learned, or for the truths he thinks it has exemplified. When John Stuart Mill wrote his own story it was a chronicle both of the abstract passions that had governed his behavior and of an educational experiment in which he regarded himself as merely typical. And when St Augustine wrote his *Confessions* it was to boast neither of the sins of his youth nor the achievements of his age, but to embody what he considered the significant truths about all human life as they had represented themselves in his own.

The autobiographer has first hand personal experience to draw on —the loves and aversions he has felt, the enthusiasms that have warmed him, the sensations and ideas that have passed through his consciousness, the people and books he has known, the events that have passed him by or swept him up into their turmoil. Twisted and self-blinded as he may be by misunderstanding or passion, everything about himself that he knows he knows. If an entirely candid and complete autobiography has never been written it is because the poor, vain, humbled, and deluded human soul, even when it can bear the spectacle of its own nakedness, cannot bear revealing it to another.

The biographer, too, can have personal knowledge of his subject. Not the internal, secret knowledge he has of himself, of course, but the knowledge one can have from talking with others, observing the tones of their voices, their gestures and fleeting changes of countenance, examining their clothes, the houses they live in, and the affections they demonstrate in their lives. And in compensation for the secret knowledge he cannot have, the biographer may learn much more certainly and completely than the subject himself may ever hope to, what others think of him and what part he plays in their lives. The biographer may weigh and compare and elicit things that his subject can never know if he even suspects. He may hear the gossip, the rumors, the scandal, the malice, the buzz that dies down when its subject enters a room; he may penetrate to places where his subject has never gone, although he has left his trace.

The biographer of a later time, who may never have met his

subject, or at the best have encountered him only in his old age, has access to still other sources of information. History—local history at least—may not have forgotten the man; and there may still be anecdotes of him among old enemies or cronies. There are the letters he has written and received, which may be extant and available, as well as other letters in which he is mentioned and discussed. Journals and diaries may be brought to light that reveal now one, now another side of his character and career. It is with such a congeries as this, of undigested and formless materials, that the biographer has to deal. The problem of the biographer's art is what use he is to make of them.

Before we try to answer the question let us stop for a moment to examine its difficulties. In the first place there may be the difficulty of sheer mass. If the writer knows so much, what is he to do with it? How is he to arrange it? on what principle of chronology or definition of themes? Is he to use it all, or eliminate some of it? and are his eliminations to be based on considerations of tautology, good taste, truth to fact, interest or dullness, reliability of evidence, or what? How is he to decide what evidence is reliable, or adjudicate between rival interpretations of a given set of alleged events? And—the converse of a plethora of conflicting evidence—what is he to do about periods or events in a life about which material is lacking, or conjectural, or scanty? How much is he entitled to guess? Finally, the complicated problem of truth and significance: what principles are to guide his course in deciding that just such and such were the deeds and qualities that gave this life its importance and meaning?

These are some of the copious problems of the conscientious biographer, and we may turn with a little relief from them to the task of noting some of the principles governing what he should try to achieve. What should a good biography be trying to attain? Primarily, I think we must say, truth—truth to the character of the human life it portrays. An absolute candor, seeking neither to blacken nor to palliate, but as clearly as may be, to understand. Such an aim necessarily involves interpretation, for a mere recital of fact will not do. Analysis must come to the aid of the deed; sometimes an entire background of social and historical color may be needed to reveal the truth about a single characteristic, and sometimes a delving into the most elusive problems of the soul.

In saying these things it becomes clear that a biography is not a psychological casebook but a work of art. If the biography must present the truth—or what seems the truth, which is as near as human achievement can come—it must do what poetry and fiction also strive after. And when we formulate the second quality of good biography we see that it is obviously a branch of literary art. For a good biography is not only true, it is the significant story of an individual life. It must have value, and not be merely a pointless and unimportant sequence of events. It must be a story, that is, a unity of events having coherence and relevance successively, not a chaos. And, lastly, the subject must be individualized. He must be shown not a puppet or figure-head of general or abstract qualities, but a living and life-like human being, colored with those traits and quirks that make him unique among men, and at the same time no monster of the imagination foreign to all the rest of the human race. Biography, in short, must accomplish the miracle of all art: that of embodying in an aesthetic form some elements of the universal through particulars.

The artist biographer must have both poetic insight and critical detachment. He must have sympathy and understanding and at the same time judgment. He must be able to enter into the darkest, most morbid, most unreally colored parts of the imagination with familiarity, and still maintain his footing in the external world. He must be a partisan or victim of no extraneous theory, drawing no sermons out of the stones where he had previously concealed them, contorting his tale into no parable to exemplify a moral morsel—or a political, or economic, or sociological one. (This is not to say, of course, that there are no legitimate uses of these disciplines as approaches to interpretation.)

And, although no biography was ever written that gave no idea of the character of the writer, he must not thrust himself into the foreground. Somewhere—shadowy, on the edge of the stage—he is bound to be, but he must not push his characters into the wings and expose himself. He must not, as many modern pseudo-biographers do, guy his subject, twist it around for satiric effect, display his own wit and cleverness on the subject-victim by making him a figure of fun. Sometimes in reading Mr Philip Guedalla we quite forget the subject through being poked brilliantly in the ribs by the author. Quips and epigrams have their place, but when they explode all over the pages of a biography, the poor subjects turn to paper dolls and fall flat on their faces.

A Rapid-Motion Panorama

Naturally enough, an awareness of the aims and methods of biography, and of the qualifications for the biographer, grew very slowly. The contemporary biographer, with all his temptations to self-display, still has the foundation of centuries of growing clarification of his task. But the earliest biographers hardly knew whether they were writing biography or history or only disordered notes of whatever events had for some reason impressed their minds. Even the best of classical biography is often mingled inextricably with legend credulously accepted in the very breath in which the writer critically analyses the type of character thus revealed; so that we find Plutarch, for example, treating the statecraft of Caesar and the mythical exploits of Theseus with little difference. And after the decay of Roman civilization the monkish chroniclers of the Christian world had to evolve painfully almost anew the difficult steps that had already been taken. Early Christian recorders are with few exceptions wandering, planless, uncritical, superstitious, and obsessed with smothering human character under thick blankets of moralizing.

The earliest English biographies were compiled by monks and schoolmen, and written, of course, in Latin. Nearly always they were concerned with the lives of saints, and from the *Historia Brittonum* (about 650) on, hagiographies and martyrologies bloom—rather bleakly—world without end. The venerable Bede drove a clear shaft of form through these often muddled compilations, and wrote with simplicity and tenderness, but even Bede continues the bad tradition of awarding ethical judgments and accepts the miraculous with monastic gullibility.

The first biography of a layman is the *Life of Alfred the Great* attributed to Bishop Asser. It conveys little real impression of Alfred's personality, giving merely a shadowy portrayal of devoutness, industry, chastity, and learning. Also there are many evasive improbabilities, much wandering from the point, and much general talk. An honorable exception to the flatness of most of the saints' lives is Eadmer's *Life of Anselm*, of which William of Malmesbury writes 'Eadmer has told everything so lucidly that he seems somehow to have placed events before our very eyes.' William of Malmesbury himself contributed other merits to the developing art. He believed in literary creation and molded his writings to definite form; 'he possessed imagination, style, and humor; above all, he was immensely inquisitive.' He delighted in vivid images and narrative detail: 'A variety of anecdote,' he remarks, 'cannot be displeasing to anyone, unless he be morose enough to rival the superciliousness of Cato.'

Among the thirteenth century chroniclers Matthew Paris was an eminent historiographer who adopted a genuinely critical attitude in the endeavor to reach historical truth. Adam of Eynsham's *Life of St Hugh of Lincoln* is noteworthy in the same century for repudiating miracles. In the age of Chaucer interest in saints' lives became more languid and even skeptical, and even the edifying legend grew less popular, so that Chaucer could teasingly allow the *Monk's Tragedies*, in the *Canterbury Tales*, to grow unbearably tedious. The Knight finally interrupts with the exclamation 'Good sir, na-moore of this!' while Harry Bailly adds 'Your tale anoyeth all this companye.'

The fifteenth century was almost devoid of biography, but in the sixteenth martyrology makes a bloodily dramatic return in Foxe's *Acts and Monuments*, usually called *The Book of Martyrs.* There are also Holinshed's chronicles, Camden's *Annals*, and that *History of Richard III* usually ascribed to Thomas More but probably by Cardinal Morton. And finally there were Roper's *Life of Sir Thomas More* and Cavendish's *Life of Wolsey*, which are the first sustained narratives of individual lives written in the English language. Both of these books go so far along the way of true biography that I shall refer to them at greater length later on.

But even when that path had been partly retraced there were still impediments enough. Izaak Walton, I believe, was the earliest English biographer to quote letters written by his characters; and William Mason's *Life of Thomas Gray* the first to make a systematic use of them as a means of showing his subject's character. The very word biography was first used by Dryden in the preface to his translation of Plutarch, where he defined it as 'the history of particular men's lives,' and went on to explain that therein 'The pageantry of life is taken away: you see the poor reasonable animal as naked as ever nature made him: are made acquainted with his passions and his follies: and find the demi-god a man.'

In Dryden's day, however, you did not see the poor creature naked as nature made him: his passions and his follies were stiffened into a fixed symmetrical pattern laid down in a series of antitheses where abstract qualities were balanced against each other. There were, perhaps, two leading reasons for this state of affairs. One was the influence of the classics; the other, related to the first, was the fascinating theory of the 'ruling passion.' North's translation of Plutarch, first published in 1579, achieved immense popularity, and paved the way for hosts of others: Holland's *Livy* and his *Suetonius*, Grenewey's *Tacitus*, Savile's *Agricola*, Heywood's *Sallust*, and, above all, Casaubon's Latin translation of the ethical characters of *Theophrastus*.

Of all these Tacitus and Theophrastus were the most influential. They led to a veritable rage of interest in typical 'characters'—that is, psychological stereotypes rather than individual temperaments, built up upon a deductive scheme of what was consistent for such and such a type to be like, rather than upon detailed observation of what a man was in fact like. Each person, so ran the theory, had one ruling passion, with all the others grouped like vassals round and swaying to its imperious motions. Any inconvenient feature of observation that didn't happen to fit, according to this method, was either firmly ignored as a mere presumptuous upstart, or else kneaded and straitjacketed somehow into the scheme. During the seventeenth century no fewer than fifty-six deliberate imitations of Theophrastus were printed, including Overbury's *Characters or Witty Descriptions of the Properties of Sundry Persons*, and Bishop Earle's *Microcosmographie*, and the method ran riot in fiction, history, and biography. Even the often glowingly etched portraits in Clarendon's *History of the Rebellion* are dramatic presentations of personified qualities, synthesized into ethical types.

Running almost underground through all this, appearing excitingly here and there in such people as John Aubrey and Roger North, there still continued what we might call the realistic tradition. It received another critical statement by the pen of Samuel

Johnson, a man of insatiable curiosity and a passionate interest in the strange manifestations of individual character. Johnson insisted on truth, on vivid detail, on psychological insight. And, with his usual hatred of cant, he perceived, and repudiated, the obituary bogey about loyalty to the dead. 'If,' says he, 'we owe regard to the memory of the dead, there is yet more respect to be laid to knowledge, to virtue, and to truth.'

Johnson's principles were brilliantly embodied in the achievement of his admiring follower, Boswell, and not unworthily represented by Macaulay's striking biographical essays and Lockhart's *Life of Scott*. Piety grew uppermost again in Stanley's *Arnold*, and panegyric irradiated Carlyle's *Sterling*, but the impulse toward realism did not die. Mrs Gaskell made an effort to present even the astringencies of Charlotte Brontë; and much later in the century Froude's courageous biography of Carlyle revived the tradition of trenchant honesty. Forster's *Dickens*, although too gently reticent about the marital career of the great novelist, is full of brilliant quotation in which Dickens characterizes himself, and Trevelyan's *Macaulay* is a triumph of character-painting in the same school. The run-of-the-mill Victorian biography, however, was not only dominated by Mrs Grundy, but pervaded by a sickly dullness. Reality was buried again and again under the heavy loam of reverence and good taste, with the twin tombstones of the official Life-and-Letters to hold it down and prevent any threatened resurrection.

Gloomy as this picture may seem, it is relieved by many bright exceptions, verdurous hollows among the crags, gleaming flesh strolling surprisingly through the grey shadows of the Elysian Fields, and living voices resounding suddenly amid the funeral utterance of galvanized corpses. Vivid among cumbrous detail we strike a passage that lights up the whole. Slyly peaking through a pious attitude we catch some glimpse of a less admirable truth that the biographer himself, perhaps, never realized was revealed. And sometimes—who knows?—while maintaining all the proprieties, a subtle writer spreads before the reader hints and fragments that enable him to fill out the whole—even what has been craftily left unsaid.

Indeed, although we may find recent biographers easier reading than their predecessors we will not find them markedly more rewarding. Contemporary writers trim their sails to a short-winded public. Mostly, they demand little depth of sympathy or understanding; even their 'subtleties' are heavily underlined. They have the obvious polish and style of writing in a technique that is as modern as an armored tractor. Their language, their allusions, are drenched in an easily recognizable present. Styles and language and conventions thus change, but when the writers of the past fail to yield their secrets to us it is not always they who have been maladroit. Sometimes we have lacked wit and insight, been impatient and obtuse. For those with some skill and patience to put themselves imaginatively in a day and a frame of mind no longer current, the spoils may be startlingly rich and suggestive. Even the luminaries of the present may dim—but it may be interesting to pursue the query in a little more detail.

Two Princes of the Church

Aside from the name George Cavendish, and the fact that he was 'Gentleman Usher' to Cardinal Wolsey, we know hardly any fact about the sixteenth century biographer of the great Churchman. Certain things we can infer about his character from the book, but the facts of his life are so dark that for long he was even confused with a cousin, William Cavendish. On the other hand we know a great deal about Mr Lytton Strachey, a brilliant writer only recently dead. We know his associates in a literary London that still flourishes, we know his enthusiasm for the French classics, we know his polished skepticism, his incisive and lapidary style. We know that Mr Strachey, more than anyone else, has been responsible for drawing attention again to the possibility that biography might be an art, a contention that he demonstrated in his own achievement; and we are familiar with the bedlam of imitators who, lacking both his scholarship and his ironic point of view, believed it a sufficient substitute to howl with mirth at grandmother's comic hats and grandfather's dusty ideas.

But suppose that, forgetting all these bits of extraneous information, and trying to ignore how much more familiar his language is to us than that of Elizabethan England, we sought to compare him and his work with that of George Cavendish. Mr Strachey has also written a life of a Cardinal: Henry Manning, whose career stretched through almost all the nineteenth century. Manning, like Wolsey, was a political ecclesiastic; Mr Strachey remarks of him that he 'seemed almost to revive in his own person that long line of diplomatic and administrative clerics that, one would have thought, had come to an end with Cardinal Wolsey.'

The hint comes from the modern writer; where could we find a better one? What may we learn of the art of biography and its fluctuations by examining these two works? What may we learn of the two writers and the qualities in the development of their art which they represent? Two churchmen, both administrators; two biographers, one at almost the beginning of the art in English, the other only recently lost to the world at the height of his prestige.

At the beginning it is clear that their aims and scopes are very different. To the eighty-five years of Manning's life Strachey devotes something like 36,000 words; the stately pace of Cavendish takes 84,000 to cover a life shorter by more than a score of years. The life of Wolsey is conceived on a grand scale as a tragedy of fortune, and it is built in such a way as to make us both anticipate and look with foreboding to the dread downfall that is to come.

Strachey's *Cardinal Manning* is–what? a drama, an apologue, a comedy? If it is a drama, the excitement is dependent upon accident, for the character is known, and the character never changes. Only in the struggle between the inner principle and outer circumstance can anything occur, never in the heart. If it is an apologue, the fable is dark and not easily applied to any conclusion, unless it be that there are natures at once supple and as hard as granite. If it is a comedy, it can be presided over only by George Meredith's Spirit of Comedy, who 'will look humanely malign and cast an oblique light' whenever men are 'self-deceived or hoodwinked . . . . whenever they offend sound reason, fair justice, are false in humility or mined with conceit.' One might even characterize Mr Strachey's handling of his characters as a laboratory demonstration or a dissection, if it did not seem every now and then to turn into a flaying.

The opening is skilful. A few details, and the outline of Manning's character is ineradicably impressed. The little episode in which he outwits a school master who finds him out of bounds, by fetching a circle and riding off on the master's horse; his taking orders after his father's bankruptcy had made a political career impossible; the facility with which, forgetting the lady he had been in love with, 'he married his rector's daughter' and stepped into the rector's shoes when he died—these things need to complete them only the sentence at the end of the chapter, 'In after years, the memory of his wife seemed to be blotted from his mind.' We already know Henry Manning.

The chapter on the Oxford Movement is a fine piece of bravura writing, irresistibly comic and at the same time presenting sufficiently an outline of events to show how Manning became entangled in them. From the point of view of perfect art the personality of the writer is perhaps too intrusive, the material is somewhat too ruthlessly laughed at, and there are places where the sneer becomes even rather cheap. (Dr Pusey was startled at the outcry that greeted his article on fasting. 'I thought serious-minded people at least supposed they practiced' fasting in some way; 'we live and learn' comments Mr Strachey, 'even though we have been to Germany.') But how wittily presented the conscientious struggles and the metaphysical problems of Hurrell Froude, how delicious the absurd quotations from *Tracts for the Times*, and, in the following chapters, how hilariously funny the combination in W. G. Ward of a priori dialectic and Opéra Bouffe! What is left unexplained, except for a misty implication of the all-coveringness of human silliness, is why such doings should ever have begun a significant movement.

Manning began to play a double game. The pretensions of the new teachings attracted him by exalting the dignity of priesthood; on the other hand a neighboring, and influential, Archdeacon was violently low-church. He wrote an article on Justin and began, secretly, holding confession. But when alarms circulated he preached a virulent Protestant sermon at Oxford. On the day after, he walked out to Littlemore 'in the hope of being able to give a satisfactory explanation' to Newman, but that was beyond even Manning's skill. Dr Newman was not at home. Manning did not forget the rebuff.

Newman was converted, after fearful wavering, to Rome. Manning, too, agonized, in elaborate tables with numbered heads and subheads, over the temptation that was for him, he knew, 'the most subtle and terrible of all temptations.' Were his ambitions really for 'an elevation into a sphere of higher usefulness' or were they vanity? He rejected, after bitter self-examination, the office of sub-Almoner to the Queen, but 'in all this Satan tells me I am doing it to be thought mortified and holy,' and then came gnawing regret. He fell ill, and spent his convalescence in Rome, where he had a long interview with the Pope. In all the detailed pages of his *Diary* for the time the only mention made of this event is 'the bald statement: "Audience to-day at the Vatican."' Two years later he was received into the Roman Catholic Church. Fourteen years later he 'was Archbishop of Westminster and the supreme ruler of the Roman Catholic community in England.'

In London he had made himself useful to Cardinal Wiseman, had defeated the Old Catholics and Dr Errington, the Archbishop of Trebizond and Coadjutor of Westminster; had separated Cardinal Wiseman from his confidant, Monsignor Searle, and 'touched with a deft finger the chord of the Conversion of England'—the Cardinal's great dream. In the Vatican he had made a friend of Monsignor Talbot, whose humble door at the top of a little winding stair had singular communications with Pio Nono. When Wiseman died, Manning, by a Pontifical act, became Archbishop of Westminster. Talbot wrote: '*My* policy throughout was never to propose you *directly* to the Pope. . . . This I say, because many have said that your being named was all my doing. I do not say the Pope did not know that I thought you the only man eligible; as I took care to tell him over and over again what was against all the other candidates. . . . Nevertheless, I believe your appointment was specially directed by the Holy Ghost.'

In his new dignity the implacable fighter proved all magnanimity. But one thing irked him still: 'a figure which, by virtue of a peculiar eminence, seemed to challenge the supremacy of his own. That figure was Newman's.' 'Since his conversion, Newman's life had been a long series of misfortunes and disappointments.' And then, at the age of sixty-three he wrote his *Apologia pro Vita Sua.* It 'was recognized at once as a classic, not only by Catholics, but by the whole English world. From every side expressions of admiration, gratitude, and devotion poured in.' Proposals were made that an oratory be established at Oxford, with Newman at the head. Manning poured comment into Monsignor Talbot's ear. Monsignor Talbot quite agreed: 'Blande suaviterque' Newman was to be deterred. The Oratory was immediately quashed.

Years passed. Manning served busily at the Council that, almost at the moment the Pope lost his Temporal Power, proclaimed his Infallibility. He was made a Cardinal; 'he ruled his diocese with the despotic zeal of a born administrator'; he lectured; he sat on committees; his name appeared on public documents immediately below that of the Prince of Wales. Monsignor Talbot was by now confined within padded walls in a Home at Passy. In neither speech nor writing did Manning ever mention him again. Pius IX died; Leo XIII ruled in his place. And once again Newman's name came up. Manning delayed sending a letter for six months, and even when a Cardinalate was definitely offered to Newman, and almost accepted, he tried yet one more trick. But the little room on the winding stair was empty; the voice that had whispered in the Papal ear was stilled, and the ear was that of another Pope. This time it failed.

Once, long after, the two Cardinals met. 'What do you think Cardinal Manning did to me?' Newman asked. 'He kissed me!' And after Newman's death: 'Poor Newman!' Manning exclaimed. 'He was a great hater!'

Manning had made a brilliant showing at the Oxford Union, but he had taken orders because his father's bankruptcy had closed the triumphs of politics to him. For Wolsey, however, the son of a poor man (a butcher, by some rumors), the Church was the only possible entry to a career of wealth and power. As chaplain to the Treasurer of Calais, he speedily drew himself to the attention of Henry VII. When the young Henry VIII, 'lusty, disposed all to mirth and pleasure,' and 'nothing minding to travail in the busy affairs' of the realm, came to the throne, Wolsey was already Almoner and a member of the Council. 'Full of subtil wit and policy,' the crafty cleric showed himself 'most earnest and readiest . . . to advance the king's only will and pleasure, without any respect to the case.' His 'filed tongue and ornate eloquence' soon advanced him.

With tremendous energy he arranged all the details of sending and supplying the King's army in France, and his favor grew. In a single year he was made Bishop of Tournai, Bishop of Lincoln, and finally Archbishop of York. But Canterbury stood in his light: the Primate of All England, before whom even York must 'abate the advancing of his cross.' Wolsey pulled strings, and became Priest Cardinal and Legatus de latere. But the purple pall was sent by a mean messenger, without pomp; and Wolsey's triumph must be public. The messenger was stayed, appareled 'with all kind of costly silks,' and then received at Blackheath with 'great assembly of prelates and lusty gallant gentlemen.' The investiture took place at Westminster, in the presence of bishops and abbots 'in rich mitres and copes.' Presently Warham, the Archbishop of Canterbury, was dismissed from the Chancellorship, and Wolsey took the Great Seal.

Glorious now was his state. The benefices of Durham and Winchester swelled his revenues; Bath, Worcester, and Hereford added their incomes to the flood. In his kitchen a Master Cook 'went daily in damask satin, or velvet, with a chain of gold about his neck.' When the Cardinal stirred abroad a numerous train of gentlemen and yeomen 'in livery coats of crimson velvet of the most purest colour' accompanied his progress, and he was preceded by two silver pillars and two great crosses of silver borne by tall and comely priests. Clad in 'crimson satin, taffety, damask, or caffa,' 'a round pillion, with a noble of black velvet' on his head, and 'a tippet of fine sables about his neck,' he paraded his garden pestered with suitors and smelling a fair vinegar-orange as a protection against the pestilent airs; or took his barge to Greenwich from his own privy stairs to dine richly and entertain the King. In his magnificence he did not forget old scores. A Sir Amyas Pawlet who had once put the young priest in stocks was sent for, greeted with 'sharp and heinous words,' and made to dance attendance on the Council for six years.

'Thus passed the cardinal his life and time.' But the King began to cast amorous glances on Anne Boleyn, and to his rage it was uncovered that young Lord Percy had dared to make love to her. Henry spoke to Wolsey and the rash youth was sent for. 'I marvel not a little,' Wolsey bullied, 'of thy peevish folly, that thou wouldst tangle and ensure thyself with a foolish girl yonder in the court, I mean Anne Boleyn.' The young man tried to defend himself. 'Lo, sirs,' Wolsey roared, 'ye may see what conformity and wisdom is in this wilful boy's head.' Percy was hectored with threats of the King's anger; his father, the old Earl of Northumberland was sent for to add his intimidations. 'Son,' he began, 'thou hast always been a proud presumptuous disdainful, and a very unthrift waster,' and threatened with disinheritance if the boy did not yield his 'lewd fact.'

Under all this pressure the young man weakened, he departed from the court, and Mistress Anne Boleyn was sent to the country. 'She smoked' with rage at the Cardinal, for she thought it all his doing, having no idea of the King's 'secret mind.' When she knew 'the King's pleasure, and the great love he bare her in the bottom of his stomach, then she began to look very hault and stout.' With her the jealous lords of the Council conspired 'to take the Cardinal in a brake.' Wolsey's doom was near.

Henry demanded action. On Wolsey's motion the Universities debated whether the King's marriage to his brother's widow was legal, and finally a court was appointed by the Pope, presided over by Wolsey and Cardinal Campeggio, to try the cause. At Blackfriars the crier called 'King Henry of England, come into the court,' and the King answered 'Here, my lords!' Queen Catherine kneeled at his feet, and prayed: 'Sir, I beseech you for all the loves that hath been between us, and for the love of God . . . take of me some pity and compassion.' She had been 'a true humble and obedient wife,' and when he had her first, she swore, 'a true maid, without touch of man.' She begged that the trial be put aside. Ending thus, she left the court.

Henry made a speech of extraordinary and cynical hypocrisy. He would declare unto them all, he said, 'that she hath been to me as true, as obedient, and as conformable a wife as I could in my fantasy wish or desire.' But his 'scrupulous conscience' had been pricked in respect of her marriage with the late Prince Arthur, so 'that it bred a doubt within my breast,' which 'pricked, vexed, and troubled so my mind . . . that I was in great doubt of God's indignation.' Was not the fact that the marriage had produced no heir male a sign of God's anger? Out of consideration for 'the estate of this realm,' therefore, he thought to 'take another wife in case that my first copulation with this gentlewoman were not lawful,'—which, he added, 'I intend not for any carnal concupiscence, ne for any displeasure or mislike of the queen's person or age,' but only out of holy concern for God's laws.

The trial dragged on. One day the Bishop of Carlisle, wiping his brow, complained of the heat. 'Yea,' said Wolsey, 'if ye had been as well chafed as I have been within this hour, ye would say it were very hot.' At last Cardinal Campeggio refused to give a decision without presenting the arguments to the Pope himself, and dissolved the court. The King raged, and the Duke of Suffolk stepped forth from his side. 'It was never merry in England,' he said opprobriously, 'whilst we had cardinals among us.'

Going down to Grafton to the King, Wolsey found no lodging appointed for him, and it was late when 'he came by torchlight' to improvised lodgings at Euston. Suddenly a blow fell. He was deprived of the Great Seal, his goods seized, and himself ordered from the Court. He made an inventory of his rich stuffs and velvets, the cloth of gold and silver in his great galleries, the gorgeous vestments, the plate and jewels and books to be handed over, and took his leave. At the water-stairs were 'a thousand boats full of men and women of the city of London, *waffeting* up and down in Thames,' supposing that he was being sent to the Tower, 'whereat they rejoiced.'

At Esher, still in hope of reinstatement, he abode a while 'without beds, sheets, table cloths, cups and dishes to eat our meat, or lie in.' 'In a white rochet upon a violet gown' 'floods of tears distilled from his eyes' in the sight of his servants; and 'fountains of water' gushed out of their 'faithful hearts down their cheeks.' The devoted Thomas Cromwell defeated an attainder of treason in Parliament, but a writ of premunire deprived Wolsey of all the income from his benefices. He threw himself on the King's mercy: 'The king's highness knoweth right well whether I have offended his majesty and his laws or no.' But, though he might justly stand on trial, he ended, he would not do so, but 'confess the offense in the inditement, and put me wholly in the mercy and grace of the king.'

The rich endowments of the Church once seized, however, Henry was not staying. Perhaps his anger with his former Chancellor had vanished; his greed had not. York Place (which belonged to the Bishopric) was taken and the Cardinal ordered to his See. Ailing, but still humbly protesting, the hunted man removed from Esher to Richmond and from Richmond to Oxford, where he 'washed, wiped, and kissed' the feet of fifty-nine poor men on Maundy Thursday. At St Oswald's Abbey he confirmed children, and was waiting at Cawood the arrangements for his formal installation at York when he was arrested. The Earl of Northumberland arrived; the sick priest greeted him with cringing courtesy. In the bed chamber, 'the Earl trembling said, with a very faint and soft voice,' laying his hand on Wolsey's arm: 'My Lord, I arrest you of high treason.'

His illness grew worse in confinement, 'with a thing that lieth overthwart my breast,' he said, 'as cold as a whetstone.' At last he knew there was no hope. 'Master Kingston,' he told the Constable of the Tower, 'all these comfortable words which ye have spoken be but for a purpose to bring me into a fool's paradise.' He died in 'an excoriation of the entrails,' saying 'If I had served God as diligently as I have done the king, he would not have given me over in my grey hairs . . . This is the just reward that I must receive for my worldly diligence.'

So the ruthless, glittering, and broken career ended. As Cavendish tells it, it is both a tragedy and a pageant of Renaissance magnificence. Time and again we are surrounded by the glow of gold, the sparkle of jewels, the shimmer of rich stuffs worn by all 'fair ladies that bare any bruit or fame of beauty in all the realm,' whose lovely forms seemed 'more angelic than earthly made of flesh and bone.' We are told of noble feasts which, the narrator says, 'I do lack wit in my gross old head, and cunning in my bowels to declare,' and from which the guests 'were fain to be led to their beds.'

But running through all this display there is an ominous note that sounds more often as the pomp grows overwhelming. The great ecclesiastic, glorying in his power, offensive in his pride, ruthless and domineering in his control, haughtily unforgiving in memory, commits again in all of these the tragic sin of hubris. Hubris was the sin of Agamemnon and Oedipus; hubris is the Cardinal's overweening pride. Tragic is the cause of his undoing as well, for it is precisely that 'king's only will and pleasure' that he had himself fostered 'without any respect to the case.'

So Cavendish bathes in all the colors of tragedy the fall of his disastered lord. At the end he breaks into a valediction, the theme of which has been running implicitly throughout: 'Who list to read and consider, with an indifferent eye, this history, may behold the wondrous mutability of vain honour, the brittle assurance of abundance; the uncertainty of dignities, the flattering of feigned friends, and the fickle trust to worldly princes. Whereof this lord cardinal hath felt both of the sweet and the sour in each degree . . . O madness! O foolish desire! O fond hope! O greedy desire of vain honours, dignities, and riches! Oh what inconstant trust and assurance is in rolling fortune!'

There is no color in Mr Strachey's handling of Manning, only a clear, cold intellectual atmosphere, dramatic enough, indeed, but stark. I can recall only two places where he uses any description at all, and both are for analytic purposes. One is when the astute priest observes that Newman has changed into grey trousers, and knows thereby that he no longer considers himself in Anglican orders. The other is the picture of Newman's tears outside the Church at Littlemore. It signalized the fact that blande suaviterque Newman's spirit had been crushed. Strachey lights his administrative cleric with an acid luminance. His analysis makes it clear enough that he regards Manning as one 'who had won by art what he never would have won by force,' who had 'managed to be one of the leaders of the procession less through merit than through a superior faculty for gliding adroitly to the front rank.'

Further, it is another of Strachey's triumphs that he gains his effects with great economy of means. There are no superfluous strokes, every sharp paragraph, every brief quotation, bites deep in the hewing. Compared with this stripped speed, this fierce pressing on the goal, Cavendish seems like the armor-plated tortoise. He winds through long and loosely constructed sentences, as unperturbed for breath as King Henry was in the intricate mendacity of his speech before the court of divorce. And sometimes, in fact, Cavendish is longwinded; in occasional stretches positively dull. He places before us none of those tingling draughts whose bitter flavor we have come to relish. He is not astringent. But—rotate the prism a few degrees, let the noble colors dissolve, and gaze again. Does not the harsh character that appears seem almost identical with Strachey's hawklike old man?

If Manning is a schemer, a subtle player upon the emotions of men, so is Wolsey. He had early estimated the nature of Henry VIII, and used it for his ends. 'Rather than he will either miss or want any part of his will or appetite, he will put the loss of one-half his realm in danger.' At first the King had wanted pleasure, freedom from the drudgery of state, pomp and display. Wolsey had given them to him, the Field of the Cloth of Gold, pageantry, military strutting; and taken on himself the intrigues of state. As the King grew interested in the game of power, Wolsey undertook his embassies for him. He profited by all.

Like Manning, Wolsey is ruthless and determined in his own ambitions. Witness how he gets himself made Cardinal in order to outrank Canterbury. (He accomplished it by holding in the Tower, in spite of repeated remonstrances from Rome, the deputy collector of Adrian, Bishop of Bath, whose influence he demanded.) Like Manning, Wolsey is vindictive to those who had baulked him —as the unfortunate Sir Amyas Pawlet learned. And like Manning he is wily in human nature. Cavendish asked him why he had confessed himself guilty of premunire when it was untrue. Once the King had seized all his goods and possessions, Wolsey replied, 'rather than yield, or take a foil in the law, and thereby restore to me all my goods again' the King would 'imagine my utter undoing.' And besides this 'if I had been found stiff necked' Anne Boleyn, a continual 'serpentine enemy' (he also calls her 'the night crow') would have breathed poison into Henry's ear and his favor been lost forever. Wolsey had observed them both well. For all her cajoleries when she needed him, Anne Boleyn had never forgiven the Cardinal. And Henry—defy that deep-jowled egoism and his rancor would be implacable. Wolsey knew. But what he could not guard against was the rapacity which, once it had plunged its fangs into the juicy flanks of the Church's revenues, would never relinquish them.

Cavendish places the Cardinal's worldly knowledge beyond all possible doubt. The administrator who raised, equipped, dispatched, and maintained a victorious army in France, the diplomat who successfully conducted the most intricate negotiations again and again, the statesman who pulled with his sensitive fingers the threads of all Henry VIII's entangled foreign policy and made England a power in Europe, the flatterer who held the fickle favor of that monarch for twenty years, was a master of his craft.

The two Cardinals are almost startlingly alike. It is significant, then, to note the contrast in the methods by which they are revealed. Both churchmen are assuredly, as Mr Strachey puts it, among those who 'have been distinguished less for saintliness and learning than for practical ability,' and the fact that Wolsey's career ended in disaster does not really destroy the parallel. But all Wolsey's traits, clearly shown as they are by Cavendish, are unobtrusively and as it were innocently revealed. If we wish to observe them, we must keep our eyes open and our minds alert. He is not underlining and pointing his material for us, as Strachey is. He may even be at some pains not to be too obvious.

We are seldom unaware while reading *Cardinal Manning* that the author is a very clever man. His pen is dipped in the inkwell of Voltaire. He flashes the instruments of his wit, the evidence of his research, before our eyes; the dexterity is admirable, and we can hardly fail to realize clearly the purpose of the whole demonstration. There is the scalpel, and if it perform a scalping, how neat! But always we are as aware of the performer as we are of Manning, and we realize gradually that he is out to 'get' Manning. The proof seems convincing, certainly, we murmur; yes, Manning must have been so, there are these and these quotations from veritable documents, and yet–! The animus is palpable, the writer brilliant–he has proved it beyond cavil–may the facts perhaps be, we wonder, not fabricated, but–*manipulated*?[1] We may rejoice thus in Mr Strachey's writing as a piece of delightful literary virtuosity, but we end by feeling dubious of how far he tried to live up to his professed aim: 'Je n'impose rien; je ne propose rien; j'expose.'

But so retiring is Cavendish that we are seldom aware of him at all, except when one of his phrases strikes a modern ear as quaint, or when he is making some deprecatory remark about his 'gross old head.' This simplicity is deceptive. He is by no means as innocent as he appears. It is no simpleton who depicts the tortuous ramifications of several of Wolsey's missions, and who gives that marvelously perjured speech of the King's from which I have quoted. The naiveté of the colloquy in which he asks Wolsey to explain why he submitted to the King's injustice is only a dramatic device. The wits that understood and remembered the explanation for over twenty years were no 'gross old wits.'

There is a tremendous skill in the way he tells us all those prideful doings of Wolsey's prime, even those that depict him as unprincipled, revengeful, and hard. When he reaches the stage of

[1] Mr Strachey is not here accused of any factual duplicity, but of the aesthetic failure of losing the reader's confidence.

Wolsey's decline we already believe in the honesty of the man who has not hesitated to show his master's faults, and so we accept his account of the conspiracy that leads to Wolsey's ruin, and sympathize with the meekness, the sorrow, and the too-late piety that then appear. If these things are deliberately done, as I believe them to be, they are more skilful than Mr Strachey's attainment. The clever modern writer has left us dubious of his trustworthiness, and has failed to remove the signs of his personality from the scene. The unobtrusive gentleman usher retains our faith and is usually in the background unnoticed.

The issue here is not whether either writer is actually coloring the truth; it is one of literary tact. Cavendish clearly avoids writing an apologia, although his mood is sympathetic. He makes no apparent effort to conceal or palliate Wolsey's flaws. They had raised up enemies, and had left him naked to them in his age. His fall is just, but who could withhold the feeling of awe and pity? Sympathy in such case demands no excuse, for it makes no defense.

Attack, however, requires double and three times the strength that forgiveness does. Biography is not diatribe, and it must guard itself against all suspicion of being. When animus lies in one scale, if the writer be skilful the other must be heaped to overflowing. With the reader a seemingly unchivalrous foe defeats himself. So Mr Strachey mercilessly at his victim loses the confidence an author less on the scene might have retained. Readers have often said that Mr Strachey was subtle, but in all such genuine attributes of subtlety Cavendish is clearly superior.

Strachey is ironic (a quite different thing from subtlety), he is sharp, harsh, and witty, in a way that Cavendish neither attempts nor could achieve. There is a spark of the romantic in the older writer; the realism of the other is almost sinisterly bleak. Cavendish is magnificent, although sometimes wordy; Strachey is always bare. And, last, Mr Strachey's art almost ostentatiously makes us aware that it is art. Cavendish, in his serene manner, takes all that by the way. That both have made penetrating, and curiously like, portraits, will not be denied. That Cavendish presents some obstacles to the impatience of the modern reader is also probably true, but mostly the obstacles are not his, only the detritus of time. That the sixteenth century biographer suffers in comparison with his modern rival is very dubious indeed.

A SHEAF OF SIX BIOGRAPHERS
16th and 17th Centuries

II

A SHEAF OF SIX BIOGRAPHERS
16TH AND 17TH CENTURIES

On Understanding the Past

QUEEN ELIZABETH's favorite oath was 'God's death!' but it is no stranger than various exclamations that may be found in popular magazines today. Nor is it more normal for women now to smoke cigarettes than for those of earlier times to take snuff. And still we are constantly tempted to regard such differences of time as proofs of our own superiority, and to be discomposed by what seem to us the oddities of the past—in dress and in manners, in ideas and diction, in rhythms and ways of thought.

Especially in literature these obstacles are often more or less in our paths. We are more familiar with the nineteenth century and with our own time than with the sixteenth century, and more familiar with certain modernisms of tone and overtone than with those of Tudor England. And so we may find it easier at first to read Strachey than Cavendish, although the latter is as vivid and as sound in portraiture as his modern rival, and perhaps fuller and richer in background.

But in approaching any older writer we may feel such difficulties. The world has so changed in even these last few hundred years that we live veritably in a mist of ignorance about bygone days. It is hard for us, often, to understand the very fabric of our ancestors' minds. Loyalties and passions for which their hearts flamed may be only old wives' tales to us. Geographical exploration and discovery, political and economic change, new inventions and ways of living, altering religious and philosophic views—all these place us in a vastly different world from that of no more than a hundred years ago.

Should we flounce impatient shoulders and pass on? If we do, we shall miss a great deal that is wonderful, moving, and revealing. Under the outward changes men have not grown really strange to what they once were, and it is not too hard to strip the masks. There is wisdom in history. Only by exploring the past can we know that our tastes are not parochial, our truths not a whim or passing fashion. Our enlightenment, if real, we shall see as mostly the fortune of heritage rather than personal insight. 'The dead writers are remote from us,' some one claims, 'because we know so much more than they did.' 'Precisely, and they are that which we know.'

The sixteenth and seventeenth centuries are not so remote that we cannot approach their biographers as human beings. If we do, they will illumine the past and revive its life. They will also clarify the aims of biography. The biographers in this chapter, ranging from the time of Cavendish to the end of the seventeenth century, are not treated in strict chronological order and they are not exhaustive. I wanted to avoid implying that they represent a 'development' of biography, with each learning from his predecessors and avoiding their errors. It is possible that North and Aubrey may not even have read Cavendish or Roper. The six biographers chosen here are presented only as illustrations of different efforts and different degrees of success in handling their problems.

Some of them are failures as biographers. There are two reasons why a writer may be a bad biographer: one, pure incompetence; the other, lack of intent. Sometimes the incompetent writer is turgid and empty. Sometimes he lacks any conception of character or depicts a stiff and lifeless paragon. Sometimes he is wandering or over-minute, or intrudes himself into the narrative, or is a melancholy and pompous bore. Nothing can mitigate such complete failure in biography. But in other cases the writer was not trying to produce biography. He may have done something highly interesting in itself, that is in a way the raw material of biography. Some of these diverse aims appear now, and others—the chroniclers, the memoir-writers, and, at their best the most vivid of all, the diarists—appear in later chapters.

Blood and Smoke

Few modern readers are acquainted with John Foxe's *Book of Martyrs*. And yet it is a work that used to be found in countless households where its only companions were the Bible and *Pilgrim's Progress*. First published in 1563, it went into four editions in Foxe's lifetime, and remained tremendously popular for long afterwards. In its great success we may find perhaps a mingling of piety and the Old Adam, for if it was intended for Protestant edification it also gave plentiful satisfaction to an impulse which was very shortly later to revel in the piled-up corpses of *The Spanish Tragedy* and the barbarities of *The Jew of Malta*.

The material of the work is the progress of Reformation, and its method is partly biography, partly chronicle. Beginning with a rather cursory sketch of the persecutions of the early Christians and outlining the career of the Emperor Constantine, who first adopted Christianity as the religion of the Roman Empire, it focuses attention upon such reformers as Wickliff and the Lollards in England, John Huss in Bohemia, and Martin Luther in Germany, and then returns to the England of Foxe's own day with detailed accounts of the burnings of hundreds in the bloody reign of Mary Tudor.

Sometimes the narrative is vivid and powerful. But only too often it is tedious beyond bearing. In the first place Foxe has no conception of literary architectonics. He tells his story chronologically under each reign until one of his heroes comes on the scene. Then he pulls up, goes back, and tells his biography from his birth: and then resumes the main line of narrative until the next interruption. He almost invariably gives all the details of the martyrs being examined before their judges, with all the points of theological controversy, no matter how many times they may virtually duplicate previously quoted trials. Worse than these faults, the prevailing tone of undiscriminating piety is such that hardly any of the characters stand out as individuals. Latimer and Tyndale cannot be separated in one's mind from John Hooper; one may recall what happens to them, but not how they differ from each other.

Occasionally, however, there is a flash of characterization. In examining Dr Rowland Taylor, we are told, Gardiner, Bishop of Winchester and Lord Chancellor, 'according to his custom reviled him, calling him knave, traitor, heretic, with many other villainous reproaches,' and this dialogue takes place. Gardiner demands:

> 'How darest thou look me in the face for shame?'
>
> 'If I should be afraid of your lordly looks, why fear you not God? . . . With what countenance will ye appear before the judgment-seat of Christ and answer to your oath made first unto King Henry the Eighth of famous memory, and afterward unto King Edward the Sixth his son?'
>
> 'Tush, tush,' [the Bishop responds] 'that was Herod's oath, unlawful; and therefore worthy to be broken' [and when Taylor argues this point, loses his temper and bursts out]
>
> 'I see thou art an arrogant knave, and a very fool.'
>
> 'My Lord,' [Taylor replies] 'leave your railing at me, which is not seemly for such a one in authority as you are.'

Both men are clearly revealed in this scene, and it is not without parallels. Probably the best of all the narratives is that of Cranmer, which skilfully evokes his milk-mildness and obedience to the King and his mingling of simplicity and spiritual subtlety—perhaps more skilfully than its author knew. We are introduced to his intricate argument that 'the Bishop of Rome had no such authority, as whereby he might dispense with the Word of God,' and Henry's jubilant exclamation, 'That man has the sow by the right ear!' There is even a sort of humor in the Protestant delight with which Foxe tells the story of the Pope offering his foot to be kissed by Henry's ambassadors. The Earl of Wiltshire, one of the envoys, had a spaniel, which while his master made no move, 'straightway went directly to the Pope's foot, and not only kissed the same unmannerly, but took fast with his mouth the great toe of the Pope, so that in haste he pulled in his feet: our men smiling in their sleeves.' Comedy and drama mingle in the episode of Cranmer consulting the Suffragan of Dover and Dr Barber while he has their treacherous letters in his bosom, and getting them to condemn themselves as worthy to be hanged.

Under Queen Mary comes his fall, and we see the trial speed apace, with the judges gagging the prisoner's efforts to plead: 'Short arguments, master doctor! short arguments!' and later we see Cranmer desperately wriggling in the net of recantation and counter-recantation. Indeed, as Foxe says, if 'a bishop ought not to be stubborn,' with that vice 'this archbishop in no wise ought to be charged.' But when at last 'the archbishop began to surmise what they went about,' his wavering ended. The final scene on the scaffold is superb: the cunning of Cranmer's declaration, couched until almost the end in such innocuous terms of repentance and profession of faith that the officials have no intimation of what is coming: 'As my hand offended, writing contrary to my heart, my hand shall first be punished therefore; for, may I come to the fire, it shall be first burned. And as for the Pope, I refuse him, as Christ's enemy, and antichrist, with all his false doctrine.' Consternation follows, while doctors 'yelp and bawl': 'Stop the heretic's mouth!' Foxe observes in satisfaction, 'I think there was never cruelty more notably or in better time deluded; for they looked for a glorious victory and a perpetual triumph by this man's retractation.'

If there is no other single story that has the dramatic completeness of this one, there are terrible episodes in many others, such as this of the deaths of Latimer and Ridley:

> Master Ridley took his gown and his tippet, and gave them to his brother-in-law, Master Shipside. . . . He gave away, besides, divers other small things to gentlemen standing by, pitifully weeping, as to Sir Henry Lea a new groat; and to divers of my Lord William's gentlemen some napkins, some nutmegs, and rases of ginger; his dial, and such other things as he had about him. . . .
>
> Master Latimer very quietly suffered his keeper to pull off his hose, and his other array, which was very simple: being stripped into his shroud, he seemed as comely a person to them that were there present, as one should see; and whereas in his clothes he appeared a withered and crooked old man, he now stood bolt upright, as comely a father as one might lightly behold. . . .
>
> Then the smith took a chain of iron, and brought the same about both Dr Ridley's, and Master Latimer's middles: and as he was knocking in a staple, Dr Ridley took the chain in his hand, and shaked

> the same, and looking aside to the smith, said 'Good fellow, knock it in hard, for the flesh will have his course.'
>
> Then they brought a faggot, kindled with fire, and laid the same down at Dr Ridley's feet. To whom Master Latimer spake in this manner: 'Be of good comfort, Master Ridley, and play the man. We shall this day light such a candle, by God's grace, in England, as I trust shall never be put out.'
>
> When Dr Ridley saw the fire flaming up towards him, he cried with a wonderful loud voice, 'Lord, Lord, receive my spirit.' Master Latimer, crying as vehemently on the other side, 'O Father of heaven, receive my soul!' received the flame as it were embracing of it. After that he had stroked his face with his hands, and as it were bathed them a little in the fire, he soon died (as it appeareth) with very little pain or none.
>
> By reason of the evil making of the fire unto Master Ridley, because the wooden faggots were laid about the gorse, and over-high built, the fire burned first beneath . . . that it burned clean all his nether parts, before it once touched the upper [so that he cried] 'Let the fire come unto me, I cannot burn.' In which pangs he labored till one of the standers by with his bill pulled off the faggots above, and where he saw the fire flame up Master Ridley wrested himself to that side. [Presently he stirred no more.]

The glare and horror of passages like these do much to explain the fascination of the book. What though there are hundreds of 'godly martyrs' burned in the fires of Smithfield of whom one learns no more than that 'altogether in one fire most joyfully and constantly' they 'ended their temporal lives, receiving there-fore life eternal'? What though repetition, wanderingness, and monotonous iteration of holy rhetoric fill page after page? When the narratives speed toward their dreadful ends and the flames rise around the figures bound in chains, piety and debate are consumed in the smoke. The Martyrologist is a forerunner of the tragedy of blood, and the ingredients of his drama are blood and fire.

Chancellor of Utopia

More nearly satisfactory as biography than Foxe is William Roper's life of his father-in-law, Sir Thomas More. Although this work was probably written long before *The Book of Martyrs*, some time after the Chancellor was beheaded in 1535, it was not published until 1626. It is a fairly lucid telling of More's life story, colored with vivid reminiscence, but weakened by being determinedly encomiastic, so much so that his subject is presented to us only in solemn lights. This might not be wrong, in itself, if we did not have some evidence of More's liveliness of disposition and quickness of wit, neither of which appears in Roper. John Aubrey tells us that More's 'discourse was extraordinarily facetious,' and that he enjoyed playing tricks on people. He gives us an anecdote illustrative of the Chancellor's ingenuity: musing on the top of a tower, he was surprised by an escaped madman who 'had a Mind to have thrown him from the battlements, saying Leap, Tom, Leap.' More said shrewdly, pointing to his little dog, 'Let us first throw the dog down, and see what sport that will be.' The luckless animal was tossed; 'This is very fine sport, sayd my Lord, Let us fetch him up, and try once more.' The trusting lunatic descended, and More was able to fasten the door and call for help.

In More's *Utopia* it was a law that young people were to see each other naked before marriage, so that they might conceal no physical defects and make sure they had no mislike of each other. According to another of Aubrey's tales, the Chancellor was so far consistent as to exemplify his own theory, and when a suitor arrived (according to the story, this very William Roper), More 'carries Sir William into the chamber' where both his daughters are sleeping in a truckle-bed, 'and takes the Sheete by the corner and suddenly whippes it off. They lay on their Backes, and their smocks up as highe as their armepitts. This awakened them, and immediately they turned on their bellies.' Thus the suitor saw both sides and More showed himself unconventionally willing to act on his own plan.

Now it may be that these anecdotes are apocryphal, or it may be that Roper, if he was concerned in the latter of them, had no mind to tell how he took Megge More to wife. He was, Mr Nicolson remarks, 'not very intelligent,' and it may have been that in his partisanship for More he believed such things would be damaging (which they should not be), but he does not even give any indication of the traits of character they exemplify. His picture of More is solemn, worshipful, and idyllic. He tells us of the days when the Lord Chancellor and his King were on so friendly terms that 'after dinner in a faire garden' they would walk together with the King 'holding his arme about his neck.' There is a pleasant scene of More hauling the King up on the leads by night, 'there to consider with him the diversities, course, motions, and operations of the Stars and Planetts.'

More's evil days came upon him, and from the Tower he wrote his daughter letters telling how he answered the Secretary, 'I do nobody no harm, I say none harm, I think none harm, but wish everybody good; and if this be not enough to keep a man alive, in good faith I long not to live.' Roper handles this part of the narrative with skill. There is a tragic farewell between Megge and her father when he is condemned, and another between him and his more practical spouse. Lady More has come to the Tower to urge that he be not obstinate, but yield to the King. More asks, characteristically, 'Is not this house as nigh heaven as mine own?' She feels impatient at this high-flown question and replies:

> 'Tille valle, Tille valle.'
> 'Howe say you, Mistress Alice, is it not soe?'
> 'Bone Deus, bone Deus, man, will this geere never be left?'

More was unaltered by this brusquerie, or, as Roper says, 'So her persuasions moved him but a little.'

In spite of the merits of such bits, the book as a whole is disappointing, and intellectually it is especially faulty because it throws no light at all on all the more lofty and significant aspects of More's character, and leaves untouched the strange paradox of his career. We find in Roper's book nothing of the splendid dawn of the Renaissance, with the new pulsations of vitality in art and architecture, and the luminous beacon of the humanities. He gives us nothing of the communion with Erasmus, and the high, disappointed hopes to which Erasmus had dedicated *The Praise of Folly*. The gentle and wise and brave-minded iconoclast of the *Utopia* is unknown to him.

On the other hand Roper does try to glorify More in the respects he does understand. He makes him out more independent as Speaker than he really was. A great many of his activities as Chancellor are untouched. How, we wonder, did More reconcile his speculative idealism in political theory with doing the dirty work of Henry VIII's diplomacy; how did the enlightened tolerance which pleaded complete religious freedom in his *Utopia* issue in the black religious cruelty that led Foxe to call him a 'bitter persecutor of good men'? Roper does not begin to answer these queries; he remains silent.

Dark Reflective Glass

If Roper fails because he is over-reverential and undercomprehending, the same reasons cannot be given for the pallid characterization of Philip Sidney in the *Life* by his friend, Fulke Greville. That strange, dark, and saddened poet and philosopher was simply not trying to write biography. It is true that he 'observed, honoured, and loved' his friend much, and that he intended in his book to 'stir up my drooping memory touching this mans worth, powers, wayes, and designes: to the end that in the tribute I owe him, our nation may see a Sea-mark, rais'd upon their native coast, above the levell of any private Pharos abroad: and so by a right Meridian line of their own, learn to sayl through the straits of true vertue, into a calm, and spacious Ocean of humane honour.' These are the words of panegyric, and where Greville remembers Sidney, he adheres to them. But mostly he is off on another enterprise, which is likewise stated in his title. After the words '*The Life of the Renowned Sir Philip Sidney*' come these:

'With The True Interest of *England* as it then stood in relation to all Forrain Princes: And particularly for suppressing the power of *Spain* Stated by Him.' And the copious page goes on to promise an account of the governmental maxims of Queen Elizabeth as well. This book, then, is a sort of combination of biography (a very little) with statecraft, in which Greville uses the prestige of his dead and reverenced friend to enforce the principles and policies he lays down. There is an introductory chapter about Sidney's boyhood, education, travels, and poetry (interrupted by 'reflections on fainéant kings'), and two chapters of testimonials to his merits, followed by an account of his embassy to the Emperor Rudolph—but then comes a disquisition on European relationships under the *form* of Sidney's arguments against Elizabeth marrying the Duke of Anjou. Another two chapters of narrative are followed by a survey of the whole state of continental politics, in which Greville tries to remind the reader at intervals that it is Sidney who is supposed to be speaking by parentheses like 'said Sir *Philip*' and 'saith he.' By the middle of the book Greville has told of Sidney's wound at Zutphen, his lingering illness, and death;

and from then on talks frankly of such topics as Queen Elizabeth, her governmental practices, how he himself came to write poetry, and the 'Object, arguments, and style' of his tragedies.

Although there is little of either Sidney's actions or his character in this odd treatise, it is not without interest, even to the passing reader, if he have a feeling for the mysterious harmonies and associations of words. Strange vibrations tremble in Greville's rhythms, and in his long and almost wandering periods images pass and repass, seen, darkly, as in a glass (to use one of his own favorite similes), sometimes illumined and sometimes obscured by the writer's intricate or melancholy wit. 'But many times it pleaseth God,' he says, 'by the breaking out of concealed flashes from these fatall cloudes of craft, or violence, to awake even the most superstitious Princes out of their enchanted dreams'; and Satan he calls 'the dark Prince, that sole author of dis-creation, and disorder, who ever ruines his ends with over-building.' He speaks of 'hypocriticall sacrifices upon the Altar of death, as peace-offerings from pride to the temple of fear, or smoaks of a dying diseased conscience choked up with innocent blood.' The tyrannical encroachments of conquerors 'carry the images of Hell, and her thunder-workers, in their own breasts, as fortune doth misfortune in that wind-blown, vast, and various womb of hers.' From true poetry one who passes 'through any straights, or latitudes, of good, or ill fortune' may 'see how to set a good countenance upon all the discountenances of adversitie, and a stay upon the exorbitant smilings of chance.' Crowding upon each other, one ingenuity suggesting another, wandering through the 'careless-ordered garden' of his fantastic mind, the images elaborate themselves; an occasional sardonic humor appears and glimmers gone again; puns and contrasts of sense and sound echo and fade. It is not mere verbal juggling, because running through it although uncontrolled there is a deeply pensive spirit. That spirit leaves behind it a richness haunting and profound.

Pure Crystal Water

A real biographer, in his own curious way, was John Aubrey: an indefatigable collector of curious fragments and details of people's lives, which he was always intending to reduce to order and never got around to doing. And yet Aubrey's disjecta membra contain the very flesh and blood of the matter, and often enough the spirit too. His notes on his own life are not the least curious and fascinating of his data. Born a country gentleman, in the county of Wiltshire, he spent his youth, he tells us, in 'an eremiticall solitude' and was sent to his 'beloved Oxon' for his education. 'But now Bellona thundered' in the Civil Wars, and his father sent for him home. Presently, however, he returned again to the felicitous scene ('ingeniose youth, as Rosebudds, imbibe the morning dew,' he says) but soon misfortune darkened. His father died, leaving him debts and lawsuits, and, always a muddler and luckless besides, he saw his estates melt away. His love-affairs went badly too; by 1666, he notes, 'all my businesses and affairs ran kim kam'; and at last even his birthplace, with its 'jedeau,' its grotto, and its 'volant Mecury', was sold. He had lost everything.

But there were two alleviations. His pride had been pleased by his election as a Fellow of the Royal Society in 1662, and he had friends in town and country who delighted in his conversation and who were charmed to offer him food and shelter. Chatting with Sir Christopher Wren in London, drinking with Edmund Wylde in Shropshire, gleaning strange observations for the Royal Society, he found himself serene: 'I had never quiett, nor anything of happiness,' he wrote, 'till divested of all.'

The range of his enquiries was striking. 'He was learned,' Lytton Strachey remarks, 'in natural history, geology, Gothic architecture, mineralogy, painting, heraldry; . . . he was a profound astrologer, and a learned geometrician.' Cookery also had no mysteries for him, and his labors included 'a collection of approved receipts.' So he passed busily a happy enough life. Only one thing disturbed him: he 'wished monastrys had not been putt downe, that the reformers would have been more moderate as to that point.' There should be 'provisions for contemplative men'; and he imagines 'What pleasure 'twould have been to travel from monastery to monastery.'

Among his other activities he collected biographical data for his friend Mr Anthony Wood, who was compiling materials for short biographies of the graduates of Oxford. Everything that came to him was fish to his net. Personal descriptions, physical oddities, traditional stories, scandalous anecdotes, all were taken down in short and sometimes formless notes. Little by little a pride of authorship became involved. At last he sent Wood a huge manuscript. Wood rudely tore out a chunk of it, and returned the undesired remainder to its author. Aubrey was hurt, gently hurt; it seemed impossible for him to be angry; he wrote a pathetic note complaining that he had been ill 'of a surfeit of peaches,' but that Wood's 'unkindness and choleric humour was a great addition' to his illness. 'I thought you so deare a friend that I might have entrusted my life in your hands, and now your unkindnes doth almost break my heart . . .'

Some excuse there was for Wood's omissions, but not for the barbarous manner of making them. Three-quarters of Aubrey's work 'is an accumulation of fragmentary sentences and old dry broken facts'; he often wrote after drinking debauches with Edmund Wylde, and many of his notes are only 'marks made to remind himself to remember better.' For example, entries like this:

> James Harrington, Esq., borne the first Fryday in January, 1611, neer Northampton; the son of Sir Sapcote Harrington, of ———, in the countie of ———, by ———, daughter of Sir ——— Samuel, was borne at Upton (Sir ——— Samuel's house in Northamptonshire) anno ———.

In still other cases Aubrey's zeal had gone beyond wisdom; he had included scurrilous and libellous matter that might indeed, as Wood had once told him, be 'things that would cutt' his throat. For Aubrey, honest fellow that he was, held back nothing, concealed nothing; and in his simplicity everything that he heard from a friend he believed. 'I here laye downe to you,' he wrote to Wood, '(out of the conjunct friendship between us) the trueth, and, as neer as I can and that religiously as a poenitent to his confessor, nothing but the trueth: the naked and plaine trueth, which is here exposed so bare that the very *pudenda* are not covered, and affords many passages that would raise a blush in a young virgin's cheeke.'

These qualities, which frightened Wood, are the very essence of Aubrey's merits as a biographer. Aubrey's honest simplicity was so great that everything in him is purified to the impersonality of art. He gave no lewd snickers to a scandalous story about one of his subjects; he listened, and wrote it down in such a way as to reveal clearly that it was told just for what light it threw upon his subject. 'Ben Johnson had one eie lower than t'other, and bigger, like Clun the player; perhaps he begott Clun.' The importance of this, as Mr John Collier points out, is not whether Jonson actually did or not, but that it is at once clear he was capable of it. Some of Aubrey's tales may thus be those inspired fictions in which a man's true character is caught by his contemporaries with a perfection that no moment of actuality has attained. E. F. Benson points out the same quality in a story about the Oxford don, Oscar Browning, returning from London, where he had met the Emperor Wilhelm III, and saying he was 'quite one of the nicest emperors I ever met.' Aubrey's mind was in fact, as he says of it, 'very cleer; phansie like a mirrour, pure chrystal water': it reflected without distorting, even in the medium of fiction.

Further than that, he had a kind of artistry that managed to catch out of a long life 'just the two or three episodes which show us all the man.' What a vivid flash we get of Richard Corbet, Bishop of Oxford, for example, in the scene where, confirming some country people, being about to lay his hands on the head of a very bald man, 'he turns to his chaplaine Lushington, and sayd, Some Dust, Lushington, (to keepe his hand from slipping). There was a man with a greate venerable Beard: sayd the Bishop, You, behind the beard.'

In his descriptions of people and their traits, he gives us just those details of person or idiosyncrasy that illumine their characters. It is striking to be told that Francis Bacon would often drink some strong beer before going to bed, to quiet a too active mind that would otherwise keep him awake; and that he had 'a delicate, lively, hazel eie,' 'like the eie of a viper.' Milton, Aubrey says, 'pronounced the letter R *(littera canina)* very hard,' and adds, a 'certaine signe of a satyricall Witt.' Sir Walter Raleigh had 'an exceeding high Forehead, long-faced and sour eie-lidded, a kind of pigge-eie,' and 'spake broad Devonshire.' Once he took a 'perpetuall Talker' and sealed up his mouth, '*i. e.* his upper and neather beard,' with sealing wax. In a racier passage we are told of his 'getting up one of the Mayds of Honour against a tree . . . who seemed at first boarding to be something fearfull.' She began crying 'Sweet Sir Walter, what doe you me ask? Will you undoe me? Nay, sweet Sir Walter! Sweet Sir Walter! Sir Walter! At last, as the danger and the pleasure at the same time grew higher, she cryed in the extacy, Swisser Swatter! Swisser Swatter!'

Even more interesting than these are some of the episodes in the brief careers he gives of certain of the characters. There is Dr William Butler, the great physician, who cured a man of an overdose of opium by placing his body into the warm belly of a just-slaughtered cow, and who responded to the low bows of a courtly Frenchman by whipping his leg over the man's politely bowed head and going away. Dr Butler used to get drunk at the tavern and be called for by a servant named Nell, to take him home. She called him a drunken beast, and then stumbled herself, whereupon he called her a drunken beast; 'and so they did drunken beast one another all the way till they came home.'

The accumulation of Aubrey's biographical data is collected together mostly in his *Brief Lives*. Formless as they are in total, they are works of art. The choice of material, the honest love of reality, the limpid style, all combine to make them at their best little masterpieces: or at the least, the stuff out of which masterpieces might come. Aubrey has the eye for detail, the love of a good story, the flair for character, and the unfalsifying selflessness of the genuine enthusiast for the lives of men. I cannot go so far as Mr Strachey, who says: 'A biography should either be as long as Boswell's or as short as Aubrey's. The method of enormous and elaborate accretion which produced the *Life of Johnson* is excellent, no doubt; but, failing that, let us have no half-measures; let us have the pure essentials–a vivid image, on a page or two, without explanations, transitions, commentaries, or padding.' The vivid image Aubrey does have, and the golden ore of biography, and his own artless art. He reveals what can be done with brevity and selection. To Aubrey's gifts we need only add the sense of form, of development, and of story.

Cloistral Images

These three things, on the other hand, Izaak Walton had, and, although he was no painstaking grubber into the minutiae of a man's life, honesty of intention and accuracy to fact as well. And yet, in a very grave way, Walton was inaccurate in essence, for his own nature inclined him to a devoutly reflective existence and a serenity in which he falsely bathes all his subjects. 'There is no doubt,' says Professor Saintsbury, 'about the strange flood of light which the book pours on the more contemplative side of English life in the seventeenth century.' But who were the subjects of Walton's *Lives?* A tormented and ambitious sensualist, a worldly diplomat, the learned author of *The Laws of Ecclesiastical Polity*, a courtly aristocrat who became a rural saint, and a celebrated casuist. Now all these people had their contemplative side, of course, and they were all sincerely devout, but the point is that they were not all alike. Nevertheless, save for occasional hints or insinuations, Walton subdues them to a curiously marmoreal sameness: despite the varying incidents of their lives, and despite the occasional hidden humor of the narration, they are like memorial images posed in the stillness of a chapel or set in the greenery of a college cloister.

Even from their youth Walton begins molding them to his inclination. As a student Donne 'gave great testimonies of his Wit, his Learning, and of his Improvement'; Wotton, during his childhood paid his mother for her pains 'with such visible signs of future perfection in Learning, as turned her imployment into a pleasing-trouble'; Hooker as a young scholar was notable for 'a remarkable Modesty, and a sweet serene quietness of Nature, and with them a quick apprehension' that made his elders believe him 'to have an inward blessed Divine Light'; '*George Herbert* spent much of his Childhood in a sweet content'; and Robert Sanderson began 'a meek and innocent life' by dedicating himself from youth to 'Piety and Vertue.' Such uniformity of zeal as an outstanding trait seems hardly in nature; and throughout the lives the unobtrusive but decided hand of Walton is ever shaping, clipping, and smoothing.

Naturally such interference requires considerable art. Walton has art, and delightfully. He consciously composed biography; he arranged his material with beautiful literary construction; his style is serene and translucent; he can flash scenes and episodes before you with a bright vividness; for all his assumed simplicity, he is urbane and subtle, with a touch here and there of exquisite faint raillery. Beyond these things, his writing has the quality of intimacy, the flavor of being really and deeply at home with his subjects when he knew them personally; and in the one case where he did not, that of Richard Hooker, it has been noted that 'he is clearly ill at ease' through being unable to convey a sense of familiarity. Biographers have presented their subjects more fully and accurately; few have given the impression of being more affectionately at one with them.

And still, as I have implied, this is sometimes more atmosphere than truth. Nowhere in the *Life of Donne* do we find an open dealing with the sensual, passionate, and disillusioned soul of that tortured man. The ambitions—and vices—of his youth are passed over with hardly a hint, the struggles to discipline himself to resignation in missing worldly power are presented only as humble doubts of his fitness for the priesthood, his alternations of rejoicing in his salvation and feeling the blackest despair are portrayed as the signs of a saintly piety. That Donne had piety I do not mean to deny, only that Walton reveals him with anything like completeness or due perspective. Where is the rebellious victim of passion who describes love as 'the tyran Pike, our hearts the Frye,' and who furiously uncovers in his own heart

> *The spider love, which transubstantiates all,*
> *And can convert Manna to gall——*

who alternates between shouting to his mistress 'For Godsake hold your tongue, and let me love' and trying to believe that whereas

> *Dull sublunary lovers love*
> *(Whose soule is sense) cannot admit*
> *Absence*

his passion is 'Like gold to ayery thinnesse beate'? All that Walton says about this aspect of Donne is, astonishingly, that it was 'as if nature and all her varieties had been made only to exercise his sharp wit and high fancy'; and that in these 'facetiously Composed' writings 'it may appear by his choice Metaphors, that both *Nature* and all the *Arts* joined.' This is strangely tempered comment on the author of *Loves Infinitenesse*, *The Canonization*, *The Will*, and *The Extasy*.

Nor does his presentation of the religious poet seem to me much better. Professor Saintsbury finds 'a curious kind of awe' therein; and some awe I suppose there is, but not of a kind to suggest the poetry, nor are the quotations the best for the purpose. His declining age, Walton says, was 'witnessed then by many Divine Sonnets, and other high, holy, and harmonious Composures.' And he quotes the *Hymn to God the Father*, beginning 'Wilt thou forgive that sin where I begun.' How much more of Donne there is in 'Batter my heart, three person'd God,' and the sonnet to Death, with its marvellous listing:

> *Thou art slave to Fate, Chance, kings, and desperate men,*
> *And dost with poyson, warre, and sicknesse dwell,*

and the magnificent opening of another:

> *At the round earths imagin'd corners, blow*
> *Your trumpets, Angells, and arise, arise*
> *From death, you numberlesse infinities*
> *Of soules, and to your scattered bodies goe.*

Almost the only thing in Walton's depiction of Donne, in fact, that would enable us to penetrate into the tangled heart of the man, if we were unacquainted with his poems and sermons, is the occasional quotation of a letter. The mourning lamentation, for example, of the following:

> 'tis now Spring, and all the pleasures of it displease me; every other tree blossoms, and I wither: I grow older and not better; my strength diminisheth and my load grows heavier; and yet I would fain be or do something; but, that I cannot tell what is no wonder in this time of my sadness; for, to chuse is to do; but to be no part of any body, is as to be nothing; and so I am, and shall so judge myself . . . my fortune hath made me such, as that I am rather a Sickness or a Disease of the world than any part of it . . . Sir, I profess to you truly, that my lothness to give over writing now seems to myself a sign that I should write no more——
>
> Your poor friend, *and*
> Gods poor patient
> JOHN DONNE

The man who felt himself 'a Sickness or a Disease' of the world has in him more of the saddened spirit of John Donne than the 'angel from a cloud' whom Walton elsewhere emphasizes.

Sir Henry Wotton spent nearly all his years as a diplomat, having been Ambassador to Venice and to several of the German Princes, and Envoy Extraordinary to the Holy Roman Emperor Ferdinand, and closed his career as the Provost of Eton. He seems thus to have united in his character the nature of man of action and that which Walton sympathized with so much more, man of reflection.

'Sir *Henry* who had for many years (like *Sisyphus*)' says Walton, 'rolled the restless stone of a State-imployment; knowing experimentally, that the great blessing of sweet content was not to be found in multitudes of men or business' pleaded with King James, and, in true diplomatic style, made use besides of 'a piece of honest policy'—'which,' Walton remarks in parenthesis, 'I have not time to relate'—and obtained the grant that placed him in his last haven.

Although it is this part of Wotton's life that his biographer has most sympathy for and devotes most space to, the earlier part of his story is not without liveliness and characterization. From his youth he showed the true diplomat's quality. After hearing of the arrest of Essex, for example, he did 'very quickly, and as privately glide through *Kent* to *Dover*, without so much as looking toward his native and beloved *Bocton*' until, sixteen hours later, he landed in France and heard subsequently that his patron was beheaded and his friend Henry Cuffe hanged. We are told that he endeared himself to the Venetians 'by a fine sorting of fit Presents, curious and not costly Entertainments, always sweetned by various and pleasant Discourse.' There is both tact and wit in his aphorism for serviceable negotiations: The envoy 'should always, & upon all occasions, speak the *truth* (it seems a *State-Paradox)* for, says *Sir Henry Wotton, you shall never be believed;* and by this means, your truth will secure your self, if you shall ever be called to any account; and 'twill also put your Adversaries (who will still hunt counter) to a loss in all their disquisitions and undertakings.'

One could wish that Walton had given more examples of Wotton's facetious wit, which sometimes displays a kind of oddity. The stone over his grave he directed to be inscribed in Latin:

Here lies the first Author of this Sentence

THE ITCH OF DISPUTATION WILL PROVE THE SCAB OF THE CHURCH

Inquire his name elsewhere

And even more odd is that unfortunate slip that infuriated King James, of his writing in a gentleman's album, in Germany, the sentiment that 'An Embassador is an honest man, sent to *lie* abroad for the good of his Country.'

For that matter, when once examined, there appears a certain oddity in all Walton's characters. There is the gloomy oddity of

Donne posing upon his urn in a winding-sheet, with his eyes shut, and his hands placed as dead bodies are usually fitted, while a painter thus depicted him in a portrait that he kept by his bedside. There is the quaintness of Dr Sanderson's very notable good memory yet never working for the recollection of his own sermons, because 'he had such an innate, invincible fear and bashfulness,' so that he always had to read them and disastrously failed on the one occasion he was persuaded not to. Perhaps strangest of all is the unworldliness of Hooker, who, allowing his landlady at an inn to persuade him that what he needed was a wife to take care of him, empowered her to choose one for him, and was surprised but not rebellious when she chose her own daughter. This young woman, Walton tells us, 'brought him neither Beauty nor Portion,' her conditions indeed being 'too like that Wife's which is by *Solomon* compar'd to a *dripping house*.'

These oddities lead us to another aspect of Walton's writing: what has been termed his 'peculiar suppressed humour.' For Walton was sly, and it is often by no means certain that he is not making fun of his characters, and sometimes quite sure that he is laughing at himself. When he tells us that Mr Danvers had so great an affection for George Herbert that 'he publickly declar'd a desire that Mr *Herbert* would marry any of his Nine Daughters' we are on the scent; but we get his full flavor in the statement that one of the daughters, Jane, 'became so much a Platonick, as to fall in love with Mr *Herbert* unseen.' At their first meeting Love 'entered into both their hearts, as a Conqueror enters into a surprized City' and 'made there such Laws and Resolutions as neither party was able to resist,' so that Jane 'chang'd her name into *Herbert*, the third day after this first interview.'

Quieter still in character is his comment on the struggle between the Pope and the Venetian state, in which the latter suspended the powers of the Inquisition; 'and the Flood-gates being thus set open,' scoffing and libels against the Pope became safely indulged in: and 'very pleasant to the people.' Of another episode in Wotton's life, when his uncle, the Dean of Canterbury, dreamed that he would be involved, if he were not prevented, in a project ruinous to the family, we are told that the good man besought Queen Mary to imprison his nephew for a while. This was done, and Wotton protected thus from losing his life in Sir Thomas Wyatt's conspiracy, which he would infallibly have done 'if his Uncle had not so happily dream'd him into a *Prison.*'

Nor is Walton more averse to playing with himself and his own actions. He knows that he has a tendency to be digressive, and is often begging the reader's pardon for taking so long, and promising that he 'shall presently lead him back' to the subject. In the *Life of Dr Sanderson* this becomes a sort of game; he brings the reader to Dr Sanderson at Boothby Pannel, deserts him there for several digressions, comes back again, and goes away, telling us 'I cannot lead my Reader to *Dr Hammond* and *Dr Sanderson* where we left them at *Boothby Pannel* till' he has made an historical digression, and only then, at last, decides to 'return to *Boothby Pannel,* where we left *Dr Hammond* and *Dr Sanderson* together, but neither can be found there'! For while Izaak has been talking the one has gone to London and the other been seized and committed to prison by the Roundheads. In the *Life of Herbert* we find another example of his slyness of phrase when he tells how the Rector of St Andrews, a man of 'unruly wit' and 'furious Zeal,' was so insolent to the King that he was committed to the Tower, 'where he remained very angry for three years.'

In some ways the *Life of Herbert* is one of the most skilfully handled of the five. We receive intimations of the yearning for worldly glitter that enticed the poet for some time: 'the love of a Court-conversation,' his favor with the King and being granted the very '*Sine Cure*' that Queen Elizabeth had given Sir Philip Sidney, his wit, as he himself described it, 'like a Pen-knife in too narrow a sheath, too sharp for his body.' Here, faint perhaps, but recognizable, are the outlines of the ardent temperament that exclaimed:

I smote the board, and cried No more;
I will abroad!
What! shall I ever sigh and pine?

* * * * *

Is the year only lost to me?
Have I no bays to crown it,
No flowers, no garlands gay? all blasted,
All wasted?
Not so, my heart; but there is fruit
And thou hast hands.

But equally strong in Herbert from the first was the holy vocation that 'heard one calling Child'; and replied 'My Lord.' After the death of King James he retired to Kent, and 'had many Conflicts with himself, Whether he should return to the painted pleasures of a Court-life, or betake himself to a study of Divinity.' Presently he beheld the Court 'with an impartial Eye,' and saw that it was 'made up of *Fraud*, and *Titles*, and *Flattery*, and many other such empty, imaginary Pleasures,' and became installed in the parsonage of Bemerton, where he lived such 'an almost incredible story, of great sanctity' as Walton hardly knows how to prepare the reader to receive. The short remainder of his life was one of devotion, piety, and deeds of gentleness and kindness that he found 'Musick to him at Midnight.'

This life, indeed, shows Walton's character as a biographer. What he knows he does not conceal, but he does manipulate it. He is a panegyrist at bottom after all, and the personality that emerges from his handling represents a will to show his friends and admired subjects in a favorable light. That light, for him, was a tone of calm and meditative goodness. He will not lie: 'Honest Izaak,' his friend the Bishop of Chichester addresses him, and the epithet is justified. He will only arrange, so that if we know what to look for, in many cases there is more to be found than meets the casual eye. In this sense, none of the lives is more revealing than the life of John Donne.

The three qualities most emphatic in Donne's character were his ambitions, his sensual passions, and the fierce vacillations of his religious feelings. If we peruse Walton's account looking for these things they will stand out on almost every page. And something else will stand out too: the strange way in which, while recognizing his talents, everyone steadily refused him political dignities. Donne's first studies were in law, and during the several years of his foreign travels 'he made many useful observations' of the 'lawes and manner of Government' of the realms he visited. On his return he became a part of the household of the Lord Chancellor, who designed him 'to some more weighty Employment in the State.' How fortunate that, having been educated a Roman Catholic, he had some years before changed his religion! Truth, says Walton, 'hath too much light about her to be hid from so sharp an Inquirer; and he had too much ingenuity not to acknowledge he had found her.' So what would have been the insuperable obstacle of his religion no longer stood in the way. Besides this, he 'had a strange kind of elegant irresistible art' in his manner.

Why, with these advantages, wit, learning, personality, was his marriage to the daughter of Sir George More so 'immeasurably unwelcome' to that gentleman that he was in transports of anger? Walton supplies only hints, which we must cull here and there from the whole story. In Donne's taking orders, we are told, the English Church had 'gain'd a second *St Austine*' and a St Ambrose as well, for 'if his youth had the infirmities of the one, his age had the excellencies of the other.' In his later years Donne was wont to lament the excesses of his life. When we recall many of his poems, and take Walton's remark that his 'youth, and travels and needless bounty, had brought his estate into a narrow compass,' we may guess the reasons in 'dear-bought Experience' for his being strongly distrusted.

Those who might advance his career proved equally chary. Lord Ellesmere did nothing for him; King James, who 'had also given some hopes of a State-imployment,' remained apathetic; many who 'were powerful at Court,' and 'watchful and solicitous for him,' still did him no good. Dr Morton, the Bishop of Durham, tried to solicit him into the Church, beginning significantly, 'I know your expectation' of a political career, 'and I know too, the many delays and contingencies that attend Court-promises.' Could Dr Morton have received any hint that these hopes were destined to be fruitless? This can only be conjecture, but if we entertain it for a moment how significant the narrative at this point: 'Mr *Donne's* faint breath and perplext countenance gave a visible testimony of an inward conflict.' John Donne had a subtle and intricate mind. He too may have guessed in this solicitation more than met the ear. His refusal was couched in the proper terms of reverence; he was not too good for the priesthood in his own estimation, but feared that 'some irregularities' in his life 'visible to some men' might cast the sacred calling into dishonor. He still waited, hoping for preferment from the King. But at last the time came when 'the King gave a positive denial to all requests.' The political channel was closed.

His abilities were recognized, but some lack must have been felt in him—of sobriety or steadiness?—that the toils of ordination might supply. James 'descended to a persuasion, almost to a solicitation,' and 'at last forced him to a compliance.' Once the step was taken it must needs be good. The life of power became for Donne 'this wilderness of the many temptations, and various turnings of a dangerous life.' He had 'required a temporal, God gave him a spiritual blessing.' 'Be it with thy servant as seemeth best in thy sight.' 'Lord, who am I, that thou art so mindful of me?'

The step had been taken, and it must needs be good. He became a 'Preacher in earnest' 'like an Angel from a cloud, but in none,' and still his friends that had often witnessed his 'free and facetious discourse' could ask him, 'Why are you sad?' He might deny it, but at other times he would grant 'that he long'd for the day of his dissolution.' His sermons were full of the vision of sin and death. Sometimes he saw plainly that it was God's 'hand that prevented me from all temporal employment; and that it was his Will I should never settle nor thrive till I entred into the Ministry; in which, I have now liv'd almost twenty years (I hope to his glory)'; and then again he groaned, 'I were miserable if I might not dye.'

So much we may guess out of Walton's account. The proud and bitter man lusted after the fleshpots all his life, but it could not be borne that he had failed of everything his ambition demanded. God had favored him by denying what he wanted; indeed he had been blest, and he was a sinner to go on being recalcitrant in his heart; no, he would *not* be stubborn. But his years were embittered to the end. Is this the truth about Donne? We cannot tell, but it fits in better with the intricate poems and the terrible and magnificent sermons than the placid contours in Walton of which the quotations I have made are only buried fragments.

So we return to the thesis with which we opened. Walton, musing by his pensive stream, transmutes everything into an autumn calm. Beneath the brown waters we may perceive flittingly a kind of streak now and then that enables us to guess at deeper and fiercer eddies than ever reach the unflurried surface, but we must be quick. Now it is gone, and we are on our way to rejoin Dr Sanderson at Boothby Pannel or being carried to Heaven in holy raptures while Dr Donne leans over the pulpit at St Paul's. It is only a strain of a certain kind of truth that permeates here, nothing fierce or passionate, not even too deep love, for love 'is a flattering mischief, that hath denied aged and wise men a foresight of those evils that too often prove to be the children of that blind father, a passion! that

carries us to commit *Errors* with as much ease as whirlwinds remove feathers.' Walton prefers that our souls and bodies should be purely, as he says of Donne's, 'a *Temple of the Holy Ghost*,' which, he adds, 'is now become a small quantity of *Christian dust:*
'But I shall see it reanimated.'

Without Lilies and Roses

Commemoration was also the motive of Roger North's *Lives* of his three brothers, Francis Baron Guilford, Sir Dudley North, and Dr John North, but the writer's vivacity, his natural honesty, and his curious inquiringness combine to frame a much greater achievement than pious laudation. Roger North had, in fact, what we may call the biographical instinct, and even when reason and sense of duty unite to lead him astray, his natural soundness sets him right. Strictly speaking, he is not a seventeenth century writer, most of his work having been done in the earlier part of the next century, but the three brothers he chronicles were all dead by the last decade of the seventeenth, so we shall consider him of the period he deals with.

North's *Lives* were commemorative, and they were written with an affection that often shows itself, whether he be writing with pride of 'His Lordship'—'their best brother,' as he often lovingly designates the Lord Keeper—or 'the Merchant,' that gay and slightly unscrupulous Turkey trader, or 'the Doctor,' the timorous young scholar whom North every now and then apologizes to the reader for so dignifying before he had actually been honored with the degree. But even so his zest for truth will not permit him to falsify the case; 'a Life,' he says, 'should be a Picture; which cannot be good, if the peculiar Features, whereby the subject is distinguish'd from all others, are left out. Nay, Scars and Blemishes, as well as Beauties, ought to be expressed; otherwise it is but an outline fill'd up with Lillies and Roses.'

Nor are these only mouth-protests. Summarizing the career of his brother Dudley in Turkey, he says, 'I must allow that, as to all the Mercantile Arts, and Stratagems of Trade, which could be used, to get Money from those he dealt with, I believe he was no Niggard; but as for Falsities, such as cheating by Weights or Measures . . . even with *Jews* or *Turks*, he was as clear as any Man living . . .

But as to Women, while he was in *Turky* (barring the Excess) I mean such Looses and Escapes, as almost all Men, there, are more or less guilty of, I cannot altogether wipe him clean.' And he has given evidence to support these conclusions.

In the life of the Lord Keeper, and, to a higher degree, in the *Examen*, an important Tory political document with which we shall not be concerned, North encountered the difficulty of separating historical writing from biography. As one of the great jurists of the day, Francis North was intimately involved in political events. Roger North was fully aware of the boundaries and difficulties. 'If the History of a Life,' he observes, 'hangs altogether upon great Importance, such as concern the Church and State, and drops the peculiar Oeconomy, and private Conduct of the Person that gives Title to the Work, it may be a History, and a very good one: but of any Thing rather than of that Person's Life.' North understood the problem, and mostly he solves it well. Only sometimes his sense of historical obligation overwhelms his skill as a narrator, and produces longueurs, such as the too protracted account of the Turkish *Avanias* (unjust demands made upon merchants) and the long examination of some of the legal decisions of the Lord Chief Justice Hales, which could be of interest only to a lawyer or historian. But even in such passages the author's sprightliness leaps out occasionally, as when he describes one of the decisions as being 'upon a metaphysical Notion, hard to the Party that lost it,' and admits 'this Matter is somewhat dark to me.'

Such strokes of nature are always appearing, even in the midst of passages dictated by his sense of duty, but although North apologizes for the character-drawing and the historically trivial but picturesque detail, he knows well that it is good. 'I fancy myself a Picture-Drawer,' he tells the reader, and goes on to point out that the leaves and branches of a tree, for example, are much harder to describe than the solid trunk, but if they were left out 'it would make but a sorry Picture of a Tree.' So, life-writing is 'the Pourtrait, or Lineament, and not a bare Index or Catalogue of Things done; and without the How and Why, all History is jejune and unprofitable.' In such details, almost as brilliant and characteristic as Aubrey's, combined with a feeling for narrative sequence only less than Walton's (his digressions are not so skilfully arranged, and sometimes obscure the clarity of outline), his peculiar ability lies.

The least extraordinary of the narratives is the comparatively placid one of the highly respectable lawyer Francis North. Leading a 'Spider-kind of Life' in his chambers, the young man worked assiduously, studying hypothetical problems when he was not working on real ones ('No Man could be a good Lawyer, that was not a Put-Case,' he used to say). By the combination of industry and the recommendations of his friends, he went 'loping into Preferments' until his practice 'flowed in upon him like an Orage.'

Although he had strong passions, he had schooled himself so that he was hardly ever observed to speak or act except under perfect control, and the worst libel his enemies in later years were able to invent of him was that he had frivolously climbed up upon the back of an enormous rhinoceros, 'than which a more infantine Exploit could not have been fasten'd upon him.' At this 'impudent buffoon Lye,' (to which the biographer recurs indignantly several times in the course of his narrative) 'His Lordship was much roiled'; his brothers had never seen him in such a rage; and as for those who came to inquire if the scandalous tale was true, 'he sent them away with Fleas in their Ears.'

Lord Guilford was a virtuoso, too, 'one of the neatest Violists of his Time,' and even did some theorizing about the mathematical relations involved in the vibrations of musical notes. He liked nothing so well as to foregather with a few friends for 'a petit Supper, but ample Feast of Discourse.' Sometimes these gatherings were at the house of Mr Weld, 'a rich Philosopher' of Bloomsbury, whose dwelling was a 'Sort of Knick-knack-atory,' and sometimes with Mr Longueville, whose 'fluent, witty, literate, copious, and instructive' discourse led those who 'did not understand him' to think 'he talked too much.'

So passed his life, worried somewhat, it is true, by the machinations of the court and by sad prognostications about what would happen to the realm and to the crown if the prerogative were not upheld. And then there was King James: 'So strong were his Prejudices, and so feeble his Genius': what was a conscientious Lord Keeper to do? His last illness came on; with 'Axes and Hammers and Fireworks in his Head' he nevertheless insisted on making out a long memorial to the King, dealing with all these evils. So he died. All his public acts had been 'without any affected Lustre, or Handles to Fame.' 'No wonder he is so soon forgot.'

Sir Dudley North, the Turkey merchant, showed an early disposition to the trade for which he was destined, and even at school 'drove a subtle Trade among the Boys, by buying and selling.' In other ways, too, he revealed the trader's spirit: he was wont to bet on cock-fights, borrowing to pay his losses. 'But he had some dormant Sparks of Honour that galled him cruelly,' so he made out for his parents 'counterfeit Bills of Expences . . . only enlarging a little, and inserting some choice Items.'

These experiences stood him in good stead in his later dealings in the East, where he learned that in lawsuits 'a false Witness was a surer Card than a true one,' for an honest witness can easily be confused by 'captious Questions,' whereas the cheat, prepared for such handling, 'can clear himself, when the other will be confounded.' He also dealt there in jewels and loans, 'ordinarily twenty or thirty *per cent.*', giving part of the loan not in cash but in goods, and thereby 'getting off his rotten Cloth and trumpery Goods, which were not otherwise vendible.' Aside from little harmless tricks like these, the merchant was quite honest.

He was a lively man, fond of jokes. We hear him making burlesque complaints on his first voyage of how the 'Motion of the Vessel raiseth a Tempest in my Guts,' so that when he lightens the ship he has 'enough to do to keep back Entrails, Heart and all'; and finding the White Sea most unfitly named, for it looks like nothing so much as 'dead Beer.' He was fond of food, 'particularly what was savoury, as Cavear, or Anchovies, sufficient to relish a Glass of Wine or two before he went to Bed,' and on such diet 'began to grow fat' and 'well-whiskered' till he looked jolly as a Turk.

Meanwhile he was not neglecting affairs. He had begun at Smyrna, but was then called into a partnership at Constantinople, where, so loosely had things been done, the partners 'found themselves in a Miz-Maze.' Mr North began setting things aright. But one of the partners 'had no Brains to understand what was done, and his Drink made him rude' to the Merchant, and 'more fastidious to him than all the Toil of the Whole Day.' 'This was a Wolf by the Ears, which the Merchant scarce knew how to hold, or to let go.' Finally he wrote the principals in England, explaining the case and separating himself from the enterprise, and most of its business remained with him. Year by year he waxed richer; in 1680 he began his voyage home.

In England he settled down, became the man of business for his family, played politics for a time, married and removed to the country, and there enjoyed a calm old age. From a friend he learned 'a little Algebra' and 'was extremely pleased with this new kind of Arithmetic, which he had never heard of before.' 'If Time lay on his Hands, he would assist his Lady in her Affairs,' and was once found 'very busy in picking out the Stitches of a dislaced Petticoat.' He was fond of carpentry and stone-hewing and working in iron, although he allowed his brother, being a lawyer, 'to be the best Forger.'

The Life of Dr John North, of which Lytton Strachey has given so lively a condensation in his *Portraits in Miniature*, is little more than a memoir, but it is packed full of lively and revealing details. He was a grave and docile youth, a trait that usually 'argues Imbecility of Body and Mind,' his brother remarks; but fortunately did not do so in his case. He soon became an accomplished scholar, doing readily all that his tutors laid upon him and more. If he had a fault, it was a certain timidity, so that even when he had gone to Cambridge he was 'afraid in the dark,' and 'when he was in Bed alone, he durst not trust his Countenance above the Cloaths.' Once his tutor, with whom he slept for a time, came home late, and 'indiscretely enough, pulled him by the Hair; whereupon the Scholar sunk down . . . and at last, with a great outcry . . . sprung up, expecting to see an enorm Spectre.'

This strange timidity extended to remarkable lengths. He had been presented with a living in Wales, a sinecure, and visiting it was received with great enthusiasm by his parishioners, who 'came about and hugged him, calling him their Pastor, and telling him they were his Sheep.' This was too much for the Doctor, who 'got him back to his College as fast as he could.' All his enormous studies led to no tangible works. He became Professor of Greek early in his career, and Master of Trinity at thirty-two, but all that he published was a small volume of commentary on Plato's *Dialogues*. His multitudinous notes were all to be burnt, and in a small notebook which he dreaded losing he had written 'I beshrew his Heart, that gathers my Opinionn from any Thing he finds wrote here.'

His appearance strangely belied this fearfulness of nature, 'for his Face was always tinct with a fresh Colour,' 'his Looks vegete and sanguine,' 'his Features were scandalous, as shewing rather a Madam *entravestie*, than a bookworm,' and he had 'a florid Head of flaxen Hair.' He liked 'to refresh himself with the Society of the young Noblemen,' and was often seen 'as merry as a Schoolboy with a Knot of them, like the Younglings about old Silenus.' 'But his Flesh was strangely flaccid and soft, his going weak and shuffling, often crossing his Legs, as if he were tipsey.'

This meticulous and eccentric being had an odd 'Entertainment in his House besides Books; and that was keeping of great House-Spiders in wide mouthed Glasses.' 'He supplied them with Crumbs of Bread' but 'their Regale was Flies, which he sometimes caught and put to them,' observing curiously how they avoided coming near 'a great Master Flesh Fly' ('for he had Claws sharp as Cats') but wound him first in a web. Indeed, some kinds of eccentricity run in this family, too, and the Lord Keeper so far shared his younger brother's timidity that he could not bear coming into a public place alone, and used to wait for others to enter 'behind whom . . . he might be shaded from the view of the Rest,' and would sometimes 'stand dodging at the Screen' thus for a considerable period, 'for it was Death to him to walk up alone in open View.' Sir Dudley, who had the habit of disciplining himself, used to enjoy clambering in high places, and once, in the tower of Bow Church, being unable to go between the columns and the wall because of his stoutness, 'took the Column in his Arm, and swung his Body about on the outside,' and so all around the colonnade. He and Roger used to go on visits to houses being erected, where they 'almost turned into Rope-Dancers, and walked' merely for enjoyment 'familiarly upon Joice in Garrets, having a View, through all the Floors, down to the Cellar.'

The Doctor, who would have shivered at such exposure, was also mightily afraid of 'Gravel and Rheumes.' But his real danger was being paralytic and epileptic. He caught a slight cold and, with his usual docility, obeyed all the orders of the physicians, physic 'enough to have purged a strong Man from off his Legs' and amber 'as Tobacco, in Pipes,' and astringent powders 'in Quills, blown into his Mouth.' This reduced him to 'extreme Weakness' at once, and he appeared 'helmeted in Caps upon Caps,' with a meagre countenance. He was fearful of stirring abroad after sunset, and distressed about his diet: 'Grapes, and Peaches, being full of Humidity, were Poison.'

Admonishing some students, very acrimoniously, during this illness 'down he dropt' in a fit; and the physicians, after reviving him, insisted 'that if he fell asleep, he would never wake more.' 'A Consort of Tongs, Firegrate, Wainscote Drum, and dancing of Curtains and Curtain Rings, such as would have made a sound Man mad' provided a 'perpetual Noise and Clangor.' His mother, the dowager Lady North, put a stop to this tintinnabulation, and nursed him in quiet. 'The Physicians were exceedingly surprised' that he recovered, but 'his Mouth and Face was drawn up on the lame Side, and his left Arm and Leg altogether enervous.' He lingered on, oddly changed in disposition (you must consult his brother to know how), but the doctors had been too much for him. He did not live long.

All these details are told in a racy, flowing language, highly copious and sometimes a little over-indulged. Our quotations hardly indicate to the full how often his choice of words is not only vigorous but almost inventively slangy. Telling of his Lordship being placed with a tutor as a small child, he describes the habit in the tutor's family of making all their scholars kneel to pray by their bedsides. 'But this petit Spark was too small for that Posture, and was set upon the Bed to kneel with his Face to the Pillow.' One of his masters in college, a very learned scholar, had been 'a famous Man indeed' 'if his Heart could have been shewed without a Microscope.' An uncle is characterized as kind to the boy 'Teeth outwards' and the later opponents of the successful lawyer are 'these Fourbs.'

Besides these, North had gifts of vivid description and caustic remark. A Mr Sydersin is portrayed as having a 'Hatchet Face and Shoulder of Mutton Hand, and he walked splay, stooping and noddling.' Commenting on the scheme to retire the Lord Keeper and advance Lord Jeffreys, he notes that no help could be expected for his brother from the court: 'The rising Sun hath a charming effect, but not upon Courtiers as upon Larks; for it makes these sing, and the other silent.' Throughout these troublous times his Lordship 'all along trod upon Eggs,' and there is hardly an extended passage that does not give some example of an individual richness unparalleled by anyone in his time.

He loves anecdotes. No considerations of dignity or piety seem to hold him back from telling amusing ones. His whole account, for example, of the rising lawyer's wooings, is irrepressible. First there was the daughter of an 'old Usurer of *Gray's Inn*,' but the father offered no marriage settlement, and his Lordship, 'glad of his Escape,' resolved 'never to come near the terrible old Fellow again.' Next there was the widow of a former friend, who held him 'at the long Saw above a Month' until he tired of being 'held in a Course of bo-peep Play with a crafty Widow,' and retired. (Roger, in the margin, comments with typical exuberance, 'Courted a Widow, and was little better than jilted.') The third prospect was a lady reputed to have £6,000, which shrank on negotiation to £5,000. His Lordship withdrew; presently the father offered £500 more on the birth of the first child. Disgusted by 'such screwing,' his Lordship exclaimed that 'he would not proceed if he might have £20,000.' Such scenes are not only amusing and brilliant in themselves, but they are in fact the very fragments in which character is mirrored clear.

Of all our six biographers, only Aubrey and North had purely biographical aims, for only they seemed to remain uninfluenced by the desire to glorify their subjects. Foxe was really a chronicler blended with a hagiographer; Roper was trying, within his limitations, to defend the memory of his father-in-law; Greville was not really writing, or even trying to write, biography at all, and Walton, who was consciously composing biography, was deflected from his aim by influences, apparently, of personal temperament.

Nevertheless, they all wrote works that embodied some biographical materials. Much as Foxe is a jumble, as we have seen, there are parts where the action is exciting and significant and the characters suddenly real; there are even fragments of dramatic construction. Roper, too, although all the higher reaches of Sir Thomas More's character were above his understanding, caught something of the affectionate and affection-inspiring man. Therein, inferior as he was to Lord Brooke in intellect, he proved superior as a biographer, for the latter in his grave political fervor really forgets to limn Sidney at all. His was a wandering and confusion of aims, each straining against the other. With singleness of purpose he might have composed a fine biography: he was a poet, and he knew his friend. We cannot tell, but it might well have been penetrating and wise.

Walton had honesty, and style, and a feeling for form, and intelligence and humor, and yet, as we have seen, his achievement as a biographer was seriously at fault. His preference for the contemplative colors all his work; the calm folds of Walton's personality cover every turbulence. In him the nature of the author obliterates the people he deals with until they all become variegated echoes of himself.

Not so either Aubrey or North. Aubrey's transparency, North's serious exuberance, are guarantors of essential accuracy in every morsel. Aubrey had both professedly and really no purpose except honest delineation; North was professedly an apologist, but he couldn't maintain the rôle. They are the only biographers we have considered so far in whom we do not feel any trace of ulterior influence. And of the two it may be that Aubrey, being almost pure anecdotalist, is sometimes more interesting in detail; but North is as clearly superior in every other relevant way. Both are individual stylists, but North has a sustained narrative skill and an ability at complete and complex projection that Aubrey, of course, never essayed.

Save for occasional dullnesses introduced by his sense of historical obligation (for although North distinguished in his mind between history and biography he did not quite succeed in keeping them apart in practice), North's tale moves smoothly and logically and interestingly along. We might, in fact, so long as we do not think of him as actually *learning* from Aubrey and Walton—for we have no evidence that he had read either—consider him as combining their characteristic merits, Walton's vision of the life as a connected whole, and Aubrey's shining vignettes of reminiscence and character.

Historically all these writers are highly illuminating, even more in comparison than when read alone. Even minor details of daily life and manners suddenly gleam into life for us: Sir Dudley not being too high and mighty to pick the stitches out of his wife's petticoat; the domestic intimacy that could allow Dr Butler, the great physician, to be called for in his cups by a servant and to exchange abuse with her about their inebriation on the way home; the screen at which Francis North in his timidity stood dodging and which existed to keep the wintry drafts out of large public rooms. There is the typical John Bull scorn of the middle-class Englishman for French courtliness, expressed in whipping the leg over the deeply bowing foreigner, and crude rough-and-tumble in even a Raleigh stopping a too loquacious talker by forcibly sealing his beard with wax. Sir Dudley's little brotherly jokes about lawyers and forging show us one way in which human nature and opinion have not changed.

We have only to shift our gaze a little and we are seeing the 'knick-knack-atory' of Mr Weld, that rich philosopher of Bloomsbury, enjoying his 'ample feast of discourse,' and hearing the strains of 'one of the neatest violists of his time.' Or from the dilettantism of Guilford and the fantastic enquiringness of Aubrey we may go to More pacing the leads and discoursing to the King on the stars, the learned speculations of the Royal Society, and the enormous if unproductive erudition of Dr John North. The College of Physicians prescribes amber and astringent powders, and Donne tries to strangle his tortured emotions in coils of scholastic ingenuity. Bacon fastidiously makes all his servants go shod in Spanish leather because he can not bear the smell of neats' leather, and meanwhile sends his mind out on shining voyages of Utopian speculation, oblivious of the hand closing over a bribe and the darkening jealous storm.

There is a rich variety in the revelation of sexual manners. Always frank-spoken (even Walton has his joke about the conditions of Hooker's wife being too like a dripping house), the biographers show us the range from the Platonizing idealism of the chivalrous tradition to the 'looses and escapes' of violent sensuality. There are the bourgeois humors of Francis North's unsuccessful courtships, the vaguely hinted excesses of Donne, the Platonic Jane falling in love with Mr Herbert unseen, Ben Jonson 'perhaps' begetting Clun, Sir Walter Raleigh, that brusque 'boarder' of Maids of Honour—indeed 'the very pudenda are not covered.' And from married life we have the commonsense brusquerie of Lady More, the easy domesticity of Sir Dudley and his wife in the country, the metaphysical devotion of Donne 'like gold to aery thinnesse beat.'

But more than anything else we receive a sense of the fierce religious prejudices and the yawning political pitfalls of the age. The flaming fires of Smithfield and the grim 'Short arguments, Master Doctor, short arguments,' are found not only in Foxe, but everywhere—in Walton, in Aubrey, in North. Even in Greville there is a grave political fervor, a passion of diplomatic reasoning, that shows us how much almost every gentleman and courtier of the period was a politician and a watcher of the stage of diplomacy. If Walton pours 'a strange flood of light' upon 'the more contemplative side of English life in the Seventeenth century,' he has curious subdued sideglances at the hidden shoals in the life of the government and court. Those 'imaginary painted pleasures' are mined with tortuous plots by which one may be brought to the executioner's block and disembowelled. The King's favor may be forfeited by an ill-advised pun or the Tower yawn upon an 'unruly wit.' Only the discretion of his friend Wood saved Aubrey from revealing 'things that would cutt' his throat for him; and during the reign of James II, even through the deliberations of the Royal Society we hear the howling fury of Papist Plots, the bellowing ferocity of Jeffreys, and the violent prejudices of the King. Savagery and scholarship go side by side, through both centuries, and More, with all his Utopian tolerance, could be a 'bitter persecutor of good men.'

Such are the sinister undertones of the entire period. We can hardly hear them or believe in them when we find ourselves in some of the serene abodes of learning or science; they seem out of key with the 'high, holy, and harmonious Composures' of John Donne, or Herbert finding his good deeds 'music at midnight' to him. It seems very remote from Sir Dudley learning 'a little algebra' and enjoying this 'new kind of arithmetic.' In the academic cloisters where Dr North carries on petty feuds with disgruntled Fellows, or in the convivial bouts of Aubrey and Wylde in Shropshire we can hardly credit these rancors and cruelties. But perhaps violence and some kinds of urbanity will seem less incongruous if we remember certain scholars of Harvard finding no flaw in the condemnation of Sacco and Vanzetti, and well-bred gentlemen in their clubs growing bitter about the need of making a fish-peddler burn.

AUTOBIOGRAPHY AND PERSONALITY
17th and 18th Centuries

III

AUTOBIOGRAPHY AND PERSONALITY
17TH AND 18TH CENTURIES

Pitfalls for Sincerity

HONESTY is the greatest stumbling-block of the autobiographer. The resolution to tell the truth about oneself takes a spartan rigor of character, and the ability to do so requires a more than common insight. There have been few if any autobiographers who have told no untruths. The degrees of truthfulness, moreover, go beyond the letter; those stern spirits who would scorn any suppressio veri may fall into an unconscious suggestio falsi. The subtler forms of self-deception lie all around us, and never do they lie more temptingly at hand than when the subject is our own character with all its merits and the extenuations of its infrequent errors. The reader of an autobiography is in much the same relationship with its writer as we are with a living acquaintance: if he wishes not to be deceived he must be on his guard against even those innocent strokes of ingratiation that may give him a quite wrong impression of character. It may be noted, too, that the errors are not always in the same direction. The writer who tells his own life-story, like the acquaintance, may have an unfortunate manner or a disagreeable surface to prejudice us against a character fundamentally worthy and even admirable. The plausible knave and the man of maladroit virtue are in print as well as in the flesh. There is no substitute for judgment and perception in the reader.

Autobiographers reveal, however, a curious desire to tell the truth about themselves. 'The man who writes his own life,' Schopenhauer notes, 'surveys it as a whole, the particular becomes small, the near becomes distant, the distant becomes near again, the motives that influenced him shrink; he seats himself at the confessional, and has done so of his own free will; the spirit of lying does not easily take hold of him here, for there is also in every man an inclination to truth which has first to be overcome whenever he lies, and which here has taken up a specially strong position.'

When the story has not been called forth as a defense against any specific ill-fame, as an apology to a man's contemporaries for actions still conceived to be in the public eye, when there is no more worldly advantage to be gained in changing the minds of his living fellows —then, it would seem, a man ultimately looks on himself with enough dignity so that he desires to lay bare the truth. Perhaps he believes that the lights will more than balance the darkness, perhaps he believes the explaining circumstances will show him more than justified. He may believe the free confession of error and penitence in a way dissociates him from the evils he sees he has done. He may even take a pride in feeling that his moral courage makes him superior to other men, that he at least is free from the hypocrisy that makes them conceal what he openly confesses. Whatever the reasons, seldom, and then only in the most painful deeps of humiliation, the most searing of shames, has the autobiographer at the end of a lifetime been led into conscious lying about external facts. Coloring and omission are more frequent; against them only what insight we possess can enable us to guard. And the degree to which the writer avoids even them is largely determined by the depth and purity of his purpose.

If the autobiographer has purity of purpose he wants to tell us the story of his life and to paint a portrait of his character as it appears to him. Only those elements he wants to emphasize, or, at least, that he is willing to have there, will be consciously included:

the sort of man, with the sort of activities and interests, he wants to be taken for. Any other emphases we must either find in unconscious revelation or seek from other sources than his own testimony, but the degree to which his self-portrait approximates what he really believes himself to be is the degree to which his work is pure in motivation and not a piece of propaganda. His perception of himself, however, may be blurred, superficial, or otherwise faulty. If so, only by means of that blessed fairy of the unconscious, which we have already invoked several times, will we be able to see many aspects of the real man which lie further down than the surface image. How deep the man's insight into himself goes, then, will determine the fundamental truth of his self-portrayal. Only those autobiographies that have purity of purpose and depth, as here defined, are of the highest quality.

These criteria are counsels of perfection. If they preserve us from valuing too highly those autobiographies in which they are but slightly regarded, their absence should not prevent our enjoyment of many more superficial kinds of interest or excitement. The writer of impure purpose or shallow perception may still be highly revealing—sometimes more revealing than he knows—and the writer held by a powerful distortion may plumb stranger depths than are possible to the Lucretian gods in their elegant detachment. We shall see some of these distortions and impurities coloring the work of a few seventeenth and eighteenth century autobiographers. They will show a number of the influences and uncertainties operating upon the writer who narrates his own life in the same way as the preceding chapter showed some of the problems of the biographer.

Favorite of Heaven

One of the earliest English autobiographies is that of Lord Herbert of Cherbury (1583-1648). Unearthed with chuckles of glee by Horace Walpole and printed sumptuously at Strawberry Hill for the delectation of his friends, the work is a curious and amusing example of a book often interesting in another fashion than its author knew. For Edward Herbert, whose fame is now far outshone by his younger brother George Herbert, author of *The Temple*, was in his day a diplomat of no mean talents and a philosopher respected by Descartes and Gassendi. But hardly any suggestion of these things appears in the autobiography. Although written at the age of sixty, it chronicles with a naive egoism and complacency his youthful triumphs in wit, bravery, politeness, and knight errantry, and stops short at the age of thirty-seven, when he had just published the *De veritate* which was his chief contribution to philosophy.

How is it that a man who was a grave pioneer in the development of freedom of thought and a penetrating observer of men and governments shows himself to us as a childish issuer of challenges to mortal combat and an ingenuous boaster about his own beauty, charm, and success? Was it perhaps that the old man, contemptuously forgotten by the Court, the glory and triumphs of his youth vanished from the minds of all but himself, comforted himself by remembering those glittering times, and put down his pen, sick at heart, before he reached the days of reversal and oblivion? Or was it, as Professor Herford suggests, that we find in him a divided character 'who may be called with equal plausibility the last of the knights errant and the first of the deists, in whom the fantastic extravagances of medieval chivalry seem to join hands with the prosaic reason of the eighteenth century'? Certainly, although the self-conscious and self-important young man dominates the autobiography, there are pages in which his graver and elder companion looks over his shoulder or even borrows the pen.

'His Life is delightful and amusing,' Professor Herford remarks, 'precisely because he himself seems to have no humour at all. We laugh at his "Quixotic" adventures, and he himself appears as devoid of humour as the Don.' Whether he is threatening a gentleman with corporal punishment for playfully snatching away the hair-ribbon of a little girl (an episode that his chivalrous imagination sees as an affront to a lady's honor) or charging a gang of robbers single-handed in his nightshirt, his life presents itself to him, Edmund Blunden points out, as a series of vindications of knighthood, of evil or impolite people punished, according to the best rules, by himself. The touches of self-credit, so punctiliously recorded, are among the most enjoyable features of his autobiography. 'This Motto by me.' One learns to look for that decorous 'by me' either in words or implied: The Spanish ambassador Gondomar astonished by the Englishman's power handsomely to refuse a request; Monsieur de Luynes being put in his place 'by me'; the grave maladies he has cured after physicians had given the cases up; the ladies who have admired his person and keep portraits or miniatures of him (although always with the utmost purity of character and behavior).

At times we hear a deeper tone. 'I much approve those parts of logic which teach men to deduce their proofs from firm and undoubted principles, and show men to distinguish betwixt truth and falsehood, and help them to discover fallacies, sophisms, and that which schoolmen call vicious argumentations,' but it is not needful to spend much time in learning 'the subtleties of logic' which fits people 'for little more than to be excellent wranglers.' But 'a virtuous man may not only go securely through all the religions, but all the laws in the world, and whatsoever obstructions he meet, obtain both an inward peace and outward welcome.' And once he appeals sadly to his readers 'whether any worldly felicity did so satisfy their hope here, that they did not wish and hope for something more excellent, or whether they had ever that faith in their own wisdom, or in the help of man, that they were not constrained to have recourse to some diviner and superior power, than they could find on earth, to relieve them in their danger or necessity; whether ever they could place their love on any earthly beauty, that it did not fade and wither, if not frustrate or deceive them, or whether ever their joy was so consummate in anything they delighted in, that they did not want, much more than it, or indeed this world can afford, to make them happy.'

Presently, however, the hortatory opening passed by (for the book was written, astoundingly enough, 'to relate to my posterity those passages of my life, which I conceive may best declare me, and be most useful to them'), we are hearing the characteristic tone again. As an infant he knew how to talk long before he spoke a word, but 'did forebear to speak, lest I should utter something that were imperfect or impertinent.' Seeing him when he was a youth, Queen Elizabeth swore 'her usual oath' and opined it a pity that he had married so young. At the siege of Juliers he tried conclusions in bravery with Balagny, one of the most celebrated French officers, by springing into the open space between the trenches and walking round. The garrison opposite opened fire on these amiable idiots, and Balagny, admitting 'It is very hot here,' suggested going back. 'You shall go first,' Herbert retorted, 'or else I will never go' and thereupon, Herbert says, 'he ran with all speed, and somewhat crouching towards the trenches; I followed after, leisurely and upright.' And 'no doubt,' comments Edmund Blunden, 'he believed he did.'

It is hardly possible to exhaust or to be exhausted by Herbert's accounts of the victories, gallantries, and repartees, 'by me.' Perhaps the highest achievement of all is that on which Heaven itself set the seal of approval. The philosopher argued that supernatural revelation was an idle fallacy, but when he was doubtful whether or not to publish his book, 'one fair day in the Summer, my Casement being opened towards the South, the Sun shining clear and no Wind stirring,' he took his book in hand, kneeled, and prayed for some sign, which was no sooner done than 'a loud though yet gentle Noise came from the Heavens (for it was like nothing on Earth) which did so comfort and cheer me, that I took my petition as granted and that I had the Sign I demanded . . .' In this devout and approved position let us leave him. Heaven decreed that he should be more handsome, more valiant, more witty, more inspired than other men.

Lurid Stage

Herbert's life and character, so external, so worldly and even trivial in the interests he mostly reveals to us, form a strange contrast with the next life we are going to consider. John Bunyan's *Grace Abounding* is a spiritual autobiography. Of his parentage, his education, his outward career, we learn almost nothing: all is concentrated on the inward drama, the crucial struggle of his life. We are told that he played cat as a boy (a game placed with a ball), that he used to ring the bells in a church steeple, that he became a preacher, that his enemies slandered him with the imputation of loose living, that he was imprisoned for his religious views, but hardly any other external facts at all.

Herbert's career as depicted by himself was all the easy assertion of a right never doubted; Bunyan's was all an agony in seeking, a suffering under temptation to betray, a martyrdom for bearing witness to an awful truth. If that truth ultimately sustained him, it was not his weakness that triumphed, but the might of God. The urbane and courtly Herbert, even the philosopher, achieved with ease a pleased serenity about matters that to Bunyan were a flame consuming his being.

No book gives a deeper insight into the fiercer, the more tormented aspects of English Puritanism, not even the fiery apocalyptic sermons and dark predestinarianism of Jonathan Edwards. The humble Bedford tinker struggled through the actual smoke and stench of hell's flame, with the Devil a real presence by his side and divine voices sometimes sounding in his ears. The story he tells in *Grace Abounding* is a Dostoyevskyan drama of dread and horror and damnation and repentance, communicated in a voice of tense and terrible conviction. It is a confession not to be read casually; if the effect is to be felt it must be with a full realization of the appalling sincerity of every stage. The Biblical imagery and turns of phrase are no easy rhetoric strung out with conventional unction. The hasty and obtuse reader who fails to realize that they came burning out of Bunyan's heart will miss the intensity of the struggle. In the small lurid center of the stage, lit with flares, Bunyan struggles with the Devil for his soul, and around all the rest is darkness, the darkness of perdition, with no glimpse of the sunlit English scene. Not until years later did he attain the serenity of the Interpreter's House, the fair vision of the Delectable Mountains, and the shining City of God.

It was while he was playing that game of cat as a boy that the conviction of sin first came on him: 'a voice did suddenly dart from heaven into my soul, which said, Wilt thou leave thy sins and go to heaven, or have thy sins and go to hell?' and looking to heaven it was as if he had 'with the eyes of my understanding seen the Lord Jesus looking down . . . as being very hotly displeased . . .' The sinfulness of playing games struck deep into his conscience; Jesus was no pitiful savior filled with divine compassion, but a stern and implacable judge. Brooding on this, 'despair did so possess my soul, that I was persuaded I could never attain to any other comfort than what I should get in sin.' Heaven was already lost, so he might as well take his fill of sin, 'studying what sin was yet to be committed' to 'taste the sweetness of it' and fill his belly 'with its delicates.'

But presently he 'fell to some outward reformation' and began to think how he 'had taken much delight in bell-ringing,' which 'practice was but vain,' and yet his mind hankered so that he would still go to the steeple-house and look at it. So doing, the thought came, 'How, if one of the bells should fall?' so he stood to one side under a beam for shelter until he thought that the bell might fall with a swing and rebound from the wall upon him, killing him despite the beam, and then he stood in the thickness of the door. But 'How if the steeple itself should fall' in punishment? and 'I durst not stand in the steeple door any longer, but was forced to flee, for fear the steeple should fall upon my head.'

Satan tempted him that 'there was no way for me to know I had faith but by trying to work some miracle,' and he was mightily impelled to 'say to the puddles that were in the horse-pads' on the the road, 'Be dry; and to the dry places, Be you the puddles.' In dreams he saw himself freezing in cold snow and dark clouds, and a wall between him and the saved on the sunny side of a high mountain. 'I durst not take a pin or a stick, though but so big as a straw, for my conscience now was sore, and would smart at every touch'; he found himself 'as on a miry bog that shook if I did but stir.' 'Darkness seized upon me, after which whole floods of blasphemy, both against God, Christ, and the Scriptures, were poured upon my spirit.'

He believed himself actually possessed by the devil, borne away: 'Kick sometimes I did, and also scream and cry; but yet I was bound in the wings of temptation, and the wind would carry me away.' Sometimes the temptation to shout blasphemies was so strong that 'I have been ready to clap my hand under my chin, to hold my mouth from opening' or 'to leap with my head downward, into some muck-hill hole or other, to keep my mouth from speaking.' He felt the devil behind him pulling at his clothes, saying to him at the time of prayer, 'Break off, make haste, you have prayed enough.'

For years these torments continued. Sometimes he would hear a voice of comfort which said 'Thou art my love; and nothing shall separate thee from my love,' and he felt so glad that he could have spoken of God's love and mercy 'even to the very crows that sat upon the ploughed land'; sometimes the voice would sound so loud that he turned his head to see if one had really called from a distance. But soon Satan was at him again, urging him to sell Christ, so that 'I could neither eat my food, stoop for a pin, chop a stick, or cast mine eye to look on this or that, but still the temptation would come, Sell Christ for this or sell Christ for that; sell him, sell him.' He put his very body into resistance, 'pushing or thrusting with my hands or elbows, still answering as fast as the destroyer said, Sell him; I will not, I will not, I will not; no, not for thousands of worlds.' 'But at last, after much striving, even until I was out of breath, I felt this thought pass through my heart, Let him go, if he will!' 'Now was the battle won, and down fell I, as a bird that is shot from the top of a tree, into great guilt, and fearful despair.' Horror overwhelmed him, and like a hot thunderbolt he felt the conviction that he had sinned the unpardonable sin. 'I could feel . . . my very body, as well as my mind, to shake and totter under the sense of the dreadful judgment of God' for 'that most fearful and unpardonable sin,' and it seemed as if his 'breast bone would have split in sunder.'

Rescue came at last. A text fell into his mind: 'Return to me,' it would cry aloud, 'Return to me, for I have redeemed thee,' and he would 'look over my shoulder behind me, to see if I could discern that the God of grace did follow me with a pardon in his hand,' but then 'all would be dark and clouded again' until once more 'it did holloa after me.' Finally a voice commanded a silence 'of all those tumultuous thoughts that before did use, like masterless hell-hounds, to roar and bellow, and make a hideous noise within me.' 'See,' it said, 'that he refuse not him that speaketh'; and a 'sudden rushing wind was as if an angel had come' bringing 'a great calm in my soul.'

There were later struggles and temptations, but the great battle was won. Never again was the vision of damnation and despair so awful; never again did the nightmare of irrevocable sin draw him into the blackness.

It is easy enough to dismiss Bunyan as unbalanced, and there can be no doubt that he suffered from hallucinations. But the author of *The Holy War*, *The Life and Death of Mr Badman*, and *The Pilgrim's Progress* was something more than merely unbalanced, and shares his visions with other men of greatness and purity of heart. Even the mundane Herbert heard the sound from Heaven approving his enquiry into truth, and Socrates had his daemon to guide him.

The religious possession that drove Bunyan almost crazed has passed again and again, in various forms, through whole communities, and Bunyan's is a valuable and penetrating record of the form it took in a simple heart. If he was never as sinful, in his bell-ringing and his cat-playing, as he believed, he stabs his dread and repentance home to us with words of blood. The strange interior drama has more of truth than most displays of the outer world: a truth narrow and limited, but of unfathomable depth.

Whip-Syllabub of Wit

With Colley Cibber's *Apology for His Life* we return to the light and frothy surface of things again. The dark interior world of the Puritans condemned the stage as vain when it was least harmful, and found it ungodly and licentious at its worst. Colley Cibber, as player and as playwright, spent his entire life in the service of the stage. His life as narrated by himself is almost as devoid of personal and private action as Bunyan's own, but for a very different reason. To Bunyan, absorbed in the fierce drama of salvation, whom he had married and the character of his wife and all the gentler feelings of daily life, faded into triviality; to Cibber it may have seemed none of the public's business what his private life had been, or it may have been that the lively pleasure of theatrical reminiscence and of letting his tongue rattle at will on any topic that came into his head made him almost forgetful of the less brilliantly lighted stage of domestic life.

For indeed, save in the sense that it gives a vivid picture of the man, Cibber's apology is very little a real autobiography. Instead it is a collection of theatrical memoirs, of brilliant dramatic portraits and skilful analyses of the actor's art; an informal and gossipy history of the stage during his time; a gallimaufrey of philosophic reflections, anecdotes, witticisms, genteel moralizings, and good humor; all as light and trivial and gay, and as sensible and keen in an everyday, worldly way as its author.

It must be emphasized that clear and well-lighted as the image of Cibber stands before us, it is the social image we behold, never anything more profound. In a way this reticence (if it was reticence and not a lack of deeper interest) is typical of the eighteenth century; intimate gossip about the less seemly aspects of a man's behavior there might be, but seldom any speculation about his inward nature; scandal about his weaknesses, respect for his virtues of action or strength of thought, but hardly ever any probing into the dark hidden springs, the half-lights and obscurities of the spirit. It is for this reason that the eighteenth century, its poetry, its thought, and its character, so often seem dry and sapless to people who feel the need of bathing life in more romantic and deeply moving hues. The earnestness and enthusiasm and feeling of the eighteenth century (and it had all these) were allowed to appear only decently clothed in a garb of the didactic or cerebral, and even then wore often the mask of light carelessness.

So it is with Cibber. Chattering away, the pert, lively creature, he gives us a glimpse of a sensible and warm-hearted man underneath the coxcomb and the rattle, lets us see a hardworking and penetrating technician in the art of the theatre, a generous appreciator of talent in his fellow-actors, a frequently witty observer of life and manners. But all these are things that any reasonably keen spectator of his public life might have noticed—The curtain falls: And what of the man? we ask; the real, inner Cibber?—Ah, ladies and gentlemen, he has gone home.

To say so much is not to derogate from the clearness and vivacity of the public image Cibber has, in fact, drawn, nor from its sincerity on its own level of truth. He begins with a gay avowal of folly: 'But why make my follies publick? Why not? I have passed my time very pleasantly with them, and I don't recollect that they have ever been hurtful to any other man living.' Further, when a man 'has pass'd above forty years of his life upon a theatre, where he has never appeared to be himself' people may naturally like to know 'what he really was, when in nobody's shape but his own.' And consequently he promises 'as true a picture as natural vanity will permit,' for to promise no vanity might, 'like a looking-glass too large . . . break itself in the making.' From this we pass to a little outline of his birth and early schooling, but are soon, by way of the dislike his wit aroused in his schoolmates, proceeding on a brisk digression about the disadvantages of superior wit unaccompanied by great discretion, and thence to an argumentative defense of folly, but 'all this my parade, and grimace of philosophy, has only been making a mighty merit of following my own inclination.'

From then on the game of digression and return is merrily played. A few speculations about how he might have entered Cambridge and become a celebrated preacher, or joined the army during the Revolution of 1688 and become a great soldier (for Cibber infuriates the prosaic-minded by his bland assumption that he would have shone in these professions as well as in his own), are followed by an account of how the theatre fascinated his youthful imagination, and then by a lively imitation of an adverse critic damning his book. Little fragments of narrative alternate with bits about his indifference to being satirized (and he had occasion, for the great Pope had made him the comic hero of *The Dunciad*), and these in turn mingle with reflections on the sad inferiority of the actor's place in society, the state of the theatre in 1690, the talents of its several leading lights, and his own early fortunes therein. By the eleventh chapter the sport is demurely admitted: 'But as I have no objection to method, when it is not troublesome,' he remarks after a more than usually long digression, 'I return to my subject.'

Witticisms and aphorisms are frequent. In vulgar repartee, he notes, 'he that has the least wit generally gives the first blow.' 'Praise, though it may be our due, is not like a bank-bill, to be paid on demand . . . If compulsion insists upon it, it can only be paid as persecution in points of faith is, in a counterfeit coin.' It 'would be a sort of tyranny in wit for an author to be publickly putting every argument to death that appear'd against him . . . praise is as much the reader's property, as wit is the author's.' Of an actress who had appeared very often in virtuous rôles he remarks that she came to feel herself really the sort of character she played 'to such a height that she was, very near, keeping herself chaste by it.'

His anecdotes are often pleasant. We have King Charles, himself of swarthy complexion, complaining of the way villains and scoundrels were so often represented in plays as black and menacing in appearance: 'Pray, what is the meaning that we never see a rogue in a play, but, godsfish, they always clap him in a black perriwig? when, it is well known, one of the greatest rogues in England always wears a fair one?' We have the mild reproof of a great personage to his chaplain, who was noted for the dissoluteness rather than the purity of his life. He told him 'with a smile of good-humour, that if to the many vices he had already, he would give himself the trouble to add one more . . . his reputation might still be set up again.' The chaplain desiring to know what it was, received the reply, 'Hypocrisy, doctor, only a little hypocrisy!' And when he is speculating why 'the celebrated Waller' was employed to alter the end of *The Maid's Tragedy* so that Evadne no longer murders the king in his bed, he remarks that this dénouement 'was shewing a too dangerous example to other Evadnes, then shining at Court, in the same rank of royal distinction; who, if their consciences should have run equally mad, might have had frequent opportunities of putting the expiation of their frailty into the like execution.'

All these passages are in his lightest key. He strikes a more serious note on the subject he feels most seriously about, the art of acting; and in his analyses of the talents of Betterton, Monfort, Nokes, Mrs Barry, Mrs Verbruggen, Mrs Bracegirdle, and numerous other actors he is not only always generous and appreciative, but truly skilful in the way he puts them before us. There is Betterton as Brutus in the quarrel scene: 'his spirit flew only to his eye; his steady look alone supply'd that terror, which he disdain'd an intemperance in his voice should rise to. Thus, with a settled dignity of contempt, like an unheeding rock, he repelled upon himself the foam of Cassius.' Monfort's men of wit 'had a particular talent, in giving life to *bons mots* and *repartees*' so that they 'seem'd always to come from him *extempore*, and sharpen'd into more wit from his brilliant manner of delivering it'; but when he did 'the false, flashy pretender' he was another person in 'the insipid, soft civility, the elegant and formal mien; the drawling delicacy of voice, the stately flatness of his address, and the empty eminence of his attitudes.'

His description of the comic actor Nokes is masterly. 'When he debated any matter by himself, he would shut up his mouth with a dumb studious powt, and roll his full eye into such a vacant amazement, such a palpable ignorance of what to think of it, that his silent perplexity' was as eloquent as the most absurd speech. As Sir Martin Mar-all, where he played a blunderer afraid of his governing servant and counsellor,

> what a copious, and distressful harangue have I seen him make with his looks (while the house has been in one continued roar, for several minutes) before he could prevail with his courage to speak a word to him! Then might you have, at once, read in his face vexation—that his own measures which he had piqued himself upon, had fail'd. Envy—of his servant's superior wit. Distress—to retrieve, the occasion he had lost. Shame—to confess his folly: and yet a sullen desire, to be reconciled and better advised, for the future! What tragedy ever shew'd us such a tumult of passions, rising, at once, in one bosom! or what buskin'd heroe standing under the load of them, could have more effectually mov'd his spectators by the most pathetic speech, than poor miserable Nokes did, by this silent eloquence, and piteous plight of his features?

No less brilliant are his appreciations of the beauties of some of the ladies of the stage. When Mrs Bracegirdle acted Millamant, 'all the faults, follies, and affectations of the agreeable tyrant, were venially melted down into so many charms and attractions' 'that few spectators that were not past it, could behold her without desire' and every audience were 'half of them her lovers, without a suspected favorite among them.' Mrs Monfort as Melantha calls forth another vivacious picture. She has just received from a gallant a letter in which her father recommends the young man to her good graces as an honorable lover. There is no modesty in her reception:

> No, sir; not a tittle of it: modesty is the virtue of a poor-soul'd country gentlewoman; she is too much a court lady, to be under so vulgar a confusion; she reads the letter, therefore, with a careless, dropping lip, and an erected brow, humming it hastily over, as if she were impatient to outgo her father's commands, by making a compleat conquest of him at once: and that the letter might not embarrass her attack, crack! she crumbles it at once into her palm, and pours upon him her whole artillery of airs, eyes, and motion; down goes her dainty, diving body to the ground, as if she were sinking under the conscious load of her own attractions; then launches into a flood of fine language, and compliment, still playing her chest forward in fifty falls and risings, like a swan upon waving water; and, to complete her impatience, she is so rapidly fond of her own wit, that she will not give her lover leave to praise it. Silent assenting bows, and vain endeavors to speak, are all the share of the conversation he is admitted to, which, at last, he is relieved from by her engagement to half a score visits, which she *swims* from him to make, with a promise to return in a twinkling.

Nowhere is Cibber more ingratiating than where he speaks of the shafts of satire that were so often aimed at himself. 'Shall I be sincere, and own my frailty?' he amiably asks. 'Its usual effect is to make me vain! For I consider, if I were quite good for nothing, the pidlers in wit would not be concerned to take me to pieces . . .' And as for the critics of greater fame, 'Not our great imitator of Horace himself can have more pleasure in writing his verses than I have in reading them, tho' I sometimes find myself there (as Shakespear terms it) *dispraisingly* spoken of.' 'When I therefore find my name at length in the satyrical works of our most celebrated living author, I never look upon those lines as malice meant to me (for he knows I never provok'd it) but as profit to himself'; and 'as a little bad poetry is the greatest crime he lays to my charge, I am willing to subscribe to his opinion of *it*.' Surely never was Pope's slashing onslaughts met with more good humor.

Roman Profile

The same public character we have noted in Cibber's portrayal of himself may be seen in a work of considerably more formal dignity. Edward Gibbon saw himself as the author of *The Decline and Fall of the Roman Empire*, and as such it seemed to him fitting that those who knew his reputation as an eminent man of letters should have a full length narrative of those parts of his life that might satisfy a legitimate curiosity. 'He had written a magnificent history . . .' says Augustine Birrell: 'It remained to write the history of the historian.' The word history is well-chosen. Gibbon approached his *Autobiography* with the same weighty dignity he gave to the panorama of a crumbling civilization, and although he tells us that he is 'reviewing the simple transactions of a private and literary life' in a style 'simple and familiar' it was hardly possible for him to regard the subject as of less moment than the Roman Empire.

'Truth, naked, unblushing truth, the first virtue of more serious history,' he had remarked in the same passage, 'must be the sole recommendation of this personal narrative.' And truth, on the whole, Gibbon told. But it was truth tempered by the considerations of a certain concern for propriety. The propriety of Gibbon, however, was not of a conventional or moral kind: he had no squeamishness about the detached admission of youthful excesses in 'the taverns and bagnios of Convent Garden' or about giving the name of that Oxford tutor who 'well remembered that he had a salary to receive and only forgot that he had a duty to perform.' His propriety is neither a tactful avoidance of offense to individuals nor a whitewashing of his own character, but a feeling of what it is too personal or vulgar to dilate upon. 'Of the various and frequent disorders of my childhood my own recollection is dark; nor do I wish to expatiate on so disgusting a topic.' The odor of the sickroom must not be permitted to offend the nose of the fastidious reader. But still other matters were none of the reader's business, and Gibbon announced plainly that such was the case. 'I shall not expatiate on my economical affairs, which cannot be instructive or amusing to the reader. It is a rule of prudence, as well as of politeness, to reserve such confidence for the ear of a private friend, without exposing our situation to the envy or pity of strangers.'

Gibbon's portrait of himself is, in fact, a good deal like the one painted by Sir Joshua Reynolds on which Charles James Fox describes him 'casting a look of complacency'—'that wonderful portrait, in which, while the oddness and vulgarity of the features are refined away, the likeness is perfectly preserved.' But Gibbon manages to retain even the oddity and the touch of ostentation that made his contemporaries sometimes regard him as vulgar, and eliminates only those details of fact or feeling that are too 'private' or 'disgusting.' And if the elegant mirror chills a little the warmth of affection in the man, it reflects faithfully many little touches of peculiarity and innocent vanity that its maker may not have been completely aware of.

Of the warmer aspects of his character it may be desirable to speak here, because he brings it out so little himself. His relation with his father he dismisses in few words; from the time he returned from abroad they were 'on the same terms of easy and equal politeness.' The stepmother whom he had first been disposed to regard with displeasure was 'an amiable and deserving woman' admirable for 'her understanding, her knowledge, and the elegant spirit of her conversation': and moreover 'her polite welcome, and her assiduous care to study and gratify my wishes, announced' that all 'suspicions of art and falsehood' were unjustified.

From these tempered commendations it would be difficult to guess the depth of his feelings. But he felt the tenderest devotion to the aunt who had cared for his childhood; and his stepmother, even as a very old lady, adored her stepson. In what proved to be the closing weeks of his life he hurried home from Lausanne, although stout and gouty, and in spite of the dangers of the French Revolution through which he had to pass, to join his friend Lord Sheffield, whose wife had just died, and who, he felt, needed his presence. These, however, are perhaps among those personal feelings which he felt to belong to his friends rather than to the curiosity of the public, and an autobiography that understates the sensibility of its subject errs in a way that is little blameworthy.

Gibbon was fully aware of what he was doing in his autobiography, and the form in which we have it is perhaps proof that in his own mind he had not quite solved its problems. 'It would most assuredly be in my power,' he wrote, 'to amuse the reader with a gallery of portraits and a collection of anecdotes.' (In a way, what Cibber did do.) 'But I have always condemned the practice of transforming a private memorial into a vehicle of satire or praise.' We find very few set pieces, therefore, in the book. Further, as it is usually printed, it does not represent Gibbon's own final rendition of his story, but is a synthesis of six different sketches, partly overlapping and on different scales, put together after his death by Lord Sheffield. The problem of scale is a special one, too complex and irrelevant for our present purposes; and fortunately for those purposes the tone—of formal and somewhat reserved portraiture—is a single one. But the six sketches are not so much signs of egoism as of literary artistry seeking for the right handling.

The handling that we find, in the separate sketches and in Lord Sheffield's fusion of them, is, as I have tried to make clear, definitely the rendition of himself as the eminent man of letters. The choice of details and their tone are everywhere dictated by that purpose. Some traces of pride of family appear, qualified by a philosophic awareness that it is not altogether rational: 'the longest series of peasants and mechanics would not afford much gratification to the pride of their descendants,' but 'we should learn to value the gifts of nature above those of fortune.' Therefore, to Gibbon personally 'the family of Confucius is . . . the most illustrious in the world.' We are speedily brought, however, into an account of his intellectual growth, the devouring of works of history and geography in such incoherent masses that he 'arrived at Oxford with a stock of erudition that might have puzzled a doctor, and a degree of ignorance of which a schoolboy would have been ashamed.'

The University, then at a low ebb in its intellectual vitality, aided him little. 'The schools of Oxford and Cambridge were founded in a dark age of false and barbarous science; and they are still tainted with the vices of their origin.' They were 'supposed to be schools of science, as well as of education; nor is it unreasonable to expect that a body of literary men, devoted to a life of celibacy, exempt from the care of their own subsistence, and amply provided with books, should devote their leisure to the prosecution of study . . .' But 'The fellows or monks of my time were decent easy men, who supinely enjoyed the gifts of the founder . . . From the toil of reading, or thinking, or writing, they had absolved their conscience; and the first shoots of learning and ingenuity withered on the ground, without yielding any fruits to the owners or the public.'

Unaided by the Professors, he fell in with the works of Bossuet in defense of Catholicism and was easily persuaded by that 'master of all the weapons of casuistry' that 'the ten-horned monster' was indeed 'the milk-white hind, who must be loved as soon as she is seen.' He was expelled from the University, and sent abroad by his father to Lausanne, where he was put under the tutelage of a Calvinist minister charged with the duty of reconverting him. We have a verbal picture of him at the time: 'a thin little figure, with a large head, disputing and urging, with the greatest ability, all the best arguments that had ever been used in favour of Popery.' Slowly he was weaned away from the pernicious creed and back into a formal profession of faith in Protestantism. But the experience had exhausted his capacity for religious fervor, and the gradual expansion of his philosophic reading completed the attitude of ironic scorn with which he thereafter regarded the subject. Of a friend of his aunt's, Gibbon remarks that he might have ranked high as a writer 'had not his vigorous mind been clouded by enthusiasm.' The mature Gibbon was in little danger of that error.

Once, however, in a different realm than that of religion, he approached it. He fell in love, a passion by which he means 'the union of desire, friendship, and tenderness, which is inflamed by a single female, which prefers her to the rest of her sex, and which seeks her possession as the supreme or sole happiness of our being.' The lady, Mlle Susan Curchod (who later became Mme Necker and the mother of Mme de Staël) was 'learned without pedantry, lively in conversation, pure in sentiment, and elegant in manners.' The combination proved irresistible: 'I saw and loved.' But Gibbon's father 'would not hear of this strange alliance' with the daughter of a poor clergyman. 'After a painful struggle I yielded to my fate: I sighed as a lover, I obeyed as a son; my wound was insensibly healed by time, absence, and the habits of a new life. My cure was accelerated by a faithful report of the tranquility and cheerfulness of the lady herself, and my love subsided in friendship and esteem.'

These passages, especially in their almost complacent serenity, reveal the difference between the private and the public man that we have commented on. In fact, as his *Diary* reveals, 'he was deeply mortified at the time by the calmness with which the lady had accepted the rupture. He heard with resentment that she shared in the social amusements of Lausanne' and 'was surrounded by admirers.' Her amusements, he said, convicted her 'of the most odious dissimulation, and if infidelity is sometimes a weakness, duplicity is always a vice. This episode, curious throughout, has been of great use to me; it has opened my eyes to the character of women, and will serve me long as a preservative against the seductions of love.' His youthful chagrin melted away, and he was in later years on gay and friendly terms with ladies, but he never seriously considered matrimony again.

Meanwhile he had continued reading on a monumental scale. He had long since remedied the ignorance of Latin and Greek that he had brought to Oxford, and had already become a serious scholar at the age of twenty-two. 'I cannot forget the joy with which I exchanged a bank-note of twenty pounds for the twenty volumes of the *Memoirs of the Academy of Inscriptions;* nor would it have been easy, by any other expenditure of the same sum, to have procured so large and lasting a fund of rational amusement.' The qualification of the noun is significant. Living in the country with his father and stepmother, 'I never handled a gun, I seldom mounted a horse; and my philosophic walks were soon terminated by a shady bench, where I was long detained by the sedentary amusement of reading or meditation.' Once, the ill-advised step of offering their names as volunteers in the Hampshire militia, which they had never expected to come to anything, involved him and his father in two years of bothersome military service uncompensated for 'by any elegant pleasure.' There may have been some alleviation, however, in the fact that the 'discipline and evolution of a modern battalion gave me a clearer notion of the phalanx and the legion.'

The days when the historian would begin his work were approaching fast. In a visit abroad, the grand project was born. 'It was at Rome, on the 15th of October, 1764, as I sat musing amidst the ruins of the Capitol, while the barefoot friars were singing vespers in the Temple of Jupiter, that the idea of writing the decline and fall of the city first started to my mind.' A dozen years later the first volume appeared. 'I am at a loss how to describe the success of the work, without betraying the vanity of the writer. . . . My book was on every table, and almost on every toilette'; Robertson and Hume added their discriminating praise to the approbation of the polite world. The last volume was finished eleven years later still, in 1787. 'I wrote the last line of the last page, in a summer-house in my garden. After laying down my pen, I took several turns in a *berceau,* or covered walk of acacias, which commands a prospect of the country, the lake, and the mountains. The air was temperate, the sky was serene, the silver orb of the moon was reflected from the water, and all nature was silent.' His first emotion of joy and pride 'was humbled, and a sober melancholy was spread over my mind' by realizing that he had taken his leave 'of an old and agreeable companion' and that the historian probably had not much longer to live.

But his temper was naturally cheerful and moderate; he felt that he had 'drawn a high prize in the lottery of life'; his health, since the illnesses of his childhood, was good; he was a rich man, 'since my income is superior to my expense, and my expense is equal to my wishes'; he had spent twenty happy years 'animated by the labour of my *History,*' and its success had given him a name in the world. He might still hope on a reasonable estimate for about fifteen years more of life, he thought; and he was entering 'the period which, as the most agreeable of his long life, was selected by the judgment and experience of the sage Fontenelle.' With such feelings of peace and complacence he laid down his pen.

Periods and Self-Portrayals

Our four autobiographers show us a sort of historical panorama, from the fantastic chivalry and braggadocio of Lord Herbert (which has in it much of the more exuberant side of Elizabethan life), through the dark and Puritan agonizings of Bunyan to the fluttering gaiety of Cibber and the characteristic elegance and eighteenth century classicism of Gibbon.

If Herbert seems at times a comic parody of the ideals of Sir Philip Sidney, in many ways he still represents the versatility of the Renaissance man that attained such splendor in the many-sided activities of a Leonardo or even a Raleigh. And, although drier and more circumscribed, there is in him also much of the tremendous craving for intellectual expansion with which Bacon took all knowledge for his province.

In Bunyan the reverberations of the Protestant Reformation penetrate to the humbler classes, and mingle with some of that moral rigor that shattered Cavalier armies before Cromwell's Ironsides. The country gentlemen and all the more urbane supporters of Puritanism retired before the wave of licentiousness that came in with the restored Stuart throne. Bunyan and his fellows in their shabby meeting houses, persecuted by the authorities and harried by their own soul-searchings, stubbornly protested the duties of a kingdom that was not of this world.

And, although not strictly contemporaneous, Cibber gives the other side of the same period: its skepticism, its lack of moral earnestness, its relaxed mood of frivolity. He reveals also the slightly cynical worldliness, not always unkindly, and the materialism that led Charles II to declare that he would never set forth on his 'travels' again.

With Gibbon the hedonism of the Restoration has changed to the Epicureanism of the Classic Age. Its worldliness is no less, but is tempered by sobriety, balance, and calm. Not averse to enjoyment, it feels that there is also a serious side to life, and grows interested in philosophy, in scholarship, in progress. In these four autobiographies we have sampled characteristic flavors of their time.

They not only flash light on salient qualities of the periods in which their authors lived, however; they illuminate as well the problems of autobiography as an art. I think it will be agreed that all of them partially succeed in their purpose, in the sense that none is dull or lacking in a feeling of personality. The degrees and ways of their success, and the nature of their limitations, are instructive.

In Herbert of Cherbury, for all his verve and aplomb, I think we feel a serious lack of both depth and purity of purpose. The man whom Descartes regarded as the most serious English philosopher after Francis Bacon could hardly, even as a youngster, have been nothing but the harebrained and quarrelsome boaster he usually paints himself. Nor, even as a youngster, is it likely that his career was so uniformly prosperous as he tells us, although it may be that the charm and beauty of his youth graced a tendency to contentiousness that was not so easily forgiven as he grew older. But we are forced to believe that there were qualities in the boy and man that he did not perceive—and of one so ready to envision his own merit as Herbert that seems unlikely—or, that he chose not to reveal.

Possibly the temptation to daydream about his youth and dramatize his character to a secret, and curiously shallow, vision of himself proved too strong to be mastered. That he told the story of only half his life is perhaps a mechanical accident; that he knew or told only a part of his personality in that half is fundamental. It does not prevent many passages of unconscious revelation, but even that unconscious revelation fails to show us nearly all of what in him commanded respect. If the autobiography in spite of all has freshness and delight, it attains them often enough by the not altogether admirable means of arousing the reader's amusement at the author. This pleasure Herbert would have been little gratified to know he produced; and pleasure achieved so, through self-complacence, is of a trivial kind.

Of none of these faults can Bunyan be accused. Instead of the shallow stage without perspective or chiaroscuro, we seem to have a cavernous depth of darkness and lurid glares. Peering into that bleak inferno of the conscience, we cannot doubt, nay we see, deeps beyond deeps, plumbed as darkly and fearfully as Bunyan explored them and struggled with their monsters himself. Nor is the purity of his intention more dubious; the frightful sincerity of the man dominates every sentence. But if the vision was deep and sincere, it was terribly distorted, distorted well-nigh to madness. All the light and air of every day is lost in *Grace Abounding*, all the love of wife and children which in one fleeting passage even Bunyan confesses to be irrationally dear to him, all the stir and pleasant distractions of life and business, of soldiering and tinkering, which even Puritanism knew, and the serene visions of the Land of Beulah and the loveliness in a flower that Bunyan himself came in the end to know. The stark and bitter principle of selection governed all; it ruled out half of life, and left a story that was true, but bare of all everyday and external fact, and bare of all those milder thoughts and feelings that failed to burn with the red heat of a crisis.

It needs no great insight to perceive that there is little depth in Colley Cibber's *Apology*. We are given a cheerful and good-humored creature with a considerable knowledge of the surfaces of men's conduct, agreeable, tolerant, wise enough in those kinds of judgment called knowing the world, generous and appreciative of the kind of merit, in the restricted realm of the theatre, he is especially interested in. He was wise enough to know that he was far better fitted for acting the butterfly rôles of farce and comedy than the tragic conceptions of Hamlet and Othello; but he did play, and successfully, the characters of Iago, Wolsey, and Richard the Third, which, even though tinged with melodrama, are not devoid of shading. Where the shades were hidden in him that answered to those powerful distortions we can only guess. He shows merely the bright and witty intelligence.

His purity of purpose, within limits, is less to be arraigned. The social image of the man, as we have said, he perceived and rendered clearly; if it was less than he perceived, it was all he intended to tell, and there is neither deception nor intention of deception. There is no specious air of inward revelation. All is frankly on the surface alone. Of either organization or completeness we find hardly a trace. The events of his life are only sketchily referred to. He mentions his marriage, but without naming his wife, and an announcement of his almost annual parenthood appears only while he is telling us that his muse was nearly as prolific. The book is, what Gibbon disclaimed desiring his to be, 'a gallery of portraits,' mainly irrelevant to the story of Cibber's life, however glittering in themselves. Cluttered thus with irrelevance in a way found neither in Herbert nor in Bunyan, for so bright a picture of the surface man to appear is a triumph of vivacity that owes nothing to either depth or form.

Gibbon's lack of depth in certain ranges of his life is undoubtedly the result of deliberate choice. Some little falsifications vanity may have produced, but no 'enthusiasm' clouded his vision even of himself; the round and rather pompous little man in his flowered velvet was as sharply aware of his own nature as was even the partisan malice of Boswell. But those perceptions were part of his 'private' character; they did not belong in, because he did not see that they affected, the character of the great historian. The nature and the depths of the historian Gibbon saw, and rendered. For this reason we can say that, within its limitations, Gibbon's purity of purpose was sustained. It was not the naked man he was painting, but 'the history of the historian.' As a historian he well knew his qualities and his debts: his irony, he tells us, was consciously formed on the *Lettres Provinciales* of the great Pascal. If, in our modern tendency to ride the hobby-horse of psychoanalysis, we feel some relationship between his youthful resentment at Mlle Curchod's cheerful acquiescence in his loss and the calm with which his history narrates wholesale rape, Gibbon was hardly to blame if he was unaware of it.

As a literary structure, his work surpasses any of the others we have here examined. It neither stops short midway, like Herbert's, nor confines itself to one significant struggle and crisis, like Bunyan's, but is the whole story of the historian carried into the autumn of life, past his struggles and triumphs, almost to the end of his days. Unlike Cibber's, which is formless and scattered in purpose, there is no particle of irrelevance. A social image, like Cibber's, it is fuller and better planned, and has more shading, if not all that would have been possible in the delineation of the inward man. Completely untinged by Romantic passion, it is a work of Classic art.

MEMOIR AND DIARY

17th Century

IV

MEMOIR AND DIARY
17TH CENTURY

Their Character and Flavor

MEMOIRS and reminiscences are a rather miscellaneous class of personal writing. Diaries are somewhat more sharply defined. But both are the raw materials out of which biography and autobiography may be shaped more often than they are clearly formed works of art themselves. The very words, reminiscence and memoir, imply a certain informality of nature and purpose; they are what the writer can remember at the time of writing. They pretend to no effort at filling in blanks or correcting false impressions or achieving any perspective of reasoned judgment; they make no claim to have consulted documents or other people, nor to the discipline of remembering better.

And, whatever blanks and jerks of movement there may be in a diary, it is conversely a day-to-day record. In all sorts of moods, in fair fortune and in ill, the writer put down whatever struck him, deeds, gossip, public events, impressions of other people, possibly all helter-skelter. He promises nothing in the way of bringing together scattered judgments or feelings into any singleness of vision. Violent contradictions may flow from him unchecked, as the entry of one day is written in hate, another in love, one in high spirits and another in grief.

Unified plan seldom exists in such writings. If they achieve striking effects of singleness, if they are bathed in any strong light of personality, it is apt to be less through the organization of their several parts than the stamp of their maker's character upon them. The nature of a man may dye so deeply the texture of everything he writes that the mere color of his work, as it were, is suffused with him. Or a complex impression of personality may be built up, bit by bit, in a bright mosaic of minute touches, as multitudinous as the tiny hints from which we shape our idea of a man's character in life. Informality may run riot here, and even if there be a system it may well be shaped on a different plan than those of biography and autobiography.

The appeal of any of these forms of writing may be biographical or autobiographical in nature. The memoirist may train his attention upon some figure whose personality and doings he projects from the magic-lantern store of memory. Or, like a string of shining beads, he may show us in turn experiences and encounters with a host of others associated only by having been known to him. In this sense, Colley Cibber's *Apology*, although it is strung upon a loose thread of life-narrative, is rather more a volume of memoirs than an autobiography; and indeed he does not call it his life-story, but an apology for his life. Even the diarist may be read sometimes with more interest in the events he observed, as we do in Samuel Pepys's account of the festive return of Charles II to England, and sometimes with more interest in the man there unveiled, as we do in other, slyer passages of that exhilarating work.

Our line of distinction, then, between these writings and history, biography, or autobiography, is a slim and fluctuating one. Evelyn's *Diary* is so complete and characteristic that it tells almost all the story of his life; and although only nine years is covered by the *Diary of Samuel Pepys* it gives us a brilliant full-length portrait of the man. The *Memoirs of the Life of Colonel Hutchinson* are hardly distinguishable from a formal biography. The naming in such case is more a matter of arbitrary choice than of correctness. Usually, however, memoirs and reminiscence are apt to lean heavily on anecdote, episode, and character-sketch, isolated fragments rather than connected narrative. The memoirist sometimes analyzes his subject under an abstract psychology, or presents us with a stiff panegyric, or a group of Theophrastian characters. When plan does exist it may be one of these rather than that of following events in their sequence of time.

In writings so little defined hardly any formal rules of excellence are to be found. Scattering and diversity are almost in their nature. Vividness and truthfulness of effect they should have. But even here, a monumental boaster, like Benvenuto Cellini, or a scandalous talemonger, like Brantôme, may achieve what we may call the truth of characteristic falsehood through a cloud of prevarication or hyperbole. Sometimes the drama of men and events, and always their character, we may legitimately look for. The criteria of depth and purity in such things are still relevant. But organization and any save a superficial continuity, if we find them, are added gifts.

Featherwit and Cavalier

The Civil War into which the obstinate royal folly of Charles I precipitated his realm split England in two. Poetry and drama has often presented it as a struggle of Cavaliers and Roundheads, the gay, courtly, long-curled gentlemen, rhyming, wining, and wenching, and all loyal to their King, and the dour Jeremiah Spintexts, in sad drab clothes, moralizing rebellion and regicide. It was not really so, although it is true that republicanism and puritanism usually went together, and that most of the lighter wits, the Lovelaces and the Sucklings, fought for the King. In the desperate struggle that sharpened to civil conflict, the claims of interest or conscience divided members of the same family, and brother fought against brother. Not the least of the interest in the *Memoirs of the Life of Colonel Hutchinson* and *The Life of the Duke of Newcastle* resides in the way they show us opposing sides during those trying times.

Margaret Lucas, who became Duchess of Newcastle, was no more than twenty-four years of age when the King was beheaded in 1649 and during nearly all of the struggle she was abroad, first as Maid of Honour to the Queen and later as the second wife of her exiled Lord. But he himself had played a prominent rôle in command of the King's forces before the fatal defeat at Hessom-moor.

It was partly in defense of his generalship that her book was written.

Lucy Hutchinson was born the daughter of Sir Allen Apsley, Lieutenant-Governor of the Tower. Only seven years, at most, the senior of the Duchess of Newcastle, her marriage brought her from the first into the thick of hostilities. Her father and his family were Royalists, but Colonel John Hutchinson, a man of serious, almost puritanic disposition and of republican sentiments, had speedily declared himself on the side of the Parliament. He took a leading position both in military and legislative opposition to the King.

Both the ladies were women of some originality, and hesitate not to lay claim thereto. The Duchess had a fertile invention, attested by a copious bibliography beginning ambitiously at the age of twenty-seven with a work entitled *Philosophical Fancies*, and running through poems, orations, 'sociable letters,' comedies, tragedies, and observations upon experimental philosophy. 'I have heard,' she says, that Aristotle 'was a great philosopher,' but also that 'his memory failed in his writings, for that he sometimes contradicted himself.' She had not read his works, because she 'had a naturall stupidity towards the learning of any other language than my native tongue,' but she 'swore if the schools did not banish Aristotle' and read her instead 'they did her wrong.' 'Some should say,' she tells us, 'my wit seemed as if it would overpower my brain,' but she believes her brain to be even stronger than her wit. In speech she may not be quite appreciated, for she fears that when she has spoken to people it has not always been 'according as their capacities lay.' And even in writing she doubts that she can do herself justice, for 'the several wayes my thoughts move in are much smoother than the tongue in my mouth, from whence words flow, or the paper on which my pen writes,' and therefore the swiftness of her fancy 'is many times lost.'

There is much evidence that her mind outstrips her pen, leaving that exhausted implement almost gasping in the effort to hold the pace. In a single sentence she speaks of her father's death, her mother's grief, the way the rebels plundered them of plate, corn, jewels, and cattle, her mother's majesty of carriage, her beauty, and her affection for her children, who are thus described: 'three sons and five daughters . . . not any one crooked, or any ways deformed, neither were they dwarfish, or of giant-like stature, but every ways proportionable; likewise well-featured, cleer complexions, brown hairs, but some lighter than others, sound teeth, sweet breaths, plain speeches, tunable voices, I mean not so much to sing as in speaking, as not stuttering, nor wharling in the throat, or speaking through the nose, or hoarsly, unless they had a cold, or squeakingly, which impediments many have: neither were their voices of too low a strain, or too high, but their notes and words were tunable and timely': and from thence the voluble sentence runs on for another full page of variegated topics.

The same qualities she reveals in her account of herself appear in her life of the Duke. Samuel Pepys read it, and was roundly contemptuous. 'March 18 [1668],' he writes. 'Thence home, and there in favour to my eyes, staid at home reading the ridiculous history of my Lord Newcastle, wrote by his wife; which shows her to be a mad, conceited, ridiculous woman, and he an ass to suffer her to write what she writes about him and of him. So to bed, my eyes being very bad.' Somewhat more curtailed and less Molly-Bloomish in syntax than her own *Memoirs* (possibly the Duke's more scholastic eye overran the pointing), it is almost equally without system, and what system it has is bad.

The *Life* is divided into four books. The first two are narrative, dealing with his life until his departure from England, and his life in exile and after the Restoration. The Third Book celebrates his notable qualities under a series of such headings as 'Of His Prudence and Wisdom,' 'Of His Natural Wit and Understanding,' 'Of His Discourse,' 'Of His Outward Shape and Behaviour,' and 'Of His Diet.' The Fourth Book consists of 'Several Essays and Discourses Gathered from the Mouth of My Noble Lord and Husband.'

Such a method is admirably calculated to divorce action from character: in one part of the book we are told, almost barely, what the Duke did; in another, entirely separated, what he thought or said about such things. We alternate between a nearly colorless catalog of narrative and the dry sawdust of empty generalization and unpointed anecdote.

If people like Charles Lamb have admired the Duchess, his 'fantastical and original-brained, generous Margaret Newcastle,' it has perhaps been because she has tickled their fancy by the cloud-capped pinnacles of her vanity and the unpredictable nature of her observations. She hopes her readers will not think her vain for writing her life, 'since there have been many that have done the like, as Caesar, Ovid, and many more, both men and women, and I know no reason I may not do it as well as they:' but in another place we are told that she does not regard 'carping tongues, or malicious censorers, for I despise them.' All readers may know she writes 'for my own sake, not theirs'; but she would not like it if 'after-ages should mistake, in not knowing . . . I was second wife to the Lord Marquess of Newcastle; for My Lord having had two wives, I might easily have been mistaken, especially if I should dye and My Lord marry again.'

Although a rival to Aristotle, her 'serious study could not be much, by reason I took great delight in attiring, fine dressing, and fashions, especially such fashions as I did invent myself, not taking that pleasure in such fashions as was invented by others . . . for I always took delight in a singularity . . .' Pepys bears testimony to this, for he records that 'all the town-talk is now-a-days of her extravagancies, with her velvet-cap, her hair about her ears; many black patches, because of pimples about her mouth; naked-necked, without anything about it, and a black *juste-au-corps*.' But, for all these 'antique fashions' and fantasies, she had as soon enclose herself 'like an anchoret, wearing a frize gown, tied with a cord about my waste.'

The fantastic creature begins her life of her husband with some ostentation, dividing the kinds of history into '(1) A general history. (2) A national history. (3) A particular history . . . The first is mechanical, the second political, and the third heroical . . . This History'—like Caesar's *Commentaries*, she tells us—'is of the third sort.' Therefore it cannot be expected 'that I should here preach of the beginning of the world' nor give 'tedious moral discourses'; and a number of other ways of 'swelling the bulk' of her work are also denied her, so that she cannot 'make this book larger.' And with this we are in full cry of panegyric and celebration of misfortune.

When His Majesty was so 'unjustly and unmannerly treated' by Parliament, her Lord raised an army of eight thousand foot, horse, and dragoons, and as a general some time later won a tremendous victory at Atherton-moor, 'notwithstanding he had quitted 7000 men to conduct Her Majesty': 'about 3000 were taken prisoners.'

But 'There was such jugling, treachery, and falsehood in his own army' that it was impossible for him to be prosperous. 'In all actions and undertakings where My Lord was in person himself, he was always victorious . . .; but whatsoever was lost or succeeded ill, happened in his absence . . .' There was no doubt of the Duke's gallantry and courage; it was only in the fantasy of his wife, however, that he was a military tactician.

Abroad he lived on credit till the Restoration. The return was not so glorious as had been hoped. Some of his estates had been in the rebels' hands and were in ruins; Welbeck and Bolsover were unrepaired and almost pulled down; his parks were nearly all destroyed and their timbers cut: all told his losses, including revenue from the estates for those sixteen years, she indignantly totals as £941,303. And His Majesty was not as grateful as he should have been; some of his estate her Lord could not get back at all, in spite of all his services to the crown, including two magnificent entertainments given years ago to Charles I, at Welbeck, with a splendid feast and a masque by Ben Jonson.

But he bore it all with equanimity, for 'My Lord may justly be compared to Titus the Deliciae of Mankind, by reason of his sweet, gentle, and obliging nature.' He engaged, by virtue of a natural wit and judgment, in philosophical discussion, although he had not much scholarship, and supplied Mr Hobbes, the philosopher, with a number of valuable ideas the latter used in his *Leviathan.* He took great delight in the exercise of weapons, but even more in the 'art of Mannage,' or riding the warhorse, in which he was so pre-eminent that he wrote a dignified treatise thereon. 'The rest of his time he spends in musick, poetry, architecture, and the like.'

The delight of Charles Lamb in the feather-brained author of this work was a mixture of affection and amusement, and his sense of humor has fathered an entire school rather less amiable than he was, for in Lamb the amusement was tempered by a lively awareness of the way in which the lady epitomized the follies of humanity, including himself. Some of the modern admirers of the Duchess smirk knowingly at her unconscious absurdities, and enhance their own sense of superiority by a supercilious enjoyment. It is no such admirable wit to perceive that a rattle-pate is a rattle-pate, and the pleasures of unintended humor the civilized reader should easily exhaust. Margaret Newcastle was an amiable creature, but her achievements in the life of her husband and the memoir of herself are slight and mostly accidental.

Regicides and Puritans

Lucy Hutchinson is a more serious person altogether. If she too has the vanity of telling us how she outstripped her brothers in the study of Latin as a child, and of remarking that her husband first became interested in her because he thought one of her sonnets showed 'something of rationality . . . beyond the customary reach of a she-wit,' she amply justifies her own good opinion by her narrative. It has vividness of phrase, skill in construction and characterization, clarity and depth in judgment. Although blemished by a few very occasional longueurs, and some repetitious pieties of language, it moves with drama and force. Her admiration for her husband was high, and it may be that she represents him as a little more invariably right than any human being is likely to be. Many others, however, admired him almost as highly and his deeds tell their own objective story. The writing is full of the flavor and color and feeling of the times. Lucy Hutchinson has been called a sour and disagreeable bluestocking, but her book seems to me to reveal a very pleasing youthful romanticism in its earlier pages and a serious serenity in many of its later.

We begin with her birth. 'The land was then at peace . . . if that quietness may be called a peace, which was rather like the calm and smooth surface of the sea, whose dark womb is already impregnated with a horrid tempest,' and we are reminded ominously that the throne of England was the heritage of a 'Norman usurper, who partly by violence, partly by falsehood, laid here the foundations of his monarchy, in the people's blood, in which it hath swam about five hundred years, till the flood that bore it was ploughed into such deep furrows as had almost sunk the proud vessel.'

But meanwhile all was calm. Her mother, 'while she was with child of me,' dreamed that she was walking in a garden and a star came down into her hand: and the child was talented in languages, music, dancing, and writing. Although piously brought up, the young girl 'thought it no sin to learn or hear witty songs and amorous sonnets or poems, and twenty things of that kind.' Presently Mr Hutchinson came to hear of 'how reserved and studious' she was, and found some of her Latin books in a closet, and his desire of seeing her was inflamed. For, though he 'practised tennis' for exercise and had 'a great mastery on the viol,' he was a serious young man himself. He had already resisted the advances of ladies who were handsome, witty, wealthy, and 'set out with all the gaiety and vanity that vain women put on to set themselves off,' including one whose beauty 'would have thawed a rock of ice.'

All these he passed by, but falling strangely infatuated with this lady whom he had not yet seen, on hearing a rumor that she was married, he 'turned pale as ashes, and felt a fainting to seize his spirits.' The rumor proved untrue, and they presently were made acquainted. The story of their courtship 'would make a true history of a more handsome management of love than the best romances describe.' But 'There is only this to be recorded, that never was a passion more ardent and less idolatrous,' and that 'she was a very faithful mirror, reflecting truly, though but dimly, his own glories on him' until he was gone, and then 'was only filled with a dark mist, and could never again . . . return any shining representation.' Find among the noblest of the Cavaliers a deeper romanticism!

The shining and carefree days soon passed. 'About the year 1639, the thunder was heard afar off rattling in the troubled air, and even the most obscured woods were penetrated with some flashes, the forerunners of the dreadful storm . . .' For Charles I, though he 'was temperate, chaste, and serious,' encouraging 'men of learning and ingenuity in all arts,' was proving 'a worse encroacher upon the civil and spiritual liberties of his people by far than his father. He married a papist, a French lady, of a haughty spirit, and a great wit and beauty, to whom he became a most uxorious husband.' 'He was the most obstinate person in his self-will that ever was, and so bent upon being an absolute, uncontrollable sovereign, that he was resolved either to be such a king or none.' Strafford and Laud were powerful instruments of tyranny, but in November, 1640, the Long Parliament convened and the two were convicted of high treason and sent to their deaths. But the King would abide by no covenants. Open rebellion at last broke out.

Mrs Hutchinson's account of events has been called bigoted and intolerant. Harold Nicolson accuses her of regarding the Royalists simply as 'debauchees' and 'ungodly,' and of speaking continually of '*their* darkness and *our* light.' It may be interesting to compare her characterization of the Earl of Newcastle (as he then was) with what she says of some of her own party. His 'great estate, his liberal hospitality, and constant residence in his country' had 'so endeared them to him, that no man was a greater prince in all that northern quarter; till a foolish ambition of glorious slavery carried him to court, where he ran himself much into debt, to purchase neglects of the king and queen, and scorns of the proud courtiers.' This is adverse, but not without respect for his merits and loyalty; and she tells of his magnanimous behavior much later when Colonel Hutchinson was under arrest. 'Colonel,' said he, 'they say you desire to know your accusers, which is more than I know,' and showed him a letter from the Duke of Buckingham accusing him of a plot; 'which my lord was so satisfied the colonel was innocent of, that he dismissed him without guard to his own house, only engaging him to stay there one week, till he gave account to the council . . .'

Her severity to her own side is no less than her moderation to the other. 'When puritanism grew into a faction, the zealous distinguished themselves, both men and women, by several affectations of habit, looks, and words' which were only a pretense and a hypocrisy. The troops of Sir John Gell, one of the Parliament men, she characterizes as 'good stout, fighting men, but the most licentious, ungovernable wretches,' and Sir John himself as 'a foul adulterer,' unjust, revengeful, and malicious. Millington and White, two leading members of the Puritan party, 'were so ensnared that they married a couple of alehouse wenches,' a course especially scandalous in the former, 'a man of sixty, professing religion, and having but lately buried a religious, matronly gentlewoman.' There is not much in these passages of '*their* darkness and *our* light.'

Indeed her history is full of the evils produced by dissensions within her own camp. As Governor of the town and castle of Nottingham, Colonel Hutchinson was constantly harassed by the jealousies of his associates. At last, hating these 'secret heartburnings,' he was obliged to call them together and tell them that if his power was in any way disagreeable to them he would decline serving, but if they wished him to continue he would not brook 'any thwarting or crossing of powers and commands.' But although they answered with smooth words, they continued to be obstructive, and the whole cause everywhere suffered much from 'secret enemies and refractory friends.' Sometimes their treasurers cheated the soldiers out of their rewards and pay, so that the men were close to mutiny and difficult to make obey orders; sometimes wandering detachments of troops used such 'saucy language' that once the Colonel was provoked to 'beat them out of the house and town'; and the factions of presbyterians and independents into which the party had split gave courage to the King and his party, and 'hardened him and them to their ruin.'

At last there seemed only one resort. The King was brought to trial, charged with 'betraying the public trust' and 'being an implacable enemy to the commonwealth.' He disowned the authority of the court, and the charges of all the blood spilled by his misdeeds, 'he heard with disdainful smiles, and looks and gestures which rather expressed sorrow that all the opposite party to him were not cut off, than that any were . . .' He was sentenced to death, and beheaded at the block.

'But now had the poison of ambition so ulcerated Cromwell's heart' that he began 'moulding the army to his mind, weeding out the godly and upright-hearted . . .' 'The colonel saw through him, and'—rather irritatingly—' forebore not to tell him what was suspected of his ambition, what dissimulations of his were remarked,' and how destructive 'to the most glorious cause' these things would be if true. Cromwell wore 'the most open face' of friendship, although the Colonel knew he resented it. Ultimately he made himself tyrant under the title of Lord Protector, 'only, to speak the truth . . . he had much natural greatness, and well became the place he had usurped.' Although solicited to do so by the Lord Protector himself, Colonel Hutchinson refused to act in any office, and retired to his house at Owthorpe, where he busied himself arranging his paintings, sculptures, and engravings, in improving his estate, in the enjoyment of music with his viol, 'and entertaining tutors for the diversion and education of his children.'

With the death of Cromwell the Commonwealth fell to pieces and at last confusion could think of no better solution than to recall the Stuarts. Bonfires burned rumps in scorn of that Rump Parliament which had crept back after the shadow of Cromwell, and when Charles II came by water to London, seeing 'all the nobility and gentry of the land flowing in to him,' he asked 'where were his enemies.'

The Colonel, however, remained unchanged in his principles.

'If he had erred,' he said in his defense before Parliament, 'it was the inexperience of his age, and the defect of his judgment, and not the malice of his heart'; if the sacrifice of him were for the public good, he would submit to it; and as for the death of Charles I, 'he desired them to believe he had that sense of it that befitted an Englishman, a Christian, and a gentleman.' The art and dexterity of this address, respectful without retraction, temporarily effected his safety, and it seemed that by the Act of Oblivion he was freed of future danger.

But the King was reported to have said that if the Colonel were unrestrained he 'would do the same thing for him that he had done for his father,' and efforts were made to terrify him into betraying his late associates. On a 'bitter, stormy, pitchy, dark, black, rainy night' he was illegally arrested and guarded in 'a most vile room.' After a brief release he was again arrested, confined in the Tower, and then sent to Sandown Castle. Here 'the bleak air of the sea' and the tide washing 'the foot of the castle walls' made the chamber 'so unwholesome and damp, that even in the summer' things were covered with mould and rain seeped through the cracks in the walls.

The Colonel had long been unwell, and at last, coming home to jail after a walk by the seaside, he 'found himself aguish, with a kind of shivering and pain in his bones, and going to bed did sweat exceedingly: . . . after that he slept no more till his last sleep came upon him . . . When some named Mrs Hutchinson, and said "Alas, how will she be surprised!" he fetched a sigh, and within a little while departed; his countenance settling so amiably and cheerfully after death, that he looked . . . as he used to do when best pleased in life.' He was brought home to Owthorpe 'with honour to his grave through the dominions of his murderers, who were ashamed of his glories, which all their tyrannies could not extinguish with his life.'

Mrs Hutchinson's narrative is not only a valuable historical document but a vivid personal record. If she does not color the actions of the King and the opposing party with the fervor of loyalty and prerogative they might use in their own minds, she is remarkably fair and restrained as a partisan writer. However noble the devotion of some of the Cavaliers to their sovereign, and however pathetic their sufferings, their opponents clearly had justice with them. And if there were zealots and fanatics who blackened the name of Puritan with intolerance and gloom, the calm and serious cheerfulness and the moderation of those like the Hutchinsons all show plainly enough that Puritanism too had its more gracious side. The squabbles between Colonel Hutchinson and the committee of Nottingham we can hardly adjudicate, and the Colonel seems at times almost annoyingly right in a sea of wrongheadedness and self-seeking. But it is noteworthy that many leading Royalists, and a Parliament that could agree on hardly anything else, united to exempt him from the measures taken against the other regicides. These facts confirm our belief that the loving prejudice of the wife very little exaggerated the merits of the man.

Pepys the Man

The voice of Samuel Pepys is heard just a little while before that of Mrs Hutchinson falls silent. He tells us of the festivities that hailed the end of the Rump Parliament. 'In Cheapside there was a great many bonfires, and Bow bells and all the bells in all the churches as we went home were a-ringing . . . and all along burning, and roasting, and drinking for rumps. There being rumps tied upon sticks and carried up and down. The butchers at the May Pole in the Strand rang a peal with their knives when they were going to sacrifice their rump . . . At one end of the street you would think there was a whole lane of fire, and so hot that we were fain to keep still on the further side merely for heat.' And only that morning he had lain long abed, had a roasted pullet for dinner, enjoyed singing with Mr Chetwind, and drunk sundry half pints of wine in a number of alehouses.

Thus, characteristically, the *Diary of Samuel Pepys* starts speaking to us. He had begun it on the New Year of 1660, and this was only the eleventh of February, but already he had recorded a number of representative adventures. We have been to church with him and heard that Mr Gunning 'made a very good sermon' on the text 'That in the fullness of time God sent his son, made of a woman &c.' We have seen him buy a dozen bottles of sack, play cards at Will's, spend a little time 'at our viols,' be troubled by a swelling nose, and come home late at night to find 'my wife and maid a-washing. I staid up till the bell-man came by with his bell just under my window as I was writing of this very line, and cried,

"Past one of the clock, and a cold, frosty, windy morning." I then went to bed, and left my wife and the maid a-washing still.'

The strange thing is that such trivial details can body forth the inner subleties of the man who wrote them. We not only have the man in the round, in a way much more familiar with the flavor of daily life than any of our autobiographers, but somehow the singing with Mr Chetwind and the wife and maid washing late at night while he goes to bed are the unpretentious signs by which we read much that ordinarily goes unnoted. These daily annotations give us Pepys in spiritual undress in a way that even the least ostentatious autobiography is not apt to achieve.

Mr Pepys was, for example, as we have already seen, fond of music. The autobiographer would be liable, even with no intention of 'impressing' his readers, to generalize a bit about his musical development and tastes: 'at this time,' he would say, 'I was fond of such and such and went much to . . .' and there would almost necessarily be a slight self-consciousness about his handling of the subject, a heightening of dignity and a loss in the real living quality of his enjoyment. Through trying to choose what is profoundly significant out of so much, a kind of freshness is lost.

But, says Pepys, 'Thence we went to the Green Dragon, on Lambeth Hill, both the Mr Pinckneys, Smith, Harrison, Morice, that sang the bass, Sheply and I, and there we sang of all sorts of things, and I ventured with good success upon things at first sight, and after that I played on my flageolet, and staid there till nine o'clock, very merry and drawn on with one song after another till it came to be so late.' We do not know what songs Mr Pepys and his friends sang in the Green Dragon, but we do know the flavor of their enjoyment, and we relish the air of innocent vanity with which he congratulates himself on the not altogether expected triumph of his sight-reading. We feel sure that they had a very gay melodious time indeed.

The difference in quality is a result of a very delicate adjustment in the nature of the details chosen. Precisely through the fact that he has not tried to choose things weighted down with significance for the heavy entity a man is apt to be for himself, he attains an artlessness that tells us even more. If Colley Cibber and Edward Gibbon in their varying ways were drawing their public selves for us, Samuel Pepys is as clearly unveiling the private man, for whose image a swelling nose is sometimes more important than the influence of Pascal. If Gibbon had seen himself as an almost spherical little figure, tapping his snuff-box while he formed his periods, and 'His mouth, mellifluous as Plato's, a round hole, nearly in the center of his visage,' how much clearer an image of the man as well as the historian he would have given us!

For those aspects of Gibbon we must depend on the outside observer; Samuel Pepys is the observer, and sometimes even the eavesdropper, on himself. He curiously devotes the same attention to his privacies as most autobiographers devote to their public achievements, and his references to his public life are almost as casual and accidental as their revelations of the secret man. 'Did business, though not much at the office,' he says, or 'Busy all morning writing letters'; but then he must go to dinner, or there is a new 'coloured silk suit very fine, and my new periwigg' to be tried on, and the less enticing subject disappears.

It was not that he had no business of importance to perform. At the time of the Restoration he was twenty-seven years of age, a graduate of Magdalene College, Cambridge. His worldly prospects largely depended on his being a protégé of the Earl of Sandwich, who presently obtained him a minor post in the Admiralty. He became Clerk of the Acts in the same year, and, as Secretary of the Admiralty, did almost all the work of the Admiralty during the plague.

Mainly through his ability and conscientious labors the British navy became soundly organized and efficiently administered; and during a Parliamentary investigation of charges of corruption Pepys not only destroyed the accusations but scored a resounding personal triumph. His complete grasp of all naval affairs was acknowledged, but he retired from office when William and Mary came to the throne. Two years later, in 1690, he published his *Memoirs relative to the State of the Royal Navy*.

He was not only an able public servant, but a man of taste and scientific curiosity as well. He was a member of the Royal Society, its President from 1684 to 1686, and a friend of the eminent connoisseur, Mr John Evelyn. His valuable library of about three thousand volumes, including his *Diary* in six volumes bound in calf and stamped with his crest and arms, was bequeathed to Magdalene College.

But the public figure that looms so large in other men's recordings of themselves is no more than on the margin of Pepys's *Diary*. The doings he sets down with endless exuberance are the ephemerae that make up nine-tenths of life. Therefore his *Diary* is alive in a way seldom attained by others. And it is not only the things recorded that give his entries their peculiar life. It is the strange white light of absolute honesty in which they are bathed. Pepys seems to have written with no idea of any other eyes than his ever reading his pages, and to have been singularly free from the temptation of posing before himself. Blame himself he often did, but a strength or an equanimity underlying all enabled him to view the naked man without palliation; although sometimes the embarrassed wrigglings of conscience forced him to resort to a jargon of bastard French or Spanish: a not incurious trait. But never is there a hint of the kind of embarrassment or disingenuousness that might proceed from the thought of his intimate life being seen.

Whether this purely private character was true in fact we can only guess. The *Diary* was kept from 1660 to 1669, and was written in a sort of cipher or shorthand the key to which is found in a treatise called *Tachygraphy*, by Thomas Shelton. This volume is in the Pepysian Library. Undoubtedly Pepys did not intend his *Diary* to be read by any of his companions or house-mates. Perhaps he wrote it entirely for himself, and it was merely left unread or unreadable among the mass of books he willed the College. Perhaps in later years (for he survived the last entry he wrote by thirty-four years) he decided that what had been intended for himself alone should be given a chance to meet the eye of posterity. Whatever the truth, it was not so revealed until 1825, when it was first published by Lord Braybrooke. It had taken a young Magdalene undergraduate three years, working twelve to fourteen hours a day, to decipher it.

Mr Pepys enjoyed the theatre, especially works of comedy if they were not too fanciful (for he shared some of the narrow Gallic classicism of his day) and tragedy done in the grand style. 'To the Opera,' he writes, 'and there saw "Hamlet, Prince of Denmark," done with scenes very well, but above all, Betterton did the prince's part beyond imagination.' But *Midsummer's Night's Dream* was 'the most insipid ridiculous play that ever I saw in my life. I saw, I confess, some good dancing and some handsome women, which was all my pleasure.' Indeed the introduction of women on the stage is a great sensation to him. 'Saw "Argalus and Parthenia,"' he notes, 'where a woman acted Parthenia, and came afterwards on the stage in men's clothes, and had the best legs that ever I saw, and I was very pleased with it.' *Macbeth* he approved, and *The Feign Innocence, or Sir Martin Marr-all*, by the Duke of Newcastle. 'It is the most entire piece of mirth, a complete farce from one end to the other, that certainly was ever writ . . . I laughed till my head [ached] all the evening and night with laughing; and at very good wit therein, not fooling.' But *The Silent Woman* was 'the best comedy, I think, that ever was wrote; and sitting by Shadwell the poet, he was big with admiration of it.'

The theatre, too, was often the scene of adventures with the fair sex, of whom Mr Pepys was an ardent admirer. At a performance of *The Lost Lady*, 'sitting behind in a dark place, a lady spit backward on me by mistake, but after seeing her to be a very pretty lady, I was not troubled at it at all.' But he was somewhat discomposed when he and Captain Cooke were received with more intimacy than he had anticipated at the house of Mr Glanville, where they 'sat talking and playing with Mrs Penington, whom we found undressed in her smocke and petticoats by the fireside, and there we drank and laughed, and she willingly suffered me to put my hand in her bosom very wantonly, and keep it there long. Which methought was very strange, and I looked upon myself as a man mightily deceived in a lady, for I could not have thought she could have suffered it, by her former discourse with me; so modest she seemed and I know not what.'

Indeed, beauty was never far from the yielding heart of Mr Pepys. Whether at an inn where he 'kissed the daughter of the house, she being very pretty,' or letting himself be overcharged for a pair of gloves trimmed with yellow ribbon, because 'she is so pretty, that God forgive me, I could not think it too much,' he is always thrilled by feminine loveliness. Of a new housemaid he remarks glumly that she is ugly to look at (his jealous young French wife perhaps took care of that), even if satisfactory in other respects. When the sermons were dull at divine worship, his imagination (like ours) was apt to go sliding up some graceful leg or sinking into a pretty bosom; and he tells us of his experience standing by a maid in St Dunstan's Church 'whom I did labor to take by the hand and body' until she was forced to repel his attentions by taking 'pins out of her pocket to prick me if I should touch her again—which seeing I did forebear and was glad I did spy her design.'

Lady Castlemaine, the lovely mistress of Charles II, however, was the far-off goddess of his dreams. Even the sight of her lingerie hung to dry is thrilling to him. 'And in the Privy-garden saw the finest smocks and linen petticoat of my Lady Castlemaine's laced with rich lace at the bottom, that I ever saw; and did me good to look upon them.' His *Diary* saddens when she is rumored out of the King's favor, and 'strange it is,' he confesses, 'how for her beauty I am willing to construe all this to the best and to pity her wherein it is to her hurt, though I know well enough she is a whore.'

These same romances of his, whether they were confined to timorous reverie or found outlet in stray caresses, gave him sufficient trouble at home. For Mrs Pepys knew or suspected the susceptible nature of her husband and had a violent temper herself. And, like many another husband, Pepys did not care to extend to his wife that liberty he conferred on himself. At Mrs Hunt's, he 'found a Frenchman, a lodger of her's, at dinner, and just as I came in was kissing my wife, which I did not like . . .'

And the woman persisted in wearing garments which, while attractive on other women, on his wife were brazen. This occasioned quarrels: 'she fell all of a sudden to discourse about her clothes and my humours in not suffering her to wear them as she pleases, and grew to high words between us . . .' Seeing that the storm was going to continue for some time Mr Pepys, enragingly, 'fell to read a book (Boyle's Hydrostatiques) aloud . . . and let her talk till she was tired and vexed that I would not hear her,' and so they became friends again, 'and to bed together the first night after 4 or 5 that she hath lain from me by reason of a great cold she had got.'

All told, 'poor wretch,' she made him fond of her, and although only the Sunday before he had stayed in the church 'door to gaze upon a pretty lady, and from church dogged her home' to near Tower Hill, he notes of 10 October, 1664: 'This day, by the blessing of God, my wife and I have been married nine years . . . bless God for our long lives and loves and health together, which the same God long continue, I wish from my very heart!'

The *Diary* is a rich mine of information about domestic manners in the period. We have him whipping their boy-of-all-work with a rod, but so small that 'it did not much hurt to him, but only to my arm . . .' The servants dwell not only in the house but sometimes sleep in the same room with their masters, and they often join in the music and song which were so frequent in the home. His wife and her maids quarrel, appealing to him for judgment: 'Before going to bed Ashwell began to make her complaint . . . I do perceive she has received most base usage from my wife, which my wife sillily denies, but it is impossible the wench could invent words and matter so particularly, which my wife has nothing to say but flatly to deny.' Meals are always copious: 'a dish of marrow bones; a leg of mutton; a loin of veal; a dish of fowl, three pullets, and two dozen of larks all in a dish; a great tart; a neat's tongue, a dish of anchovies; a dish of prawns, and cheese.'

Sometimes we are given a glimpse into the intricacies of business. One piece of policy is suggestive. Pepys had obtained for a Captain Grove 'the taking up of vessels for Tangier,' and consequently he did not immediately open the letter of acknowledgment from that gentleman. Waiting till he reached his office, 'there I broke it open, not looking into it till all the money was out, that I might say I saw no money in the paper if ever I should be questioned about it. There was a piece of gold and £4 in silver.'

But if he now and then accepted a small present, Pepys was a painstaking public servant who did not spare himself. 'Up at four o'clock in the morning and at five by water to Woolwich there to see the manner of tarring, and all the morning looking to see the several proceedings in making of cordage'; and then a surprise descent on Deptford, where he 'discovered many abuses, which we shall be able to understand hereafter and amend.' In Waltham Forest he discovered how the King was cheated in the timber he bought. His knowledge and alertness were constantly on the increase. In 1665 he had been elated by Albemarle's praise 'that I was the right hand of the Navy here . . . At which I was (from him) not a little proud.' But a few years later, when the same nobleman was given a vote of thanks for his conduct of the Dutch War, Pepys exclaims 'I know not how, the blockhead Albemarle hath strange luck to be loved, though he be, and every man must know it, the heaviest man in the world, but stout and honest to his country.'

Mr Pepys was present on many historical occasions. He heard the King's speech on the Bill for Repealing the Triennal Act, and comments frankly 'he speaks the worst that ever I heard man in my life . . .' The great naval victory over the Dutch is noted with excitement and jubilation. 'Admirall Opdam blown up, Trump killed . . . all the rest of their admiralls, as they say, but Everson are killed . . .' The great Plague is described in poignant entries: 'how empty the streets are and melancholy; so many poor sick people in the streets full of sores . . .' And, although Pepys was no saint himself, we find him recording that 'the King and Court were never in the world so bad as they now are for gaming, swearing, whoring, and drinking, and the most abominable vices that ever were in the world . . . the Court is in a way to ruin all for their pleasures'; and Sir George Carteret had 'taken the liberty to tell the King the necessity of having, at least, a show of religion in the Government, and sobriety.'

In every situation the figure of Mr Pepys is a pleasant one. Whether burning '*L'escholle des filles*, a mighty lewd book,' so that 'it might not be among my books to my shame,' or having his annual feast to celebrate the successful operation he had undergone for the stone, or listening to Dr Tearne deliver a lecture on 'the kidneys, ureters, &c., which was very fine,' he is a pleasant talking-companion. But unhappily his eyes were beginning to trouble him. All the reading he had done and this writing in cipher late at night were threatening him with blindness. So 'I must now forebear: and therefore, resolve, from this time forward, to have it kept by my people in long-hand, and must therefore be contented to set down no more than is fit for them and all the world to know . . .'

'And so I betake me to that course which is almost as much as to see myself go into my grave: for which, and all the discomforts that will accompany my being blind, the good God prepare me!' So he ended, a little more than ten years after he had begun. It is good to know that he did not grow blind after all, but lived another third of a century in respect, activity, and good cheer.

The Model Virtuoso

On the 4th of June, 1679 Mr John Evelyn had dinner with Mr Pepys. The circumstances were somewhat peculiar, for Pepys was a prisoner in the Tower of London, where he had been thrown charged with misdemeanors while he was Secretary of the Admiralty. 'I believe he was unjustly charged,' Evelyn wrote stoutly, and proceeding to send him a piece of venison somewhat later, 'went and din'd with him' again. As we already know, Pepys triumphantly refuted the charges against him, but the entry and even more the action are indices to the character of John Evelyn. He was a more serious-minded man than Mr Pepys, and his sense of right and wrong was strongly developed. Diplomatic enough to avoid giving offense (for during this same time he was conferring with the new Commissioners of the Admiralty), he adhered too firmly to principle to desert a friend whom he believed innocent. He had managed himself with similar skill on previous occasions. Since the time, in 1649, when his translation *Of Liberty and Servitude* had given offense ('for the Preface of which I was severely threatened'), Evelyn had behaved with great circumspection. He was a Royalist, but during the Protectorate, he says, he never took the Covenant, and yet succeeded in retaining his estates and even obtained permission to travel abroad.

Evelyn had, in fact, the happy secret of getting on with everybody. He was so sincerely and indefatigably interested in everything, his curiosity was so endless, he was so eager to hear whatever you had to say, and so restrained in his gentlemanly capacity for avoiding the least suggestion of disapproval, that it was no wonder both the King and his mistresses were no less pleased to have Mr Evelyn being polite to them than were Sir Thomas Browne and Monsieur Zulichem, 'the great mathematician and virtuoso,' 'inventor of the pendule clock, and discoverer of the phenomenon of Saturn's annulus.' It was not that Evelyn was a sycophant. He was well-informed and intelligent, he was an interesting talker and at the same time modest, he was a man of the world. He would not do violence to his conscience, but his conscience was not so exigent that it demanded his being rude to those in great stations. For these, almost as much as Monsieur Zulichem and Sir Thomas Browne, could add to those stores of knowledge he was always insatiably collecting.

His appetite for facts was enormous and his memory for them no less. When he traveled he noted down detailed accounts of the arts, architecture, literature, commerce, state of manufactures, activities in science, public buildings, gardens, and inventions in foreign lands: everything that could be discovered by enquiry or observation. He wrote books on the state of France, sculpture, forestry, numismatics, gardening and topiary work. He was a fellow of the Royal Society, a member of its council in 1662, and Secretary in 1672. His diplomatic talents obtained for it the great Arundelian Library in 1678. When St Paul's Cathedral was to be repaired just before the Fire of London his architectural knowledge led to his being one of the Commissioners. In the same year he was on a Commission for regulating the manufacture of saltpetre. As Treasurer of Greenwich Hospital he did an enormous amount of work. His industry was as inexhaustible as his curiosity.

And everything that he learned, saw, and did, he recorded in his *Diary*. He began keeping it in detail in the year 1641 (the entries before that date are occasional and summary) and continued it in a very small, close hand until he reached the end of a 700 page quarto in 1697, and thence carried it on in a smaller book till within three weeks of his death in his eighty-sixth year. He recorded everything–that is to say, everything of public interest or of intellectual curiosity.

His personal or private adventures and emotions, save on the solemn occasion of a death, he seldom mentions. The flow of instructive or curious facts is endless, current history finds him nearly always on the very spot, sometimes an eccentric anecdote brightens his pages: but there are none of the graceless revelations we find in Pepys. If John Evelyn ever misbehaved his *Diary* does not know of it. Therein we find the gentleman, the Christian, and the man of learning, but the serious pages are never disfigured with even a moment of embarrassment or of absurdity.

Only once can I recall a bit of even unconscious humor, when he records, with some dismay, that 'In the night a cat kitten'd on my bed, and left on it a young one having six ears, eight leggs, two bodys from the navil downwards, and two tayles.' Even here the scientific curiosity soon overbalances the displeasure. Evelyn is always impeccable. He is therefore sometimes a little tiresome.

His even perfection and elevation are real, but either they are not all the man or else he is a man of regrettable solemnity. As he appears in those restrained pages of his, he lacks the charm of Mr Pepys. If he ever had a moment of self-doubt, we feel, it must have been like a debate in some marmoreally lofty Senate: grave, weighty, and imbued with the underlying assurance that ultimately the right decision would be made, unlike the remorses and humiliations of Samuel Pepys. A cheerful and amiable companion in his lifetime he may have been, and possibly—although his *Diary* shows no evidence thereof—even witty, but of any capacity for unbending, for foolery, he shows not a single trace.

It is in the intellectual and historical realms that his *Diary* is especially valuable. When he visited Antwerp he described the Church of the Jesuits 'wholly incrusted with marble, inlay'd and polish'd into divers representations of histories, landskips, flowers, &c.' with 'the Statue of the B. Virgin and our Saviour in white marble' on the altar, and the pulpit 'supported by foure angels and adorn'd with other carvings.' And then, ascending the tower of Notre Dame d'Anvers, 'a venerable fabriq, built after the Gotick manner,' he speculates on the nature of the moon: the bright reflection of the sun's rays from the surface of the earth confirmed his 'opinion of the moon's being of some such substance as this earthy globe consists of; perceiving all the subjacent country, at so small a horizontal distance, to repercuss such a light . . .' On the way to Brussels he admired a canal 'carried on an aqueduct of stone so far above' another which it intersected 'that the waters neither mingle nor hinder one another's passage,' and in Brussels he 'was pleas'd with certain small engines by which a girl or boy was able to draw up, or let downe, great bridges. . . .'

He visited the silk-manufacturing at Tours, 'went to see the wonderful engine for weaving silk stockings, said to have been the invention of an Oxford schollar 40 years since'; and followed a trip to Lambeth, 'that rare magazine of marble,' to order chimney-pieces for the house of his friend Mr Godolphin by a visit to 'the Duke of Buckingham's Glasse-worke, where they made huge vases of mettal as cleare, ponderous, and thick as chrystal; also looking-glasses far larger and better than any that come from Venice.' 'At the Hospital of La Charité I saw the operation of cutting for the stone. A child of 8 or 9 yeares old underwent the operation with most extra-ordinary patience . . .' During the second war with the Dutch he saw a sailor's leg amputated, 'the stout and gallant man enduring it with incredible patience, without being bound to his chaire as usual on such painful occasions. I had hardly courage enough to be present. Not being cut high enough, the gangreen prevail'd, and the second operation cost the poore creature his life.'

He dined at 'that most obliging and universally-curious Dr Wilkins's, at Wadham College,' and was shown the 'hollow statue which gave a voice and utter'd words,' and all the Doctor's collection of 'shadows, dyals, perspectives, and many other artificial, mathematical, and magical curiosities, a way-wiser, a thermometer, a monstrous magnet, conic and other sections . . .' In Paris 'I went to see a Dromedarie, a very monstrous beast . . . and the water-spouter, who drinking only fountaine water, rendred out of his mouth in severall glasses all sorts of wine and sweete waters, &c. For a piece of money he discover'd the secret to me.' It is characteristic of Evelyn that even a magician's trick he insists on understanding. It interested him hardly less than the rare collection of 'that famous scholar and physitian, Dr T. Browne, author of the "Religio Medici," and "Vulgar Errors" &c, now lately knighted.' He was fascinated to be told by Captain Baker, who had been looking for the North West Passage, of the 'prodigious depth of ice, blew as a sapphire, and as transparent.' He listened to Sir Kenelm Digby's tale of how Lady St Ledger had 'such an antipathie' to roses that, 'laying but a rose upon her cheeke when she was asleep, it rais'd a blister'; but this was a shade too much, and 'Sir Kenelm,' he writes, 'was a teller of strange things.'

Unlike his friend Mr Pepys, he was not fond of the theatre. He 'saw Hamlet, Prince of Denmark played, but now the old plays began to disgust this refined age,' and he disapproved that display of feminine charm that aroused the susceptible Pepys. The playhouses, he noted, 'were abused to an atheistical liberty, fowle and undecent women now (and never till now) permitted to appeare and act, who inflaming severall young noblemen and gallants, became their misses . . . to the reproch of their noble families, and ruine of both body and soul.' The King's mistress, Mrs Barlow, he had dismissed wrily as 'a browne, beautifull, bold, but insipid creature,' and the even more celebrated Louise de Querouaille as 'a childish, simple, and baby face'; but he was scandalized at the King exchanging pleasantries with Nell Gwyn, 'an impudent comedian, she looking out of her garden on a terrace at the top of the wall, and [he] standing on the greene walke under it.' He adds that the

King left her to join the Duchess of Cleveland, 'another lady of pleasure, and curse of our nation.'

The more solemn events of history found him present and observant as well. He 'beheld on Tower Hill the fatal stroke which sever'd the wisest head in England from the shoulders of the Earle of Strafford; whose crime coming under the cognizance of no human law, a new one was made not to be a precedent, but his destruction.' The famous windows of Canterbury he saw before they were destroyed by Roundhead fanatics. At Whitehall 'I got privately into the council of the Rebell Army . . . where I heard horrid villanies.'

He saw the return of Charles II: 'the wayes strew'd with flowers, the bells ringing, the streetes hung with tapistry, fountaines running with wine; the Maior, Aldermen, and all the Companies in their liveries, chains of gold, and banners; Lords and Nobles clad in cloth of silver, gold, and velvet; the windowes and balconies well set with ladies; trumpets, music, and myriads of people flocking,' and 'I stood in the Strand and beheld it, and bless'd God.' He describes the coronation of the King, in all its pageantry, and the punishment of the Regicides: 'I saw not their execution, but met their quarters mangl'd and cutt and reeking as they were brought from the gallows in baskets on the hurdle.'

He devotes vivid pages to the Fire of London, with 'nothing heard or seene but crying out and lamentation, running about like distracted creatures, without at all attempting to save even their goods,' and 'all the skie of a fiery aspect, like the top of a burning oven,' 'the noise and cracking and thunder of the impetuous flames,' and 'the fall of Towers, Houses, and Churches like an hideous storme' with clouds of smoke computed to reach fifty-six miles. In the streets 'the stones . . . flew like granados, the mealting lead running downe . . . in a streame, and the very pavements glowing with fiery rednesse . . .'

Save when he deals with regicide or harlotry, Evelyn's opinions are usually tolerant enough. He felt strongly about Milton's defense of the execution of Charles I, but he employed Milton's nephew Edward Phillips, who 'was not at all infected with his principles,' as a tutor for his own son. He was a devout member of the Church of England, but he was able to speak calmly of the Church of Rome. Even from the first he was not infected by the hysteria of the nation in the alleged Catholic Assassination Plot, and distrusted the testimony of the notorious Titus Oates. Only once a little insular prejudice leaps out of him, when, obviously remembering Jeanne d'Arc as well, he speaks of the Church of St Genevieve in Paris as 'dedicated to another of their Amazons.'

So Mr Evelyn lies embalmed in his own pages for us: the perfect model of an English gentleman (except that he is more curiously enquiring than an English gentleman absolutely needs to be), restrained, intelligent, correct. His feelings and principles are unobtrusive but proper. He is much more like the nineteenth century ideal exemplified by the Prince-Consort than he is like the madrigal-loving and emotional Englishman we find in the annals of English history from the times of Henry VIII to the country squires of Fielding. As we read, the mind is continually stimulated, but the emotions are almost unstirred and the sense of personality is consequently rather thin.

The Color of the Times

Although the Duchess of Newcastle called the work we have examined *The Life of the Duke of Newcastle*, its scattered and fragmentary treatment and its eccentric plan clearly place it among the memoirs and reminiscences. And although Lucy Hutchinson modestly laid claim to no more than writing memoirs of her husband, she remembered so clearly and in such detail that there is little to distinguish her book from formal biography. Both ladies were eulogistic rather than entirely scientific in their aim, Mrs Hutchinson much more convincingly than the Duchess. Historically Mrs Hutchinson is invaluable, so much so that the only fault we might be inclined to find with the formal merit of her work as biography is that it so often becomes history, and is therefore a mingling of two genres. Even so, her history is so sharply etched and brilliant in itself, so revealing in its delineation of aspects of Puritanism we seldom do justice to, and so often justified by the commanding position Colonel Hutchinson took in public events, that we can be grateful for the historical inclusions. Our view of those times would be gravely distorted by Restoration satire if we did not have some few like Mrs Hutchinson.

It can hardly be said that the Duchess of Newcastle gives us a similar insight into the Cavalier side of the Rebellion. The self-absorbed lady enables us to deduce a fairly clear portrait of her own fantastic self, but beyond that circle of radiance all is blurred, and we perceive neither the royal cause nor the years of exile, neither the high devotion nor the gleaming triumph of return. As for the Puritans, they do not appear at all: they are heaps of captured and slain after one of the Duke's victories or they have just retired from the stage, having ruined his manorial parks. The ego of the Duchess is a bright cloud obscuring the insignificances of mere history. Mrs. Hutchinson not only gives us a firm and convincing outline of the Parliamentary cause, and numerous vignettes of its leaders, but sometimes ventures even into the Royalist camp with an acid but not altogether unfair sketch.

Their success as biographers seems to me all in favor of Mrs Hutchinson. Noble—too noble—as the image of Colonel Hutchinson may seem, it is there. The man is realized. His life at Owthorpe is painted, the red cloak in which he went to Ireton's funeral, his squabbles with the committee at Nottingham, his slightly over-ostentatious frankness, the finesse and bravery with which he defended himself under cross-examination, the bleakness of Sandown and his death in fever. Scenes and actions are not left to be assumed: they are presented. But what a vague bundle of unvisualized perfections is the Duke of Newcastle! The method the Duchess employed gives us an occasional humorous morsel, but mostly a mist of panegyric and generalization. By ingenious cogitation we can sometimes hazard a shrewd guess as to what the man really was like, and how he differed from the faint outline of the Duchess's adulation, but the reward is slight. Many other sources than the Duchess would need to be consulted for anything like an adequate picture of that somewhat insouciant amateur-general, luxurious prince, horse-fancier, and gentleman-farce-writer.

The contrast between Pepys and Evelyn is less to the latter's disadvantage than that of the two ladies is to the Duchess's. In spite of their difference in length (and Evelyn covers sixty years on almost the same scale as Pepys's ten), both are detailed enough to give us full-length portraits of their authors. Pepys, with his ever-busy psychological curiosity, and his alternations of complacence and humility, analyzes himself in a way Evelyn never seems to think of attempting, and gives us an infinitely more intimate feeling. But it was equally natural, I imagine, for Evelyn not to delve within himself in such ways; he was less introspective if also less truly sociable, and one feels that even his emotions were more often dictated by cerebration and deep rational conviction than by any merely instinctive spontaneity such as always wells up in Pepys. He liked being with people, but more for what they could tell him than through gregariousness. Pepys is full of personal anecdote, his gaieties, amours, triumphs, humiliations, excitements, self-examinations, enthusiasms, discoveries. Evelyn's reticence about himself is perhaps as significant to reflection as the volatile chatter of Pepys, but it gives us the impression the man may well have created in life, of being a kind and benevolent man, but one not easily known. If this is not so, and those who knew him in real life felt close and warm and affectionate with the man, then Evelyn's *Diary* is less translucent to personality than that of Pepys.

The society they reveal—and the ten years of Pepys fall almost midway in the more than sixty of Evelyn—is of course the reflection of their individual differences. The world of Pepys is filled with eating and drinking and bedding and singing and buying new clothes and squeezing pretty girls: all activities that Evelyn gives no verbal evidence that he ever performed. We have numerous comments on the plays Pepys went to see and the books he purchased and read—either in private, like *L'escholle des filles*, or aloud to his young wife. Evelyn, as we have seen, disapproved of the theatre, and although there is evidence that he was a well-read and even an erudite man, he seldom mentions reading a book in his *Diary*. His world is a compendium of facts, meetings of learned societies, conversations with virtuosos and savants, general speculations, and brief notes of the trend of the times.

It is not strange that Pepys and Evelyn should paint very similar pictures of the Fire and the Plague, for men do not differ profoundly in their responses to great natural calamities. But there may be some wonder, considering how different they were in temperament, at their revealing even a very similar view of public events. The one was so much interested in personalities and the other so much in things, the one so free and easy and the other so almost priggish, we should have imagined their interpretations would show wide divergences. But here is how Evelyn tells of the dismissal and disgrace of the Earl of Clarendon: 'Visited the Lo. Chancellor, to whom his Majesty had sent for the seales a few days before; I found him in his bed-chamber very sad. The Parliament had accus'd him, and he had enemies at Court, especially the buffoones and ladys of pleasure, because he thwarted some of them and stood in their way; I could name some of the cheife.' And Pepys: 'This business of my Lord Chancellor's was certainly designed in my Lady Castlemayne's chamber; . . . when he went from the King on Monday morning, she was in bed, though about twelve o'clock, and ran out in her smock into the aviary . . . and stood there joying herself at the old man's going away.' Pepys is, as usual, more dramatic and pictorial, and less discreet in the way he mentions names, but both men trace the event to the same causes.

Such agreement in men so different would not always exist, and is not altogether easy to explain. Partly it may be that they were not deeply engaged in these events (and undoubtedly the King and Lord Clarendon would have given different explanations of the dismissal), partly that the stage of politics was less crowded with actors and the whole more confined to a narrow and intimate group than it is today, partly that in the small world of seventeenth century England the complexities of economics and sociology were less confusing than they are now, and partly that the instruments of falsification and propaganda were not as well developed as those of our newspaper-lords. When the enquiring intellectual looked for explanations he did not have to ferret his way through a maze of false scents, and when the eager gossip nosed about he was not led through a muckheap of mass-suggestion. The intelligent observer, providing he were not deceived by his own prejudices or loyalties, could more easily arrive at a fair conclusion.

And so, different as they are in spirit and in emphasis, the worlds of Pepys and Evelyn are obviously the same world. It is not merely that they often mention the same names and comment on the same events. Pepys, although so much the emotional and animal man, was a man of intellectual curiosity as well. In his virtuosity, he often plunges us into the world of Tillotson and Newton, where Evelyn more habitually dwelt. And Evelyn, for all that he so often impressed us as an almost disembodied intelligence, lived in the social atmosphere of his times, and fragments of it cling to his academic dryness. His descriptions of glass-works and the carvings of Grinling Gibbons and the planning of Greenwich Palace and his laborious activities in behalf of the Hospital and finding the Lord Chancellor in bed and the innumerable convivial dinners with which men of learning enlivened their graver deliberation—all these are deeply infused in the life of that busy and chaotic and yet narrow world of seventeenth century London. Evelyn reflects, a little bit chillily, the color of that warm and active life; and Pepys, in the midst of his concerts and wenching and toiling at the Admiralty and feasting, scoops up typical fragments of the life of the learned world which goes on nearly in an eddy of the other. Their two diaries supplement each other, almost like a stereopticon, the difference of focus giving the shape of history atmosphere and depth.

HEYDAY
OF THE LETTER-WRITERS

V

HEYDAY OF THE LETTER-WRITERS

The Coming of the Post

THE art of letter-writing develops relatively late in any civilization. In early days nobody save a king, a great noble, or a member of some priestly hierarchy had the means of sending written messages over great distances; and even these were more likely to confine their correspondence to the necessities of state-craft and diplomacy or to questions of ecclesiastical administration and theology than to exchange any merely friendly news or greetings. When correspondence had to be maintained by special courier service or private messenger only interchanges of grave import could take place.

During the early Renaissance some of the great Florentine bankers and some of the merchants of the Hanseatic League had correspondents in the leading cities of other countries, but these again were utilitarian and bore mainly on those events, political and economic, that might presumably affect business. Such letters were really news-bulletins. Only if society is relatively stable and secure, and travel moves constantly over many highways, does it become possible for letters to be delivered inexpensively enough to serve individuals who are not great nobles or men of enormous wealth.

But the means of communication are not enough. There must be a class of people, relatively comfortable and prosperous if not wealthy, whose lives allow them sufficient leisure to write each other. They must move around freely so that they become scattered in places not easily or often reached in person. And they must be well enough educated so that writing has for them no purely mechanical difficulties, so that the labor of forming written symbols with their fingers or the difficulty of 'thinking of what to say' does not overwhelm them. Letter-writing requires a certain ease, a tinge of urbanity, some ability really to see yourself and things around you: not necessarily great depths of culture or profound reflective powers, but a little of the capacity to stand aside for a while from the heat and rush of activity and realize imaginatively what your experience has been.

Only when the means of communication have thus existed simultaneously with a group of such people has letter-writing flourished. In Rome under the Caesars there were a few men of wealth, country gentlemen, great landowners or urban patricians, who wrote each other and used their slaves as messengers. We have letters of Cicero and of Pliny, the naturalist, but either the Romans wrote in an extremely formal style or else their letters, as we have them, were not real letters at all, but a kind of literary exercise intended to show their command of rhetorical eloquence and striking reflections. From the Middle Ages few letters have survived; and probably few were written, for conditions were unstable and the lives of most men parochial. Monastic communications there were, and the dispatches of nobles and diplomats, but seldom personal letters. Those attributed to Abélard and Héloïse are among the few that have come down to us.

With the Renaissance communication became easier and literacy outside the clergy a little more widespread. We have many occasional letters of celebrated personages and sometimes those of relatively obscure people. In the fifteenth century there are the letters of the Paston family, useful to the historian, but rather dull. The sixteenth century shows a considerable body of scholarly correspondence, the letters of Roger Ascham and of John Lyly, and some of those between Sir Philip Sidney and his friend Languet.

A little later royal posts became established in France and England (the first inland post was inaugurated by Charles I). Although they were intended largely for the carrying-on of public business many people connected with the government or in lofty stations were given franking privileges and extended the service to their friends by allowing letters to be sent under their own seal.

Especially in the clear and well-ordered world of the late seventeenth and the eighteenth centuries, nearly all the gentry at least had access to somebody's franking privilege if they desired it, and through them men of letters and polite learning as well. The nobility of France, rotating in the glittering orbit of Louis XIV, became a polite miniature world where everyone was known to all the others. Attached to these splendid gyrations there were all the attendant brilliances of poets, dramatists, musicians, savants, virtuosos, philosophers, and princes of the church. In the grand salons of Versailles and the less magnificent but equally luxurious drawingrooms and boudoirs of noble ladies they met according to the rules of a stately ritual. Out of these highly artificial conditions, a sort of narrow and hot-house culture, came some of the finest letters ever written: the wonderful letters of Madame de Sévigné, which are so often referred to in the pages of Marcel Proust.

The Gallicized courtiers of Charles II brought back French manners and French standards with them. Their comedies sparkled with borrowed brilliants intermingled with bursts of native wit, and their manners were refined sometimes to an exquisite foppery derived partly from the Hôtel de Rambouillet. Although all over the countryside booby squires like Fielding's Squire Western and Goldsmith's Tony Lumpkin, and simple-minded country gentlemen like Sir Roger de Coverley, were to linger for many a long decade, the tone of English society became more polished and urbane. The England of Elizabeth and James, for all its blaze of learning and genius, had had no such general diffusion, even among those at court, of education and poise.

But after the unsettled conditions produced by the fanaticism and obstinacy of James II had cleared into the relative security of the succeeding reigns, the life of the upper classes became increasingly stable and unified. Londoners especially, and those among the country gentry urbane enough to spend part of their time in London, developed a closely knit social life. Communication became ever cheaper and easier. A halfpenny post was established in London in 1708, and by 1783 there were mailcoaches that would carry a letter twenty miles for fourpence and three hundred miles for a shilling. Through the eighteenth century these influences spread over the whole countryside. And correspondingly during this period there is a spread of refined and versatile letter-writing.

The Most Personal Art

There is some difficulty in isolating those merits that peculiarly belong to a letter, and that letters do not merely have in common with other kinds of good writing. When Gregory, in a letter to Nicobulus, remarks that 'we neither ought to be long when there is not much to say, nor brief when there is a press of matter,' he is saying something true, but it is equally true of a Greek tragedy or a treatise on determinants.

There is no hard and fast rule to show when a piece of writing is too long or too short. A letter may be spun out into the frailest Venetian glasswork of whimsy or deliberate absurdity, and no matter how slight its intertwining and translucent threads may be, if their shapes and colors charm the attention it is not too long for its matter. And the weightiest of subjects may exhaust the capacity a feeble writer brings to them long before he has ceased elaborating truisms and prodding a Pegasus that falls down in the stable.

The same deficiencies are to be found in the statement that letters should have variety and interest. A letter may be a potpourri or it may have a single theme. But it need say nothing very original, nor is it likely that it often will, for most situations have occurred so many times before that nearly all reflections have been made. There need only be some newness and life in the way old things are apprehended: no invention of strange and hitherto unimagined things nor any vaudeville-succession of themes. Variety is a matter of delicate changes of tone or rhythm even more than a delicatessen of subjects. It is a waste of time to say to the writer, 'Be varied.' If he can, he will. It is pointless to tell him, 'Be interesting.' Interest is a possession of the reader's, which not Merlin nor Trismegistus may command. Variety and interest are indefinable merits of all good writing.

Other touchstones that have been suggested are those of general appeal and familiar style. These notions seem to me without foundation. A letter is not a public performance. (Or if so, it is really a bulletin, a proclamation, or a harangue masquerading as a letter.) Letters are written to single persons, or, at most, to small groups. They should be fitted to the tastes, understandings, and sympathies of their recipients, and that is all. There is no more literary obligation for letters to be intelligible to the unlearned, if they were not sent to the unlearned, than for Hegel, Lobachevsky, or Brahms to be received with lucid delight by an alderman.

Is there anything to distinguish a good letter from any other form of good writing? We may reasonably look in a letter, it would seem, for a quality, or at least a degree, of ease and spontaneity somewhat more than we invariably expect elsewhere. Unless the letter be written with the desire to goad or madden, we write to please, and a letter can give little pleasure that bears visible signs of having been dragged out with difficulty.

This is not true of all other forms of writing. Certain kinds of song and lyric we expect to have spontaneity, and many more forms of writing to have grace, but seldom in quite the same seemingly artless way as in the letter. Many a work of art shows formidable signs of its maker's struggles with his conception, erosions of contour that only enhance our awe at the genius able to wrestle with such problems and tear their solution from them. Those coagulations of language in Meredith and Browning, and even more, certain obstructions in the utterances of Blake and Nietzsche, are not idiosyncratic, but the pangs of labor entailed in tremendous struggles of birth. We can be grateful for what they give us with no more feeling of personal responsibility than we have in accepting an inoculation against some dread disease which men lost their lives to discover. But we should be distressed if these heroes of science told us personally, 'We are dying of anthrax, of rabies, of cancer, and we are enduring these torments for *you*.'

And, in its lesser realm, we want to feel that a letter written for our enjoyment cost its author no onerous pains to write. The letter may in truth have been exquisitely polished, but it should bear no signs of its workmanship. The novelist and the tragic dramatist may compose themselves to observe every painful detail of an experience, they may agonizingly dissect it down to the last dark and trembling fibre, and they may stumble and fall in the effort to make its remotest inward meaning waver before us. They reveal the obscure to us, but we have no personal bond, and the author is for us even in his suffering only one of the vast almost anonymous army of martyrs to the exploration of consciousness. But the letter-writer who sought bitterness in order to wound his friends with it would be going beyond the bounds, and even when bitterness comes to him a letter is not appropriate for the travail of discovery.

We may also look for one other quality. Letters are personal communications. Therefore they should have the flavor of personality. We should be able to distinguish between the tone of Lincoln's letter to Mrs Bixby and the Gettysburg address, not because the one is informal in tone and the other not, but because in the one a man is speaking his own heart to a bereaved woman and in the other he is trying to voice the emotion of a people.

The word personality, however, we must use with care. All works of imagination, and even works of history and philosophy, have about them a flavor which is the personality of their authors. But there is a direct intimacy that is not merely permissible but desirable in a letter, and that is apt to be either an intrusion or an artistic blunder in any other form of writing.

Of course, the personality of any good writer is always present in his work. The personality of Flaubert is as much responsible for the seemingly 'objective' rendering of *Madame Bovary* as the personality of Thackeray, making its little bow and delivering its stageman's speech, in the pages of *Vanity Fair*. The charming and witty personal intrusions of Fielding into the pages of his novels we may relish because they are so ingenious and so consciously impudent; and the brilliant egomania of Byron parading his bleeding heart may enamour an era or inflame the enthusiasm of the young. But these are unusual victories; we forgive the violation of the principle because we are offered so much in compensation. Usually we resent an author who insists on displaying himself in a formal work of literature, to the exclusion of his alleged subject.

In a letter, however, the precise opposite is true. The subject of the letter is the writer, and his personality has everywhere the right to appear. In his pages who speaks and what he feels about things is central; part of our pleasure is tasting the suffusion of personality even in every phrase and turn of epithet. The direct presence of the writer's personality, by whatever magical touches he can use to conjure his breathing self up before us, is the very aim and heart of the enterprise. In the glimmering sequence of moods, in gossip or admonition or nonsense, in news or words of sympathy, in personal narration or reflective interludes, a character should take shape before us: the character of the man who wrote there.

Two Ladies, a Dean, and Some Others

Two of the earliest noteworthy letter-writers were women. The Marquise de Sévigné was a member of that world of pageantry and fashion that shone so brightly in the rays of Le Roi Soleil; and from Paris and Versailles, where the comedies and ballets of Molière darted their arrows of satire, from Chantilly at the Duc de Rochefoucauld's mansion, from her country home at Les Rochers, she let fall the clear manna of her letters: wit, vivacity, taste, gossip, sentiment–all deliciously mingled, in the purest of styles, and perfectly translucent to the spirit of the age. Madame de Sévigné died when Lady Mary Wortley Montagu was a little girl of six, but the latter was to be a rival to her talents. A daughter of Evelyn Pierrepont, Esq. (afterward Duke of Kingston), a young lady of wit and fashion, a toast of the famous Kitcat Club, and until some mysterious quarrel a friend of Alexander Pope, the young lady formed a romantic runaway match with Mr Edward Wortley Montagu, traveled abroad with him while he was Ambassador to Constantinople, and unfolded in the letters of fifty years a character strong, sensible, penetrating, and worldly, but not without depth and sensibility. They are a little harder and dryer than the letters of Madame de Sévigné. They do not have her sometimes exquisite tenderness, her delicate perceptiveness of the refinements of feeling. The one is thinking and feeling in prose, and the other, for all her balance and restraint, is feeling in poetry. Lady Mary's style is sharp and brilliant like a black-and-white, Madame de Sévigné's transparent like a water-color.

Even the trivial gossip of more than two centuries ago Madame de Sévigné can infuse with the glow of life: 'I am going to tell you of an event which is the most astonishing, the most surprising, the most marvellous, the most miraculous, the most magnificent, the most bewildering, the most unheard-of, the most singular, the most extraordinary, the most incredible, the most unexpected, the greatest, the least, the most rare, the most common, the most public, the most private till today,'—how adroitly Madame provokes our curiosity by the antitheses of the last three pairs!—'the most brilliant, the most enviable . . .; an event which we cannot believe in Paris (how then can it be believed in Lyons?), an event which makes everybody exclaim, "Lord have mercy upon us!" . . . an event, in fact, which will take place on Sunday next, when those who are present will doubt the evidence of their senses; an event which, though it is to happen on Sunday, may perhaps not be accomplished on Monday. I cannot persuade myself to tell you. Guess what it is! I give you three guesses. Do you give it up? Well, then I must tell you. Monsieur de Lauzun is to be married next Sunday at the Louvre—guess to whom! I give you four guesses, I give you ten, I give you a hundred. Madame de Coulanges says, "It is not very difficult to guess, it is Madame de Vallière." You are quite wrong, Madame. "It is Mademoiselle de Retz, then." No, it is not; you are very provincial.

'"Dear me, how stupid we are," you exclaim, "it is Mademoiselle de Colbert, of course." You are farther off than ever. "Then it must be Mademoiselle de Créqui." You are no nearer. Well, I find I must tell you.' And so, after another paragraph of lively delay, to the momentous announcement—to 'Mademoiselle, first cousin to the King.' The thing that is noteworthy about these flowing and glancing sentences is not their dénouement, of course, but the delicious way in which they build up their suspense, until we are well nigh as eager to know as Madame de Grignan must have been herself. And there are the faint touches, besides, by which we are given a slyer taste of the period. That slightly naughty 'which, though it is to happen on Sunday, may perhaps not be *accomplished* till Monday'; and the pretended patronage of the dry 'you are very provincial,' in answer to one imagined guess. The whole, by the lightest touches in the world, is as alive in its airy way today as it was when it was written. Who will write of any fashionable wedding in our time and be assured of making it as charming to read two centuries hence?

Sometimes her wit has a hint of malice. 'Madame de Brissac was ill today, and remained in bed, with her hair dressed so beautifully, and looking so handsome, that she was fit to turn everybody's head. I wish you could have seen how prettily she managed her sufferings, her eyes, her arms, and her cries, with her hands lying helplessly in the quilt, and looking for the sympathy she expected from all bystanders. I was quite overcome with tenderness and admiration . . .' And how prettily the Marquise manages her little cat-stroke of insinuation for us. We too are quite overwhelmed with admiration. But she can turn that little claw in upon herself as well: 'I have grown rather more unceremonious than you, for the other day I let a carriageful of the Foneseul family go home through a tremendous rain for want of a little pressing them with a good grace to stay . . .' We have the entire picture implied, of the somewhat boring family, wanting to be urged to stay, and being urged, but not quite enough, so that off they go—and although there is a dig for the social absurdity that insists on being urged and urged again, there is also a bit of compunction at the omission: for it was a breach! A whole background of manners and standards is shadowed in those few words.

Through the lady of wit, however, the tender-hearted woman and mother is easily to be seen. She tries to rationalize her sorrow at the departure of her son for Lorraine: 'You know how it vexes me to see the breaking up of an agreeable party, and how delighted I am when I see a carriage driving off with people who have wearied me to death all day; upon which we might make the observation that bad company is more desirable than good.' And she goes on to say, 'I recollect all the odd things we used to say when you were here, and all you said yourself, and all you did; the thought of you never leaves me; and then, again, I suddenly remember where you are, my imagination represents to me an immense space and a great distance . . .' Family affection, indeed, is never far from Madame de Sévigné's heart. Madame de Brissac's illness reminds her: 'My child, when I remember with what simplicity you are ill, and the calmness in your pretty face, you seem to me a mere bungler!' And always, 'Love, love your daughter, my dear child; it is the most natural and delightful employment in the world.'

Letter-writing flourished in England as well as in France. Lady Mary Wortley Montagu was not the first to follow in the footsteps of her distinguished foreign predecessor. The earliest published collections of personal letters were those of Bishop Hall (1574-1656) and the *Familiar Letters* of James Howell (1594-1666). Pope's letters in some curious way had been pirated by the publisher Curll in 1737, and the injured poet had felt himself obliged to bring out a personally supervised edition, correcting Curll's misprints, omissions, and falsifications. Pope was vain of his epistolary talents, and the piracy may not have been completely unauthorized: indeed many of the letters have a suspiciously formal and elaborated style, with conceits both of language and concept that smell strongly of manufacture for publication, or, at least, of ex-post-facto revision. Swift's *Journal to Stella* (a name he did not use, supplied by his cousin, the first editor) was written as a series of journal-letters between 1710 and 1713, and not published until 1769—twenty-four years after his death.

Many other occasional and collected letters of the seventeenth and eighteenth centuries have been preserved and are now available in print, but none attain the bulk or the importance of some of those I have mentioned. A few samples of such fugitive correspondence may prove interesting. Here is a letter to Charles II:

> King Charles,—One of your subjects, the other night, robbed me of forty pounds, for which I robbed another of the same sum, who has inhumanly sent me to Newgate, and he swears I shall be hanged; therefore, for your own sake, save my life, or you will lose one of the best seamen in your navy.
>
> JACK SKIFTON

The condescending monarch replied:

> Jack Skifton,—For this time I'll save thee from the gallows; but if hereafter thou art guilty of the like, by God I'll have thee hanged, though the best seaman in my navy. Thine,
>
> CHARLES REX

There are some charming domestic letters of Sir Richard Steele, that manage in their few lines to distil much of the affection and carefreeness and devotion of the man.

> Dear, lovely Mrs Scurlock,—I have been in very good company, where your health, under the character of the woman I lov'd best, has been often drunk, so that I may say I am dead drunk for your sake, which is more than I die for you. Yours,
>
> R. STEELE.

And only two days later, from St James's Coffee-House, comes this:

> Madam,—It is the hardest thing in the world to be in love and yet attend to businesse. As for me, all who speak to me find me out,

> and I must lock myself up or people will do it for me. A gentleman ask'd me this morning what news from Lisbon, and I answer'd she's exquisitely handsome. Another desir'd to know when I had been last at Hampton Court, I reply'd 'twill be on Tuesday come se'nnight. Prithee allow me at least to kisse your hand before that day, that my mind may be in some composure . . .

They were married 'Tuesday come se'nnight,' and we have thereafter little showers of one- and two-line notes written in the course of business and sent home to her. 'I desire, my dear, that you have nothing else to do but to be a darling,' and 'Dear Prue,—I am very sleepy and tired, but I could not think of closing my eyes' until 'From the Press' at one in the morning he had sent this note of affection. Here is one written in 1712—five years later:

> Dear Prue,—I thank you for your kind billet. The nurse shall have money this week. I saw your son Dick, but he is a peevish chit. You cannot conceive how pleased I am that I shall have the prettyest house to receive the prettyest woman who is the darling of
>
> RICHARD STEELE.

Compared with the freshness and gaiety of these, the journal-letters in the *Journal to Stella* are wooden indeed. Important to the political historian for the light they throw on the partisan warfare of the Whig and Tory parties, and the struggles of Harley and Bolingbroke to control the country, they are of rather less value to the spiritual historian. They are without the artificiality and decorative elaborateness of Pope's letters, it is true, but they have little liveliness of observation or comment, and alternate between a bare and fatigued abstract of where he has been and whom he has seen, and the repetitious puerilities of the 'little language' he used to show affection for his two correspondents. The Stella, Cadenus, and Vanessa entanglement has been romanticized in a way that throws fictitious glamor on the *Journal;* but a person who reads it for light on that dark realm of Swift's life will find little, and even of politics little but the bones of fact: no color of characterization or blazoning of issues.

Sometimes we find a detail that enables us to reconstruct something of the age. On his way to Sir Godfrey Kneller's, the painter, he 'met the electors for parliament-men: and the rabble came about our coach, crying A Colt, A Stanhope, &c. we were afraid of a dead cat, or our glasses broken, and so were always of their side.' We have short accounts of dinners with Rowe and Prior and other celebrities, and frequent glimpses of Harley, the celebrated politician, who became Earl of Oxford.

In spite of their different political affiliations Swift wanted to be helpful to Steele; he went to make suggestions about it to Addison, 'but found Party had so possessed him, that he talked as if he suspected me, and would not fall in with anything I said. So I stopt short in my overture, and we parted very dryly; and I shall say nothing to Steele, and let them do as they will; but if things stand as they are, he will certainly lose' his place 'unless I save him . . .' But, as for Addison, at the coffee-house 'I behaved myself coldly enough' and 'I shall not alter my behaviour to him, till he begs my pardon, or else we shall grow bare acquaintance.'

There is a description of the witty Congreve, who had burned the candle at both ends and who was now, although younger than Swift, a decrepit man. He 'is almost blind with cataracts growing on his eyes; and his case is, that he must wait two or three years until the cataracts are riper, and till he is quite blind, and then he must have them couched; and besides he is never rid of the gout, yet he looks young and fresh, and is as chearful as ever . . . He gave me a pain in the great toe, by mentioning the gout.'

The hypochondria of this last comment is a frequent quality, and so is the parsimony about trifles which is so striking a contrast to Swift's generous charities. 'I find all rich fellows have that humour of using all people without any consideration for their fortunes,' he grumbles; 'but I'll see them rot before they shall serve me so.' And the occasion for this?—'Lord Halifax is always teazing me to go down to his country house, which will cost me a guinea to his servants, and twelve shillings coach hire; and he shall be hanged first.' And during a rainy spell, he frets, ' 'Tis plaguy twelve-penny weather this last week, and has cost me ten shillings in coach and chair hire.' He is fond of a dubious turn of phrase, even with his two feminine correspondents, and says, a propos his first appointment with Harley for a Saturday afternoon, 'I will open my business to him; which expression I would not use if I were a woman;' and then adds, chucklingly, 'I know you smoakt it;' (saw the meaning of it) 'but I did not till I writ it.'

His occasional letters to his friends, however, reveal much more of the proud and bitter and witty and affectionate man than is to be found in the curtailed notes of the *Journal*. Writing to Pope, for example, while he was finishing the revision of Gulliver, he says: 'But the chief end I propose to myself in all my labours, is to vex the world, rather than divert it; and if I could compass that design without hurting my own person or fortune, I would be the most indefatigable writer you have ever seen without reading.' (His *Tale of a Tub* had long since ruined his chances of ecclesiastical advancement in the time of Queen Anne.) '. . . I have ever hated all nations, professions, and communities; and all my love is towards individuals . . . But principally I hate and detest that animal called man, although I heartily love John, Peter, Thomas, and so forth. This is the system upon which I have governed myself many years (but do not tell), and so I shall go on until I have done with them.

'I have got materials toward a treatise proving the falsity of that definition *animal rationale*, and to show it should be only *rationis capax*. Upon this great foundation of misanthropy (though not in Timon's manner) the whole building of my travels is erected; and I never will have peace of mind till all honest men are of my opinion.'

Many letters to Pope, to Arbuthnot, to Gay, and others–show that he spoke truly in claiming his love 'towards individuals.' Only three years before the melancholy insanity in which he ended his days, he wrote to Pope that he had learned 'with great concern that you were taken ill. I have heard nothing since; only I have continued in great pain of mind; yet for my own sake and the world's more than for yours; because I well know how little you value life both as a philosopher and a Christian . . . If you are well recovered, you ought to be reproached for not putting me especially out of pain, who could not bear the loss of you; although we must be for ever distant as much as if I were in the grave . . . I have nobody left now but you. Pray be so kind as to outlive me; and then die as soon as you please; but without pain . . .'

In a livelier mood, he jested with Miss Hoadly, one of the young ladies whom he had always had the ability to fascinate with his raillery. 'Madam,–When I lived in England, once every year I issued an edict, commanding that all ladies of wit, sense, merit, and quality who had an ambition to be acquainted with me, should make the first advances at their peril; which edict, you may believe, was universally obeyed.' And he proceeds to 'wonder how you came so long to neglect your duty,' and to thank her for some gifts recently dispatched in these words: 'I have heard of a judge bribed with a pig, but discovered by the squeaking; and, therefore, you have been so politic as to send me a dead one, which can tell no tales. Your present of butter was made with the same design, as a known court practice, to grease my fist that I might keep silence. These are great offences, contrived on purpose to corrupt my integrity . . . However, I have two ways to be revenged: first, I will let all the ladies of my acquaintance know [that you] understand housewifery; which every girl of this town, who can afford sixpence a month for a chair, would scorn to be thought to have the least knowledge in; and this will give you as ill a reputation as if you had been caught in the act of reading a history, or handling a needle, or working in a field at Tallagh;' and second, he will swear that her letter is 'written in a fair hand, rightly spelt, and good plain sense,' which will make 'every female scrawler . . . spread about the town that your writing and spelling are ungenteel and unfashionable, more like a parson than a lady.'

Many of Pope's letters, as I have already mentioned, were probably not real letters at all, but formal literary compositions arbitrarily cast into the letter-mold; and even those that were actually sent to people were often revamped for publication. Nearly all have a set elegance, a highly wrought Augustan polish, a striving for effect, that sometimes produces an air of insincerity and at the best hides the man beneath the fashionable garments of paradox and elaboration. His *Letter to a Noble Lord* is a brilliant piece of irony and invective, but it was really a studied public insult to Lord Hervey, and not a letter at all; and the same is true of a number of Pope's other letters. Although they were designed to find their way into print by seeming accident, they were really prose satires, having no more of the personal in them than any other such work. It need not be denied that there was sincerity and gentleness in Pope, but these are qualities that seldom appear with much convincingness in his letters. Here is part of one to Lady Mary Wortley Montagu, which is self-explanatory:

> I prodigiously long for your sonnets, your remarks, your Oriental learning; but I long for nothing so much as your Oriental self . . . I expect to see your soul as much thinner dressed as your body; and that you have left off, as unwieldy and cumbersome, a great many damned European habits. Without offense to your modesty

be it spoken, I have a burning desire to see your soul stark naked, for I am confident it is the prettiest kind of white soul in the universe . . . But if I must be content with seeing your body only, God send it to come quickly: I honour it more than the diamond-casket that held Homer's Iliads; for in the very twinkle of one eye of it there is more wit, and in the very dimple of one cheek of it there is more meaning, than all the souls that ever were casually put into women since men have had the making of them.

I have a mind to fill the rest of this paper with an accident that happened just under my eyes, and has made a great impression upon me. I have just passed part of this summer at an old romantic seat of my Lord Harcourt's, which he lent me. It overlooks a common-field, where, under the shade of a hay-cock, sat two lovers, as constant as ever were found in romance, beneath a spreading beech . . . a terrible storm of thunder and lightning arose, that drove the labourers to what shelter the trees or hedges afforded. Sarah, frightened and out of breath, sunk on a haycock, and John (who never separated from her) sate by her side, having raked two or three heaps together to secure her. Immediately there was heard so loud a crack as if heaven had burst asunder. The labourers, solicitous for each other's safety, called to one another: those that were nearest our lovers, hearing no answer, stepped to the place where they lay: they first saw a little smoke, and after, this faithful pair; —John, with one arm about his Sarah's neck, and the other held over her face, as if to screen her from the lightning. They were struck dead, and already grown stiff and cold in this tender posture. There was no mark or discolouring on their bodies, only that Sarah's eyebrow was a little singed, and a small spot between her breasts.

And to the letter he adds an epitaph on the lovers:

When Eastern lovers feed the funeral fire
On the same pile their faithful fair expire;
Here pitying Heaven that virtue mutual found,
And blasted both that it might neither wound.
Hearts so sincere th' Almighty saw well pleas'd
Sent his own lightning and the victims seiz'd.

Think not, by rigorous judgment seiz'd
A pair so faithful could expire;
Victims so pure Heaven saw well pleas'd
And snatched them in celestial fire.

The rather strained pastoralism of this sentimental effusion bespeaks it much more the occasion for quoting his epitaph than any spontaneous flow of feeling. The whole episode has been manufactured, wrought up, as a literary production; and the letter is therefore a kind of set piece designed to display the talents of the author rather than the feelings of the man. Lady Mary, who nowhere shows her good sense more than by the quiet way she ignores his artificial professions of gallantry towards herself, reacts from the pseudo-Arcadianism of these raptures into a tone of bald insensibility: 'I must applaud your good nature in supposing that your pastoral lovers (vulgarly called haymakers) would have lived in everlasting joy and harmony, if the lightning had not interrupted their scheme of happiness. I see no reason to imagine that John Hughes and Sarah Drew were either wiser or more virtuous than their neighbors. That a well-set man of twenty-five should have a fancy to marry a brown woman of eighteen is nothing marvellous . . . His endeavoring to shield her from the storm was a natural action, and what he would have certainly done for his horse, if he had been in the same situation.' And she makes up her own epitaph on the same event:

Here lies John Hughes and Sarah Drew;
Perhaps you'll say, what's that to you?
Believe me, friend, much may be said
On this poor couple that are dead.
On Sunday next they should have married;
But see how oddly things are carried!
On Thursday last it rain'd and lighten'd;
These tender lovers, sadly frighten'd,
Sheltered beneath the cocking hay,
In hopes to pass the storm away;
But the bold thunder found them out.

. . . . . .

Who knows if 'twas not kindly done?
For if they had seen next year's sun,
A beaten wife and cuckold swain
Had jointly curs'd the marriage chain;
Now they are happy in their doom,
For P. has written on their tomb.

'I confess these sentiments are not altogether as heroic as yours; but I hope you will forgive them in favor of the two last lines.'

The ironic worldliness of this passage is an admirable foil to Pope's literary ecstasy, and the deliberately prosaic tone of her epitaph is neatly joined to the concluding compliment. A certain sharpness and common sense, far removed from a poetic romanticism, such as she reveals here, are what we ordinarily find in her letters. She has a sane disillusion about the world and human society, penetrating if slightly cynical judgments on character and motive, an intellectual vitality that is close to wit, and a sustained capacity for keen and inclusive observation.

Even in her earliest letters she displays little of the affectation one might expect in an attractive and much flattered young lady with a reputation for wit and fashion to justify. The letters to Mr Wortley Montagu before their marriage show much warmth and steadiness of feeling. Although theirs was a runaway match, it was neither heedless nor impulsive, but was undertaken only after much reflection had convinced them it was the only solution.

We find him wondering at first if she were not too frivolous and fond of pleasure to be a suitable companion to one as sober as himself, and her writing, 'Give me leave to say it, (I know it sounds vain,) I know how to make a man of sense happy; but then that man must resolve to contribute something towards it himself. I have so much esteem for you, I should be very sorry to hear you was unhappy; but for the world I would not be the instrument of making you so; which (of the humour you are) is hardly to be avoided if I am your wife.'

He praised some of her qualities and frankly blamed others; she replied: 'I suppose . . . I should thank you for the wit and beauty you give me, and not be angry at the follies and weaknesses; but, to my infinite affliction, I can believe neither one nor t'other. One part of my character is not so good, nor t'other so bad as you fancy it. Should we ever live together . . . you would find an easy equality of temper you do not expect, and a thousand faults you do not imagine.'

A struggle of wills went on between them, and she handed him his entire freedom, although with no animosity or pretence of indifference. 'After all I have said, I pretend no tie but on your heart. If you do not love me, I shall not be happy with you; if you do, I need add no farther. I am not mercenary, and would not receive an obligation that comes not from one that loves me.' But, although she was not mercenary, financial obstacles lay between them. Her father would not consent to the marriage without a settlement on their children that her lover would not consent to. Lady Mary was agitated with both: 'I writ you a letter last night in some passion. I begin to fear again; I own myself a coward . . . I am afraid you flatter yourself that my F. [father] may be at length reconciled and brought to reasonable terms. I am convinced . . . he never will.' Finally they resolved to defy opposition, and we have a cry of uncertainty the night before they ran off; 'I tremble for what we are doing.—Are you sure you will love me for ever? Shall we never repent? I fear and I hope.'

She is never more attractive than in the combination in these letters of good sense and sincere feeling, of modesty and an occasional very slight teasing coquettishness, deepening as their intimacy deepened, into a direct truthfulness of statement worthy of high esteem.

Edward Wortley Montagu was appointed ambassador to Constantinople, and she followed him on that difficult journey. Her letters from there are full of vivid details about Turkish life and manners. She speaks highly of the kindness with which slaves are treated, and denies the fiction of Mohammedan contempt for women. 'I assure you it is certainly false . . . that Mahomet excludes women from any share in a future happy state.' He denies a Paradise only to 'virgins, who die virgins, and the widows who marry not again, dying in mortal sin' by not fulfilling their office 'of multiplying the human race.' If St Catherine and St Theresa are 'judged by this system of virtue,' she humorously adds, they will be found 'infamous creatures, that passed their whole lives in most abominable libertinism.' And, so far is the Turkish lady from being confined or enslaved, 'I have not seen any such prudes as to pretend fidelity to their husbands,' although 'No woman dares appear coquette enough to encourage two lovers at a time.'

She gives a full account of the Turkish method of inoculation against smallpox, which she had the courage to practise on herself and her children, and was responsible for introducing into England. An 'old woman comes with a nutshell full of the matter of the best sort of smallpox,' she writes, and pricks several veins at your choice, inserting into them 'as much venom as can lie upon the head of her needle, and after binds up the little wound with a hollow bit of shell . . .' The illness is very slight, lasting only a week, and never leaving any mark. 'Every year thousands undergo this operation; and the French ambassador says pleasantly, that they take the smallpox here by way of diversion, as they take the waters in other countries.'

Her comments on other countries are often striking. 'All the country villages of France,' she says, 'show nothing else' but misery. 'While the post-horses are changed, the whole town comes out to beg, with such miserable starved faces, and thin tattered clothes, that they need no other eloquence to persuade of the wretchedness of their condition. This is all the French magnificence till you come to Fontainbleau. There you begin to think the kingdom rich when you are shewed one thousand five hundred rooms in the King's hunting palace.' This was in 1718, but the French Revolution was already germinating in these starved hamlets.

Again, she pictures the field of Carlowitz, scene of Prince Eugene's great victory over the Turks: 'The marks of that glorious bloody day are yet recent, the field being strewed with the skulls and carcases of unburied men, horses, and camels. I could not look without horror, on such numbers of mangled human bodies, and reflect on the injustice of war, that makes murder not only necessary but meritorious. Nothing seems to be a plainer proof of the irrationality of mankind . . .' If the style here is cool, the sentiments are just.

The truth is, Lady Mary's mind was nearly always well in control of her feelings. But the feelings were usually well-grounded; if she and her husband ultimately disowned their son, he was a scamp who richly deserved it; and she displayed a constant affection for her daughter, who became the Countess of Bute. Her common sense disposes of most problems in short order. There is Mr–, who demands that his wife shall suckle their newly born son, instead of giving it cow's milk, and argues that breast-feeding is according to Nature. 'Indeed, if Mrs– was a buxom, sturdy woman, who lived on plain food, took regular exercise, enjoyed proper returns of rest, and was free from violent passions (which you and I know is not the case), she might be a very good nurse for her child; but as matters stand, I do verily think that the milk of a good comely cow, who feeds quietly in her meadow, never devours ragouts, nor drinks ratafia, nor frets at quadrille . . . would be [more] likely to nourish the young squire . . .'

In her youth we are often treated to fashionable gossip. 'Mr Sterne, the *titular* bishop,' she could write as a young lady, 'was last week married to a very pretty woman, Mrs Bateman, whom he fell in love with for falling backwards from her horse leaping a ditch, where she displayed all her charms, which he found irresistible.' And even later she found it hard to resist a juicy morsel, like the story of the Duke of Bedford, 'who by the care of a pious mother, certainly preserved his virginity to his marriage bed,' where he was so much shocked at what was expected of him 'that he already pukes at the very name' of his bride, and determined 'to let his estate go to his brother, rather than go through the filthy drudgery of getting an heir to it.' 'This comes,' Lady Mary adds, 'of living till sixteen without any competent knowledge either of practical or speculative anatomy, and literally thinking fine ladies composed of lilies and roses.'

But in her later years she becomes less addicted to scandal, and, always something of a bluestocking, comments on philosophy and books, tells what she thinks of Shaftesbury and Bolingbroke, discusses the novels of Richardson and Sterne, of Fielding and Smollett. 'I was such an old fool as to weep over Clarissa Harlowe, like any milkmaid of sixteen.' But she knew well that Richardson's whole view of society was so absurd and ignorant as to make it clear he 'was never admitted into higher company, and should confine his pen to the amours of housemaids.'

The merits of her own letters she was well aware of. 'The last pleasure that fell in my way was Madame Sévigné's letters,' she writes; 'very pretty they are, but I assert, without the least vanity, that mine will be full as entertaining forty years hence.' She was guilty of a serious underestimation there, finding no more than 'a lively manner and fashionable phrases, mean sentiments, vulgar prejudices, and endless repetitions. Sometimes the tittle-tattle of a fine lady, sometimes that of a nurse,' but 'well gilt over by airy expressions, and a flowing style.' Today we do not prize Lady Mary quite as highly as we do her chosen rival, but she commands our respect and admiration. And it may be that only Madame de Sévigné's more charming depths as a person lead us to praise her more.

HEYDAY
OF THE LETTER-WRITERS

(Continued)

VI

HEYDAY OF THE LETTER-WRITERS

Eighteenth Century Ideal

NO WRITER of didactic letters has ever given so clear a portrait of his own character as the Earl of Chesterfield. This is probably because Chesterfield almost alone was wholeheartedly intent on inculcating an attainable result, and one that he really believed in. Didactic letters there have been, doubtless, by millions, on all subjects from the perfect epistolary style to the nature of the faultless knight—but mostly they have been marred either by an unworldly insistence on the ideal or by the author's feeling that he must pretend to embody all the virtues he praised. These deformities have given nearly all such works an air of unavoidable priggishness or of moral unreality.

Lord Chesterfield set a standard high but not ineffable. As much as any man, he had lived by the principles he laid down, which were therefore tried by practice; and even the respects in which, as a young man, he had failed to exemplify his later injunctions, he did not hesitate to use as object-lessons in error. With no shadow of pose, he threw himself into his task of shaping a human character: and the *Letters*, which are the strokes devoted to that task, are also the image of the man.

Philip Stanhope, to whom they were addressed, was the Earl's illegitimate child. He was an awkard and shy little boy, and these traits, for all the advice and example of the letters, did not entirely leave him when he became a young man. Early his father realized that ease and grace in society were the respects in which the boy was especially lacking. If the letters seem to labor these points more than they do those needful to a virtuous character it was not because of any cynical disregard of virtue in the father's mind, but because the problem was more one of external than of inward grace.

Chesterfield was a man of the world: he wanted his son to be a good man (not an impossible, namby-pamby paragon, but good as might be reasonably hoped), and, quite as much as this, he wanted him to be a successful man. The grand aim of the letters is not to form the young man into a graceful and useless coxcomb, but to enable him to achieve those graces of manner and those solid traits of character that may further a serious and valuable career.

For these purposes it is essential that one have charm of manner; for that, rather than virtue, is what most people judge by. 'Virtue and learning, like gold, have their intrinsic value; but if they are not polished, they certainly lose a great deal of their lustre; and even polished brass will pass upon more people than rough gold.' One should begin with grace of carriage, and Chesterfield draws a lively caricature of 'an awkward fellow' coming into a room, stumbling over his sword, letting his hat fall down, and in retrieving it, throwing down his cane. 'At dinner his awkwardness distinguishes itself particularly, as he has more to do: he eats with his knife to the great danger of his mouth, picks his teeth with his fork, and puts his spoon, which has been into his throat twenty times, into the dishes again . . . Besides all this, he has strange tricks and gestures; such as snuffing up his nose, making faces, putting his fingers in his nose, or blowing it and looking afterwards in his handkerchief, so as to make the company sick. His hands are troublesome to him . . . and he does not know where to put them . . .'

These pitfalls avoided, there are graces of conscious behavior to be attended. One should be attentive in company: 'What is commonly called an absent man, is commonly either a very weak, or a very affected man:' and in either case 'a very disagreeable man in company.' It might be permissible in a Newton or a Locke, immersed in intellectual tasks, but only a few people 'since the creation of the world, have had a right to absence, from that intense thought which the things they were investigating required'; a young man deservedly earns his exclusion from good society by such behavior. His language must be well-chosen and correct, neither vulgar nor pedantic: 'Proverbial expressions and trite sayings are the flowers of the rhetoric of a vulgar man. Would he say that men differ in their tastes; he both supports and adorns that opinion, by the good old saying, as he respectfully calls it, that *what is one man's meat is another man's poison.* If anybody attempts being *smart*, as he calls it, upon him, he gives them *tit for tat*, ay, that he does.' Equally undesirable, however, is an ostentatious display of scholarship. 'Speak the language of the company that you are in; speak it purely, and unlarded with any other . . . Wear your learning, like your watch, in a private pocket, and do not merely pull it out . . . to show you have one.'

Even handwriting and little things like dancing are worth a gentleman's care: 'Dancing is in itself a very trifling, silly thing; but it is one of those established follies to which people of sense are sometimes obliged to conform; and then they should be able to do it well.' 'Frequent and loud laughter is . . . the manner in which the mob express their silly joy at silly things . . . True wit, or sense, never yet made anybody laugh; they are above it; they please the mind, and give a cheerfulness to the countenance . . . I am neither of a melancholy, nor a cynical disposition; and am as willing, and as apt, to be pleased as anybody; but I am sure that, since I have had the full use of my reason, nobody has ever heard me laugh.' Therefore 'I could heartily wish that you may be often seen to smile, but never heard to laugh while you live.'

If in this last bit of advice Chesterfield carries a fashionable idea of the day to an excessive degree, there is nevertheless much ingenuity and shrewdness in what he says. And when he goes beyond these superficial matters, his worldly wisdom is penetrating. Men 'will much sooner forgive an injustice than an insult.' 'Never yield to that temptation, which to most young men is very strong, of exposing other people's weaknesses and infirmities . . . You may get the laugh on your side by it, for the present; but you will make enemies by it for ever; and even those who laugh with you then will, upon reflection, fear, and consequently hate you.'

'Have a real reserve with almost everybody, and have a seeming reserve with almost nobody; for it is very disagreeable to seem reserved, and very dangerous not to be so.' Open looks, thoughts restrained—volto sciolto, pensieri stretti—is one of his favorite sayings. Even people capable of reasoning 'live and die in a thousand errors, from laziness; they will rather adopt the prejudices of others, than give themselves the trouble of forming opinions of their own.' But the man of judgment should analyse his impressions both of things and people; he should study human nature. 'Search every one for that ruling passion' 'to which the others are subordinate.' Use the ruling passion to move a man by, but 'remember never to trust him where that passion is concerned.'

Especially study the ruling passions of women, for 'their suffrages go a great way towards establishing a man's character in the fashionable part of the world': but never take them seriously. 'Women . . . are only children of a larger growth; they have an entertaining tattle and sometimes wit; but for solid, reasoning good sense, I never in my life knew one that had it, or who reasoned and acted consequently for four-and-twenty hours together . . . A man of sense only trifles with them . . . but he neither consults them about, nor trusts them with, serious matters; though he often makes them believe he does both . . . No flattery is either too high or too low for them. They will greedily swallow the highest, and gratefully accept of the lowest; and you may safely flatter any woman, from her understanding down to the exquisite taste of her fan . . .'

'But these are secrets which you must keep inviolably, if you would not, like Orpheus, be torn to pieces by the whole sex . . .'

It would be foolhardy indeed, after being so expressly warned, to quote these sentiments with any appearance of approbation, but perhaps they may be allowed to stand by virtue of their insistence on the importance of feminine influence. Whether 'from the weakness of men' or other causes that Chesterfield does not analyze, that influence is probably as strong today as then. And, in any case, no outline of Chesterfield's character would be veracious unless it allowed room for an opinion to which he more than once recurs.

A central feature of his social strategy is playing on the weaknesses of others. Though he nowhere advises the despicable arts of a Bel-Ami, an adroit use of flattery is one of the graces by which a man advances his career. And his career is always the paramount concern. For it he cultivates the Graces whom Chesterfield is ever invoking. The Graces! The Graces! senza di noi, ogni fatica é vana. But beneath the winning air there must always be the determination of iron. Suaviter in modo—another favorite saying—fortiter in re.

It would be an error, however, to believe that Chesterfield fixes his attention exclusively on worldly success, or that he has no principles other than those that conduce to getting on. It has already been shown that he despises the mere man of fashion almost as much as he does the Man of Pleasure, whom he early in his letters stigmatizes as 'a beastly drunkard, an abandoned whoremaster, and a profligate swearer and curser.' He speaks with disgust of the way he was misled in his own youth into drunkenness 'because I then considered drinking as a necessary qualification for a fine gentleman.' Wine and play in moderation are not evils; but, letting others do as they will, one should 'stop short of the pains inseparably annexed to an excess' of drinking, and one should 'play for trifles' only, conforming to custom, but not venturing sums it would be painful to lose.

Indeed, the law of moderation governs all wisdom, and even every virtue carried to excess becomes a vice. 'Generosity often runs into profusion, economy into avarice, courage into rashness, caution into timidity . . .' 'The sure characteristic of a sound and strong mind is, to find in everything those certain bounds, *quos ultra citraque nequit consistere rectum* . . . In manners, this line is good breeding; beyond it, troublesome ceremony; short of it, is unbecoming negligence and inattention. In morals it divides ostentatious puritanism from criminal relaxation. In religion, superstition from impiety; in short, every virtue from its kindred vice or weakness.'

His feeling for merit is strong, and his essential contempt for merely fortuitous honors consistent. 'The penetration of Princes,' he remarks, 'seldom goes deeper than the surface' (princes are 'about the pitch of women; bred up like them, and are to be addressed and gained in the same way'). Their suffrage, like that of society in general, is worth intrinsically nothing, but is one of those worldly influences without which no great aim can come to fruition. Therefore they must be cultivated in season, but the only really good company is that of men of personal distinction. 'I used to think myself in company as much *above* me, when I was with Mr Addison and Mr Pope, as if I had been with all the Princes in Europe.' (My italics.) His judgment of the course of events was as sound as his evaluation of merit. 'I foresee,' he wrote in 1752, 'that before the end of the century, the trade of both King and priest will not be half so good a one as it has been.'

Chesterfield's letters are always instructive, and they never fail to be interesting and full of character as well. Their style is as easy and well-bred as he was urging his son to be, shaped to the highest elegance but never either empty or ornate; and in these letters the style is indeed the man. They have intellectual power and urbanity, they have judgment and poise. Although he was much a man of his age, he was not incapable of decided personal judgments as well. 'Homer's hero, Achilles, was both a brute and a scoundrel . . .; he had so little regard for his country, that he would not act in defense of it because he had quarrelled with Agamemnon about a whore; and then, afterwards, animated by private resentment only, he went about killing people basely, I will call it, because he knew himself invulnerable . . .' His wit constantly concentrates itself into epigram, and his choice of individual words is often brilliant. 'A constant smirk upon the face, and a whiffling activity of the body are strong indications of futility.' The word whiffling, here, has just the silly and undignified air of useless fussiness he wants to evoke.

His standards are worldly, but they are not contemptible. Nothing could be less true than Dr Johnson's biased statement that the *Letters* 'teach the morals of a whore and the manners of a dancing-master.' Dancing, as we have seen, Chesterfield despised sufficiently, and he never failed to warn against debauchery and vice. He took the world, however, as he found it, and if it was unfortunate that young men could hardly be expected to remain quite chaste, he was concerned to ensure that his son be no libertine. Above all, his fundamental principles were sound; the best company is that of 'people of sense and learning,' the best life one of serious endeavor, knowledge, and moderation. Many sages have taught no more than this polished gentleman and man of the world.

Glass of Fashion

When Lady Mary Wortley Montagu was in Florence in 1740, she met 'Horry Walpole,' as she calls him in one of her letters, and she speaks of him as 'particularly civil' to her. The favorable impression was not reciprocal, for although he grants her 'wit and style superior to any letters I ever read but Madame Sévigné's' he had a low opinion of both her character, as avaricious, and her mentality, as précieuse. During that very stay in Florence he wrote: 'On Wednesday we expect a third she-meteor. Those learned luminaries the Ladies Pomfret and Walpole are to be joined by the Lady Mary Wortley Montague . . . Only figure the coalition of prudery, debauchery, sentiment, history, Greek, Latin, French, Italian, and metaphysics; all, except the second, understood by halves, by quarters, or not at all.' And when she actually arrived he was no less hard on her person: 'She wears a foul mob, that does not cover her greasy black locks, that hang loose, never combed or curled; an old mazarine blue wrapper, that gapes open and discovers a canvas petticoat.' The white paint on her face 'for cheapness she has bought so coarse, that you would not use it to wash a chimney.'

These two passages are characteristic of the feline and rather malicious wit of Walpole. Youngest son of the great prime minister, a dilettante in literature, the arts, mediaeval lore, old books, Gothic architecture, and half a dozen other subjects, he lived a life of dabbling and tasting, moving gracefully in the highest society of England and the Continent, clever, alert, urbane, just a little bit shallow, but not devoid of a capacity for loyalty, sound judgments, and sincere affections. He was a connoisseur of paintings, etchings, and engravings. He built a sham-Gothic castle at Strawberry Hill, and installed a printing-press where he ran off limited editions of the odes of his friend Gray and of rare finds like the *Life* of Lord Herbert of Cherbury. He wrote, himself, a mystery-thriller of supernatural goings-on, called *The Castle of Otranto*. And from everywhere—Strawberry Hill, London, Florence, Paris—he wrote his friends letters that were vivacious, brilliant, scandalous, full of observation and amusing comment.

His wit plays over almost every subject he touches. Talking of the coldness of the Italian climate, he says: 'The men hang little earthen pans of coals upon their wrists, and the women have portable stoves under their petticoats to warm their nakedness, and carry silver shovels in their pockets, with which their Cicisbeos stir them—Hush! by them, I mean their stoves.' During a period of widespread earthquakes, which the clergy were attributing to heavenly disapproval of the luxury of the age, he remarks ironically of a cancelled masquerade that 'the Bishops . . . have made an earthquake point of it,' and had it postponed. General Wolfe he describes as 'a commander whom a child might outwit, or terrify with a popgun.' Meeting Lady Mary, years later, he finds 'Her face less changed in twenty years than I could have imagined; I told her so, and she was not so tolerable twenty years ago that she need have taken it for flattery, but she did, and literally gave me a box on the ear. She is very lively, all her senses perfect, her languages as imperfect as ever, her avarice greater.' As he grew older, like many who age, he found a decay in manners, a growing brusquerie his formal training led him to disapprove, but even this he phrased with his usual sprightliness: 'This sublime age reduces everything to its quintessence; all periphrases and expletives are so much in disuse, that I suppose soon the only way of making love will be to say "Lie down."'

As son of Sir Robert Walpole, he knew everybody, went everywhere, and commented on everything, from the witticisms of Lord Chesterfield or the trial of a noble murderer to the American War and the loot of India. He notes the passing of a celebrity of the last generation: 'Old Marlborough [Sarah, the Dowager Duchess] is dying—but who can tell! last year she had lain a great while ill, without speaking; the physicians said "She must be blistered, or she will die." She called out, "I won't be blistered, and I won't die." If she takes the same resolution now, I don't believe she will.' He tells how, when Lord Lovat was going to his trial for rebellion, 'a woman looked into the coach, and said, "You ugly old dog, don't you think you will have that frightful head cut off?" He replied, "You damned ugly old bitch, I believe I shall."'

Walpole's letters are a running commentary on all public events.

Braddock's defeat he describes at some length, including how the 'common soldiers in general fled; the officers stood heroically, and were massacred; our Indians were not surprised, and behaved gallantly. The General had five horses shot under him . . . What makes the rout more shameful is, that instead of a great pursuit, and a barbarous massacre by the Indians . . . not a black or white soul followed our troops, but we had leisure two days afterwards to fetch off our dead. In short, our American laurels are strangely blighted!'

The War against the American Colonies he both disapproved and thought unlikely to bring them to obedience, and says ironically, 'The war with America goes on briskly, that is as far as voting goes. A great majority in both Houses is as brave as a mob ducking a pickpocket. They flatter themselves they shall terrify the Colonies into submission, and are amazed to hear that there is no such probability.' And a little later: 'I hear the Congress have named General Washington Generalissimo, with two thousand a year and five pounds a day for his table; he desired to be excused receiving the two thousand. If these folks will imitate both the Romans and Cromwellians in self-denial and enthusiasm, we shall be horridly plagued with them.'

The earlier, constitutional stages of the French Revolution he approved; it was only later, as violence and outrage flamed out, that he swung around to agreement with the mournful diatribes of Burke. At first it all seemed benevolent and orderly; M. Turgot began several reforms and then retracted them: Madame du Deffand remarked, 'Dans les bons vieux tems on reculoit pour mieux sauter, au lieu que Mons. Turgot saute pour mieux reculer.' The King was amiable, and his ministers not disposed to 'let their master's benevolent disposition rust.' Corvées were to be abolished, 'but the *country gentlemen*,' Walpole keenly foresaw, 'that race of interested stupidity,' would baffle the attempt. Malesherbes himself gave Walpole an account of freeing the prisoners in the Bastille, and told how one man who had been a prisoner fifteen years, and had nothing left, refused to leave unless he received a pension. 'M. de Malesherbes reported it to the King, who replied, "*C'est juste*," and the man has fifteen hundred livres a year and his freedom.'

Walpole's judgments on public questions, indeed, are usually humane and sound. He perceived clearly enough that the empire of trade created war, and says, 'I have no public spirit, and don't care a farthing for the interests of the merchants. Soldiers and sailors who are knocked on the head, and peasants plundered or butchered, are to my eyes as valuable as a lazy luxurious set of men, who hire others to acquire riches for them; who would embroil all the earth, that they may heap or squander; and I *dare* to say this, for I am no minister. Beckford is a patriot because he will clamour if Guadaloupe or Martinicio is given up, and the price of sugar falls. I am a bad Englishman, because I think the advantages of commerce are dearly bought for some by the lives of many more.'

The plunderer of India he often alludes to with special anger. 'We are Spaniards in our lust for gold, and Dutch in our delicacy of obtaining it . . .' General Clive, 'the *heaven-born* general,' Walpole bitterly echoes Pitt's encomium of him, 'knows of a part of India where such treasures are buried, that he will engage to send over enough to pay the National Debt.' And, three months later, when Clive came to London, 'General Clive is arrived all over estates and diamonds. If a beggar asks charity, he says, "Friend, I have no small brilliants about me."'

The sharp dealing used in seizing the Americas aroused his equal indignation: 'At present my chief study is West Indian history. You would not think me very ill-natured if you knew all I feel at the cruelty and villainy of European settlers: but this very morning I found that part of the purchase of Maryland from the savage proprietors (for *we* do not massacre, *we* are such good Christians as only to cheat) was a quantity of vermilion and a parcel of Jews'-harps!'

Sometimes his views have a trace of superciliousness or of fashionable affectation. 'The French affect philosophy, literature, and freethinking: the first never did, and never will possess me; of the two others I have long been tired,' he writes languidly. 'Freethinking is for one's self, surely not for society; besides one has settled one's way of thinking, or knows it cannot be settled, and for others I do not see why there is not as much bigotry in attempting conversions from any religion as to it . . . For literature, it is very amusing when one has nothing else to do. I think it rather pedantic in society; tiresome when displayed professedly . . .' The effete patricianism of this attitude is largely pose; it is classic taste playing at being hellenistic. The sentiments of the educated man of the age are found in his opinion of Wesley, the preacher, whose performance he called an 'opera,' with hymns to 'Scotch ballad tunes . . . so long, that one would think they were already in eternity . . .' Wesley himself was 'as evidently an actor as Garrick,' and his sermon had 'parts and eloquence in it; but towards the end he exalted his voice, and acted very ugly enthusiasm, decried learning, and told stories': all very vulgar and repulsive.

If enthusiasm was plebeian, and the airs of a world-weary aesthete enjoyable, there was nevertheless much that was understanding in Walpole, and even more that was tender and loyal. Certain fetiches of his day he did not worship at all. If all his training and tastes led to his despising vulgar beliefs, he was no blind camp-follower of his own class. 'Lord Byron has killed a Mr Chaworth in a duel at a tavern. I, who should like the trial of a Laud or a Strafford, as a wholesome spectacle now and then, am not interested about an obscure Lord, whose birth alone procures his being treated like an overgrown criminal.' But his gentle heart was harrowed by the way dogs were run over in the London streets: 'a very picture of the murder of the innocents–one drives over nothing but poor dead dogs! The dear, good-natured, honest, sensible creatures! Christ! how can anybody hurt them?'

When his friend Conway was deprived of his offices for independence in using his vote in the Commons, Walpole begged to be allowed 'to make your loss as light as it is in my power to make it: I have six thousand pounds in the funds; accept all, or what part of it you want. Do not imagine I shall be put off with a refusal . . . You have ever been the dearest person to me in the world. You have shown that you deserve to be so. You suffer for your spotless integrity. Can I hesitate a moment to show that there is at least one man who knows how to value you?'

The generosity and the other virtues of Walpole had their roots, of course, in a world of privilege and sinecure. The public offices which he held were not graced by his presence; clerks paid by the public did all of his work. It was the custom of his age, and Walpole never even thought of thinking of it. He despised the 'interests of the merchants,' and 'the *heaven-born* general' looting the poor Indian filled him with rage, but he did not realize that his disinterestedness could hardly have existed without such instruments of imperialism. He would have been far in advance of his time if he had. Instead, the kindhearted, dandified creature played with his toy Gothic castle, his books and his pictures, looked on at the entertaining spectacle of life and formulated his reflections and sentiments about it in letters where pungency, sensibility, playfulness, insight, and persiflage are mingled in an incomparable entertainment.

Elegy and Burlesque

His friend Thomas Gray, the poet, is more of a scholar than Walpole, more serious, perhaps less the man of the world if that term be regarded as implying enjoyment of the beau monde. Pensive and with a love of solitude, Gray's wit shines less brightly and constantly than Walpole's, and he is urbane with a difference: for it is not so much fashionable society that he has mingled with as chosen society. Walpole laughs at the absurdities of the world he dwells in, but he dwells there. Gray retired from it. After going to Eton and Cambridge, spending a short time in London, and traveling on the continent with Walpole from 1739 to 1741, he made Cambridge his headquarters for the remainder of his life. Three years before his death he was appointed Regius Professor of History and Modern Languages at Cambridge, but otherwise his life was entirely devoted to reflection, friendship, study, and literature.

Friendship is more especially displayed in the letters of Gray than in those of Walpole, for Gray was a reserved man, opening out only to those of whom he felt fond, whereas Walpole scattered letters everywhere among his acquaintance. Gray's 'rare and marvellous quality of sympathy' is shown not merely in those letters written to his friends to comfort them in times of sorrow, but in his ability to feel with them and adapt himself to them in all the variations of mood. Writing to Walpole in London he is gay and whimsical, to his mother on a bereavement he is gently philosophical, to Wharton serious and literary, and to all of them any of these by turns, with modulations suited to their different natures.

The same quality of sympathy appears in his literary judgments, combined with a critical acumen that makes his discussions of the writings of his contemporaries both revealing and, usually, sound. And, although he was so retired a scholar, he was no mere bookworm, but had enough practical wisdom and knowledge of the world to spice with urbanity and wit the judgments of the man of learning. Of the academic community in which he dwelt he thought poorly enough: 'The Masters of Colledges are twelve grey-hair'd Gentlefolks, who are all mad with Pride,' he wrote; 'the Fellows are sleepy, drunken, dull, illiterate Things; the Fellow-Commoners are imitatours of the Fellows, or else Beaux, or else nothing: the Pensioners grave, formal Sots, who would be thought old; or else drink Ale, & sing Songs against ye Excise. The Sizers are Graziers Eldest Sons, who come to get good Learning, that they may all be Archbishops of Canterbury . . .'

He endured 'lectures daily and hourly since I came,' but he felt in himself no talent for metaphysics or mathematics, all of which these people seemed to know 'and more, and yet I do not know one of them who inspires me with any ambition of being like him. Surely it was of this place, now Cambridge, but formerly known by the name of Babylon, that the prophet spoke when he said, "the wild beasts of the desert shall dwell there, and their houses be full of doleful creatures, and owls shall build there, and satyrs shall dance there; their forts and towers shall be a den for ever, a joy of wild asses."' Idleness and pedantry have ever elbowed themselves into the homes of scholarship; the satire of a Gray needs remembrance in our time.

He is equally amusing in a parody of University tittle-tattle: 'Cambridge . . . is, as it was, for all the World; & the People are, as they were; and Mr Trollope is as he was, that is, half ill, half well. I wish with all my heart they were better, but what can one do? there is no News, only I think I heard a Whisper, as if the Vice-Chancellour should be with Child (but I beg you not to mention this, for I may come into trouble about it); there is some suspicion that the Professor of Mathematics had a Hand in the thing. Dr Dickens says the University will be obliged to keep it, as it was got, in Magistru.'

Turning to the more serious realms of literary criticism, we find him praising the characters in *Joseph Andrews* as having 'a great deal of nature,' and Fielding's reflections upon high and low people, and 'misses and masters' as being very good, although 'The incidents are ill-laid and without invention.' But Fielding's painting of human nature he considers 'as weighty and much more useful than your grave discourses upon the mind, the passions, and what not.' The vogue of Lord Shaftesbury as a philosopher he can explain only in the following way: 'First, he was a Lord; 2dly, he was as vain as any of his readers; 3dly, men are very prone to believe what they do not understand; 4thly, they will believe anything at all, provided they are under no obligation to believe it; 5thly, they love to take a new road, even when that road leads nowhere; 6thly, he was reckoned a fine writer, and seemed always to mean more than he said. Would you have any more reasons?' This may not be sufficient as a permanent analysis of Shaftsbury's importance, but it is a shrewd statement of some of the influences of fashion.

Addison, he thought, 'had . . . not above three or four notes in poetry, sweet enough, indeed, like those of a German flute, but such as soon tire and satiate the ear with their frequent return.' Johnson's *London* was 'one of those few imitations that have all the ease and spirit of an original.' Macpherson's *Ossian* he was 'gone mad about,' but could not quite decide on its authenticity; he made enquiries and received answers so 'ill-wrote, ill-reasoned, unsatisfactory, calculated (one would imagine) to deceive one, and yet not cunning enough to do it cleverly' that he could not but regard the poem as counterfeit, but the work itself was so admirable he 'resolved to believe' it 'genuine, spite of the Devil and the Kirk.' Rousseau's *Emile* 'abounds with his usual glorious absurdity' and its 'scheme of education' is 'an impracticable chimera: yet there are a thousand lights struck out, a thousand important truths better express'd than ever they were before . . .'

In his amused comments on the failures of his readers to understand *The Bard* there is an air of dandified patronage that reflects some of the superciliousness of his fashionable friends. He had really not expected many to understand the poem, but 'The Συνετοι appear to be still fewer, than even I expected.' He dismisses criticism of the gnomic language of the prophecy: 'Mr Fox, supposing the Bard sung his song but once over, does not wonder if Edward the First did not understand him . . . though it had been sung a hundred times under his window, it was impossible King Edward should understand him; but that is no reason for Mr Fox, who lives almost 500 years after him. It is very well; the next thing I print shall be in Welch,—that's all.'

The wit of his personal comments is often superior. His friend Ashton was deciding on marriage, but 'two things he is terrified at,' lest his wife 'should not breed, and lest she should love him:

I comforted him by saying, there was no Danger of either.' The use of the word comforted is a Walpolian touch. And to Walpole he writes, in burlesque anger at not having heard from him, 'Gadsbud! I am provoked into a fermentation! when I see you next I'll firk you, I'll rattle you with a Certiorari: let me tell you; I am at present as full of wrath & choler as—as—you are of wit & good-nature; though I begin to doubt your title to the last of them, since you have balked me in this manner . . .' He parodies Walpole's scandalous gossip with an account of 'an amour carried on almost under my window between a boar & a sow, people of very good fashion, that come to an assignation, and squeak like ten masquerades; I have a great mind to make you hear the whole progress of the affair, together with the humours of Miss Pignies, the Lady's Confidente. . .'

Burlesque, in fact, is one of his favorite figures, and he uses it gorgeously in his letters from abroad during his two years of European travel. The Duke of Modena's palace draws the following description: 'Imprimis, a house, being in circumference a quarter of a mile, two feet and an inch; the said house containing the following particulars, to wit, a great room. Item, another great room; item, a bigger room; item, another room; item, a vast room; item, a sixth of the same; a seventh ditto; an eighth as before; a ninth as abovesaid; a tenth (see No. 1); item, ten more such, besides twenty besides, which, not to be too particular, we shall pass over. The said rooms contain nine chairs, two tables, five stools, and a cricket. From whence we shall proceed to the garden, containing two millions of superfine laurel hedges, a clump of cypress trees, and half the river Teverone, that pisses into two thousand several chamberpots. Finis.'

Even more hilarious is his prospectus for printing a volume of travels:

Proposals for printing by Subscription, in

THIS LARGE
LETTER,

THE TRAVELS OF T: G: GENT:

which will consist of the following Particulars.

CHAP: 1:

The Author arrives at Dover; his conversation with the Mayor of that Corporation; sets out in the Pacquet-Boat, grows very sick;

the Author spews, a very minute account of all the circumstances thereof; his arrival at Calais; how the inhabitants of that country speak French, & are said to be all Papishes; the Author's reflexions thereupon. . . .

3

. . . a Cut of the inside of a Nunnery; its Structure, wonderfully adapted to the use of the animals, that inhabit it: a short account of them, how they propagate without the help of a Male, and how they eat up their own young ones, like Cats and Rabbits, supposed to have both sexes in themselves, like a Snail. Dissection of a Dutchess with Copper-Plates, very curious. . . .

7

Goes into the country to Rheims in Champagne, stays there 3 Months, what he did there (he must beg the reader's pardon) he has really forgot.

8

Proceeds to Lyons. Vastness of that City. Can't see the Streets for houses. how rich it is and how much it stinks. Poem upon the confluence of the Rhône & the Saône, by a friend of the Author's; very pretty!

9

Makes a journey into Savoy, & in his way visits the Grand Chartreuse; he is set astride upon a Mule's back, & begins to climb up the Mountain. Rocks & Torrents beneath; Pine-trees, & Snows above; horrours, & terrours on all sides. the Author dies of the Fright.

11

Sets out the latter end of November to cross the Alps. he is devoured by a Wolf, & how it is to be devoured by a Wolf . . . how he lights among a certain fat nation, call'd Clouds: how they are always in a Sweat, and never speak, but they f—t. how they flock about him, & think him very odd for not doing so too . . .

12

. . . locked out of Parma in a cold winter's night: the author by an ingenious stratagem, gains admittance. despises that City, & proceeds through Reggio to Modena. how the Duke, & Duchess lie over their own Stables, and go every night to a vile Italian comedy; despises them, & it; & proceeds to Bologna. . . .

15

Arrival at Florence . . . Account of the City, & manners of the inhabitants. A learned Dissertation on the true situation of Gomorrah . . .

And here will end the first part of these instructive & entertaining

> voyages. the Subscribers are to pay 20 Guineas; 19 down, & the remainder upon delivery of the book. N: B: A few are printed on the softest Royal Brown paper for the use of the Curious.

In many ways the letters of Gray, no less than his more formal writings, are portents of the change of taste that was coming over the eighteenth century. His admiration for the rude Ossianic fragments, his own delving in Celtic and Iceland sagas, the incipient romanticism transfusing the classic form of his *Elegy* and his *Odes*, the leaning toward the mediaeval he shared with Horace Walpole, the changing attitude toward wild scenes in nature: all are to be found in Gray. Crossing Mount Cenis, although he still speaks in the earlier way of 'the savageness and horror of the place,' he is awed by the 'immensity of the precipices, the roaring of the river and torrents that run into it, the huge craggs covered with ice and snow, and the clouds below you and about you;' and on another occasion he says, 'None but those monstrous creatures of God know how to join so much beauty with so much horror.'

Romanticism, indeed, breaks out again and again in Gray, and he is always writing of his garden or of landscape with a seeing eye that shames the classic use of standardized epithet. 'The sea,' he says, '. . . mixes its white transient sails and glittering blue expanse with the deeper and brighter greens of the woods and corn'; and though he adds apologetically, 'this last sentence is so fine, I am quite ashamed: but, no matter! you must translate it into prose,' the picture remains.

The loving heart of the man appears in many ways. Here is part of a letter to Norton Nicholls: 'It is long since, that I heard you were gone in haste into Yorkshire on account of your Mother's illness, and the same letter informed me she was recovered; otherwise I had then wrote to you, only to beg you would take care of her, and to inform you that I had discovered a thing very little known, which is, that in one's whole life one can never have more than a single Mother. You may think this obvious, and (what you call) a trite observation. You are a green Gossling! I was at the same age (very near) as wise as you, and yet I never discovered this (with full evidence and conviction, I mean) till it was too late. It is 13 years ago, and seems but yesterday, and every day I live it sinks deeper into my heart.'

One might quote endlessly from Gray's letters. Though in his early days he spoke lightly of erudition, and denied possessing any talent for metaphysics or morals, he made them, and criticism, science, history, and antiquarianism, all a part of his knowledge; and his acquaintance with them was not superficial. He loved voyages and travels, and had taste in painting, prints, and architecture. A year after his death, the Reverend William Temple described him as not only 'perhaps the most learned man in Europe,' but, more than that, 'a good man, a well-bred man, a man of virtue and humanity.' And Dr Johnson, who had no very high appreciation of Gray's talents as a man of letters, save for the *Hymn to Adversity* and the *Elegy*, saw that 'he was a man likely to love much where he loved at all.' There is hardly a letter in which that fact may not be read plain.

Twilight Landscape

In minor keys the still and gentle life of William Cowper echoes many of the tones we have heard in the life of Gray. Most of his days were passed in quiet retirement first in the little village of Olney and then in Weston Underwood: even more rural retreats than Cambridge and Stoke Poges. His correspondents, Lady Hesketh and Lady Austen, Joseph Hill, William Hayley, a few old schoolfellows, and various quiet country clergymen, were not brilliant luminaries like Madame du Deffand, Conway, Sir Horace Mann, and Walpole; but the first three named among Cowper's friends lived among London gentlefolk, and Hayley was a literary man rather over-famous in his day.

Neither as poet nor as scholar was Cowper so notable a figure as Gray, but his scholarship was solid enough to make his translation of Homer both more exact and more noble in language than that of Pope, and his own poetry is full of charm and gentle humor. Cowper's nature was affectionate and lovable, although inclining to melancholy. In this respect, indeed, his life strikes sadder notes than that of Gray, for if Gray had a leaning to twilight pensiveness he experienced no unusual sorrows, and in Cowper there was an obscure religious melancholia that always hung over him and threatened to envelop him in insanity.

His first seizure had come upon him when he was thirty-two,

and a struggling barrister hoping for an appointment as Clerk of the Journals to the House of Lords, to which his uncle had the reversion. He tormented himself with the thought that he desired the Clerk in possession to die, and brooding on his sin and failure, he fell prey to suicidal mania. He was ill for two years, and on his recovery his relatives placed him in the retirement in which most of the rest of his life was passed. His delicate balance was continually threatened by periods of despair, and times came when he was again insane. For a golden stretch of sixteen years he was comparatively serene, and then in 1792 the clouds began to darken again, and by 1794 he was hopelessly buried in despondency. He roused a few times after that, but briefly, and died in 1800.

Out of this sombre background the homely charm and domestic ease of Cowper's letters move, with all their playfulness, serenity, and good sense. Homely and personal Cowper's letters are in the highest degree, and hardly another master of letter-writing has used his pen so exclusively on matters confined to his own direct observation. Leading a confined life in a small village, he lets his mind run humorously and easily over the mild events of his daily life, and everywhere the result is clarity and exquisite grace. No one has made so much charm out of so little.

It is strange to remember that his whimsical lightness comes to us from such depths of shadow. He tells of a visit he once made to the Isle of Thanet: 'One sight, . . . I remember, engaged my curiosity, and I went to see it:—a fine piece of ruins, built by the late Lord Holland, at a great expense, which, the day after I saw it, tumbled down for nothing. Perhaps, therefore, it is still a ruin; and if it is . . . it must have been much improved by this fortunate incident. It is hardly possible to put stones together with that air of wild and magnificent disorder which they are sure to acquire by falling down of their own accord.' Or, having no other adventure to record, he tells us, 'In the morning I walk with one or other of the ladies, and in the afternoon wind thread. Thus did Hercules, and thus probably did Samson, and thus do I; and were both those heroes living, I should not fear to challenge them to a trial of skill in that business, or doubt to beat them both.' To his friend the Reverend John Newton, visiting the seaside at Lymington, he writes: 'I am not . . . totally destitute of such pleasures as an inland country may pretend to. If my windows do not command a view of the ocean, at least they look out upon a profusion of mignonette, which, if it be not so grand an object, is however quite as fragrant: and if I have not a hermit in a grotto, I have nevertheless myself in a greenhouse,–a less venerable figure perhaps, but not at all less animated . . . '

'When I read your letters,' he says to Lady Hesketh, 'I hear you talk, and I love talking letters, especially from you.' Talking letters are the kind he writes himself, for his are full of exactly such spontaneous and amiable chatter as comes into the heads of two friends gossiping with each other. He dislikes the sort of letter that sounds like a set-piece, and makes a jesting little sermon on his own vanity, which might have made him 'as disgusting a letter-writer as Pope, who seems to have thought that unless a sentence was well-turned, and every period pointed with some conceit, it was not worth the carriage. Accordingly he is to me, except in a very few instances, the most disagreeable maker of epistles I ever met with.'

For himself this temptation had almost been a pitfall. 'Your mother communicated to me,' he wrote to the Reverend William Unwin, '. . . that you thought me entertaining and clever, and so forth:–now you must know, I love praise dearly, especially from the judicious, and those who have so much delicacy themselves as not to offend mine. But then I found this consequence . . . if my friend thought me witty before, he shall think me ten times more witty hereafter;–where I joked once, I will joke five times, and for one sensible remark I will send him a dozen. Now this foolish vanity would have spoiled me quite . . .' The true way to write a letter is just to begin and go ahead:

> . . . I have nothing to say: this seems . . . a good reason why I should not [write]. Yet if you had alighted from your horse at our door this morning and at this present writing, being five o'clock in the afternoon, had found occasion to say to me–"Mr Cowper, you have not spoke since I came in; have you resolved never to speak again?" it would be but a poor reply, if in answer to the summons I should plead inability as my best and only excuse . . . a letter may be written on anything or nothing just as that anything or nothing happens to occur. A man that has a journey before him twenty miles in length, which he is to perform on foot, will not hesitate and doubt whether he shall set out or not, because he does not readily conceive how he shall ever reach the

> end of it: for he knows, that by the simple operation of moving one foot forward first, and then the other, he shall be sure to accomplish it. So it is in the present case, and so it is in every similar case. A letter is written as a conversation is maintained, or a journey performed; not by preconcerted or premeditated means, a new contrivance, or an invention never heard of before,—but merely by maintaining a progress . . . If a man may talk without thinking, why may he not write upon the same terms?

The prescription might not work with everyone, but with Cowper the results are delicious. 'All the bees in the neighborhood resort to a bed of mignonette, opposite the window, and pay me for the honey they get out of it by a hum . . . which is as agreeable to my ears as the whistling of my linnets. All the sounds that nature utters are delightful,—at least in this country. I should not perhaps find the roaring of lions in Africa, or of bears in Russia, very pleasing; but I know no beast in England whose voice I do not account musical, save and except always the braying of an ass . . . I should not indeed think of keeping a goose in a cage, that I might hang him up in the parlour for the sake of his melody, but a goose upon a common, or in a farm-yard, is no bad performer; and as to insects . . . in whatever key they sing, from the gnat's fine treble to the bass of the humble-bee, I admire them all.'

Or he has recently 'glazed two frames designed to receive my pine plants,' and thinks of mending the kitchen windows: 'and possibly the happy time may come when I shall be seen trudging away to the neighboring town with a shelf of glass hanging at my back. If government should impose another tax on that commodity, I hardly know another business in which a gentleman might more successfully employ himself. A Chinese, of ten times my fortune, would avail himself of such an opportunity without scruple; and why should not I, who want money as much as any mandarin in China?' Or, writing to Lady Hesketh, ' I know well, my Cousin, how formidable a creature you are when you become once outrageous. No sprat in a storm is half so terrible. But it is all in vain. You are at a distance, so we snap our fingers at you.'

His literary comments are often fascinating. With Johnson's unmerciful treatment of Milton in his *Lives of the Poets*, Cowper had no patience: 'A pensioner is not likely to spare a republican; and the Doctor, in order, I suppose, to convince his royal patron of the sincerity of his monarchical principles, has belaboured that great poet's character with the most industrious cruelty . . . Churlishness in his private life, and a rancorous hatred of everything royal in his public, are the two colours with which he has smeared all the canvas . . . as a poet, he has treated him with severity enough, and has plucked one or two of the most beautiful feathers out of his Muse's wing, and trampled them under his great foot . . . Oh! I could thresh his old jacket, till I made his pension jingle in his pocket.'

This is the only time I can recall finding Cowper unjust, for Johnson's Toryism long antedated his pension; but he makes it up in his general comment: 'I am very much the biographer's humble admirer. His uncommon share of good sense, and his forcible expression, secure to him that tribute from all his readers. He has a penetrating insight into character, and a happy talent of correcting the popular opinion when it is erroneous: and this he does with the boldness of a man who will think for himself, but, at the same time, with a justness of sentiment that convinces us he does not differ from others through affectation, but because he has a sounder judgment.'

Cowper read the poems of Burns, 'and though they be written in a language that is new to me, and many of them on subjects much inferior to the author's ability, I think them on the whole a very extraordinary production. He is I believe the only poet these kingdoms have produced in the lower rank of life since Shakespeare (I should rather say since Prior), who need not be indebted for any part of his praise to a charitable consideration of his origin, and the disadvantages under which he has laboured.'

Cowper is severe on the faults of Pope's translation of Homer: 'Metaphors of which Homer never dreamt, which he did not seek, and which probably he would have disdained if he had found, follow each other like the sliding pictures in a show-box. Homer is, on occasions that call for such a style, the easiest and most familiar of all writers,' whereas Pope 'takes the most religious care that he shall everywhere strut in buckram. The speeches of his heroes are often animated to a degree that Pope no doubt accounted unmannerly and rude, for he has reduced numbers of them . . . to the perfect standard of French good-breeding.'

Sometimes on serious topics he strikes a deeper note. 'If a great man struggling with misfortunes is a noble object, a little man that despises them is no contemptible one; and this is all the philosophy I have in the world at present.' 'If you hear ballads sung in the streets on the hardships of the negroes in the islands, they are probably mine. It must be an honour to any man to have given a stroke to that chain, however feeble . . . Woe be to us, if we refuse the poor captives the redress to which they have so clear a right and prove ourselves in the sight of God and men indifferent to all considerations but those of gain.'

And sometimes we hear the melancholy undertones to his lightness. 'If I trifle, and merely trifle, it is because I am reduced to it by necessity—a melancholy, that nothing else so effectually disperses, engages me sometimes in the arduous task of being merry by force. And, strange as it may seem, the most ludicrous lines I ever wrote have been written in the saddest mood, and, but for that saddest mood, perhaps had never been written at all.' And, leaving Olney for Weston Underwood, he wrote, 'I could not help giving a last look at my old prison and its precincts; and though I cannot easily account for it, having been miserable there so many years, felt something like a heartache when I took my last leave of a scene, that certainly in itself had nothing to engage affection. But I recollected that I had once been happy there, and could not, without tears in my eyes, bid adieu to a place in which God had so often found me . . . What consequences are to attend our removal, God only knows. I know well that it is not in situation to effect a cure of melancholy like mine.'

Within a few days, though, we find him writing more cheerfully about their new home, that 'if it is not an hermitage, at least it is a much better thing; and you must always understand, my dear, that when poets talk of cottages, hermitages, and such like things, they mean a house with six sashes in front, two comfortable parlours, a smart staircase, and three bedrooms of convenient dimensions; in short, exactly such a house as this.' The shadow hovered, but there were long days of light ahead. Let us leave him before the time of utter darkness.

It is a little hard to make comparisons between letter-writers because our judgments of letters, to a much larger degree than our judgments of books, are liable to be a subjective matter, depending on our liking or antagonism to the personality displayed in them. The author of a novel may only now and then force us to be aware of his personality, and we may not make the critical effort to discern the personality that is implied in his work. But in the letter it confronts us on every page, or, if it does not, that is even worse.

Absence of personality certainly means a bad letter, we may agree. By the mysterious chemistry of repulsion or attraction, however, the very character that warms one reader to affection and admiration may enrage another. The rollicking absurdities and punsome humours of Charles Lamb, which have endeared him to many, left Carlyle certain that he was 'in some considerable degree insane': a 'pitiful, ricketty, gasping, staggering, stammering Tomfool,' 'witty by denying truisms and abjuring good manners.' This judgment in itself has humor, for there were those who remarked of Carlyle that 'if he spoke English and attended to the rules of good breeding, his charm for the mass of his admirers would disappear.' The question, then, should not be so much whether we like the personality revealed as how clearly and interestingly it is revealed.

Naturally even the realization of the danger cannot altogether banish it. If we dislike a personality very much indeed, we may make ourselves feel that it does not interest us, when in fact it interests us to the point of rage. It is possible, however, by trying hard, to allow as much as we can for such a tendency. If, so determined, we examine these letter-writers, what shall we decide? Of them all, Chesterfield is, in the superficial sense, the least intimate. He is never less than in court dress, and with only so much, sometimes, not of informality but of a polite likeness of informality, as to show that he is himself completely at ease. There is never a moment of triviality or relaxation, nothing merely frivolous or for amusement only; all the wit is put to service. No doubts or self-questionings ever for a moment appear, for all have been magisterially settled years ago. High, polished, assured, invulnerable: if he is these things to his son, we may be certain that the manner never grew more unbending. We have so sharply etched an image of Chesterfield because he was concerned to score again and again those outlines that he considered important.

Lady Mary's letters, save for many of those early ones to Edward Wortley Montagu and some of those to her daughter, have almost the same degree of reserve. Whatever hesitancies or tremors there may have been in her we do not know; it is the social image of the well-informed and shrewd lady that we have before us. Her wit, her cynicism, her worldly wisdom, her judgment, are all there, and many polite assurances of esteem and friendship; but little heartfelt warmth and as little violent hate, although sometimes a touch of cerebral malice. The stronger feelings seem to have been underneath, but they hardly move the surface of the letters.

Madame de Sévigné, on the other hand, below the smooth surface of her style, has always the movement of personal feeling. And it is not formality of phrasing that makes the difference, for her most polished sentences are pellucid to sentiment. Her mind was perhaps not so strong and positive as that of Lady Mary, but it was exquisite in the discrimination and analysis of feeling. She was ever using it for such delicate operations; and it is for this reason that we seem to know her more intimately than it is possible to know Mary Wortley Montagu.

To a much slighter degree Walpole is also a less intimate writer than those who remain for our consideration. He is witty and entertaining nearly always, but we might find as much exhilaration, and often of the same kind, in reading the comedies of Congreve or the essays of Addison or the *Philosophical Dictionary* of Voltaire. It is a wonderful thing to be so copiously amusing and interesting, but Walpole wrote letters that were both these to so many people that it is hardly to be wondered if sometimes the tone of intimacy grew faint. Only to a very few is there any true unveiling. In Gray and Cowper, however, we find the personal touch everywhere. Both maintain the decent reserve that is needful to save the feelings of their friends from being harrowed in times of disturbance, Gray even more than Cowper; but in each there is a transparency that leaves even the most trivial sentiment clear to the reader.

None of our writers is lacking in real spontaneity, although it takes different forms, from the elaborate stateliness of Lord Chesterfield to the 'divine chit-chat' of Cowper. In Lady Mary the choice of subject and the manipulation of ideas, especially of ideas of wit, seem at times to be just a little dictated by the effort to make the impression produced. I do not mean that she does not make it, but that her effort to do so is visible. In Chesterfield long practice has obviously made it completely spontaneous to write in a manner that in others would be formal and even forced. Walpole ingeniously combines the rhythm and tone of conversational speech with just enough of formal structure to give spice to a manner of perfect ease. Gray, at his most happy, is almost as good in this way; but sometimes, especially in his more critical utterance, his sentences become a little wrought. Of the clarity and ease of Cowper I have already said enough: although Coleridge's phrase, 'divine chit-chat,' was applied to his poetry, it is the perfect description for the letters as well.

Even the few quotations from the letters with which this section has been illustrated will establish beyond any possibility of doubt the richness of the letter as a self-portrayal of character. It would be hard for a biographer to give a clearer and more brilliant image of a human being than these six writers have given of themselves, and no biography of them could be successful that did not draw heavily on their letters for light and shadow. Biography, indeed, of Walpole and Cowper has been a sort of marginal commentary on their letters; stray facts and explanatory notes have been added, missing links have been supplied in those places where the subject was misinformed, uninformed, or too reticent to write himself, and inferences or psychological interpretations drawn from the evidence: but their main outlines are forever contained in the letters.

Equally rich are these letters for understanding the history of the times their writers lived in. Only a historian of the most transcendent genius could throw so clear and searching a light on the reign of Louis XIV as we may glean from a reflective reading of Madame de Sévigné, the *Memoirs* of the Duc de Saint-Simon, and the *Letters* of Pascal. And the sensitive heart of Madame de Sévigné, murmuring in the midst of the gilded salons and the marble fountains in their alleys of cypress, is no less illuminating than the Duke's withering rancor or the lonely agonies of the philosopher. In England the sharpness and intelligence of Lady Mary Wortley Montagu throws an arid light on many features of her pragmatic age.

Lady Mary really belonged in many ways to the period of Queen Anne, but she lived, busy, energetic, gossiping, traveling, and reading, into a later day. In it, Lord Chesterfield, if not so prominent in politics as he had desired to be, was a conspicuous because a representative figure. He epitomized a kind of ideal; he was the figure that many wished to be. Just as Castiglione's *Book of the*

Courtier had symbolized the ideal Renaissance aspiration of the gentleman, with his star-ranging desire to be versed in everything, from swordsmanship to poetry and music—and as Sir Philip Sidney had represented almost the attainment of that ideal for his Elizabethan contemporaries, so that Spenser had enshrined him in *The Faerie Queene* as Sir Calidore, the perfect courteous knight—so Chesterfield represents what the serious judgment of his age admired. In him the wit and grace that the English nobility had brought over from France with Charles II's restoration had lost their frivolity and vice, and become the instruments of serious purpose, the tools for carving out a career. Without a trace of the utopian and visionary (as there had been in the lofty ambitions of the Renaissance) he set up a clear and unsentimental picture of attainable ends: not contemptuous of virtue, but aiming only at the practical. The sanity and balance, the coolness and steadiness of aim, the lack of poetry and the enthronement of reason that marked the age are given a corporeal form in the Earl of Chesterfield.

The second half of the century in all its changing colors and excitements is no less clearly mirrored in our later three letter-writers. For fifty years the world of fashion, the theatre, war and politics, literature, gossip and scandal, the fine arts, scintillates in the pages of Horace Walpole's airy monologues. His gaiety, sophistication, worldliness, and dilettantism, and the dislike for 'enthusiasm' he shared with Gibbon and most of his educated contemporaries, the contempt for the visionary and the imaginative: in all he is characteristic of his age. And he is characteristic too of its first reachings-out after those very elements of romance it so robustly despised, in the fantastic gingerbread of Strawberry Hill and in the supernatural machinery of *The Castle of Otranto* with its mediaeval trappings.

The breath of the Middle Ages stirred in Gray, also, as we have seen; and a love for the awful, frightening grandeur of the Alps. The balanced judgment of the age he tempered with deep feeling, though pensive and restrained; he melted away the frozen glitter of its wit and let it grow humane.

In Cowper too some of the same mingling of elements can be seen. If all his critical judgments still partake of the dogmas of classicism, the emotional tone is again and again that of a new age. The enjoyment of fresh country sights and sounds, the wit which is playfulness rather than satire, the brooding melancholy, the passionate sympathizing with the sorrowing or oppressed, the longing for escape to 'a lodge in some vast wilderness' where his ear and heart may be no longer pained by the cruelty of 'man's obdurate heart': both in his poetry and his letters these sentiments constantly appear. In such feelings Cowper is aware of the great outer world stretching beyond the horizons of Olney and Weston Underwood. They appear and disappear amid the daily hues of rural life. Bright and sober by turns, these letters are water-colors transparent with the essence of those remotest backwaters that, as much as Walpole's swarming London, were the reality of changing England.

EIGHTEENTH CENTURY APOGEE

VII

EIGHTEENTH CENTURY APOGEE

The Doctor as Biographer

WE HAVE already heard Cowper engaged in reading Johnson's *Lives of the Poets*, subscribe himself 'very much the biographer's humble admirer.' His admiration of Johnson's critical dicta, to be sure, was somewhat tempered by indignation at the treatment of Milton, and by a number of other judgments with which he did not agree. But the sharpness of the characterization excited his enthusiasm. 'What vanity, what petulance in Pope! How painfully sensible of censure, and yet how restless in provocation! To what mean artifices could Addison stoop, in the hope of injuring the reputation of his friend! Savage, how sordidly vicious, and the more condemned for the pains that are taken to palliate his vices . . . What a sycophant to the public taste was Dryden; sinning against his feelings, lewd in his writings, though chaste in his conversation.'

Aliveness and vigor coursed through the pages of the book that could arouse such feeling comment. And, indeed, to the modern reader, the sinewy quality of Johnson's mind is one of the strongest enjoyments provided in the *Lives of the Poets;* we read as much to taste the character of Johnson as to learn the characters of Waller, Dryden, Prior, and Pope. His judgments we read with interest sometimes because they are so penetrating and sometimes because they are Johnson's. For, although Johnson was occasionally prejudiced to the degree of being fantastic, he was never merely absurd. Within even his most violent oddities there is some core of sense or reason, or, at the least, of mental power. These qualities he applied as successfully to the characters of the poets he deals with as to their muse. The result is a work bristling with trenchant and revealing comments on almost every page.

The *Lives of the Poets* is, of course, not pure biography, but biography alternating with and partly existing for the sake of literary criticism. Its fifty-two narratives, indeed, some of them running to over a hundred pages and a number to only three or four, Johnson originally wrote as introductions to a publisher's collected edition of the major English poets.

The art of biography, nevertheless, fascinated him, and he had given it much thought. Insatiably curious always about the strange manifestations of human character, he seized avidly on any trivial detail that could throw light on individual personality, and he had little interest in Theophrastian generalizations. In his passion for psychologizing, he was always turning human qualities inside out, testing them, analyzing. Mere surfaces never satisfied him; he must always probe for what they meant within. This tendency led him to realize that the biographer must often 'pass slightly over those performances and incidents which produce vulgar greatness' and 'lead the thoughts into domestic privacies, and display the minute details of daily life . . . Thus, Sallust, the great master of nature, has not forgot in his account of Catiline, to remark, that his walk was now quick, and again slow, as an indication of a mind moving with violent commotion.'

He realized the truth of Plutarch's observation that 'a short saying, or a jest,' may 'distinguish a person's real character more than the greatest sieges or the most important battles.' He noted that we may sometimes learn more of a man from 'a short conversation with one of his servants, than from a formal and studied narrative, begun with his pedigree, and ended with his funeral.' But to these perceptions Johnson added another quality of historic importance: an aversion to panegyric. In this he cut straight through a quarrel that recurred frequently in the nineteenth century and that still turns up today. For him truth was a passion; and the truth about a human being could never be unadulterated praise. Essential truth was a necessary quality in any story whatsoever. 'A story is a picture either of an individual or of human nature in general. If it is false, it is a picture of nothing.' The biography must be, therefore, so far as we can make it so, absolutely and unconditionally true.

Johnson was no painstaking grubber, to be sure, in 'the rubbish of antiquity.' He worked, he has recorded, 'in my usual way, dilatorily and hastily, unwilling to work, and working with vigour and haste.' He wrote out of a full mind, a retentive memory that had gathered and stored a tremendous mass of floating tradition, but for all the mechanical labor of verification and settlement of details he had small respect. 'To adjust the minute events of literary history is tedious and troublesome': he refused to be bothered with it. Such activities required 'no great force of understanding,' but were the drudgery of a literary termite.

The truth Johnson believed in was truth in spirit and in all larger outlines. He believed in consequence that we may not rightly conceal even the blemishes. 'There are many who think it an act of piety to hide the faults or failings of their friends, even when they can no longer suffer by their detection. We therefore see whole ranks of characters adorned with uniform panegyric and not to be known from one another but by extrinsic and casual circumstances.' No duty to the dead can justify suppression of the truth: 'If we owe regard to the memory of the dead, there is yet more respect to be laid to knowledge, to virtue, and to truth.' Palliation of the evils in a man's behavior our knowledge of the circumstances may lead to our making, but if we cannot persuade ourselves to tell the whole truth about him as we know it, we have no right to publish his biography.

These, then, are the principles and the character on which Johnson's biography are founded, insistence on truth, on vivid detail, on psychological insight. We may see how he exemplified them in his work.

The *Life of Savage* was composed long before the others as a separate work in 1744, and only later included in the larger scheme. It has a special character, for Savage was not a man of amiable disposition or of admirable character, but he had befriended Johnson when the latter was young, and loyalty was one of Johnson's strong traits. He told Boswell in his old age of another such, 'He was a vicious man, but very kind to me. If you call a dog "Hervey," I shall love him.' A conflict between truth and loyalty was set: there were ways in which Savage had been grossly ill-used by those who should have befriended him, and yet his own conduct was so very bad that perhaps it made understandable their reluctance to help him. Johnson's essential honesty is nowhere more tried than in his dealing with his friend's career.

Richard Savage claimed to be the illegitimate son of Anne Countess of Macclefield by the Earl Rivers. According to him the lady had formerly admitted and then decided to deny their relationship, and had only with reluctance paid for his early education in penurious surroundings. The relentless antagonism of this parent, indeed, would impress us as an invention of Savage's, if it were not clear that Johnson, who was not a credulous man, continued in later years to believe in it. Defrauded of his father's intention of providing for him by a lying tale of the mother's, Savage was for a time befriended by Sir Richard Steele and then estranged through the malice of a talebearer. Subsequently he drifted into a career of precarious authorship.

But misfortune still pursued him. In a coffee-house brawl a man was killed, and Savage was accused of his death. 'The witnesses which appeared against him,' Johnson writes, 'were . . . a common strumpet, a woman by whom strumpets were entertained, and a man by whom they were supported; and the character of Savage was by several persons of distinction asserted to be that of a modest, inoffensive man, not inclined to broils or to insolence, and who had, to that time, been only known for his misfortunes and his wit.' The judge, however, was prejudiced, and, according to Savage, harangued the court against him: 'Gentlemen of the jury, you are to consider that Mr Savage is a very great man, a much greater man than you or I, gentlemen of the jury; that he wears very fine clothes, much finer clothes than you or I, gentlemen of the jury; that he has abundance of money in his pocket, much more money than you or I, gentlemen of the jury; but, gentlemen of the jury, is it not a very hard case, gentlemen of the jury, that Mr Savage should therefore kill you or me, gentlemen of the jury?' Whether he was guilty or no, this dispassionate handling of his trial resulted in a conviction.

He was pardoned, however, by the intercession of Queen Caroline. For a while Lord Tyrconnel became his patron, but Savage—the 'modest' and 'inoffensive'—introduced riotous companions to his Lordship's wine-cellar and sold books stamped with his arms, 'it being usual with Mr Savage, when he wanted a small sum, to take his books to the pawnbroker.'

Generous and compassionate as Johnson tells us he was by nature, it was his unfortunate habit to make too free with the possessions of his friends. Favors he asked of them 'without the least submission or apparent consciousness of dependence,' and looked 'upon a compliance with his request' as no great obligation; 'but a refusal was resented by him as an affront, or complained of as an injury; nor did he readily reconcile himself to those who . . . gave him afterwards any intimation that they expected to be repaid.' As a house-guest he 'would prolong his conversation till midnight, without considering that business might require his friend's application in the morning;' but, once in bed, it was equally difficult to arouse him for dinner.

Of traits like these Lord Tyrconnel ultimately tired. Though there must, Johnson says, have been intimations of 'coldness, peevishness, or neglect' for some time before the break, 'everyone that knew Savage will readily believe that to him it was sudden as a stroke of thunder—that though he might have transiently suspected it, he had never suffered any thought so unpleasing to sink into his mind.' In the few strokes of this characterization almost the whole man is palpable.

Various projects for improving his circumstances occupied him, but he was unable to direct his own conduct—'an irregular and dissipated life made him the slave of every passion.' 'By imputing none of his miseries to himself, he . . . was never made wiser by his sufferings, nor preserved by one misfortune from falling into another. He proceeded throughout his life to tread the same steps on the same circle; always applauding his past conduct, or at least forgetting it, to amuse himself with phantoms of happiness which were dancing before him; and willingly turned his eyes from the light of reason, when it would have discovered the illusion, and shown him, what he never wished to see, his real estate.' He sank lower and lower, and died ultimately of a fever in a debtors' prison.

'His mind was in an uncommon degree vigorous and active.' 'His judgment was eminently exact both with regard to writings and to men'—although he never arrived at a realization of how men would respond to his own insolencies and aggressions. His manner was ingratiating, and to this fact much of the forbearance of others may be laid. 'He was never vehement or loud, but at once modest and easy, open and respectful . . .' 'He was compassionate . . . but when he was provoked (and very small offences were sufficient to provoke him), he would prosecute his revenge with the utmost acrimony . . . His friendship was therefore of little value . . .' But his abilities were better than either his fortune or his capacity for discipline; and his faults 'were not easily to be avoided by a great mind, irritated by perpetual hardships . . .' A wise man would not 'presume to say,' Johnson concludes, ' "Had I been in Savage's condition, I should have lived or written better than Savage." '

Such are the main outlines of his characterization. The qualities in it that tend to produce compassion are the numerous instances that are given of the ways in which Savage's hopes were disappointed, his schemes balked of success, or his friends and protectors disgusted with him. However justified their conduct, the steadily increasing burden of misery is affecting. The tone is one of philosophic generalization, which by weighing and explaining seems to extenuate without denying the vices which are plainly stated. So judicious, in fact, is this tone that we may need a little reflection to realize that, for all his brilliance and specious charm, Savage was an ingrate and a dissipated scoundrel. But the sympathy of his friend, although it weights the style, never impairs the rightness of the judgment. Johnson's gentleness of feeling leads neither to the hiding of a single harsh fact nor to the slightest unbending of his rigid morality.

I have examined the *Life of Savage* in some detail because it is a crucial test of Johnson's devotion to truth in biography. If there was ever any temptation for him to soften the truth it was in dealing with Savage. Against the temptations of antagonism, however, although he tried to be on his guard, it was difficult for him to be altogether proof. There were few poets more calculated to move him to rage than Milton. Johnson was a devout believer in the Church of England, and Milton had been an independent who attacked the bishops of that Church; Johnson was a Tory and a Royalist, and Milton had justified the beheading of a king whose memory Johnson revered. Johnson's literary taste was strongly classical and 'correct'; Milton had wrested the genius of English into a highly individual idiom and even syntax of his own. On all these counts Johnson was prejudiced against Milton, and he seldom misses an opportunity for laying open his defects.

Milton had found it unbecoming that men designed for orders should act in loose comedies, 'writhing and unboning their clergy limbs to all the antic and dishonest gestures of Trinculos, buffoons, and bawds . . .' 'This is sufficiently peevish,' Johnson comments, 'in a man who . . . relates with great luxuriance the compensation which the pleasures of the theatre afford him. Plays were therefore only criminal when they were acted by academics.' This outburst overlooks the fact that Milton's condemnation is of their acting in certain kinds of performance; and surely what it may be permissible to see it may not be fitting that one in a position of moral responsibility present.

For Milton's republicanism Johnson can find no explanation but 'an envious hatred of greatness,' (ignoring Milton's loyalty to Cromwell), 'a sullen desire of independence,' a 'petulance impatient of control,' and a 'pride disdainful of superiority.' 'It has been observed,' Johnson goes on ironically, 'that they who most loudly clamour for liberty do not most liberally grant it'; and he finds in Milton's writings 'something like a Turkish contempt for females,' and accuses him of being 'severe and arbitrary' with his daughters that they 'might not break the ranks.' And, indeed, though there is some exaggeration in the conclusion that 'He thought women made only for obedience, and man only for rebellion,' the paradoxical accusation is not entirely unfounded.

Vanity and frugality in bestowing praise are also scored against Milton: He 'considered his mention of a name as . . . a certain preservative from oblivion;' and 'scarcely any man ever wrote so much, and praised so few.' It becomes, however, almost ludicrous to behold the Doctor belaboring Milton for returning home at the beginning of the Parliamentary struggle and setting up a school.

'Let not our veneration of Milton forbid us to look with some degree of merriment . . . on the man who hastens home because his countrymen are contending for their liberty, and, when he reaches the scene of action, vapours away his patriotism in a private boarding-school.'

And then, conscious that his antagonism has carried him too far, but unable to persuade himself to cancel the sentence, he adds that there is no need to 'excuse an act which no wise man will consider as in itself disgraceful. His father was alive; his allowance was not ample; and he supplied its deficiencies by an honest and useful employment.' 'Milton was not a man who could become mean by a mean employment.' If Milton's needs forced him to supplement his allowance, there is nothing so laughable in 'vapouring away his patriotism' in earning a living instead of perishing in public spirit. Johnson could not resist the fling; he could repair it, however, and he did so. His basic honesty conquered again, and he gives us the means of seeing through his own misrepresentation.

In his flashes of description he limns character again and again by the tersest of means. Addison, at the first production of Cato, 'frighted lest he be thought a promoter of insurrection,' and wandering 'through the whole exhibition behind the scenes with restless and unappeasable solicitude'; Pope, who would have men believe that it diverted him to be satirized by others, reading a pamphlet by Colley Cibber, 'his features written with anguish'; Swift's reply to an angry accusation of being the author of a certain lampoon: 'Mr Bettesworth, I was in my youth acquainted with great lawyers, who, knowing my disposition to satire, advised me that if any scoundrel or blockhead whom I had lampooned should ask, "Are you the author of this paper?" I should tell him that I was not the author; and therefore I tell you, Mr Bettesworth, that I am not the author of these lines'—what a flood of light each of these small episodes pours on the man of whom it is told!

And Johnson does not do this once, he does it repeatedly. There is Addison's calm arrogance in explaining his unreadiness in conversational wit by the remark that 'he could draw bills for a thousand pounds, though he had not a guinea in his pocket.' There is the witty story of Prior at the Paris opera silencing his enthusiastic companion who had persisted in singing with the performer: the poet 'fell to railing at the performer with all the terms of reproach he could collect,' till the Frenchman was moved to expostulate; 'I know,' said Prior, 'mais il chante si haut, que je ne sçaurois vous entendre.' There is the picture of the unfortunate Gay, about to read his tragedy *The Captives* before the Princess of Wales, and so nervous with reverence that, advancing to her he 'stumbled at a stool, and falling forwards threw down a weighty Japan screen.'

Not only the episodes, but the formal characterizations and the intimate details of the habits, physical idiosyncrasies, and appearance of his subjects are admirable. Pope's spider-like shape, 'protuberant behind and before,' his thin legs, which he enlarged 'with three pairs of stockings . . . drawn on and off by the maid,' his bodice of stiff canvas, without which he could barely hold himself erect, his extreme sensibility to cold, which forced him to wear a fur doublet under his shirt: how vividly Johnson makes us see the distorted and pathetic figure, humanized by the brilliance of the animated and glowing eyes! The deathbed scene is painted circumstantially, with its blurring of his vision and his plaint of 'inability to think.' 'Bolingbroke sometimes wept over him in this state of helpless decay, and being told' that during the intervals of delirium Pope 'was always saying something kind either of his present or absent friends, and that his humanity seemed to have survived his understanding, answered, "It has so." . . . At another time he said, "I have known Pope these thirty years, and value myself more in his friendship than"—his grief then suppressed his voice.'

Johnson's comments on his subjects are often witty and penetrating. Pope had been obliged to construct a subterranean passage to a garden across a public road, and had proceeded to decorate its walls and call it a grotto. 'A grotto is not often the wish or pleasure of an Englishman, who has more frequent need to solicit than exclude the sun; but Pope's excavation was requisite as an entrance to his garden, and, as some men try to be proud of their defects, he extracted an ornament from an inconvenience, and vanity produced a grotto where necessity enforced a passage.'

His characterization of the metaphysical poets, in the biography of Cowley, is famous: 'If . . . that be considered as wit which is at once natural and new, that which, though not obvious, is, upon its first production, acknowledged to be just; . . . to wit of this kind the metaphysical poets have seldom risen. Their thoughts are often new, but seldom natural; they are not obvious, but neither are they just; and the reader, far from wondering that he missed them, wonders more frequently by what perverseness of industry they were ever found . . . The most heterogeneous ideas are yoked by violence together; nature and art are ransacked for illustrations, comparisons, and allusions; their learning instructs, and their subtlety surprises; but the reader commonly thinks his improvement dearly bought, and, though he sometimes admires, is seldom pleased.'

The paragraphs that follow go on to redress the balance of these vigorous antitheses which, by themselves, would constitute a somewhat biased description of the poetical achievements of Donne, Herbert, Vaughan, or Crashaw. His comparison of Pope and Dryden is equally famous and much more penetrating: Dryden's mind, he says, had a larger range, and his education was superior; 'Dryden knew more of man in his general nature, and Pope in his local manners.' 'Dryden's page is a natural field, rising into inequalities, and diversified by the varied exuberance of abundant vegetation; Pope's is a velvet lawn, shaven by the scythe, and levelled by the roller.' Of genius, with some hesitation he decides that Dryden had more, but not that Pope had only a little; and if Dryden 'has brighter paragraphs, he has not better poems.' Dryden's composition was hasty and careless; Pope's slow and cautious, accumulating 'all that study might produce or chance might supply. If the flights of Dryden therefore are higher, Pope continues longer on the wing. If of Dryden's fire the blaze is brighter, of Pope's the heat is more regular and constant. Dryden often surpasses expectation, and Pope never falls below it. Dryden is read with frequent astonishment, and Pope with perpetual delight.' No more brilliant words have ever been written on this subject.

Both in the biographical and the critical parts of his work in the *Lives of the Poets*, Johnson shows himself easily equal to nearly all the demands the subjects make upon him. There were places, among the very minor figures, where neither his interest nor the information he presents is great, but in almost every important instance his ability rises to the occasion.

Johnson's work, furthermore, is a magnificent anticipation of a kind of biography that, especially in recent years, has become of increasing importance. This is the critical biography, by now almost a separate genre, which centers its attention on the development of a man's artistic career. Sometimes, like Mr Van Wyck Brooks' study of Mark Twain, it may employ a psychoanalytic method; sometimes, like that of Mr Bernard De Voto, it may be sociological and deny the psychoanalytic. Again, like Mr Newton Arvin's *Hawthorne*, it may fuse both methods. But in any case, the primary emphasis is not upon the man as man, but upon the man as literary artist. His career is examined to see how it explains the artist, and the elucidation and evaluation of his work is the central aim. Now, in a less formal way, these are certainly dominant among Johnson's purposes. Anecdotes there are, introduced for their own sakes, but mostly in revealing the character of their subject they also illuminate the poet. And nearly always the biographies build up to and support the critical observations with which they conclude.

All the major qualifications of the biographer Johnson had in an eminent degree. He was honest. With some effort he could hold his prejudices within bounds. He had enormous grasp and powers of memory. His judgment was strong, clear, and decided. He had reflected on the principles of biography and knew his own mind about it. His powers of construction were marked. He possessed psychological insight and a flair for the revealing trait or episode. With all these abilities of the biographer, Johnson, if he had tried, might have written formal biography of the highest eminence. Even in the short and hastily written *Lives of the Poets* he is always interesting and often richly rewarding.

The Mystery of Mr Boswell

When James Boswell was presented to Dr Johnson, he was a young man of twenty-three and the distinguished writer was already fifty-four. Boswell has described the meeting himself. It took place in the back parlor of Mr Thomas Davies, a bookseller. 'I was much agitated; and recollecting his prejudice against the Scotch, of which I had heard much, I said to Davies, "Don't tell where I come from."—"From Scotland," cried Davies roguishly. "Mr Johnson," said I, "I do indeed come from Scotland, but I cannot help it." I am willing to flatter myself that I meant this as a light pleasantry to soothe and conciliate him, and not as a humiliating abasement at the expense of my country. But . . . he seized the expression "come from Scotland," which I used in the sense of being of that country; and retorted, "That, Sir, I find, is what a very great many of your countrymen cannot help." This stroke stunned me . . .'

The episode is characteristic of both men. There is the elephantine and crushing pleasantry of Johnson, which, without being really conclusive, is delivered with the force of a detonation. There is the absurdity of Boswell, no less exquisite in his assurance to the reader that he meant no disloyalty to the land of his birth than in the feeble effort to ingratiate Johnson. His triumph, however, tickled the Doctor a good deal, and Boswell ultimately encouraged himself enough to wait on him at his home. So the celebrated friendship began which lasted for the remaining twenty-one years of the older man's life, and which enabled Boswell to write his monumental work.

Johnson's life not only supplied Boswell with the materials of his biography, his example supplied a suggestion of the method and his writings and conversation provided instructive rules and principles. In the very opening pages of the *Life*, Boswell quotes those generalizations of Johnson on the art of biography that I have included in the preceding section of this chapter. Several passages in the *Life* record sayings of Johnson on the subject, and there can hardly be much doubt that Johnson developed the theme on occasions that Boswell may not have written down. Johnson's appetite for episode and character was insatiable. 'I love anecdotes,' he remarked to Boswell at Edinburgh, and he was forever telling or listening to them. He had read a good deal of Boswell's *Journal of a Tour to the Hebrides*, in which Boswell essayed the method later used in the *Life*, and had given Boswell the benefits of his criticism. Boswell was no fool; he had profited by much speculation on all these points.

For the controlling design of his work he had gone thus to Johnson's own rule and example. Gathered within the firm sweep of the plan we find a circle of further merits. The use of letters and original documents which the complaisance of Boswell led him to attribute to Mason, in his *Life of Gray*, had of course been seen before; for example, in Walton's *Lives*. The conversational anecdote we find in Spence giving brilliance to the circle of Alexander Pope; but Johnson's remarkable powers as a talker and Boswell's unusual memory for the very idiom and manner of his friend enable the *Life of Johnson* to outshine by far anything of the kind ever attempted. His style, finally, without being striking or spectacular, is easy, flowing, and unobtrusive. Indeed, Boswell's style is deceptive, for it has no flowers of rhetoric, and is still singularly fitted to its purposes, amazingly just in its choice of the word that will be found quietly right, and sometimes exceedingly subtle in its use of suggestion or insinuation.

Boswell was no fool, I have said, and yet perhaps this statement needs to be amplified. For to many he has seemed an eccentric and a buffoon, whose success might be explained on the ground of mere luck: the luck of having an acute verbal memory, and the luck of association with a man whose conversation was a rich expression of his personality. Macaulay regarded him as a fool. Mr Harold Nicolson, while laboring his silliness and his lack of dignity, decides that he was neither a fool nor a genius; but maintains the odd thesis that biography 'does not require genius; it requires only a peculiar form of talent.' The distinctions between these two indefinables I am unable to appreciate.

Lytton Strachey, with more ingenuity, concludes that Boswell's snobbery, his absence of personal pride and shame, his unconventionality, his asininity—that these qualities were precisely necessary to the achievement of his work. 'Boswell triumphed,' he writes, 'by dint of abandoning himself, through fifty years, to his instincts.' If he had not been a snob, he would not have attached himself—or tried to attach himself—successively to Paoli, Wilkes, Jean-Jacques Rousseau, Lord Chatham, and a host of others. If he had had either pride or shame he could not have endured the personal humiliations so often inflicted on him by the sharp rebukes of Johnson and could not have persuaded himself to reveal those shameful scenes to his readers. If his mind had not possessed a certain freedom from convention, an unusual flexibility of opinion, that pleased Dr Johnson's own vigorous contempt of cant, that old lion might not have been able to bear with his vices and absurdities. Add all these things together, Strachey concludes, and you have the nature uniquely necessary to Boswell's unique performance.

The paradox is attractive, and yet—is it true? Can a great literary achievement be explained as the fortuitous result of a happy combination of vices? Professor Walter Raleigh thought otherwise: 'The accident which gave Boswell to Johnson and Johnson to Boswell,' he admits, 'is one of the most extraordinary pieces of good fortune in literary history.' But then—'Boswell was a man of genius; the idle paradox which represents him in the likeness of a lucky dunce was never tenable by serious criticism. . . He had simplicity, candour, fervour, a warmly affectionate nature, a quick intelligence, and a passion for telling all that he knew.' And for Sir James Stephen, Boswell was 'the prince of biographers,' and 'a man of true genius however coarse his feelings and however flagrant his self-conceit.'

Now it certainly cannot be denied that Boswell was often silly, and that he had all the other vices attributed to him, and nearly all of them in ludicrous and sometimes contemptible ways. He was a drunkard, a wastrel, and a libertine. In vain he tried to reform, taking under 'a venerable yew' an oath to abstain, to limit himself to four glasses of wine at dinner and a pint afterwards. His numberless and preposterous love-affairs are solemnly narrated in his letters to his friend Temple, who was a quiet Devonshire clergyman. 'One progresses with marvellous exhilaration,' says Mr Strachey, 'from Miss W—t ("just such a young lady as I could wish for the partner of my soul") to Zelide ("upon my soul, Temple, I must have her"), and so to the Signora, and the Moffat woman ("can I do better than keep a dear infidel for my hours of Paphian bliss?"), and the Princess ("here every flower is united"), . . . and La Belle Irlandaise ("just sixteen, formed like a Grecian nymph, with the sweetest countenance, full of sensibility, accomplished, with a Dublin education"), and Mrs Boswell ("I am fully sensible of my happiness in being married to so excellent a woman"), and Miss Silverton ("in the fly with me, an amiable creature who has been in France. I can unite little fondnesses with perfect conjugal love"), and Miss Bagnal ("a *Ranelagh girl*, but of excellent principles, in so much that she reads prayers to the servants in her father's family, every evening. 'Let me see such a woman,' cried I") . . . and—but the catalogue is endless.' His health grew enfeebled, his wife died, his estates melted away, his drunkenness became confirmed, his humiliations piled up. But he had been the friend of Paoli and of Dr Johnson; he had the most extraordinary confidence that the biography of his great friend would make his reputation. Through poverty and drunkenness he toiled on. Seven years after Johnson's death the task was accomplished. He survived its completion four years.

But if Boswell was sensual, drunken, extravagant, and inclined to maudlin self-pity and melancholy, he had other qualities without which he would not for long have been tolerated in the Johnson circle. Indeed, the man who could draw Rousseau into a correspondence, make a friend of Paoli, and obtain the affection of Johnson is by those very facts proclaimed a man of mark. Boswell fitted well into the 'Literary Club,' even though he tells us he was almost blackballed at first. The only one of its members who did not like him—a dislike that was reciprocated—was Gibbon. Boswell was what Johnson called a 'clubbable' man, a man easy and pleasant to be with, either alone or in a group. It was a quality Johnson, who hated loneliness, prized highly.

He was free from conventional opinions, in some ways even more so than Johnson himself. One of Johnson's favorite injunctions was, 'Free your mind of cant, Sir,'—do not repose in merely conventional authority, but strive to pierce to the bottom of things with your reason. With few was it so seldom needful to shout that command as with Boswell. 'You and I,' Johnson commended him, 'do not talk from books.'

He had a tremendous zest for life, always enthusiastic, always interested, willing to canvass and discuss any subject, willing to conceive any hypothesis, able, in the fantasy of his imagination, to propound even absurdities and nonsense. The aliveness of Boswell's intelligence is everywhere in his books, even when he is being a clown. And although as a lawyer he let his practice fall to pieces, and idled away his time in London, of his literary industry there can be no question. There he worked with an earnestness and a sense of form that placed his biography in the supreme rank it occupies.

Eighteenth Century Lion

Boswell's *Life of Johnson* has sometimes been dismissed as no more than a mosaic of quotations fitted together in date order, achieving no form, and presenting of its central figure a characterization either blurred or contradictory. But Boswell's own statement that he made a choice of the most illuminating out of vast accumulations of materials is substantiated by recent scholarship; and those who find contradictions in Johnson beyond what we should normally expect in a man are guilty of incomprehension. Any man of whose conversation so much was recorded would be bound to present some contradictions, and to have said some things he did not really mean. Johnson himself confessed, 'Nobody, at times, talks more laxly than I do.' But the bulk of Johnson's opinions are consistent and solid. A modern reader may disagree with them, but if he examines them with any effort at understanding he can hardly find them eccentric, prejudiced, or absurd, as they have often been accused of being. To do so is to show lack of historical imagination.

Johnson was a Tory. Toryism has gone out of fashion since the eighteenth century, but its philosophy is not therefore completely unsound. A Tory is simply a person who believes that the bad in human nature is held down (even to the degree it is) by such uncertain restraints that he thinks it wiser to accept a certain number of evils in our institutions than through change to risk overthrowing the habits of discipline. The evils of mechanical adjustment that develop from time to time, institutions themselves have been devised to deal with, and their authority should not be impaired by what the Tory would consider a flighty-minded tinkering with their operations. Only when all the resources of the accumulated wisdom and tradition of civilization have been drained and proved fruitless will he approve a very careful innovation. Violent and hasty changes release the most destructive passions, and Dr Johnson, had he lived until the French Revolution, would have pointed with triumphant indignation to its excesses as a vindication of his position. Now obviously much can be said for these contentions, and indeed the chief question is to exactly what degree the normal course of people's behavior may be unsettled by a proposed change, and at exactly what point an evil becomes so vicious that humanity demands risking the change. The answer must be different at different times, but it is not an answer easily arrived at.

Such was Johnson's Toryism. He thought there was very little reason to prefer one set of institutions to another, but that settled institutions were a necessity. 'I would not give half a guinea,' he said, 'to live under one form of government rather than another . . . If a sovereign oppresses his people to a great degree, they will rise and cut off his head. There is a remedy in human nature against tyranny, that will keep us safe under every form of government.' He lived himself under a monarchy, and thought the monarchy should be retained; had he lived in a republic it would no less have engaged his defense. Degrees of merit in governments he thought very slight. Political events in his own time drew from him a comment on the lack of superiority in public life. All governments, he thought were apt to be administered in a muddling way by the venal or incompetent. The only real test of a good government was the degree of solicitude it displayed for the poor.

For social position he had little respect. Dukes might be, and often were, blockheads; character and sense might be found in the lowest ranks. But it was better for society that a duke should remain a duke and a porter a porter than that any attempt be made to upset things by levelling ranks. Besides this, he disbelieved in the sincerity of 'levellers.' He had proposed to a democratic lady who tried to argue him into a belief in equality that she allow her footman to join them at dinner: 'She has never liked me since. Sir, your levellers wish to level *down* as far as themselves; but they cannot bear levelling *up* to themselves. They would all have some people under them; why not then have some people above them?'

Again, marriage, as an institution, he approved of, but the details were less important than that the contract have an understood meaning and responsibility. 'I believe marriages would in general be as happy, and often more so, if they were all made by the lord chancellor, upon a due consideration of the characters and circumstances, without the parties having any choice in the matter.' Education based on arousing competitive passions he strongly disapproved: 'by exciting emulation and comparisons of superiority, you lay the foundations of lasting mischief' in people's characters. Superiority should proceed from enthusiasm for the thing done, not from a mean desire to humble others.

We may not agree with all or even many of these views. But they are not merely absurd, and they are completely consistent with each other.

Johnson's religion firmly supported his social opinions. He was a devout member of the Church of England. He believed in original sin, and that belief reinforced his conviction that it was dangerous to tamper with the restraints that held man's lower nature in check. There was an underlying sadness in his heart of which his sad philosophy was a true expression. He prized his own life little, but he feared death; his deep consciousness of the sinfulness of the human heart made the after-life he believed in a thing of dread. 'His thoughts upon this awful change,' Boswell says, 'were in general full of dismal apprehensions. His mind resembled the vast amphitheatre, the Coliseum at Rome. In the centre stood his judgment, which, like a mighty gladiator, combated those apprehensions that, like the wild beasts of the *arena*, were all around in cells, ready to be let out upon him. After a conflict he drives them back into their dens; but not killing them they were still assailing him.'

Like the elder Mill, however, he believed that life was a poor thing at best. 'Man never *is*, but always *to be* blest,' he quoted Pope; and asserted that 'happiness was very rare in human life.' Asked if a man was not sometimes happy in the present, he replied, 'Never, but when he is drunk.' He disliked those who asserted that they were happy. 'It was all *cant*,' he would cry; 'the dog knows he is miserable all the time.' To a friend whose wife's sister had supported the statement that she was happy, he replied, 'If your sister-in-law is really the contented being she professes herself, Sir, her life gives the lie to every research of humanity; for she is happy without health, without beauty, without money, and without understanding.'

Perhaps it was this underlying melancholy that made Johnson so avid for company. He was unhappy alone, and would stay up for hours postponing the time of parting. 'Sir,' he told Boswell, 'I am obliged to any man who visits me.' Under the stimulus of companionship, his vigor of mind sustained him, controversy kept him active, his native gusto awoke. For, although he was sad, he had also a tremendous zest for experience; in spite of some infirmities his physical vitality was enormous; instinct made him savor the richness of enjoyment.

A mere scene of bustling activity pleased him, and he and Boswell united in extolling the cheerfulness of Fleet Street, although Johnson felt that 'the full tide of human existence is at Charing Cross.' The infinitely varied stimuli of the metropolis made him feel that it was the only great school of life, the only environment for a man of intellectual activity. 'When a man is tired of London, he is tired of life; for there is in London all that life can afford.' And to Boswell's provocative remark, 'Sometimes I have been in the humour of wishing to retire to a desert,' Johnson flashed back sarcastically, 'Sir, you have desert enough in Scotland.'

All manifestations of life in a rich and copious form pleased him. He ate greedily and with immense relish, and 'he talked of good eating with uncommon satisfaction.' 'Some people,' he remarked, 'have a foolish way of not minding, or pretending not to mind, what they eat. For my part, I mind my belly very studiously, and very carefully; for I look upon it, that he who does not mind his belly will hardly mind anything else.' Once when he and Boswell were sculling on the Thames and treated to a shower of Billingsgate from some boatmen, Johnson enjoyed their hearty vituperation, and gave them back oath for oath. No less did he enjoy the humors of human nature. Remarking to a lady once that he had known all the wits from Mrs Montague to Bet Flint, and learning that she had not heard of the latter, he described her: 'Oh, a fine character, madam; she was habitually a slut and a drunkard, and occasionally a thief and a harlot.'

His vitality showed itself most in his delight in argument. He hated self-deception and intellectual dishonesty, and his arguments were usually directed against those tendencies in his opponents. The Arcadian romanticizing of the wild life of the Indian, for example, which was fashionable in his day, filled him with disgust. A gentleman quoted with approval the following reflection: 'Here am I, free and unrestrained, amid the rude magnificence of Nature, with this Indian woman by my side, and this gun, with which I can procure food when I want it: what more can be desired for human happiness?' Johnson: 'Do not allow yourself, Sir, to be imposed upon by such gross absurdity. It is sad stuff; it is brutish. If a bull could speak, he might as well exclaim,—Here am I with this cow and this grass; what being can enjoy greater felicity?'

Vulgar notions repeated by rote annoyed him. 'My dear friend,' he would say, 'clear your *mind* of cant. You may *talk* as other people do; you may say to a man, "Sir, I am your humble servant." You are *not* his most humble servant. You may say, "These are bad times; it is a melancholy thing to be reserved to such times." You don't mind the times. You tell a man, "I am sorry you had such bad weather the last day of your journey, and were so much wet." You don't care sixpence whether he is wet or dry. You may *talk* in this manner; it is the mode of talking in society; but don't *think* foolishly.'

The effort to separate conventional opinion from sense occupied much of his attention. People expressed horror at gambling; Johnson: 'Depend upon it, Sir, this is mere talk. *Who* is ruined by gaming? You will not find six instances in an age. There is a strange rout made about deep play; whereas you have many more people ruined by adventurous trade, and yet do not hear such an outcry against it.' He would not bear with any attempt to put an amiable face on human selfishness. 'The Irish,' he said, 'are a *fair people;*—they never speak well of one another.' 'To act from pure benevolence is not possible to finite beings. Human benevolence is mingled with vanity, interest, or some other motive.'

When Johnson thought people were wrong-headedly opposing him, he was apt to carry rudeness to a fantastic degree. To a gentleman who said he could not understand one of Johnson's arguments, he replied, 'I can provide you with an argument, Sir; but I cannot provide you with an understanding.' He would cut people short with 'You don't see your way through the question, Sir,'—'I perceive you are a vile Whig, Sir.' Commenting to Boswell once that they had enjoyed a rousing discussion the previous night, he was answered, 'Yes, Sir, you tossed and gored several people.' And to a rather foolish remark of Boswell's about Pope's *Dunciad*, he exclaimed, 'It was worth while being a dunce then. Ah, Sir, hadst *thou* lived in those days!'

There are occasional examples of credulity to be found in Johnson, but they are very few. The often-quoted hearsay opinion that swallows 'conglobulate together, by flying round and round and then all in a heap throw themselves under water and lie in the bed of a river' is balanced in the same conversation by his skepticism about the common belief that the scorpion commits suicide. His disposition to suspend judgment about the Cock-lane ghost imposture has been unfairly quoted against him, for Johnson there was merely of opinion that there had not been enough decisive evidence about apparitions in general to deny this one a priori; and he later detected the cheat himself.

But, although Johnson was severe in his denunciations of error, he voiced them without real indignation unless there was intention to deceive. It was customary with him to say, 'Sir, he lies.' Truth was so devious and hard to discover that it was a natural thing for a man to lie often in his account of things. But when the lie was made deliberately and with knowledge that it was falsehood, then Johnson roared, 'Sir, he lies, and he knows that he lies.'

Although he was harsh to those who ventured to controvert him, he was tender and affectionate to his friends. He never forgot a kindness; we have already heard his gratitude to the memory of Hervey. Though easily angered, he was readily brought to forgiveness by a few words of contrition; and when reflection convinced him that he was the offender he was not slow to make amends. The stout, redfaced, and middle-aged wife, who had seemed absurd to his friends, he loved with the sincerest devotion and mourned after her death for the remainder of his life. Boswell quotes a prayer found after Johnson's own decease: 'O Lord! Governor of heaven and earth, in whose hands are embodied and departed spirits, if thou hast ordained the souls of the dead to minister to the living, and appointed my departed wife to have the care of me, grant that I may enjoy the good effects of her attention and ministration, whether exercised by appearance, impulses, dreams, or in any other manner agreeable to thy government. Forgive my presumption, enlighten my ignorance, and however meaner agents are employed, grant me the blessed influences of thy Holy Spirit, through Jesus Christ our Lord. *Amen.*'

Such are the leading outlines of the character Boswell presents to us. Of the more obvious physical characteristics, the rolling and puffing figure, the snortings and noises, the slovenliness, the convulsive movements, it is hardly necessary to speak: they have been canvassed by all commentators from Macaulay to the present. It is enough to remark that by an adroit insertion of bits of description from time to time, by dropping a word here and there about his manner, his gait, his intonations, or way of pronouncing his words, Boswell makes us as vividly aware of the outward man and his oddities as we are of his inward disposition. The minute pictorial touches by which our overwhelming consciousness of Johnson's physical presence is implanted in us are among the most subtle and brilliant in Boswell's whole technique.

And Boswell is dramatic, too. With so slight variations in Johnson's fortunes to narrate (for Boswell met him when he was already old and famous, and the bulk of his book deals with the later years), Boswell makes capital of the slightest things. Johnson does not all at once become clear to us, but disengages himself from the vague and reverential image of 'the Sage' only little by little, as skilfully embedded details make their contributions. Johnson's horror of death, for example, tempered by his religious faith, Boswell does not generalize upon until there have been several conversations in which Johnson expresses the utmost agitation at the continuance of the subject. His oddities, like the collection of orange peel (the purpose of which he refused to divulge) and his superstitious touching of lamp-posts, are introduced casually before they are made the basis of comment. And equally skilful is Boswell's use of Johnson's friends and acquaintances, and Johnson's tilts with them, to achieve miniature dramas.

His description of Goldsmith sulking on a sofa, pretending to be uninterested while Johnson related what had passed during his meeting with George III is one of these. Goldsmith refused to be curious, Johnson went on; presently Goldsmith became ashamed of his jealousy, and sprang up: 'Well, you acquitted yourself in this conversation better than I should have done,' he burst out; 'for I should have bowed and stammered through the whole of it.' Deeply fond of his older friend as Goldsmith was, Johnson's greater conversational talents often roused in him a peevish resentment.

Sometimes, however, Goldsmith scored a victory, notably on the occasion when Johnson laughed at his analysis of how to write good animal fables. The little fishes, he had said, who petitioned Jupiter to be changed into birds should be made to 'talk like little fishes.' Observing Johnson shaking his sides, he exclaimed, 'Why, Dr Johnson, this is not so easy as you seem to think: for if you were to make little fishes talk, they would talk like WHALES.'

One of the most dramatic of Boswell's stories is that of how he brought Johnson and Wilkes together. Wilkes had had a stormy political career; his election to Parliament as member for Middlesex had been three times annulled, and Johnson had called him 'a retailer of sedition and obscenity.' Aware that if he had asked, 'Sir, will you dine in company with Jack Wilkes?' Johnson would have flown into a passion and answered, 'Dine with Jack Wilkes, Sir! I'd as soon dine with Jack Ketch,' Boswell bided his time, and conveyed an invitation from Mr Dilly the bookseller to dine with him on Wednesday next. Johnson: 'Sir, I am obliged to Mr Dilly. I will wait upon him–'

'Provided, Sir, I suppose,' Boswell interrupted, 'that the company which he is to have is agreeable to you?'

'What do you mean, Sir? What do you take me for? Do you think I am so ignorant of the world as to prescribe to a gentleman what company he is to have at his table?' Boswell innocently suggested that Mr Dilly might possibly have 'some of what he calls his patriotic friends with him.'

'Well, Sir, and what then? What care *I* for his *patriotic friends?* Poh!'

'I should not be surprised to find Jack Wilkes there.'

'And if Jack Wilkes *should* be there, what is that to *me*, Sir? My dear friend, let us have no more of this. I am sorry to be angry with you; but really it is treating me very strangely to talk to me as if I could not meet any company whatever . . .'

The evening arrived. One of the guests was Mr Arthur Lee, who 'could not but be very obnoxious to Johnson, for he was not only *a patriot*, but an *American*.' 'Too, too, too,' Johnson made one of his habitual mutterings under his breath. 'And who is that gentleman in lace?'

'Mr Wilkes, Sir.'

'This information,' Boswell tells us, 'confounded him still more,' and he took up a book and pretended to read it in order to compose his feelings.

Dinner was announced; Wilkes sat by Johnson's side, and overwhelmed him with civilities. He helped him to some fine veal. 'Pray give me leave, Sir–It is better here–A little of the brown–Some fat, Sir–A little of the stuffing–Some gravy . . .'

'Sir; sir; I am obliged to you Sir,' cried Johnson, bowing, and turning his head to him. And by the end of the meal Johnson and Wilkes were such friends that they joined to make teasing jokes about Scotland at Boswell's expense.

This anecdote is a notable instance of Boswell's skill in bringing out character as well as of his use of suspense. It brings into one climactic flash, as many lesser moments that have preceded it have made ready for his doing, the statement that Johnson was not always free from 'the spirit of contradiction.' It has been glimpsed sometimes in Johnson's repartee, and now and then in his fractiousness in argument; here it achieves the prominence of an entire little story, with preparation, conflict, uncertainty of outcome, and dénouement.

One more quotation I cannot refrain from giving, the innocent remark of a Mr Edwards, an old fellow-collegian of Johnson's. They had not seen each other since 1729; in the meanwhile Johnson had become old and famous. The two elderly men sat exchanging reminiscences, and Edwards said, 'You are a philosopher, Dr Johnson. I have tried too in my time to be a philosopher; but, I don't know how, cheerfulness was always breaking in.'

Flemish Portrait

Never has a man in his very habit and daily appearance been rendered more vividly or more fully than Johnson in Boswell's pages. Boswell had indeed not only written what he claimed, one of the most entertaining books in the world; he had portrayed a living man in living words. The achievement, as I have already pointed out, was no accident, but the result of forethought, labor, and amazing skill. The method, although not original in any one detail, was startlingly original in totality, and Boswell knew it to be so. 'It appears to me,' he wrote, 'that mine is the best plan of biography that can be conceived; for my readers will as near as may be accompany Johnson in his progress, and, as it were, see each scene as it happened.' And that is exactly what he gives us: a series of brilliant pictures, so well colored, with the highlights and shadows so skilfully arranged, that, flashing them before us in rapid succession, he gives us the illusion of actual presence and movement.

> Instead of melting down my materials into one mass, and constantly speaking in my own person, [he writes] . . . I produce, wherever it is in my power, his own minutes, letters, or conversation, being convinced that this mode is more lively, and will make my readers better acquainted with him, than even most of those were who actually knew him, but could know him only partially; whereas there is here an accumulation of intelligence from various points, by which his character is more fully understood and illustrated.
>
> Indeed, I cannot conceive a more perfect mode of writing any man's life, than not only relating all the most important events of it in their order, but interweaving what he privately wrote, and said, and thought . . . I will venture to say that he will be seen in this work more completely than any man who has ever yet lived.
>
> And he will be seen as he really was, for I profess to write, not his panegyrick, which must be all praise, but his Life; which, great and good as he was, must not be supposed to be entirely perfect.

> To be as he was, is indeed subject of panegyrick enough to any man in this state of being; but in every picture there should be shade as well as light, and when I delineate him without reserve, I do what he himself recommended, both by his precept and his example.
>
> What I consider as the peculiar value of the following work, is, the quantity it contains of Johnson's conversation . . .
>
> I am fully aware of the objections which may be made to the minuteness on some occasions of my detail of Johnson's conversation, and how happily it is adapted for the petty exercise of ridicule, by men of superficial understanding and ludicrous fancy; but I remain firm and confident in my opinion, that minute particulars are frequently characteristick, and always amusing, when they relate to a distinguished man. I am therefore exceedingly unwilling that anything, however slight, which my illustrious friend thought it worth his while to express, with any degree of point, should perish. . . .

Out of the vast bulk of his materials Boswell painstakingly preserved, pieced, and arranged the extracts from Johnson's journals, his letters, his conversation—all that had 'any degree of point'—skilfully interlarding them with remarks and reminiscences by others—thereby showing his subject from varying points of view and with differing perspectives—and molded them all into a structure with his own lucid narrative and often wonderfully revealing comment. His task was no slight one. It was not merely that his information was so copious as to require a mind with unusual powers of synthesis to draw from it any living and unified picture. His information was rich and full in an embarrassingly spotty way, and discouragingly scant in others. Out of the seventy-five years of Johnson's life, Boswell knew by personal acquaintance less than a third. During their twenty-one years of friendship Boswell spent a total of only 276 days with Johnson, scattered over various times of which the longest consecutive period was probably their tour together in Scotland.

How has Boswell managed to give us the feeling in his book of knowing Johnson by spending long periods of time month after month in his company? How are we prevented from feeling the blanks when Boswell is away and cannot give us those snortings and bludgeonings of conversation we know the man by? How are we made almost unaware of the discrepancy between the bulk of the material dealing with Johnson's comfortable old age and the paucity of that concerned with his years of struggle, discouragement, and poverty? How has Boswell managed so to weight his picture for us that our image of Johnson is never that of the thin, proud, hungry, and morose young publisher's hack; but the Johnson he knew by sight: the heavy-set old man in his dusty and wrinkled clothes, with his woollen stockings, his rolling figure the strange combination he made of the venerable and the grotesque?

Nor are these discrepancies merely imaginary. To the first fifty-four years of Johnson's life—the period preceding their acquaintance—Boswell devoted only one-fifth his entire book. The remaining one-third of Johnson's life occupies four-fifths of the biography. Largely these startling proportions are concealed by the adroitness with which Boswell gradually exchanges one scale of treatment for another. For the early years of Johnson's life he had little material. But he not only had fuller information from Johnson's own lips as he drew nearer to the time he knew himself, he obtained reminiscences from others. He inserted a larger and larger proportion of anecdote, of reminiscence, of quotations from letters, as he came to that day in 1763 when he was drinking tea in Mr Davies's back parlour and the great man made entrance. And so artistically did he blend the two parts of his narrative into each other that we hardly notice at what point anecdotes and conversation begin to be reported, hardly notice when it begins to be Boswell himself who was present and reports them. There we are at the Mitre or the Club, with Goldsmith sulking or Mr Gibbon rapping his snuffbox, and the peremptory sage shouting 'Clear your mind of cant, Sir!' And we are only dimly aware of the starveling blackbrowed youngster in the background as an occasional explanation of the sad, courageous, and lovable old bully Boswell has given us.

In somewhat the same way Boswell has masked the hiatuses when he was in Scotland struggling with his uncongenial duties at the bar, trying to conciliate his father, the old Laird of Auchinleck, trying to show how sensible he was of his 'happiness in being married to so excellent a woman' as Mrs Boswell. There are letters that Johnson wrote to him and to others, extracts from Johnson's journal, reports of his sayings and doings gleaned from Kemble, Goldsmith, Bennet Langton, and Dr Burney; and presently the Doctor and Bozzy are rolling down Fleet Street together again, exclaiming on its wonderful animation, or discussing the engaging topic of gentlewomen in liquor. The absence has been managed so well and unobtrusively that we are hardly aware it has existed.

On the marvelous skill with which Boswell conveys the drama of purely intellectual struggles, the violences of controversy, I have already commented. What is even more remarkable is that the liveliness of a very lively book is for the most part provided by such means alone. We can see this all the more clearly, if we compare Boswell's book with some other great life-narratives. Take Lockhart's pathetic story, for example, of the riches and acclaim of Scott and the sad aftermath of the Constable failure; or Trevelyan's portrayal of Macaulay as the Fairy-Tale Prince mounting from triumph to triumph. Against the tale of marvellous success Boswell can place only his Flemish painting of an old man living on a moderate pension and talking day after day among his boon companions and admirers. The hardships and desperate struggles were over by the time Boswell knew him; and although he was Dictionary Johnson, the Grand Cham of English Literature, his success had never been so widespread nor so brilliant as either Scott's or Macaulay's was to be. Against the clouding mind, the loneliness, and the broken hopes of Scott's last days Boswell has only the image of a man whose labors are nearly done, drinking tea in a comfortable haven at last. But Boswell is still the most entertaining of all biographers. His lively mind flashes light even within his subject, and gives his portrayal the excitement of exploration. The massive strength, poise, and sanity of the Doctor's mind make his life great and profound; and, through Boswell, we know no one in the past more completely and livingly than we know Dr Johnson.

ROMANTIC LETTER-WRITERS

VIII

ROMANTIC LETTER-WRITERS

Journey to the Inner World

THE awareness of man moves between the inner world of feeling and imagination and an outer world of material things and observation. Peering into the dark abyss of the human heart, through mists and shadow-shapes, we find revealed regions of horror and mystery and realms of serene luminosity, breathing essences moving between the darkness and the light. But turning from that inner world, which is sometimes so clear and again so nebulous, our physical eyes see trees and mountains, houses and busy thoroughfares and factories, truckdrivers and motion-picture sirens. To our ears there come the sounds of human voices, brass-bands, and rumbling trains—many things that seem to be objective facts, existing quite independently of whether we are there to notice them or not, that seem in no way affected by the inner world.

In reality these two worlds are probably continuous, intermingling with each other. The world of material fact often appears to mold the events of the inner world, and those inward essences that are part of ourselves to color and shape our vision of the physical universe. We know times when one or the other seems to predominate in us. There are people in whom one seems to have the ascendent. And there have been ages when mostly one seemed uppermost.

The elements in mankind are too intricately blended for any age ever to be all of a piece, any more than any single human being is so completely unified in character as to have no conflicts, no wanderings of purpose, no uncertitudes within himself. But as we gather together all we know of Periclean Athens, or the Roman republic, or Rome in the days of the Empire, or the France of Louis XIV, it seems to us that in each certain qualities are outstanding, that they group themselves into an approximate unity, and we feel able to say, 'The Athenian, the Roman, or the Frenchman of those times was like *that*.'

In such ways the eighteenth century has come to figure in our minds as the Age of Reason, and the earlier decades of the century that followed as the Age of Romanticism. And if we examine these terms a little more carefully we will see that they correspond to saying that in the former period men emphasized more the influence and importance of the outer world, and that in the latter they felt with renewed force the authority of the inner.

The eighteenth century, Preserved Smith has said, was the period of prose; but he might have added that within it was germinating a renewal of poetry. Not that there was no poetry written in the eighteenth century. Its poetry, however, was subjected to the genius of prose. Its taste demanded that poetry should exhibit cleverness, reflective powers, ingenuity, or common sense; that it should be restrained and held in check by the intellect, and follow those rules of construction and treatment that were prescribed by the intelligent suffrage of the informed. If we analyze these requirements, they will tell us much more of the eighteenth century than what its poetry was like, for its poetry was a brilliant miniature of its entire globe.

We have seen how such diverse men as Gibbon and Walpole agreed in finding that 'enthusiasm' left a wry taste in their mouths. Enthusiasm is the opposite of restraint; and much in eighteenth century ideals was founded on restraint. Restraint meant the subordination of the individual to society, and restraint meant the rule of the emotions by the reason. Both of these meant order. Order: everything in its place and functioning as it was supposed to do in the physical world; order: everything classified, clearly arranged, sharply outlined and understood in the inner world as well. Everything subject to law, and law completely intelligible to the mind. These were the eighteenth century's ideals.

The universe of Newton was a machine in which astronomical bodies following the fixed laws of attraction spun around in the vastness of space with clockwork precision. Once set in motion in the remote backward and abysm of time—a disagreeably mystic concept which the mind did not have to contemplate—they might roll on forever with no unwelcome attention from their Creator. The laws of physics and chemistry showed a pleasing capacity for being stated in mathematical terms, and doubtless even those realms of knowledge that had not yet been reduced to formulae—so eighteenth century optimism flattered itself—would ultimately become so. Locke's analysis made the mind into a blank tablet etched with the impressions of experience. Anticipating the genius of the century, Newton and Leibniz tinkered with the notion of a mechanical language that would make the operations of thought automatic and arrive at new discoveries by pure manipulation of its elements.

The study of comparative religion resulted from an effort to find the common elements of 'natural' religion in all religions, what the enquiring mind could arrive at for itself without the dubious aid of revelation. Such study led to a growing temper of skepticism and of antagonism to any unscientific emphasis on miracles. Ultimately the clergy themselves began to soft-pedal the miraculous and to devote themselves more and more to making of religion a scheme of intelligible morals. And to a considerable extent, perhaps, even the humanitarian passion that began to protest vigorously against injustice and exploitation, the sufferings of the poor and the cruelties of slavery, may be traced to an impatience with the unintelligence of a social order that made so many suffer, and to an ex hypothesi elaboration of doctrines about the nature of man and the origin of human society. Progress seemed so glowing an ideal to the Encyclopaedists because it was illogical that Man should continue to be tyrannized over by the superstitious heritage of the Dark Ages.

But if reason so dazzled the minds of the eighteenth century philosophers and their followers, it alone was the only excuse for differing from one's fellow-men. The light of reason was available to all alike; if some cowered or with morose obstinacy chose to remain in darkness that was their own fault, for the demonstration they closed their minds to could have convinced them. The truth was the same for all men. Ignorance might blind them or interest lead them to deny it; the new enlightenment would gradually change all that. For a man to differ in his essential values, however, from the community was either presumptuous or deranged. Crotchets, manias, enthusiasms, eccentricities—all departures from the common sense of the community—were despised and derided. The common sense of the community—the sense that was common to the community—governed all; the man of sense conformed to that governance except when he believed he could prove it contrary to reason; even then, he often conformed unless it seemed a matter of unescapable principle. There were the laws of motion, the laws of logic, the laws of good breeding, the laws of poetry and art: all well-nigh equal in authority.

Such was the eighteenth century world we have been sampling. In the clear and somewhat hard intelligence of Lady Mary Wortley Montagu; in the urbanity, grace, and conformity that Chesterfield mingled with well-concealed contempt; in the coolness, detachment, and irony of Gibbon; in the acrid wit of Swift; in the robust and sturdy penetration (for all his oddities) of Johnson; in the clear, cheerful, and limited horizon of Cibber; in Walpole's gaiety, sophistication, and dilettantism: in all of these we have different facets of the same world. Even if they did not often mention the same names and events it would not be hard to discern that they have many more things in common, even when they sneer at each other, than they have in common with the age that follows. Chesterfield and Johnson would have been equally blind to the light that never was on sea or land; Pope and Cibber would have cared equally little where Alph, the sacred river, ran; Swift and Lady Mary would both have been incredulous if told, 'Truth is Beauty' is 'all ye need to know.'

The eighteenth century world is very clear and well-defined. There are few or no uncertain boundaries or dark corners; everything is spread before one in an uncolored cerebral light. All is neat and tidy; mystery and wonder have been shown out at the back door, and the drawing-rooms and salons have only polite and periwigged facts making their bows. Out in the street, to be sure, there are Mohocks and young bloods pulping out the eyes of nocturnal travelers for sport; traitors are disembowelled on the scaffold, and highwaymen hang from the gallows; negro slaves sweat in the Barbadoes, noble statesmen flee to France when detected negotiating with the Pretender, and government is the monopoly of a privileged class wrangling with each other over the spoils. But these details are no more mysterious than the others; they are part of the prosaic and expected nature of things. 'To Lord Chesterfield and to Pope, to Prior and to Horace Walpole, there was nothing at all strange about the world; it was charming, it was disgusting, it was ridiculous, and it was just what one might have expected.'

Their world is all wonderfully clear and orderly, but after a time there it begins to seem a bit limited and close. There are no vistas, no distant horizons. We are hemmed in by the external pressure of people and cities and systems. Men began to find its air somewhat stifling, and longed for the desert air and the dark unfathomed caves of ocean. Out of that longing the Romantic revolt was born.

Even before the end of the century the change was making itself felt in queer stirrings among those who were otherwise its characteristic children. The strange edifice that Horace Walpole erected at Strawberry Hill, with its turrets, its vaulting, and its gingerbread, although it was only a bastard-Gothic, showed that the word Gothic was ceasing to be an epithet of scorn and disgust. The Middle Ages, indeed, were undergoing a metamorphosis in men's judgments; their barbarism was assuming glamor, and taking on the gallant colors of the Crusades, prancing steeds, courtly knights, and jousts at arms. Bishop Percy collected popular ballads; Chatterton and Macpherson forged ancient fragments; Gray studied the relics of Erse, and Welsh, and Icelandic bards, and used in his own poems their tales of old savage exploits. *The Castle of Otranto* drew a scene full of the mediaeval trappings of romance: portcullises, battlemented towers, dungeon keeps, windy corridors, ghosts and gloomy chapels. The dust of the Dark Ages, even in such papier-mâché presentments, came to life again in wild and irregular passions; and its breath was strangely sweet in the lungs of those who had choked over the aridity of common sense.

The search for distant horizons ventured into the past and the supernatural, and began pressing into realms remote from the oppressive society of man. Nature had long been for men only a painted backdrop against which was enacted the much more important drama of mankind. When nature was domesticated into clipped hedges and garden paths, pollarded trees, flowers in geometrical beds, terraces and fountains with jets, it might be praised and admired: it was but a symbol the more of how man dominated the world. And in the orbits of the planets, the precession of the equinoxes, the rotations of the celestial globe, there were to be seen again on a tremendous scale the reign of law and reason.

But in between the scale of the garden sundial and the solar system nature assumed other forms not so easily assimilable to control and order. There were tempests, strewing wreckage and death, with lash of seething water; and mountains ribbed in ice, mist enshrouded, howled around by savage gales, 'horrours & terrours on all sides.' These monstrous and unsubduable things, for most of the century, had been uncouth and disgusting. Their wildness was menacing, and lay outside the safe realms of control. Journeys over the Alps were told in terms of discomfort, revulsion, and horror.

Only as the century moves on, and the longing for the unknown rises in men's hearts do we find some realization of grandeur and stark beauty in the craggy forms. The Sublime appears in criticism, and there is enjoyment of the picturesque. The mind retires to distant huts on rainy slopes and gazes over the intervening vale at 'hamlets brown and dim-discovered spires' and watches twilight draw over all her 'gradual dusky veil.' On the eve of the nineteenth century Wordsworth's *Lines Written Above Tintern Abbey* proclaim Nature 'the guide, the guardian of all my moral being,' and finds there

> *a motion and a spirit that impels*
> *All thinking things, all objects of all thought,*
> *And rolls through all things.*

Nature thus became for the Romantic Period an awe-inspiring manifestation of the vast and mysterious forces of the world. The Unknown lured without and within. The water like a witch's oils burned blue and green and white around the marooned bark of the Ancient Mariner, the blue and green mountains of ice growled like noises in a swound amid the desolation of antarctic waters; but they were only signs and symbols of the desolation and turmoil within his heart. The universe of infinite and eternal things lay even more in the misty depths of the spirit of man than in the outer world. In the measureless caverns of those Xanadus who could tell what pleasure domes and caves of ice might dwell? The inner world reasserted its sway. Imagination (which Coleridge distinguished from Fancy) held the key to the absolute. Veux-tu découvrir le monde? Ferme tes yeux, Rosemonde!

Thus for the Romanticist the values of the Age of Classicism became inverted. Fancy, the faculty for giving ingenious forms or applying superficial decoration to the known, was a trivial craft of the intellect. Only by plunging into the deep well of intuition, where the transmutations of association took place, could Imagination discover the verities of existence. All knowledge melts into the unknown—Omnia exeunt in mysterium; but introspection might plumb the depths.

And so the individual becomes the lawgiver for society. The Romanticist looked into his own heart and found there the intuitions of truth. Where society stood in the way or failed to conform to his vision, society was wrong, and he, the seer, was there to set it right. There was small need of argument, as there had been in the previous era, for it was not by syllogisms that one found revelation but by the insight of the creating imagination. Sympathy and pity and indignation the individual found in his heart when he surveyed oppression and suffering; they burst from him in blasts of anger or despair. The Classicist had tried to condemn where he disapproved by appealing to the suffrage of thinking mankind. The Romanticist fiercely told the world that it was wrong.

In summing up thus the development from the middle of the eighteenth century through the earlier decades of the nineteenth, I am of course speaking in parables. Only the outstanding spirits thought and felt so; the sturdy, beef-eating tradesmen, the party politicians, farmers and yokels and factory-owners, constables and merchants, went on living and acting in their average-stupid, average-kindly, and average-selfish way. But Godwin's noble worship of justice inspired a Shelley; Wordsworth spoke his grave and lofty sentences; Byron's burning soul now flamed in humane indignation and now darkened in pride or guilty shame; Coleridge voyaged on strange seas of idealism; Keats struggled to understand 'the love of good and ill'; many others joined the great adventure. The spirit of an age is in its grandest attainments as well as in its meanest. Slowly somewhat of the fervor of the leaders made its way down into the other ranks of society, and took shape as humanitarianism, reform, love of nature, the breaking of old molds of habit and custom.

Individualism took uglier shapes too. As laisser-faire it enslaved thousands to noisome and life-breaking toil in hideous factories. Under a battle-cry of liberalism, money bought the votes and packed the legislatures. In the old régime there had been misery enough for those who never glimpsed the gold and red salons where their betters drank, listened to the harpsichord, gambled, conversed, and bowed. But at least some in those salons had been aristocrats responsive to the tradition of signorial responsibility. The new dispensation of Manchester and Birmingham let loose a horde of rapacious money-grabbers who had no tradition and recognized no law except the law of Devil take the hindmost. The feudal system, as, even after the Revolution of 1688, it had lingered on through the eighteenth century, had retained evils enough; but they did not compare with the evils that attended the birth of democracy and industrialism. Although individualism had nobler forms as well, it brought a spawn of foul things with it, of which those that have been mentioned were only the most widespread.

The Romantic revolt against the immediate past was, even more than most periods, one of transition. The old synthesis was crumbling, no new one had as yet received even a clear outline. The appeal to the emotions, of which Rousseau had been the prophet, emphasizing the inner world of the spirit, and denying the rule of external law, whether of the reason or of the community—that appeal had results its pleaders never foresaw. They bruised themselves against the world, and wounded and even destroyed others in the course of the changes they were partly instruments in bringing about. The inner world of feeling and imagination transformed the world of material things.

Anger and Pride

Wordsworth and Coleridge were the two great forerunners of revolt. Both had been filled with enthusiasm by the outbreak of the French Revolution, which seemed to them to promise freedom for the spirit of man from all the tyrannies of tradition and custom and fusty-dusty delving in the dry sands of argumentation. It was not until years later that they gradually retreated to intricately qualified and rationalized Toryisms.

Meanwhile they blew a magical wind of release over the human spirit. Wordsworth's great philosophic poem *The Prelude* and his lyrics are really his autobiography, exploring with wonderful delicacy and insight the development of his own character, and tracing the influences of awe and reverence and beauty evoked by the elemental forces of nature upon his strong and sensitive nature. Some of the mistiest chambers of the human soul became luminous beneath his serene and penetrating gaze.

The world of Coleridge was the world of magic and enchantment, the realms in which the spirit seems enclosed by enchantment, held in by webs and mists grown strong as iron. The caverns measureless to man where the will was held imprisoned helpless, the spell of evil that muted the tongue of Christabel, the wicked whisper that turned the heart of the Ancient Mariner as dry as dust and the spring of love that at last gushed through his heart, the mysteries that lurked in the deep well of the unconscious—he struggled painfully through them, for he had been imprisoned by them all.

Lord Byron, like Wordsworth, has written his best autobiography in his poems. Through *Childe Harold*, *Lara*, *The Corsair*, *Manfred*, and *Cain*, the same figure moves always under different names and always basically the same. Sometimes on the green reaches of the ocean, tossed like its flying spray, wild as its howling storms; sometimes in lonely deserts carrying a heart arid as their burning sands; then high among the crags and precipices of glacier-girded mountains, with a pride as stony and frozen and lofty as their peaks; or hiding a dark and mysterious sense of guilt in the desolation and blackness of dense forests.

These heroes of Byron's, with their terrible arrogance, their high scorn of humanity, their tortured nobility and despair, their broken grandeur and inward stain, are Byron's portrait of himself. In them intellectual eminence and moral greatness of character have somehow been warped and tarnished, whether through some internal blemish spreading within them or through contagion from an evil world without is never made plain. Potentially highest, they are most sinful; they all bear the brand of Cain. Self-exiled to far-off solitudes, they stand aloof, scorning and deriding the world from whence they are cast away, hating all its evil, and scourging its evil in themselves. Perhaps in a nobler world they would be among the noblest, but this world can give them only corruption or banishment.

Such is the Byronic hero, and the outlines of his character are also the formula for Byronism, which may be defined as disillusion turned upon itself within. The Byronic character speedily discerns the selfishness and vice that permeate society. He has in himself enough of good to scorn and hate the ill; but not enough to forgive it. He repays the world for disillusion with contempt and cynicism.

Unhappily for his complacency he cannot stop there. For intelligence as well as potential good exists in him. Intelligence ferrets out and forces on his awareness the very evils he has loathed in the outer world coiled like serpents in his own heart. He refused to forgive the world; justice now forbids that he forgive himself. Hatred turns inward, gnawing. Pride and humiliation wrestle bitterly with each other. Ultimately in cynicism and a kind of despair, the Byronic man turns erratic. Generous impulses still arise in him, and lead to noble action, movements of love and sacrifice, admiration of the best. They are corroded by self-indulgence, impatience, suspicion, rage. Capable of highest things in flashes, he is capable of meanest depths. Disgust and self-disgust turn everything he tastes to Dead Sea fruit.

In Byron himself high animal spirits and piercing wit even to the end sustained and enlivened experience. Bitter were the depths, but desire still flared high, and ambition, and the savor of seeing clearly and describing with acid brilliance. To the end he enjoyed the possession of a healthy body, plunging into the iciest currents and swimming for hours; he still enjoyed eating and dressing well. He enjoyed feeling cynical about the conquests made by his handsome person and engaging address; he enjoyed despising his own prestige. The swift movements of his mind were sources of pleasure. As long as a vice or an absurdity could be made fantastically ridiculous or exploded in some sharp epigram, there was relish to life: just to feel his faculties so alive and vigorous within him. If Byron had lost the joy of satire and become merely misanthropic, despair would have been dark indeed.

Byron's sensibility was romantic; his wit derived from the eighteenth century. Even in one of his earliest letters, written when he was twenty, we find him using the balanced antithesis and the dry cerebral statement as a means of gaining his effects; and the tone of jesting self-scorn he assumes is prophetic: 'I once thought myself a philosopher, and talked nonsense with great decorum; I defied pain, and preached up equanimity. For some time this did very well, for no one was in *pain* for me but my friends, and none lost their patience but my hearers. At last, a fall from a horse convinced me bodily suffering was an evil; and the worst of an argument overset my maxims and my temper at the same moment: so I quitted Zeno for Aristippus, and conceive that pleasure constitutes the το καλον!' We can see him delighting in his own emancipation in his first letters from the Near East: 'I see not much difference between ourselves and the Turks, save that we have foreskins and they have none . . . that they have long dresses, and we short, and that we talk much, and they little. They are a sensible people.'

That delight in his own wit, despite all other disappointments, he carried with him to the end. His poems were composed to bursts of enjoyable inspiration, written at top speed. 'You ask me,' he wrote to Murray in 1819, 'for the plan of Donny Johnny:' (notice the almost affectionate gaiety of the diminutive for his title) 'I *have* no plan; I *had* no plan; but I had or have materials; though if, like Tony Lumpkin, I am "to be snubbed so when I am in spirits" the poem will be naught, and the poet turn serious again. If it don't take, I will leave it off where it is, with all due respect to the Public; but if continued, it must be in my own way. You might as well make Hamlet (or Diggory) act mad in a strait waistcoat as trammel my buffoonery, if I am to be a buffoon: their gestures and thoughts would only be pitiably absurd and ludicrously constrained. Why, Man, the Soul of such writing is its license; at least the *liberty* of that *licence* . . . You are too earnest and eager about a work never intended to be serious. Do you suppose that I could have any intention but to giggle and make giggle?—a playful satire, with as little poetry as could be helped, was what I meant: and as to the indecency, do, pray, read in Boswell what

Johnson, the sullen moralist, says of *Prior* and Paulo Purgante.'[1]

Like most representative young men of his generation, Byron was by enthusiasm a radical, or, at least, a reformer. The bad mixture of pride in him led him to despise those of plebeian birth when he found them 'above their stations,' but he had an even greater contempt for a brainless lout if he chanced to be a lord. In the early days, we find him sympathizing with the rebellion of peasants and factory operatives against their oppressors; and even, in a speech delivered in the House of Lords, defending the riots in which manual laborers smashed the machines that were destroying their livelihood.

> I consider the manufacturers, [he wrote Lord Holland—meaning those who did the *work* of manufacturing in the mills] as a much injured body of men, sacrificed to the views of certain individuals, who have enriched themselves by those practices which have deprived the frameworkers of employment. For instance;—by the adoption of a certain kind of frame, one man performs the work of seven—six are thus thrown out of business. But it is to be observed that the work thus done is far inferior in quality, hardly marketable at home, and hurried over with a view to exportation. Surely, my Lord, however we may rejoice in any improvement in the arts which may be beneficial to mankind, we must not allow mankind to be sacrificed to improvements in mechanism. The maintenance and well-doing of the industrious poor is an object of greater consequence to the community than the enrichment of a few monopolists . . . I have seen the state of these miserable men, and it is a disgrace to a civilized country. Their excesses may be condemned, but cannot be subject of wonder.

His liberalism did not prevent his being dazzled by the glamor of Napoleon. When that corsair of genius made himself Emperor, Beethoven in a rage tore up the page on which his *Eroica* had been dedicated to the First Consul, but many others were blinded by his energy and fascination. And especially when all the nations of Europe were banded against him, there were isolated spirits who admired his courage in the uneven struggle, and who 'hoped he would win—at least beat back the invaders.'

But even this hero, for Byron, turned to an idol with feet of clay. To be overcome would have had grandeur—but to abdicate! 'Na-

[1] 'There is nothing in Prior that will excite to lewdness. If Lord Hailes thinks there is, he must be more combustible than other people.'

poleon Buonaparte has abdicated the throne of the world. "Excellent well." Methinks Sylla did better; for he revenged and resigned in the height of his sway, red with the slaughter of his foes—the finest instance of glorious contempt of the rascals upon record. Dioclesian did well too—Amurath not amiss, had he become aught but a dervise—Charles the Fifth but so so—but Napoleon worst of all. What! wait till they were in his capital, and then talk of his readiness to give up what is already gone!! "What whining monk art thou—what holy cheat?" 'Sdeath!—Dionysius at Corinth was yet a king to this. The "Isle of Elba" to retire to!' Once more another hollowness stood exposed.

Many dark and scandalous half-hints have been strewn about Byron's amatory career, from Lady Caroline Lamb's entry in her diary on first seeing him, 'Mad, bad, and dangerous to know,' to the efforts of various kindly biographers to fasten the imputation of incest upon him. The secret causes of the separation from Lady Byron, little more than a year after their marriage, aggravated such efforts; and even in his own day Byron was accused of 'every monstrous vice.' What the facts were that made reconciliation seem impossible, whether mere incompatibility or suspicions of insanity, are unknown, but their very ambiguity has vastly whetted the lust of psychoanalysts. The fantastic nature of Caroline Lamb should, however, have expunged her testimony from the record. Her career before and after her acquaintance with Byron, the almost unbalanced character of her caprices, the wild absurdity of that entry in her diary and the pertinacity with which she then pursued and threw herself into the arms of the fascinating fatality; all should make it clear that any testimony from her was completely unreliable.

Byron yielded to Lady Caroline's importunities, but then found her extravagant behavior highly embarrassing. Her mother implored her to leave London, Byron was appealed to by Lady Melbourne to break off the affair. They brought the pressure of circumstance to bear on Lady Caroline, and a letter Byron wrote her is evidence of a kindliness that could soften farewell with affection and with the pretence that she had herself responded to a call of duty: 'God knows, I wish you happy, and when I quit you, or rather you, from a sense of duty to your husband and mother, quit me, you shall acknowledge the truth of what I again promise and vow, that no other in word or deed, shall ever hold the place in my affections, which is, and shall be, most sacred to you, till I am nothing. I never knew till *that moment* the *madness* of my dearest and most beloved friend . . . Do you think *now* I am *cold* and *stern* and *artful?* Will even *others* think so? Will your *mother* ever—that mother to whom we must indeed sacrifice much, more, much more on my part than she shall ever know or can imagine? "Promise not to love you!" ah, Caroline, it is past promising.'

But women pursued the man, and he found it difficult to resist them. Clare Clairmont wrote him, confessing herself in love with him, called at his rooms, pursued him abroad. We find him writing his half-sister, Augusta Leigh, that 'as to all these "mistresses," Lord help me—I have had but one. Now don't scold; but what could I do?—a foolish girl, in spite of all I could say or do, would come after me, or rather went before—for I found her here—and I have had all the plague possible to persuade her to go back again; but at last she went. Now, dearest, I do most truly tell thee, that I could not help this, that I did all I could to prevent it, and have at last put an end to it. I was not in love, nor have any love left for any; but I could not exactly play the Stoic with a woman who had scrambled eight hundred miles to unphilosophize me.'

No, he could not play the Stoic, and presently in a gayer vein we find him writing Thomas Moore the burlesque carnival-episode with Marianna Segati. The lady was out for the evening with her husband, when the door opened, and in came a handsome blonde girl of nineteen 'who informed me that she was married to the brother of my *amorosa*.' The conversation lasted but a few minutes, however, before in flew Marianna Segati herself, 'and after making a most polite courtsey to her sister-in-law and to me, without a single word seizes her said sister-in-law by the hair, and bestows upon her some sixteen slaps, which would have made your ear ache only to hear their echo.'

Amid screaming the visitor fled, and Marianna 'went into fits in my arms; and in spite of reasoning, eau de Cologne, vinegar, half a pint of water, and God knows what other waters besides, continued so till past midnight.' In the midst of this, in comes Signor Segati, 'and finds me with his wife fainting upon the sofa, and all the apparatus of confusion, dishevelled hair, hats, handkerchiefs, salts, smelling bottles—and the lady as pale as ashes, without sense or motion. His first question was, "What is all this?"' But Venetian husbands were easily appeased in those days, and the whole affair blew over.

By this time Byron had given up the hopes he had once entertained of reconciliation and reunion with Lady Byron. Whatever the reasons, her resentment continued unabated, and took the form of trying to deprive him of all legal rights over their child. Byron wrote, 'You and yours might have been satisfied with the outrages I have already suffered, if not by your design, at least by your means. I know your defense and your apology—duty and Justice; but *Qui n'est que juste, est dur* . . . Throughout the whole of this unhappy business, I have done my best to avoid the bitterness, which, however, is yet amongst us . . . the man who has been sacrificed in fame, in feelings, in every thing, to the convenience of your family, was he whom you once loved, and who—whatever you may imagine to the contrary—loved you.' And in a letter written near the end of his course we find him thanking her for a lock of their daughter's hair, and adding, 'I also thank you for the inscription of the date and name, and I will tell you why; I believe that they are the only two or three words of your hand-writing in my possession.' The others were all returned, the later ones destroyed because they contained vindictive words.

Meanwhile his life went on, superficially gay, but at heart 'the most melancholy of mankind.' Shelley died. Four months before Byron had written to Moore, 'Shelley is to my knowledge, the least selfish and mildest of men—a man who has made more sacrifices of his fortunes and feelings for others than any other I ever heard of.' Now Shelley was gone, and the world still threw slime upon his name. 'You were all brutally mistaken about Shelley,' he wrote, 'who was without exception, the *best* and least selfish man I ever knew. I never knew one who was not a beast in comparison.'

There had been only Shelley. The rest, including himself, were beasts. But he had lost faith in goodness; one good man was not sufficient to keep it in credit. He could tolerate men's meannesses, now, and emulate them too, although the melancholy was always there. He behaved with cruel unreliableness to Leigh Hunt. And then, at last, he was off to Greece, to redeem his life by one unselfish blow for freedom. The fevers of Missolonghi took him; the burning heart was stilled on the Aetolian shore.

Such is the story we may read in the letters—told with less than the passion and glowing color of the dramas and poems, but with more of the light of the everyday. The caldron of burning thought and feeling is not there as it is in the hurrying and impetuous lines of the verse, there is none of the interior monodrama, or the long brooding passages of introspection and sorrow and despair that throbbed therein so often, or the lovely interludes in which he tried to assuage his sadness by mingling with the swell of moving waves or rising to the peaks of the calm and eternal mountains. But it is the same story, and if some of the passion is lost, it has the solidness of fact.

There is no more of deliberate writing for effect in his letters than there is in the poems; whatever attitudinizing Byron may have indulged was mostly unconscious and deceived himself perhaps more than it did others. They are written with the same racing pen, free from forethought and afterthought. If they evade, except in passages of witty disillusion, his underlying scorn of himself and men, that is because he was a gentleman and would not inflict his darkest moods upon a friend. Byron the letter-writer is almost as eloquent as Byron the poet; and in the end the two are obviously the same.

The Aspiring Heart

Byron and Shelley had met in Italy. Shelley's estimate of the slightly older man reveals how uncomprehending is the view that Shelley was a mere luminous visionary deluded about the world around him by his radiant dreams. He found Byron 'deeply discontented with himself; and, contemplating in the distorted mirror of his own thoughts the nature and destiny of man, what can he behold but objects of contempt and despair?' No contemporary saw deeper into the nature of Byron's malady; and the speculation he added to these words was prophetic: 'I do not doubt, and, for his sake, I ought to hope, that his present career must end soon in some violent circumstance . . .'

As he came to know Byron more he understood him even better. In his character, Shelley said, 'the wit and poetry which surround, hide with their light the darkness of the thing itself. They contradict it even; they prove that the strength and beauty of human nature can survive and conquer all that appears most inconsistent with it.' But in spite of that strength and beauty, Byron was one of those men, 'however excellent, from whom we would never receive an obligation, in the worldly sense of the word.'

The shallow fancy, indeed, that Shelley the man lived in a universe as ethereal as the realms of speeding wind and pearly cloud, of spirits and dreams and visions, of shining and enchanted song, that gleam in his poetry is altogether false. Men overlook the fact that Shelley died at thirty, and that his noblest and most powerful poetic utterance is the work of his last few years, when he was visibly growing maturer in his judgments, clearer in mental grasp. They confuse the enthusiastic youth with the experienced man. The excited emotion of the youth cooled and strengthened into an emotion no less strong, but more balanced and controlled. The principles that swirled through the fervid oratory of the youth still, for the most part, guided the man, but with less fanaticism and more assured knowledge of human nature, tempered by more worldly wisdom in their application.

The letters of the youthful Shelley, indeed, are immature enough. Metaphysical questions tumble out one after another in a rush of incoherence; objurgations and exclamations mingle in a heat of eagerness; excitement is shrill in underlinings and dashes. 'Why are we here?' he enquires. 'What does man exist for. Surely not for his own happiness, but as a more perfect instrument of that of others . . . How, then, obligations! Surely one being is not *obliged* to another for a performance of his duty never the most rigid.' Obligation can only arise from doing 'an unrequited, unrequitable kindness.' Reward, however, already exists in the pleasure of the act itself. 'What! two rewards for one simple performance of evident duty . . . This is far too much.–I thought there were some souls which soared above the mean prejudices of the world. *I* am but a novice in it.' And from here he goes on to pointing out how ignoble is a pride that refuses aid, and from thence to the conclusion that revealed religion is responsible for 'murder, war, intolerance,' and that consequently he rejects it entirely. All these arguments, moral sentiments, pour forth at top speed in a sort of strangulated hysteria of emotional enthusiasm.

Many of the ideas were derived, of course, from Godwin, whose *Political Justice* he had taken almost as a Bible. The intermingling of rationalism and romanticism is nowhere more clearly shown than in this work, where, by purely a priori methods, the author deduces from the nature of man the nature of society, and arrives at an ideal picture of anarchy in which the fundamental goodness of man is uncorrupted by the superstitions of religion or the oppressions of magistrates and kings. Freed from the selfishness of priests and tyrants by the clear light of reason, the world's great age may begin anew, and the golden years return. Inspired by this gospel, we see Shelley inveighing against the filth of commercialism: 'Vile as aristocracy is, commerce–purse-proud ignorance and illiterateness–is more contemptible.' 'I still see Religion to be immoral.' Its edifices are 'gigantic piles of superstition.' Marriage, as such, is an evil, because it is 'monopolizing, exclusive, jealous': 'a law to compel you to hear' music only in the company of one person 'appears to me parallel to that of Marriage.' Nevertheless a great and general reformation in morals is necessary, he adds, before the evil of marriage may be remedied.

His antagonism to Christianity was relentless, not because of any real quarrel with the spirit of its founder, but because of its application by professing Christians. It had been converted into a system of punishments and vindictive cruelty; its adherents far more often modeled their behavior on the Pharisee than on the Samaritan. Shelley found a poor woman wandering through the snow barefooted, and about to give birth to a child; he gave her his own shoes, wrapped her in his own coat, and tried to persuade the nearest householders to take her in while he went to seek medical attention. They all refused. A portly old gentleman alighting from a carriage remarked that there were too many imposters roaming the country, and wound up his refusal with a 'Sir, your conduct is extraordinary.' Shelley exploded. 'Sir, I am sorry to say *your* conduct is *not* extraordinary . . . It is such men as you who madden the spirits and the patience of the poor and wretched; and if ever a convulsion comes in this country (which is very probable), recollect what I tell you: you will have your house, that you refuse to put the miserable woman into, burnt over your head.'

Terror and cruelty, he had concluded, were the real foundations of Christianity, and we find him describing Michelangelo's *Last Judgment* with emphatic revulsion. 'God is leaning out of heaven, as it were eagerly enjoying . . . the infernal tragedy . . . The bottom of the picture is divided by a lofty rock, in which there is a cavern whose entrance is thronged by devils, some coming in with spirits, some going out for prey. The blood-red light of the fiery abyss glows through their dark forms. On one side are the devils all in hideous forms, struggling with the damned, who have received their sentence at the Redeemer's throne, and chained in all forms of agony by knotted serpents, and writhing on the crags in every variety of torture. On the other are the dead, coming out of their graves—horrible forms.'

Of such a religion he could not believe in the Deity—he became an atheist. But his later belief, and the one more truly representing his feelings, seemed to be that perhaps such a god did exist, and that if so he was a tyrant of monstrous cruelty, scourging the world and inspiring his devotees to their own deeds of evil emulation. His passionate idealism could not surrender, however, the idea of a force of divine good, which he conceives of as in eclipse but destined to dethrone the demon who poses as Benevolence and Wisdom. Shelley identifies himself with the rebels, with Prometheus and Satan, spirits that question and revolt, and the serpent becomes in his mythology the symbol of goodness and knowledge.

The roots of all these things he found in Godwin. We have his first letter to the eminent philosopher. 'The name of Godwin,' he wrote, 'has been used to excite in me feelings of reverence and admiration. I have been accustomed to consider him a luminary too dazzling for the darkness which surrounds him. From the earliest period of my knowledge of his principles, I already ardently desired to share, on the footing of intimacy, that intellect which I have delighted to contemplate in its emanations.

'Considering, then, these feelings, you will not be surprised at the inconceivable emotions with which I learned your existence and your dwelling. I had enrolled your name in the list of the honourable dead. I had felt regret that the glory of your being had passed from this earth of ours. It is not so; you still live, and, I firmly believe, are still planning the welfare of mankind.'

Shelley was destined to a sad disillusion. Godwin was full of abstract benevolence, but he was a poor man and his radical reputation had injured him. He earned his bread by a desultory journalism, and he had compromised his belief in freedom to the point of marrying Mary Wollstonecraft instead of risking the obloquy of a free union. His belief in the duty of extending aid to any who were in need without expecting any sense of gratefulness or obligation (which he had generously acted upon when he had the means) he now gave his friends full opportunity to display toward him. Godwin was always in need, and Shelley had informed him that he was the heir to £6,000 a year.

Godwin's mind was as clear and luminous as ever, his principles unchanged, his syllogisms brilliant and surprising, his epigrams explosive. Shelley felt enchanted, and nothing was more natural than that he should help the necessities of the sage whose writings had taught him the duty of general benevolence. Nothing more natural also than that he should act on Godwin's principle of the freedom of sexual unions by eloping with Godwin's beautiful and gifted daughter. The sage was in a mighty indignation, and wrote Mary that Shelley was 'a disgraceful and flagrant person,' but he could not resist begging in the same letter for more money in addition to the £4,700 Shelley had given him already.

When the death of Harriet Shelley later on permitted a marriage, a ceremony was quietly performed, and Godwin and his son-in-law became reconciled. But although 'added years,' Shelley later wrote, 'only add to my admiration of his intellectual powers, and even the moral resources of his character,' Shelley's steadily growing maturity enabled him in the end to judge Godwin with more justice than Godwin could judge himself. His final estimate of their relationship, and the mutual failures of both, is absolutely sound:

> I have given you within a few years the amount of a considerable fortune, and have destituted myself, for the purpose of realizing it, of nearly four times the amount. Except for the *goodwill* which this transaction seems to have produced between you and me, the money, for any advantage it ever conferred on you, might as well have been thrown into the seas. Had I kept in my own hands this £4,000 or £5,000 and administered it in trust for your permanent advantage, I should have been indeed your benefactor. The error, however, was greater in the man of mature age, extensive experience, and penetrating intellect than in the crude and impetuous boy. Such an error is seldom committed twice.

Meanwhile he had taken up his abode in Italy, and his letters, although as philosophic as ever, breathe an increasing serenity of mind and understanding of the obstacles to social change, without ever losing their fervor for the welfare of humanity or their indignation at all cruelty. The grandeur and loveliness of nature always moves him, and the monuments of Roman civilization often lead him to comparison with the present. Vesuvius impressed him; it had not

> the radiant beauty of the glaciers; but it has all their . . . tremendous and irresistible strength . . . you wind up the mountain, and cross a vast stream of hardened lava, which is an actual image of the waves of the sea, changed into hard black stone by enchantment. The lines of the boiling flood seem to hang in the air, and it is difficult to believe that the billows which seem hurrying down upon you are not actually in motion. This plain was once a sea of liquid fire. [On foot they ascended the cone to the summit,] a kind of irregular plain, the most horrible chaos that can be imagined; riven into ghastly chasms, and heaped with the tumuli of great stones and cinders, and enormous rocks blackened and calcined, which had been thrown up from the volcano upon one another in terrible confusion. In the midst stands the conical hill from which volumes of smoke, and fountains of liquid fire, are rolled forth forever. [From the erupting mountain] a thick heavy white smoke is perpetually rolled out, interrupted by enormous columns of an impenetrable black bituminous vapour, which is hurled up, fold after fold, into the sky with a deep hollow sound, and fiery stones are rained down from its darkness, and a black shower of ashes fell even where we sat.

The ruins of Pompeii and Herculaneum, with their garden porticos, their mosaics, and their frescoes, gave him images of ideal life. 'The public buildings,' he wrote, 'whose ruins are now forests, as it were, of white fluted columns, and which then supported entablatures, loaded with sculptures, were seen on all sides over the roofs' of the one-story private dwellings. 'This was the excellence of the antients. Their private expenses were comparatively moderate; the dwelling of one of the chief senators of Pompeii is elegant indeed, and adorned with most beautiful specimens of art, but small. But their public buildings are everywhere marked by the bold and grand designs of an unsparing magnificence.' How could humanity not be inspired, or 'every human being' fail to catch 'a splendour not his own,' when, unlike 'the inhabitants of the Cimmerian ravines of modern cities,' he was surrounded by such grace and able to see on every side the glorious scenery, with the moon high behind Vesuvius, and the sun setting 'in the sea, tremulous with an atmosphere of golden vapour, between Inarime and Misenum'?

Under such skies, Shelley, the serious, could sometimes grow even irresponsibly frivolous. Mr Gisborne's nose was 'something quite Slawkenbergian–it weighs on the imagination to look at it,–it is that sort of nose which transforms all the *g's* its wearer utters into *k's*. It is a nose once seen never to be forgotten, and which requires the utmost stretch of Christian charity to forgive.' When Shelley could unconsciously use the word Christian in a traditional sense he was softened indeed. 'I, you know,' he continues, 'have a turn-up nose; Hogg has a large hook one; but add them both together, square them, cube them, you would have but a faint idea of the nose to which I refer.' Much like schoolboy humor as this description is, it is significant of the mellowing that was taking place in Shelley that he essays any passage of purely nonsensical, non-satiric humor at all.

And yet the shining image of a world of goodness seemed further off than ever. Sometimes, surrounded by the melancholy beauty of the clouds, or remembering the high clear song of the skylark with its ringing freedom from pain, or hearing the long soughing chords of the west wind as it swept the dead leaves before it and made the vegetation of the sea-floor shiver with its power, there seemed room for nothing but surrender and despair. The Titan must ever suffer torments on his lonely peak in the Caucasus, and Asia weep forever unredeemed.

But then his hopes and courage awake again. The west wind would sow his dead thoughts over the universe like seeds of the new world that was to be; the incantation of his verse would be a spell awakening men to nobility and splendor; perhaps not in his time, but dawning, and he too would be a bringer of light. Gazing into the future he saw crumbling faiths and empires gleam like wrecks of a dissolving dream. Their crashing ruins were a glory. But did even the golden age contain the seeds of renewed strife and hate? would the dark cycle of guilt bring always the fate of the House of Atreus, the violences of Laian rage? He closed his eyes to the dreadful vision; no, the golden years return . . .

Meanwhile there was serenity and melancholy and strength and hope; there was courage and disheartenment, moments of gaiety and love of lofty things. There was good to be done: a servant so ugly that no one else would give him anything in going away, so that Shelley, in spite of loathing the man's ugliness, or perhaps because of it, must make him a gift in parting. There was Keats, who was coming to Italy desperately ill; Shelley could not surrender the gratification of taking care of him. 'Where is Keats?' he wrote. 'I am anxiously expecting him . . . I consider his a most valuable life, and I am deeply interested in his safety. I intend to be the physician both of his body and his soul, to keep the one warm, and to teach the other Greek and Spanish. I am aware, indeed, in part, that I am nourishing a rival who will far surpass me; and this is an additional motive, and will be an added pleasure.'

But when Keats landed in Naples he was beyond the ministrations of Shelley. He struggled up to Rome, and lay down there in the bed that warmed for a few months his last sparks of life. Less than a year later the storm arose on the blue Bay of Spezzia in which Shelley was drowned.

The translucent and almost liquid loveliness in which Shelley steeped nearly all his poetic utterance has hidden from many people the fact that his mind was so largely concerned with social problems. The symbols and myths in which his imagination clothed the syllogisms of Godwin veil with luminous cloud the sharp clarity of his vision, soften the fierce shock of his iconoclasm. His letters, however, full of the eager play of dialectic (even though somewhat confused in the most youthful of them) and busy with denunciation and praise, should make unequivocally clear that the central interest of Shelley's life was the relationship of man to society and the abolition of injustice among men.

To that central issue the brief lyric outbursts of amatory exaltation or grief that figure in most anthologies are merely peripheral. Love could hardly be the thing of splendor it might be hoped as long as the very tissues of society were permeated with the evils of tyranny, exploitation, and possessorship, poisoning the hearts of men and women in their most intimate relationship. The fruitless search for ideal love accompanies the campaign of social reform. The poet's intuitions of beauty and justice and love are being called on to instruct the world of other men. What those intuitions meant outside the realm of poetry Shelley's life tells, and his letters are a vivid record of that life.

The Love of Good and Ill

If the symbolism and the cloud-splendor of Shelley's imagery have hidden for some the fact that he was a rebel against society even in his poetry, the sensuousness of Keats's poetry has in the same way hidden the fact that he was a philosopher among poets. Men remember the dramatic question in *Lamia*, 'Do not all charms fly at the mere touch of cold philosophy?' and, forgetting the part it plays in the emotional development of the poem, assume that it gives Keats's personal attitude, whereas it is really a foreshadowing of the anguished cry of Lycius on losing his beautiful illusion. Keats never wrote an elaborate cosmological poem like Lucretius or Dante, but the careful reader of his letters may see in them again and again a grappling with problems that the poems robe in garments of rich imagery. The reader who has merely luxuriated in the verbal texture and gleaming pictures of the *Ode on a Grecian Urn*, and never tried to explore the depth of meaning in

> *'Beauty is Truth, Truth Beauty,'—that is all*
> *Ye know on earth and all ye need to know—*

that reader has failed to reach to the heart of Keats.

'I am convinced more and more every day,' Keats wrote, 'that (excepting the human friend Philosopher) a fine writer is the most genuine Being in the World. Shakspeare and the Paradise Lost every day become greater wonders to me.' But woven all around these dominating and deepest colors of his reverence for the poet and the philosopher—the *human friend* philosopher—there are the golden and rainbow-hued threads of Keats's darting fancy and the tragic colors of his personal life. I know of no letters more beautiful, or more revealing of a great and beautiful character, than those of Keats.

'If,' said Harry Buxton Forman, 'to be true, interesting, attractive, witty, humorous, idealistic, realistic, speculative, discursive, and gossippy in turns is the note of a good letter-writer, then indeed Keats was one. If to tell one's friends just what they want to know about one's doings and thoughts, and about the doings and thoughts of mutual friends, is to be a good letter-writer—that is where Keats, of all men of genius in the last century, excelled. If consideration for the feelings of others in the manner and degree of presenting misfortunes or disagreeables be an epistolary virtue, then Keats was largely dowered with that virtue. If to present a true picture of the essential qualities of one's personality is a valuable art, Keats manifested that art in a high form in his letters. And if, when wrung by disease and misery, it is better to leave some record for a pitying posterity than to carry a ghastly secret into the oblivion of the grave, then in this also Keats excelled others who have made the world richer with their letters. Lastly, the man is not dissociated from the poet in them. Not only is the poetic mode of thought frequently the ruling mode in the prose fabric of these letters; but they are set with gems of verse of all waters, dashed in just as they were composed, a part of the man's life enacting and reflected throughout . . .' These are words of high praise, but they are not too high.

We find him on a tour of Scotland describing the island of Staffa, with its surface like a roof 'supported by grand pillars of basalt standing together as thick as honeycombs'; and Fingal's Cave 'entirely a hollowing out of basalt Pillars. Suppose now the Giants who rebelled against Jove had taken a whole Mass of black Columns and bound them together like bunches of matches—and then with immense Axes had made a cavern in the body of these columns—of course the roof and floor must be composed of broken ends of the Columns—such is Fingal's Cave except that the Sea has done the work of excavations and is continually dashing there—so that we walk along the sides of the cave on the pillars which are left as if for convenient Stairs' and behold 'the sea through the large Arch at the entrance,' green between columns of 'a sort of black with a lurking gloom of purple therein.'

Farther south, at Ireby, he watches the country-dances of the peasants: 'they kickit and jumpit with mettle extraordinary, and whiskit, and friskit, and toed it, and go'd it, and twirl'd it, and whirl'd it, and stamped it, and sweated it, tattooing the floor like mad. The difference between our country dances and these Scottish figures is about the same as leisurely stirring a cup o' Tea and beating up a batter-pudding. I was extremely gratified to think that, if I had pleasures they knew nothing of, they also had some into which I could not possibly enter.' That kindly gratification, with its large sympathies, paints one of the loveliest qualities in the man.

In a rollicking mood he writes a mad letter from Devonshire. He has heard, he says, 'that Milton ere he wrote his Answer to Salmasius came into these parts, and for one whole Month, rolled himself, for three whole hours in a certain meadow hard by us—where the mark of his nose at equidistances is still shown.' And in another place we find him improvising a gay and slightly scandalous little rhyme about maidenheads,—

O blush not so, O blush not so
Or I shall think ye knowing;
And if ye smile, the blushing while,
Then maidenheads are going.
There's a blush for won't, and a blush for shan't
And a blush for having done it,
There's a blush for thought, and a blush for naught
And a blush for just begun it.

Or, in a letter in which he has included the first draft of *La Belle Dame Sans Merci*, explaining

And there I shut her wild wild eyes
With kisses four—

'Why four kisses—you will say—why four? because I wish to restrain the headlong impetuosity of my Muse—she would fain have said "score" without hurting the ryhme—but we must temper the Imagination as the Critics say with Judgment. I was obliged to choose an even number that both eyes might have fair play: and to speak truly I think two a piece quite sufficient. Suppose I had said seven; there would have been three and a half a piece—a very awkward affair and well got out of on my side—'

In Ireland, though, he felt heartsick at the poverty he saw, 'the worse than nakedness, the rags, the dirt and misery of the poor common Irish. A Scotch cottage, though in that the smoke sometimes has no exit but at the door, is a palace to an Irish one . . . We had the pleasure of finding our way through a Peatbog, three miles long at least—dreary, flat, dank, black, and spongy—here and there were poor dirty Creatures, and a few strong men cutting or carting Peat.' On his return to Donaghadee from Belfast 'we met a sedan—the Duchess of Dunghill . . . Imagine the worst dog-kennel you ever saw, placed upon two poles from a mouldy fencing. In such a wretched thing sat a squalid old woman, squat like an ape half-starved, from a scarcity of biscuit in its passage from Madagascar to the Cape, with a pipe in her mouth, and looking out with a round-eyed, skinny-lidded inanity; with a sort of horizontal idiotic movement of her head—squat and lean she sat, and puffed out the smoke, while two ragged, tattered girls carried her along.'

Alive as he was thus to the misery, the jollity, the beauty, and the grandeur of the world, the central thing for him was being a poet. It was a thing of trembling and wonder; 'I have asked myself so often why I should be a Poet more than other Men,–seeing how great a thing it is,–' and he felt almost afraid, 'the Idea has grown so monstrously beyond my seeming Power of attainment.' 'There is no worthy pursuit but the idea of doing some good for the world,' he said: how grand was the benefaction of giving men the richness and fullness of beauty! The poet must enter into the fullness of all experience, knowing it as it is known to the experiencer and even as the experience is in its own inmost essence, not hiding or withholding any of it because of his own intellectual prepossessions or judgments: his mind must 'be a thoroughfare for all thoughts' and feelings. The mind of the true poet, in a way, he said, has *no* character, 'it has no self–it is everything and nothing . . . it enjoys light and shade; it lives in gusto, be it foul or fair, high or low, rich or poor, mean or elevated–It has as much delight in conceiving an Iago as an Imogen.'

It was this that made Shakespeare so great and the lack of this that made Wordsworth in the end an inferior poet. Wordsworth tried, through the medium of his poems, to force his own philosophy into Nature. 'We hate poetry,' Keats exclaims, 'that has a palpable design upon us . . . Poetry should be great and unobtrusive, a thing that enters into one's soul, and does not startle it or amaze it with itself but with its subject. How beautiful are the retired flowers! how would they lose their beauty were they to throng into the highway crying out, "admire me I am a violet!" ' Wordsworth's poetry was the 'egotistical sublime,' but the real poetic quality, which 'Shakespeare possessed so enormously,' is '*Negative Capability*'–being able to remain 'in uncertainties, mysteries, doubts, without any irritable reaching after fact and reason,' being able to reflect in forms of beauty all things that exist in the world without inflicting on them the violences of personal judgment.

For this reason the poet must know suffering as well as joy, evil as well as good, taking them deep into his being, knowing their very heart and core. The poet is a symbolic man, scaling the heights humanity may climb to, plumbing the blackest pits of suffering and despair. 'A Man's life of any worth is a continual allegory, and very few eyes can see the Mystery of his life—a life like the scriptures, figurative—which such people can no more make out than they can the hebrew Bible. Lord Byron cuts a figure—but he is not figurative— Shakespeare led a life of allegory: his works are the comments on it.' The poet, for Keats, was such a symbolic man, and his life a life of allegory. It pierced into the deeper meaning of truth for all humanity. And perhaps it even revealed the truth about the mystery of evil, the reason for sorrow and frustration, that has so troubled the hearts of men.

As a poet, a man must know and understand the griefs of humanity. But why do they exist? What is really good and what is evil? Was the development of man as a moral being, capable of responding to stimuli of beauty and nobility, purely accidental in a universe where his organism stumbled, to its weal or pain, on mechanical laws? Or did the existence of evil have a place in the universe, explainable, understandable, and capable in the end of eliciting moral consent? Such questions have troubled men's minds since Job's rebellion was answered from the whirlwind. Most philosophers have tried to answer them with their minds alone, submitting all their other faculties as much as they possibly could, to the checkrein of reason. Keats brought to it openly and consciously the full vitality of his eager emotions and his vivid imagination.

He began by being sure of one thing: that truth was a matter of emotional acceptance, that things received their meanings from the value they had for the observer. 'I am certain of nothing,' he exclaimed, 'but of the holiness of the Heart's affections and the truth of Imagination—What the imagination seizes as Beauty must be truth—whether it existed before or not.' The will or the desire of man explores the domain of experience, and his mind is the instrument only, powerless without the motivation. 'I have never yet been able to perceive how anything can be known for truth by consequitive reasoning . . . Can it be that even the greatest Philosopher ever arrived at his goal without putting aside numerous objections.' In this way 'every mental pursuit takes its reality and worth from the ardour of the pursuer—being in itself a nothing.' The statements poets and philosophers make do not even begin to have real meaning for us until they touch on experiences that have awakened our feeling, or call to emotions we have known. Even 'axioms in philosophy are not axioms until they are proved upon our pulses. We read fine things, but never feel them until we have gone the same steps as the Author.'

And in the effort to make clear how the problem of evil arises for us, Keats uses an image in which life is 'a large Mansion of Many Apartments, two of which I can only describe, the doors of the rest being as yet shut upon me.' The first is the chamber of childhood, where we remain a long while, although the doors of the second chamber are open and bright. We enter the second, 'which I shall call the Chamber of Maiden-Thought,' upon 'the awakening of the thinking principle within us'; and there we grow 'intoxicated with the light and atmosphere' for a while.

Gradually there we become aware that 'the world is full of Misery and Heartbreak, Pain, Sickness and oppression—whereby this Chamber of Maiden-Thought becomes gradually darken'd and at the same time on all sides of it many doors are set open—but all dark—all leading to dark passages.' This is when we feel 'the burden of the Mystery' that Wordsworth labored with in *Tintern Abbey;* 'and it seems to me,' Keats writes, 'that his genius is explorative of those dark passages. Now if we live and go on thinking, we too shall explore them.'

But meanwhile the imagination, 'Lost in a sort of Purgatory blind,' is saddened and bewildered by the darkness and the pain. 'Oh never will the prize, High reason, and the love of good and ill Be my award?' Keats cries in a verse-letter to Reynolds. 'The love of good and ill': how indeed is the heart of man to grasp that hard necessity? Out of this nettle pain, we pluck this flower courage. The imagination must be taught in some way to feel the need and the beauty of evil too, and then it will have learned 'the love of good and ill,' then 'what the imagination seizes as Beauty' will indeed be truth, beautiful in pain. How is this to be done?

Keats had an intimation of it in an early letter: 'The first thing that strikes me on hearing a Misfortune having befallen another is this —"Well, it cannot be helped—he will have the pleasure of trying the resources of his spirit."' There is 'an electric fire in human nature tending to purify,' and thence pain and suffering continually bring about 'some new birth of heroism.' A world in which there were no suffering, a world with mankind perfected, would still have Death, and 'the whole troubles of life' would then be accumulated in the terrors of those few last days, the more terrible because of the paradise of all a happy life.

'But in truth I do not at all believe in this sort of perfectibility . . . The point at which Man may arrive is as far as the parallel state in inanimate nature and no further.' The sun that warms and nourishes a rose may glare upon it till it wilts, the cold wind that kills it may sow the seeds of further blooms. Such is 'the use of the world' for human beings; its evils are the means of spiritual enrichment. Our intelligences at birth 'are atoms of perception' to be wrought upon by the world and made into souls. They are emanations of God which are 'to have identity given them—so as ever to possess a bliss peculiar to each one's individual existence.' Thus Keats has arrived at 'a system of Spirit-creation.'

Spirits are created, he says, 'by three grand materials acting the one upon another for a series of years.' These are 'the *Intelligence* —the *human heart* (as distinguished from intelligence or Mind)— and the *World* or *Elemental space* suited for the proper action of *Mind* and *Heart* on each other for the purpose of forming the *Soul* or *Intelligence destined to possess the sense of Identity*.' And finally, 'Do you not see,' he cries, 'how necessary a World of Pains and troubles is to school an Intelligence and make it a Soul? A Place where the heart must feel and suffer in a thousand diverse ways.' And so we arrive at the identity of Beauty and Truth. 'What the imagination seizes as Beauty must be truth,' because the imagination will at last perceive the justification of suffering and evil, and, clasping 'the *love* of good and ill,' find the beauty in pain. Truth is Beauty, because without the whole arsenal of bitterest truths, beauty itself could not be.

The story of Keats's love has been told too often before to need telling again. From it he learned long passages in the lesson of pain —that lesson he was so triumphantly transforming into beauty in his poems, and reducing to understanding in the letters where we have found him struggling to learn it. 'The very first week I knew you I wrote myself your vassal,' he exclaims, and the early hours of that dawn are all full of intoxication. 'I want a brighter word than bright, a fairer word than fair.' 'Why may I not speak of your Beauty . . .? I cannot conceive any beginning of such love as I have for you but Beauty.' 'You are always new. The last of your kisses was ever the sweetest; the last smile the brightest; the last movement the gracefullest.'

But there were gathering troubles. His health was precarious, and they could not be always together. Gay, thoughtless, capricious, she wounded him by her love of other pleasures. 'My greatest torment since I have known you,' he wrote, 'has been the fear of you being a little inclined to the Cressid.' Meaningless gallantries from his friend Brown cut him to the heart. 'I cannot forget what has pass'd. What? nothing with a man of the world, but to me dreadful . . . Brown is a good sort of Man–he did not know he was doing me to death by inches.' And there was the difficulty of his livelihood; how was he to make a career? There was nothing but poetry, which so far had not been a financial success, and he *would* not write down to the public or 'run with that most vulgar of all crowds, the literary.'

'Knowing well that my life must be passed in fatigue and trouble,' he wrote her, 'I have been endeavoring to wean myself from you: for to myself alone what can be much of a misery?' But the need returned again and again, and made his 'heart now seem made of iron.' 'I am not happy enough for silken Phrases and silver sentences,' he says bitterly, and then bursts out 'Forgive me for this flint-worded letter.' His health grew worse; he coughed blood. 'I know,' he said to a friend, 'the color of that blood,–it is arterial blood–I cannot be deceived in that colour; that drop is my death-warrant.'

His friends insisted on his going abroad in the hopes that a southern clime might enable him to recover. He went, but in the certainty that he was doomed. He would never see her again. 'I dare not fix my Mind upon Fanny, I have not dared to think of her.' 'Everything that I have in my trunks that reminds me of her goes through me like a spear.' 'I can bear to die–I cannot bear to leave her. O, God! God! God!'

The shortness of his career also weighed heavily upon him. None of the work he had done so far seemed more than a prelude to what he had really intended. "If I should die," said I to myself, ' "I have left no immortal work behind me–nothing to make my friends proud of my memory–but I have lov'd the principle of beauty in all things, and if I had had time I would have made myself remember'd."' The *principle* of beauty in all things! It was indeed what he had loved, and sought; the principle binding together beauty and truth and pain. 'Perhaps,' he was heard to say when near the point of death, 'I may be among the English poets when I die.' Matthew Arnold replied to that question: 'He is; he is with Shakespeare.'

Pictures of a World

In Byron and Shelley and Keats the awareness of a tension between the inner and the outer world is a dominating presence, and each regards the inner world as infinitely more important. The inner world is not more real than the outer, for each exists, and there are elements in the outer world that are in no way malleable to the desires of the inner; but ultimately for all three it is the inner world that endows the outer with such values of good or ill as it contains. It is the inner world—the spirit of man—that holds authority in the realm of value. Beside that realm the brute facts of the external universe are insignificant.

In Byron, for all the passionate fire and intensity of his nature, the conflict existed on a relatively superficial plane. His letters are full of scorn for society; they flame with the hatred of rebellion. But his anger is more often aroused by personal frustration than by social injustice, and his strictures easily subside into the smartness of the scoffer. In him a violently selfish ego was pitted against society, and in the resulting struggle the ego lost self-respect and fell prey to bitterness without yielding in its imperious desires. Sullied by the same vices that stood in its way, and that it despised in others, Byron's character was very little superior to the world it derided; and the slight superiority it had was only enough to add hatred of self to hatred of the external world.

The scenes of nature which his letters describe, with which he felt in sympathy, and with which he tried to identify himself, were those that the anthropomorphic imagination could feel to be either coldly indifferent or destructive to man. Oceans and storms and icy desolations were killing to the human vitality, the human will that he hated almost as much in himself as in others; forests and desert sands and mountain pinnacles and the remote chill light of the stars were outside the realm of humanity altogether, terrible forces and entities unaware of the puniness of man creeping about them. Filling his horizon and his mind with such existences he could forget the conflict within himself, where the most ignoble elements of the outer world that aroused his scorn had almost stifled the best.

Shelley's letters too reveal a conflict between the outer and inner world, but in him the effort is to bring the selfish elements in man's nature into subjection to his higher moral being, and thereby change the machinery of society and bring it into agreement with moral law. Even those enthusiastic incoherences he poured out to his correspondents in adolescence glow with that fervor. Whereas Byron's conflict was that of a strongly self-centered ego with an indifferent society, Shelley's is that of a generous and altruistic ego with an antagonistic world. His later letters are full of the harmonious grandeur of nature, alternating with a lofty pity and indignation at human failures. And in their philosophic passages there is sometimes an almost Platonic clarity of movement. They employ a passionate and exalted dialectic, but his appeal in the end is always to the springs of nobility he is sure exist even in the most stained and corroded of hearts. He stakes everything on his conviction that the inward nature of man is harmonious and is capable of imposing order on the external world: capable even of bringing its unruly passions, if they were not fed into evil strength by evil institutions, into agreement with the inmost laws of goodness and love.

Keats does not so much deal with a conflict between the external and the internal worlds as triumphantly move the whole significance of the external world into the human heart. In his letters he germinates a philosophy; the poems are its fruit. He is not a mere passionate rebel like Byron, who would probably have been proudly miserable in any society, and he is not a reformer of institutions like Shelley, because his fundamental problem made the conflict of Shelley appear superficial to him. The gentleness and the lofty heart that moved Shelley's behavior he admired, and the innumerable deeds of goodness that starred his career; but in the Utopian vision of a world where men would experience no evil and make no acquaintance with griefs he had no belief. Not abolition of pain and frustration and despair he aimed at, but understanding and accepting their existence, realizing the way in which they were ministers to all those noblest attainments of human nature, those most shining manifestations of beauty, that he as much as Shelley loved and worshipped.

And these three romantic poets taken together wonderfully supplement each other in the picture with which we may conceive the new world that glimmered among the fragments of the classic synthesis. They are pioneers in the path Wordsworth began to blaze—pioneers in the effort to shake loose the shackles of that rigid law-ridden and reason-ridden society that still lingered in an only half-broken dominance over the realms of religion, and law, and government, and social relations. The inner world of Byron was still clogged by the muddy and violent and obstinate flesh. The inner world of Shelley was fired by the warm and aspiring heart. The inner world of Keats was illumined by the understanding spirit.

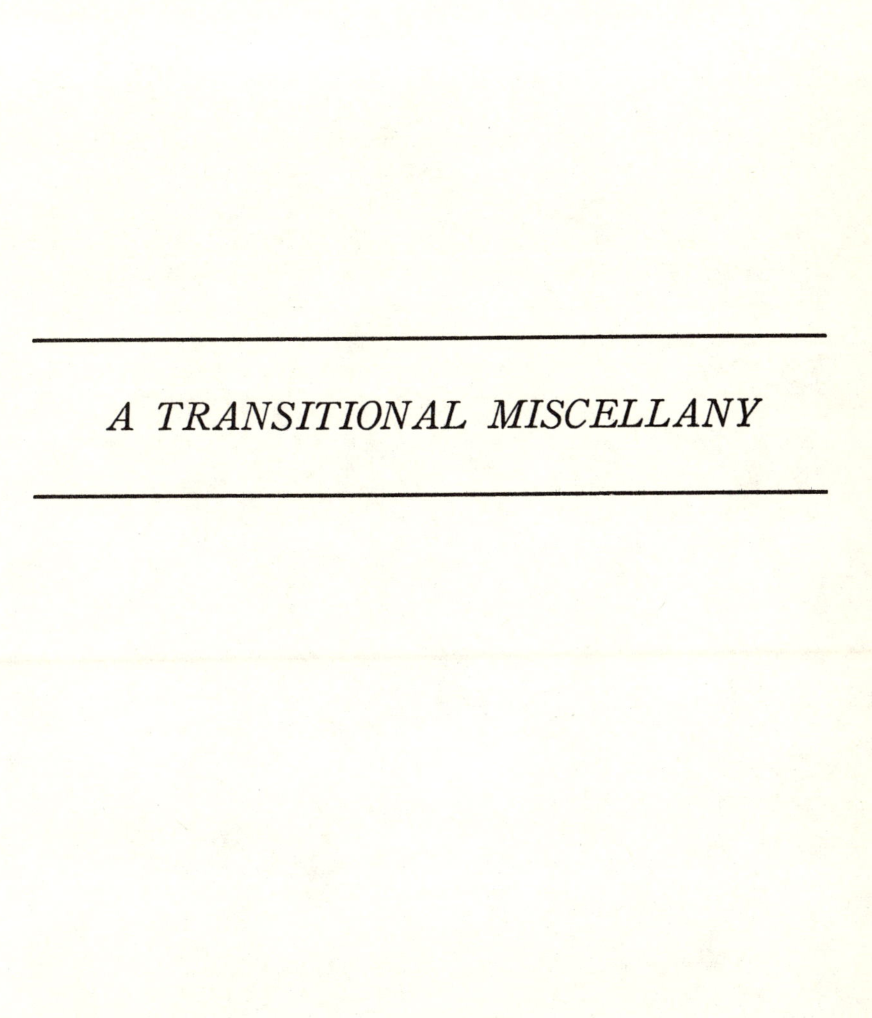

A TRANSITIONAL MISCELLANY

IX

A TRANSITIONAL MISCELLANY

Citizen of the World

IN the preceding chapter we have explored something of the spirit animating and underlying the age of romanticism. Here we shall turn to some of its outer manifestations—what its legislators were doing, and the turmoil of the political scene, what people were reading and talking about, the artists and philosophers and scandals they knew, and how the hum of change was swelling to a roar. In all possible ways people were telling ever more copiously what they thought of things. We shall select a few varied examples out of this flood: some reminiscences, a memoirist and an autobiographer, a couple of journals, and several writers of letters. Taking them all, we may derive a feeling both of their personalities and of the activities of the age.

The long life of Henry Crabb Robinson includes and stretches far beyond the days of Shelley's revolutionary hope and Byron's despair. When he was born in 1775, Johnson was in the warm sunset of his age and the full splendor of his prestige; Sir Joshua

Reynolds was painting in the Grand Style, Gibbon perfecting his irony. When he was a boy Burke flashed the angry sword of his eloquence in the impeachment of Warren Hastings, and the Estates General were being convened in France. In his young manhood he heard Wesley preach, a reverend old man with 'long white locks' and a 'feeble voice,' the excesses of enthusiasm that had revolted Walpole long since bathed in admiration and love.

Enthusiasm was indeed the order of the day. Robinson himself flamingly defended the anarchistic doctrines of William Godwin. During the repressive anti-Jacobin administration of William Pitt he visited Wakefield and his publisher in the prison to which they had been condemned for sedition. Leigh Hunt was jailed for libeling the Prince Regent as 'a violator of his word, a libertine over head and ears in disgrace, a despiser of domestic ties, the companion of gamblers and demireps;' and Robinson had heard Hunt say 'pleasantly enough, "No one can accuse me of not writing a libel. Everything is a libel, as the law is now declared, and our security lies only in their shame." '

Robinson was forty when the Battle of Waterloo was fought (and on the field only a few weeks later). He was a friend of Lamb, Wordsworth, and Coleridge. He lived through the agitations of the Reform Bill of 1832 and the European disorders of 1848. He followed with deep concern the progress of the American Civil War —he had always been a fervent abolitionist—and he felt bitterly the 'spirit engendered by slavery' that flamed in the assassination of Lincoln, 'the noblest person in America.' In the last half year of his old age he read of the Battle of Sadowa, which broke the power of Austria and enabled Bismarck to make Prussia dominant in Germany.

These ninety-two years, extending from his birth to within a few days of his death in 1867, are vigorously recorded in a tremendous mass of varied documents. There are brief journals covering his life through 1810, there are thirty-five manuscript volumes of his *Diary*, about thirty volumes of travel journals at home and abroad, reminiscences reaching to the year 1844, and large numbers of letters and miscellaneous papers. The bulk of material reveals the enormous vitality that is in Robinson an outstanding trait. After visiting friends in the country, for example, he decides to walk home, and when he reaches his chambers is surprised to note that he feels 'rather fatigued, though my walk was not a long one—only eighteen or twenty miles.' Wordsworth in later years called him 'a healthy creature who talked of coming again in seven years as others would of seven days'; and in his seventieth year his friends found him 'as much a boy as ever.'

His flow of high spirits was no less marked. He keenly appreciated pronounced character in others, he loved being with people, he was a tremendous talker. At one of Samuel Rogers's breakfast parties the host said, 'Oh, if there is any one here who wishes to say anything, he had better say it at once, for Crabb Robinson is coming.' And so little was he aware of his own vibrant energy that when his doctor told him once that he had been using his brain too much, he exclaimed, 'That is absurd!'

He thought of himself as an idle man. It was true, indeed, that he did not expend his powers in the ways that usually make for spectacular achievement. He was the third son of a moderately well-off family of Dissenters who destined him to the Bar. But his real interests were literature and philosophy, and in London he speedily fell in with a circle of literary men who included Godwin, Holcroft, and William Hazlitt. He did not have great literary abilities, however, and soon realized the fact. Vacillating about his career, he put off the hour of decision by going to Jena as a student, and remained in Germany for five years.

Goethe was then 'the idol of the German literary public,' Robinson wrote his brother. Readers declared that the sacred fire had burned to perfection only in the art of Homer, Cervantes, Shakespeare, and Goethe; some asserted that 'the three great "tendencies" of the late century' were 'the French Revolution, the Fichtian philosophy, and "Wilhelm Meister's Lehrjahre."' Robinson studied Kant and Goethe, and gave Madame de Staël the introduction to German philosophy that she later used in her *L'Allemagne*. But he was unable 'to make her feel the transcendent excellence of Goethe,' and an irreverence of which she was guilty provoked him to 'a very rude observation': 'Madame, vous n'avez pas compri Goethe, et vous ne le comprendrez jamais.' The lady's eyes flashed, 'she stretched out her fine arm, of which she was justly vain,' and exclaimed, 'Monsieur, je comprends tout ce qui mérite d'etre compris; ce que je ne comprends n'est rien.' (Robinson, indeed, is rather severe on the blue-stocking daughter of Suzanne Curchod; years later he enters in his *Diary* an anecdote of her pressing Talleyrand for an opinion of her *Delphine*, in which she was supposed to have portrayed him in the character of a woman. 'That is the work, is it not,' Robinson reports Talleyrand's response, 'in which you and I are exhibited in the disguise of females?')

Returned to London in 1805, Robinson became for a while Foreign Editor of *The Times*, and was a correspondent in Spain during part of the Peninsular Campaign. But he still hesitated to adopt a career until his sister-in-law spoke sharply to him. He reports it in his *Reminiscences*: 'For a man who has the repute of having sense, you act very like a fool. You decline reporting because that might be an obstacle to your being called to the Bar, and yet you make no steps towards being called to the Bar. Now, do one or the other. Either take to newspaper employment, or study the Law at once, and lose no more time.' When he was thirty-eight, he finally began to go on circuit. But at fifty-three, having put by enough to satisfy his moderate needs (a net income of £500 per annum), he told his friends that he had made up his mind to discontinue his practice in the absence of 'other inducements than those of mere money-making.'

He dined and talked with everybody, he traveled everywhere, and noted many of the main currents of the times. He deepened an affectionate friendship with Charles Lamb. After the death of Southey, with whom he had also been friendly, he saw his revered friend Wordsworth become Poet Laureate, and set off from Rogers's for the Queen's Ball 'with sword, bag-wig, and Court-dress.' The years went on; by now in his seventieth year, Robinson was beginning to 'consider old age commencing.' But he was still active in University College, of which he was one of the founders and a trustee. He helped establish resident scholarships as memorials of the Dissenters' Chapels Bill; he made nearly all the arrangements for having the collected works of the artist Flaxman preserved in a gallery at the College. The only sign of age was an absent-mindedness that distressed him: he would go off with a friend's hat instead of his own, and paying a call on his way to return it, blunder again by making another unconscious exchange.

He dined out and read as much as ever. Carlyle's *French Revolution* he liked as 'rhapsodies—not a history,' although 'Some one said, a history in flashes of lightning.' He enjoyed *Henry Esmond* more than he had *Vanity Fair*, telling his brother in a letter that it did 'not exhibit in disproportion all the *parties honteuses* of our mixed nature.' He read it in the library of the Athenaeum all the day of the Duke of Wellington's funeral, only now and then leaving the fire to take 'a peep from the drawing-room window' and see 'the noble troops, and the mourning coaches, and the banners.' The following spring, on his way to hear a lecture at University College, his *Diary* records, he was knocked down by a cab-horse and stunned, 'but in a few minutes recovered,' and, all muddy, proceeded to the lecture.

His friends were dying around him. Wordsworth's widow died in 1859, and Robinson sadly reflected that he would probably never see Rydal Mount again. Everywhere doors were closing. He made his last continental tour in 1863, spending his time chiefly at Heidelberg, and giving up the idea of visiting Frankfort. He seldom cared to read *The Times* now; many hours were spent in sifting over old letters. In 1866 he resigned as Vice-President of the Senate of University College. At his last visit to the theatre he saw *King John*, but he could not distinguish the actors' faces from each other, though he was in the front row of the orchestra-stalls.

He was in his ninety-first year. On 31 January, 1867, he was commenting in his *Diary* on Arnold's *Essay on Criticism*, when he suddenly drew a dash and wrote, 'But I feel incapable to go on.' For several days he dozed through an almost painless illness, and talked cheerfully to friends. 'Then came the cloud of insensibility,' and on 5 February he passed out of the world.

There are ways in which Robinson's diaries and journals remind us of John Evelyn, but he is narrower in some of his interests and broader in others than Evelyn. Robinson has none of Evelyn's unquenchable curiosity about processes, manufacturing, industry, and craftsmanship. When he descended once into a mine at St Andreasberg he found it so 'fatiguing and particularly uninstructive and uninteresting' that he sympathized 'with the vulgar inscription of an English "My lord" in the album: "Descended this d—–d old hole." ' He seldom notices the developments of science, although he does record his sensations on first taking a railway journey, and was never weary of lauding the beneficent effect of chloroform, which was used in lancing a swelling on his back when he was sixty-nine. In his diaries and correspondence there is seldom much to parallel Evelyn's detailed accounts of architectural monuments and works of art.

But like Evelyn he is almost entirely external in his interests. Hardly at all introspective, he is engrossed by the world around him, political and social questions find in him an interested commentator. He did not have Evelyn's connections in government or diplomatic circles, but he is often able to throw a strong oblique light by salvaging a report or comment. He knew nearly all the outstanding writers and many of the artists of his day, and delighted in observing their personalities no less than in absorbing their ideas.

In this he goes far beyond Evelyn, whose *philosophic* curiosity was slighter and whose interest in people was almost limited to what they could tell him. Robinson, on the contrary, delights in individuality, and relishes all expressions of it. 'All his conversation,' he said of one acquaintance, 'is ostentatious egotism; and yet it is preferable to the dry talk about the weather, with which some men torment me.' He could accommodate himself to all kinds of men, and without any trace of sycophancy could often please those who began by disliking him. A horse-riding country squire who took a prejudice against him was quite won over when Robinson cited 'that *fine and wise saying*' of Lord Herbert of Cherbury: 'A fine man upon a fine horse is the noblest object on earth for God to look down upon.'

His interest in personality places among Robinson's more valuable entries his comments on the eminent men of whom he made friends. Blake, whom he hardly knew whether to call 'artist, genius, mystic, or madman,' his *Diary* describes with vividness and candor. 'He is now old (sixty-eight), pale, with a Socratic countenance, and an expression of great sweetness,' entirely matter-of-fact about his visions, saying simply, 'The Spirit told me.' Blake's wife put in a word of reminder: 'You know, dear, the first time you saw God was when you were four years old, and he put his head in the window, and set you a-screaming.' Everyone, Blake told him, was immortal, 'all co-existent with God, members of the Divine body.' Jesus was 'the only God. But then,' Blake added, 'and so am I, and so are you.' The greatest of evils was 'endeavoring to explain to the rational faculty what the reason cannot comprehend.' It led to Atheism, for 'Everything is Atheism which assumes the reality of the natural and unspiritual world.' Blake concluded one conversation by observing, 'I know what is true by internal conviction. A doctrine is told me. My heart says, "It must be true." ' In these few sayings of Blake's, Robinson gives us the heart and essence of romanticism.

At his first meeting with Goethe, the poet 'rose, and with rather a cool and distant air beckoned us to take seats.' Then about fifty-two, and beginning to be corpulent, Goethe was still 'one of the most oppressively handsome men I ever saw,' and his hauteur chilled Robinson so greatly that he made no further effort to see his idol. But in 1804, at the theatre, Benjamin Constant introduced him again, and Goethe 'with a smile as ingratiating as his ordinary expression was cold and forbidding, said, "Wissen Sie, Herr Robinson, dass Sie mich beleidigt haben?"—"How is that possible, Herr Geheimrath?"—"Why, you have visited every one at Weimar excepting me." ' Robinson begged him to imagine any cause except 'want of reverence,' and two days later was invited to dinner. In later years he visited Goethe as a friend, and in 1828 Goethe sent him two pairs of medals in token of esteem.

The glorious, rainbow-hued, and mist-spun eloquence of Coleridge also enchanted Robinson. Early, however, he realized and pitied the poet's unhappy weakness for wandering from the point and losing himself in the abstract empyrean. In one of his lectures Coleridge ran on from one irrelevancy to another, and Lamb whispered to Robinson, 'This is not much amiss. He promised a lecture on the Nurse in *Romeo and Juliet*, and in its place he has given us one in the *manner* of the Nurse.' And, brilliant as Coleridge's gifts of theorizing were, Robinson noted that in argument he could 'be easily unsaddled'; 'one may obtain from him concessions which lead to gross inconsistencies.' In truth, Coleridge had 'neither the readiness nor the acuteness required by a colloquial disputant.'

Sometimes, however, he had a power of happy retort. At his Bristol lectures a man sneered at him 'for professing public principle,' asking why, then, he took money at the door. 'For a reason,' replied Coleridge, 'which I am sorry in the present instance has not been quite successful—to keep out blackguards.'

But his inability to give direction to his life ruined him. Lecturing on *Hamlet*, he said, 'Action is the great end of all; no intellect, however grand, is valuable, if it draw us from action and lead us to think and think till the time of action is passed by . . .'

Robinson wrote to his friend Mrs Clarkson, 'Somebody said to me, "This is a satire on himself."—"No," said I, "it is an elegy."' The weak and grand spirit sank more and more, growing dependent on the kindness of friends whose patience he often outwore. He said to Robinson, 'I fell asleep, and fancied I was surrounded by my friends, who made me marvellous fine promises. I awoke and found these promises as much a dream as if they had actually been made.' In his retired old age, guarded by Mr Gilman at Highgate, Robinson visited him and thought he had never heard him so eloquent, though it was painful on reflection to find that few of the gleaming phrases seemed really memorable. But when he died Robinson lamented 'the dear, good, Coleridge.'

Robinson's cosmopolitanism is unusual in an age when foreign disorders were keeping most English gentlemen at home. Haydon, in his *Autobiography*, notes that the French looked on him in 1814 as if he 'had dropped out of the moon, and we upon them as if we were dropping into it . . . We had thought of France from youth as forbidden ground, as the abode of the enemies of our country.' He had been 'born, nursed, and grew up hating and to hate the name of Frenchmen.' Robinson's freedom from this insularity makes him a valuable witness to historic events. At Hochheim, on a walking tour, he cautiously admitted to three officers of the invading French army that he was an Englishman, and they laughingly refrained from arresting him. But he talked freely about Bonaparte and endeared himself to the Germans. One gentleman begged him to ride in his carriage, for 'It will do my heart good,' he said, 'to talk with an Englishman about that vile people and their vile Emperor, who have thrust my nation into such misery.'

After the battle of Waterloo Robinson feared that even that victory would 'not so affect the French people as to occasion a material defalcation from Bonaparte'; but it was followed so promptly by the taking of Paris that less than two months later he was on the celebrated field. 'There were arms of trees hanging down, shattered by cannon balls, and not yet cut off. And there were ruined and burnt cottages in many places, and marks of bullets and balls on both houses and trees; but I saw nothing in particular to impress me, except that in an inn near the field I had a glimpse of a lady in weeds, who was come on a vain search after the body of her husband, slain there.' It might almost have been Amelia Sedley, desolated for her faithless George.

At home in England, the Tory government had long been running things with a high hand that disgusted reflective people. In 1808, Robinson remembered, 'Southey said that he and Coleridge were directly opposed in politics. He himself thought the last administration (Whig) so impotent that he could conceive of none worse except the present; while Coleridge maintained the present Ministry to be so corrupt that he thought it impossible there could be a worse except the late.' Publishers were fined and imprisoned for printing liberal or deistic works. Robinson saw the publisher of Paine's *Age of Reason* in the pillory and heard the sympathetic exclamations of the people: 'Pillory a man for publishing a book! Shame!' 'Religious liberty!' 'Liberty of conscience!'

With the course of years, to be sure, Robinson had ceased to be a disciple of Godwin. But, unlike Southey and Wordsworth, who grew more and more intolerantly conservative, he remained, although sometimes a little dubiously, a liberal. At the time of the Reform Bill he wrote in a letter, 'I was always a moderate Reformer; and, now that success seems at hand, I think more of the dangers than the promises.' But when he went among the anti-Reformers and heard 'the worse cant and more odious impostures of the old Tory party,' he was '*righted*,' and joined the crowd again.

He disapproved of the 'dangerous speculations of Fourier,' and regarded the Saint-Simonian movement as 'very national, very idle, very ridiculous, possibly well-intentioned on the part of its leaders, whose greatest fault may be unconscious vanity.' He judged it 'destined to be very short-lived, unless it can acquire a political character.' Intolerant rigidity of opinion he disliked, and quoted with approval Douglas Jerrold's reply to the query, What is dogmatism?—'Puppyism full grown.' But he thought vehement radical opinion not unbecoming in a young man, and to one such in 1848 he said, 'I like you better for not thinking as I do now.'

The revolutionary flames of 1848 disquieted him, as they did many others who were not unsympathetic to reform and change. It seemed to them, with the *Annual Register*, that 'the foundations of the great deep of political society have been suddenly and violently broken up.' Matthew Arnold had dark fears: 'The spectacle of France is likely to breed great agitation here, and such is the state of our masses that their movements can now only be brutal, blundering, and destroying.' In London, the American Ambassador wrote, 'the aristocracy are overwhelmed with gloom.' Robinson feared the outbreak of European conflict; the acts of the French Provisional government read 'like a continuation of the proceedings of the National Convention, as if fifty years were annihilated.' He only hoped the Ministry would 'be prudent enough to keep aloof.' Carlyle's voice was almost alone in seeking to make people understand the radical 'organization of labour.'

But Robinson had not read the signs of the times as clearly as Carlyle, although, like the author of *Heroes and Hero-Worship*, he feared mob passions in government. He felt that the problem of his age was to put shackles on the hasty decisions of the people and at the same time enable them to hinder every attempt at tyranny or exploitation. But he was well in advance of most opinion in his day by insisting that the reason the populace were not to be trusted was that they had not been regarded by their governors: 'The *real* criminals are the legislators and magistrates, who have made no provision for the masses.'

This, also, and not natural depravity, he insisted, is the cause of vice and violations of the law. 'What is the measure of the guilt of a poor child bred in a night-cellar . . . with thieves and prostitutes?' Such a child, 'being sent out by his parents to beg or steal, is flogged if he comes home at night without anything, and rewarded by their praises, or perhaps a dram or other luxury, when he brings home plunder. He has never heard property spoken of but as something which gentlemen have got, and which he ought to get from them if he can. Of law and magistrates, and right and wrong, he knows nothing but what he has heard from thieves and prostitutes. It is sheer cant and nonsense to say that his natural conscience should have taught him better . . . the guilt is to be imputed to the mass of society, which has not given him an education.'

If Robinson was not in the vanguard in all the movements of his day, he was vividly aware of nearly all except those of science, well abreast of a good many, and in the rear of general opinion in none. His lively and vigorous mind runs over innumerable topics, from gossip to politics, from literature to philosophy. Although neither subtle nor profound, his intelligence nevertheless has a strength and sanity that make his observations occasionally more penetrating than those of deeper minds. No diaries or letters of his time cover a broader expanse of awareness or give us a livelier sense of its thronging vitality.

Elia in Laughter and Flight

In comparison with the multitudinous general interests of Robinson, the bookish enthusiasms of his friend Charles Lamb seem to be musings from a retired backwater indeed. Although more than half his life was passed in the employment of the East India Company, neither his essays nor his letters show any stirring of interest in its far-flung empire; and although the corruption of its Indian administration was often under attack, Lamb's connection with the gigantic corporation is commemorated only in a few pages of quaint reminiscence about India House and his fellow clerks. Lamb's *Letters* reveal hardly any more curiosity about public affairs than might be felt by the Arabian Astrologer in his underground palace.

But there was no enchanted princess to lull Lamb's reveries with melody, for although he had offered his heart to Frances Kelly, the actress, she had rejected him; and indeed there were reasons sad enough for hesitating to marry Lamb even had there not been the 'early and deeply rooted attachment' she pleaded. The hollow unfilled by the princess had to be taken by friends and humorous nonsense, by devotion to his dear and afflicted sister Mary, and by appreciative communings with old authors: Burton, and Sir Thomas Browne, and the more obscure Elizabethan dramatists. And in the fantastic absurdities and exaggerations of his letters, in their desperately feeble puns (for Lamb propounded the theory that the worst puns were the best ones), and even more in the growing and jestingly defended inebriation of his later years, a sensitive reader may often feel a sort of flight from the dark central despair around which his life was built.

The nature of that distress is well known. In a letter to Coleridge written when he was twenty-one, Lamb announced 'the terrible calamities' that had fallen on them: 'My poor dear, dearest sister, in a fit of insanity, has been the death of her own mother. I was at hand only time enough to snatch the knife out of her grasp. She is at present in a madhouse, from whence I fear she must be moved to a hospital. God has preserved to me my senses: I eat, and drink, and sleep, and have my judgment, I believe, very sound.'

'Some have hinted, one man has pressed it on me,' he wrote two months later, 'that she should be in perpetual confinement: what she hath done to deserve, or the necessity of such an hardship, I see not; do you?' Though his heart ached when he remembered 'the little asperities of temper' with which he had sometimes given his mother pain, he would not allow his sister to be shut away from his tenderness and care; he had determined that he was 'wedded to the fortunes of my sister, and my poor old father.'

His situation was not easy. His father was much shaken, and sometimes when Lamb felt ill able to bear it, in order not to be teased he would have to play cards with the old man all day long. Their Aunt Hetty had been taken off his hands by an 'old hag of a wealthy relation' who presently summoned him to fetch her home again because she was 'indolent and mulish'; and, straitened as they were, Lamb felt obliged 'to transplant the poor old creature from the chilling air of such patronage.' Mary's insanity recurred at intervals, and when its signs made their appearance, the two, weeping, would set off together for the hospital.

And still he depended on her sane guidance so that in her absence 'I dare not think, lest I should think wrong; so used am I to look up to her in the least and biggest perplexity . . . She is older and wiser and better than I, and all my wretched imperfections I cover to myself by resolutely thinking on her goodness.' And then he would upbraid himself bitterly that, unable to bear all the strain, he had 'been wasting and teasing her life for five years past incessantly with my cursed drinking and ways of going on.'

But with such burdens it is hardly cause for wonder that sometimes he would get 'drunk for two days running,' and 'find my moral sense in the last stage of consumption, my religion burning blue and faint as the tops of burning bricks. Hell gapes and the Devil's great guts cry "cupboard" for me. In the midst of these infernal alarums, conscience (and be damned to her) barking and yelling as loud as any of them.'

Jests and old tomes were also sources of distraction. 'Wither is like an old friend, whose warm-heartedness and estimable qualities make us wish he possessed more genius, but at the same time make us willing to dispense with that want.' And *The Jew of Malta*, he wrote to Southey, was a very fine old play, with Barabbas saying

As for myself, I walk abroad a-nights,
And kill sick people groaning under walls.
Sometimes I go about, and poison wells . . .

'Now,' says Lamb, 'hear Ithamore, the other gentle nature.'

ITHAMORE
(A comical dog)

. . .

One time I was hostler at an inn,
And in the night time secretly would I steal
To traveller's chambers and there cut their throats.

. . .

To which Lamb was delighted to have Barabbas reply judiciously, 'Why, this is something.' And then there were the entire theological works of Thomas Aquinas recently picked up, 'of whom I have often heard and had dreams, but never saw in the flesh—that is in the sheepskin—' how he would 'revel in his cobwebs and subtleties, till my brain spins!' And how delightful was Burnet's *History of His Own Times*, 'Full of scandal, which all true history is,' and with 'None of the cursed philosophical Humeian indifference, so cold, and unnatural, and inhuman.'

Besides these, there were friends to be loved and gently laughed at. Even Wordsworth was not to be exempt: 'He says he does not see much difficulty in writing like Shakespeare, if he had a mind to try it. It is clear that nothing is wanting but the mind.' And there was dear, foolish, gentle George Dyer. Dyer's poetry, Crabb Robinson tells us, inspired 'an epigram that I fear I thought was just . . .'

The world all say, my gentle Dyer,
Thy odes do very much want fire.
Repair the fault, my gentle Dyer,
And throw thy odes into the fire.

Lamb was never tired of chuckling at George's absurdities. A learned acquaintance had 'set George's brains mad about old Scotch writers,' and returning home, 'George kept wondering and wondering, for eight or nine turnpike miles, what was the name, and striving to recollect the name, of a poet anterior to Barbour. I begged to know what was remaining of his works. "There is nothing *extant* of his works, Sir; but by all accounts he seems to have been a fine genius!" . . . Poor Dyer! his friends should be careful what sparks they let fall into such inflammable matter.'

A few days later, hearing mentioned Wilkie's *Epigoniad*, a tenth-rate epic copied from Homer, no sooner did 'the sound of *Homer* strike his pericranicks, than up he gets, and declares he must see that poem immediately . . . for he had touched pretty deeply upon that subject in his criticisms on the Epic'; and thereupon Lamb has a good deal of fun with the absurd phrase, touch pretty deeply. But when Dyer's *Poems* were published his 'phrenitis came to a head': there were eighty pages of preface, and he had just discovered 'that in the very first page of said Preface he had set out with a principle of Criticism fundamentally wrong . . . The Preface must be expunged, although it cost him £30 . . . In vain have his real friends remonstrated against this midsummer madness. George is as obstinate as a Primitive Christian, and wards and parries off all our thrusts with one unanswerable fence:—"Sir, 'tis of great consequence that the *world* is not *misled!*" '

Sometimes Lamb's letters are exercises in pure whimsy. He asks P. G. Patmore anxiously how Dash is. 'I should have asked if Mrs Patmore kept her rules, and was improving; but Dash came uppermost. The order of our thoughts should be the order of our writing . . . All the dogs here are going mad, if you believe the overseers; but I protest they seem to me very rational and collected. Try him with hot water: if he won't lick it up it is a sign he does not like it.' Then, after a good deal more nonsense, comes a scratched-out passage which, he explains, was 'a German quotation, from Lessing, on the bite of rabid animals; but I remember you don't read German. But Mrs P—— may, so I wish I had let it stand. The meaning in English is—"Avoid to approach an animal suspected of madness . . ." . . . The Germans are certainly profounder than we.' Or, again, to his friend Thomas Manning, who has gone to China, he writes, as if he had been away for scores of years, 'There's your friend Tuthill has got away from France; you remember France? and Tuthill?'

He cannot resist teasing Wordsworth by pretending to find no beauty in nature and exaggerating his love of London:

I have no passion (or have had none since I was in love, and then it

> was the spurious engendering of poetry and books) for groves and valleys. . . . Your sun, and moon, and skies, and hills, and lakes, affect me no more, or scarcely come to me in more venerable characters, than as a gilded room with tapestry and tapers, where I might live with handsome visible objects. [But, on the other hand,] The rooms where I was born, the furniture which has been before my eyes all my life, a book-case which has followed me about like a faithful dog, (only exceeding him in knowledge,) wherever I have moved, old chairs, old tables, streets, squares, where I have sunned myself, my old school,—these are my mistresses. . . . So fading upon me, from disuse, have been the beauties of Nature, as they have been confinedly called; so ever fresh, and green, and warm are all the inventions of men, and assemblies of men in this great city.

But although he quizzes he also cherishes his friends; and we find him pleading with one of them to attend Coleridge's new series of lectures: 'He is in bad health, and worse mind: and unless something is done to lighten his mind he will soon be reduced to his extremities; and even these are not in the best condition.' Twelve years later, writing to another friend, he exclaims, 'How you frighted me! Never write again, "Coleridge is dead," at the end of a line, and tamely come in with "to his friends" at the beginning of another. Love is quicker, and fear from love, than the transition ocular from line to line.'

The years were moving on, and death was not improbable. After 'thirty-three years' slavery,' he was retired on a pension of £450 a year. 'I came home FOR EVER on Tuesday in last week. The incomprehensibleness of my condition overwhelmed me. It was like passing from life into eternity . . . I wandered about thinking I was happy, but feeling I was not. But that tumultuousness is passing off . . . Mary wakes every morning with an obscure feeling that some good has happened to us.' Mary's illnesses, however, encroached more and more with time. 'I look back upon her earlier attacks with longing: nice little durations of six weeks or so, followed by complete restoration . . . ' Now, 'half her life she is dead to me, and the other half is made anxious with fears and lookings forward to the next shock.'

The alleviations of many years had still to serve. People might say

> that it is not a seemly sight for an old gentleman to go home a pick-a-back. Well, maybe it is not. But I have never studied grace. I take it to be a mere superficial accomplishment. I regard more the internal

> acquisitions. The great object after supper is to get home, and whether that is obtained in a horizontal posture, or perpendicular (as foolish men and apes affect for dignity) I think is little to the purpose. . . . I have just sense enough to remember I was very happy last night, and to thank our kind host and hostess, and that's Sense enough, I hope.

The world was going painfully with him, but he still had Mary after all. 'When she is not violent, her rambling chat is better to me than the sense and sanity of this world. Her heart is obscured, not buried; it breaks out occasionally; and one can discern a strong mind struggling with the billows that have gone over it.' His own struggle had very little longer to last.

Despite the pathos of some of these letters, and the even deeper pathos ever behind them, despite Lamb's glancing humor and absurdities, his charm, his tenderness and bravery, although we may pity and admire, we do not feel in the end that Lamb's are among the best of all letters. And Lamb himself, lovable and gentle and brave as he was, still was not brave in meeting his dreadful problems as Keats was in meeting his. Lamb had in his younger days, to be sure, spent six weeks in a madhouse himself, and the possibility of a recurrence of that insanity always hung over him. But Cowper had also been insane, and was to be so again, yet his saner days show a kind of struggle to transcend his personal life that Lamb does not reveal. Cowper took a living interest in the world around him, he was pained by slavery and man's inhumanity to man, his heart was roused by liberty and justice. Keats dissolved his own pain and frustration in the whole beauty of the world. But Lamb was ever haunted by his own disaster, and in his letters, if he often looks it in the face, he even more often flees from it to the refuge of ancient volumes and their archaic eloquence or to coverts of whim and nonsense and grotesquerie. We may follow him, perhaps, and forget the tears almost entirely in the delicious mirth. And still, deeply as we sympathize with that seeking for oblivion, his letters give us a sense of something evaded rather than overcome.

'The Mad Painter Haydon'

Among the several appearances Lamb makes in the *Autobiography* of Benjamin Robert Haydon, none is more characteristic than one at a party for Wordsworth on 28 December, 1817. Haydon had allowed a stranger to come who told him 'he was a comptroller of stamps, and had often had correspondence with the poet.' Immediately after the introductions, the gentleman solemnly asked Wordsworth, 'Don't you think, sir, Milton was a great genius?' Uncertain that he had heard this absurd question aright, Lamb enquired, 'Pray, sir, did you say Milton was a great genius?' 'No, sir, I asked Mr Wordsworth if he were not.' 'Oh,' said Lamb, 'then you are a silly fellow.' 'Charles! my dear Charles!' protested Wordsworth, and there was an embarrassed confusion.

'After an awful pause' the comptroller tried again: 'Don't you think Newton a great genius?' This was too much for them all; several stifled their mirth; Lamb took a candle and said, 'Sir, will you allow me to look at your phrenological development?' and then turning his back began to sing

Diddle diddle dumpling, my son John
Went to bed with his breeches on,

presently returning to exclaim, 'Do let me have another look at that gentleman's organs.' He was hurried into the next room by Haydon and Keats, who immediately gave way to a hysteria of laughter. Haydon returned to soothe the wounded dignity of his guest, but all the while they 'could hear Lamb struggling in the painting-room,' and shouting 'Who is that fellow? Allow me to see his organs once more.'

The boisterous episode is full of the flavor of Haydon's story as well: a life of furious energy, courageous shouts, panting struggle, and roars of conflict. If Crabb Robinson is energetic, Haydon is nothing less than galvanic; blue sparks seem to flash sizzling out of whatever he touches, and his world is a dizzy maelstrom of violent activity. And not only is everything about him violent, everything about him is huge. He paints enormous canvases, his moments of revelation are tremendous, his triumphs magnificent, his downfalls cataclysmic. There were, alas, few enough triumphs. In an age of indifference to fine art, Haydon was enthralled by the ideal that England should regard art as a glorious necessity. The artist, Haydon said proudly, should be at the command of his genius, not of patronage; and he exhausted himself crusading for these ends.

Unhappily he was little fitted to realize them in his own person.

Sincere as was his devotion to art, 'his fierce passion for fame' seemed to ordinary eyes more like enthusiasm for his own employment. And, for all his fury, his paintings are too often monotonous expanses where gigantic historical figures are displayed on canvases too large for any walls. He was interested only in historical painting, and always he had these monumental delusions of grandeur; his cry, as Edmund Blunden says, was, 'Here is grand art, and if you argue, here is another square mile; yield!' Nor was he able to see in his defeats anything but cant, prejudice, meanness, and lack of imagination. He lived in a world of vindictive rivals, ignorant connoisseurs, venomous academicians, and blind vulgarians. He defied the Academy, insulted the connoisseurs, upbraided the government, struggled with his creditors, saw his debts grow staggering and his children die and his hopes melt away, as he drew nearer and nearer the abyss.

But there were others who believed in him in his day, as he believed in himself. Leigh Hunt had called him a 'painter indeed,' fit to be numbered in succession to Michelangelo and Raphael; John Hamilton Reynolds had hailed him in a sonnet as 'born to Immortality!' Keats and Wordsworth had written sonnets in his praise, and Elizabeth Barrett hymned his portrait of Wordsworth upon Helvellyn:

> *A noble vision free*
> *Our Haydon's hand has flung out from the mist!*
> *No portrait this, with Academic air!*
> *This is the poet and his poetry.*

The celebrated painter Fuseli praised his youthful efforts. Lord Mulgrave offered to buy his first picture. Even Sir George Beaumont, the friend of Garrick and Sir Joshua Reynolds, seemed disposed in his favor. But the lack of tact that Haydon was often to display in the future soon made its appearance in a way that nettled Sir George even though it did not entirely alienate him. 'Like all men of fashion,' Haydon tells us, Sir George 'had a way of saying pleasant things without the least meaning,' and was always full of invitations to visit him at Coleorton. Finally Lord Mulgrave shamed him into making the invitation real. When Haydon arrived, and was walking in the garden with him, Sir George hoped he would be able to stay a fortnight. ' "Oh" said I, perceiving the motive, "a month if you wish it, Sir George!" '

Later still, Sir George having retreated a little unscrupulously from an agreement about a painting Haydon was to do for him, Haydon showed acquaintances the letters that demonstrated how ill-treated he was. Presently he was invited to one of the Beaumonts' brilliant dinners; the host talked about Pope, and his letters, and letter-writing, and then:

> "It is very strange," said Sir George, "but I have a great aversion to people showing letters; nothing, you know, is so indelicate." "Certainly," I replied, "but there are cases, you know, Sir George, which oblige a man to show letters in his own defense." "Certainly," said the company, without knowing one *iota* of the dispute. Wilkie grew paler than ever, paler than death. I chuckled, and passed the claret. . . . Lady Beaumont began to stammer, a way she had when she wished to be peculiarly interesting. . . . [In the drawing-room, Lady Beaumont] rallied me on the propriety of docility in early life. "Yes," I replied; "but is there not a docility amounting to servility?"

Such a man was little likely to commend himself to the snobbery that Ruskin was to castigate as one of the destroyers of British art. The directors of the Academy withdrew their offers of three prizes for historical paintings in order to devote the money to buying 'a large feebly painted picture of Christ healing the Blind' that had not even been submitted to them, and offered Haydon 'thirty guineas!—that I might not be out of pocket for my frame which cost me sixty.' In a fury he 'tore up their note.'

He was unable to pay his landlord, he was unable to buy his dinner. It seemed to him that the servants at the house where he ate on credit were inattentive; 'I thought the meat was worse. My heart sank as I said falteringly, "I will pay you tomorrow" '; and, 'escaping with a sort of lurking horror,' he was appalled to be told that the master wished to see him. But the good man, his forehead perspiring from embarrassment, wanted to offer credit till the ill-used artist could afford to pay. Haydon sent for his landlord and offered to vacate, explaining that if he stayed he would be unable to pay until he had finished his next picture. How long would that be? Two years. ' "What, two years more, and no rent?" "Not a shilling." ' The landlord rubbed his chin and muttered, and then gave Haydon his hand on two years more, saying, ' "Then, sir, we'll consider what is to be done; so don't fret, but work." '

He did work, with violence, as he did everything. Looking 'fearlessly at my unblemished canvas in a species of spasmodic fury,' he would 'fly' at it and 'dash down the first touch.' He 'seizes' his maulstick, paints 'like a tiger' or as if 'with air-balloons tied under my armpits,' becomes so absorbed that he does not take in the meaning of a letter telling of the death of his father, and clenches his teeth so tightly in his abstraction 'that my gums became painfully sore.' His mind dealing with a new painting is like 'a steam-boiler without valve, boiling, struggling, and suppressing'; and when the idea is born 'All of a sudden a great flash comes inside your head, as if a powder-magazine had exploded without any noise. Then come ideas by millions–'

So he goes on. He attacks Knight, the celebrated authority 'on taste,' for denying the originality of the Elgin marbles and attributing them to journeymen, and covers him with derision: 'In no other profession is the opinion of a man who has studied it for his amusement preferred to that of him who has devoted his soul to excel in it. No man will trust his limb to a connoisseur in surgery;– no minister would ask a connoisseur in war how a campaign is to be conducted . . . I most sincerely trust that this fatal proof of Mr Payne Knight's complete want of judgment in refined Art' will impress people 'with this truth, that by listening to the authoritative dictates of such men, they risk sharing the disgrace of their exposure.'

The Academy was hardly better, being merely a trade-union of portrait-painters, having little to do with Art. 'Wherever the British settle, wherever they colonize, they carry . . . trial by jury, horse-racing, and portrait-painting.' Intrigue was all that could be expected of such gangsters of art. No matter how noble the cause, 'If you ask their assistance they thwart the best plans by diplomacy; if you leave them out they destroy the best prospects by malignity.' No wonder, after such exposures, the academicians 'slunk by, pale and contemptible'!

Despite their jealousy, Haydon managed to make a success of his large painting *Christ's Entry into Jerusalem* by exhibiting it himself. He cleared a profit of almost £1300 in London and about £900 in Scotland, and refused £1000 for the canvas. Debts were paid and a new canvas of *Christ raising Lazarus* immediately started. 'My room was thirty feet long, twenty wide, fifteen high. So I ordered a canvas nineteen long by fifteen high, and dashed in my conception, the Christ being nine feet high.' The triumphs were few, however, and the years were rolling on. The Elgin Marbles had been purchased for the nation, and the new Houses of Parliament were, at last, to be decorated with historical paintings. But his cartoons were rejected; 'He was seen in a coffee-house weeping most bitterly.'

He had almost accepted defeat. He developed a 'line' of Napoleon musing, and in March, 1844, he records, 'I have painted nineteen Napoleons.' By December he could add, 'Began and finished a Napoleon in two hours and a half; the quickest I ever did, and the twenty-fifth.' Charitable assistance was well-nigh exhausted, and in 1846 the public went to see Tom Thumb in the Egyptian Hall instead of his paintings of *The Banishment of Aristides* and *Nero Playing his Lyre whilst Rome is Burning*. Through the heat of that June he could hardly paint any longer. At noon on the 22nd his daughter found him in his painting-room, 'his white hairs dabbled in blood, a half-open razor smeared with blood, at his side, near it, a small pistol recently discharged, in his throat a frightful gash, and a bullet wound in his skull.' His family would be happier, he had written, 'released from the burden of my ambition.'

The *Autobiography* reaches no further than 1820, but his *Journals* trace this long tragedy almost to its desperate end. Although few people today would rate his artistic achievements highly, his failures grew even more out of deficiencies of character than out of inferiority of talent. But the first half of the nineteenth century in England was an ill time for painters; even the genius of Turner was misunderstood in his wild and apocalyptic later style until he was championed by Ruskin. We need not tarry on those faults Haydon did have—to judge them severely 'is as unnecessary as it would be towards the sea-bird dashing at the lighthouse lamp.'

If all that wild energy resulted in his personal achievement being nothing more than those miles of gigantic Romans and Greeks, those figures from sacred history, and those pictorializations of scenes from Shakespeare's tragedies, there were larger orbits in which his influence was felt. His eloquent panegyric shamed the British nation into acquiring the Elgin marbles. His vigorous polemic undermined the claims of pretentious authority. And his tumultuous spirit had one triumph that it never knew. If he was a failure in art, there was a sister-art in which his portraits are brilliant and dramatic, his historical figures full of the fire of life, his whole world breathing with the violent vitality that is his. That art he exhibited in his *Autobiography* and his *Journals.*

The Governing Classes

The government that Haydon bombarded with demands for recognition of the national duty toward High Art was agitated by struggles that made it largely indifferent to those claims. Castlereagh was repressing the radicals, and then the Duke of Wellington and Sir Robert Peel were resisting the encroachments of financiers and manufacturers on the landowning aristocracy; later still Lord Grey was adjusting the exact needful measure of middle-class reform. During the Regency and until the stately pomposities of Victorian liberalism under Russell and Gladstone, the fashionable and political worlds were in turmoil, with Romanism and rebellion, government corruption, and luxurious debauchery among the royal family dividing attention among them. Although George IV gave Haydon five hundred guineas for his *Mock Election* in 1828, neither royalty nor aristocracy were interested in the welfare of the arts; they were far too immersed in the squabbles of the Royal Dukes, their insulting behavior to all the nobility, and the scandals of their marital and extra-marital lives.

This intermingling of petty tittle-tattle and open shame in high places with intrigue and the gravest problems of government is nowhere more brilliantly revealed than in two of the political and social memoirs of the times. *The Creevey Papers* consist largely of letters to and from Mr Creevey, although they are supplemented here and there by journals and sometimes commented on in reminiscence. *The Greville Memoirs* are almost pure journal, at times summarizing the events of a considerable interval and infrequently dotted with later comment. Greville abounds in anecdote and scandal, but he is always dignified, sometimes even pompous; Creevey is delighted *chronique scandaleuse* in lively undress. There are no great names for him: George IV is always Prinney; the Duke of Wellington, the Beau; the Earl of Durham, King Jog (because he had once said a man 'could jog along on £40,000 a year'); Lady

Holland, Old Madagascar; Lord Brougham sometimes Beelzebub or the Arch-fiend, sometimes merely Bruffam.

Of Creevey's origins we know little. Penniless, but a gay and entertaining talker, he was put into Parliament by a Duke, and spent his life traveling from the hospitality of one Whig mansion to another. Although a Whig reformer, and incensed with the villainy of the Tories, Creevey's life was a career of privilege: he began in Parliament as representative of a pocket-borough, and after a lifetime in opposition the triumph of his party enabled him to wind up as the holder of a sinecure. He was an intimate of the Prince of Wales and Mrs Fitzherbert before the Regency, when the Prince wined and gambled with Sheridan and Fox. He was among the gay crowd at the Pavilion; he gnashed his teeth at the perfidy and 'infinite meanness' of Canning and the 'intellectual confusion and mental dirt' of Huskisson; and he lived to see 'little Vic,' now Queen of England, gobbling her food, laughing, and 'showing not very pretty gums' at Brighton.

Charles Cavendish Fulke Greville, Clerk of the Council under George IV and William IV, is a more solemn figure than Mr Creevey, and from the nature of his permanent office less of a partisan than Creevey. Related to any number of noble families, he first obtained a sinecure through the influence of his grandfather, the Duke of Portland, and then became Clerk of the Council in 1821, discharging the duties of that office for nearly forty years. In Creevey's pert and impish vocabulary, Greville was 'Punch,' but the grave pictures of high circles in *The Greville Memoirs* reinforce Creevey's disrespectful familiarities.

The characters of the royal family were indeed disgraceful. 'By God! you never saw such a figure in your life,' the Duke of Wellington said of the Regent, who was by now a fat and corseted old rake. 'Then he speaks and swears so like old Falstaff, that damn me if I was not ashamed to walk into a room with him.' The Prince arrived at Lady Salisbury's 'from his own dinner beastly drunk,' and if he went abroad unprotected 'nothing can equal the execrations of the people who recognize him.' Of the proceedings against Queen Caroline Creevey writes that the title of the Bill ought to be changed to 'A Bill to declare the Queen a whore, and to settle her upon the King for life, because from his own conduct he is not entitled to a divorce.' And the Princes, Wellington told Creevey, had 'insulted—

personally insulted – two-thirds of the gentlemen of England.'

Greville adds his testimony. The Duke of York 'is the only one of the princes who has the feelings of an English gentleman.' As for George IV, he was a 'contemptible, cowardly, selfish, unfeeling dog,' who was 'degraded as low as he could be already.' At Drury Lane, though he was acclaimed, some shouted 'the Queen'; 'A man in the gallery called out, "Where's your wife, Georgy?"' Going over his effects after his death, they found a 'prodigious quantity of hair–women's hair–of all colours and lengths, some locks with the powder and pomatum still sticking to them, heaps of women's gloves, *gages d'amour* which he had got at balls, and with the perspiration still marked on the fingers, notes and letters in abundance.'

William IV, the new King, was perhaps less scandalous, but assuredly more ridiculous. Suddenly elevated from 'obscurity and neglect, in miserable poverty, surrounded by a numerous progeny of bastards, without consideration or friends,' Greville says, now he could not stir 'without a mob, patrician as well as plebeian, at his heels'; at the late King's funeral 'they were all as merry as grigs.' Mr Creevey describes 'Billy 4th,' as he calls him, at the Opera: 'a more *Wapping* air I defy a king to have–his hair five times as full of *poudre* as mine, and his seaman's gold lace cock-and-pinch hat was charming. He slept most part of the Opera,' but the Princess Victoria, who was with him, 'looked like a very nice little girl indeed.'

Lady Grey described to Mr Creevey an evening at Windsor Castle around a mahogany table, 'the Queen knitting or netting a purse–the King sleeping, and occasionally waking for the purpose of saying:–"Exactly so, ma'am!" and then sleeping again.' But the King's ridiculous qualities asserted themselves more and more; 'If he was not such an ass that nobody does anything but laugh at what he says,' Greville remarks, his undiplomatic speeches on foreign affairs might have had very serious consequences. But then, 'What can you expect from a man with a head like a pineapple?'

Meanwhile there were the more important events of history. The excitements of Waterloo were over, but Mr Creevey had been on the spot. In Brussels, before the fight, the Duke had exclaimed to him confidently, 'By God! I think Blücher and myself can do the thing,' and pointing at a private, he added, 'it all depends on that article whether we do the business or not. Give me enough of it, and I am sure.' And we hear him immediately after the battle: 'It has been a damned serious business. Blücher and I have lost 30,000 men. It has been a damned nice thing—the nearest run thing you ever saw in your life.' Creevey asked if the French had fought better than he had ever seen them do before. 'No,' Wellington said, 'they have always fought the same since I first saw them at Vimeira.' Then after a pause, 'By God! I don't think it would have done if I had not been there.'

Creevey also had a front seat at the trial of Queen Caroline, whence he observed 'a few straggling ringlets' on the neck of 'this much-injured princess,' 'which I flatter myself from their appearances were not her Majesty's own property.' He was closely acquainted with Brougham, the Queen's Attorney-General, and followed the shifts and stratagems of 'Old Wickedshifts' with excited interest.

This strange figure, with his plaid trousers and his flexible nose, half charlatan, half encyclopaedia, was like a strong wind blowing over English politics for thirty years. While he was still an undergraduate his scientific papers were published by the Royal Society; at twenty-five he was one of the founders of the *Edinburgh Review;* as a radical Whig he fought the slave trade until its abolition, defended the Hunts in their trials for free speech, and campaigned violently for the unpopular causes of factory legislation, free popular education, abolition of flogging in the army, and many others. 'He attacked not only starvation and high prices but showed their relationship to the viciousness of the court, political dishonesty, and the need of parliamentary reform, coming up repeatedly against the tremendous force of deliberate reaction that swept the country after the Napoleonic Wars.'

Brave crusader as he was, however, there was a curious taint of unscrupulousness and self-interest in him that repelled people at the same time that his talents extorted unwilling admiration. It was evident enough that Brougham was using the whole affair of the Queen's trial for his own advantage, and building up a position from which he could either dominate or blackmail his party. Greville, who regarded him as base and unprincipled, was overpowered by his eloquence and intellectual powers, and quotes Rogers: 'this morning Solon, Lycurgus, Demosthenes, Archimedes, Sir Isaac Newton, Lord Chesterfield, and a great many more went away in one post-chaise.' Much later he adds an account of a visit to the British Museum, where Brougham 'would not let anybody explain anything, but did all the honours himself. At last they came to a collection of minerals,' but here too Brougham took the words out of their conductor's mouth, 'and dashed off with as much ease as if he had been a Buckland or a Cuvier.'

With the change of government in 1830, Brougham's stature was portentous. He had Lord Grey's cabinet 'in a dreadful fright' by 'all but declaring a hostile intention to the future administration'; he 'flourished his reform *in terrorum* over their heads; he was affronted and furious because he fancied they neglected him.' 'It is pretty clear,' Greville summarized, 'that this eccentric luminary will play the devil with their system.'

But a few days later all the danger was over. Holding in his hands 'questions which he could employ to thwart, embarrass, and ruin any ministry'; able 'to domineer in the House of Commons and to gather popularity throughout the country by enforcing popular measures of which he would have all the credit'; he had yet been so thoughtless as to swallow the bait of the Great Seal that had been dangled before him. As Lord Chancellor he could no longer be in the House of Commons: 'all men feel that he is emasculated and drops on the woolsack as on his political deathbed; once in the House of Lords, there is an end of him, and he may rant, storm, and thunder without hurting anybody.' His political lightnings chained, Brougham subsided into long years of almost innocuous distinction.

Then came the excitements of the Reform Bill. The ignorant workers, deluded with the belief that it would do some good to them, or be extended to them, rioted over the countryside. 'Wherever there has been anything like fighting,' Greville records with aristocratic prejudice, 'the mob has always been beaten, and has shown the greatest cowardice.' These same riots aroused the indignant pity of Carlyle. And on 23 March, 1831

'Majority for our Bill
☞ *I* ☜'

Creevey wrote Miss Ord in jubilant diagram. Soon, however, he winced when the Committee appointed by his own Government to revise the scale of salaries, reduced his own emoluments as Treasurer of the Ordnance. 'Have you seen how that damned retrenching Committee have docked my office of £200 a year?' he asks his step-daughter.

But meanwhile his social life was going on pleasantly enough. At country houses he was as much a favorite as ever. The new dining room at Knowsley, he noted, was '53 feet by 37,' and had 'two great Gothic church-like doors the whole height of the room'; General Grosvenor asked, 'Pray, are those great doors to be opened for every pat of butter that comes into the room?' At Thorp Perrow one of the drawing-rooms was fifty feet long, 'with a great bow furnished with rose-colored satin,' and every night at half past ten a fat butler wheeled a 'barrel of oysters and a hot pheasant, &c.' into the room. Raby was magnificent with gold plate and a band of music during dinner; at Goodwood the rooms were in 'brightest yellow satin.' Always the fare was sumptuous and the wine praiseworthy. After heavy drinking, 'five or six glasses of light French wine' made an admirable restorative; 'at midnight, when the talk began to flag . . . what could be more rejuvenating than to ring . . . for a broiled bone?' And ladies still gathered around him everywhere. 'How agreeable you have been!' Lady Cleveland would exclaim, or Lady Grey, 'Oh, thank you! Mr Creevey; how useful you have been!' And 'Lady Georgiana told me last night that she had laughed out aloud in bed at one of my stories.'

He was getting to be 'old Creevey' now, and wore woolen stockings under his silk ones to keep warm in the evening. But he dined out as much as ever—with Lady Holland, who was 'very complaining, and eating like a horse,' with Lord Grey, Melbourne, and Palmerston, and some 'minor poets,' with Samuel Rogers, whom he disliked as 'a sour, snarling beast' too much inclined to talk 'about the grandees he lives with—*female* as well as male.' New celebrities were coming into prominence. Greville sat next at dinner to 'a common looking man in black,' of a vulgar and ungainly appearance: 'not a ray of intellect beams from his countenance,' Greville wrote. When he learned that it was the eloquent Macaulay, whose genius and astonishing knowledge he had heard so much of, feeling as if his thoughts could be read, Greville was embarrassed into a profuse perspiration. Macaulay turned out to be indeed extraordinary, but, Greville thought, 'he has none of the graces of conversation, none of that exquisite tact and refinement which are the result of a felicitous intuition, or a long acquaintance with good society.' Mr Creevey dismissed the new luminary more briefly as a 'noisy vulgar fellow.' Less spectacular was 'young Mill,' whom Greville found slow in conversation, seeming to be 'always working in his mind propositions or a syllogism.' None of the younger men were as polished and entertaining as the older generation of Sheridan or Brougham.

The stage was slowly filling with the actors in a new age. William IV was quarreling with the Duchess of Kent; he passionately exploded at a birthday dinner with the hope 'that my life may be spared for nine months longer, after which period, in the event of my death no regency would take place.' The Princess Victoria would then succeed to the throne without any authority being 'in the hands of a person now near me . . . who is herself incompetent to act with propriety in the station in which she would be placed.'

The character of the young Princess was entirely unknown. She had been kept in jealous seclusion by her mother, 'never having slept out of her bedroom, nor been alone with anybody but herself and the Baroness Lehzen.' Finally the King died, and the slender girl entered the room where the Council were assembled and 'read her speech in a clear, distinct, and audible voice, and without any appearance of fear or embarrassment.' The new age had begun.

Mr Creevey lingered a little while, and was presented to the Queen, who could not get her glove off, and 'blushed and laughed and pulled,' until at last he kissed her hand. But he was seventy years old, and soon he slipped from the scene. Greville, like Crabb Robinson, was to live for another quarter of a century into the changing Victorian world, but, unlike Robinson, he was to be more and more a relic of the past.

It would not be highly profitable to consider these records we have glanced at as literary art. The diaries and journals, indeed, have only the qualities of occasional writing, falling sometimes into grey fogginess, and again glinting here and there with a precious stone or shining for whole passages with vitality. Greville is sometimes heavy and prosaic, and even Creevey's lively chatter may now and then be about trivialities unseasoned by the spice of wit or scandal. Crabb Robinson is at times so impersonal in his entries as to verge on the dry and barren. Lamb's letters have achieved higher fame in the literary world than any of these, but numbers of them are devoted to the kind of not-shining trifles that fade away after the moment that called them into being. Haydon's *Autobiography*, although it stops abruptly with the year 1820, is perhaps the most truly among them all a work of literary art. The writing is full of Haydon's vigor and quickness of movement, drenched in his honest, noisy, and bombastic personality.

But if we look in all these for the sense of being alive in their time, how richly are we rewarded! Mr Creevey fighting in committee against 'this infernal nuisance—the loco-motive monster . . . navigated by a tail of smoke and sulphur,' or Crabb Robinson riding on it and being impressed by the way engines going in the opposite direction whizz by at twenty miles an hour; Haydon disgusted at Hazlitt for having the frivolity to admire his own features in a room where 'Milton had conceived, and perhaps written, many of his finest thoughts'; Greville finding Strawberry Hill just as 'old Horace Walpole left it,' or telling how the Spanish Ambassador paid a droll compliment to Madame de Lieven by finding the young beauties at a ball 'trop fraiche,' and adding with a tender look, 'J'aime les femmes un peu passées.'

It is the same when Lamb tells us of a blue-stocking 'Miss Benjay or Benje' who questions Mary in French, 'possibly having heard that neither Mary nor I understood French.' Robinson, too, is full of such moments—for example, Lord Thurlow's reception of the committee seeking his support to repeal the Corporation and Test Acts. He heard the committee 'very civilly,' and then said, 'Gentlemen, I'm against you, by God. I am for the Established Church, damme! Not that I have any more regard for the Established Church than for any other church, but because *it is* established. And if you can get your damned religion established, I'll be for that too!' These little episodes, and a thousand others, flash us in a second upon the scene with their actors. And they not merely transport us to the early nineteenth century world of Greville and Creevey, of Lamb and Robinson and Haydon; they are full of human nature as it has been in all times.

TOWARDS VICTORIANISM

X

TOWARDS VICTORIANISM

Prologue to an Age

THE Victorian Period has often been portrayed as darkened by a deadly cloud of respectability and evangelicalism. Horsehair sofas, whatnots, wax flowers under glass, antimacassars; heavy Sunday dinners and heavy Sunday afternoons; a rather gloomy earnestness, relieved only by spasms of self-gratulation at the monstrous increase in the number of steel knives turned out at Sheffield and the miles of iron rails laid end to end. In the realm of biography a pained silence is supposed to have reigned over any doings not suitable for juvenile conversation. Eminent men were commemorated in earnestly stodgy two-volume lives written in a uniform style of elegiac reverence and reticence. In deference to Mrs Grundy, truth went padded in black bombazine and swathed in heavy veils, as respectable as the Queen.

This caricature is not totally lacking in a basis of fact, but it is violently exaggerated. To begin with, reticence carried even to the point of practical dishonesty was no trait singular to the Victorians.

Sprat, in his *Life of Cowley*, in the eighteenth century, even refused to quote Cowley's personal letters on the ground that in them his character appeared 'undressed,' and therefore not fit 'to go abroad into the streets.' In our own time Mrs Martha Dickinson Bianchi grimly holds on to the secret, whatever it may have been, of Emily Dickinson's love-life, but thriftily doles out a few more poems every now and then. Nor was it in any way a surprise some years ago to see a determined effort by the Church of Christ Scientist to suppress Edwin Framden Daiken's *Life of Mary Baker Eddy*.

Our contemporary biographers are very gay in heaving brickbats at P. T. Barnum or Mark Hanna or General Grant. But their iconoclasm might find itself curiously tempered in dealing with the living General MacArthur. And when John Middleton Murry, a few years back, wrote a study of D. H. Lawrence, then only recently dead, and ventured on some rather painful criticisms, the howls of reviewers rose to heaven at his bad taste, and a whole platoon of lady worshippers who agreed about Lawrence in no other respects united to fling hand grenades at Mr Murry. Our enlightenment, then, is not so great as we have flattered ourselves. It enables us to sneer at George Washington or give a Freudian wink at the domestic character of Henry VIII, but we are not above demanding that any recent life be seen couleur de rose.

Now it should be recalled that in the nineteenth century biography was not yet so professionalized as it has grown today. A great deal of our biography is concerned with figures of the past, reconstructed out of books and other records. They are free from any concern for personal feelings. But the Victorian biographer was usually telling the life of one very recently dead, personally known to himself, perhaps a friend. He was bound by all the ties of affection for the dead and for the living who were still involved. The legal possibilities of libel also hedged him about. When the nineteenth century biographer ventured into the past, as in Monk's *Bentley* or Churton Collins's *Bolingbroke*, he showed considerable freedom in handling the less shining aspects of a character. And even in dealing with his contemporaries, he was by no means as frightened as we have pretended. Lockhart's *Life of Scott* traces in—faintly, but with determined honesty—some of the weaknesses of that kindly man. Mrs Gaskell made a brilliant effort to depict 'even the slight astringencies' of Charlotte Brontë. And Froude's *Life of*

Carlyle sharply contrasts the rugged intellectual honesty of the man with his selfishness and blindness to most interests other than his own.

Undoubtedly it is easier for the conscientious biographer today to deal forthrightly with the uglier aspects of his subject than it was during a good deal of the last century. Protests are now less frequent, perhaps, and there is usually a vigorous opposition to any effort at shutting the mouth of the writer. But this is not all gain. The Victorian biographer had a sense of moral responsibility forced on him. He could not wallow in lubricity and sensationalism. Although moral squeamishness leads inevitably to whitewashing, prudery, and suppression, it keeps within bounds the attempt to cheapen and degrade, and makes it impossible for prurience to wear the disguise of emancipation. The Victorian biographer who defied the code of silence—and not a few did—was fortified by sobriety and courage. They gave a strength to his work never achieved by professional denigration.

The Wizard of the North

John Gibson Lockhart was the son-in-law of Sir Walter Scott. The *Life* in which he devoted himself to displaying the character of the great novelist is one of the triumphs of English biography. Leslie Stephen ranked it next to Boswell; Professor Saintsbury called the *Life of Johnson* 'its only possible rival.' Andrew Lang has said that in Lockhart's biography 'we have the full portrait of a man; the defects are blazoned by the intense light of genius and goodness . . .' He does not rank the book higher than Boswell's, 'for Boswell's hero,' he says, 'appears to myself to be of a character more universally human, a wiser man, a greater humorist, his biography a more valuable possession than Sir Walter and Sir Walter's *Life*. But it were childish to dispute about the relative merit of two *chefs-d'oeuvre*. Each work is perfect in its kind and in relation to its subject.'

Thomas Carlyle, who reviewed the book when it was being published between 1836 and 1838, expressed more qualified praise. It was too long, he said,—it was originally issued in seven volumes—and it was 'not so much a composition as what we may call a compilation well done.' There is a vast stretch of eighty-four chapters, and in their endless accumulation of letters, diaries, journals, extracts from prefaces, Carlyle felt, the character of Sir Walter is sometimes obscured. The materials for the portrait lie there unworked, a precious ore, but it is left for the reader to dig them out. Such is Carlyle's view, and he concludes, 'Scott's biography, if uncomposed, lies printed and indestructible here, in the elementary state, and can at any time be composed, if necessary, by whosoever has a call to it.'

That the biography is too long and leisurely may be admitted. There are places where the reader's appetite flags, and the piling up of detail is needlessly extended on points that have long since been proved to the hilt. That the character emerges dimly or confusedly I do not think true. There is a steady progression and deepening of the strokes by which Scott's character is drawn, and if some of the strokes prove supererogatory, they do not muddle the portrait. On other points Carlyle gives more commendation, and his brilliant defense of Lockhart is worth quoting:

> One thing we hear greatly blamed in Mr. Lockhart, that he has been too communicative, indiscreet, and has recorded much that ought to have lain suppressed. Persons are mentioned, and circumstances not always of an ornamental sort. It would appear that there is far less reticence than was looked for! Various persons, name and surname, have "received pain." Nay, the very hero of the biography is rendered unheroic; unornamental facts of him, and of those he had to do with, being set forth in plain English; hence "personality," "indiscretion," or worse, "sanctities of private life," &c. How delicate, decent, is English biography, bless its mealy mouth! A Damocles' sword of *Respectability* hangs forever over the poor English life-writer. . . . The English Biographer has long felt that if in writing his biography he wrote down anything that could by possibility offend any man, he had written wrong. The plain consequence was that, properly speaking, no biography whatever could be produced.

Instead we get 'some vague ghost of a biography, white, stainless, without feature or substance.'

Now these censures of Lockhart, he goes on to say, are really his highest praise. 'He is found guilty of having said this and that, calculated to be not entirely pleasant to this man and that,' to give him 'a living set of features,' instead of leaving him 'vague in the white beatified ghost condition.' Whereupon men cry out, ' "See, there is something written not entirely pleasant to me!" Good friend, it is pity, but who can help it? They that will crowd about bonfires may sometimes very fairly get their beards singed; it is the price they pay for such illumination; natural twilight is safe and free to all. For our part, we hope all manner of biographies that are written in England will henceforth be written so.'

He concludes with a discussion of the 'censure of Scott being made unheroic.' 'Your true hero,' he writes scornfully, 'must have no features, but be a white stainless, impersonal ghost hero!' There had been malicious theories that Lockhart disliked Scott, and chose 'an underhand treacherous manner to dishero him!' Nothing could be more stupid: 'If Mr Lockhart is fairly chargeable with any radical defect, if on any side his insight entirely fails him, it seems even to be in this, that Scott is altogether lovely to him, that Scott's greatness spreads out before him on all hands beyond the reach of eye, that his very faults become beautiful, and that of his worth there is no measure.'

Here, again, Carlyle travels perhaps a little too far in reaction against the common view he was combatting. It certainly was not true that Lockhart's attitude toward Sir Walter had a single grain of meanness; it *was* true that he loved and admired him. Scott perhaps respected too highly the gradations of rank and he strove overheartily, it may be, for material rewards. Lockhart's affection lessened his awareness of these faults; it may have blinded him entirely to others. But faults, he knew, existed, and those he was aware of he drew. 'A stern sense of duty–' he wrote, 'that kind of sense of it which is combined with the feeling of his actual presence in a serene state of elevation above all petty terrestrial and temporary views–will induce me to touch the few darker points in his life and character as freely as the others which were so predominant.' The fundamental outlines of Lockhart's portrait of Scott no subsequent biography has seriously altered, although a thorough study of the evidence now available through Grierson's magnificent collection of Scott's letters, the unexpurgated edition of his Journals, and other still unpublished sources would undoubtedly suggest modifications.

The book makes no significant departure from the Boswell method. Lockhart does not, indeed, follow Boswell in reporting conversation, partly because Scott did not excel in repartee and dialogue, but rather in narration and anecdote, and partly because he recognized that he himself lacked Boswell's flair for regaining the flavor of spoken words. Only now and then does he repeat some joke or short sentence that lingered in his memory. He follows Scott into the outdoors where so much of his time was spent in riding and hunting and walking and fording streams; he catches the nature of the man in action, in his relations with other men, in his laughter and his kindnesses, and in the sentiments he expressed, rather than in the manner of a spoken interchange. But in all the other details of his documentation he follows Boswell's example. He even has much of Boswell's skill in the arrangement of those characteristic episodes that are needed to make a personality proclaim itself. He is especially admirable in conveying the warm and comfortable flavor of Scott's life at Ashestiel and Abbotsford, and the sweetness and intimacy of his relations with his friends.

The work begins with an autobiographic fragment left by Scott. He was a frail little boy, and lame besides, so that he used to be left alone on a knoll where he could watch the clouds and the trees. Once he was forgotten while a thunderstorm was coming on, and the aunt who ran to fetch him 'found him lying on his back, clapping his hands at the lightning, and crying out, "Bonny! bonny!" at every flash.' In an otherwise childless household with his grandfather, he learned to talk much with his elders, and once the parish clergyman exclaimed in exasperation, 'One may as well speak in the mouth of a cannon as where that child is.' At the age of four he was taken to his first play, *As You Like It*. 'I made, I believe,' he confesses, 'noise more than enough, and remember being so much scandalized at the quarrel between Orlando and his brother in the first scene, that I screamed out, "A'n't they brothers?" A few weeks' residence at home convinced me, who had till then been an only child in the household of my grandfather, that a quarrel between brothers was a very natural event.'

As a school boy, he 'glanced like a meteor from one end of the class to the other, and commonly disgusted my kind master as much by negligence and frivolity as I occasionally pleased him by flashes of intellect and talent.' His memory was wonderfully acute, and 'seldom failed to preserve most tenaciously a favourite passage of poetry, a playhouse ditty, or, above all, a Border-raid ballad;' but it was capricious—'names, dates, and the other technicalities of history escaped me in a most melancholy degree.' In mathematics and science he did poorly: 'through every part of my literary career,' he writes regretfully, 'I have felt pinched and hampered by my own ignorance.' 'But all that was adventurous and romantic I devoured without much discrimination, and I really believe I have read as much nonsense of this class as any man now living.'

Bishop Percy's *Reliques of Ancient Poetry* inspired him with enthusiasm, and presently we find him as a young man 'raiding' the countryside for border ballads and staying with the Scotch farmers over night. 'Eh me!' said one of his tramping companions, 'sic an endless fund o' humour and drollery as he then had wi' him! Never ten yards but we were either laughing or roaring and singing. Wherever we stopped, how brawlie he suited himsel' to everybody! He ay did as the lave did; never made himsel' the great man, or took ony airs in the company. I've seen him in a' moods in these jaunts, grave and gay, daft and serious, sober and drunk . . . but drunk or sober, he was ay the gentleman.' His *Minstrelsy of the Scottish Border*, a result of these 'raids,' established him as a writer of erudition and charm.

Meanwhile he had been studying law and been called to the bar. His first case was an unsuccessful defense of a minister against 'charges of habitual drunkenness, singing of lewd and profane songs, dancing, and toying at a penny-wedding with a "sweetie wife" '—a traveling vender of gingerbread, etc. His defense of a poacher in the Jedburgh criminal court was rewarded by the gift of a hare the next morning; but he had less success with a notorious housebreaker, who, in gratitude for his efforts, however, advised him to keep a little yelping terrier within doors rather than a mastiff without, and to use big, heavy locks on his house instead of 'nice, clever, gimcrack locks.'

Outside of term time his days were active. He rose at five and wrote until breakfast, wrote again from breakfast till noon, and the afternoon was open for riding and enjoyment. There was coursing with greyhounds, and salmon-spearing in the Tweed, sometimes renewed by the aid of torches at night. 'Burning the water,' it was called, and sportsmen often had icy baths in some dark pool or barked their shins in the blackness. Sometimes they climbed the wild tracts to the tarn of Loch Skene, losing themselves in a thick fog, or blundering their way through bogs and sloughs of peaty mud and water; from the gloomy loch, as they approached, 'a huge eagle heaved himself . . . and rose right over us, screaming his scorn.' During the fears of French invasion in 1807, he joined the volunteers, and in intervals of drilling could be seen galloping his black steed furiously past the surge on Portobello sands.

He had been made Clerk in the Court of Session, and was simultaneously earning a name for himself in poetry. *The Lay of the Last Minstrel* had been followed by *Marmion*, both enormously successful, but the reception of *The Lady of the Lake* was unprecedented. 'The whole country rang with the praises of the poet,' Lockhart writes, '—crowds set off to view the scenery of Loch Katrine, till then comparatively unknown; . . . every house and inn in that neighborhood was crammed with a constant succession of visitors.' Soldiers in the trenches in Spain, lying prostrate on the ground, listened to their captain read the battle in Canto VI, interrupting him only 'by a joyous huzza whenever the shot struck the bank close above them.' But Scott himself admired 'neither his own nor any modern popular style of composition especially'; what pleased him most was Johnson's *London* and *The Vanity of Human Wishes*. His little daughter was asked what she thought of *The Lady of the Lake*, and replied, 'Oh, I have not read it: papa says there's nothing so bad for young people as reading bad poetry.'

Waverley, published anonymously in 1814, created even more furore than any of the poems had done, but the later verse-tales were proving less successful. The violently colored and daring compositions of Lord Byron made inroads on their popularity, and Scott was disappointed by the comparative failure of *The Lord of the Isles*. Meanwhile Scott had assumed his fatal silent partnership in the Ballantynes' printing firm. Both James and John Ballantyne loved and revered their friend, but they had serious deficiencies as business men; already, in a flurry of panic in 1813, Scott had been worried into crying, 'For Heaven's sake, treat me as a man, not as a milch-cow.'

At the moment, however, all was well. Stout, mock-majestic James gave grandiose aldermanic banquets to celebrate each new novel. Amid a wealth of turtle and venison, iced punch, ale, and Madeira, he would rise pompously to give the toast, 'his eyes solemnly fixed on vacancy . . . in the sort of whisper by which a stage conspirator thrills the gallery—"*Gentlemen, a bumper to the immortal Author of Waverley!*"' Then he would lament the modest obscurity in which this illustrious man chose to conceal himself. Raffish little hopping John Ballantyne, whom Scott affectionately called Rigdumfunnidos, would be grinning at the board, and a number of others in the secret. 'The cool demure fun of Scott's features during all this mummery was perfect; and Erskine's attempt at gay *nonchalance* was still more ludicrously meritorious.'

The flow of his imagination seemed endless and magical. In hardly more than a year he had written *Ivanhoe*, *The Monastery*, *The Abbot*, and *Kenilworth*. Why should the springs ever run dry? The post-Napoleonic disorders slipping into the past, England was riding a wave of luxuriousness and extravagant speculation. The great bookseller Constable gave munificent advances on novels not only as yet unwritten, but unconceived, by their author. John Ballantyne collected objets de vertu; Scott had reared a magnificent new dwelling on his estate of Abbotsford, where he dispensed a baronial hospitality. But all this prosperity was built on quaking ground. The booksellers were tied together by loans and agreements, and their capital was intricately involved in South American mines, gas companies, and other unstable enterprises. When the great crash came, it was whispered, all would go down together.

By December, 1825, the increasing tremors in London could not be ignored; hysteria broke out in the City. Scott's first thought was of those dependent on him in Abbotsford, and of the cottagers on his estate. He must give up Abbotsford. 'My dogs will wait for me in vain . . . Poor Things! I must get them kind masters!' Offers of financial assistance from devoted friends poured in upon him—£500 offered by his daughter's harp master—'probably,' says Scott's *Diary*, 'his all;' and an anonymous offer of £30,000. He refused them all. The ultimate indebtedness reached the sum of £130,000, for which Scott assumed entire responsibility. Only, he insisted, he must retain Abbotsford for his heirs. If his creditors demanded a sale, he would go into bankruptcy, and they would get no more than his present estate would bring. If they abstained, he would apply his future literary labors to paying them in full.

The offer was accepted, and he began the long toil of earning the enormous sum with his pen. He worked nights now, as well as days; it was a severe winter and he got chilblains in his fingers. His little grandchild was ill, and Scott's heart was full of foreboding. Lady Scott, too, sickened, and in spite of her daughter's faithful nursing, grew worse. In the soft air of May, with the leaves glittering, 'she raised herself in her bed, and tried to turn her eyes after me, and said, with a sort of smile, "you have all such melancholy faces." These were the last words I ever heard her utter . . . ' 'For myself, I scarce know how I feel—sometimes as firm as the Bass Rock, sometimes as weak as the water that breaks on it. I am as alert at thinking and deciding as I ever was in my life. Yet, when I contrast what this place now is, with what it has been not long since, I think my heart will break. Lonely, aged, deprived of my family—all but poor Anne; an impoverished, and embarrassed man . . .'

The secret of the authorship of the Waverley Novels, of course, was widely known now, and was at last openly acknowledged at a banquet in February, 1827. 'The clouds have been dispelled,' Lord Meadowbrook said, '—the *darkness visible* has been cleared away—and the Great Unknown—the minstrel of our native land—the mighty magician who has rolled back the current of time, and conjured up before our living senses the men and manners of days which have long passed away, stands revealed to the eyes and hearts of his affectionate and admiring countrymen.'

But such triumphs were few. Illness grew upon him. As long ago as 1817 he had complained, 'how the deuce can I make Rob Roy's wife speak, with such a *curmurring* in my guts?' Now headaches and hemorrhages afflicted him, and sometimes in the work of dictation 'he paused and looked around him, like one half-waking from a dream, mocked with shadows . . . Then came the strong effort of aroused will—the cloud dispersed as if before an irresistible current of purer air—all was bright and serene as of old—and then it closed again in yet deeper darkness.' Sometimes he would gaily begin a story to a friend, 'but before he reached the point, it would seem as if some internal spring had given way—he paused and gazed around him with the blank anxiety of look that a blind man has when he has dropped his staff.' Then in some way the thread would be supplied him, and 'with his habitual smile of courtesy' he would go on.

The evils of the times distressed him. He had seen the misery of poverty in Manchester: 'God's justice is requiting,' he exclaimed, 'and will yet further requite, those who have blown up this country into a state of unsubstantial opulence at the expense of the health and morals of the lower classes.' But, a convinced Tory, he distrusted democratic remedies, and his opposition to the Reform bill led to his being hooted and interrupted at a public meeting. Riotous artisans hissed, and he exclaimed, 'I regard your gabble no more than the geese on the green.' Leaving the assembly, he was hissed again; he bowed 'and took leave in the words of the doomed gladiator,' 'MORITURUS VOS SALUTO.' During the elections, his carriage was pelted with stones, and a woman spat upon him from a window; 'but this last contumely,' Lockhart adds, 'I think he did not observe.' Scott's *Diary* notes, 'I left the borough in the midst of abuse, and the gentle hint of *Burk Sir Walter*. Much obliged to the brave lads of Jeddart.'

As his health vanished, his mind weakened. He began to fancy that all his debts were paid, and at last he believed it implicitly. But now and then he dimly realized his condition. He felt, he wrote, 'some mental confusion, with the extent of which I am not, perhaps, fully acquainted . . . I neither regret nor fear the approach of death, if it is coming. I would compound for a little pain instead of this heartless muddiness of mind.'

In the hope that a trip abroad would restore his health, the British government placed the frigate Barham at his disposal to convey him to the Mediterranean. The splendors of Abbotsford were revived briefly before his departure by a reunion at which Wordsworth was present. The poet wrote a sonnet on the forthcoming voyage:

A trouble, not of clouds, or weeping rain,
Nor of the setting sun's pathetic light
Engendered, hangs o'er Eildon's triple height:
Spirits of power assembled there complain
For kindred power departing from their sight;
While Tweed, best pleased in chanting a blithe strain,
Saddens his voice again, and yet again.
Lift up your hearts, ye mourners! for the might
Of the whole world's good wishes with him goes;
Blessings and prayers, in nobler retinue
Then sceptred King or laurelled Conqueror knows,
Follow this wondrous potentate. Be true,
Ye winds of Ocean, and the midland Sea,
Wafting your charge to soft Parthenope.

But the rest came too late. In Naples and Pompeii he longed for home. Finally the return journey was begun. During its last stages he seemed not to perceive his surroundings, and those around him wept bitterly. 'Thus surrounded by those nearest to him, he alone was unconscious of the cause or depth of their grief, and while yet alive seemed to be carried to his grave.' But as the carriage bore him along Tweedside he began to murmur the names of familiar places, and on beholding his own towers 'he sprang up with a cry of delight.' Presently he was in his chair in the dining room— the dogs 'began to fawn upon him and lick his hands, and he alternately sobbed and smiled over them, until sleep oppressed him.' The next day, being wheeled about his home, 'I have seen much,' he kept saying, 'but nothing like my ain house.' After a few days he thought he would write again, but the pen dropped from his fingers. 'He sank back among his pillows, silent tears rolling down his cheeks;' and when, later in the day his friend Laidlaw said, 'Sir Walter has had a little repose,'—'No, Willie,' he replied, 'no repose for Sir Walter but in the grave.'

He sank lower and lower, his mind hopelessly obscured, but dwelling, it seemed, 'on serious and solemn things; the accent of the voice grave, sometimes awful, but never querulous . . . Now and then he imagined himself to be administering justice . . .' And a few times 'his fancy was at Jedburgh—and *Burk Sir Walter* escaped him in melancholy tones.' On the 17th of September his faculties returned again, and he sent for Lockhart. 'I may have but a minute to speak to you,' he said. 'My dear, be a good man—be virtuous—be religious—be a good man . . . God bless you all.' Two days later, on a serene and warm afternoon, with the gentle ripple of the Tweed coming through the open window, he breathed his last. His eldest son kissed and closed his eyes.

Such is the close of Lockhart's narrative. Scott's life was splendid in its material triumphs, full of glory and acclaim; but there was more grandeur in the sickness and struggle of the last years. He had involved himself, without sufficient knowledge or supervision, in the tangled convolutions of the publishing business. If his carelessness was culpable, he paid bravely for it. Before he died almost all the huge debt had been paid, and ultimately the earnings of his novels settled every penny of it. The fault was a too easy willingness to assume that all was well rather than dishonesty, but it was aggravated by the fact that there had been ominous symptoms long before the final crash. Lockhart makes nearly all these factors plain, and orients them in the general confusion of the bookselling trade; a muddle that involved Constable and scores of others in a widespread disaster of financial collapse. Only by a higher standard of behavior than business men apply to themselves could Scott be blamed. That standard he measured himself by, and instead of allowing himself to be cleared, as he might easily have done—as Constable and the other booksellers involved did do—by a declaration of bankruptcy, he pledged the earnings of books still unconceived to wipe out the debt.

The other blemishes on his character are slight. He exulted in worldly success, and took a childlike delight in his fame and the luxurious indulgences it brought him. He liked playing lord of the manor at Abbotsford, and took a rather absurd pride in his dignity of birth. 'I have my quarters and emblazonments,' he boasted; 'free of all stain but Border theft, and High Treason, which I hope are gentlemanlike crimes.' He had an undue regard for those above himself in rank. His reverence for royalty led him into an almost subservient respect for even that rake and reprobate, George IV.

He believed in the feudal organization of society, but he accepted the responsibilities of feudalism as well as its privileges. Bitter was his indignation against those who selfishly oppressed the poor. Charitable interferences in the lives of the peasantry he hated. 'I dislike all such interference,' he said, 'all your domiciliary, kind, impertinent visits;—they are all pretty much felt like insults, and do no manner of good: let people go on in their own way, in God's name. How would you like to have a nobleman coming to you to teach you how to dish up your beefsteak into a French kickshaw? Let the poor alone in their domestic habits: protect them, treat them kindly, trust them; but let them enjoy in quiet their dish of porridge . . . ' Especially you should beware, Scott felt, of doing anything that can 'make them lose their precious feeling of independence.' His own relations with his dependents were affectionate and intimate. Going up a ravine at Abbotsford, Scott remarked to his servant, Tom Purdie, 'This will be a glorious spring for our trees, Tom!'—'You may say that, Shirra,' Tom replied, and then, 'My certy,' he added, scratching his head, 'and I think it will be a grand season for *our buiks* too.'

His friendliness to the poorest was balanced by his ability to see and correct a fault in the highest–save, to be sure, those chartered vices in which royalty has usually been privileged. When some ladies of rank showed a disposition to make Mrs Coutts, the widow of the great banker, feel uncomfortable because she had formerly been a provincial actress, Scott waylaid the highest in rank, the Marchioness of Northampton, and spoke plainly to her. 'It is, I hear, not uncommon,' he said, 'among fine ladies in London to be very well pleased to accept invitations, and even sometimes to hunt after them, to Mrs Coutts's grand balls and fêtes, and then, if they meet her in any private circle, to practice on her the delicate *manoeuvre* called *tipping the cold shoulder*. This, you agree with me, is shabby; but it is nothing new either to you or me, that fine people will do shabbiness for which beggars might blush, if they once stoop so low as to poke for tickets.' The behavior of the ladies in his house, he went on, was 'a sin of the same order. You were all told a couple of days ago that I had accepted her visit . . . Now if any of you had not been disposed to be of my party at the same time with her, there was plenty of time for you to have gone away before she came.' The lady apologized, she dropped a word to the others, and for the remainder of her stay Mrs Coutts had a delightful time.

Scott's conversational charm lay more in ease and liveliness than in sententiousness or wit; he was not so much a debater, as most Edinburgh society was in his day, as a felicitous and poetic story-teller. The 'mournful aspect' of his eyes 'when he told some dismal and mysterious story' had a 'doubtful, melancholy, exploring look, which appealed irresistibly.' 'Occasionally, when he spoke of something audacious or eccentric, they would dilate and light up with a tragi-comic, hare-brained expression, quite peculiar to himself.' 'The first dawn of a humorous thought would show itself . . . by an involuntary lengthening of the upper lip, followed by a shy sidelong glance at his neighbors, indescribably whimsical, and seeming to ask . . . whether the sparks of drollery should be suppressed or allowed to blaze out. In the full tide of mirth . . . he could go on telling or descanting, while his lungs did "crow like chanticleer," his syllables, in the struggle, growing more emphatic, his accent more strongly Scotch, and his voice plaintive with excess of merriment.'

His relation with his children was ideal. 'Like their playmates, Camp and the greyhounds, they had at all times free access to his study; he never considered their prattle as any disturbance . . . and when they, unconscious how he was engaged, entreated him to lay down his pen and tell them a story, he would take them on his knees, repeat a ballad or a legend, kiss them, and set them down again to their marbles or ninepins, and resume his labour . . .' He 'made his kind informal instructions to blend so easily and playfully with the current of their own sayings and doings that so far from regarding him with any distant awe, it was never thought that any sport or diversion could go on in the right way, unless *papa* were of the party, or that the rainiest day could be dull, so he were at home.'

Two unkindnesses that he remembered doing troubled him sorely. He had been angry at Constable for trying to get him to borrow money on the security of Abbotsford when he must have known that such a sum could no longer be of any aid; and he had refused to meet the broken-down man again. His conscience reproached him with that: 'To nourish angry passions against a man whom I really liked,' he wrote in his *Diary*, 'would be to lay a blister on my heart.'

And there was the brother with whom he had refused to communicate because of an early act of cowardice: after he was dead, Scott mourned his own cruelty. The character of Connachar, in *The Fair Maid of Perth*, was 'a sort of expiation,' he said, 'to my poor brother's manes. I have now learned to have more tolerance and compassion than I had in those days.' Lockhart reminded him of Samuel Johnson standing bareheaded in the market-place of Uttoxeter to do penance for a youthful irreverence to his father. 'Well, no matter,' said Scott, 'perhaps that's not the worst thing in the Doctor's story.'

But although a single or occasional failure of the nerves should not be judged so harshly as he had done his brother's, courage was the key virtue to all the rest. 'Without courage there cannot be truth; and without truth there can be no other virtue.' It was no shallow insight, and it was one he had learned to the core. He did not have Johnson's depth and breadth of perception. His Toryism was much more a thing of loyalty and traditional faith than a reasoned philosophy, as Johnson's was. But the vivid imagination and the kind heart had laid hold on a few brave and simple truths. He lived those truths out to the end.

Lockhart had over Boswell one tremendous advantage: the story he had to tell. Not only was it a dramatic story, with grand contrasts of splendor and melancholy downfall; it was a tragic story, in which the darkness of the end could be directly connected with the carelessness of his hero's prime. And the materials Lockhart had at his disposal were almost as full for every period, instead of being, as Boswell's were, insignificant and scanty for two-thirds of a career and over-full for the end. If the total outline of Lockhart's story is more exciting than Boswell's and if the dark end, as it unrolls before us in his seventh volume, is grand and heartrending, the one fact is Lockhart's good fortune but the other is all his high achievement. Boswell has no such heightening of emotions to choke the reader's throat, but he has been almost continually enticing. No one ever reached the end of Lockhart's *Life of Scott* without struggling through weary and interminable passages in the middle; and rare is the man who can open Boswell at random and not be impelled to turn the page and continue reading where he began. Lockhart's is one of the most moving of all true stories, and Boswell's perhaps the most unremittingly fascinating.

Darkness over Haworth

Elizabeth Cleghorn Gaskell's *Life of Charlotte Brontë*, although published in 1857, has resemblances to some of our modern fictionalized biographies. Mrs Gaskell was a novelist, the author of *Mary Barton* and *Cranford*, and she approached the biography of her friend not only with personal devotion but with something of the novelist's art. She painted the lonely moors around the village of Haworth in colors darkly appropriate to her tale, and called down the bleak moorland winds to move chill and dark through her pages. She saw the story of Charlotte Brontë in tragic tones, like a Brontë novel.

But Mrs Gaskell was conscientious. She would not knowingly invent or tell a falsehood, although sometimes she accepted statements on unreliable testimony, and in one crucial episode left out a part of the story altogether. But mainly she was true to the conception of Charlotte Brontë's character that she held. Although she loved her dead friend, she knew there had been 'astringencies' in her disposition. These she did not suppress. Her loyalty and her imagination joined forces, however, to explain them, in terms that involved some unintentional falsification, not so much of Charlotte as of others.

Thus she sees the early life of the Brontë children as repressed by a stern and at times stormily wrathful father, and scruples not to employ the testimony of a nurse to that effect. Charlotte's unhappy memories of her loneliness at Cowan Bridge school gave birth to a distorted image of a house pervaded by 'the odour of rancid fat' and dirty and unwholesome food. Mrs Gaskell repeats these distortions as facts. Emily, wild, fierce, and lonely, passionate and mystical, fares ill in her pages; and Branwell is a disgraceful and melodramatic pseudo-Byronic figure. Worse than any of these distortions of her subsidiary characters, Mrs Gaskell deletes altogether those parts of Charlotte's letters that reveal her to have fallen in love with Monsieur Héger, the head of the school she attended in Brussels, and allows homesickness to seem the cause of her despair.

How, with all these counts against her, is it possible to refer to Mrs Gaskell as 'conscientious' and to praise her biography? There are two reasons. The important episode she left out did not alter the outlines of Charlotte Brontë's character; it occurred when those outlines had already become firmly drawn, and did not change them. The carelessness in verification and the misunderstanding of Mr. Brontë and Emily and Branwell did not injure her portrayal of her central figure. And that central figure, for all the surrounding circumstances in which she went wildly wrong, she understood. 'When all the old rubbish has been sifted,' wrote May Sinclair; 'when all the old letters in that frail diminutive handwriting have been unearthed and published; . . . when all the silly tittle-tattle has gone the round of the literary parish, we shall come back to Mrs Gaskell's *Life* with the certainty that we shall find there the truth about Charlotte Brontë, all that was most profoundly and essentially she.' In spite of mistakes of fact the real personality of Charlotte Brontë is alive in Mrs Gaskell's book.

And part of that result emerges from the conception of the *Life* as a sombre and tragic novel. From the beginning 'the air is dim and lightless'; 'vegetation does not flourish, it merely exists'; and what crops there are 'consist of pale, hungry-looking grey-green oats.' The road to Haworth rises steep between stone dykes, 'with a background of dun and purple moors,' wild, bleak, and solitary, oppressive and monotonous. The grey stone parsonage leans steeply against the sharp winds at the top of the narrow street. 'The white pinched faces of the motherless children' look out over the few elder and lilac bushes at the rain-blackened tombstones in the graveyard. And from there we move into the church, with its high angular pews of black oak and the tablets of the dead Brontës whose lives we are to read: HERE LIE THE REMAINS OF: five times funereally repeated. And outside, the moors, bleak and bare, with the four winds of heaven 'tearing round the house as if they were wild beasts striving to find an entrance.'

Such is the opening. The Brontë children 'were grave and silent beyond their years.' Mr Brontë would not have them indulged; he had burned some colored boots that had been given them because he regarded them as 'too gay and luxurious for his children.' His temper was silent but volcanic: he would not speak when annoyed, but worked off his anger by firing pistols out of the back-door. The children, though precocious, were timid with him, and thinking to relieve them of this timidity he had them wear a mask while he submitted them to interrogation, and speak out from under its cover. Thus protected, to the question what a child like her wanted most, Anne (aged five) replied, 'Age and experience.' Emily (age seven), when asked how to make Branwell behave, said, 'Reason with him, and when he won't listen to reason, whip him.' The oldest child, Maria, was asked what was the best mode of spending time. 'By laying it out in preparation for a happy eternity.'

The children could all read at an early age. They were intensely interested in politics, being permitted to see the newspapers and periodicals Mr Brontë took. Charlotte was especially fascinated by the Duke of Wellington, and made him the hero of many of the romances she was already composing at the age of twelve. All the children were playing a game known as *Islanders*, in which they each took an island, settled it with an imaginary population drawn from the celebrities of their day, and invented for it institutions, geography, and a dramatic history; and from these developed a whole group of sagas that soon took written form about the secret lands of the Angrians and the Gondals.

Literature seemed the foreordained career of Branwell. It was a little more dubious whether it could be so for the girls. They might have to be governesses or teach school, although how they were to do so, wretchedly shy as all of them were and miserable when away from home, was a problem. Charlotte was so near-sighted that she read with her nose almost touching the book, and the presence of any stranger at all disconcerted her to agony. And, deep within her, Charlotte nourished literary hopes after all. At the same time that Branwell was writing to ask Wordsworth's opinion of some of his poetry, she was writing to Southey.

The Poet Laureate replied, kindly but discouragingly, although he felt that it was 'not a pleasant task to cast a damp over the high spirits and generous desires of youth.' It was not that he thought her talent contemptible, but literature was no profession for a woman. 'The day dreams in which you habitually indulge are likely to induce a distempered state of mind; and in proportion as all the ordinary uses of the world seem to you flat and unprofitable, you will be unfitted for them without becoming fitted for anything else.' He would not discourage her from exercising her gift, but she must 'Write poetry for its own sake; not in a spirit of emulation, and not with a view to celebrity.'

Charlotte replied, with what may have been some irony, that it was kind of him to allow her to write. She did not think that she neglected any of her duties in pursuing 'that single, absorbing, exquisite gratification.' 'In the evenings, I confess, I do think, but I never trouble anyone else with my thoughts.' Nevertheless, his answer discouraged her, and she put aside for the time all ideas of literary enterprise. But her secret heart was hot with craving for success, grandeur, admiration, passionate intensities. She tried to stifle these 'evil, wandering thoughts,' to put a damper on her 'corrupt heart, cold to the spirit and warm to the flesh,' that heart which was 'a very hot-bed for sinful thoughts.' Suppression was an agony to her.

Suppress them she did, however, and turned her thoughts in another direction. If they were ever to be anything better than governesses, she and Emily and Anne must fit themselves for more. Perhaps they might establish a school at Haworth. But for this they must be prepared to teach more than reading, ciphering, and needlework. They must be able to give instruction in history, art, foreign languages. For this, especially the last, they would need training abroad. Finally Charlotte argued her Aunt Branwell into putting up the money to send her and Emily to Brussels, where they would study at the pensionnat Héger. Presently, in spite of a misery of loneliness, almost sick for home, there they were established. They studied hard with their master, M. Héger, and acquitted themselves well (M. Héger 'rated Emily's genius as something even higher than Charlotte's'), but Emily was too unhappy away from home to stay beyond the year they had agreed on.

Charlotte continued as a teacher-pupil for an additional period, but she too was unhappy. She had fallen in love with M. Héger, who 'was good to her'—much to the embarrassment of that well-meaning man, who showed his wife all the letters she wrote him (but Mrs Gaskell does not tell us this part). The internal struggle with herself was severe. Finally she tore herself away, but it seemed as if something in her was 'tamed down and broken. I have fewer illusions; what I wish for now is active exertion—a stake in life.'

In July, 1844, they sent out the prospectus of the little school for which all this had been endured. August, September, October, went by; but no pupils were offered. The whole enterprise had failed.

Branwell had also been unsuccessful. A tutor in a private family, he had fallen in love with his employer's wife, and been dismissed. Always self-indulgent, Branwell began to drown his humiliation in drink. The husband died, and Branwell infatuatedly expected to be called to the lady's side. A message was sent him at the Black Bull. 'More than an hour elapsed' after the messenger departed; 'then, those outside heard a noise like the bleating of a calf, and, on opening the door, he was found in a kind of fit . . .' She had forbidden him to try to see her again.

He succumbed to repeated drunkenness, and began taking opium. His fits of delirium tremens kept his father up late into the night while the trembling sisters listened below. ' "The poor old man and I had a terrible night," ' Branwell would whine; ' "he does his best —the poor old man! but it's all over with me;" (whimpering) "it's *her* fault, *her* fault." ' Remembering her own grim and secret struggle with her passion for M. Héger, Charlotte felt contemptuous of this blubbering self-pity. When he died her affection had been completely eaten away by the acid of her scorn for his weakness.

Meanwhile a strange accident had revived her literary projects. Charlotte came upon a private manuscript volume of Emily's verse, and found in the poems 'a peculiar music, wild, melancholy . . .' Emily was outraged at this violation of her privacy, but finally she yielded to Charlotte's browbeating, and a volume of poems by the three sisters appeared under the pseudonyms of Currer, Ellis, and Acton Bell. Unsuccessful financially, the venture nevertheless stimulated the old fervor, and all three were soon furiously composing novels. But the household had changed. Emily hid her work from the prying hand of Charlotte, and Charlotte worked alone. Mr Brontë ate by himself; Emily's savage dog Keeper skulked through the silent rooms; the sisters scribbled all alone. Only when *Jane Eyre* was published did Mr Brontë learn what they were doing. Then Emily's *Wuthering Heights* appeared, but its wild, eerie, and lamentable beauty was not so highly acclaimed as the more human passion of Jane for Rochester.

Emily was ill, but she would not admit it or allow any attention to be paid her. 'Many a time did Charlotte and Anne drop their sewing, or cease from their writing, to listen with wrung hearts to the failing step, the laboured breathing, the frequent pauses, with which their sister climbed the short staircase; yet they dared not notice what they observed, with pangs of suffering even deeper than hers.' Keeper followed her around the house, which now she never left. But she refused to see a doctor even when he was in the house; 'and the medicines which he sent she would not take, denying that she was ill.' Pained by the estrangement between them, Charlotte went out on the moors in December to find for her a little spray of the heather she loved. But Emily would not regard it. Her breath rattled, and still she would not give in. At last she could only whisper in gasps. She died a few days before Christmas. For days and days Keeper howled at her chamber door.

Anne did not live long, and now Charlotte was alone in the house with her father. She wrote and tied up papers or letters in little bundles. 'No one comes to the house; nothing disturbs the deep repose; hardly a voice is heard; you catch the ticking of the clock in the kitchen, or the buzzing of a fly in the parlor . . .' 'The great trial,' Charlotte wrote, 'is when evening closes and night approaches. At that hour we used to assemble in the dining room—we used to talk. Now I sit by myself—necessarily I am silent.' And later still, as she sat there, all alone, 'On windy nights, cries, and sobs, and wailings seemed to go round the house, as of the dearly-beloved trying to force their way to her.'

Then the gloom lifted. The Reverend Arthur Nicholls, her father's curate, proposed marriage to her, and after a first surprise and hesitation she accepted him. Her father was in a rage, then finally he consented to the marriage and a day was set. But on the night before the wedding Mr Brontë had a fit of temper and announced that he would not go to the church. 'What was to be done? Who would give the bride away?' Mr Brontë obstinately stayed in bed, and an old friend was obliged to take her father's place.

She fell in love with her husband. What Arthur felt and believed and said became paramount. Then the following January she fell ill, and grew weaker and weaker. Late in March, waking from delirium, 'she saw her husband's woe-worn face, and caught the sound of some murmured words of prayer that God would spare her. "Oh!" she whispered forth, "I am not going to die, am I? He will not separate us, we have been so happy." ' Soon the five tablets that lay heavily across the opening chapter were complete in the bare church, and the wild winds whose voices Emily loved howled round the lone grey house.

Mrs Gaskell never understood the secret and unearthly passions Emily hid beneath her moody reserve, and her sympathies were all with Charlotte in the coldness that grew between the two. But even here, her touch was more successful than she knew; and the reader can understand how Emily revolted at Charlotte's dictatorialness, how painfully she felt herself violated by Charlotte's callous intrusion into her poems. And Mrs Gaskell even hints something of Emily's sympathy for Branwell, and her resentment of the cruel scorn which Charlotte did not even trouble to conceal from her brother.

But most effective of all is Mrs Gaskell's rendering of Charlotte herself and the atmosphere of that bleak parsonage. Charlotte's passionate hidden romanticism and her brusque self-discipline; her glowing, fleshly emotion and her stern practicality; her agonized shyness and her unbending determination; her devotion and her intolerance;—all are vividly seen. Filled with affection herself, Mrs Gaskell does not hide those humanizing weaknesses of Charlotte's domineering loving heart. She irritates, and she compels our pity and respect.

Both Lockhart and Mrs Gaskell struggle effectively with their temptations to partisanship. Mrs Gaskell is unsympathetic to Emily and melodramatically imaginative about Branwell, but she tries to be rigidly just in depicting the angularities of Charlotte. It is possible, of course, that more of these tone the picture than Mrs Gaskell knew or revealed by intent. Lockhart is still more successful than Mrs Gaskell in painting a complex portrait, even though he tends to see Scott as a grander figure than he was. But, again, his slight and loving bias does not blind the reader, and we see Scott as he was, not blameless, but despite all faint blemishes, beautiful and noble.

Mrs Gaskell surpasses Lockhart in building and controlling her story. Lockhart's, as we have noted, is long-winded, and attention falters. Mrs Gaskell, working on the scale and with the technique of the novelist, does nothing to excess; she does not weaken the dramatic effect of a single stroke by redundance. It must be admitted that her story is stark and bleak in a way that gains by brevity, and that Lockhart's allows a certain comfortable lingering over details, a human friendship that encourages us to return and bathe in Scott's warm companionship. We should not care so much to loiter over a cup of tea with Charlotte in the cold steep parsonage at Haworth.

To speak of them in these terms, however, is to reveal how vividly both authors have achieved their primary aim, revealing the personalities of their subjects. To think of sitting in the bare dining-room with Charlotte, to picture ourselves wandering along the Tweed with Sir Walter, is to regard them as real human beings. That we can do so constitutes the triumph of Lockhart and Mrs Gaskell.

TWO MONUMENTS of the LIFE-AND-LETTERS METHOD

XI

TWO MONUMENTS OF THE LIFE-AND-LETTERS METHOD

If the Muse of Biography has her own special fountain of inspiration, it can only be the stream of personal records. For the life-writer, diaries, reminiscences, letters, and personal narratives are the springs of personality. Since the time of Boswell, the purest draughts of living personality have been distilled only by such biographers as have dipped deeply in those springs. And of all personal records letters are most often available. They are more often written than diaries, memoirs, or autobiographies; and even a modest degree of eminence is enough to ensure numbers of a man's letters being preserved. And although even distinguished writers have sometimes written bare and colorless letters, a letter is as likely as anything a man leaves behind him to breathe with his personality.

So it is not strange that of all biographical forms the life-and-letters came during the Victorian period to be the dominant one. Boswell and Lockhart had used other materials as well, but they had given clarity to the method. The trail they blazed was followed by almost every biography, great or insignificant, during the century. Brilliant as its triumphs might be in the hands of an artist, it was not proof against mediocrity. Too easily in the imitators it degenerated into a series of chronologically arranged epistles cemented together by slabs of flabby narrative to bridge the gaps. Lacking selection, design, or style, and smeared over with the disheartening treacle of panegyric, it could produce the conventional two-volume 'authorized life' that Lytton Strachey complained of—'as familiar as the *cortège* of the undertaker,' and with 'the same air of slow, funereal barbarism.'

The truth is, of course, as G. M. Trevelyan remarks, that, 'It takes two to give excellence to any man's *Life and Letters:* the author of the *Life* and the author of the *Letters* . . .' If the letters are not vivid, interesting, and personal, there is no sound reason for printing them. They may even muffle and obscure a character whose sparkling highlights, glowing colors, and profound depths they reduce to the dimness of a sunstruck photograph. And the life-narrative must at least be clear, well-proportioned, and well-arranged; it must have movement and grasp of character not clouded by idolatry.

The two biographies I am going to discuss in this chapter are nineteenth century triumphs in the method. Their subjects, Charles Dickens and Thomas Babington Macaulay, although not among the greatest of all letter-writers, are sparkling, vigorous, interesting, and clear. And their authors are men who united to organizing ability and intelligence an intimate knowledge of the lives they narrate. John Forster was Dickens's lifelong friend; Sir George Otto Trevelyan, the son of Macaulay's best-loved sister.

Both employ 'the method of enormous and elaborate accretion which produced *The Life of Johnson*' and *The Life of Scott*, but with more discretion in length, for neither runs to over a thousand pages. Even on that scale, however, we must address ourselves to them inductively, inasmuch as they are both more concerned with documenting character vividly than with generalizing about it. Neither Trevelyan nor Forster is preeminently interested in reducing his task to a few characteristic flashing outlines or establishing a simple pattern of motivations. They give us a broad and varied panorama with all the features of the countryside indicated in clear and unmistakable perspective: but we must draw our own map. They do not psychologize; if we wish to understand the springs of conduct we must look beneath the surfaces. We shall find them there, but not in any hints or nudges from the authors.

Neither Forster nor Trevelyan is entirely free from Victorian restraints in delineation. Trevelyan is confident that if Macaulay ' "were now living he would have sufficient judgment and sufficient greatness of mind" '—he is quoting Macaulay's own words—'to wish to be shown as himself'; and announces that he will 'suppress no trait in his disposition, or incident in his career, which might provoke blame or question.' And Trevelyan's son points out that the biography does indeed show us the 'occasionally uncouth violence of his dislikes of particular men and books, his failure to be just to Croker or pitiful to Robert Montgomery,' and 'the limitations of his literary sympathies to the literature of the past, more or less exclusive of all that was going on in his own age.'

Considerations of tact led to the suppression of proper names in some situations, and the withholding of certain letters in which public events or personages were lampooned for the amusement of the family. At the time such minor omissions of materials which might have been misunderstood was quite permissible. Less easily to be defended is the refusal to quote a witty repartee of Macaulay's 'too strictly classical'—by which I suppose he means too classically indecent—'for reproduction in these pages.' One of the not entirely pleasant traits in Macaulay is a certain priggishness that a few such witticisms might go far to mitigate.

Forster is unsatisfyingly vague about Dickens's troubled marriage. The story is unhappy, but not at all monstrous. Dickens and his wife were unsuited in temper, lived unhappily together for many years, and at last agreed to separate. Subsequently, the evidence now available strongly suggests, Dickens lived during the remainder of his life with a young woman with whom he had fallen in love. Belated as the separation may have been, and impossible as it was for Forster to tell the whole at the time, he surrounds these events with an atmosphere of mysterious and evasive reticence that leads the reader to suspect much darker and more noisome evils than were ever there. But these are only slight blemishes on a book that in no way falsifies the main outlines of Dickens's character and that gives a clear and striking portrait. And the letters, 'those sparkling, clear, and sunny utterances of Dickens's own,' as Carlyle calls them, are indeed 'bits of *auto*-biography unrivalled in clearness and credibility.'

Macaulay's letters, too, as they appear in his nephew's selection, 'are much too good to miss,' and often in a few lines tell us 'more about Macaulay than a page of psychological analysis.' And Trevelyan's narrative is in vividness superior to Forster's, which is sometimes pedestrian and lacking in sparkle. It must be admitted, however, that there are places where Forster's narrative sequence is clearer. Trevelyan's story sometimes gets a little ahead of the letters, and then the weaving back and forth of dates is apt to be confusing; and sometimes an important event is hidden allusively in a letter and not dealt with directly in the narrative at all. In characterization, Trevelyan contributes more that is valuable to his subject than Forster, who in the main is content to allow Dickens's letters to speak for themselves.

In the more detailed narrative discussion that follows, I am first rendering the presentation of the two authors, and then basing certain interpretations of character upon them. Those interpretations are mine, not theirs: they have no responsibility for them, save insofar as a critical reading of their biographies lends its support.

The Inimitable Boz

He was a queer small boy, too sickly to play cricket or prisoner's base, and never very skilled at marbles or peg-top. But in a little back room there were *Roderick Random*, *Peregrine Pickle*, *Don Quixote*, *Gil Blas*, the *Arabian Nights*, 'a glorious company' who suggested marvelous games. 'I have been Tom Jones (a child's Tom Jones, a harmless creature) for a week together . . .' And then, again, 'armed with the centre-piece of an old set of boot-trees,' he was a captain in the Royal British Navy 'beset by savages and resolved to sell his life at a great price.' And there was the marine parade at Chatham (his father was in the navy pay-office); the little boy loved 'the gay, bright regiments always going and coming, the continual paradings and firings, . . . the ships floating out in the Medway, with their far visions of the sea . . .'

Then his father came to be involved in trouble about money (it was tied up with something mysterious called 'the deed') and the child had to take a long stage-coach journey alone in a dreary rain from the bright port to a mean tenement in Camden Town. He cleaned his father's boots for him now; there was 'not too much for dinner; and . . . at last my father was arrested.' The little boy had to work for six shillings a week in a blacking-factory where 'old grey rats swarming down in the cellars' made 'their squeaking and scuffling' audible through wainscotted rooms with rotten floors and staircase. He wandered through the London streets and ate alone: sometimes he could not resist 'the stale pastry put out at half-price on trays at the confectioners' doors in Tottenham Court Road,' and then he had to do without dinner.

At last his misery was more than he could bear. He wept when he saw his father, now released from the debtors' prison. 'I do believe he had never thought . . . about it,' Dickens wrote, years later, but now he began to feel 'it was not quite right.' 'I do not write resentfully or angrily; . . . but I never afterwards forgot, I never shall forget, I never can forget, that my mother was warm for my being sent back.'

There was a brief interval as a day scholar at a private school, and then we find him as an office-lad in an attorney's office, groping his way blindly through a system of shorthand with 'marks like flies' legs' and 'arbitrary characters; the most despotic characters I have ever known.' At nineteen he was a Parliamentary reporter and contributing occasional sketches signed 'Boz' to the *Evening Chronicle*. In 1836 a new series of sketches was suggested. Dickens says, 'I thought of Mr Pickwick.' Within fifteen weeks the demand for each number was more than forty thousand.

The young author was full of health and high spirits. He was forever sending his friend Forster little notes proposing jaunts in the country. 'What a brilliant morning for a country walk!' he would write, not adding another word. Or, 'Is it possible that you can't, oughtn't, shouldn't, mustn't, *won't* be tempted, this gorgeous day!' Meanwhile his prolific invention was turning out *Oliver Twist*, *Nicholas Nickleby*, *The Old Curiosity Shop*, and *Barnaby Rudge*.

The amazing and unexpected success of these early writings made him resentful of the not entirely advantageous terms on which they were brought out. He finally forced his publishers to a new financial arrangement. So fortified, Dickens and his wife (he had married Catherine Hogarth in 1836) set out for a vacation tour of the Highlands. The inns were small—'There isn't a basin in the

Highlands that will hold my face; not a drawer that will open after you have put your clothes in it; not a water-bottle capacious enough to wet your toothbrush'—and the weather was rainy—'the sky is a vast waterspout that never leaves off emptying itself.' Glencoe was 'perfectly *terrible*. The pass is an awful place. It is shut in on each side by enormous rocks from which great torrents come rushing down' and 'scores of glens, high up, which form such haunts as you might imagine yourself wandering, in the very height and madness of a fever.'

One part of the journey was even more noteworthy. 'If you should happen to have your hat on,' he wrote to Forster, 'take it off, that your hair may stand on end without any interruption.' 'Through the whole glen, which is ten miles long, torrents were boiling and foaming, and sending up in every direction spray like the smoke of great fires. They were rushing down every hill . . . and tearing like devils across the path, and down into the depths of the rocks. Some of the hills looked as if they were full of silver, and had cracked in a hundred places.' Presently their carriage had to ford a swollen stream. Once in the water, 'The carriage went round and round like a great stone, the boy was pale as death, the horses were struggling and plashing and snorting like sea-animals, and we were all roaring to the driver to throw himself off . . . when suddenly it came all right (having got into shallow water) and, all tumbling and dripping and jogging from side to side, climbed up the dry land.'

Soon, however, he was experiencing even wilder adventures. It was proposed that he travel in America, and keep a notebook of his impressions. In January, 1842, he embarked on the Britannia. Sea-voyaging was rough in those days. 'Four dozen plates,' he wrote, 'were broken at dinner. One steward fell down the cabin stairs with a round of beef, and injured his foot severely. Another steward fell down after him, and cut his eye open. The baker's taken ill; so is the pastry-cook . . . Twelve dozen of bottled porter has got loose up on deck, and the bottles are rolling about distractedly, overhead.'

His early impressions of America were favorable. 'There is no man in this town, or in this State of New England, who has not a blazing fire, and a meat dinner every day of his life. A flaming sword in the air would not attract so much attention as a beggar in the streets.' The people were 'friendly, earnest, hospitable, kind, frank, very often accomplished, far less prejudiced than you would suppose, warm-hearted, fervent, and enthusiastic.' Only one queer little trait he noticed at first: the national vanity. The newspapers always described him when he appeared in public as being 'very pale,' 'apparently thunderstruck' at all he saw; and one 'gravely expressed its conviction' that he had never been in such society before, and 'that its high and striking tone' could not 'fail to make an indelible impression on his mind.'

Then Dickens ventured to comment on the dishonest habit American publishers made of pirating foreign books. There was a loud outcry!—he was 'no gentleman,' he was a 'mercenary scoundrel.' 'The notion that I, a man alone by himself, in America, should venture to suggest to the Americans that there was one point on which they were neither just to their own countrymen nor to us, actually struck the boldest dumb!' The howl disillusioned him: 'I believe there is no country, on the face of the earth, where there is less freedom of opinion . . .'

As he traveled in from the coast, ill impressions multiplied. Spitting was universal. In the railway train, 'The flashes of saliva flew so perpetually and incessantly out of the windows all the way, that it looked as though they were ripping open feather-beds inside . . . There are spit-boxes in every steamboat, bar-room, public dining-room, house of office, and place of general resort . . . I have twice seen gentlemen at evening parties . . . spit upon the drawing-room carpet. And in every bar-room and hotel passage the stone floor looks as if it were paved with open oysters.' On the canal boats the ladies were content 'with smearing their hands and faces in a very small quantity of water'; the men made 'a hasty use of the common brush and comb.' People blew their noses with their fingers upon the carpets.

Intolerance of opinion on the slavery question was rampant. 'They won't let you be silent. They *will* ask what you think of it;' and then explode with rage and hatred at adverse comment. The prosperity of the coast cities did not extend to the settlements. In their forlorn and desolate cabins, 'Old hats, old clothes, old boards, old fragments of blanket and paper, are stuffed into the broken glass' of the windows. And, in spite of all these distressing circumstances, 'The national vanity swallows up all other countries on the face of the earth.' The United States despised art and literature. '"Our people don't think of poetry, sir. Dollars, banks, and cotton are our books, sir." And they certainly are,' Dickens adds, 'for a lower average of general information than exists in this country on all other topics, it would be very hard to find.'

But in spite of this discouraging experience of democracy, Dickens was still a radical. When he was a child he had been told that *the radicals* were 'terrible banditti,' 'whose principles were that the prince regent wore stays; that nobody had a right to any salary; and that the army and navy ought to be put down.' But as he had grown older, and become acquainted with 'the debtors' prisons described in *Pickwick*, the parochial management denounced in *Oliver*, and the Yorkshire schools exposed in *Nickleby*,' as he had heard the bitter cry of the children in the factories and observed the gin-drowned miseries of the poor, his indignation rose. He wrote angry rhymed squibs on the Tories and their doctrines:

I'll sing you a new ballad, and I'll warrant it first-rate,
Of the days of that old gentleman who had that old estate;
When they spent the public money at a bountiful old rate
On ev'ry mistress, pimp, and scamp, at ev'ry noble gate,
In the fine old English Tory times;
Soon may they come again!

The good old laws were garnished well with gibbets, whips, and chains,
With fine old English penalties, and fine old English pains;
With rebel heads and seas of blood once hot in rebel veins:
For all these things were requisite to guard the rich old gains
Of the fine old English Tory times;
Soon may they come again!

. . .

The bright old day now dawns again; the cry runs through the land,
In England there shall be—dear bread! In Ireland—sword and brand!

And poverty and ignorance, shall swell the rich and grand,
So rally round the rulers with the gentle iron hand,
Of the fine old English Tory days;
Hail to the coming time!

Fifteen years later, during the Crimean War, he was even more embittered. Political aristocracy and tuft-hunting, he thought, were 'the death of England.' In spite of all, he pressed on: 'every movement for practical reforms, to obtain more efficient sanitary legislation, to get the best compulsory education practicable for the poor, and to better the condition of laboring people, he assisted earnestly to his last hour.' And still there loomed the 'enormous black cloud of poverty in every town,' a 'non-working aristocracy,' Parliament 'the dreariest failure and nuisance': he was disheartened with democracy. The machinery of representative government seemed to him altogether broken down.

Travel on the Continent deepened the darkness of the scene. The evils of poverty were even worse in Italy and France than in England. The lazzaroni were 'mere squalid, abject, miserable animals for vermin to batten on; slouching, slinking, ugly, shabby, scavenging scarecrows!' And the paupers' burial place in Naples, the 'great paved yard with three hundred and sixty-five pits in it,' one of which was 'opened every night in the year' and the bodies 'flung in uncoffined' to the quicklime from a cart whose red lamp glared through the streets! Amid this misery, speculation was high. On the Bourse there were constant crashes, disaster elbowing luxury: 'thoroughbred horses without end, and red velvet carriages . . . go by all day long;' speculators 'all howling and haggard'; 'Concierges and people like that perpetually blow their brains out . . .' A sordid landscape.

But not all his time was passed in these melancholy observations of social evils. Forster shows him still writing at breakneck speed, living with gusto, playing games with unbounded vitality, sightseeing. He went up the Great St Bernard pass and saw the monastery by its 'black lake with phantom clouds perpetually stalking over it. Peaks, and points, and plains of eternal ice and snow . . . Everything ironbound, and frozen up. Beside the convent, in a little outhouse with a grated iron door . . . are the bodies of people found in the snow . . . standing up, in corners and against walls . . .'

In Paris he attended luxurious dinners with Augier and Sandeau; in Boulogne he had a villa for a time, where he describes an exciting war to preserve a pet canary from two marauding cats. Nothing could keep them out of the house. They hid away 'in the most terrific manner: hanging themselves up behind draperies, like bats, and tumbling out in the dead of night with frightful caterwaulings.' The household blazed away with shotguns; they lay in ambush in bushes; 'the tradesmen cry out as they come up the avenue, "Me voici! C'est moi–boulanger–ne tirez pas" '–and immediately after they had been firing in the front garden a cat would enter 'in the calmest manner, by the back window.'

Even Dickens's immense vitality, however, was beginning to give way under the pressure of his laborious writing and lecturing and traveling. He developed coughs and was stethoscoped, rubbings were ordered for his chest. A restlessness springing from domestic unease kept him forever moving. He felt a 'vague unhappy loss or want of something' that he did not care to clarify further. But secretly he knew what it was. 'Why is it, that with poor David, a sense comes always crushing on me now, when I fall in low spirits, as of one happiness I have missed in life, and one friend and companion I have never made?'

At last he concealed it from himself no longer. 'I find that the skeleton in my domestic closet is becoming a pretty big one.' The truth was, he wrote Forster, 'Poor Catherine and I are not made for each other, and there is no help for it . . . She is exactly what you know, in the way of being amiable and complying; but we are strangely ill-assorted for the bond there is between us. God knows she would have been a thousand times happier if she had married another kind of man . . .' Finally it was decided that they should separate. 'The eldest son went with his mother . . . and the other children remained with himself, their intercourse with Mrs Dickens being left entirely to themselves.'

His restlessness did not diminish, and he continued the lecture-readings from his works that he gave with such energy and dramatic force. But he began to be subject to attacks of faintness and often he was unable to sleep at night. He was in a terrible railway accident that shook him up a great deal, and from then on he had curious feelings of soreness in his body. Nevertheless he insisted on undertaking a second American tour in 1867, and everywhere his arrival was a sensation among a people who had long forgiven or forgotten their fury at the *American Notes* of 1842. People stood in lines eight hundred long to buy tickets for his readings: 'Members of families relieved each other in the queues; waiters flew across the streets and squares from the neighboring restaurants, to serve parties who were taking their breakfast in the open December air; while excited men offered five and ten dollars for the mere permission to exchange places with other persons standing nearer the head of the line.' But he was unable to get rid of a hacking cough for a good part of the tour, even with the aid of the 'Rocky Mountain Sneezer' of brandy, rum, and snow given him by his landlord in New York.

At last he got back to England. He rested awhile and then began another series of readings. With terrible exertion and gruesome effect he would read the scene of Sikes murdering Nancy. A gradual and unconscious suicide was taking place beside the imaginary murder, but nothing would induce him to give up. The readings came to an end at last, and he returned to his home at Gadshill Place. But the strain had gone on too long. At dinner on 8 June, 1870, his sister-in-law saw that he looked ill; when he tried to rise he almost fell. 'Her effort was then to get him to the sofa, but after a slight struggle he sank heavily on his left side.' All aid was useless. 'There was an effusion of the brain; and though stertorous breathing continued all night,' and all the next day, 'there had never been a gleam of hope . . .'

Such is Forster's telling of the tale. Why is it that we feel, through all the blare and glitter of success, that the queer small boy had never really gotten what he wanted? His life had been full of high spirits and gusto, bursting grotesquely out of the novels, and revealed again and again, as we have seen, in his letters. He had made a great name for himself; he had grown wealthy and bought Gadshill Place, which it used to be a treat of his childhood to come and look at. But none of these things had really satisfied him. Over and over again there was the cry for that 'vague unhappy loss or want of something,' the restlessness that drove him forever with insatiable energy. What was it that was wanting? was it love?—the young sister of his Catherine, whom he had not married, and whose shade had stood dimly between them? Or was that failure a result of something else?—a something growing out of those early years of shabby indigence, the shame of the blacking-warehouse his mother 'was warm for his being sent back' to, the humiliations of childhood corroding his pride?

To escape those years he had been obliged to exert tremendous powers of will. In doing so, he became, Forster confesses, 'hard and aggressive' with 'almost the tone of fierceness.' He had forced his earliest publishers to make a new financial arrangement with him, when they had every right to insist on his standing by his agreement. But Dickens simply maintained with the vehemence of a grievance that he would not be able to write if he felt himself so unjustly treated. In many other ways he displayed a like ruthlessness. His resolves were 'insuperable, however hasty the opinions on which they had been formed.' And yet, mingled with this hardness there was an intense sensibility 'and the most eager craving for sympathy.'

He longed to be loved, but the 'stern and even cold self-reliance' to which he had schooled himself made it hard for him to yield himself utterly, as he desired. Warm and generous in nature, he could overflow in loud games and horseplay or let himself go in the disguises of theatricality; but the call of deeper feelings found him constrained, knotted up within. 'What it was that in society made him often uneasy, shrinking, and over-sensitive,' Forster observes, 'he knew; but all the danger he ran in bearing down and overmastering the feeling he did not know.'

The youthful hardships had left still other marks. 'Pray, Mr Dickens,' someone had asked his father, 'where was your son educated?'—'Why, indeed, Sir—ha! ha!—he may be said to have educated himself.' He had; and, for all his glowing success, there were distressing gaps. It was only the earliest days of David Copperfield that were autobiographic. The education at Canterbury, the serene years with Mr Wickfield, were the longed-for that had never been. He had read copiously but erratically: the many things a cultivated man knew and that he did not know were sources of embarrassment to him. There were many things *he* knew, to be sure, that the cultivated man did not. But they did not alleviate the feeling of discomfort that had to be overmastered.

There was in Dickens also a kind of social insensitivity, a want of taste, that sometimes made him crude and inconsiderate. He did not mean to pain Leigh Hunt by taking some of his most noticeable oddities and using them in the character of Harold Skimpole, in *Bleak House;* it did not occur to him that people would also attribute the less airy and whimsical qualities in the character to Hunt. And brilliant as is the portrayal of Mr Micawber, it is a success 'obtained,' Professor Saintsbury remarks, 'a little in the teeth of the fifth commandment.'

His skill in painting the 'everyday vulgar, shabby genteel, or downright low' was the fruit of a certain congeniality as well as of observation. Forster reluctantly admits 'his occasional preference for what was even below his level over that which was above it.' He was not quite sure he was a gentleman. He was not quite confident of his own manners. It made him hate aristocracy and sentimentalize the virtues of the poor. He satirized in *Barnaby Rudge*, through the character of Mr Chester, the polished manners of a Chesterfield, but the fear of being thought not a gentleman did not altogether leave him. In the background were the blacking-warehouse and the debtors' prison, which he must try to forget. They produced those sensations of uneasiness and shrinking in society that he had to bear down on and overmaster.

The great artist, the potent magician who had created a hundred living beings, never freed himself from a middle-class shame for the poverty, the disgrace, and the educational scantiness of his childhood. They had forced him to queer shifts, and brought him into contact with queer types who had never been elevated into art before. As an artist he was indeed the product of his starved childhood and striving youth: two people in his past had made his triumph sure. The queer small boy exulting in the marine parade or playing at being Tom Jones, shamed by being put to menial tasks, had brought imagination and sensitiveness. The smart pushing young reporter observing the rookeries of the poor and the horsey characters around inns had contributed determination, humor, and a new range of subject-matter.

But the same two had taken the full sweetness of victory away from him. How they mingled humiliation and loud confidence; tenderness, robust imagination, and gusto; shrinking and pride! Then, with exuberant release, the old vulgar enjoyment of Sam Weller or Mr Pickwick would sweep over him in waves of rollicking humor; or the monstrous images of Fagin and Sikes would build themselves up horribly; or he would brood tenderly over the pathos of little Miss Flite. Fearfully interwined they lay, the 'sparkling, clear, and sunny utterance,' and, 'deeper than all, . . . dark, fateful, silent elements, tragical to look upon, and hiding, amid dazzling radiances as of the sun, the elements of death itself.'

Child in Armor

'Often, in newspapers and elsewhere,' writes Macaulay's grand-nephew, G. M. Trevelyan, 'I notice references to Macaulay as the "typical" Victorian, with all the merits and limitations of that down-right and optimistic period incarnate in his person.' There is much to be said for the identification. He was a middle-class intellectual in a day when the middle-class was dominant. As a Whig, from the moment he entered politics he rode on the triumphant crest of liberalism and reform. He had all the ardors of the battle combined with the refreshing certitude of being not only in the right but destined to succeed.

Like the age itself, he looked with complacency on its material progress. Tremendous as was his reading and devoted as he was to literature, his admirations were centered largely in the past, in the artistic fait accompli. Otherwise, like the manufacturers of Manchester and Birmingham and the politicians who represented them, he was largely anaesthetic to art. He shared the insular conviction of his fellows that in the concert of nations God intended the voice of England to be paramount; he had no doubts that the backward portions of the globe were the white man's burden.

His judgments were dogmatic and without subtlety; but they were affirmed and defended with courage. Self-confident and impregnable to outward view, his personal affections were of an extreme, a vulnerable susceptibility. He hid within himself the sentimentality that was the other face of Victorian hard-headedness and imperialism.

His life was of a piece with the character of the age. Everyone is familiar with the splendid public career, marching from triumph to triumph without a single shadow of failure, and crowned in harvest maturity with the honors of the man of letters and historian. At three the precocious child was already reading incessantly, with a book in one hand and a piece of bread-and-butter in the other; and at eight, Trevelyan reports, his compositions had the lucidity and scrupulous accuracy in mechanics that characterize his mature works. At Cambridge he twice gained the Chancellor's medal for English verse and the prize for Latin Declamation, and became a Fellow of Trinity. When he was no more than twenty-five his essay on Milton in the *Edinburgh Review* made him famous. The following year he was called to the bar, and soon after was made a Commissioner of Bankruptcy, with an income of nine hundred pounds a year. On the very eve of the great Reform Bill agitation, in 1830, he entered Parliament.

The temper of the age cried out against the scandals of borough representation, the manipulation of the small band of electors by means of the patronage of India, the gagging of the press, the ruinous fines and protracted imprisonments for those who spoke their minds. The manufacturing interests must be represented, the rotten boroughs abolished, India cease to be the spoils of a party. 'On the 1st of March, 1831, Lord John Russell introduced the Reform Bill amidst breathless silence, which was at length broken by peals of contemptuous laughter from the Opposition benches as he read the list' of the boroughs sentenced to death.

Macaulay defended the Bill in an eloquent speech. Trevelyan quotes his peroration: 'Now, therefore, while everything at home and abroad forbodes ruin to those who persist in a hopeless struggle against the spirit of the age, now, while the crash of the proudest throne of the Continent is still resounding in our ears, now, while the roof of a British palace affords an ignominious shelter to the exiled heir of forty kings, now, while we see on every side ancient institutions subverted and great societies dissolved . . . take counsel, not of prejudice, not of party spirit . . . but of history, of reason, of the ages which are past, of the signs of this most portentous time . . . The danger is terrible. The time is short. If this bill should be rejected, I pray to God that none of those who concur in rejecting it, may ever remember their votes with unavailing remorse, amidst the wreck of laws, the confusion of ranks, the spoliation of property, and the dissolution of social order.'

The Bill passed, Macaulay's office was reformed out of existence, but presently he was one of the Commissioners of the Board of Control, which represented the Crown in its relations to the East India Company. Samuel Rogers gave the last proof of esteem by asking him to the celebrated breakfasts. He dazzled high society as well. Holland House echoed to his floods of informative conversation, and the aristocratic cosmopolitanism of the great Whig families put him in touch with the culture and affairs of the great world. He blossomed into a boyish dandyism, with a 'wardrobe . . . enormously overstocked,' and wearing 'perfectly new dark kid gloves' that were much too tight.

Meanwhile reorganization of the Indian service was being pressed. The East India Company 'was relieved of its commercial attributes, and became a corporation charged with the function of ruling Hindoostan; and its directors remained princes, but merchant princes no longer.' Macaulay was asked to be a member of the Supreme Council which would govern the Eastern Empire. His family's fortunes were strained; if he accepted this appointment it would put them beyond any possible want. At Calcutta he could live in splendor for half his salary of ten thousand pounds a year, and save the remainder. It would involve four years of exile, but he could return at the age of thirty-nine with a fortune of thirty thousand pounds.

Only he could not bear the separation alone; his homesickness would be too great; he begged his favorite sister Hannah to go with him. 'I can bribe you only by telling you,' he pleaded, 'that, if you will go with me, I will love you better than I love you now, if I can.' Hannah consented to accompany him on an expatriation which, Trevelyan affirms, 'he would never have faced without her.' In February, 1834, they set sail.

In India he labored assiduously. He had spent the voyage out in mastering the principles of jurisprudence, which had bored him as an advocate but fired his imagination now that he had to take on the responsibilities of the law-maker. As President of the Committee on Public Instruction he outlined an entire system of education, began vigorously to create the machinery for bringing it into existence, and threw himself into the task of administration and control. He became President of the Law Commission; and most of the Indian Penal Code was his personal work. Of it, his successor, Mr Fitzjames Stephen, said, 'It is to the French "Code Pénal," and, I may add, to the North German Code of 1871, what a finished picture is to a sketch.'

In 1838 he left India for home. He entered Parliament again as member for Edinburgh. During Lord Melbourne's government he held the Secretaryship at War. But the defeat of the government in

1841 gave him the leisure he had desired for resuming his literary career. His *Lays of Ancient Rome* were greeted almost immediately 'with a paean of hearty, unqualified panegyric.' Christopher North seized the opportunity to depreciate the reigning verse-writers of the day. The 'Young Poets' was his invidious epithet for them. The 'Young Poets,' he said, were 'rather ignorant; his knowledge is great': they 'dally with their subject; he strikes its heart': they 'steal from all and sundry, and deny their thefts; he robs in the face of day. Whom? Homer.'

Meanwhile he continued the monumental labors of erudition on which his history was built. To verify a few paragraphs about the size of Leeds in 1685 he carried on a whole correspondence and consulted innumerable records. He 'expended on the pointing of a phrase as much conscientious research as would have provided some writers, who speak of Macaulay as showy and shallow, with at least half a dozen pages of ostentatious statistics.'

Finally the first two volumes appeared. 'I shall not be satisfied,' he had written cockily in 1841, 'unless I produce something which shall for a few days supersede the last fashionable novel on the tables of young ladies.' But he had his desire. Within ten days the *History* sold three thousand copies; of the third and fourth volumes, in 1855, the whole first edition of twenty-five thousand copies was ordered in advance, and the stock for printing it weighed fifty-six tons. His prestige became enormous. At the zoological gardens 'two damsels were just about' to enter and see the hippopotamus, he reports in a letter, 'when I was pointed out to them. "Mr Macaulay!" cried the lovely pair. "Is that Mr Macaulay? Never mind the hippopotamus." '

His health was wavering, but he continued, although not very actively, to represent Edinburgh in Parliament. On the rare occasions when he addressed the House, though, members broke into a run and crowded through the door, wigs and gowns appeared, pressmen hurried to the galleries. Bills that had gone unopposed through all their stages but the last were thrown out by majorities of over a hundred when Macaulay, in a house grown still as death, stood up to speak against them. In 1856 the ill-health that was gaining on him led to his resignation. In 1857 he was offered a peerage and became Baron Macaulay of Rothley.

In his chambers in the Albany, and later at Holly Lodge, in

Kensington, he constantly saw all his young nephews and nieces, and was in almost daily contact with his sister Hannah. Her marriage while they were in India had only added Trevelyan as a brother to his family. But in 1859 Trevelyan was offered the Governorship of Madras, and Macaulay brooded unhappily over the separation it would mean. Whenever he reflected on it, the thought left him in tears. A little after Christmas, his sister, hearing that he was more than usually melancholy, came to spend the night with him. 'As we drove up to the porch . . . the maids ran crying out into the darkness to meet us, and we knew that all was over.' He had been in his library and told the butler he was tired. 'The man proposed his lying on the sofa. He rose as if to move, sat down again, and ceased to breathe.'

'He died as he had always wished to die;' Trevelyan says, '—without pain; without any formal farewell; preceding to the grave all whom he loved; and leaving behind him a great and honourable name, and the memory of a life every action of which was as clear and transparent as one of his own sentences.'

'One of the happiest lives that it has ever fallen to the lot of a biographer to record,' is his nephew's valediction. His life had indeed been like that of the Prince in a fairy tale. There had been the brambled wood to pierce, but the thorns had parted before him; and the glass mountain to scale, but he had ascended with ease. There had never been a Princess to be won, but he had not seemed even to notice her absence. Never disappointed in his affections, brilliant, confident, acclaimed, successful—what more could be asked? And yet, as we gaze on him, we wonder if the fairy tales have told the whole story after all. Maybe Prince Charming, also, from long-continued triumph, became a little too self-assured? Perhaps his feelings, unrefined by suffering, although still just and sensible on the whole, came to lack delicacy, shading—subtlety of perception?

Certainly Macaulay often seems to us a little bit hard and metallic, his edges too angular and obtrusive. He was kindly and sympathetic. Those whom he loved he loved tenderly, even tremulously. But outside the charmed circle so drawn his perceptions hardened into unimaginative rigidity. He was impatient of people who bored him: 'fools he by no means suffered gladly,' but voiced his antagonism decidedly and loudly.

His judgments, so quick and dogmatic, have often a cocksure superficiality. Chesterfield's *Letters*, he said, 'are for the most part trash,' and borrow their celebrity from the fact that Chesterfield had such a reputation for wit that at last it became the custom 'to laugh whenever he opened his mouth, without waiting for the *bon mot*.' Walter Scott he condemned severely: 'In politics, a bitter and unscrupulous partisan; profuse and ostentatious in expense; agitated by the hopes and fears of a gambler; perpetually sacrificing the perfection of his compositions, and the durability of his fame, to his eagerness for money . . .' Haydon, he wrote, 'was exactly the vulgar idea of a man of genius,' and 'as poor, commonplace a creature, as any in the world'; his paintings 'huge daubs' and his character all disdain and ingratitude. Macaulay's own disdain for the paintings blinds him to the electricity of the man; and even his 'huge daubs' is no credit to his perception, being no more than a conventional echo. Macaulay had little responsiveness to art or literature save as they emanated from the past. For all his knowledge, and his immense efficiency and grasp, he often misses the important qualification, the significant depth.

But if there was an unlovely severity in his judgments of others, his own course was uncompromising. Though he had been brought up almost in luxury, his father's prosperity was short-lived, and the young man unhesitatingly took up the burden of providing for the welfare of his brothers and sisters. 'At a time when his Parliamentary fame stood at its highest he was reduced to sell the gold medals which he had gained at Cambridge.' Despite his father's debts and the ruin it might bring on himself to defy his party, loyalty to his father's anti-slavery principles made him oppose the West India Bill which his government brought up.

As a politician he was remarkably independent. He refused to canvass for votes: 'To request an honest man to vote according to his conscience is superfluous. To request him to vote against his conscience is an insult.' Nor would he pledge himself 'to make or support any particular motion.' His actions as a legislator must always be in accordance with his growing knowledge of the nation's needs, not hampered by agreements in advance. And although he was always a man of the Industrial Revolution, completely in sympathy with its material course and objects, from the beginning he protested against exploitation. Of the Peterloo Massacre he wrote to his father,

'When I cease to feel the injuries of others warmly, to detest wanton cruelty, and to feel my soul rise against oppression, I shall feel myself unworthy to be your son.' The other side of his intolerance was his unbending probity.

But he was not all solemn rectitude. He had high spirits as well as high principles. Even the precocious small boyhood had been 'as playful as a kitten,' and 'at any period of his life [he] could literally spend whole days playing with children.' During school holidays the house overflowed with noise and frolic. 'Games of hide-and-seek, that lasted for hours, with shouting and the blowing of horns up and down the stairs and through every room, were varied by ballads, which, like the Scalds of old, he composed during the act of recitation,' and attributed 'to an anonymous author whom he styled "the Judicious Poet."' An acquaintance who had the unfortunate habit of detaining clergymen by their buttonholes was celebrated in a long saga:

Our friend has filled a mighty trunk
With trophies torn from Doctor Monk,
And he has really tattered foully
The vestments of Archbishop Howley.
No button could I late discern on
The garments of Archbishop Vernon,
And never had his fingers mercy
Upon the garb of Bishop Percy,—

And so on for stanzas. His liveliness overflowed through all his life in jokes and humor. He was physically clumsy to a degree where he never shaved without cutting himself. Once he had hurt his hand, and was obliged to send for a barber. When he asked what was the charge, 'Oh, Sir,' said the man, 'whatever you usually give the person who shaves you.' 'In that case,' said Macaulay, 'I should give you a great gash on each cheek.'

From India one of his letters illustrates the same boyishness. An Englishman had accosted him:

"Pray, Mr. Macaulay, do not you think that Buonaparte was the Beast?" "No, Sir, I cannot say that I do." "Sir, he was the Beast. I can prove it. I have found the number 666 in his name. Why, Sir, if he was not the Beast, who was?" This was a puzzling question, and I am

> not a little vain of my answer. "Sir," said I, "the House of Commons is the Beast. There are 658 members of the House; and these, with their chief officers,—the three clerks, the Sergeant and his deputy, the Chaplain, the doorkeeper, and the librarian,—make 666." "Well, Sir, that is strange. But I can assure you that, if you write Napoleon Buonaparte in Arabic, leaving out only two letters, it will give 666." "And pray, Sir, what right have you to leave out two letters? And, as St John was writing Greek, and to Greeks, is it not likely that he would use the Greek rather than the Arabic notation?" . . . The man looked at me as if he thought me a very wicked fellow; and, I daresay, has by this time discovered that, if you write my name in Tamul, leaving out T in Thomas, B in Babington, and M in Macaulay, it will give the number of this unfortunate Beast.

There is not only humor in Macaulay's life; there is pathos. Even in the precocious childhood there is a kind of touching, unchildlike maturity, as if the poor little fellow in his green coat with red collar and cuffs, his frill at the throat, and his white trousers, had never really been a child at all, but always a little man. When he was a pretty, light-haired boy of four, some coffee was accidentally spilled on his legs, and when he was asked, somewhat later, how the burn felt now, he looked up and replied, 'Thank you, madam, the agony is abated.' And when a housemaid threw away the row of oyster-shells that marked out as his own a little plot of ground at the rear of the house, he walked into the drawing-room where his mother was entertaining visitors, and said very solemnly: 'Cursed be Sally; for it is written, Cursed is he that removeth his neighbor's land-mark.'

His childhood was not unhappy, 'for all testimony declares' that he was very 'lively and merry.' But it has the pathos of seeming to miss in some ways the simplicity of childhood. His mature affections seem conversely to have some of the dependence of the child. Beneath all the vigorous self-reliance of the public figure, for his family and friends 'his affections were only too tender, and his sensibilities too acute.' The thought of his exile in India, half a globe away from them, was so painful to him that he was unable to face it without the comforting presence of his sister. It was a severe effort, when Trevelyan fell in love with her, to refrain from discouraging the attention. 'I could easily have prevented it,' he wrote another sister, 'by merely treating Trevelyan with a little coldness, for he is a man whom the smallest rebuff would completely discourage . . . What I have myself felt it is unnecessary to say. My parting from you almost broke my heart . . . Now I have nothing except the resources of my own mind, and the consciousness of having acted not ungenerously.'

His forebodings were unjustified. He and the Trevelyans formed a single household where 'his existence was passed amidst a bright atmosphere of domestic happiness.' In the last months, to be sure, before his sister was to follow her husband back to India, Macaulay was unhappy enough. He was 'fully convinced that, when he and his sister parted, they would part for ever.' He thought of how he would die when she was thousands of miles away. Reading Arthur's farewell, in *The Idylls of the King*, his misery overwhelmed him; 'I cried over some passages . . .' And, a little later, he wrote: 'A month more of such days as I have been passing of late would make me impatient to get to my little narrow crib, like a weary factory child.' During the last few days of his life he had no longer the force to suppress the outward signs of grief. 'I have shed no tears during some days, though with me tears ask only leave to flow, as poor Cowper says. I am sensible of no intellectual decay;—not the smallest.' Seven days later he was released by death.

So the little boy with the powers of a man melts into the man with the sorrows of a child. His abiding love of boyish jokes and noisy games played with children, his exclusive centering of his emotional life in childlike dependent affection for his family, his crude and forthright likes and dislikes and snap judgments, his failure ever to feel the need of sexual companionship or the enchantment of romantic love: all reveal the psychology of a boy.

Through his public life the man concealed the child like one hidden in armor. He was indomitable because his vulnerability was all hidden within. He was a boy playing a game: playing it with all the intensity, vigor, and earnestness of a boy. The mechanical, efficient style, with all its sharp contrasts of lights and shade, its hardness of outline, and the hammer blows with which it makes its points, was the same, almost from the start, in man and child. Its emphasis on action, its lack of nuance, are characteristic. Undisconcerted from the first by the fierce light of public life, the young prodigy began talking in his loud confident voice, pouring out that flood of vehement language, remorseless, undeviating, swift. In untiring precision it classified and disposed of facts. But at home he romped and played noisy games of hide-and-seek, wept with a child's despair at being separated from a beloved sister, and then at last, like a tired child, went to his 'little narrow crib' in the dark.

TWO NINETEENTH CENTURY EDUCATIONS

XII

TWO NINETEENTH CENTURY EDUCATIONS

New Lamps for Old

ONLY within the last century have autobiographers tried to throw a flood of light on their educations. Even serious autobiographers like Herbert of Cherbury and Gibbon think of the world more as a stage for their achievements than as a school where they have learned by application. They see themselves as *essences;* youth and young manhood brought them to the full realization of themselves, they had emerged from the chrysalis, and although isolated discoveries might well up in the future, they were what they were, in a clear and unchanging world.

But increasingly in modern times autobiographers have come to feel themselves explorers, successful or thwarted, in worlds but gradually realized. Anthony Trollope, Charles Darwin, John Ruskin, John Stuart Mill, Thomas Huxley, Henry Adams, and, in recent years, H. G. Wells and Lincoln Steffens, form a continuous series of those who have regarded their lives as a search. Now these preoccupations merely reflect a process of educational questioning that has been almost constant in our time. Criticism is sharpened by the fact that modern history has been a period of transition and change, of warring creeds and cries of mortality.

In a stable social order, education is more or less taken for granted. Whatever principles or rules of thumb served our fathers, we are apt to assume, fulfill their purposes equally well for ourselves. If they lead to tragedy and disaster, it is easy to believe that these grew out of weaknesses in the individual rather than deficiencies in society or in his education. But in periods of widespread change, the concepts of education too are subjected to critical overhauling. Since Rousseau wrote *Emile* in 1762 men have wrinkled their brows more and more over the problem of how to fit the individual to the world he lives in and how to remold that world itself closer to the heart's desire.

The nineteenth century, with its clamor of new machinery and its pushing new classes scrambling for their interests and creating hundreds of new problems, resounded with debate over the difficulty. Thomas Arnold set himself to developing Christian English gentlemen at Rugby, where the future statesmen and Governor Eyres of Britain's colonial imperialism were modeled to the worship of athletics and good form; and Cardinal Newman anxiously elaborated the problem of what a gentleman really was, and how the universities were to produce him. Industrialism and democracy made the absence of proper education glaring and dangerous. In apocalyptic tones Carlyle denounced the governing classes with the wrath of God for not knowing how to govern, but could find no better solution than falling back upon the aid of a fascist dictator-hero because the clamoring masses were too weak and gullible to guide themselves. Matthew Arnold fastidiously recoiled from the philistine crassness of the rising manufacturing powers and their faith in machinery, and warned them that only culture, the study of perfection, could save the desperate field. How to attain an education was the Sphinx query to the Oedipus of modern times.

It is not strange, therefore, to find the query echoed in individual lives. The need that was disturbing all thoughtful men when they looked at the world around them made itself felt in their personal struggles for adjustment. Had the education they had themselves received really fitted them to grapple with the problems that confronted them? and where it failed, how had it failed and why? How could they employ for the benefit of their children the knowledge won from their own difficulties and failures? How could they build into the framework of society devices for reducing the toll of frustrated strivings?

Men of dogmatic shallowness might still believe themselves in the best of all possible worlds, and posture to themselves in triumphant poses; the serious minds of the times were aware that they lived in a changing world in which only a radically changed technique of education could conquer the new problems. Considerate parents bent their efforts to finding more than the conventional means of preparing their children for the world.

Education so emphasized became an outstanding element in people's minds. Again and again in modern autobiography we find the writer devoting great attention to his education. In such a contemporary autobiography as that of Henry Adams the interest becomes dominant, and we see the author regarding his whole career as a vain and long-drawn-out pursuit of education. In the nineteenth century, too, the attention of the autobiographer is frequently concentrated on his education, whether it be to detail the pure misery and uselessness which was all Anthony Trollope could recall of his schooldays at Harrow or to record the unique experiment in education of which John Stuart Mill knew himself to be the result. And there are numerous other autobiographies in which, even when the theme is not so explicitly introduced by the author, it hovers significantly over all the earlier pages and many later ones as well.

Among these, none is more striking than John Ruskin's 'Outlines of Scenes and Thoughts Perhaps Worthy of Memory in My Past Life,' to which he gave the title *Praeterita*. It may be profitable to compare Ruskin's sketches of his former years with the *Autobiography* of John Stuart Mill.

Both were, and knew themselves to be, the products of unusual childhood trainings. Both were outstanding men of their day. The circle in which Mill's name has been known, either then or now, is much smaller than the sphere of those dazzled by the eloquence of Ruskin, but it might be debatable whose influence has been the larger. And although the colored splendor and moving rhythms of Ruskin's prose made his prestige more brilliant than any that Mill ever commanded, we may wonder which of the two was really the more successful.

For Mill's career, though it had its griefs, and even a period of despair, was largely one of growth, expanding powers, and vigorous conviction of purposeful and effective activity; but Ruskin, all of whose fame as an art critic came to him so easily, nevertheless achieved it from depths of emotional frustration that made it all dead sea fruit, and was filled in later years by the ever-present bitterness of battering himself in vain against the obduracy of a world both evil and mad. The world did not do all that John Stuart Mill wished it to do, but it did much that at first it seemed set against doing, and it appeared disposed to be led ultimately to do even more.

The world listened to John Ruskin's beautiful words and admired the paintings he told it to admire. When he pleaded with it, however, that its way of life was uncomely and cruel, it turned on him savagely and broke his heart. All who knew him have commented on the sweetness of Ruskin's disposition, and yet his personal relationships were largely unhappy, and the more deep and intense they were the more they entangled him in misery and defeat. Mill's intimacies were few, but he worked effectively with many other people, even when they were markedly different from himself, and the deep bonds of affection he did have were sources of unalloyed sustenance to him.

Here are two careers, then, both of outward decorum and public achievement, but the inner life of one relatively serene while that of the other is anguished and tormented over the verge of insanity. Were the things that made this internal difference merely fortuitous, accidents of circumstance? Or did they proceed from differences in the characters of the two men? And, if their characters are the solutions to the problem, to how great a degree were those characters made what they were by the unusual education that each received? It is to these significant questions that their autobiographies hold the key.

'*A Reasoning Machine*'

John Stuart Mill was a child of theory. Chosen by his father James Mill, and his friend Jeremy Bentham, to be their successor in the dissemination of Philosophical Radicalism, he was also to be 'an indubitable testimony to the validity of the psychology upon which' the Benthamite faith was founded. He was to be the flesh-and-blood proof of the omnipotence of education. It is this experiment in education of which Mill was the result. His autobiography is written in part to leave a 'record of an education which was unusual and remarkable,' and which proved how much more might be taught even in early childhood than was commonly supposed. But, furthermore, the mind which was the product of that education 'was always pressing forward' in later years, 'equally ready to learn and to unlearn either from its own thoughts or from those of others.' In an age of transition in opinions, confused with the problems of education, Mill thought, both these aspects of a life-long education might be of interest and benefit.

It began when he was an infant of three. 'I have no remembrance,' he writes, 'of the time when I began to learn Greek.' His father, naturally one of the most impatient of men, spared himself no more than he did his small son; and while he was writing his *History of India*, with John studying at the desk by his side, submitted to the incessant enquiries about the meaning of Greek words which the non-existence of Greek-English lexicons made necessary. The little boy also studied arithmetic, a less congenial topic, and in his eighth year began Latin. For enjoyment he was allowed to read history: Robertson, Hume, Gibbon, 'but my greatest delight, then and for long afterwards, was Watson's Philip the Second and Third,' with its heroic defense of the Knights of Malta against the Turks.

Even these, however, were made a vehicle for education, for in before-breakfast walks with his father through the green lanes and wild flowers near Hornsey, he gave his father an account of what he had been reading, making notes on slips of paper in order to do so. His father used these talks as a means of explaining ideas about 'civilization, government, morality, mental cultivation, which he required me afterwards to restate to him in my own words.' By his eleventh year, aided by his father's comment, he was able to read Mitford's *Greece* and be on his guard 'against the Tory prejudices of this writer, and his perversions of facts for the white-washing of despots, and blackening of popular institutions'; and he even compiled a history of Roman government himself, stressing the contentions between the patricians and plebeians, vindicating the Agrarian Laws, and upholding the Roman democratic party.

This was the first stage of his education, that of storing the mind, which Locke had taught to be only capable of passive receptivity in early years, with multitudes of facts. In John's thirteenth year, James Mill judged that the time had come for criticism, generalizing, and evaluation. He started the boy on Aristotle's *Organon*, the Schoolmen, and Hobbes. Precocious as this training was, Mill felt in later years that no part of his education had been more valuable. 'The first intellectual operation in which I arrived at any proficiency was dissecting a bad argument, and finding in what part the fallacy lay.' Mathematics was not its equal, for in mathematics 'none of the real difficulties of correct ratiocination occur.' By his father's close drilling in this exercise he came to 'attach a precise meaning to words and propositions,' and not to be 'imposed on by vague, loose, or ambiguous terms.' He made such progress that his father put in his hands Ricardo's *Principles of Political Economy*, and they discussed all the points it raised in their daily walks.

One other feature of his early training is noteworthy. He was 'brought up from the first without any religious belief.' His father, educated in the creed of Scotch presbyterianism, had rejected all belief in revelation, and come to look on traditional religion with aversion, not merely as a 'mental delusion' but as 'a great moral evil.' His own convictions partook of the Stoic, the Epicurean, and the Cynic. 'In his personal qualities the Stoic predominated. His standard of morals was Epicurean . . . taking as the exclusive test of right and wrong, the tendency of actions to produce pleasure or pain. But he had (and this was the Cynic element) scarcely any belief in pleasure . . . He thought human life a poor thing at best, after the freshness of youth and unsatisfied curiosity had gone by.' If life were what it might be made by good government and good education, it might be worth having: 'but he never spoke with anything like enthusiasm even of that possibility.' For their own sakes alone, he praised justice, temperance, truthfulness, perseverance, laborious exertion, and dedication to the public good. These views 'he conveyed in brief sentences, uttered as occasion arose, of grave exhortation, or stern reprobation and contempt.'

The elder Mill's demands upon the boy were always severe. He never gave explanation until after his son 'had felt the full force of the difficulties.' 'He was often, and much beyond reason, provoked by my failures in cases where success could not have been expected;' and was indignant when the boy failed to detect the fallacy that a thing true in theory may need correction in practice. But he not only drilled much knowledge into his son, he made him think about it instead of parroting adult opinions. 'At a later period I even occasionally . . . altered his opinion on some points of detail: which I state to his honour, not my own.'

John was anxiously guarded from self-conceit by being kept out of the way of hearing himself praised. He thought, if anything, that he was rather backward, since he never came up to what his father seemed to expect. He did not hesitate to argue and contradict, for his father encouraged the free expression of opinion, and therefore he sometimes impressed his elders as disagreeably self-important. But in reality he had no notion of his own superiority at all. The proud father had to tell him, on the eve of a long visit to Sir Samuel Bentham's, in Toulouse, that he had been taught many things which youths of his age did not commonly know; and warned him that he must not be vain or boastful on this account, for it was no merit in him, but entirely the product of his unusual advantages.

The entire emphasis of the boy's education had been upon the intellectual and moral. He had no association with children other than the younger members of his own family, for his father was bent on his escaping the 'corrupting influence which boys exercise over boys' and 'the contagion of vulgar modes of thought and feeling.' He played no games, although from much walking he grew up hardy and healthy.

To this lack he later ascribed a certain physical clumsiness, although it did not equal that of his fellow-prodigy Macaulay, who never learned to tie his cravat. There was no tenderness in his father's behavior, not from want of feeling, Mill came later to believe, but from embarrassed restraint. He would have valued his son's affection, but he must have felt 'that fear of him was drying it up at its source.' If he did not inspire his son's love, however, 'I was always loyally devoted to him.'

The Spartan régime, nevertheless, had not destroyed Mill's emotional nature. 'The middle-age architecture, the baronial hall, and the spacious and lofty rooms' of Jeremy Bentham's summer home at Ford Abbey were 'a sort of poetic cultivation' to him; and he felt the romantic appeal of the Abbey grounds, 'which were riant and secluded, umbrageous, and full of the sound of falling waters.' There was a similar charm for him in *The Lady of the Lake* and *Marmion*, which he was now allowed to read and which he eagerly devoured; and in Campbell's *Gertrude of Wyoming* he found 'the perfection of pathos.' During a trip to the Pyrenees with Sir Samuel Bentham's family the sublime and awful mountain scenery 'made the deepest impression' on him. The severe intellectual training had only overlaid and established the forms of his sensibility.

But to the outside observer, the young hope of Philosophical Radicalism seemed 'a mere reasoning machine.' Introduced in 1821, at the age of fifteen, to Bentham's 'principle of utility,' he felt as if the keystone of an arch were falling into place and giving unity to all his detached and fragmentary ideas. It was a creed, a grand conception of the improvement of mankind. Bentham's demonstration that phrases like 'law of nature,' 'right reason,' 'the moral sense,' and 'natural rectitude,' were merely disguises of dogmatism burst upon him with 'all the force of novelty.' His program for the amelioration of human life was a clarion call.

The rising liberalism of the times made them seem ripe for reform. The oppressions of the government and the trial of Queen Caroline had roused widespread hatred, and the leadership of the Burdetts and Cobbetts was making radicalism formidable. In this movement James Mill's vigorous eloquence and his mental resources made him a powerful force. The youthful Mill flung himself into the struggle with enthusiasm, retorting with the epithets 'sentimentality' and 'vague generalities' upon those who denounced utilitarianism as sordid calculation. He formed the Utilitarian Society to debate popular questions, an organization that included among its members such celebrities as Macaulay, Praed, Wilberforce, and Bulwer Lytton. He contributed controversial articles to the *Westminster Review*, and at the age of twenty was already in the center of his party's councils.

Then suddenly in the midst of all this, the 'reasoning machine' broke down. In a moment of enervation the question occurred to him: 'Suppose that all your objects were realized; that all the changes of institutions and opinions which you are looking forward to, could be completely effected at this very instant: would this be a great joy and happiness to you?' The 'No' that welled up in him filled him with profound despair. The cloud grew thicker and darker as the days passed; life was weary, stale, flat, and unprofitable. It was

A grief without a pang, void, dark, and drear,
A drowsy, stifled, unimpassioned grief,
Which finds no natural outlet or relief
In word, or sigh, or tear.

The books that had once inspired him now left him uncharmed; his father, whom he would have consulted in any other trouble, was the last person to help in this. 'My education . . . was wholly his work . . . and I saw no use in giving him the pain of thinking that his plans had failed, when the failure was probably irremediable, and, at all events, beyond the power of *his* remedies.'

His despair grew deeper as he became convinced that the flaw in his own life 'must be a flaw in life itself.' Pains and pleasures, he had been taught, were the results of association, and 'the habit of analysis has a tendency to wear away the feelings' by revealing the unessential character of the associations. Those about him had convinced him 'that the pleasure of sympathy . . . and the feelings which made the good of others . . . were the greatest and surest sources of happiness; but to know that a feeling would make me happy if I had it, did not give me the feeling.' His education had failed to give him feelings 'in sufficient strength to resist the dissolving influence of analysis,' and all his training had made analysis 'the inveterate habit of my mind.'

From this state of congealed grief he was aroused by a burst of tears over a moving passage in Marmontel's *Mémoires*. From this time his burden grew lighter, and in the autumn of 1828 the 1815 edition of Wordsworth's poems helped him even more. He found that Wordsworth too 'had felt that the first freshness of youthful enjoyment of life was not lasting; but that he had sought for compensation, and found it' not in mere outward beauty, but in 'states of feeling, and of thought coloured by feeling, under the excitement of beauty.' With Wordsworth he came to hear again

The still, sad music of humanity

and to know that

The clouds that gather 'round the setting sun
Take a sober colouring from the eye
That hath kept watch o'er man's mortality.

And although happiness was indeed 'the test of all rules of conduct, and the end of life,' it could not be attained directly. 'Ask yourself whether you are happy, and you cease to be so.' 'Those only are happy,' he thought, 'who have their minds fixed on some object other than their own happiness.' And finally even the pitfalls of analysis ceased to appear dangerous to him. He emerged from the waste land of those who believe that knowledge and reason destroy emotional values. That modern temper which feels the dignity of man to be grounded in illusion no longer darkened his heart. 'The intensest feeling of the beauty of a cloud lighted by the setting sun,' he realized, was 'no hindrance to my knowing that the cloud is vapour of water, subject to all the laws of vapours in a state of suspension;' nor did the knowledge of those physical laws destroy his ability to feel the 'distinction between beauty and ugliness.'

With this harmonious resolution of the conflict between his rational and emotional natures, he made rapid strides forward in his beliefs. He came to see 'the wonderful power' in Carlyle's writings as 'poetry to animate' instead of the 'insane rhapsody' his father always found them. Comte's doctrine 'of the natural succession of three stages in every department of human knowledge'—the theological, the metaphysical, and the positive, or scientific stage—seemed to him profoundly illuminating. In the end, though, he was to recoil from Positivism as 'the completest system of spiritual and temporal despotism which ever yet emanated from a human brain.' He was much attracted by the Saint-Simonians, whose principle of everyone being required to take a share in the labor of the community and remunerated according to his works seemed to him 'a far superior description of Socialism to Owen's,' and he was pleased by 'the boldness and freedom from prejudice with which they treated the subject of the family,' which scarcely any reformer had had the courage to touch.

He had come to feel that 'all questions of political institutions are relative, not absolute, and that different stages of human progress not only *will* have, but *ought* to have, different institutions.' But although representative democracy thus ceased to be an absolute principle with him, being merely a political instrument like any other, he 'was as much as ever a radical and democrat for Europe, and especially for England,' in his own time. The predominance of the noble and the rich was 'an evil worth any struggle to get rid of.' It demoralized the country by gross immorality in government, by degrading the position of the masses of the people, and by making wealth and the display of wealth the only things really respected. In this frame of mind, the French Revolution of July found him, and aroused his utmost enthusiasm.

The year 1830 brought an even more powerful influence into his life, the friendship with Mrs Taylor, who after an intimacy of twenty years finally became his wife. But at the time Mr Taylor was still alive, 'a most upright, brave, and honorable man,' Mill calls him, 'of liberal opinions and good education, but without the intellectual or artistic tastes which would have made him a companion for her.' Of Mrs Taylor Mill writes in terms of the highest romantic devotion. Her friendship was 'the honour and chief blessing' of his existence, 'the source of a great part of all' that he has attempted or hoped for human improvement. Only Shelley was like her, he says, but Shelley 'was but a child compared with what she ultimately became.' Her mind 'a perfect instrument,' her feelings and imagination those of 'a consummate artist,' eloquence, knowledge of human nature, unselfishness, the passion for justice warmed by profound loving-kindness: he pours out all virtues upon her memory. 'The benefit I received was far greater than any which I could hope to give.'

For years during Mr Taylor's life they conducted themselves with the greatest propriety, for although they 'did not consider the ordinances of society binding on a subject so entirely personal,' they did feel bound not to wound the worthy husband. Ardently as he loved her, Mill would have foregone the privilege of marrying her for ever, 'rather than owe it to the premature death of one for whom I had the sincerest respect, and she the strongest affection.' But in 1849 Mr Taylor died, and two years later Mrs Taylor became Mill's wife. 'For seven and a half years that blessing was mine; for seven and a half only! I can say nothing which could describe, even in the faintest manner, what that loss was and is.' 'Her memory is to me a religion, and her approbation the standard by which, summing up as it does all worthiness, I endeavor to regulate my life.'

This was the man whom his less discerning contemporaries regarded as 'a mere reasoning machine'! The Carlyles, sniggering with each other in Cheyne Row, found no such genius in Mrs Taylor, but Mill consulted her in everything, discussed with her the ideas of all his books, and wrote many passages as the outcome of her direct suggestion. They looked forward into the future together, and under her inspiration Mill became even more radical. 'The social problem of the future we considered to be, how to unite the greatest individual liberty of action, with a common ownership in the raw material of the globe, and an equal participation of all in the benefits of combined labour.'

In 1845 even before the revolutions of 1848, Mill's own thought grew steadily more revolutionary. In the chapter 'On the Probable Futurity of the Labouring Classes,' added on his wife's impulsion to his *Principles of Political Economy*, Mill revealed these developments clearly. 'If . . . the choice were to be made between Communism with all its chances, and the present [1852] state of society with all its sufferings and injustices;' if the rewards of labor under private property are necessarily apportioned in inverse proportion to the labor, so that the most exhausting and unpleasant bodily labor can hardly earn a meager living, as is now the case: 'if this or Communism were the alternative, all the difficulties, great or small, of Communism would be dust in the balance.'

They did not fear that the selfishness of human nature would prevent changing institutions. 'Education, habit, and the cultivation of the sentiments, will make a common man dig or weave for his country as readily as fight for his country . . . The deep-rooted selfishness which forms the general character of the existing state of society, is *so* deeply rooted, only because the whole course of existing institutions tends to foster it . . .'

In 1865 the electors of Westminster asked Mill to be their candidate for Parliament. He specified that he would not canvass from house to house nor incur any election expenses, forewarned them that he would give no time to purely local interests, and outlined his general political principles to them, including his belief in women's suffrage. In spite of these conditions and declarations they begged him to stand, and he was triumphantly elected. At an election meeting an effort to discredit him with the working classes by asking him if he had written that they were generally liars brought cheers from his audience of workers when he courageously replied, 'I did.'

In Parliament he spoke in favor of a broader basis of suffrage than was provided in Gladstone's Reform Bill, defeated a bill to prevent public meetings in parks, led the prosecution of Governor Eyre for the lawless violence with which he had suppressed the uprising in Jamaica, and helped defeat an Extradition Bill which would have led to the surrender of political refugees to the governments against which they had rebelled. He favored a proportional representation scheme in which people would be given votes in accordance not with their wealth but their degree of education, and secured seventy-three votes for an amendment to the Reform Bill giving the franchise to women. But Mill had none of the arts and dodges of the politician, and his refusal to work for the individual interests of his borough later told against him. In 1868 he was defeated of re-election, and although offered several other constituencies, decided to retire from Parliament.

He went to Avignon, where he spent the last five years of his life. His *Logic*, his essays *On Liberty* and *Utilitarianism* were the product of earlier years, but he had still to write *The Subjection of Women* and his *Three Essays on Religion*, which includes the advanced and wise essay on *Nature*. His life was retired, by deliberate choice. 'General society, as now carried on in England,' he wrote, 'is so insipid . . . that it is kept up for any reason rather than the pleasure it affords. All serious discussion on matters on which opinions differ, being considered ill-bred, and the national deficiency in liveliness and sociability having prevented the cultivation of the art of talking agreeably on trifles . . . the sole attraction of what is called society to those who are not at the top of the tree, is the hope of being aided to climb a little higher in it . . .' The last few years of his life he devoted to a comprehensive examination of Socialism which, unfortunately, his death left unfinished. In it, he recommended a Fabian policy, a gradual reform of private ownership working toward the establishment of some system of Communism.

Mill had, indeed, as he said of himself, never been static but 'always pressing forward.' There were deficiencies in James Mill's system of training, but it *had* developed an intellectual honesty and a critical open-mindedness that led his son at last far from doctrinaire Benthamism. John Stuart Mill modified his father's psychology, became sensible of a range of emotional values to which his father was blind, deepened his philosophy of history far beyond the depth James Mill and Jeremy Bentham had sounded, and pierced with radical foresight into the social problems of the coming century. Few nineteenth century minds were so constantly growing.

'The Loneliness Was Very Great'

John Ruskin's education was also one carefully planned and supervised in its every detail, but it may be described as one looking not so much to the future as to the past, and not so much the product of logic as of temperament. It was not that James and Margaret Ruskin were 'temperamental' in the ordinary sense of that term, but they were not two philosophical radicals trying to fashion a mind that should be a perfect instrument; they were a respectable and honest sherry-merchant and his very sober, evangelical, and sternly upright wife. And Margaret Ruskin had, as she later told her son, 'solemnly "devoted me to God" before I was born; in imitation of Hannah.' Ruskin adds, 'Very good women are remarkably apt to make away with their children prematurely in this manner': what it meant was that he was to be bred for the Church.

James Ruskin was not so devout as his wife, but he was extremely conscientious, and he was dominated by her. His father had let his business fall to pieces and gone into debt, which, after his death, it took the son nine years to pay. He sacrificed health, ease, and society to that task, and only when it was accomplished did he and the 'exemplary Croydon cousin' who had been waiting for him finally marry. Inferior in station and cultural training to her husband, she felt, her son tells us, that 'it was a great delight to be allowed to love him'; and she tried 'to cultivate her powers of mind, and form her manners, so as to fit herself to be the undespised companion of a man whom she considered much her superior.' She was a 'faultless and accomplished housekeeper, and,' her child adds, 'a natural, essential, unassailable, yet inoffensive prude.' John Ruskin was the only son of this couple.

Few things are stranger in autobiography than the almost detached objectivity with which Ruskin thus analyzes them. From the distance of later years he sees very clearly the strangeness of that family group, and probes into its hidden relationships with an almost painful minuteness. That two intelligent and conscientious people should have maimed the life of their dearly beloved son is more than usually tragic. The tragedy is even deeper when we reflect on what Ruskin achieved in spite of all, and try to imagine the noble beauty his life might in happier circumstances have attained.

But the tragedy was still years in the future. The blue-eyed little boy sat on a low stool by his mother's skirts, and learned long chapters of the *Bible* by heart, from Genesis to the Apocalypse. Presently at half past four Papa came home from the City, where he had been writing his customers 'that if they found fault with their wine, they did not understand it, and if they wanted an extension of credit, they could not have it.' He dined solemnly in the front parlor.

In the evening, while Mamma knitted, Papa would read *Waverley* or *Don Quixote* or *Lear* or *Marmion*: 'his sense of the strength and wisdom of true meaning, and of the force of rightly ordered syllables made his delivery' of 'the *best* poetry and prose' 'melodiously grand and just.' Once he threw down *Count Robert of Paris* with an 'intense expression of sorrow mixed with scorn,' partly for the book itself, 'but chiefly of the wretches who were tormenting and selling the wrecked intellect, and not a little, deep down, of the subtle dishonesty which had essentially caused the ruin.'

When little John was not reading the Bible with Mamma, he looked out of the window at 'a marvellous iron post, out of which the water-carts were filled, through beautiful little trap-doors, by pipes like boa-constrictors,' with a 'delicious dripping.' He was not allowed to have any toys except a cart and a ball and two boxes of wooden blocks. Once when an aunt gave him a radiant scarlet and gold Punch and Judy for his birthday, good manners constrained his mother to accept them, but afterwards she 'quietly told me it was not right that I should have them; and I never saw them again.' Still, he was happy enough, on the whole, watching the hydrant, and looking at the colors of the carpet, and later among the lilacs and laburnums of Herne Hill, their new home, he might go into the garden—although he must not eat the gooseberries or cherries—and lead 'a very small, perky, contented, conceited Cock-Robinson Crusoe sort of life.'

The household was serious but it was not gloomy. His mother had 'a hearty, frank, and sometimes almost irrepressible laugh.' There was even a Smollettesque turn in her, so that during their evening readings she extremely enjoyed *Humphrey Clinker*, for all its earthiness. His father liked an edge of irony in a jest, and as the boy got older both father and son 'rejoiced in all the sarcasm of *Don Juan*.' But, even so, there was a feeling of being hemmed in; and when Mr Northcote, the painter, asked what he would like in the background of his portrait, the child said, 'Blue hills.'

He endured the horror of being still in the bottom of the pew during long sermons on Sunday, and delighted his mother when he was little by preaching a sermon 'at home over the red sofa cushions,' 'some eleven words long,' and beginning with the words, 'People, be good.' On Sunday evenings their reading was restricted to *Pilgrim's Progress*, or *The Book of Martyrs*, or Mrs Sherwood's *Lady of the Manor*—'a very awful book to me, because of the stories in it of wicked girls who had gone to balls, dying immediately after of fever.'

So his childhood passed. With his curious detachment Ruskin enumerates its blessings. He 'had never heard his father's or mother's voice raised' or even 'seen an angry . . . or offended, glance' in their eyes, or been made aware of any trouble or disorder in the household. He had learned to obey implicitly, without idea of resistance. Nothing was 'ever promised me that was not given; nothing ever threatened me that was not inflicted; nothing ever told me that was not true.' Peace, obedience, faith, and to these he adds the habit of attentiveness.

And then, with the same detachment, he lists its 'dominant calamities.' His parents were only 'visible powers of nature' to him; he did not love them, and he did not love God. Never having learned to love, 'when affection did come, it came with violence, utterly rampant and unmanageable.' He had nothing to endure, no danger or pain to teach patience and fortitude. He was never placed on his own responsibility, never out of 'bridle and blinkers.' And he concludes that his education 'was at once too formal and too luxurious; leaving my character, at the most important moment of its construction, cramped indeed, but not disciplined; and only by protection innocent instead of by practice virtuous.'

Years later he wrote his father bitterly, 'Men ought to be severely disciplined and exercised in the sternest way in daily life—they should learn to lie on stone beds and eat black soup, but they should never have their hearts broken . . . The two terrific mistakes that Mamma and you involuntarily fell into, were the exact reverse . . . you fed me effeminately and luxuriously . . . But you thwarted me in all the earnest fire of passion and life.' What justification there was for these cruel reproaches will be more clear in the parts of the story that are still to come.

He saw little of other children. At the age of nine he was writing verse in a maddeningly efficient imitation of Pope, and he began to draw in the style of Prout, and then of Turner. He was taught by a private tutor until almost fourteen. The two years he then spent at a boys' school did not much help his shyness, for he walked down to the school with his father after breakfast, carrying his blue bag of books, and came home to half-past-one dinner. Finding him 'what boys could only look upon as an innocent,' the other boys 'treated me as they would have treated a girl; they neither thrashed nor chaffed me . . .'

On their visits to the seashore, little John was 'not allowed to row, far less to sail, nor to walk near the harbor alone; so that I learned nothing of shipping or anything else worth learning,' but simply spent his time in 'staring and wondering at the sea.' When they sent him to a riding school in London, he was put on big, rearing horses and fell off, and was 'a burning shame and misery to myself.' But he 'might have got some inkling of a seat' if only no fuss had been made about him. Instead, each day brought searching scrutiny into his disgraces, and he 'merely got more nervous and helpless after every tumble,' until this branch of his education was abandoned.

In summer, he and Mamma and Papa were off in a roomy post-chaise and pair, touring England, Wales, and a great deal of lowland Scotland, Papa combining business and pleasure by calling on his country customers. Later still, they went abroad, going in their own traveling carriage, but they 'no more partook of the life about them than do the curious who go under the sea in a diving bell.' They were tourists, not travelers; they went primarily for the picturesque, instead of in the spirit of the eighteenth century, when a gentleman went abroad to observe the arts, manufactures, and government of other nations and to mingle with its celebrated men.

Never did young Ruskin really mix with his fellow beings.

Once only they came out of their bell, when they were invited to dinner by Monsieur Domecq, Mr Ruskin's foreign partner, and the boy met his daughters, Diane, the lovely Adèle-Clotilde, Cecile, and little Elise. The elder sisters did not choose to trouble themselves with the shy red-haired boy who spoke only halting French, but Elise, 'being of entirely benevolent and pitiful temper, came across the drawing-room to me in my desolation, and leaning an elbow on my knee, set herself deliberately to chatter to me mellifluously for an hour and a half by the timepiece . . .'

Subsequently the young girls came to Herne Hill for a visit. 'The arrangements were half Noah's ark, half Doll's house, but we got them all in'; and Ruskin fell violently in love with Adèle-Clotilde. Miserably self-conscious, completely unused to feminine society, he either 'sat jealously miserable in company,' or tried in tête-à-tête to entertain his 'Spanish-born, Paris-bred, and Catholic-hearted mistress with my own views on the subjects of the Spanish Armada, the Battle of Waterloo, and the doctrine of Transubstantiation.' 'Virtually convent-bred more closely than the maids themselves,' Ruskin was completely helpless: thrown into 'the fiery furnace, or fiery cross, of these four girls,' in four days he was reduced 'to a mere heap of white ashes.'

How could his parents 'allow their young novice to be cast into the fiery furnace of the outer world in this helpless manner'? But they saw little harm in it. Monsieur Domecq saw that Ruskin 'had some seedling brains,' and, if any of his daughters liked Ruskin, was perfectly willing to have them marry 'in the interests of the business.' James Ruskin was of much the same mind; and Mrs Ruskin regarded his 'marrying a Roman Catholic as too monstrous to be possible' and 'too preposterous to be even guarded against.' She was annoyed, 'as she would have been if one of her chimneys had begun smoking,—but had not the slightest notion her house was on fire.' 'The *Mercredi des cendres*,' Ruskin sorrowfully adds, 'lasted four years.'

Adèle laughed or was bored, and Ruskin went up to Christ Church, Oxford, and constrained himself to study hard, but externalized his feelings by composing gruesome poetry. His father complained of the 'slaughter-house atmosphere' of his Newdigate prize poem *Salsette and Elephanta*, and through all his verse there is a feeling of hollowness that is distressing when we remember the youth and brilliance of the author. When Adèle was eighteen she and her sisters came to England again. Ruskin immediately saw that she was not so pretty as she had been at fifteen, but 'my love was much too high and fantastic to be diminished by her loss of beauty.' 'And day followed on day, and month to month, of complex absurdity, pain, error, wasted affection, and rewardless semi-virtue.' Later he wondered how he would have turned out if 'Love had been with me instead of against me.' But he concluded that 'such things are not allowed in this world': 'The men capable of the highest imaginative passion are always tossed on fiery waves of it.'

Trying to subdue his pain, he worked at Oxford. His father's ideal of his future was that he 'should enter at college into the best society, take all the prizes every year, and a double first to finish with; marry Lady Clara Vere de Vere; write poetry as good as Byron's, only pious; preach sermons as good as Bossuet's, only Protestant; be made, at forty, Bishop of Winchester, and at fifty, Primate of England.' The wine merchant's son was received good-humoredly among the young blades: 'an inoffensive little cur' among 'the dogs of race at the gentlemen commoners' table.' And he was tolerated in spite of the fact that his mother came to Oxford with him, and took lodgings in the High Street, where he reported every evening for tea.

One gang broke into his rooms with the object of ragging him; Ruskin received them in his dressing-gown. 'Gentlemen,' he said, 'I am sorry I cannot entertain you now as I should wish, but my father, who is engaged in the sherry trade, has put it in my power to invite you all to wine tomorrow evening. Will you come'? His sweetness and courtesy won them over. And even Bob Grimston, the boxer and racing man, had a sort of pitying affection for him, and took him to a tavern to learn some points about the horses entered for the Derby, 'an object only to be accomplished,' Ruskin writes, 'by sitting with indifference on a corner of the kitchen table, and carrying on a dialogue with careful pauses, and more by winks than words.'

One evening he felt a curious taste in his mouth, 'which I presently perceived to be that of blood.' The doctors diagnosed it as consumptive, and recommended that the autumn and winter be spent abroad. His father, 'to whom the business was nothing, but for me, left his desk, and all other cares of life, but that of nursing me.' His illness was almost as much unhappiness and despair, however, as it was weakness of the lungs. They went abroad, Ruskin gloomily determined to enjoy nothing. In Rome, the Capitol was a 'rubbishy square of average Palladian,' the Forum 'a good group of smashed columns,' the Colosseum a public nuisance. The Ruskins met Joseph Severn, the friend and death-bed nurse of Keats, who liked the father and mother, but was appalled by these heresies in the son. But the cough improved, and in May, 1842, he went back to Oxford to take his degree as Bachelor of Arts.

What he was to do now was still vague. It was becoming clear that he would not ever be Bishop of Winchester, but aside from some talent for drawing and writing and an analytical faculty still pretty much in embryo he could not say what his vocation might be. His father was utterly indulgent: should he travel? 'Perhaps it may deserve some dim praise that I never seriously thought of leaving my father and mother . . .' On the other hand, he 'had not the least love of adventure, but liked to have comfortable rooms always ordered, and a three-course dinner ready by four o'clock.' And, 'finally, though I had no rightly glowing or grateful affection for either father or mother, yet as they could not well do without me, so also I found I was not altogether comfortable without *them.*' Finally the whole problem was deferred by another family tour, while the servants at home were moving the Turners, the Titian, the Sir Joshuas, the solid furniture, the silver plate, and, very carefully, the sherry, from Herne Hill to their new house at Denmark Hill.

And suddenly a piece of work presented itself. Turner, for years a celebrated painter, was refusing to stay put. An elderly academician, he was nevertheless in a wild mood, experimenting in groping, feverish, apocalyptic pictures which much disturbed the critics. The *Athenaeum* critic described them as painted 'with cream or chocolate, yolk of egg, or currant jelly'; and Ruskin, furious, resolved to vindicate Turner by setting forth the principles that underlie painting. At the age of twenty-three he began work on the first volume of *Modern Painters.* The book was an enormous success. The Brontës, Elizabeth Barrett Browning, Miss Mitford, were in raptures; Tennyson, too poor to buy it, took infinite pains to borrow it; Wordsworth told everyone that its author was a brilliant writer; a little coterie of painters read it aloud to each other. They included William Morris, Burne-Jones, and Holman Hunt. Its author was immediately famous.

Artist friends came down to Denmark Hill, 'and when the candles came, and the good jests, over the nuts and olives, there was "frolic wine" in the flask at every right hand.' But John Ruskin still felt an emptiness in his life. He had recovered from Adèle, and Charlotte Lockhart was in a way of bewitching him. Unhappily Scott's grand-daughter seemed little charmed at a dinner party by his disputing the state of prisons in Naples across her with Mr Gladstone, and Ruskin was doomed to disappointment again.

Seriously perturbed, the elder Ruskins laid their heads together. A distant cousin, Euphemia Gray, was invited to the house, with every intention that their son should marry her. Ruskin took her to art galleries and exhibitions, and Effie showed a tireless interest in being lectured to. Presently his mother horrified him by assuring him that he was in love with his cousin. Ruskin denied it, but soon his mother was at him again, telling him that 'though he did not recognize the fact himself, she and his father were convinced that he was deeply enamoured.' Ruskin fought a losing fight. His parents were relentless: 'They saw in a marriage with Euphemia,' says one of his biographers, 'the means by which they might gain a daughter and not lose a son.' At last he capitulated and the ill-matched pair were wed.

It is significant that Ruskin never mentions a single circumstance of his marriage in *Praeterita*. They traveled, they took a house in London and went to a great many parties which Effie liked and Ruskin did not, and he worried about the agitations of 1848 and wrote his *Seven Lamps of Architecture*, which he later disliked violently. 'The utterly useless twaddle of it, the shallow piety, and sonorous talk,' he wrote, 'are revolting to me.' He was beginning to feel that art could not be divorced from the economic framework of society; he was disturbed by religious doubts, hearing the 'dreadful hammers' of the geologists clinking 'at the end of every cadence of the Bible phrases'; he was growing radical about the Corn Laws. The whole question, he said, was 'whether the landed property in England is to lose part of its value, or whether that value is to be maintained by making the poor pay more for their bread.'

Effie danced away at parties, and Ruskin was hideously bored: 'Horrible party last night—stiff—large—dull—fidgety—strange—run-against-everybody-know-nobody sort of party. Naval people. Young lady claims acquaintance with me. I know as much of her as Queen Pomare. Talk. Get away as soon as I can—ask who she is—Lady Charlotte Elliott—as wise as I was before. Introduced to a black man with chin in collar. Black man condescending . . . Go away and ask who black man is. Mr Shaw Lefevre—as wise as I was before.'

Effie danced her way into the heart of John Everett Millais, the painter, and Ruskin did not seem to notice, or if he did, did not care. At last Effie ran off to her parents in Scotland, and subsequently a court decided that the marriage had been one only in name. Years afterward Ruskin told a friend that he would have felt it wrong and horrible that it should be more unless he could love her, which he was sure he could never learn to do. Old James Ruskin was furious, and Ruskin had to smuggle Millais's portrait of himself out of the house to prevent the old man slashing his penknife through it. The narrative of *Praeterita* begins to note events in Ruskin's life again without even revealing the gap.

Little John Mill had at least had the companionship of his own brothers and sisters to fit him for mingling with people. What with keeping their son solitary, indulging him, restraining him, giving him no responsibility, fussing over him, worshiping and distrusting him, failing to help him adjust himself to love, and forcing him into marriage with a girl he did not love, Ruskin's two devoted parents had made a dreadful mess of his life.

He took refuge in work, He wrote, and he lectured eloquently in a beautiful voice that enchanted his listeners. More and more, though, the world afflicted him with 'great fits of vexation'; he felt that he lived 'the life of an old lady in a houseful of wicked children.' He was 'always howling and bawling the right road to a generation of drunken coachmen,' his head up through the trapdoor and his face all over mud, and 'no right road to be got gone upon after all.' When he was called on to give evidence before a parliamentary committee for improving the usefulness of art galleries and libraries, he testified that the laboring day in England oppressed the workman and broke him down so that it was 'not refreshment to use his mind,' and that 'the principles on which our commerce is conducted are every day oppressing him and sinking him deeper.' When the chairman, worried by the radical sound of it, remarked that he was sure Ruskin did not mean to cast a slur upon competition, Ruskin rejoined fiercely that he not only intended to cast a slur, 'but to express my excessive horror of the principle of competition in every way.'

Such ways of writing and talking distressed his father. Ruskin commented, 'his whole life is bound up in me, and yet he thinks me a fool—that is to say, he is mightily pleased if I write anything that has big words and no sense in it . . . This form of affection galls me like hot iron, and I am in a subdued fury whenever I am at home, which dries all the marrow out of every bone in me.' But when he was away from home, he wrote or telegraphed his parents every day.

In *Unto This Last* and *Fors Clavigera* he gave free rein to his anger at social injustice, and loosed violent blasts of sarcasm. Carlyle applauded exultantly 'the pincergrip (red-hot pincers) you take of certain bloated cheeks and blown-up bellies.' All the evils of capitalist imperialism one by one came under the molten rain of his invective. Instruments of warfare and war-profits: 'Two nations may go mad, and fight like harlots—God have mercy on them—you, who hand them carving knives off the table, for leave to pick up a dropped sixpence, what mercy is there for you?' The conventional defense of interest on capital he subjects to a brilliantly destructive analysis. Interest is (1) reward for abstinence, (2) compensation for risk of loss, (3) wages for labor of superintendence. He has himself, he says, £15,000 in the Bank of England, 'but I have never received the slightest intimation from the directors that they wished for my assistance in the superintendence in that establishment.' As for risk of loss, he put the money there 'because I thought it exactly the safest place to put it in.' And 'reward for abstinence': if he did not have his £15,000 he might be a good deal more abstinent still and nobody would talk of rewarding him. 'It might indeed be possible to find even cases of very prolonged and painful abstinences, for which no reward has yet been adjudged by less abstinent England.'

But people paid no attention to him, or they angrily cried out against what he wrote as insane ravings. Unaffrighted he went on; his mind had always, as he said, been analytical; and as he saw how one hideous phenomenon was connected with another, he hewed through them all. At last he was prepared to declare that 'indeed I myself am a Communist of the old school, reddest also of the red.'

More and more, however, the bottomless pit of indifference into which his protests seemed to fall was preying upon his mind. There were times when he was delirious and out of his senses. 'The doctors say I went mad from overwork . . . I went mad because nothing came of my work. People would have understood my falling crazy if they had heard that the manuscripts on which I had spent seven years of my old life had all been used to light the fire like Carlyle's first volume of *The French Revolution.* But they could not understand that I should be the least annoyed, far less fall ill in a frantic manner, because, after I had got them published, nobody believed a word of them.'

He recovered, but 'the loneliness was very great.' Then, at intervals, there would be 'another bite or two of Nebuchadnezzar's bitter grass.' By 1889 he could hardly ever collect his mind, although he longed to add to *Praeterita* the chapter he called 'Joanie's Care' in token of his gratefulness to the young cousin who nursed his weakness.

All the defeats of his strivings, the memory of Rose La Touche, his young love for whom he had hoped since he was forty-five, and who had been estranged from him and died when he was fifty-six, the triumphs that had come so easily and proved so empty, the domination of his mother that had enchained him for over fifty years: they had broken him down. He wrote no more; his beautiful voice was no more than a whisper. He looked venerable and benign with his long white beard, but when people spoke to him 'he only said yes, or no, or smiled, or bowed his head.' When he was eighty, he looked at his thumb and finger, and said, 'They will never hold pen again.' Then he smiled softly, and added, 'perhaps it's as well, they have brought me into so much trouble.'

Benjamin Jowett, who had once disliked him, had grown devoted in later years. 'He is the gentlest and most innocent of mankind,' Jowett said, 'of great genius, but inconsecutive, and he has never rubbed his mind against others, so that he is ignorant of very obvious things.' Burne-Jones was another dear friend. One night, on his way to bed, Ruskin stopped and nodded his venerable head at his portrait, 'That's my dear brother Ned.' The next day Burne-

Jones was dead. Ruskin himself had only one year longer to live.

Sereneness and Defeat

Whether Ruskin's public strivings might have been crowned with more success if his education had been conducted differently is of course debatable, and whether the more immediate triumphs of inaugurating social changes should outweigh the permanent fame he now has may also go unanswered. The drift of his ideas has been misunderstood by people who have considered him only as an art critic with a flair for purple passages and a weakness for wandering from the point into dogmatic generalizations about God and morals. Nevertheless, a dim and misunderstood immortality he assuredly has, and his flaming indignation is there to be read, where at any time it may fire and quicken.

But that his personal life was unhappy and defeated, and that those distresses were largely the bitter fruit of his education we can hardly doubt. Sweet-tempered and high-aspiring, 'the gentlest and most innocent of mankind,' he had 'never rubbed his mind against others.' He had not only never been taught, but had been prevented from learning 'very obvious things.' Striving to guard their son in cotton wool against all dangers, James and Margaret Ruskin had unfitted him for the give-and-take of existence. He could not be a member of a group or work with a group, but could only either talk at people or have deep, almost confessional intimacies. He longed for feminine sympathy and companionship, but all his life he achieved them only with older women or with little girls who regarded him as something between a saint and an uncle. He could neither yield nor persuade, and he could draw no strength of resignation from his defeats, only gangrenous mortification and lonely pride. As he himself realized, he was both bridled and indulged; and his parents wove around him an emotional tyranny which they used with deadly kindness.

John Stuart Mill's father had come very near destroying *his* son's happiness in an opposite way. If Ruskin had been made too inward, too entangled in a morbid and secluded family intimacy, Mill had been given no normal outlet for his affections at all. James Mill, in a shamefast diffidence, had discouraged displays of emotion, and as a philosopher he had feared that emotion might be a support for illogical prejudice. There can be no doubt that the melancholy and discouragement into which Mill fell at the age of twenty was the revenge of his unfilled heart crying out for warmth and sympathy.

But the error was not so fatal in Mill's case as were the errors in Ruskin's. His feelings welled up of themselves, and found their natural objects, and attained a balance. If in him reason was always to be at the helm, again and again when he was deeply moved his sentiments were to voice themselves in a grave and lofty eloquence. And in his love he achieved the deepest romanticism. 'For seven and a half years that blessing was mine; for seven and a half only!'

Although James Mill had made no effort to develop his son's emotions, even dammed them back partly, he had given him habits that made even the days of despair something that could be borne with stoicism. He had taught him self-imposed discipline, taught him to work steadily whether he wished to or no. He had deprived him of a childhood, as much as the Ruskins had deprived their son of a childhood, but he had not clamped him in solitary confinement with two elders. Little John Mill had always had his brothers and sisters, and he had had to adapt himself to their needs, for he was their tutor, passing on to them what he learned from his father. Thus, unconsciously, perhaps undirectedly, he picked up the arts of adjustment to others which Ruskin never really learned. Even when as the precocious young hope of philosophical radicalism he was impressing others as conceited, he nevertheless managed to work in harmony with his colleagues and to edit *The London and Westminster Review.*

Mill's intellectual development was more consistent and more temperate than Ruskin's, and that too we can trace to his education. Mill did not continue to believe as his father did, any more than Ruskin, but although he was careful not to wound his father by making their differences obtrusive if he could honestly avoid it, he felt no sense of guilt in changing his views. Ruskin did feel so, and his exacerbation then made him stab his father with reproaches. Mill moved by gradual modifications from the Utilitarianism of Bentham to a reasoned, humanistic, and libertarian Communism; Ruskin leaped violently almost at once to an emotional Communism, 'reddest of the red.' It was as drastic as his love for Adèle-Clotilde and for Charlotte Lockhart, and as much a source of despair.

Their autobiographies reflect their personalities. *Praeterita* has passages of eloquence and pathos and sarcasm and beauty. Mingled with the hurt and bitterness there are sweetness and understanding too. It abounds in passages of strange insight, and it dissects all those old wounds with a curious penetration almost impersonal. But there are the significant hiatuses of the marriage that was no marriage, and there are long-winded passages of wandering from the point, of eccentricity of thought and fantastic intrusion. These things ultimately build up in some readers' minds a mood of impatience that overshadows its deep and touching revelations. Numbers have told their own stories more connectedly, but no nineteenth century autobiographer so touches the hidden springs.

Mill's *Autobiography* does not; it is all a clear, severe concentration on his intellectual development. It is logical and restrained, all the emotion almost banished, at most discernible as a sort of underglow to the course of statement, save in occasional passages of sympathy or tribute. There is no outcry about himself, little color or movement of anecdote. Carlyle read it in his lonely old age, remembering the man whom in his mature manhood he had loved, and was bitterly disappointed. 'It is wholly the life of a logic-chopping engine, little more of human in it than if it had been done by a thing of mechanized iron. Autobiography of a steam-engine, you may sometimes read it . . . The thought of poor Mill altogether, and of his life and history in this poor muddy world, gives me real pain and sorrow.' Carlyle's judgment was unjust. There is real feeling in Mill's *Autobiography*, but it is muted and subordinated to the educational development.

That educational development is the most deeply significant part of it all. The education of Mill and Ruskin proceeded throughout their entire lives, and embraced the central decades of their century. That Mill's was carried on with sobriety and hope, and Ruskin's in grief, madness, and despair, is a comment on the earlier training of each. That, with all their differences of mind and feeling, they so nearly agreed on the overwhelming problem of their age and its solution, is a lesson for modern society. One worked toward it gradually, reaching his convictions as the fruit of a serene and well-spent life. The other rounded fiercely upon Mammon with the burning diatribe of an Old Testament prophet. But the lonely child of the sherry-merchant and the product of experimental philosophy looked toward the future and saw the same light.

VICTORIAN SUNDOWN

XIII

VICTORIAN SUNDOWN

Nineteenth Century Waste Land

NOT only Ruskin and Mill wrestled with the Sphinx-problem of nineteenth century fate. Almost every great and clear mind of the period was troubled by its perils; they seemed treading from precipice to abyss. The chimneys of the factories and the cancerous slums of the great cities; commercial rapacity engulfing Egypt, the Sudan, South Africa, China; 'spheres of influence,' rival imperialisms, demands for 'a place in the sun'; the struggling nationalisms of Greece, Spain, Germany, Italy, Poland; democracy and illiteracy, privilege and corruption; decaying traditional morals and the impotence of the church; science placing deadly weapons in the hands of children and maniacs, unsettling habits, destroying past authority, and leading—where?—answering no questions save with more questions, an endless and fearful vista!

Problems enough to frighten the most courageous, it is not strange that on those sensitive enough to perceive but not strong enough to overcome, or at least stand unconquered, they produced a paralysis and despair. Through the music and literature and art of the nineteenth century there runs a ground-tone of weltschmerz, sometimes a subdued theme in minor keys, sometimes crashing into grand chords of cosmic futility or defiance. The lesser intellectuals, the followers and disciples, were led into these impasses and lost, they became the spiritually disinherited. There were no authoritative answers to their problems. The industrial revolution and material science were racing too fast to be controlled or assimilated. Minds reeled. Uprooted, but feeling still the need of stability, they were left without guide or compass.

John Sterling was one of these. A boy of enthusiastic and impetuous turn, like many of the brighter and more ardent young men of his time, he had been unsettled in his convictions by the political and spiritual radicalisms that surrounded him. He tried to pull out some of his roots and plant them elsewhere, but discovered they would not grow there; desperately replanted them in traditional soil, with equally unhappy results. Too much the product of his class, and too little an individual, to find sustenance in other worlds or to make his own world, he wandered lost

between two worlds
One dead, the other powerless to be born.

He was the nineteenth century disinherited intellectual.

He and his fellows were both like and unlike those in our own times, who have seen the orgies of inflation and the sinking contortions of finance capitalism. Unlike our desperate revelers of the Jazz Age, they were too sober to pursue oblivion in dissipation; and unlike the hollow men sinking into impotence and decay, they earnestly believed in the importance of—of—they did not know exactly what. The dust of the waste land had not choked their faith in striving, in nobility and grandeur, but it had undermined their certainties about what to strive for. They were left a prey to vacillation of the will. Sterling was among these a representative, but hardly a heroic figure. He thus achieves a certain symbolic importance in his age.

This is the man Carlyle celebrates in his *Life of Sterling*. It is a strange thing, remembering Carlyle's blame of Lockhart for allowing Scott to be 'altogether lovely to him,' to survey Carlyle's own work in the field of biography. For we discover that nearly all

Carlyle's endeavor was one of heroizing and wiping away the faults of his subjects. His *Life of Cromwell* is more a history of the Rebellion and Commonwealth and Protectorate than it is a biography, and is consequently somewhat beyond our scope; and the same is true of his monumental work on Frederick the Great of Prussia. But in both these productions Carlyle betrayed a determined effort to whitewash almost every one of the actions of his heroes, and to find their 'greatness spread out before him on all hands beyond reach of eye.' He makes them ultimately, in fact, into two of those Great Men whom he was always exhorting the public to obey and worship.

It is perhaps not surprising, then, that in his *Life of Sterling* we find him attempting the same feat. If he cannot translate Sterling into a great man, he can try at least to reveal him as a great man manqué: one who had, however feebly, the seeds of greatness in him: and who might have accomplished more if he had lived longer.

Yet, as we have seen, the external facts about Sterling are hardly impressive. Moved, doubtless, by high and noble purposes, he divagated sadly. He had glimmering thoughts of a parliamentary career, and gave them up. He thought of literature, wrote an unsuccessful novel, and gave it up. He fell under the spell of Coleridge's insidious magic and mystic idealism, and became lost in the wandering wood of metaphysics. He outfitted a ship to help the Spanish refugees stage a revolt, which failed. After all his skepticisms he blundered into the clergy, and then, realizing that it was not his vocation after all, straggled out again. He made other attempts at literature, founded the Sterling Club for discussing public questions, and finally died of tuberculosis.

Sterling had a great deal of liveliness, debater's skill in argument, and personal charm. But he lacked any such intellectual powers as might have led him at last to a significant goal. Lost in luminous idealistic mists, his abilities were insufficient to arrive at clear conclusions. He ceased to believe in the gentlemanly deity of the Church of England, but replaced him with a vague, anti-materialistic, beatified, but otherwise undefined, *faith*.

It is this amiable wanderer whom Carlyle's biography hymns for us in seraphic terms as 'the noble Sterling, a radiant child of the empyrean, clad in bright auroral hues in the memory of all that knew him.' And, by a quaint enough turn, in the very volume where Sterling, who accomplished nothing, is portrayed with panegyric in excelsis, Coleridge, whose contributions to nineteenth century thought and poetry were innumerable, is satirized in a brilliantly malicious chapter for his weakness and failure! It was easy for those seduced by the charm of the younger man to believe, if they wished, that he might have attained something if he had lived. (Although Mrs Carlyle had discerned readily enough that he was 'a little flighty.') But it was clear that the sage of Highgate Hill had never harnessed the half of his powers. That was what ruined his credit with the prophet who championed the gospel of work.

Coleridge alone in England, Carlyle says ironically, 'knew the sublime secret of believing by "the reason" what "the understanding" had been obliged to fling out as incredible'; and sat there, in 'his Dodona oak-grove . . . whispering strange things, uncertain whether oracles or jargon . . .' 'No talk in his century, or in any other, could be more surprising,' but it was 'aimless, cloudcapt, cloud-based, lawlessly meandering,' misty and disembodied. 'One right peal of concrete laughter at some convicted flesh-and-blood absurdity, one burst of noble indignation at some injustice or depravity, rubbing elbows with us on this solid Earth, how strange it would have been in that Kantean haze-world, and how infinitely cheering amid its vacant air-castles and dim-melting ghosts and shadows!'

So he leaves Coleridge, whose life 'amid the ghosts of defunct bodies and unborn ones' had given birth to the *Ancient Mariner*, *Christabel*, and the *Biographia Literaria*, to praise Sterling, who financed an unsuccessful revolution, wrote an unsuccessful novel, experienced an unsuccessful religious conversion, and succeeded mostly as a failure. It may not be impossible, however, to discover why Carlyle thus idealizes him. Sterling's earlier spiritual history had echoed, less sulphurously, Carlyle's own: he had gone through the same torments Carlyle recorded in The Everlasting Nay and The Everlasting Yea of *Sartor Resartus*. And, like Carlyle, Sterling had submerged his doubts in a pious reconversion of mystical hope. Unlike Coleridge, he could be led, he could be a disciple; perhaps, if he had lived—who knows?—the beloved disciple? Certainly, then, 'a radiant child of the empyrean'!

The chaos of that waste land they had both dwelt in Carlyle

eloquently describes. It is not, like T. S. Eliot's, an arid desert of old men and drought; that is too static for Carlyle's furious genius. His waste land is a hell hurtled through by the wild and melodramatic ride of demoniac valkyrie:

> A world all rocking and plunging, like that old Roman one when the measure of its iniquities was full; the abysses and subterranean and supernal deluges, plainly broken loose; in the wild dim-lighted chaos all stars of Heaven gone out. No star of Heaven visible, hardly now to any man; the pestiferous fogs, and foul exhalations grown continual, have, except on the highest mountain-tops, blotted-out all stars: will-o'-wisps, of various course and colour, take the place of stars. Over the wild-surging chaos, in the leaden air, are only sullen glares of revolutionary lightning; then mere darkness, with philanthropistic phosphorescences, empty meteoric lights; here and there an ecclesiastical luminary still hovering, hanging on its old quaking fixtures, pretending still to be a Moon or Sun,–though visibly it is but a Chinese Lantern made of *paper* mainly, with candle-end foully dying in the heart of it. Surely as mad a world as you could wish!

What is the young soul to do, with 'noble human valour, bright intelligence, ardent proud veracity' in him, when he comes into 'this waste-weltering epoch of Sterling's and ours?' Carlyle enquires. In threading such gulfs of uncertainty, sloughs of despair, in truth, Sterling was at a dreadful disadvantage. He had mental agility, but none of the strength or solidity of a careful thinker. How could he deal with the problems of a disintegrating world in which it was hard for ideals to find a home? 'I likened him often, in my banterings,' Carlyle says, 'to sheet-lightning; and reproachfully prayed that he would concentrate himself into a bolt, and rive the mountain-barriers for us, instead of merely playing on them and irradiating them.'

But Sterling had no such electric power. Agile in controversy, 'when the blows of contradiction came too thick,' instead of bearing their battering, 'he could with consummate dexterity whisk aside out of their way; prick into his adversary on some new quarter; or gracefully flourishing his weapon, end the duel in some handsome way.' As a game it was delightful. But it would rive no mountain-barriers, outshine no false luminaries. And he was just a little too apt to resort to plausible claptrap, catchwords. '"Flat Pantheism!" urged he once . . . as if triumphantly, of something or other, in the fore of a debate . . . "It is mere Pantheism, that!"'

But his opponent in this argument was not to be taken in by any such name-calling: '"And suppose it were Pot-theism?" cried the other: "if the thing is true!"'

For all the shimmering lights in which this picture is painted, Sterling's lack of weight and solidity is clear enough. But he had the merit, for Carlyle, of having denied the materialism of the age. For at last, despite all those false ecclesiastical luminaries pretending to be Moon and Sun, he had found his religion. He painfully shaped it together for himself, 'out of the abysses of conflicting disbelief and sham-belief and bedlam delusion.' By this Carlyle means that he was gradually drawn into the orbit of Carlyle's own Sun, the Carlylean gospel. Thus his lot, for all that he accomplished little else, became 'victory and not defeat . . . an impressive emblem of his time, and an instruction and a possession to his contemporaries. For, I say, it is by no means as a vanquished *doubter* that he figures in the memory of those who knew him; but rather as a victorious *believer* . . .'

An impressive emblem Sterling may well seem to us. But surely he is so in the very opposite sense to that which Carlyle says. Doubt may be a mighty and affirmative weapon; such it never was, but only a source of wavering, in Sterling. And his belief was not achieved in the teeth of doubt, meeting and overthrowing every argument doubt could advance, but an ostrich-belief that at last merely closed its eyes, head hidden in the sand, and said, I will believe; a belief, furthermore, in no-thing, bound no-where, but merely nebulous, formless, white-ghost-like belief. Sterling was vanquished by doubt and vanquished by belief; he was defeated by his time, and his surrender of doubt was the last surrender. Beside this empty and luminous belief what a mighty thing is Ruskin's despair!

From first to last *The Life of Sterling* violates Carlyle's every principle, as he voiced them in his review of Lockhart. He bathes Sterling in shining rainbow colors of ideality. Overkindly to Sterling, finding excuses for all his shortcomings and weaknesses, blurring them in a mist of fine writing, he is pitilessly intolerant to others, above all Coleridge. There can be no justification of this violent partisan, who realizing clearly what the aims of biography should be, wrote a book that is all diatribe or idyll.

It is a marvelous triumph of eloquence. But that through the effulgence of rhapsody Sterling emerges with any personality at all is one of the irrational victories of art over its votaries. Carlyle shows us what Sterling really is, through and despite his efforts to surround him with light. That real identity gives him his importance for us. He was not one of the heroes, but he wandered, stumbling and distracted, through the drifting smoke of the battle. Carlyle shows us the battle, and the no-man's land in which it was taking place. For all the difference in time, we recognize that shell-torn field.

Ikon of a Prophet

The modern reader may find it hard to understand the poisonous clamor that surrounded the appearance of Froude's *Life of Carlyle.* The accusations of vile taste that had greeted his publication of the *Reminiscences* in 1881 were followed by louder screams of rage, in which the words traitor, scavenger, and ghoul were virulently shouted. But these sounds of fury were signs not so much of Victorian squeamishness as of the strange eminence Carlyle had assumed in his later years—from which, with the publication of these volumes, he suddenly crashed. The Sage of Chelsea, he had become something remote, prophetic, godlike, speaking oracular words of gnomic wisdom. He dwelt in an august and blinding cloud. The biographical revelations that showed him as a fallible being destroyed an idol; and the man who had done it was charged with betraying and befouling 'the memory of the man whom . . . he had loved and revered as he had loved and revered no other of the sons of men.'

Froude had indeed himself been one of the worshippers, and with a devotion that demanded the very unveiling for which he was execrated. Carlyle had in a thousand words of violent scorn protested against the decorous dressing-up of truth in conventional biography. Idealizing of him, 'to whom untruth of any kind was abominable'! Froude could not do it. Such a course would go counter to Carlyle's most positive injunction. Had he not consulted Carlyle on what to do about a passage in one of Mrs Carlyle's letters, in which an eminent living person was judged in terms 'more just than flattering'? Carlyle had said, 'It will do him no harm to know what a sensible woman thought of him.'

It would have been easy to do, no doubt, by 'recasting the entire material, by selecting chosen passages out of his own and his wife's letters, by exhibiting the fair and beautiful side of the story only,' and this 'without suppressing a single material point.' 'When the Devil's advocate has said his worst against Carlyle, he leaves a figure still of unblemished integrity, purity, loftiness of purpose, and inflexible resolution to do right . . .' But the honesty Carlyle himself enjoined would not permit manipulation: 'If he was to be known at all, he chose to be known as he was, with his angularities, his sharp speeches, his special peculiarities, meritorious or unmeritorious, precisely as they had actually been.' But the Victorian public, comments Lytton Strachey, 'unable to understand a form of hero-worship which laid bare the faults of the hero, was appalled, and refused to believe what was the simple fact—that Froude's adoration was of so complete a kind that it shrank with horror from the notion of omitting a single wart from the portrait.'

But in saying so much, Mr Strachey has himself gone a little beyond the truth, and in a way somewhat surprising in a writer noteworthy for the brilliance with which he flashes the blade of irony. It is true that Froude revered Carlyle's memory and regarded him as a great teacher, and yet——! There were strange depths and reservations, curious half-thoughts stirring in the heart of Froude, and sometimes they come to the surface in little flashes of almost Stracheyan innuendo. There is the passage, for example, in which he comments on Carlyle's *Journal* revealing that he 'was putting himself through a severe cross-examination,' and discovering that he was too intolerant, too contemptuously indifferent to others, and wanting in courtesy. Then Froude says quietly:

'One discovery came on him as a startling surprise.

' "On the whole art thou not among the *vainest* of living men? At bottom the very *vainest?*" '

Something other than hero-worship spoke in that single sentence, and what it was the shrewd reader may sooner or later discern for himself. For against the pricklinesses and acerbities of Carlyle there is one figure that does stand out as 'white' and 'stainless': the image of Mrs Carlyle. If Froude revered the sage, he was even more bewitched by the enchanting Jane; and in all the tangled story of that ill-assorted pair she beglamors Froude's memory, subtly weighing down his judgment. Even his anecdotes of her childhood, which he did not know, are filled with the fascination of 'little

Pen,' her daring and her mimicry, her temper and her charm. Froude describes her as an accomplished and beautiful young girl of twenty, with 'black hair, large black eyes shining with soft mockery, pale complexion,' and a figure 'slight, airy, and perfectly graceful.'

The mature, clever, discontented woman he had come to know; she fascinated him as she fascinated even Tennyson with her vivacity and wit. In imagination he could see her blacking the grate on the bleak farm at Craigenputtock while her lord and master went off for a walk by himself, just as he now saw her in later years suffering illness and loneliness while Carlyle wrote in his silent upper room or attended a party at Lady Ashburton's, to which his wife had not been invited. No; it was not a pretty picture, and possibly Mrs Carlyle, in a quiet way, had made the most of it. It is not surprising that in their domestic infelicities Froude should be her partisan.

Her unhappiness was perhaps exaggerated. It is natural that a clever and pretty woman whose famous husband is obliged to leave her often alone should feel a bit sorry for herself; and even more natural that she should sometimes hint a little pathos to a devoted friend of the family whom she knows she can twist around her finger's end. And whatever distortions there may have been in Froude's perspective were deepened and rendered indelible by the last years of Carlyle's life, when the saddened old man, yearning for his lost darling, tortured himself with lamentable exclamations and sharpened his misery with a self-accusing remorse that darkened every circumstance to monstrous blackness.

But if Froude was unjust he neither knew nor intended it. And his injustice operated within a limited range—the small theatre of domestic intimacies. In all the larger outlines of Carlyle's career and personality his judgment is generous and understanding, his portrayal sharply etched and convincing. Although he was terribly careless, it is true, in transcribing manuscript, and made sometimes culpable blunders, in Froude's biography Carlyle is alive, and is the real Carlyle. There have been many corrections of fact, and there have been differences of shading or emphasis. But in hardly a single essential feature has any biographer since his time altered Froude's portrait.

That portrait is founded on Carlyle's heredity. A 'stern, laborious, plebeian family of Lowland Scots—with its remote Teutonic affiliations, its coarseness, its narrowness,'—so Havelock Ellis describes the Carlyles. The father, James Carlyle, a stonemason in the tiny village of Ecclefechan and a somberly religious man, had withdrawn from the Kirk to a stricter dissenting sect. Although unlettered, he awed his family as a man of mental power with his 'bold glowing style,' 'full of metaphor, though he knew not what metaphor was,' his son said, and 'all manner of potent words.' 'In anger, he had no need of oaths; his words were like sharp arrows that smote into the very heart.' He was severe in manner: 'We all had to complain,' Carlyle wrote, 'that we dared not freely love our father. His heart seemed as if walled in.'

Is it possible not to see in this forbidding figure, with its conscientiousness, its sternness, its wounding invective, the explanation of Carlyle's own character? 'When he was excited,' Froude tells us, his eloquence 'was like the eruption of a volcano, thunder and lightning, hot stone and smoke and ashes. He had a natural tendency to exaggeration,' with 'flashes of Titanesque humour'; and 'his invectives when they burst out piled themselves into metaphor so extravagant that they ended in convulsions of laughter with his whole body and mind.' Havelock Ellis, indeed, finds in Carlyle 'the Scotch Aristophanes, as Rabelais is the French and Heine the German Aristophanes.'

But to himself, Carlyle was a moralist, with the denunciations of Isaiah and the lamentations of Jeremiah ever springing to his lips. The Calvinist theology of his father, to be sure, had not survived the doubts born of his student days in the University of Edinburgh, whither his family had painfully sent him. Gibbon's *Decline and Fall*, with its 'winged sarcasms, so quiet and yet so conclusively transpiercing and killing dead,' proved to him 'that Christianity was not true.' But though the Calvinist theology was slain the Calvinist spirit lived on in him. Life became a nightmare. 'To me the universe was all void of life, of purpose, of volition, even of hostility: it was one huge, dead, immeasurable steam-engine, rolling on in its dead indifference, to grind me limb from limb. Oh, the vast, gloomy, solitary Golgotha and mill of death!'

So it lasted for him 'as in bitter, protracted death-agony through long years. The heart within me, unvisited by any heavenly dewdrop, was smouldering in sulphurous, slow-consuming fires.' At last it suddenly occurred to him to ask himself: 'What *art* thou afraid of? wherefore, like a coward, dost thou forever pip and whimper, and go cowering and trembling? Despicable biped! what is the sum total of the worst that lies before thee? Death? Well, death; and say the pangs of Tophet too, and all that the devil and man may, will, or can do against thee!' And, reflecting thus, 'there rushed like a stream of fire' over his soul; and from that time the temper of his misery was changed: 'not fear or whining sorrow was it, but indignation and grim fire-eyed defiance.'

From then on Carlyle never lost his sense of vocation. He must dedicate himself to his mission, the mission of finding in his spirit a new evangel for humanity. Every moment spent otherwise than in spiritual travail was a shirking. 'For these many months,' he wrote to Jane Welsh, 'the voice of every persuasion in my conscience has been thundering to me as with the Trump of the Archangel: Man! thou art going to destruction. Thy nights and days are spent in torment; thy heart is wasting into entire bitterness. Thou art making less of life than the dog that sleeps upon thy hearth. Up, hapless mortal! Up, and rebuild thy destiny if thou canst!' He was willing to sacrifice himself to the hard endeavor; he was willing also to sacrifice the woman he was asking to be his wife.

He was to be a moral leader. And everywhere he saw plentiful signs that he was needed. In London there were many people, 'some of them kind and influential,' he said, 'almost all ignorant enough'; and, 'let him be crossed in argument' by these or any others, Froude tells us, 'let some rash person, whoever he might be, dare to contradict him, and Johnson himself was not more rude, disdainful, and imperious.' He looked about him with the censorious eye of the prophet. Fashionable London was so futile that if he 'were doomed to exist as a man of fashion' he would 'swallow ratsbane, or apply to hemp or steel before three months were over.' Paris was even more degraded, physical luxuries in the midst of 'noise and stink,' 'the chosen abode of vanity and vice,' and the French were indeed, as Voltaire had called them, 'tigres-singes (tiger-apes).'

Individuals fared as ill in his judgments as classes and nations. Thomas Campbell had the smirk of an auctioneer, the eye 'of a conceited worldling;' he was a 'literary dandy,' and his talk was 'small, contemptuous, and shallow.' Coleridge was 'flat, flabby, incurvated . . . with a watery mouth, a snuffy nose, a pair of strange brown, timid, yet earnest-looking eyes, a high tapering brow, and a great bush of grey hair.' 'He has no resolution'; he stoops, he shovels and slides in walking, he has to make 'strong and frequent inhalations' to keep 'the water of his mouth from overflowing'; his conversation is wandering, unprofitable, and tedious. Macaulay was 'a sophistical, rhetorical, ambitious young man' who made 'flash speeches'; Moore 'a lascivious triviality of great name'; Rogers 'an elegant, politely malignant old lady.' Poor Lamb was 'a confirmed, shameless drunkard; *asks* vehemently for gin and water in strangers' houses, and is only not thrown out of doors because he is too much despised for taking such trouble with him. Poor Lamb! Poor England, when such a despicable abortion is named genius.'

The Prophet of God pulling down the idols of the heathen, Carlyle found a certain grim amusement in these onslaughts. He dramatized himself as 'a wild, monstrous Orson,' smashing 'everything to pieces.' 'The very sound of my voice is savage-prophetic. I am as a John Baptist girt about with a leathern girdle, and whose food is locust and wild honey.'

The picture is prophetic in more ways than one. So arrogant a Daniel among the London lions might hesitate little to throw even his wife to far other lions if it would enable his voice to sound in the ears of men.

At first, indeed, all the advantages lay with Jane, and there seemed not even the faintest of possibilities of her ever becoming his wife. She was a lady, an heiress, talented, with an imperious disposition; he awkward, uncouth, and a peasant—a peasant of genius, true, but still a peasant. He assumed charge over her reading, and was soon referring to 'those few Elysian hours we spent together lately' and writing in conclusion 'Addio Donna mia cara!' Miss Welsh speedily called a halt to these 'somewhat too ardent expressions of friendship'; she was extremely angry, and he became again merely the literary adviser.

But insensibly their correspondence grew warmer in tone once more, and although their endearments were supposed to maintain a Platonic tone we find that when his language became too specific Jane now cried, 'For mercy's sake, keep in mind that my peace of mind, my credit with my Mother, the continuance of our correspondence, everything, depends upon your appearing as my Friend, not as my Lover.'

Powerful though the fascination was, however, Carlyle was aware of the discrepancies between them. Jane, also, continued to be less then carried away. He compared her 'gay cousins' and their 'brilliant equipment' with his own 'simple exterior and scanty prospects': could he be the right man for her? 'I love you,' she wrote, 'and I should be the most ungrateful and injudicious of mortals if I did not. But I am not *in love* with you . . . my love is not a passion which overclouds my judgment.' The financial difficulties in the way of their union were discouraging. She would not curtail her mother's style of living by taking away any share of the income on which they lived together—especially in a marriage she knew her mother would disapprove—so that although her ultimate prospects were comfortable, her present income would be almost nothing.

Carlyle proposed that they settle down to farming and writing on the small property of Craigenputtock, which she owned. Jane's response was derisive. 'I would as soon think of building myself a nest on the Bass Rock.' At Craigenputtock she 'would not spend a month . . . with an Angel.' She had no prescience of the six long years from 1828 to 1834. Did he have, she demanded, 'any *certain* livelihood to maintain' her? 'any fixed place in the rank of society I have been born and bred in? No.' Only prospects and capabilities. She would promise to marry no one else, but nothing more. And this was final: if there were any change to be made 'it must be made by you, not by me.'

Carlyle admitted her objections to be well enough founded; he voiced no blame. Her maxims were prudential, but *he* must 'adopt other than common maxims,' for he was a man of destiny, which he would not betray by writing potboilers or running with the mob. If she felt that a life of labor and poverty with him would be a sacrifice, she was right to refuse. But 'the love which will not make sacrifices to its object is no proper love'; as for him, 'the union with such a spirit as yours might be, is worth all price but the sacrifice of those very principles which would enable me to deserve and enjoy it.'

Froude, here, as Greek chorus, remarks 'on the subtler forms of self-deception to which the human heart is liable.' Self-sacrifice, it is true, is a noble thing. 'But a sacrifice which one person might properly make, the other might have no right to ask or allow.'

Self-denial Carlyle was prepared to make: 'the devotion of his whole life to the pursuit and setting-forth of spiritual truth . . . But apostles in St Paul's opinion were better unwedded.'

Slowly, however, Jane's resolution weakened. 'Not many months ago I would have said it was *impossible* that I should ever be your wife,' she wrote. 'At present I consider this the most probable destiny for me, and in a year or two perhaps I shall consider it the only one.' Mrs Welsh was made to realize that, despite her opposition, despite his gaucherie and his violent tempers, the marriage was inevitable. She yielded, and, 'since the marriage was to be,' she agreed 'either to live with him or to accept him as her son-in-law in her own house and in her own circle.'

It might seem that the obstacles were now past; but no, Carlyle said this would never do. He 'would never have any right enjoyment of his wife's company' till he had her to himself in his own house; and 'the moment he was master of a house,' the first thing he would do 'would be to slam the door against nauseous intruders.' The praiser of self-sacrifice, who was willing to pay all price but the sacrifice of his principles, would not sacrifice the right to slam the door against the nauseous intrusion of her mother and her mother's friends.

Jane was deeply hurt, but her old imperiousness was dead now. She wailed in a tearful and frightened letter that they were 'already married, married past redemption. God knows in that case what is to become of us. At times I am so disheartened that I sit down and weep.' But Carlyle, although he could see that his manners had been rude, was adamantine. '*The man should bear rule in the house, and not the woman,*' he wrote, with underlining. He must be head of his own house; otherwise he would be miserable and would make all about him miserable. Mrs Welsh decided to leave her house at Haddington, and Carlyle suggested that he and Jane might live there. The 'evil of impertinent visitors' that had made him reject sharing a residence with Mrs Welsh, he now regarded with majestic serenity; the nauseous intruders were nothing; he had nerve in him to dispatch 'that sort of deer by dozens in the day.' He could not understand why Jane should find it painful to live in the home he had refused to think of while her mother was in it.

At last a house was found in Edinburgh, at Comely Bank, which they could afford. As the day of the marriage approached they were both filled with terror. Jane jested, but shivered, at what she called 'the odious ceremony,' and Carlyle tried to allay his fears by reading the *Kritik der reinen Vernunft*, but 'found it too abstruse for his condition, and that Scott's novels would answer better.' They were married in the parish church of Templand, and drove off in a post-chaise.

The circumstances were not too propitious. Jane also had a fiery temper. 'When provoked she was as hard as flint,' and 'the sarcasms flashed out from her as the sparks fly from lacerated steel.' Even in later years, when she had come into her inheritance and Carlyle was a man of renown, her letters, though often witty, show an almost continuous undercurrent of malice in their comment. Experiences, books, people, are subjected to a jesting but subacid depreciation, which, for all the pretty display of laughter, is often definitely spiteful.

At an amateur performance of *Every Man in His Humour* she describes Charles Dickens as Captain Bobadil: 'poor little Dickens, all painted in black and red, and affecting the voice of a man of six feet . . .' Old Mr Sterling, John Sterling's father, she calls 'his Whirlwindship,' and tells how he tried to cut short a visit to some boring people by ' "feeling it his duty to see poor Mrs Carlyle 'ome." His secret purpose was evidently to take himself and me back in the carriage, and leave Mrs S. to follow as she could . . .' And to one of her barbed remarks, his Whirlwindship replied, 'Do you know, Mrs Carlyle, you would be a vast deal more amiable if you were not so damnably clever.' Such mere acerbities in social intercourse would be aggravated by the closeness of married life.

But Carlyle himself was no easy house-companion. He suffered from dyspepsia, and had to swallow 'whole hogsheads of castor oil.' And, 'of all the men whom I have ever seen,' Froude writes, 'Carlyle was the least patient of the common woes of humanity . . . He saw his ailments through the lens of his imagination, so magnified by the metaphors in which he described them as to seem to him to be something supernatural; and if he was a torment to himself, he distracted every one with whom he came in contact.' Even his mother early described him as 'gey ill to live wi',' and he had not changed.

'The slightest noise or movement at night shattered his nervous system; therefore he required a bedroom to himself . . .' He was essentially solitary, and walked out by himself in all weathers, leaving Mrs Carlyle at home to keep the house in order. In the early years they were so poor that she had to cook and wash and scour and mend shoes and clothes. 'He was extremely dainty about his food.' Delicacies he did not care for, but common things had to be perfect: 'if the porridge was smoked, or the bread heavy . . . he was entirely intolerable.' So Mrs Carlyle learned to bake the bread, dress the dinner, clean the room, milk the cows. 'Nay, it might happen that she had to blacken the grates to the proper polish, or even scour the floors, while Carlyle looked on encouragingly with his pipe.'

Their marriage was not happy, Froude comments, 'in the roseate sense.' 'She had the companionship of an extraordinary man. Her character was braced by the contact with him . . . Long years after, in the late evening of her laborious life, she said, "I married for ambition. Carlyle has exceeded all that my wildest hopes ever imagined of him—and I am miserable." '

There can be no doubt that Carlyle was selfish, extremely selfish. He sacrificed himself to his work, but his household must revolve around him, and its movements must be dictated by the conditions that would make his work easiest. If Froude distorts, his distortion is not so much one of fact as of proportion; the charm in which Jane Welsh Carlyle was bathed for him made him see her, truly enough, as an exploited woman, and he remained unaware of faults that might make quite as difficult a companion as dyspepsia and selfishness could make. Froude never suspected any tendency to play the martyr in her; he never saw anything but playful cleverness in the stroke of those feline claws. Tennyson, who admired both the Carlyles, perhaps saw more deeply in one way than Froude. He could never agree with the belief that they each should have married someone else, for if they had, he said, there would have been four people dissatisfied instead of two.

But when she was dead, Carlyle himself deepened Froude's belief that the sins had been all on one side. Immeasurably drowned in misery and despair, he imaged for himself his 'lost radiant one,' and with meticulous anguish accused his conscience of all the harshnesses he had ever displayed against her. The loss 'had peeled my life all bare, and, in one moment, shattered my poor world to universal ruin. They took me out next day, to wander . . . in the green sunny Sabbath fields; and ever and anon there rose from my sick heart the ejaculation "My poor little Woman!"—but no full gush of tears came to my relief, nor has yet come; will it ever? A stony "Woe's me, woe's me!" sometimes with infinite tenderness, and pity not for myself . . .' Froude writes: 'For many years after she had left him, when we passed the spot in our walks where she was last seen alive, he would bare his grey head in the wind and rain—his features wrung with unavailing anguish.'

These words are written near the end of the two volumes in which Froude commemorates the first forty years of Carlyle's life, but the succeeding part of the biography, *Life in London*, although it deepens many of the strokes and deals with days of achievement and triumph, does not change the lines that have been already laid down. Carlyle had placed his journals and correspondence in Froude's hands 'with no instructions save that I should tell the truth about him, and if shadows there were, that least of all should I conceal them.' Froude felt that he had fulfilled his trust. Carlyle's life had been a life of battle: it had made him fierce, uncompromising, scornful, arrogant. His judgments were stern. 'The sins of passion he could pardon, but the sins of insincerity, or half-sincerity, he could never pardon.' He would not condescend to conventional politenesses. He was 'often harsh when he ought to have been merciful; he was contemptuous when he had no right to despise; and in his estimate of motives and actions was often unjust and mistaken.' He was unconscious of his own weaknesses.

'But there is another side of the account. In the weightier matters of the law Carlyle's life had been without speck or flaw.' He had ever been true in word and upright in deed. His habits were Spartan and he had been generous in helping those in need. 'It was enough if a man or woman was miserable. He did not look too curiously into the causes of it.' He had regarded his talents not as a means to aggrandizement, but as a trust. He had never written for money, never written anything he did not in his heart believe to be true.

Such is Froude's final estimate. It had been written not without internal struggle. There was loyalty to Carlyle; there was loyalty to conflicting affections; there was loyalty to truth; there was the certainty that his motives would be condemned and misunderstood.

But the task was nevertheless done. The lines were bitten deep, and Carlyle lives there before us: angular and prickly, hateful and pathetic, a figure of grotesque, self-deluded comedy and a figure of tragic woe. The lighting is as lurid, as sharply glaring in lava-flame and smoke and strange shadow, as Carlyle's own fiery apocalyptic utterance. It is a fantastic image, but it is no caricature, for Carlyle was his own caricature. Some few lines may have been out of drawing, but the entire portrait has the glow of truth.

Epilogue to an Age

The young Victoria was newly on the throne when Lockhart's final volume of the *Life of Scott* made its appearance; Froude's *Carlyle* shocked the public in 1882. Between these fall most of the others we have surveyed. Lamb, Creevey, and the hard-faced viveur Greville were products of an earlier age. Haydon, Charlotte Brontë, Sterling, and Macaulay cluster around the middle of the century. Mill, Dickens, and the vigorous Crabb Robinson almost reach its three-quarter mark; and Ruskin, sorrowful and broken, lingers on into the dawn of the nineteen hundreds. Taken together, they are a panorama of changing England.

The eighteenth century after-glow of the Regency lasted into the nineteenth century, mingling with the rainbow hopes of dawning romanticism; but slowly the tide of industrialism brought its social problems. Already in 1812, Wordsworth was haunted by the fear, Crabb Robinson reports, 'lest a social war should arise between the poor and the rich,' the danger of which he felt 'aggravated by the vast extension of the manufacturing system.' Disraeli's *Sybil*, in 1845, bore the significant subtitle *The Two Nations*—the rich and the dispossessed—and at almost the same time Robinson noted that in France the application of the words *propriêtaires* and *proletaires* had given recognition to the class distinction.

The factories of Birmingham belched smoke and the children of the poor grew pale, stunted, and rachitic, while the middle class waxed rich and smugly contented. But humanitarian hearts melted with pity; repeated waves of social protest dashed themselves against the evil; and when the filth of factory conditions led to recurrent outbreaks of cholera even the exploiters became terrified.

There were frightening implications, too, in the advances of the sciences of geology and biology; religion and science seemed to be looking on each other with hostile gaze. The face of nature grew cruel and implacable with the struggle for existence. The world of the spirit seemed to have no place in this new universe governed by mechanical laws of determinism or chance. What sanction was there for the virtues of duty and mercy, nay, for any virtues, in that 'vast, gloomy, solitary Golgotha and mill of death'?

And yet, there seemed to be amelioration, there was increasing prosperity, material productivity, expanding powers, there seemed to be—positively—progress! The Utilitarians were the prophets of machine-triumph; the Manchester school of economists celebrated the march of mind; Macaulay blew trumpet-blasts of rejoicing over material growth. But the novelists—Dickens, Kingsley, Disraeli, George Eliot—noted the degradation of the poor. Carlyle thundered against it, and Mill and Ruskin tried to find solutions to the injustice of modern society. Uncertainty and doubt struggled with jubilation; amid the confusion of clanging engines and factory sirens blew the winds of doctrine carrying the sound of many voices. Where was the world-machine going? Some hearts answered with sinking hopes; others were brisk with a breathless optimism.

Such is the shifting England behind all these biographical records. It is the European world that is mirrored in them. But there are other signs of the times to be read there, less universal but significant. England was growing more provincial as it became more imperial. In the eighteenth century educated sentiment was international. Voltaire and Swift, Gibbon and Walpole, were men of the world, not subjects. Talents were employed without regard to nationality. The Prince de Ligne, a Belgian, commanded an Austrian army. The Prince of Nassau-Siegen was in the Russian navy. Sir John Acton became Prime Minister of the Kingdom of Naples, and an American, Benjamin Rumford, was Minister of State at Munich. During the Seven Years' War, Lawrence Sterne rode in Paris through cheering crowds who loved his Uncle Toby, and saw plays among a resident English colony at Frontignac. But the French Revolution and the Napoleonic Wars ended nearly all this hopeful internationalism.

The bitterness of the struggle against complete domination and absorption built up a hatred that had not existed in eighteenth century wars. The Continental System with which Napoleon fought against English power led to the Blockade, which for ten years made it difficult to travel on the Continent. The days when every young man of family made the Grand Tour were gone. Englishmen narrowed into a rigid John Bullism, despising foreigners and priding themselves on their own crotchets. National feeling ran so high that Napoleon was known as 'the atheistical usurper,' 'the Corsican monster,' the Beast of the Apocalypse; among the vulgar he was believed to devour babies.

When, after Napoleon's downfall, they did travel again, it was in a far different spirit from that of the days when Voltaire had mingled with Bolingbroke and Swift, and taken back to France an enthusiasm for the philosophy of Newton and the parliamentary form of government. The Ruskins went abroad to see galleries and cathedrals, not to observe a different society; they were not travelers, but tourists. Carlyle traveled in France with Edward Strachey in 1824, and heard him curtly refuse a pourboire to the postilion with the words, 'Nong! Vous avez drivé devilish slow.' His grandson Lytton Strachey comments, 'Fifty years earlier a cultivated Englishman would have piqued himself upon answering the postilion in the idiom and accent of Paris.'

Crabb Robinson, that citizen of the world, was a survival of the earlier period. Mill, too, was vividly responsive to Comte, to European socialism, and to Saint-Simonism as it was glowingly described by the attractive young Frenchman, Gustave d'Eichthal. But Mill was a product of philosophical radicalism, which was itself the child of eighteenth century theory; in the Victorian age he was an exception. Of that age W. S. Gilbert's burlesque really catches the flavor:

For he might have been a Roosian,
A French, or Turk, or Proosian,
  Or perhaps I-tal-i-an!
But in spite of all temptations
To belong to other nations,
  He remains an Englishman!

This spreading parochiality can be seen all through the period. The Brontës as a family were unusually well-read in current events and international affairs. Even as children, in their remote parsonage on the moors, they devoured *Fraser's* and *Blackwood's Magazine* and saw the news in the journals; they knew all about the exploits of the Duke of Wellington, the Corn Laws, the Catholic question, and Mr Peel's speech. But when Charlotte and Emily were at Brussels they took no pleasure in observing the life around them and hardly any in the architectural and historical monuments of the city. The national character of the Belgians Charlotte found 'cold, selfish, animal, and inferior,' and their principles 'rotten to the core.' For their religion she felt an intolerant hatred: its ceremonies were 'mummeries' and 'feeble childish humbug,' its priests all had an 'idiotic mercenary aspect.'

Nor are these outbursts merely a reflection of Charlotte's peculiar misery when in strange surroundings. Margaret Ruskin, although it might be well enough to have foreign partners and even to entertain them, regarded the idea of her son marrying a foreigner and 'a Roman Catholic as too monstrous to be possible.' Dickens, who had made figures of glorious farce out of the Wellers and Jingles, was horrified by a barbarous poverty in America that a contemporary French traveler, Francis Wey, found in the slums of London: whole families 'mere skeletons covered with rags of incredible dirt' and, on Saturday nights, 'Drunken women by the hundred . . . higgledy-piggledy in the mud, hollow-eyed and purple-cheeked, their ragged clothing plastered with muck.' With such spectacles before his eyes—and he was not blind to them—Carlyle reserves his choicest sneers for France, despises the French nation even more than the polite world of London, and agrees with Voltaire's epithet tigres-singes. To Macaulay, the French were 'a people which violently pulls down constitutional governments and lives quiet under despotism.'

Despite all the confusions of the changing scene, a dogmatic earnestness was becoming more noticeable in English sentiment. There had been strong convictions in the eighteenth century, but except in the privileged arena of politics, they were mostly governed by a polished concern for the amenities. A Johnson might bludgeon his opponents with abuse, but Walpole felt that it was almost inelegant to have strong beliefs and certainly ill-bred to insist on them in company. Chesterfield and Gibbon would have agreed on the desirability of a courteous restraint in voicing all opinion. Society generally was laodicean, even relaxed, lending itself in frivolous circles to polite and fashionable vices. But the nonconformist conscience, which had dominated middle-class dissent, spread in the nineteenth century, and took charge of other concerns than those of religion. Even in the literary world, book reviewers could lash themselves into a moral fury, and dismiss Hazlitt as a 'slang-whanger' and an 'angry buffoon' whose writings were 'loathsome trash,' while Keats's *Endymion* was 'calm, settled, imperturbable, drivelling idiocy.'

The change did not take place all at once. The circle of the Prince Regent, subsequently George IV, had an almost restoration tone. In the glittering life of Brighton and the Pavilion a languid elegance mingled with a cynical pursuit of every indulgence. Sir Walter Scott was a good and earnest man, but he was enough the product of an earlier age so that he ignored the unsavory scandals surrounding the Prince, allowed himself to be charmed by his elegant manners, and reverently carried home in his coat-tail the goblet in which the Prince had drunk his health. Mr Creevey, less impressed by the august presence, refers to him as 'Prinney' and notes that, no longer wearing a corset, he 'has loosed his belly, which now reaches his knees.' The same tendencies descended into less exalted circles: old Walter Welsh, Jane's grandfather, although he did not drink to excess himself, disapproved of Carlyle's unwillingness to drink whiskey punch because 'he thought total abstinence in a young man was a sign of conceit or affectation.'

By the middle of the century all this was altered. In spite of her tortured shyness, in spite of her reverence for Thackeray as 'a Titan of the mind,' Charlotte Brontë found the great man so 'cynical, harsh, and contradictory' that she was positively obliged 'to speak to him of some of his shortcomings (literary, of course).' The determined little lady ferociously cross-examined the Titan for two hours on his literary misdeeds. When her friend Harriet Martineau collaborated on a book expressing atheistical views, Miss Brontë, deeply shocked by her 'fatal tenets,' enquired 'Who can trust the word or rely on the judgment of an avowed atheist?'

Carlyle struggled with the appalling vision of the universe as a 'huge, dead, immeasurable steam-engine,' the horrible Darwinian world-machine that darkened the pessimism of Thomas Hardy's universe and James Thomson's *City of Dreadful Night.* But in spite of all, Carlyle did not lose his conviction of the august primacy of the realm of morals, of which he was the custodian. 'Deeply as he admired his German friends,' Froude explains, 'his stern Scotch Calvinism found much in them that offended him.' Schiller and Goethe appeared positively to believe that the hopes for improving mankind lay in the arts 'rather than in obedience to the old rugged rules of right and wrong; and this perplexed and displeased him.'

The world was trying to cling to traditional ways, even though, with Ruskin, it heard the dreadful hammers of the geologists at the end of every Bible cadence. Even poor Sterling, wandering helplessly between two worlds, tried earnestly to imagine for a while that he believed in orthodox Christianity, and with an equal moral earnestness declaimed against repugnant ideas as 'mere Pantheism.' A product of radicalism like Mill might have no religious faith; Swinburne and a few other neo-Pagans might garland themselves in the paper roses of rapture and vice. But mostly the Victorian age outstared the grim face of determinism, faintly trusting in the larger hope.

The lives in which we may see all these developments reflected are copious in pictures of historical events. We are in Brussels after Waterloo with Creevey, and hear Wellington: 'It has been a damned serious business!' and 'By God! I don't think it would have done if I had not been there'; and we visit the field with Crabb Robinson. Greville reports Charles X's dissolution of the French Parlement, the fighting in Paris between the people and the Royal Guard, and judges 'the game is up with the Bourbons. They richly deserve their fate.' The fires of 1848 glare through Europe, apprehensively for Robinson and Matthew Arnold, hailed with hope by Mill and Carlyle. Sadowa and the rise of imperial Germany appear on the horizon; Ruskin greets the Paris Commune after the fall of Napoleon III. The scenery is sliding into place for the dénouement of 1914.

Meanwhile Miss Brontë sees Queen Victoria flash by in her carriage during a visit to King Leopold, her uncle: 'She looked a little, stout, vivacious lady, very plainly dressed, not much dignity or pretension about her.' We are in touch with burning issues again in Scott's indignation at the distresses of the industrial revolution in Manchester, and the excitement of the Reform Bill of 1832, with the flaming partisanship that led to his being hissed in public and pelted with stones during the election. The Houses of Parliament burn to the ground, and Carlyle shows us the popular sentiment on the occasion. 'The crowd was quiet,' he says, 'rather pleased than otherwise; whewed and whistled when the breeze came, as if to encourage it. "There's a flare-up for the House of Lords!" "A judgment for the Poor Law Bill!" "There go their *Hacts!*" Such exclamations seemed to be the prevailing ones: a man *sorry* I did not see anywhere.' Later still we hear Carlyle's bitter words, describing the Peterloo massacre of the laborers: 'There lie poor sallow work-worn weavers, and complain no more now; women themselves are slashed and sabred, howling terror fills the air; and ye ride prosperous, very victorious—ye unspeakable: give *us* sabres too, and then come on a little!'

That portentous new birth, democracy, was forcing itself on men's minds, with resistance and confusion. Even when they looked at the past, now, it began to seem clear that the great events were those involving peoples, not individuals. The great and revolutionary third chapter of Macaulay's *History* was concerned, not with kings, ministers, legislatures, wars and battles, but with urban and rural populations; the state of agriculture, mining, commerce, and industry; the different classes of society—country gentlemen, clergy, yeomanry, commercial and manufacturing interests; methods of communication and travel; newspapers and periodicals; the state of art, literature, and science; theatres, amusements, and watering-places; the wages and living conditions of laborers.

So realized, history must be rewritten in terms of the real community and its welfare. What was Scott's *History of Scotland*, Carlyle enquired scornfully, but

> a series of palace intrigues and butcheries and battles, little more important than those of Donnybrook Fair; all the while that *Scotland*, quite unnoticed, is holding her course in industry, in arts, in culture . . . Strange that a man should think he was writing the history of a nation while he is chronicling the amours of a wanton young woman called queen, and a sulky booby recommended to kingship for his fine limbs, and then blown up with gunpowder for his ill behaviour! [And as for the aristocracy,] The day is coming when these our modern hyaenas (though *toothless*, still mischievous and greedy beyond limit) will (quietly I hope) *be paid off*: *Canaille fainéante, que faites-vous là?* Down with your double-barrels; take spades, if ye can do no better, and work or die!

More and more the cry against social injustice is heard. Mill finds that if the choice is 'between Communism, with all its chances,' and the sufferings under capitalism, then 'all the difficulties, great or small, of Communism would be dust in the balance.' Ruskin analyzes the relationship between the principle of competition and the evils he sees about him, and repudiates a competitive society. 'Supply and demand is not the one Law of Nature,' Carlyle cries; 'Cash-payment is not the sole nexus of man with man . . .' And in the depression of 1842 he draws the horrible picture: 'Two million shirtless or ill-shirted workers sit enchanted in Workhouse Bastilles, five million more (according to some) in Ugolino Hunger-cellars;'—What, only seven millions? say our modern Bourbons—'and for remedy, you say,—what say you? "Raise *our* rents!" I have not in my time heard any stranger speech, not even on the Shore of the Dead Sea.'

Such was the Victorian era. An age of lost certitudes and of dogmas, of new despairs and burgeoning hopes. Smug, unhappy, sentimental, cruel:—contradictory. But one still looking to the light, yearning and striving for wider horizons. To that age Goethe on his deathbed was really the prophet:

Macht die Fensterladen auf, damit ich mehr Licht bekomme!

TURN OF THE CENTURY

XIV

TURN OF THE CENTURY

AUTOBIOGRAPHY

New Lights

LIGHT was the aspiration of the age. But as the nineteenth century drew to a close and we move into the early years of the twentieth, our impression is less one of clarity than of confusion. Every new idea and discovery, instead of substituting another clearly mapped realm for the blackness of some terra incognita on the chart, brought into view still further unknown vistas disappearing in blue mist, gave rise to a hundred new complexities bristling in place of the old. The nature of knowledge and the difficulties with which humanity struggled seemed to be infinite.

These complexities are reflected not only in the bewilderments recorded in biographies; although again and again they remind us that careers and beliefs are no longer objects of serene certitude but of conscientious doubt or thoughtless drift. Complexity appears also in the very structure and point of view of the writer, in manner, attitude, scope, technique, and feeling. The fluid character of the times impels writers, whether telling of themselves or others, to seek out new channels of awareness and invent or adapt new methods. Both biographers and autobiographers are forced into devising ways of communicating the varieties of experience brought to the fore by a world of shifting values.

I do not intend to suggest that all this meant a great burst of enlightenment in biographical art. Every period has its own sensibilities and problems, which it has to find appropriate means of translating into art. Biographers and autobiographers at the turn of the century were developing ways to clarify the meaning of the personal experiences they chronicled. They have the merits fitting to the scene of rich confusion they deal with, but they are no more deep and final in their view of character or fate than Lockhart or Cavendish. The instruments of psychoanalysis or sociological theory, as they are employed by numbers of contemporary biographers, may draw our attention to profoundly significant aspects of the relationships between the outer world and the human heart. They do not transcend or invalidate other interpretations of character. Often, applied to lives even out of the past, they may throw new light; they still do not command *the* light, ultimate and veridical.

Much, and many-colored, light they nevertheless do throw. The burgeoning of new sensibilities, the splintering impact of new knowledge or new ignorance, the kaleidoscopic transformation of new attitudes resulting from them; all are to be seen intertwined in the autobiography of recent times. Shifts and glints of nuance there have always been in autobiography. Even in Lord Herbert and John Bunyan, startling glimpses of self-insight suddenly flashed into the plain and assured outline the man had of his own nature; and, in Ruskin, there is dark exploration into subtle and lamentable wounds.

But, in a way, all these autobiographical writings were classical. Their authors had a clear image of what sort of man they were, dominated by a sharp central unity of character. Save for aberrant traits floating up unawares, they saw their qualities as parts of the unity they knew as *themselves*, and they so depicted them. They were not interested in sensibility realized for itself alone, in the exploration of temperament which seized upon each nuance of feeling and savored it as an essence. But, inspired possibly by the influence of Pater, this has been the quality of various modern autobiographers, like Arthur Machen in *Things Near and Far* and W. H. Hudson in *Far Away and Long Ago*. They give us a discrete, romantic awareness of the delicate flavors of experience, their mingling, their growth, and their reciprocal influences, that has colored even the autobiographical novel in recent decades.

And the autobiography as education, or the failure of education, has grown ever more noticeable in the same period. The form of autobiography required to present life as a long search for enlightenment is very different from the forms that display it as character study or tragedy or glorious and successful romance. The sometimes dazzling and sometimes clouded vistas presented by the growth of modern technology, the baffling complexities of industrial society, the dark abysms psychology leads us to peep into but does not plumb: the crowding knowledge and the crowding uncertainties from which only the cocksure are free, all these are mirrored in the autobiographical records. They are full of the doctrinal disputes and clash of struggle in our time.

The very uncertainties created by all this new knowledge and new ignorance leads to another quality in modern autobiography. The hard-and-fast lines between what is praiseworthy and what is contemptible having in part broken down, the meaningful and the mere flotsam of experience being so confused, dignity and propriety have undergone a weakening of force. Men are not ashamed of what would once have been humiliating, or they are ashamed of being ashamed and violently ride their shame down. In *The Americanization of Edward Bok* we are told with positive complacency of the ruthless campaign by which the author badgered an autograph out of the old, feeble, and mentally-failing Emerson. Emulating the confessional frankness of Rousseau, John Middleton Murry reveals painful hypocrisies and falsehoods of which he accuses himself in the past, and tries to analyze their significance in his character.

The chaos of values makes rudeness courageous, slander witty, gossip amusing, and a hundred other things permissible in print that would once have been consigned to the smoking room or the surreptitious whisper of the powder-closet. Gossip and scandal, even when they found their way into print, were sotto voce and excluded from serious autobiography. But often enough, in modern times, the confusion of judgments leaves a character uninjured by even the public blazoning of what would once have been disastrous. With contagious gaiety George Moore in his *Memoirs of*

My Dead Life, lets us overhear the frou-frou of ladies' petticoats in his rooms, and the malicious gossip of studio and green-room. Such gains are valuable in many ways even though they may sometimes enable venom to masquerade as frankness.

Not only in making allowable what would once have been scandalous does this weakening of old restraints and judgments work. It permits the inclusion of the trivial and the undignified. Autobiographers do not fear to show themselves even in absurd lights. They may serenely regard themselves as the norm and write with no consciousness of eccentricity. They may be careless of revealing themselves in undress, aware that unbending dignity is no longer expected even of those who have distinguished themselves in the world. And, partly, besides these, there is the feeling that perhaps the trivial might after all be the important, that no clue is too slight to be without some revelation, and that perhaps the mere uncharted and undirected flow of consciousness might in its ripples and sinuous cross-currents be the most deeply significant of all. Sustained by these not entirely ill-founded suspicions, the autobiographer has frequently given a free rein to whatever has ridden into his head. Norman Douglas, not so many years ago, dipped into a bowl containing old visiting cards, and told whatever the card that came to hand brought up in his mind.

The Phooka

In so tracing the developments through the opening years of the twentieth century it may well seem to the reader that I have been describing the present rather than the work of thirty or forty years ago. But indeed, save for certain journalistic vulgarizations, there are no outstanding characteristics of contemporary biography and autobiography that were not well-defined or brilliantly anticipated by our immediate predecessors. George Moore's *Confessions of a Young Man*, which was written as early as 1888, has an engaging emancipation from conventional reticences, and the flurry of lingerie we have noted, in a naughtiness perhaps more allusive than real. His *Memoirs of My Dead Life* plays gracefully with the same insinuations of daring. Indeed in all his confessional writings Moore leaves the reader wondering if he does not tell rather more kisses than were ever exchanged. But certainly, even if he would like us to see him as amatorily a descendant of Rochester and the Cavalier poets, Moore is concerned neither with making himself admirable in readers' eyes nor with cutting a pretentious figure. He often invites us to share his amusement at his own whims or absurdities or defeats (for they seldom leave him humiliated), and he is no more sparing of his friends and associates.

Nowhere is this freedom of rendering more delightful and amusing than in his *Hail and Farewell*, the three parts of which appeared between 1911 and 1914. They are perhaps more memoirs than anything else, for although there is much that is autobiographic in them, they are filled also with digressive musings on other parts of Moore's career, with caracolings upon any number of those hobby-horses Moore delights to mount and take for a swirling flight through the airy regions of cloud-cuckoo-land; and with irreverently funny episodes in which the solemn creators of Ireland's new poetry are subjected to Shandyan confusions and revealed in the tricksy light of Moore's imagination. For indeed, although he pretends that the whole comedy he has to tell is Nature's work, and his own task confined to 'taking down her many surprising inventions,' the ghost of Sterne was hovering near while Moore held the pen. His spirit and Moore's are distilled into a single rich and teasing influence over the whole.

But Moore sedately maintains the pose. 'Nature is a sly puss,' he tells us; 'she sets us working, but we know nothing of her designs; and for many years I believed myself to be the author of *Hail and Farewell*, whereas I was no more than the secretary, and though the reader may doubt me in the sentence I am now writing, he will believe that I am telling no more than the truth when the narrative leads him to Coole Park and he meets the hieratic Yeats and Lady Gregory out walking, seeking living speech from cottage to cottage, Yeats remaining seated under the stunted hawthorn . . . Lady Gregory braving the suffocating interior for the sacred cause of Idiom.' But although Nature provided the materials, through this air of innocence the reader sees, as he is no doubt intended to, Moore arranging the stage: 'the hieratic Yeats,' and 'the esurient Edward' Martyn, devouring huge lamb chops and stewed chickens and platefuls of curried eggs, while he suffers terrific qualms of conscience, and AE—what is the adjective that will represent him? —suddenly Moore swoops upon it in triumph—'the maieutic AE!'

Then add Plunkett and Gill, and who can fail to believe that, if not Nature, certainly Ireland, and assuredly not George Moore, is the author 'of this extraordinary work'?

Nevertheless his personality plays around it. There are hints of gracious ladies who have been complaisant, and an explanation of the family prejudice that prevents him from kissing Bridget, his cousin's mistress: 'it has always been the tradition' in his family not to yield 'to such indulgences as peasant mistresses' or hot punch. At a banquet we find him 'looking up and down the long tables' and musing that not one of the men present could 'inspire passion in a woman; no one even looked as if he would like to do such a thing.'

Constantly Moore returns to sport allusively with the delicious subject. There is the yawn of Gill, the Editor of the *Daily Express.* He yawns in the Abbey Theatre, he yawns in the middle of his own speeches; 'He has been seen yawning in chapel, and it is said that he yawns even in those intimate moments of existence when—but I will not labour the point; we can have no exact knowledge on this subject whether or no Gill yawns when he—we will dismiss all the stories that have been collected about these yawns as apocryphal, restricting our account to those yawns that happen—well, in our faces.' Or he recalls a cousin who had been painting in Paris and returned to London 'with a young Frenchwoman whom he called Louise.' When the hope was expressed that he 'had turned out something,' meaning painted a picture, 'the young man had answered, I don't know if I have turned out anything, but I have turned up a good deal.' This suggestive answer, Moore pretends, 'displeased me,' but he does not fail to tell of it.

Or else Moore discusses the unsatisfactoriness of his friend Edward Martyn as a boon companion. Edward 'is not very surefooted on new ground,' and his soul demands church services, abstention from meat on Fridays, and the suppression of remarks about Moore's 'feelings towards the ladies we meet in the railway-trains and hotels when we go abroad.' The ideal boon companion would have none of these tiresome traits, he would 'know instinctively that Manet is all vase, and that Mr——'s portraits are all washtub,' and he might be apt to 'mutter that there was too much rectory lawn in Tennyson.' Moore evolves a theory that a poet who overdresses will also overdecorate his verse, and begins to test it by remembering Verlaine, Hugo, Banville—'But let us be content with the theory, and refrain from collecting facts to support it, for in doing so we shall come upon exceptions, and these will have to be explained away.'

The central elements of his pattern, however, are those dwellers in the Celtic twilight who drew him briefly into the movement of the Irish Renaissance. First of them is Yeats, that strange mixture of philosophical acuteness and symbolic mysticism. Moore tells how at Tillyra an old gentleman complained at the table that he had been unable to rest all night, 'dreaming of Neptune and surging waves.' 'Last night, said Yeats, looking up gloomily from his breakfast, I felt a great deal of aridness in my nature, and need of moisture, and was making most tremendous invocations with water, and am not surprised that they should have affected the adjoining room.'

But when Moore first met him at the Cheshire Cheese in London, they fell to dispute on Blake, and Moore 'rushed at him with all my feathers erect.' Yeats parried the blow with such ease and skill that Moore was taken aback. 'A dialectician, I muttered, of the very first rank'; we are forced to chuckle at the evaluation. But Yeats finally let him off without being worsted, 'perhaps because he did not care to humiliate me, or it may have been that he wearied of talking about a literature to one who was imperfectly acquainted with it, or'—Moore concludes these Proustian alternatives with a perky recovery of assurance—'it may have been that I made a better show in argument than I thought for.'

Presently, in Ireland, he and Yeats are deep in a plan for collaborating on a play from Irish folklore, *Diarmuid and Grania.* Their first difficulties are about the style; they must avoid, Yeats insists, 'words that recall any particular epoch,' as honor and ideal do the Middle Ages, or glory the victories of Lord Kitchener, or soldier a professional in a scarlet uniform. Moore gloomily suggested that Yeats 'begin by writing a dictionary of all the words that may not be used, and all the ideas that may not be introduced.' Next they were discussing the theory of play construction, and Yeats was irritating Moore by nonsensical generalizations that 'the first act of every good play is horizontal, the second perpendicular.'

'And the third, I suppose,' Moore interjects sarcastically, 'circular?'

But, 'Quite so,' Yeats replies unperturbed. And with gestures he explains how the first act extends from right to left (while Moore wonders whether it would not be better from left to right), and winds up eloquently showing how the third act 'could be made even more circular than the first and second were horizontal and perpendicular.'

The style, however, was still giving trouble. Moore impatiently declared that he would rather write the play in French than write within all the limitations of vocabulary imposed, and, at loggerheads, they went to bed. He was wakened by a loud knocking. Yeats had thought over his suggestion, and had decided it was good. Moore would write the play in French, Lady Gregory would translate it into English, Taidgh O'Donoghue would translate the English into Irish, Lady Gregory would then do the Irish back into English, and Yeats would 'put style upon' the final product. It was a satisfaction, Moore replied bitterly, 'to hear that you can stand my English style at four removes.' By the time morning came, however, it began to appeal to Moore's sense of humor that his play should 'be translated three times back and forwards before a last and immortal relish was to be poured upon it,' and presently he was sitting in a Paris hotel, imagining Grania couched on a bearskin in a cavern, and saying 'J'ai entendu un bruit. Quelqu'un passe dans la nuit des rochers. Diarmuid!'

Such Maeterlinckian antics as these by no means exhaust the humors of the book. A company of strolling actors was suggested as a means of inducing the people to learn Irish, but the Gaelic League was afraid the priests would be against the idea, and refused to back it. For ladies to travel about acting the feminine rôles would be opposed on grounds of faith and morals: 'So the Irish language is going to be sacrificed,' Moore fumed, 'for the sake of a little female virtue.' It was scandalous, when 'girls are seducing young men . . . and old men, too, for the matter of that, all over the world, and every hour of the night and day.'

Raging over this obstacle to Irish culture, Moore went to AE full of a revolutionary discovery: that literature and dogma were incompatible. 'He seemed to think that everybody knew that this was so; and is there anything more discouraging than to find one's daring definitions accepted as commonplace truths?' Moore comforted himself by reflecting that a Catholic would have to put up more of a defense than AE. So to a Catholic he would go, and reduce him to defeat; unless, indeed, his opponent replied 'that it was no part of the business of Catholicism to consider whether dogma tended to encourage or repress literary activities. To this defence, the true one, I should have no answer.'

So he went from one to another, making himself a good deal of a nuisance to everyone, and a bright disturbing influence in that movement which was producing *Deirdre*, and *Cathleen ni Houlihan*, *The Playboy of the Western World*, and *Riders to the Sea*. He was, indeed, as AE said of him in a symbolic little apologue, a 'Phooka.' What is the Phooka? He is a strange and iridescent being of fable, a Bird of Fire swooping out of legend into the Irish Renaissance. It was this magical and perilous being, AE said, 'who appeared some years ago, and the young people crowded about him and he smelted them in the fires of fierce heresies, and petrified them with tales of frigid immoralities, and anybody who wilted from the heat the Phooka flung from him, and anybody who was petrified, he broke in twain and flung aside,' and at last the Phooka disappeared.

Hail and Farewell is the Phooka's playful melting down of the Irish Renaissance to the stature of a bright dream-farce. Its unmalign laughter leaves no figure in its pages unteased, no character, not the Phooka's own, without its touch of the absurd. Moore's light sanity is destructive, but it is an acid-silvery washing away of inflated dignities, not the wrath of a destroying angel. And in the place of heavy memorial images he gives us glancing and flashing water-colors of living beings. If they are sometimes a bit ridiculous —well, human beings often are. Neither a scornful iconoclast nor a mean libeler, Moore brings grace and charm to the freedoms he so carelessly assumes. For vividness, facetious wit, and ease *Hail and Farewell* ranks high among the pleasantest of memoirs.

Pilgrim of Sensibility

No one would ever mistake Henry James for a Phooka. The quiet, heavily built figure clad in the most conventional of clothes, the round bullet-head emphasizing by a slight baldness the domed brow, the solid hawk-nose contradicted by eyes questing and yet a little diffident and by the reticent and sensitive droop of the mouth —all proclaim the inner world to which he gives allegiance, and deny that he could ever burn with the Phooka's mischievous flame. None of Moore's playful and rash assertiveness was possible in his conscientiously qualified and spun-out sentences, and none of those irreverent intrusions into other people's holies of holies, for he was far too fascinated by how people felt to desire disputation. He wanted to *realize* experience, and this need was far too serious for him to be flippant or jesting, although he was not without a sense of humor growing out of a full rich inner savoring. But beyond all, as the curiosity in his gaze and the down-drooping upper lip both hint, his spirit seeks complete fusion with all that it knows: the world must be taken into himself and possessed entirely, and he must reach exploring tendrils into every cranny of that world, drinking in the concentrated essence of its flavor.

James's novels have often been treated as works of cerebral analysis rather than of sensibility; and, of course, they employ analysis 'for all,' as James himself might say, diffidently scooping a popular form of diction into inverted commas, 'that it is worth.' But for James, analysis can only be an instrument in the service of emotional realization. And if many readers notice only the ingenuity, failing to capture the emotion, James is quietly certain that they can only have been careless or inattentive, for the emotion is there, subtle and refined, but of an intensity! And when he turns himself back, in *A Small Boy and Others*, upon the remembrance of his own past, these qualities of the novels prove for him a veritable divining rod for unburying once more the riches of personal experience. 'To recover anything like the full treasure of scattered, wasted circumstance was at the same time to live over spent experience itself, so deep and rich and rare,' and 'to find discrimination' well nigh impossible, 'so inseparably and beautifully they seemed to hang together.'

And so 'aspects began to multiply and images to swarm,' the world of the past began to compose itself 'out of a thin golden haze,' and we are soon sharing the life of a small boy in Albany of the 1840's on long summer afternoons, 'tasting of accessible garden peaches' and 'of strange legendary domestics, inveterately but archaically Irish.' There is also the memory of the Astor House, 'a great square block of granite with vast dark warm interiors, and a place called the Pavilion, at New Brighton, which to childish eyes was 'a great Greek temple shining over blue waters in the splendour of a white colonnade and a great yellow pediment.' A little later there was the brownstone of their house on Fourteenth Street, and the red brick of his grandfather's house on Washington Square, then still called the Parade-ground and fenced with 'ancient wooden palings,' whereas Union Square, 'at the top of the Avenue,' was more smart with iron rails and a fountain.

Before this, though, there is a vague memory of governesses. 'A bevy of these educative ladies passes before me'—among them Miss Rogers, 'who handled us literally with gloves,' for he can still see 'the elegant objects as Miss Rogers beat time with a long black ferule to some species of droning chant,' and 'a stout red-faced lady with grey hair and a large apron' suggesting 'that she viewed her little pupils as so many small slices cut from the loaf of life and on which she was to dab the butter of arithmetic and spelling.' And there is a glimmering image of his brother William, 'already seated at his task,' 'in the most exemplary manner,' 'when the attempt to drag me crying and kicking to the first hour of my education failed.'

Soon, however, school in New York was an established part of life, and the boys came home from East Twenty-Third Street past the Hudson River Railroad in course of construction to 'a riot of explosion and a great shouting and waving of red flags when the gunpowder introduced into the rocky soil was about to take effect. It was our theory that our passage . . . was beset with danger, and our impression that we saw fragments of rock hurtle through the air and smite to the earth another and yet another of the persons engaged or exposed.' But on other occasions he sees himself smelling 'the cold dusty paint and iron as the rails of the Eighteenth Street corner rub his contemplative nose'; and he makes us realize that that little figure is the forecast of all his life, demanding only that he 'somehow receive an impression or an accession, feel a relation or a vibration.'

And indeed the boy was to have none of the usual American demands made upon him. Although money-earning work was so praised and idleness so frowned upon that to the small boy the entire field of adult activity was covered 'by three classes, the busy, the tipsy, and Daniel Webster,' it was early understood that the James children had no such obligation, they needn't understand 'questions of arithmetic and of fond calculation, questions of the counting-house and the market.' They were brought up as gentlemen, although their father was careful to see that they 'were bred in horror of *conscious* propriety, of what my father was fond of calling "flagrant" morality.'

Meanwhile there were the sensations still piling up, richly to be enjoyed. There were visits to the family dentist, 'so old and so empurpled and so polite, in his stock and dress-coat and dark and glossy wig,' and poring over the pages of Godey's *Lady's Book* 'to the music of my brother's groans.' There was 'the sticky sweetness' of Isabella grapes and Seckel pears, and yellow peaches eaten with cream or 'brandied.' There were school and the dancing academy, bristling 'with Van Burens, Van Winkles, De Peysters.' There were visits with his father to *The New York Tribune*, and 'the strange steepnesses and machineries and noises and hurrying bare-armed, bright-eyed men.' There was the southern family of Norcoms who came to live next door, and who on a 'glazed southern gallery' known as 'the "poo'ch"' dispensed a profuse hospitality of hot cakes and molasses and sausages from a home-worked sausage-mill.

And, more and more, there were enticements all emanating from a source of which the young Henry was early aware. Burying his nose in books from abroad he deliciously breathed in 'the strong smell of paper and printer's ink, known to us as the English smell.' Everything conspired to give him a 'sense of Europe' that drew him on. With a 'sacred thrill' he watched the green curtain rise on *The Comedy of Errors*, his first play, and saw Mr Burton as one of the Dromios, 'his vast slightly pendulous cheek surmounted by a sort of elephantine wink, to which I attributed a remarkable baseness.' The boy's mind was soon busy imagining the glories of Madame Judith who was believed to be a possible rival to Rachel. He saw Edwin Booth, and Laura Keene, whose 'English' sweetness of speech was ravishing, and Mrs Wallack as Lady Gay Spanker in *London Assurance*.

At home, under the shade of a drooping tablecloth, he heard *David Copperfield* read aloud, undiscovered until 'the strain of the Murdstones' snapped the cord and he 'broke into sobs of sympathy,' and was dragged forth. Thackeray lectured in America on 'The English Humorists,' and calling at their house, he spied the youngster hovering on the staircase, and bent the spectacles of wonder on the brass-buttoned jacket, calling out, 'Come here, little boy, and show me your extraordinary jacket!' And then there was Thorwaldsen's enormous *Christ and the Disciples*, a confectionary sweetness of white images ranged in a semicircle of dark maroon walls. 'If this was Europe then Europe was beautiful indeed; and we rose to it on wings of wonder.' And the Düsseldorf collection in Broadway, with its huge canvas of *The Martyrdom of John Huss* almost challenged the shining newness 'of that wonderful painter B. R. Haydon,' whose *Banishment of Aristides* they were soon to see and admire in the Pantheon of Oxford Street, with all its grandiose detail down to 'the foreshortened boy picking up stones to shy at the all-too-just.'

For at last the wonderful voyage of discovery was made, in the summer of 1855, and 'the thick and heavy suggestions' of his London room were followed by 'the fond apprehension of Paris . . . from the balcony of an hotel that hung, through the soft summer night, over the Rue de la Paix.' He was just turned twelve, but every lighted window was as it were 'a word in some immortal quotation, the very breath of civilized lips,' and all the young traveler could say to himself was, 'I told you so, I told you so!' The London postmen in their red military frock-coats and black beaver hats, milk-women with short full skirts and enormous boots, footmen hooked behind coaches, and all the horrors of Cruikshank's illustrations realized in the vivid picture 'of a woman reeling backward as a man felled her to the ground with a blow in the face,' the 'queer old obsequiosities and appeals, whinings and sidlings and hand-rubbings and curtsey-droppings': they were like coming home!

And Paris was even more deeply satisfying, in the 'so-called pavilion' they lived in, with its 'diffused glassy polish of floor and perilous staircase,' its 'redundancy of mirror and clock and ormolu vase,' its white and gold panels and red damask and gilt-framed sofas and chairs. The youthful but already receptive sensibility fastened immediately on the things from which it could draw nourishment: the sense of the past, the sense of being steeped in a plenitude of association, colored with all the many-hued dyes of tradition and historical emotion. Henry James had at last seen the world with which all his young imagination had been burning.

So we reach the end of *A Small Boy and Others*. There are two things especially remarkable in these memories of his: the scenes that emerge one following another in the pages, and the exploratory deepening grasp of emotional nuance. The scenes compose themselves with a magical touch, with a translucent vividness that drenches them in appropriate tones. Whether in those hazy Albany summer afternoons or in those characteristically childish hallucinations of rocks hurtling through the danger-fraught air of Twenty-

Third Street, with something of adult amusement, James also recaptures the flavor of the childish experience; and the rendering gains in perspective by the way in which we thus dwell simultaneously in the two worlds, of luminous childish haze and sensations bright though hardly analyzed, and of later contemplative understanding. We are given at the same time the child's partly distorted vision in clear hues and, ever so tactfully, the mature corrective.

But not only this. Each scene is indeed the evocation of an experience, 'an impression or an accession,' 'a relation or a vibration,' and the feeling is perhaps more intensely realized even than the image with which it is associated. It is truly 'the very pattern and measure of all he was to demand,' feeling, as he was to do, 'that no education avails for the intelligence that doesn't stir in it some subjective passion.' James not merely paints those subjective passions for us with a rich and flowing brush, but more than that, and more revealingly than most of the subjective impressionists, he traces the developing significance of these multiplying awarenesses. Sensation grows no less dazzling but more and more clearly defined, more various, more discriminated, fuller and deeper in nuance. And all the emotional nuances interpenetrate and unify until we see even the life of the boy as no mere many-sensationed flux, but a homogeneous growth.

The grasp of awareness, as I have said, is exploratory and deepening; it constantly gives us more, and assumes direction and strength. Very delicate are the means by which this feat is accomplished, for James is too much the artist to accomplish his task by mere statement; everything must be concretized, dramatized, conveyed, and indeed he refrains altogether from pointing out expositorily the steps his demonstration has made. But by the time he leaves himself in his thirteenth year, the reader has already seen unmistakably the development of an unusual receptivity, and seen unmistakably the relationship between it and the author who across the gulf of so many years has recreated a childhood.

Twilight of an Education

There is nothing like James's rendering of atmosphere in even the childhood pages of *The Education of Henry Adams.* James deals, to be sure, only with a few years of his life in comparison with the sixty-nine covered by Adams, and in two more volumes, *Notes of a Son and Brother* and *The Middle Years,* he traces the outlines of his later life. But the comparative aridness in Henry Adams is a dryness of the soul, not an effect of concentration. Absorbing as his book is, the education or the failure of education it outlines has the desert quality of the world as Adams found it, with hardly ever an oasis of waving palms and sparkling water such as James would have come upon in even the rockiest and sandiest of landscapes. To be sure, Adams might have claimed that James's green foliage was all mirage, but it tells something of the two that one should be surrounded by life where the other finds nothing but desiccation.

From almost the earliest pages of *The Education* we feel an air of weary futility pervading the book. Possibly it reflects Adams's feeling that alone among his distinguished family he had been a failure, a feeling that may color the not unrelated feeling that modern civilization is a failure. By any ordinary standard, certainly, his career as a writer, as a teacher, and as a historian, was not a failure but a brilliant success. But in comparison with the concrete power his grandfather and great-grandfather had wielded, which even his father had handled, and which alone Adams wanted, it was nothing. And so the two parallel feelings of the failure of Henry Adams and the failure of modern society mingle in a book that is, for all its intellectual interest, a long Odyssey of futility. Like John Stuart Mill's, it is an autobiography of a life-long education; but, embittered by personal frustration, unsustained by any mood of historical faith, baffled by the chaotic multiplicity of the universe, unlike that of Mill, it runs off into lost streams, broken threads, blind alleys, and cosmic despair.

The 'ten pounds of unconscious babyhood' that was born under the shadow of Boston State House in 1838 had what seemed tremendous advantages. A family so high in the nation's councils and history, a prestige as it were ready-made, every help which education and tradition could confer, powerful intimates and associates: had the child known and understood he would probably 'have been astounded by his own luck.' But as it was to turn out, Adams assures us, this 'child of the eighteenth century' could 'scarcely have been more distinctly branded' or more 'heavily handicapped in the races of the coming century' than he was by his very advantages. But he knew nothing of this; his first conscious memory was of a yellow kitchen floor on which he sat aged three. Then came summer and winter in his grandfather's house at Quincy and his own home on Mount Vernon Street: wading in the brook or chasing muskrats or gathering nuts on the hills, and confinement, school, discipline, snows and frosts in town. They fell into duality: country and town, summer and winter, liberty and restraint. They were only the first of the dualities that were to baffle his life.

New England society, in which he breathed and felt at home, was dominated by the professions. It was an 'upper-class *bourgeoisie*' in spirit identical with the Paris 'of Louis Philippe, Guizot, and de Tocqueville, as well as the London of Robert Peel, Macaulay, and John Stuart Mill,' with which it felt 'instinctive cousinship.' It had lost the religious instinct in a mild Unitarianism, but nobody thought anything of that, nobody regarded it as a portent, 'No one, except Karl Marx, foresaw radical change.' Thus early in his story we find Adams emphasizing the limitations of class and attitude to which he was being molded. It was the straitjacket that was not only to explain and excuse why he himself was never to play a dominating rôle in the world to which he was growing up, but to explain why control was slipping from the hands of the Everetts, the Channings, the Sumners, and the Adamses, and taking strange uncouth forms. Unless they could transform themselves and cease to be Brahmins they had no part in the future.

In the spring of 1850 the boy was taken to Washington, a village with an earth-road meandering from the colonnade of the Treasury to the white marble front of the Post Office, and a 'thick odor of the catalpa trees' filling the air. A few years later he was at Harvard, which gave him little. Its only positive virtue was that it produced no intellectual distortions, because it left the intellect completely untouched. 'It taught little, and that little ill, but it left the mind open, free from bias, ignorant of facts, but docile.'

He did imbibe its enthusiasm for German philosophy and scholarship, a worship which resulted from the fact that Germany was 'a hundred years behind western Europe.' For the literary world, dimly sensing the future and therefore turning back to the past, was in revolt 'against the yoke of the coming capitalism—its money-lenders, its bank-directors, and its railway magnates.' 'The middle class had the power, and held its coal and iron well in hand, but the satirists and idealists seized the press' and followed the novelists 'in scratching and biting the unfortunate middle class with savage ill-temper.' Those who were being thrust from dominance were fighting a losing battle with words. And once again Adams gives us a significant reminder that, however little food for the mind he received, he was being molded to the pattern of a group that still had prestige, but that must be reborn if it were still to hold the substance of power: 'Four years of Harvard College, if successful, resulted in an autobiographical blank, a mind on which only a water-mark had been stamped.'

After Harvard, he went abroad to study the Civil Law. London had a certain style dignifying its grime; it was still eighteenth century. 'History muttered down Fleet Street, like Dr Johnson, in Adams's ear; Vanity Fair was alive on Piccadilly in yellow chariots . . .; half the great houses, black with London smoke, bore funereal hatchments . . .' The youth could not guess, Adams remarks bleakly, how the great city was to grow smaller as it doubled in size; 'cheaper as it quadrupled in wealth; less imperial as its empire widened.' Berlin was worse, 'German student life was on the whole the thinnest of beer.'

And increasingly we hear the note of flatness and unprofitableness, even in minor details: 'So he took a room in the household of the usual small government clerk with the usual plain daughters . . .' Would life not even vouchsafe a pretty girl, and was that what was to be expected, 'the usual'? 'Possibly one might learn something more by accident . . .' Civilization began to seem incomprehensible and pointless. 'Rome was a bewildering complex of ideas, experiments, ambitions, energies' in which 'Gibbon might have gone on for the whole century, sitting among the ruins of the Capitol' without finding anyone 'capable of telling him what it meant. Perhaps it meant nothing.' The discouraging search for a philosophy of history already makes its appearance.

Suddenly the Civil War was upon them, and Adams accompanied his father Charles Francis Adams as secretary when he was appointed Minister to England. They believed themselves going to a friendly Government, 'true to the anti-slavery principles which had been their steadiest profession.' Their ideas 'were the reverse of truth.' England's great cotton trade made the manufacturers sympathetic to the South; no one doubted that the Confederacy would win, and 'nearly all were glad of it.' Here was spread out an object lesson in economic determinism for the young student of public affairs, if only he were not too confused by a multiplicity of interests to profit by it.

Minister Adams found himself in a labyrinth of chicanery, disingenuousness, hostility, and downright falsehood, and a new stage of his son's education began. What, really, was Lord John Russell's attitude? What construction was to be placed upon Gladstone's ambiguous behavior? And how were they to thwart the undoubted hostility of Lord Palmerston? But even here education trickled off into uncertainty. For it transpired years later that Palmerston had moderated, not opposed, that Russell's assumed sympathy was dubious, and that Gladstone—but who could tell *what* Gladstone might have meant? Were these diplomats honest or dishonest? Were they Machiavellian or blunderers? All their behavior had the appearance and result of concerted intention, and yet the evidence proved that the Adamses had certainly misunderstood the turn of events. If he could not know the truth about these men whom he had watched and analyzed almost daily, with such full sources of information, how was it possible to know the meaning of any event? The puzzle was a miniature statement of the problem that balked Adams again and again. How was it possible to find the necessary sequences in history and know what they meant?

But whether Minister Adams understood what was truly going on behind the curtains or no, he knew how to deal with affairs. From a nullity he gradually made himself into a power, pushing the Government steadily into weaker positions, until in spite of the London nightmare of Abraham Lincoln as a demon served by another demon named Seward, he had stripped from Russell every rag of defense, and ended with the famous sentence: 'It would be superfluous in me to point out to your lordship that this is war!' 'After a long and desperate struggle, the American Minister had trumped their best card, and won the game.'

The end of the Civil War left Adams without a profession. 'For the law, diplomacy had unfitted him; for diplomacy he already knew too much.' He had sampled English dilettantism, and run through the study of half a dozen subjects, but there were for him fatal objections to them all. He was interested by now in history, but he would not fall into the sink of antiquarianism and a philosophy of history seemed unattainable. The attempt to find one brought him up against science, whose achievements he had to take on faith. Even when taken, however, all they seemed to mean was flux and change. Lyell's Glacial Theory introduced into geology agents quite as catastrophic as those they superseded. Evolution had far too many hiatuses and classifications in which there was an obstinate failure to evolve. What, then, became of uniformity and natural selection? He felt that he 'could prove only Evolution that did not evolve; Uniformity that was not uniform; and Selection that did not select.' If he could not be certain that he saw any authoritative and explanatory pattern in the natural sciences, how could he attain one in history, where the evidence is so much more confused, unascertainable, unverifiable? 'By rights, he should have been a Marxist, but some narrow trait of the New England nature seemed to blight socialism, and he tried in vain to make himself a convert.'

With these few words, in a book that elaborates a thousand others exhaustively, he dismisses the subject. And yet it would have been indeed illuminating to a reader to know the argument that must have taken place during those sessions when he 'tried in vain,' and to share the exploration, the scrutiny, the analysis, the efforts to persuade himself, the reasons for rejection. But no—merely 'he tried in vain.'

Socialism demanded a break with too much that had struck its roots into his nature, it demanded affiliations with which he felt no instinctive sympathy, it went counter to all the liberal tradition and background. It called for a self-surrender and dedication that this scion of individualism could not feel himself capable of. He would have liked to benefit society, to play some useful and important rôle—the desire was in his blood—but not at the cost of too great a yielding of self, and very definitely with the glory of achievement rather than devotion to the task in his mind. Individualism and skepticism—the last fruits of the liberal tradition—stood in the way, dividing him against himself in an unconquerable duality, answering a blank to every attainable pursuit of value. He had exhausted the temptations offered by politics, law, diplomacy, art, and history; and, jaundiced, he stared about and wondered what to do.

Even if politics could now have satisfied him, it was doubtful if he could have maintained a foothold among the venalities of post-Civil-War politics. The patrician group from whom the Republic had chosen its first senators and consuls had been swept along in a current directed by the claims of business privilege. His brother Charles Francis saw the handwriting, and deliberately allied himself with the new owners of the world by plunging into the intricacies of railroad finance. Henry Adams was too ambiguously the product of all his heritage to make such a choice; he could neither renounce nor affirm.

'The world, after 1865, became a bankers' world, and no banker would ever trust one' who, like himself, tempered his serfdom with mockery. Grant's administration was a scandal of corruption and incompetence, and it was clear that the political machinery of 1789 had broken down. 'Nine-tenths of men's political energies must henceforth be wasted on expedients to piece out—to patch, or, in vulgar language, to tinker—the political machine as often as it broke down.'

But Adams felt neither ability nor impulsion in himself to strive for a new system, nor faith in any principle upon which it might be built. He could only stand by, noting and analyzing the symptoms of disease.

In the academic life to which, for want of a possible alternative, he retreated, things were if possible worse. 'Several score of the best-educated, most agreeable, and personally the most sociable people in America united in Cambridge to make a social desert that would have starved a polar bear.' Adams knew 'both Congressmen and professors, and he preferred Congressmen.' But he energetically carried on his duties at Harvard, acquiring the knowledge of the Middle Ages he had lacked when he began teaching mediæval history, and watching the swarming factories of industrialism and the inevitable tread of capitalist imperialism. 'The climax of empire could be seen approaching, year after year, as though Sulla were a President or McKinley a Consul.'

And he tried constantly to find a formula which would give intelligibility to history, which would correlate 'the political and social and scientific values of the twelfth and twentieth centuries' 'in some relation of movement that could be expressed in mathematics.' Fellow-historians, less rigorous in plotting their impasse than he, or more intent on escaping the evidences of confusion, immersed themselves in the murky waters of factualization. 'All his associates in history condemned such an attempt as futile and almost immoral,' but he persisted. All he could observe, to be sure, was multiplicity, and 'History had no use for multiplicity; it needed unity.'

The pattern he at last worked out for himself, a pattern of circular futility, is the most significant thing of all, even more significant than the completeness with which, a sensitive recording instrument for all the contradictions of his position, he worked himself to stalemate. How to symbolize the movement from the twelfth century to the present? The Virgin might be used as the symbol of the power the twelfth century recognized. 'She was goddess because of her force . . .; she was reproduction—the greatest and most mysterious of all energies; all she needed was to be fecund.'

For the twentieth century, 'Among the thousand symbols of ultimate energy, the dynamo was not so human as some, but it was the most expressive.' From the Virgin, then, to the Dynamo! Everywhere in modern life he ran across complexity and multiplicity, even contradiction. Perhaps in the end 'the scientific synthesis commonly called Unity' might turn out to be the same thing as 'the scientific analysis commonly called Multiplicity.' A long slow start, and then a speeding around curves, ending in a whizz—with the only description an unthinkable fusion of contradictions. That was the tendency of history.

With this idea, he began to run his conception to earth. It took form as two contrasting studies. One was of the twelfth century, 'the point in history when man held the highest idea of himself as a unit in a unified universe.' It became his *Mont-Saint-Michel and Chartres: a Study of Thirteenth Century Unity*. The movement of the world in the intervening centuries could be measured by the other, which was entitled *The Education of Henry Adams: a Study of Twentieth Century Multiplicity*. They plotted a curve of constantly accelerating movement, of diversity and complexity that seemed very like chaos. But perhaps the new American would learn 'to think in contradictions' and 'the new universe would know no law that could not be proved by its anti-law.'

As for society, heaven knew where it was going. An elderly student pursuing the belated fragments of his education might well give it up, since he had never learned anything until it was too late for him to make anything of it but the realization that the new world would probably forever elude his comprehension. His curve of progress whizzed at infinite speed as it came down the bend of the centuries, and exploded into bewildering contradictions. Either this was the lesson of history or he had failed to learn the lesson.

What it seemed to mean was that either the history of the historian was a failure or else the history of the race he had philosophized over. But possibly beyond remoter horizons than his—Adams's humanitarian liberalism made a last gasp of hope—the values of education could be fixed or renewed. Perhaps, say, in 1938, his centenary, he might be allowed to return for a holiday; 'and perhaps then, for the first time since man began his education among the carnivores,' he 'would find a world that sensitive and timid natures could regard without a shudder.'

'Perhaps in 1938'—with these words sounding their profoundly ironic implications in the world of today *The Education of Henry Adams* closes. The author has described himself as a representative of an 'upper-class *bourgeoisie*,' and the more that classification is pondered over, and the more it is compared with his entire development, the more appropriate it seems. Henry Adams represented the upper middle classes in America, as Macaulay and Gladstone did in England. His family had long rendered distinguished services in the public business of the nation. There was no circle of associations, of endeavor, or of attainment that was barred to him. The entire culture of modern upper-class Europe and America lay open to him, and not only open but the way to its enjoyment smoothed for his feet. And his own mind was vigorous, keen, sinewy, assimilating its experience with ease, analyzing it with penetration and originality, judging independently. Adams is thus the very flower of his class and culture; to adapt a phrase Professor Irwin Edman applied to *The Last Puritan*, he is not chronologically but dialectically the last representative of the upper middle class. He is completely and perfectly its product, all its fruits ripening in him and falling at last into sterility.

For to this favored and one of the most gifted of its scions, modern culture seemed to have come to a dead end, all it had to offer tasted of ashes, and the modern world appeared a meaningless disintegration. The ideals and principles generated by upper-middle-class liberalism expanded to their full logical development, and turned into opposing dualisms checking each other: duty and freedom, individualism and conformity, dominance and humanitarianism. In a world where they could no longer be exercised in separate compartments, without clashing, and in a mind where the self-consciousness engendered of individualism forbade ignoring their conflict, they reduced their victim to impotence and confusion. It would therefore seem that the tradition he inherited had reached the end of its possibilities. It is an almost startling confirmation of the pattern that the only philosophy this child of contradiction could evolve was a philosophy of contradiction. Liberalism, if Adams were a significant figure, was moribund; only by some fresh affirmation, outside its decaying cycle, could a living scheme of values be achieved.

Still further significant for us to note is that mood of tired emptiness, the vanitas vanitatum that runs through the book. In Henry Adams the emotions generated by the industrial revolution have run through a great circle. The boundless a priori optimism of the romantic era was tempered to a tentative empiricism by the great Victorians, but sustained by an inner drive of energy and of confidence in the powers of mind to solve the problems it uncovered. The enthusiasm of Shelley and his compeers gave way to the searchings of Mill and Darwin.

But by the end of the century bourgeois culture at its most intellectually conscious and in one of its most typical as well as gifted products could see itself only as a failure and evolve a weltanschauung only of disintegration. Certainly the failure may have been in Adams, and it was tempting for him to blame his heredity and the society of which he was a part. But the identification that he himself made between the two is fundamentally just. Adams is a symbolic man; his life recapitulates the life and the end of an era, a class, a culture, and a philosophy. *The Education of Henry Adams* is the swansong of political democracy and bourgeois liberalism.

Henry Adams is thus a key personality to understanding the present. He took for signs of world-frustration the decay of his class, but that he did so suggests that the dominant orientation of nineteenth century Europe had reached the end of its fruitfulness. The modern dwellers in the waste land, the 'lost generation,' who ask themselves agonizingly if Europe was a success, lose themselves in a tissue of self-spun hesitations, and cling to an irresolute and dubious affirmation of a set of values fading away before their eyes, are his spiritual heirs. In them we see revealed the mood if not the intelligence of Adams's despair.

Generous souls have escaped that despair only by throwing out new roots in what the upper-middle-class liberalism of Adams would have regarded as no more than subjects for humanitarian benevolence. By a full spiral they have returned to Shelley's mood of affirmation, of courage, and of hope. 'Some narrow trait of the New England nature,' Adams thought, 'seemed to blight' his capacity for any such affirmation. It was not a narrowness restricted to the New England nature, it was a narrowness upper-class Boston shared with its cousins in Paris, London, everywhere. Thoughtful men transcend it today by breaking through the bonds of restricted loyalties and established molds.

TURN OF THE CENTURY

XV

TURN OF THE CENTURY

BIOGRAPHY

The Varied Stream

THE biographer was not slower than the autobiographer to dye his fabric in the colors of the age. The freedom of Moore, the delicate receptivity of James, the struggling with social change that troubled Adams: all are paralleled by the modern biographer. He too dramatizes the presentation of kinds of character and conflict not always emphasized before. He too brings the illumination or confusion of modern knowledge to the handling of biographical problems new and old. He too shows no hesitation in using whatever morsels come to his attention, sometimes in love of the tidbit for its own sake, sometimes for the colorful lighting of his portrait. And he now brings to his task instruments from other crafts—psychiatric analysis, historical criticism, a technique sharpened by the methods of fiction.

New perspectives on character such as have made most of us amateur psychoanalysts have led to forms of biography representing above all the tones and clashes of temperament. Sometimes a whole life is thereby re-viewed from the angle of such a salient quality or conflict. So Newton Arvin's *Hawthorne* attempts to reveal Hawthorne in terms of his essential *loneliness* and its hidden causes. Sometimes the biography has been sharply concentrated on certain years or crucial episodes in a life, as in Strachey's *Elizabeth and Essex.* Sometimes it has been focused not on a single character but on a relationship, the slow abrasion of one by another, or the clash of antagonism, which is the theme of Gosse's *Father and Son.* All these aims have required new limitations in range, have led to new principles in the selection and building together of materials.

The biographical problems thus stated have often been similar to the problems created in the plots of fiction. It is not strange therefore to find the biographer learning from the novelist not merely in structure, preparation, symmetry, and scale, but in the minor devices of narrative as well. More often than not he dispenses with genealogical introductions, avoids set and formal descriptions either of character or appearance. Instead he tries to make the narrative episodes *create* the impression of character he wishes to convey, and he adroitly embeds details of physiognomy or mannerism in the course of narration until the reader begins to see and hear the characters in action. If authenticated conversation is available, he stages it dramatically (and sometimes not too conscientiously even adds to or invents it). There is hardly a device of the modern novel that has not, both legitimately and illegitimately, been pressed into the service of biography.

The growth of an unconventional frankness has been marked in modern biography; in recent years it has sometimes exploited subjects with no other aim than such display. There is no question of honesty involved. Contemporary biographers who specialize in sneering or denigration are clearly as dishonest as those who conceal blameworthy truths. But biographical freedom (although, as I have shown, it has not been so rare in the past as we have sometimes assumed) has on the whole been a valuable aid not only to truth but to vividness and depth in characterization. It has enabled even the no more than average-good biography to have light and shade by adding resources its writer might not otherwise have dared to use.

Just as the autobiographer has tried more and more to understand himself in relation to the problems of his times, the biographer has tried increasingly to see more than the mere shape and outward adventures of his subject. A man's meaning, his value, his rôle in society: the degree to which the major forces of his age are embodied in the man, the degree to which he gives significance and direction to them: these problems have persistently brought the biographer close to the social historian. His endeavor to find the philosophical relation between the individual life and the spirit of the age—and, perhaps, too, the steady professionalization of biography—has led to a constant increase in historical subjects, which offer greater freedom and more enticing personalities than any present can ever provide in large numbers. Biographers have come to range over all times and lands from the Mexico of Cortez to the Haiti of King Henry Christophe.

Now this tendency had no parallel in the nineteenth century. There were great monuments of scholarly erudition, such as Spedding's *Life of Bacon*, Masson's *Life and Times of John Milton*, Aitken's *Richard Steele*, and Sichel's *Bolingbroke;* but these authors devoted all their powers to a single personality or age, and their work was almost isolated from the main stream of biography. A few, like Scott, who produced lives of Dryden and Swift, and Morley, with his eighteenth century studies of Voltaire, Rousseau, and the Encyclopaedists, explored larger domains. Even they, however, felt most at home in a single century; and they returned to the more usual mode of nineteenth century biography by dealing with their contemporaries—in Scott's *Napoleon* and Morley's *Gladstone.* Almost the only Victorian biographer to range at all widely over the past was Macaulay. His brilliant but often prejudiced biographical essays, greatly as they were admired, found no imitators.

But although the lives of eminent contemporaries still pour forth unabated, in recent years they have been swamped in the flood of historical biography. For the professional biographer the fields of the past are immeasurably the most rewarding. Although he may go astray in them, he is in much less danger there of being detected in error. If he industriously studies all the records he can obtain, he may draw from them conclusions that are unlikely to be exploded by an indignant survivor. Dark secrets and stains on characters are neither so closely guarded nor so liable to be dangerously resented as when they concern the present. If the evidence is either sparse or confused, hypothesis may well be fruitful, and many interpretations may each have their grain of truth. Furthermore, the evidence is apt to be largely documentary, and to present thereby an appearance of being fixed for all time that the biographer dealing with the contemporary can seldom hope for. The more he wishes to achieve definitive portraits the more the biographer is likely to find comparative assurance in going to the past. The more he looks for rich and dramatic examples of personality the more likely he is to find them there in abundance. All influences converge to place the emphasis of modern biography on the historical.

Tory Pioneer

Charles Whibley was one of the first writers of modern biography in this way to realize the past as a storehouse of richly various human nature. His subjects are nearly all from the pages of history: and they range in time from Petronius and Heliodorus to Lord Melbourne and Disraeli, in theme from writers, dandies, and courtiers to politicians, statesmen, and other more variously adventurous scoundrels. His interest in them all is lively. Rabelais and Robert Burton, Philippe de Comines and Casanova, Frederick the Great and Bishop Burnet—all are handled with unabated gusto, although he certainly likes a shady scoundrel like Casanova better than a canonized one like Frederick.

Whibley is not merely a historical biographer. In numerous ways he is a forerunner of tendencies we have come to regard as essentially novel in biography. His earliest volume of biographical essays, *The Pageantry of Life*, was already in print in 1900, and from then until his death in 1930, a stream of short and long biographies placed him in the forefront of the innovators. His longer lives of Thackeray and William Pitt alternated with volumes of essays that were sometimes pure biography, sometimes imaginative biography, and sometimes a mingling of literary criticism and biography. They include the lively *Book of Scoundrels, Studies in Frankness, Essays in Biography, American Sketches*, and a number of others.

He is a pioneer in the field of short biography. Most of his biographical essays average twenty or thirty pages, and only rarely attain a length of one hundred. Such compression, anticipating

Lytton Strachey's plea for 'a becoming brevity,' is achieved by excluding the redundant and stressing only the significant. And even in such miniatures as his studies of Lucian and Poe, of Sterne and Sir Thomas Urquhart, Whibley strikingly employs biography to illuminate literary criticism and criticism to illuminate biographical understanding. Many of our contemporary critical biographies of writers devote painstaking volumes to the same task of elucidation that Whibley concentrated into a brilliant essay.

It is significant, however, that if Whibley had the merits which the best of similar biographers today share with him, he had also the defects which they often reveal. Like them, he is not always entirely scrupulous in the use of his imaginative powers. Like them, he is so adroit in the manipulation of words that he is not invariably able to restrain himself from displaying a cleverness that calls attention to the author rather than to his theme. In the introduction to his *Studies in Frankness*, for example, he draws so many ingenious paradoxes and epigrams out of the statement that modesty leads ultimately to concealment, cowardice, and dishonesty that at last we begin to feel him rather pretentious and attenuated. Any three pages chosen at random might impress us as brilliantly witty, but gems tossed in such relentless profusion glitter more and more like paste.

But Whibley is more than a clever biographer; he is a biographer with a point of view. It is both his strength and his weakness. In his best work it is a source of power, giving precision and clarity to his vision. In his worst it is a trap and a distortion. Espousing a position and principles, he becomes their ill-timed apologist. So impelled, sometimes in positively irrelevant ways and in defiance of all balanced judgment, he falls into attitudes of partisan defense or attack.

In the first series of his *Political Portraits*, written in 1917, he is unable to restrain his animosity against modern Germany when he writes of Frederick the Great. His avowed purpose is to portray the unscrupulous and philosophic monarch of Sans Souci, but he breaks out again and again with irrelevant references to 'the pretentious infamies of William II.' Having broken his word to Maria Theresa by invading Silesia, Frederick endeavored to patch up a peace by promising to defend her dominions against any other aggressor; and 'being a Hohenzollern,' Whibley adds, 'he did not see that the second promise, like the first, was worth precisely nothing.' What begins as a study of Frederick ends as a diatribe against imperial Germany. We need not quarrel with the point of view to feel that it is out of place in a biographical essay.

Nor is Whibley always better advised when he deals with personalities nearer home. The British politicians who appear in both series of *Political Portraits* (1917 and 1923) are drawn with an emphasis that makes almost every essay seem less biography than a kind of special pleading. It is not merely that Whibley's ingrained Toryism is revealed in his attitude toward every figure in English politics, for conservative historians have sometimes been fair to the opposition and understood them keenly. But Whibley persistently whitewashes his own side and blackens the other. With a sneer at all the liberals and poets of the time, he defends Castlereagh even to condoning the Manchester Massacre. He minimizes or denies Bolingbroke's negotiations with the Pretender before the death of Queen Anne, and hides all the stains of treachery and venality that blacken his flight to France. He presents Bolingbroke's long years of venomous attack on Walpole as a serene and philosophical retreat from the world.

He even defends the ferocious Jeffreys. Admitted that on the bench Jeffreys 'jesting, bullied, denounced'; that 'he took for granted the guilt of every prisoner' and did not scruple to overwhelm them with 'rough humour and coarse repartee'—he was but doing his duty! which was not to administer justice, but to advance the King's business. 'In brief, Jeffreys did but adhere to the practice of his age; and he has been held up to obloquy ever since because, being incomparably better endowed in wits and style than his fellows, he has filled a larger space in history than they could ever hope to fill.' Jeffreys was a black and cruel hanging judge, but he hanged them with style! This is a strange defense of a man who took a horrible pleasure in browbeating those he was paid to hound to their deaths, and who cringed in slobbering terror when he was brought to trial himself. James II had other instruments who were ready enough to advance the King's business. But none of them did it with the bloodthirsty gusto of Jeffreys, whom Whibley will stoop to excuse.

But whereas Tories may wade in blood, Whigs must even beware of wine. Let Bolingbroke take Alcibiades for his model, and emulate the more spectacular exploits of Rochester—he is still a noble statesman. Let Charles James Fox love women and the dice-box and the bottle, *he* becomes a rake and gambler. Fox's Pharo bank is a scandal, but Voltaire's story of the exultant cry of a town harlot when Bolingbroke was made Secretary of State, 'Seven thousand guineas a year, my girls, and all for us!' is merely the slander of a licensed jester. To admire Fox for his firmness in adhering to democratic principles in an age of reaction is all 'cant,' for Fox's principles were a traitorous giving of encouragement to the enemy.

Lord Melbourne is treated somewhat more tolerantly than most Whigs. For Melbourne, Whibley is sure, was temperamentally a Tory who found himself by family tradition in the Whig fold; his loyalty (a Tory virtue) would not allow him to betray these hallowed associations. Whibley approves Melbourne's feeling that the rotten boroughs were 'a bulwark against the encroaching mob.' He is charmed when the noble statesman asks experimenters to 'moderate their zeal,' and when in Cabinet meetings he answers proposals for reform by asking, 'Why not leave it alone?' He shares Melbourne's grave disapproval of radicals urging their measures in times of danger and unrest, and his conviction that they should wait for 'a period of perfect tranquillity and security' and then try to extort concessions from a ruling class assured of its own power.

Now all these faults gravely distort Whibley's portrayals of political figures. And yet, even in the political sketches, Whibley's work has color and movement. If we know how to allow for his prejudice, it can supply us with vivid pictures of the men and their times. We see Jeffreys as an unsuccessful lawyer trying to pretend to prosperity by having his servant bring to him in coffee-houses the news of imaginary clients waiting in his chambers, so that he may reply indifferently, 'Let them stay a little; I will come presently.' There is a vivid picture of the contemptible and fantastic Bubb Dodington: his 'natural love of marble pillars and columns of lapis-lazuli, of costly furniture and Greek statues'; his corpulence, his coxcombry, and his wit; his brazen mendacity and treachery; and his five boroughs for sale to whoever would pay the highest price. Even in the essay on Fox, with its unfairnesses, there are sharp flashes, such as that of Fox as a little boy brought up in all the indulgent luxury of Holland House and having his surprising announcement to his father that he meant to smash a watch answered, 'Well, if you must, I suppose you must.'

And the secret of Whibley's success, coloring even his failures, is to be found in the sharp aliveness of his responses. Even when he is unfair, he has the vividness of a man dealing not with bookish abstractions but with live people. It enables him to cut a daring path through the conventional trammels of pedantry and caution. He does not hesitate to have an opinion about his characters, not even a strong opinion. He does not hesitate to bring them to life for us by whatever means.

He will visualize and describe a scene for which he has only a few sentences of bare narrative to draw upon, as he does, for example, in 'Young Weston,' from his earliest volume, *The Pageantry of Life:* 'The King, missing his stroke, stumbled clumsily upon the tennis-court; and, gathering up his heavy frame with difficulty, strode sullenly within. "Your Grace," cried young Weston, chuckling that another game was his, "Your Grace shall take your revenge with the dice-box." But Henry, enraged no less at his waning skill than at the loss of his money, threw not a word at his smiling favourite, who gazed imperturbably at the retreating corpulency.'

So begins his portrait of the handsome and dashing young courtier whose head ultimately fell at the behest of his jealous King. Manner, gesture, and tones of voice are all sparklingly imagined; and even the recesses of the mind may be searched into for what the characters are thinking and imagining in the significant moments of their careers. 'No wonder,' we are told, that Francis Weston 'dreamed his career a march of triumph; no wonder he believed his charm invincible. Mine, he said to himself, is the genius of success. He would royster and gamble through life, winning all those hearts which he chose to assail, and as much money as should equip him nobly for the most gallant enterprise. His childish vanity persuaded him to hope that he would bend even the stubborn King to his will, and the monarch's displeasure at another lost game irked him not a whit.'

Whibley attained maturity before the vogue of analyzing the unconscious became an obsession with biographers, but his keenness of insight often supplied the place of its fascinations. In his earliest work, indeed, he anticipated nearly all the devices of the fictionalized biography, and used them with a spirit and tact that disarms criticism of even those dubious methods. If he invents the details of typical scenes, he gives us no major ones without recorded authority. If he tells us what young Weston feels, he does it in such a way that we know well he is not pretending to report literal fact but giving us a creative interpretation of character and motive, In his later work he becomes less addicted even to these inventive liberties with fact, and perhaps less startlingly *dramatized*, but he never loses his decisiveness and his vigorous clarity.

He is always interesting and sympathetic when he is not impeded by political rancor. He moves easily from Casanova to Petronius, and from Apuleius to Montaigne. He likes to show us old Robert Burton passing his quiet life in Christ Church, content to be a scholar and escape the many melancholies of this world he so ingeniously and humorously anatomized; and he shows us the old fellow, tired of the talk of his colleagues in the common-room, going down 'to the foot-bridge in Oxford' to hear 'the bargemen scold and swear at one another, at which he would set his hands to his side and laugh profusely.' Or he tells us a story that gives us the image of the fantastic scholar lost in an ambling-minded daze: The Earl of Southampton was presented to him in a book shop. '*Mr Burton*, says the earl, *your servant. Mr Southampton*, says Mr Burton, *your servant*, and away he went.'

Whibley achieves an effect of mingled comedy and grotesque tragedy with Thomas Urquhart. The learned translator of Rabelais traced his noble descent all the way back to Adam, 'surnamed the protoplast,' and created out of red earth 'merely that he might be the forbear of all the Urquharts.' Sixteen generations after Adam came Esormon, a Prince of Achaia; in the fortieth generation Molin married Panthea, Deucalion's daughter, 'and allied the Urquharts to one of the best families in Greece'; the Queen of Sheba came late in the family's ramifications. Only during the comparative recency of the past two thousand years had the Urquharts had as their home a castle in Scotland.

The descendant of these grandeurs was one of the most learned men of a time when his fellow Scots lords were barbarians searching 'for wild fowl, wading through many waters.' But while he was plumbing mysteries of nature, 'the finding out of longitude, and the squaring of the circle,' the house of Urquhart fell upon evil days. The elder Sir Thomas had thought it 'derogating to his dignity to look too closely into his own purse'; 'Unfaithful, servants had filched much of his personal real estate; swindling bailiffs had embezzled his rents.' Then came the Civil Wars, Urquhart's father was dead; and, fighting for King Charles, the knight had his castle seized, and all his library and manuscripts were lost.

Of his tremendous output he was able to recover only a few monumental fragments in an amazing and elaborate style. In his *Trissotretras* he will tell us 'how to resolve all manner of triangles'; and his *Logopandecteision* introduces us to a universal language, invented by Sir Thomas, having eleven cases, eleven genders, and four numbers to every noun, and four voices, seven moods, and eleven tenses to each happy verb. And, best of all, there were ten synonyms to every word. Synonyms, in fact, were Sir Thomas Urquhart's strength. He had a gusto for words of all kinds and his vocabulary was enormous.

There could be no better endowment for a translator of Rabelais, but such was Urquhart's erudition, he could outdo 'even Rabelais in extravagance, thereby achieving what might have seemed a plain impossibility.' When Rabelais would seem to have exhausted every imaginable synonym for one of his lists, Urquhart is always ready to increase them from his own bottomless knowledge, and expands one list of thirteen to thirty-six. And Urquhart's vocabulary is not only learned and enormous, it is picturesque. He disliked saying 'backgate' when he might say 'some secret angiport and dark postern door'—and 'the advantage,' Whibley adds, 'both for sound and expression' is clearly with Sir Thomas. Hardly any other translator has dared such liberties with his text, and still it is true that 'every line bears the true impress of Rabelais.'

But the man who scored such a triumph was marked for every other misfortune. His 'schemes of progress and scholarship died with the brain they inhabited.' Most of his original works were lost and destroyed, and his learning became no more than a legend. He was the last of his family. His castle was so utterly demolished that even its foundation is left unmarked. His last days are buried in obscurity, save for the legend that 'he went beyond seas, where he died suddenly in a fit of excessive laughter' on being told that Charles II was restored to the throne. 'His life was marred,' Whibley concludes, 'by broken ambitions, and made by one surpassing masterpiece.'

If none of Whibley's biographical essays are surpassing masterpieces, many of them make enticing reading and are valiant forerunners of a new freedom of treatment. Sometimes he does not handle that freedom with all possible tact, but largely he justifies it. Even his partisan judgments, as we have seen, ruinous as they are to balance in presentation, do not totally destroy his merits; and many of his subjects are free from the kind of temptation he was unable to conquer. His cleverness, although sometimes obtrusive, is usually held in check. His subjects are drawn from books, sometimes from very eccentric and obscure ones, but he himself, even when filled by enthusiasm for them, is never bookish. When he wished to praise a writer, he was wont to say that his style had *life* in it. The life in Whibley's books is his own highest praise.

Journalist of Art

Frank Harris is in truth, as he says of himself, an artist-reporter in biography. There is much that is journalistic about his writing, much that is slipshod and poorly arranged, and more than a suspicion of the sensational here and there. We may sometimes feel dubious of the strange lure that impels people to confess to him their most painful and intimate secrets, displaying all manner of pitiful family skeletons to a man who could never have impressed even the most confiding as discreet. Yet Harris has a charm, too; we feel affection and loyalty of a sort in him; and it is possible after all that his confidants yielded to impulse. But in spite of all his deficiencies and all the doubts he arouses, Harris's biographical sketches often breathe with authentic character and life; even the slightest of them are apt to have some flash of personality or insight.

His five series of *Contemporary Portraits* have had more influence than his *Oscar Wilde* upon modern biography. They may almost be said to have inspired the kind of short biographical sketch which is part literature and part journalism. But Harris has no doubt that he is himself 'artist rather than reporter'; he arranges his portrait in order to compose a picture conveying the 'essence of his sitter's soul.' As the word portrait implies, he attempts no sustained narrative of an entire life, but a mingling of impressions, conversation, and narrative chosen so as to reveal character.

For these purposes he uses the devices of fiction easily and with skill. Sometimes he begins with a scene, as in his portrait of Carlyle: 'The servant girl at his house had told me that Mr Carlyle had gone for his usual walk on Chelsea Embankment, so I went off to find him. It was a Sunday in June, about midday; the air was light, the sun warm; the river shone like a riband of silk in the luminous air.' After walking only a few hundred yards he comes on the writer, who was for him at that time 'the greatest of living men.' He describes 'the shaggy, unkempt grey thatch of hair' and 'the bony, almost fleshless face' lit up 'by the deepset eyes, most human, beautiful; by turns piercing, luminous, tender-gleaming; pathetic, too, for the lights were usually veiled in brooding sadness broken oftenest by a look of dumb despair and regret; a strong, sad face, the saddest I ever studied—all petrified, so to speak, in tearless misery, as of one who had come to wreck by his own fault and was tortured by remorse—the worm that dieth not.'

During their conversation Harris notes other details: the 'long, obstinate upper lip' when Carlyle insists on maintaining that Heine was a dirty pig, and the triumphant dance of the deepset eyes when he closes an argument about Jesus by pouncing on a fatal lack—'Man, He had no humor; Jesus had no Falstaff in him; I wad na gie up the ragged company for all the disciples.' The mingling of eloquence and carping pours on, about all manner of subjects, and gathers itself to a climax in denouncing 'these days of flatulent unbelief and piggish unconcern for everything except swill and straw'; then, a moment later, it flares up again in indignation at Darwin's survival of the fittest, that 'cowardly, sneaking evasion, with its tail between its legs.' Was your 'fittest' the noblest, Carlyle demanded, or was it 'a poor servile two-legged spaniel, sneaking round for bones and fawning on his master, beslobbering his feet? Or just the greedier mediocrity among hosts of mediocrities, the slightly stronger pig or fox, eh? *Ay di me, ay di me*—the evil dreams: "Fittest," humph!' and the old man 'blinked his eyes to get rid of the unshed tears.'

'Did you tell Darwin what you thought of his new scientific creed?' Harris asked, and a quick change of mood swept a smile over Carlyle's whole face. He had, indeed, told Darwin, before an open-mouthed crowd, that it was all very interesting 'how we men evolved from apes, and all that, and perhaps true,' he saw no reason to doubt it; but what he wanted to know was, 'how we're to prevent this present generation from devolving into apes?' Enjoying his triumph, 'the old man laughed—a great belly-shaking laugh that shook him into a cough, and there we stood laughing, laughing in harmony at length with the sun which shone bravely overhead, while the silken wavelets danced . . . and the air was young and quick.'

This portrait is typical in the vividness with which it gives us the words and manner of speaking, the expressions that dart or steal over the face, the very movements of the man. Although Harris tells much in direct quotation that he could not have noted down word for word, he defends himself against the charge of fabrication. 'When I reproduce conversations in this book,' he warns the reader, 'and put the sayings of my contemporaries in inverted commas, it must not be assumed that they are literally accurate: they are my recollections of what took place.' But he insists that his memory is more than usually exact and that he has always taken pains to ensure fixing in his mind precisely what was said in any meeting with a distinguished man.

How skilfully he conveys the speaker's idiom we may see by comparing his rendering of Carlyle's language with the darting little phrases, the jerks and inversions, by which he presents Whistler to us. The artist is alluding to Frank Holl, a popular portrait painter: 'A talent, not a genius, Holl, quite English, you know; content with the colored photograph kind of thing that all the old fellows did, and some of 'em better. Art's not imitation, that's clear, eh?' Or, again, 'If you paint a young girl, youth should scent the room: a thinker, thoughts should be in the air, an aroma of personality . . . And with all that, it should be a picture, a pattern, a harmony . . . I sometimes say an arrangement in black and white, or blue and gold, don't ye know?'

It is not merely the attitudes and ideas that are different in the two men; each has a rhythm and a structure that is his own. If Harris does not remember the exact words, he certainly finds for each the characteristic *way* of arranging them which conveys the flavor of personality. And he gives us their physical appearance and their movements as well. We see Whistler's alert, wiry perkiness carrying his five feet four in height, his gleaming monocle and the waving plume of white hair and the French top-hat; we see Meredith's vivacity of expression and quick-glancing eyes, and hear his high, loud voice; see Anatole France's long oval face, somewhat like Napoleon III, with silver-grey hair and imperial, his bright eyes 'the color of coffee beans,' with 'heavy gummy bags under them.'

Harris seldom keeps himself out of his picture very long; he cannot resist telling us what *he* thought and said about his subjects, the bright improvements on their ideas he was able to add, how he out-argued them when they disagreed, and much more to the same effect. But it is all done with a sort of innocent egoism, which is not offensive and which does not hide his subjects: unlike the more subtle egoisms of some recent biographers, who do not introduce themselves personally into the scene but distract us by an incessant crackle of intrusive witticisms. Harris does, however, arouse our skepticism by his fondness for revealing well-nigh incredible confidences which it would seem that people could not resist imparting to him. There is sometimes corroborating evidence, or at least rumor, for the things themselves; it is not always they that are unbelievable, but the idea that people would so betray themselves to him by explicit confession.

One such scene is the angry clutch of the arm with which Robert Browning betrays his jealousy of James Russell Lowell being flattered and surrounded by the musical laughter of pretty women at a party while he stands aside, unnoticed and alone. But the strangest of them all is one occurring on a walk with Carlyle. It began to rain as they neared Hyde Park Corner, but Carlyle stopped 'and taking off his soft hat stood there in the rain with his grey head bowed.' It flashed over Harris that it was here Mrs Carlyle had died in her carriage while Carlyle was off in Edinburgh. 'When he put on his hat and walked on, the tears were running down his face.'

And then, Harris says, overwrought by grieving memory, Carlyle made a startling confession. Loving his wife devotedly all his life, nevertheless he 'had never consummated the marriage.' ' "The body part meant so little to me" ' he quotes Carlyle as pleading, ' "I had no idea it could mean so much to her . . . *Ay di me, ay di me* . . . Quarter of a century passed before I found out how wrong I was, how mistaken, how criminally blind . . .

' "And the worst of it all is, there is no other life in which to atone to her—my puir girlie! It's done, and God himself cannot undo it. My girl, my puir girl! . . . Man, man, it's awful, awful to hurt your dearest blindly, awful!" and the tears rained down the haggard old face and the eyes stared out in utter misery.'

How can we believe this amazing story? It is hard to imagine the episode ever took place at all. Froude has told us of that sad memorial observance at the place of his wife's death, and scandal has breathed the suspicion to which Harris gives the support of his testimony, but not with enough circumstance to make it unimpugnable. Harris tells us that the Carlyle family physician later confirmed the story; it is possible that Harris was unable to resist the temptation of giving a dramatic form to a statement he may really have received from other sources. We can hardly imagine that even in a moment of heartbroken memory such a confession could be made; and yet it is just barely possible, for strange waves of feeling sometimes overwhelm people. But things of this kind account for much of that faint dubiousness we sometimes feel in reading his *Contemporary Portraits*.

It is a dubiousness we never feel, however, in the pages of *Oscar Wilde*. This full-length life-story, although it exerted less influence than the portraits, is undoubtedly Harris's best work in biography. George Bernard Shaw wrote the author that it was 'the best life of Oscar Wilde.' It reveals a living personality for us, the gay and charming talker whose happy spirits and bright unmalicious wit often disarmed even those who were little inclined to like him; it shows a man who was incapable of real friendship and who still inspired deep affection; and it strangely invalidates our conventional assumptions about tragedy by making tragic the downfall of a man who had neither strength nor nobility of character.

And still the book has many of the faults Harris displays in his other biographical work. The opening chapter, with cheap sensationalism, is devoted to the trial for rape of Wilde's father, Sir William Wilde, an event that has little bearing on Oscar Wilde's own weaknesses. Numerous recollections of Wilde's opinions and conversation, often valuable as indications of his personality, are worked into no narrative plan, but merely strung together in a number of loosely handled chapters near the end of the book. The chronology is sometimes so vague as to be extremely confusing; in one place Harris seems to represent Wilde as receiving an allowance from his wife although she was no longer living at the time.

The writing is slipshod, and Harris is addicted to a kind of sentimental philosophizing which can betray him into writing such a sentence as, 'Love is the best of artists; the puddle of rain in the road can reflect a piece of sky marvellously.' The puddle does not love the sky, and love often fails distressingly to write even a passable sonnet. But despite all these flaws, there is no denying the veracity and power of Harris's portrait; Shaw told him, 'Wilde's memory will have to stand or fall by it.'

We see the gifted boy enchanted at school by the luxury, wit, and parade of noble names in Disraeli's romances; and the Oxford youth rhapsodizing over the 'dreaming spires and grey colleges, set in velvet lawns and hidden away among the trees,' (he was fond of stringing together and paraphrasing the purple passages of others), Oxford, 'home of lost causes and impossible ideals.' His life was all easy triumph, undisciplined by troublesome effort or athletic striving. He learned no steadfastness of will, only luxurious living and the delight of gratifying expensive tastes, and he went to London expecting to continue his victories on a more glorious scale.

His knee breeches and silk stockings, the strange flowers he wore at first nights, and above all his eager conversation, aroused gossip and gave him the entrée into the best society in London. Brilliantly witty, at the same time he was full of praise for everything. Lily Langtry was more beautiful than the Venus of Milo, Lady Archie Campbell more charming than Rosalind, Whistler an incomparable artist. Such enthusiasm mingled with his golden eloquence and sweet playful wit overcame even a slightly repellant first impression. Indeed, at first sight, for all his six feet of height and broadness of build, there was something bilious and pouchy about him; 'he looked like a Roman Emperor of the decadence'; his handshake was limp and flabby, his clothes too tight and affected. And there were sinister rumors even then, a subterranean gleam of dislike and distrust, which Wilde arrogantly outrode and defied. But pose and oiliness and dark suspicions all alike were forgotten in the light and shining flood of his charm.

At first he was no more than a privileged charlatan, but with *The Picture of Dorian Gray*, and then with the first of his plays, *Lady Windermere's Fan*, his powers were admitted. Harris wrote Wilde in praise of *Dorian Gray*, and Wilde called on him, bubbling over with content. 'How charming of you, Frank,' he cried, 'to have written me such a divine letter.' Harris reiterated that the first hundred pages placed him undeniably among the wittiest writers in English; 'How wonderful of you, Frank,' Wilde sang happily; 'what do you like so much?' The dramatic critics at first could hardly realize the success that was taking place before them. On the opening night of *Lady Windermere*, one of them sneered that he might say, 'in Oscar's own peculiar way, "Little promise and less performance." Ha! ha! ha!' It was the very opposite of Oscar's way, Harris retorted: 'It is the listeners who laugh at his humour.'

Wilde danced over the very champagne froth of success, but more and more the submerged rumors rose to the surface. He became entangled with Lord Alfred Douglas, whose aristocratic arrogance and brazenness frightened him. In the background there was Douglas's father, the Marquis of Queensberry, with his plain, heavy, sullen face, and his quick hot eyes. Wilde ate and drank more, and seemed gross and puffy. Once Harris was distressed to see him with a pair of leering rosy-cheeked Cockney boys, their hair plastered in lovelocks on their foreheads and low, cunning eyes, but he told himself that Wilde was probably observing them as literary material.

Queensberry grew more and more violent in his objections to the intimacy between Wilde and his son. He was sure there existed 'the most loathsome and disgusting relationship'; he had read it in their 'horrible features' when he saw them together. With skill Douglas flicked his father on the raw, in a telegram reading, 'What a funny little man you are!' Next, he threatened, if his father attacked them, to shoot him in self-defense, as 'a violent and dangerous rough, and I think if you were dead many people would not miss you.'

Finally Queensberry became so libelous that Douglas egged Wilde into bringing suit. It was his ruin. The case collapsed, and the police promptly arrested Wilde on a criminal charge. Bail was refused, and panicky or morally vindictive creditors brought judgments against him which led to the sale of all the possessions in his Tite Street house for less than a quarter of their value. The jury disagreed, and Harris tried to galvanize Wilde to energy for his second defense. 'Oh, Frank,' Wilde exclaimed, 'you talk with passion and conviction, as if I were innocent.'—'But you are innocent,' Harris cried in amaze, 'aren't you?'—'No, Frank,' he replied, 'I thought you knew that all along.'

A strange apathy seemed to leave Wilde's will paralyzed. Harris chartered a small steam yacht to smuggle him away to Normandy, and described it persuasively. 'There's a little library on board of French books and English; I've ordered supper in the cabin—lobster à l'Americane and a bottle of Pommery. You've never seen the mouth of the Thames at night, have you? . . . houses like blobs of indigo . . . ships drifting past like black ghosts in the misty air.' But the more importunate Harris became, the more trembling and helpless Wilde grew, 'leaning against the railing, hung up with his head on his arm, shaking.' He could not be forced into action; he would only weep and wait. When he was convicted at last, he received the maximum sentence of two years at hard labor. Outside the court, 'troops of the lowest women of the town' danced together and kicked up their heels, while policemen and spectators guffawed with delight; and Harris saw two of the men Wilde was accused of having corrupted laughing and leering as they went off in a cab together.

Prison crushed him. He was frequently ill with earache, but he grew pale at Harris's suggestion that he should send for a doctor when he was unwell. 'Why, Frank, however ill I was now,' he said in a frightened whisper, 'I would not think of sending for the doctor.' For a short while after his release he tried to work again; he wrote *The Ballad of Reading Gaol;* but Douglas got hold of him once more, they wrangled about money, and something inside him was broken. Douglas complained that he was 'getting fat and bloated, and always demanding money . . . like an old fat prostitute,' and added horribly, 'and I told him so.'

Little by little Wilde sank lower. He was unable to strengthen himself to an effort now. 'I was born to sing the joy and pride of life, the pleasure of living, the delight in everything beautiful in this most beautiful world,' he said, 'and they took me and tortured me till I learned pity and sorrow. Now I cannot sing the joy, heartily, because I know the suffering, and I was never made to sing of suffering.'

But Harris's narrative makes one inclined to agree with him rather than with Wilde, and to feel that perhaps if his wife had forgiven him, if she had not been persuaded to subject him to solitary probation after his release from prison, if he had managed to keep free of the hysterical and degrading clutch of Douglas, he might have come out of his punishment with renewed strength. Indeed, the most curious part of the story is the way in which Wilde not only provoked resentment and punishment by his carelessness and pride, but seemed positively to court them by his every action from the suit against Queensberry on. The evidence against him was too clear and too easily obtainable for him to hope for one instant that he might succeed, and yet with a sort of blind infatuation he rushed into danger. He refused to cross the Channel to safety before he was arrested on criminal charges, although he might easily have done so; and he refused to flee on Harris's yacht.

From one point of view all this is a sort of weak folly and obstinacy, but from another there is something in it curiously profound. It is perhaps not a conscious part of Harris's telling of the story, but there emerges almost a feeling that Wilde needed to *woo* martyrdom, as if he felt the need of humiliation and defeat. He had been too easily and too superficially successful; the ease with which the glitter of fame had gilded him accounts for somewhat of that flippancy and shallowness that irritates in his writings.

It is as if in the spirit of the artist, that lay submerged somewhere beneath all that mass of pose and pride, there was a deep need for the humanizing finger of sorrow, as if Wilde unconsciously knew that only so could he possibly become a great and not merely a charming and witty writer. And for the first few months after he was released from prison, indeed, it seemed to his friends that he had been strengthened and grown in depth; then, under various influences, he sank back into supineness and the self-excusings we have seen. The effort had failed, but it might have won.

Because reflections such as these are not irrelevant to the story of Oscar Wilde as it is given in Frank Harris's pages, the book is deserving of serious consideration among biographies. For all its faults, it has a depth of meaning that makes it more than a merely vivid and lively picture of a man's character. It is that, too, but in its suggestion of hidden undertones it achieves genuine seriousness. Harris does not make Wilde either nice or admirable, but he does give him glamor, and he convinces us that in Oscar Wilde deeper powers were defeated of their fruition. It is this that makes the life of Oscar Wilde a tragic thing—neither the suffering nor the spectacular plunge from the glittering pinnacle of prestige into the depths, but the fact that the sorrow was frustrated of its justification. We are not witnessing the torment of a man who was or ever had been great, but we see such potentialities of fineness as the man did have reaching out and striving to became real—almost attaining reality—and then withering.

Beside these achievements the cheapnesses and the stylistic sloppiness in the book pale into triviality. Its defects of occasional structure are lost in the stark main outlines that block out its meaning. The sensationalism of the opening is forgiven, because there is no sensationalism later on, where if Harris had been a vulgar soul who wanted to exploit it he might have found a more phosphorescent slime to delve in. Not even in the innocent way in which he sometimes intrudes into the *Contemporary Portraits* does Harris intrude here; after the first third of the book he is often on the scene, but he is never edging the principal figure off. And, above all, we never, in his *Oscar Wilde*, lose our faith in what he is telling us; we have complete belief in his veracity to the facts as he knows them. He may sometimes be confused in memory or presentation, but we never suspect him as we have elsewhere of even an approach to fabrication.

It is for these reasons, rather than out of any considerations of mere bulk or even sustained narrative, that *Oscar Wilde* is much superior to the *Contemporary Portraits*. It has exerted less influence than they—indeed one sometimes feels that Harris's successors have deliberately set out to model themselves on his less admirable qualities; that his bumptiousness, his journalistic tricks, and his possible irreverence for fact are what have commended themselves to imitators—but his *Oscar Wilde* has all the valuable qualities he reveals in his other biographical work, purged of nearly all that renders it dubious.

Conflict with a Dying Age

Although he has written other biographies, Sir Edmund Gosse will be remembered pre-eminently for but one excursion into the realm of biography. In that single foray, though, he wrote himself more significant as an artist, more striking as an innovator, than either Harris or Whibley. Few people can have realized, when

Father and Son was published anonymously in 1908, what a portent glowed before them.

That it was a fascinating book anyone could see—fascinating as a most brilliant novel. Two people were there—a sober, earnest, and desperately devoted man and an instinctively rebellious little boy—in all the sharpness and shading of life; and they were surrounded by a group of brightly sketched minor figures. There were drama, comedy, pathos; a strange mixture of hilarity and bitterness, seen as in life, and yet suffused with understanding, reflected in the serene mirror of the past. There was the spectacle of a spirit being enslaved, almost reduced to unresisting dust, by the kindliest and most noble-hearted affection; and then, by the queerest of chances, a source of strength and resistance unwittingly presented by the benevolent oppressor.

All these things might be clear enough to any reader. But the revolutionary nature of the book came from other qualities. It was hard to classify, as biography or autobiography, for in almost equal degrees it mingled the two, the narrator being the little boy so nearly crushed by his father's love. It was not the story of the father's life, and still less of his son's, but the story of a relationship and a struggle. Its details were selected with all the unerring craftsmanship of a masterly novelist, deepening the atmosphere with wash after wash of color, touched with sparkling highlights, and the crucial scenes marched with ever-increasing drama to the ultimate flare-up of defiance.

Not until twenty years later, in Strachey's *Elizabeth and Essex*, was anything like this conflict of two entangled, devoted, and yet antagonistic personalities to command the whole attention of a biography, and even then it could not have the curious insight derived from one of the contestants being the teller of the story. Clarence Day, in his reminiscences of his father, narrates the explosive but not rancorous guerilla warfare between Father and his family, but the continual outbursts of the elder Day are fireworks rather than conflict, and his son's sketches are episodic not climactic.

In all these ways the genius of Gosse has been exploratory, opening new realms with quiet authority, and, so far, transcending any of those who have followed him. The tense psychological struggle, the dramatic structure, the mingling of biography and autobiography, the stringent limitation of theme: here were blazes of new light illumining undreamed-of deeps.

And although Gosse was not alone in regarding his experience as historically significant, representative of his age (for Mill and Henry Adams, as we have seen, so rated the importance of their own lives), he is unique in finding its significance precisely in a conflict. 'This book,' he begins, 'is the record of a struggle between two temperaments, two consciences, and almost two epochs.' That struggle marked the dividing line between the non-conformist, evangelical conscience—'a state of soul once not uncommon in Protestant Europe'—and the modern mind. It is 'the diagnosis of a dying Puritanism' that Gosse presents us.

His parents were extreme Calvinists, austerely withdrawn from all ritual and ceremony. 'So far as the sects agreed with my Father and my Mother, the sects were walking in the light; wherever they differed from them, they had slipped . . . into . . . a darkness into which neither of my parents would follow them.' These two believed in the absolute truth of everything in the Bible; for them, 'nothing was symbolic, nothing allegorical or allusive . . . except what was, in so many words, proffered as a parable or a picture.' They lived absolutely alone, in the most rigid poverty, dividing their time between zoology (the profession of the elder Gosse) and the discussion of theology. To this literal-minded couple, already middle-aged when they were married, 'the advent of a child was not welcomed, but was borne with resignation,' and the unconscious infant was dedicated to the Lord.

The child was not allowed to hear or read stories: the stern conscience of his parents debarred all fictions as lies. 'I was told about missionaries, but never about pirates; I was familiar with humming-birds, but I had never heard of fairies.' It would be erroneous, however, to think of the household as a gloomy one for a child. Like the Ruskins, they were a cheerful family. His mother was ethereally pretty, with gold hair and white skin, and his parents 'were playful with one another,' his mother 'sometimes extremely gay, laughing with a soft, merry sound.' They were full of guileless mirth, and so indifferent to forms that they could even joke mildly about the surroundings of their religion.

But God, omniscient and absolute, was always with them, unseen but as solid as father, with whom the childish mind, in fact, confused Him. Not until his sixth year did the child realize that his father did not share God's knowledge. One morning his father announced some fact to them. 'I was standing on the rug, gazing at him, and when he made this statement, I remember turning quickly, in embarrassment, and looking into the fire. The shock to me was as that of a thunderbolt, for what my Father had said *was not true.*' It was merely an error of fact, but to the child it revealed the appalling discovery that his father did not know everything.

Worse was to follow. The heathen in their blindness bowed down before objects of wood and stone, and his father assured him that God would be very angry indeed if anyone in a Christian country were guilty of the sin of idolatry. When his parents were safely out of the house, 'with much labour,' he hoisted a small chair on to a table, and, his heart in his throat, knelt and prayed to it, 'O Chair!' What would God do? 'I was very much alarmed, but still more excited; I breathed the high, sharp air of defiance.' But nothing happened. He had committed idolatry, and God did not care. It did not make him question the existence and power of God; but it did 'lessen still further my confidence in my Father's knowledge of the Divine mind.'

In his seventh year his mother fell ill. When he asked the meaning of the word that told her cruel disease, he saw his parents 'gazing at each other with lamentable eyes.' In terrible pain she met her death serenely, saying to her husband, 'I shall walk with him in white. Won't you take your lamb and walk with me?' Dazed with grief, he failed to understand, and growing agitated she repeated several times, 'Take our lamb, and walk with me!' Then the child was pressed forward, and the dedication begun in his cradle was sealed at her death-bed. 'But what a weight, intolerable as the burden of Atlas, to lay on the shoulders of a little fragile child!'

In their lonely life after his mother's death, when his father would often fold him closely in his arms, the child turning up his face wonderingly 'while the large, unwilling tears gathered in the corners of his eyelids,' it became the parent's greatest desire that the child should be received into the community of the 'Saints,' the small band of brethren with whom he prayed. But how to show that a little child, his mind still unfolding, could already be in a state of grace? He believed that this had taken place in his son at so early an age that it could not be observed; useless to expect a repetition! 'The heavenly fire must not be expected to descend a second time; the lips are touched with the burning coal once, and once only.'

The congregation proved a little restive at the suggestion: 'each of themselves, in ripe years, had been subjected to the severest cross-examination' before being admitted to communion. But finally opposition was overborne. The child was submitted to examination by two of the elders, and his answers were so clear, his acquaintance with Scripture so amazing, his testimony to the principles of salvation so exhaustive, that they felt confounded.

In the midst of intense excitement, at the age of ten, he was publicly baptized. His father's joy was pathetic. 'His sternness melted into a universal complaisance. He laughed and smiled, he paid to my opinions the tribute of the gravest consideration, he indulged,—utterly unlike his wont,—in shy and furtive caresses.' When he was asked if now his son could call him 'Beloved Brother,' he laughed, and said, 'That, my love, though strictly correct, would hardly, I fear, be thought judicious!'

Despite this external triumph, there was no native ardor in the boy's heart. He was sincere in desiring to be good and holy, he did not doubt that his father indicated to him the good life, he was not lacking in candor, but there was never any spiritual joy in surrender. There was nothing but resignation, and a desperate clinging, deep within, 'to a hard nut of individuality,' almost destroyed and shrivelling away. 'My soul was shut up, like Fatima, in a tower . . . and it might really have been starved to death, or have lost the power of recovery and rebound.'

Then, suddenly, by a wild caprice, his father 'gratuitously opened a little window' in the prison-tower, 'and added a powerful telescope.' The boy had become fascinated by the geography of the West Indies; his father presented him with an old copy of *Tom Cringle's Log*, saying, 'You'll find all about the Antilles there.' It was the first work of fiction he had ever had; at first he did not realize that it was not literally true; but when his father advised him to read the descriptions of sea and mountain and skip the noisy amorous adventure, of course he did not do so. They filled his horizons with radiant glory.

When his father married a second time the boy was aided to a further gasping plunge into beauty. As a pretty kind of aftermath to courtship his father read aloud to his bride some of the poems of Scott, and, unobserved, a shudder floated down the boy's backbone when he heard the resounding words:

A sharp and shrieking echo gave,
Coir-Uriskin, thy goblin cave!
And the grey pass where birches wave,
On Beala-nam-bo.

Insensibly the stern prohibition melted away. The novels of Dickens were permitted, on the ground, somewhat odd in a newly married husband, that they expose 'the passion of love in a ridiculous light'; and the boy's shouts of laughing at the richer passages in Pickwick were almost scandalous. 'I felt myself to be in the company of a gentleman so extremely funny that I began to laugh before he began to speak; no sooner did he remark "the sky was dark and gloomy, the air was damp and raw," than I was in fits of laughter.'

But worldly gaieties were still frowned upon. Imaginative horizons, however, were widening, doors being thrown open, and they gave the boy courage to resist. When he was invited to 'tea and games' by some neighboring Browns, he evinced so strong a desire to go that his father was obliged to make it an occasion for prayer. With great fervor he asked the Lord to reveal whether or not it was his will that the boy should go to the Browns' party. 'My Father's attitude seemed to me to be hardly fair, since he did not scruple to remind the Deity of various objections to a life of pleasure and of snakes that lie hidden in the grass of evening parties.' Finally, 'in a loud wheedling voice,' his father asked him, 'Well, and what is the answer which our Lord vouchsafes?' He had no doubt of the reply, he was already planning, his son believed in later years, some little treat to make up for the loss. 'But my answer came, in the high, piping accents of despair: "The Lord says I may go to the Browns."' Speechless with horror, his father was nevertheless caught in his own trap, and there was no way for him but to retreat. 'Yet surely,' Gosse adds demurely, 'it was an error in tactics to slam the door.'

Slowly but inevitably his father's prestige and infallibility thenceforth declined. His face might blaze white with Puritan fury as he denounced the 'so-called gods of the Greeks' and likened them to those for which God poured down fire and brimstone on the Cities of the Plain: his son pored over steel engravings of serene Apollo, and Venus in her undulations, reflecting that they were too beautiful to be as evil as his father said. 'The dangerous and pagan notion that beauty palliates evil budded in my mind,' and it was not long before, in his teens, he was reveling in the sorcery of Shakespeare and the passion and music of *Hero and Leander.* And there came a moment at last when the youth broke out in open revolt. To his father's anxious questioning as to whether he was 'walking closely with God?' he responded with violence and hysteria. 'I desire not to recall the whimpering sentences in which I begged to be let alone . . . in which I repudiated the idea that my Father was responsible to God for my secret thoughts . . .'

It was the end. To London he hurried, followed close by a letter in which his father reviewed with sorrow the stages of his breaking away from God. He prayed that his son might be restored to grace, and then 'Oh! how joyfully should I bury all the past, and again have sweet and tender fellowship with my beloved Son, as of old.' It was an ultimatum that allowed no truce or compromise, and none was made. Then and there, 'as respectfully as he could,' the young man 'took a human being's privilege to fashion his inner life for himself.' Neither Father nor Son, 'to the very last hour, ceased to respect the other, or to regard him with a sad indulgence'; but 'sweet and tender fellowship' was beyond all yearning lost.

It is unusual, as Gosse says, to find a story of spiritual struggle so mingling merriment and tragic pathos. It is not only true, however, that such minglings are the very nature of life—they may have as well the unity and perfection of art. Nothing is clearer than that Gosse is telling *a story:* not a chance series of events, but a development, steady, inevitable, logical, climactic, in which all that he had to do with the materials that life presented to him was to subdue the irrelevant and bring out the dramatic movement. The scenes of comedy were no mere 'comic relief'; they were an irreducible datum of the very character and structure of his tale. Only by portraying them could he give us the full human depth and flavor of that childhood scene.

There is an immeasurable gain in realizing it in no stage-caricature rendering of a blue-nosed and strait-laced Puritanism, of mean hypocrisy and thick gloom, but as a living thing, shot through by gleams of lightness and laughter. The cheerful sereneness possible in Evangelical religion is as logical a necessity in Gosse's narrative as the series of revelations by which his spirit is led to freedom. Fate presented him with brilliant finds, but there is not one out of which Gosse's art does not wring the last drop of significance, from the hot embarrassment of the little boy looking into the fire on realizing that his father is not as God to the young man's whimpering rebellion in the orchid-perfumed hothouse. Nature had enacted a work of art, and Gosse had the power to seize and shape to lasting form what nature had provided.

In less significant only because less inventive ways Gosse is quite as noteworthy. No one who ever reads the book will forget its scenes and episodes; no one will forget the characters of the father and the mother and the little boy, although the more fluid and rapidly changing character of the youth, as is inevitable in those years when the personality is changing sometimes with airplane speed, grows less sharply defined. No one will forget the deepening sense of conflict, from the quaintness of the little boy's early skepticism about idolatry to the obsessive struggle against what is, for all its sacrificial purity, almost a spiritual vampirism. But unless we stop to reflect upon it we may not have realized the blinding new biographical possibilities that are thus thrown open in releasing biography from the leading-strings of the entire-life, birth-to-death formula, and at the same time giving it more force than the mere anecdote-enlivened character sketch. They are possibilities that few biographers have yet seen, but they are endlessly fruitful.

The deepest significance of all in *Father and Son*, as Gosse indeed realized, is its historical meaning. Not only were his parents 'perhaps among the latest consistent exemplars' in Protestant Europe of the iron Calvinism that had been so powerful a force in earlier days: their religion was to join in battle with the modern age. They were vigorous-minded people, both of distinguished accomplishment—it is these facts that give significance to 'the contrast between their spiritual point of view and the aspect of a similar class of persons today.' The elder Gosse was to find that, both in science and in the heart of his son, he was flung into desperate warfare to preserve a waning creed.

The impact of scientific materialism upon the father's career as a zoologist is told in some brilliant pages of Gosse's book. The strong mingling of pathos and absurdity so often running through it is nowhere richer than in the story of his father's unhappy 'Omphallos'-theory, which a hasty press coarsely defined as being 'that God hid the fossils in the rocks in order to tempt geologists into infidelity.' But if his conflict with the modern world embittered his professional life, he found the conflict even more painful when he was obliged to wage it over the soul of his son.

The interplay of pragmatism, paganism, and poetry in the son was like the innocent-looking waves of the sea; but they sucked and tore at the stone foundations of faith, crumbled gradually and remorselessly the joints in the rock; and in vain did the elder strive to save the edifice by damming or by striking at the individual symptoms: he might as well strike the waves on the shore. Freedom, science, skepticism, a more flexible morality, an emancipated art: against all these tendencies of the contemporary world the elder Gosse was dashing himself in vain. It was indeed a struggle between two ages, and as such we can almost see the world-process being enacted symbolically in these narrow little London lodgings and country cottages.

The great intellectual realms of politics and philosophy and sociology are almost entirely offstage, not in the center of things as they are in the autobiographies of Mill and Henry Adams, but the swirl of conflict is no less there. In *Father and Son,* quite as much as in *The Education of Henry Adams*, we are observing a world in transition, in struggle and defeat. Adams was borne further along in the flood than the elder Gosse, but he too at the end of his book is left among the flotsam and the wreckage. Gosse enables us to understand, and even sympathize with the hopes he leaves behind, and then flings us on the threshold of a life, looking forward to the new. He finds the meaning of those mid-nineteenth-century years in the conflict. The meaning is as much victory as it is defeat.

HERE AND NOW

XVI

HERE AND NOW

Kaleidoscope of Forces

As we near the present time our scene becomes international. Every year hundreds of biographies are published; scores of them appear simultaneously in more than one country. They reach an audience numbering thousands of readers. These facts exert a powerful pressure on the biographer. Not only is he aware that he may possibly command a tremendous reading public: he is brought into immediate contact with the biographical achievement of the whole modern world. In the nineteenth century a biography, even a scholarly biography, might come to a slow fruition almost isolated from all other biographical endeavor that had not been specifically devoted to its own field and subject. And if the biographer had chosen a domestic theme he was likely to find that nearly all his sources lay within the confines of his own land and language. Today he may learn that a French scholar is one of the foremost authorities on Swinburne, that an English man of letters has written an important biography of an American diplomat, and that an

American historian is the author of an indispensable life of Condorcet.

Not only are research and biographical interpretation international. New techniques in biographical art, applications to biography of new ideas and new awarenesses from many other realms, immediately make their impact. In the preceding two chapters we observed the beginnings of these tendencies, but they were merely the upper reaches of a stream that has swollen to a torrent. Let a Henry James or a Marcel Proust or a James Joyce explore in fiction some shadowy and mysterious Thibet of the spirit's sensibility, and it will not be long before biographers are swarming through its secret hills and striving to scale its cloud-veiled mountains. A French industrialist no sooner writes a romanticized life of Shelley than scores of others, taking the cue, have plunged into imaginative reconstructions of Alfred de Musset, Aspasia, or John L. Sullivan. A Lytton Strachey dissects the Victorian age with mordant irony, and a host of writers perceive that an acid treatment may be more effective than embalming in treacle, a realization that some of the more simple-minded of them translate into trying to bite grandmother's leg. Within a few months after publication, a novel experiment in biography may be read and evaluated in England, France, Russia, the United States, and South America. The use the biographer makes of all these influences will of course depend upon his receptivity, intelligence, and skill, but he cannot remain unaware of them. He dwells in a world where Unamuno, Emil Ludwig, and André Maurois are as familiar as his own countrymen. He must be, to a degree, a citizen of the world.

As such, he finds all the forces of the modern world converging upon him. He must be aware of some of the complexities and confusions of physical science, of the intricate structure of modern industrial society with its problems and menaces: and these awarenesses must color his weltanschauung. He must have a glimmering notion of the efforts made in the social sciences—economics, psychology, sociology—to clarify and solve human problems. And these too are international. Taine's analysis of the influence of climate, geography, and social organisms upon art and the individual is possibly a little too crude and slapdash, as he developed it himself, to be accepted unmodified; but no intelligent biographer would reject the approach altogether. The way in which the economic structure of society molds individual judgments and values has been pointed out from slightly different angles by Marx and Veblen, and their method has been fruitfully applied to biography. Still others—notably the psychoanalysts, Freud, Jung, Adler, Rivers; and the behaviorists, Watson, Pavlov—have approached these problems as a matter of individual adjustment and maladjustment. An alert biographer finds it hardly possible to ignore the bearings of such activities on biography.

Of them all, the Freudian and the Marxian approaches have been most widely used by contemporary biographers, and have had the most far-reaching results. Armed with the instruments thus placed within their grasp, biographers have turned again to statesmen, generals, financiers, poets, and artists, and often their conclusions have been profoundly modified. Used in a doctrinaire or careless way, such methods may result in grotesque distortions, but employed with tact they may illumine unsuspected depths. And there can be no doubt that they have added coloring and shading even to biographies in which they were not the dominant methods.

A host of influences thus tends to make contemporary biography international. To understand its ramifications we must widen our horizon and at least note the parallel developments taking place all over the modern world. If the English biographers flirt with psychoanalysis when they come again to the problems of Wordsworth and Blake and Donne, if Philip Guedalla leans on it in portraying Napoleon III, if John Middleton Murry makes it the most prominent strand in his interpretation of D. H. Lawrence, Emil Ludwig also brings it to bear on Leonardo da Vinci, Van Wyck Brooks uses it on Mark Twain and Henry James, Gamaliel Bradford on an entire company of subjects, and Joseph Wood Krutch on Edgar Allan Poe.

It will be noted how frequently these psychoanalytic efforts are directed upon artists and men of letters. In the first place to a man of letters—and a biographer is one—a man of letters is interesting as a fellow-artist, his work is there as a problem in literary criticism to be understood, and a subtle and fascinating relationship to be established between the man and his art. In the second place, the artist, and especially the literary artist, has left a record of his personality much more direct, copious, and individual than that which a general scores upon landscapes and the bodies of men with battles.

The character of Wellington may be somewhere hinted in the events of Waterloo, or the spirit of Metternich in the Congress of Vienna, but they are not charted down to almost the last dark and secret cave, as is the character of Dostoyevsky in his novels. (Elie Faure, though, in his *Napoléon,* treats his subject as a great lyric artist.) The revelation of the artist is infinitely richer, and, when the interest is primarily in character, more readily decipherable than the usually rather thin personal records of the man who is a man of action, and no more.

In no respect does contemporary biography differ more from nineteenth century biography than in this living interest in the relationship between the character of an artist and his work, between the forces at work upon his life and his responses to them in the novels, the poems, or the paintings, or the music, that he drew out of himself. The nineteenth century was interested in the man, and it was interested in his work, but it seldom occurred to the biographer to attempt any penetrating analysis of how, in what vital way, they were related to each other.

Between Lockhart and Forster we can discover no change. They each tell us what sequence the novels were written in, interpolate a few words of description or literary criticism of each novel, add some comment on how it was received, and pass on to other things. Occasionally they may note where the author heard the anecdote that gave him the idea for a particular episode, or they may tell us that certain events were autobiographic, but they make no effort to uncover the deep sources of the theme and the emotional antagonisms and loyalties it implies.

That Dickens's own unhappy childhood made him hate cruelty and oppression all his life and attack them in his novels of course we learn, but there is no extended and powerful effort to trace either the influence of his experiences and character on the novels, nor the evidence in the novels of that character. The same is true with Trevelyan's *Macaulay:* how, we may ask, did that tender and sensitive heart produce the brass and the trumpets, the trip-hammer and pile-driver strokes of his rhetoric? For the most part when the author-subject of the nineteenth century biography retires to his study to write a book, we learn little more of the relationship between the two than if it were merely squeezed out of him like toothpaste.

The modern critical biography, in trying to connect all the strands of a life with each other, thus has a significance transcending literary criticism alone, and sometimes attaining to the importance of social criticism. The problems and defeats, the aspirations and triumphs of the representative or gifted individual, become the index to the character of a period, a measuring rod by which the successes and failures of the age may be gauged, a microcosm of its entire character. Bernard de Voto violently disagrees with Van Wyck Brooks, who regards Mark Twain as a victim of the Puritanic and materialistic elements in American life in his age, but he as certainly agrees in regarding him as a representative figure by which the age can be judged.

So Professor Cazamian treats *Carlyle* as one of the signs of the times, a voice crying out in the wilderness of modern society; and so Clara Gruening Stillman regards *Samuel Butler*, not merely as a personal problem in literary psychology, but as a great force of rebellion and dissent. Mill, Ruskin, Arnold, Disraeli, Shelley, Byron, Morris, Rossetti—almost all the great figures of the romantic and Victorian periods—have been so analyzed by more recent biography. The critical biography merging into the biography of social criticism thus becomes another facet of the interpenetration of biography and history, another aspect of the effort to clarify the meaning and philosophy of history.

The psychoanalytic and the sociological both derive their deepest significance, in fact, from the bearing that both have upon the struggles of man in the society he has built or stumbled upon. When the Freudian dissects individual problems of psychosis or fixation he finds them to be illustrations of a recurrent pattern in human psychology. He must, if he is wise, try to relate them to the larger pattern of organized society in which their continued recurrence is surely no accident.

The Marxian biographer conversely applies to individual cases principles derived from a study of the entire mechanism of modern society, which enable him to display even the highest degrees of eccentricity and aberration as resultants of general forces, brilliant variations on a theme of which their very multiplicity illustrates the constant direction. 'Psychoanalysis and the new psychology of Freud and Jung,' Lincoln Steffens points out, are 'a feather in the cap of the red who had always held that to change men's minds one must first change their environment.'

Fundamentally, there is thus no necessary antagonism between the Marxian and the Freudian, despite the scorn with which they have sometimes treated each other. Indeed the wiser biographers have not hesitated to use the methods of both schools together. The point of view from which Amabel Williams-Ellis deals with John Ruskin is chiefly sociological, but she deepens her grasp by tracing the threads of that close and stifling family intimacy within which Ruskin was held and partly enslaved. Van Wyck Brooks leans heavily upon the emotional dominance of Mark Twain's mother, a dominance which he regards as transferred to his wife in later years, but he endeavors to orient Mark Twain in the tyrannous pattern of pioneer society and to relate it to the whole American scene of his day. Newton Arvin, in his *Hawthorne*, uses the sociological and the psychological in a closely mingling analysis, and makes them yield a significant portrait not merely of Nathaniel Hawthorne but of the limitations of American nineteenth century culture. As a vehicle of searching social criticism, biography has gained immensely in depth and meaning from these two methods, and nowhere more than when they have been employed hand in hand.

The social emphasis has likewise given new precision and clarity to scholarly research in biography. Such great scholars as Spedding and Aitken in the nineteenth century tell us everything that can possibly be learned about Bacon and Steele, but they either have no focus at all or else they are focused too exclusively on the man alone. Partly we are lost in a blur of too much information, partly the background remains to be supplied or left blank by the reader himself. When, occasionally, a Masson tried to repair such deficiencies he fell into the opposite excess of straying too far afield: and Carlyle remarked drily that Masson was 'very brave, for he has undertaken to write a history of the universe from 1608 to 1674, calling it a *Life of John Milton*.' Carlyle himself did hardly any better, however, in his own *Oliver Cromwell* and his *Frederick the Great*, both tremendous panoramas which are fully as much history (brilliant but rather distorted history) as they are biography.

The scholarly biography of the present seeks, not always successfully, to retain the emphasis on the personal and yet suggest the color of an age and reveal the relationship between it and the individual. Harold Nicolson's biography of *Lord Carnock*, as contrasted to his *Curzon*, is a study of an older school of European diplomacy placed beside a representative of the new. James Truslow Adams's *The Adams Family* is a panorama of four generations of America as well as of four generations of the Adams clan. Ralph Roeder, in *The Man of the Renaissance*, chooses his characters precisely to illustrate the main facets of that many-sided period; there are spectacular and pretentious digressions into historical chromo, but mainly the fusion of the two is attained. From Louis Trenchard More's brilliant *Sir Isaac Newton* and the two fascinating volumes Arthur Bryant has completed of his *Samuel Pepys* we get a richly documented picture of the political, social, and intellectual life of the age.

These biographies are all products of laborious research, but they reveal how earnestly the contemporary biographer strives not to lose himself in a narrow groove of specialization, to retain the human significance and drama of his theme. Even the scholarly biographer today is trying to be not a pedant writing for the carping of pedants, but a man writing to intelligent and well-read men. This effort, to be sure, when not curbed by discriminating judgment, has sometimes produced too many concessions to mere popularity. There are lapses into a rather foolish sprightliness in Michael Sadleir's *Bulwer*, which is offered as 'a panorama in miniature of England and of English humanity during the changing decades of the nineteenth century.' They probably resulted from an uneasy awareness of the dashing manner cultivated by the romanticized biographies which had a fashionable vogue after the publication of Maurois's *Ariel* and a series of *Vies Amoureuses* of Balzac, George Sand, Chopin, and others.

Linked to the novelized biography by a similar aim has been the now moribund school of 'debunking,' a coterie inspired by the simple formula of denying all traditional judgments of past greatness. Is Lincoln a folk hero of the American people? Then it becomes necessary to investigate these queer stories about an earlier love and his unhappiness with Mary Todd Lincoln. Was Washington the Father of His Country?—his descendants must be told that he was so far from sharing the alcoholic prejudices of the Anti-

Saloon League that he ran a profitable whiskey mill. And General Grant—he drank to excess, and had dark and underhanded dealings with Wall Street; and Mark Hanna was a cynical politician; and Andrew Carnegie was by no means merely a sanctified peace advocate!

Now the devil's advocate is a valuable figure in biography; it is desirable that our judgments should be constantly reevaluated and reinterpreted. There is no fame so holy that it must not be examined. The peerings of the biographical sleuth are valuable just to the degree that new and significant criteria can be uncovered. George Washington *should* be made into a believable human being instead of a glacial superman nine feet high; the chicanery and unscrupulousness upon which certain millionaires have reared their vast fortunes *should* be revealed. When the idols are bloated into a toplofty unreality they should be toppled from their pedestals. Such disintegrations of undeserved good fame are fundamental exercises in critical honesty. Without them biography would have no more significance than the mob in *Julius Caesar* throwing its sweaty nightcaps in the air. Whenever panegyric in biography threatens truth, destruction must prick the rainbow-bubble.

But in the nineteen-twenties, inspired partly by Lytton Strachey's acid but intelligent example, biography became for a while a dance of impish glee around scores of broken altars. No eminence was safe as long as dynamite or crowbars were anywhere to be obtained, and the search for flaws became so relentless that the price of microscopes tripled. Philip Guedalla took a cue from Victor Hugo's monumental scorn for Napoléon-le-petit, and in *The Second Empire* made a comic opera figure out of that melancholy and imperialed adventurer. R. F. Dibble deflated Admiral Dewey and Brigham Young with giggles, and, still giggling, reversed the process in a patronizing heroic portrait of John L. Sullivan. W. E. Woodward uncovered the facts about Washington's whiskey-mill, and was forced to announce regretfully that somehow, he didn't quite know how, there was something great about Washington after all. The American excesses were worse than the English ones, less restrained by taste, less judicious in irony; but both were dictated not so much by truth as by triumph.

It was this liveliness, indeed, like the exhilaration of a small boy discovering insolence, that gave debunking its ephemeral charm.

As an innovation it was startling to readers, and had some of the breathless excitement that the novelized biography achieved by treating real people as if they were characters in fiction. On its valuable side it was a rather more naive aspect of the trend toward social criticism; on its spectacular side it was sheer slapstick and surprise.

The delight of the reader grew partly out of its novelty and partly out of the wickedness that makes us all rejoice when pompous and portly gentlemen, slipping on a banana peel, describe wild arabesques against the sky. By the end of the decade, however, the skies had become a frieze of elderly and upset dignity, and the public wearied of the sport. Even such brilliant sparklers as Mr Guedalla grew more circumspect; he still sparkled, perhaps to excess, but he tried to glitter in a way suggesting great sobriety underneath. The legitimate deposit which the debunkers left behind them was a disinterested willingness to subject any reputation whatsoever, no matter how portentous and respectable, to a critical examination.

Even more than the debunking biography, the romanticized life is impelled by a search for dramatic interest. Looking with envy into the adjacent realm of the novelist, the biographer saw that the novelist was privileged to use many devices conventionally denied to biography. The novelist constantly availed himself of conversation as lively as his imagination could present him with, but people's verbal memories of even the most exciting dialogues of real life were distressingly thin and inexact. The novelist could depict his characters through pages of reverie and introspection, but the subjects of biographies have seldom recorded the flow of their sentiments when alone. A novel can be shaped to a logical and ideal development, excluding irrelevancies, digression, and anticlimax, but the facts of many lives insist on displaying all these irritating features. Why, the biographers asked themselves, should biography not emulate some of the novel's freedom?

And many of them promptly answered themselves, No reason at all! They would omit, or soft-pedal, or play up the facts in such a way as to make a more dramatic story or a more satisfactory thesis. If a man had been so tasteless as to live thirty years after the importances of his life were dead, they would leave him before the days of emptiness began. If the real events could be made more exciting by just a little alteration in their sequence, surely, some of the biographers thought, it would do no harm to change them to just that slight degree? If there was a dearth of real conversation, why could it not be invented?—it was easy enough to imagine what must have been said under the circumstances.

And, just to be completely honest and scientific about it, the biographers argued, here is what these people actually said on an only slightly different occasion in this diary, or these letters; look, we will put what they wrote here into a conversation; it is certainly what they thought, and it is much more interesting told this way. As for reverie, we all know about dream symbolism and the unconscious nowadays; very well, here is a page where this man was obviously day-dreaming in his journal, I shall elaborate its meaning according to the best rules of psychoanalysis, and here it is, presented as a reverie; here is a dream in one of his letters, oho! we all know what that means, so now we can render a passage of introspection.

Such are the arguments behind the fictional biography, and it is clear that they cover a wide variety of practices, ranging from downright dishonesty to a not illegitimate poetic coloring of a theme. Whether a given omission is suppression or selection depends on the intelligence and truthfulness of the biographer; it is not claimed that he must tell everything, but he must not omit anything that thereby presents an impression false to the facts. To invent what we may call 'typical' conversation may be a reasonable privilege, but to build up a highly elaborated and individualized conversation in any situation except where it is quite clearly indicated that it is imaginary is surely indefensible.

No paths are forbidden that any means of analysis can cut through the dark forest of the human heart, but we should not be led to believe that these inspired guesses represent actual reveries known and recorded as having taken place. Where they are employed as symbols of a real tendency, not as facts, we are not deceived, and their use is innocent. Undesirable as they are in other ways, for example, no one would be in danger of mistaking those vast, windy, Victor-Hugo-like monologues that Emil Ludwig blows around a subject for anything that Goethe, or Michelangelo, or Napoleon had left on record. Such rhapsodic pythoness-wallowings obviously proceed from Ludwig alone.

In modified form, some of the quickness and translucency of the fictionalized life are achieved by descriptive atmosphere and emotional coloring. More subtly still, it may be attained purely by suggestion, perhaps by scale alone—the relative emphasis given to one episode or quality as against another, rather than by either omission or invention. At this stage of delicacy in arranging materials it is hard to distinguish between a novelistic handling and a merely artistic one, for the choice, arrangement, and proportional space devoted to known facts must clearly be a result of interpretation. Where legitimate interpretation gives way to undue interference is a nice problem, which cannot be discussed in the abstract but only in particular cases.

The effort leads us, however, directly to what is perhaps the most significant of all contemporary developments in biography: the attempt to regard biography as definitely a work of literary art, and to write it and judge it by artistic standards. This will be the theme of the chapter following the present one.

Realms of Romance

The stream of contemporary biography has swollen into a vast flood which no longer moves past us, but deepens and deepens, exploring tortuous inlets its waters never reached before and tearing with its waves at many neighboring shores. Unlike other seas, however, it varies immensely in composition, and if we lower an exploring bucket here and there, instead of infinitesimal traces, we find heavier concentrations or deposits, of weed, of jewels, of mud, of salt, and occasionally of almost pure gold. But our samples must be more stringently limited than ever before, if we are not to lose ourselves in an endless examination. We can only take a number of characteristic specimens, chosen not entirely at random, from that cosmopolitan sea, and observe how they illustrate the developments we have reviewed.

It is characteristic that a young scion of an industrial family, escaping from the distasteful materialism of the ancestral textile mills, should sound the faery horn which claimed biography as a realm of romance. *Ariel* (a tricksy, airy name) the horn was called, and if it suggests romance less solid and four-square than the horn of Roland at Roncesvalles, it promises a lively ease and brilliant color in the moving air. It is a dream-world in which this new biography is to dwell, *Mape: The Land of Illusion* (in the original *Meipe, ou la Délivrance*), a world where Monsieur Maurois is liberated from the trammels of the everyday and commonplace, free from the choking lint of the textile mills, a world of dashing action and exciting thought, where all the periods of mechanized routine or boredom may be passed over rapidly in a few paragraphs. It is a world of release in which the biographer imagines himself successively as Shelley, as Byron, as Disraeli, or the young Goethe, personalities chosen 'in order to respond to a secret need in [the author's] own nature.'

Romantic escape, subjectivity: these are the two keynotes of Maurois's biography. But it must not be imagined that these mean complete irresponsibility. For although Maurois explores his subjects by imagining himself in the same experiences, they are selected by that secret need that makes them all in some wise masks, projections, avatars of what in other circumstances the author feels that he might have been himself. It will be noticed that his main figures—Shelley, all air, fire, and crystal; Disraeli, dandy, exquisite, wit, and poseur; Byron, despiser, cant-hater, aristocrat, lover of freedom—are all rebels, iconoclasts, daring in act, spectacular in gesture, ardent in imagination. Even Voltaire, for all his dry and cynical sanity, is a romantic figure, from the time when he learns to handle the rapier as a young man, in order to challenge the great Chévalier de Rohan, to when, as a wizened, mercenary, hypochondriacal, and yet somehow heroic old one, he defies Frederick the Great. This flamboyance, whether caught in the clear, almost gemlike flame of Shelley, or in the more sulphurous gust of Byron, and this Rostand-world of moonlight and rhodomontade, of irony, tableaux, poetry—these are Maurois's favorite rôles and scenes, and as long as he chooses subjects that are appropriate he plays them with verve.

But his carefulness goes further than choosing subjects in which he can merge himself. Although his aim is an illusion of reality, Maurois will not deceive the reader, at least not within the limits of his purpose. He is giving a sincere portrait of his subject, as he honestly believes him to be, and he has taken pains to ensure that the portrait is complete and in the round. Although he reworks the material freely in imagination, Maurois uses all the sources available to obtain his picture, and his life of *Byron* supplies detailed documentation of exhaustive research. His narrative goes contrary to no established fact, and omits no significant ones. All his details are veracious; not one is without its source in letter or picture or memoir. His work is a mosaic of the original sources, selected by an ordering sense of values, and developed with enhanced color and shading by a re-creative imagination.

Conscientiously as Maurois tries to adhere to the spirit, however, he takes daring liberties with the letter. He does not hesitate to assume an identity between an author and whatever seem to be autobiographic traits in his writings; he does not hesitate to give us soliloquy and dialogue representing what may indeed, for all we know, have been the birth of sentiments that later found their way into letter or poem.

Thus the *Epipsychidion* which Shelley declared 'an idealized history of my life and feelings' is combined with a few hints in letters and reminiscences to provide a lucid narrative of Shelley's emotional history; and acting on Shelley's confession that it is 'not easy for spirits cased in flesh and blood to avoid . . . seeking in a mortal image the likeness of what is, perhaps, eternal,' Maurois makes an amorous romance of Shelley's relations with Emilia Viviani. Again, Maurois shows us Goethe turning over in his mind the new-born idea of writing a Faust: 'Mine would be a greater character—a kind of Prometheus. Defeated by the gods, if you like, but at least because he tried to snatch their secret from them.' Shortly after, he is thinking of deserting pretty Frédérique Brion, trying in his mind to find sophistical excuses for his inconstancy, and then sweeping them away in a gust of ruthless and Nietzschean honesty. 'At this moment he imagined Frédérique in tears by the roadside and himself riding away, his head bent, not daring to look back. "What a scene for *Faust*," he thought.'

Such is Maurois's method. The leit-motiv, so to speak, of every one of these episodes is to be found somewhere, in a phrase of *Epipsychidion*, a letter to Gisborne, a page of Lewes's biography of Goethe, or an inference from *Werther*, but all have been melted down in the alembic of the imagination and poured out in a new mold, brilliant, sharply defined, full of light and shade. We must not imagine that an author necessarily transfers either real people or real events literally to his pages. Werther, Charlotte, and Albert, are not Goethe, Charlotte Buff, and his friend Kestner: 'Werther was Goethe if he had not been an artist. Albert was a slightly meaner Kestner, endowed with Brentano's jealousy and with Goethe's own intellectual powers. Charlotte was Lotte, but brought up by Frau de la Roche, and a reader of Rousseau and Klopstock.'

Nor is the use of inference from novel or poem illegitimate. Naturally our ideas of the character of a Shelley, a Dickens, a Goethe, is derived in part from his writings. The dangerous assumption is that even a modification of any scenes or reflections therein ever occurred as an acted event or as an emotion having a personal bearing. As soon as we find the author proceeding on such an assumption, we find ourselves breathing the air of romance, which has its own exhilaration but is not the air of biography. There is a gain in a certain style of vividness and immediacy, but a loss in biographical authority, for a crucial part of biography's effect is our assurance that it is all factually true. That authoritativeness vanishes as soon as we discover a significant episode portrayed as fact that could not possibly be known as fact.

It is not the use of imagination that is the error. Every biographer must use imagination. It is the violation of a subtle compact tacitly underlying the biographer's relation to his reader. That compact is that the biographer is to use his imagination in the creative synthesis of character but not in the invention of material. If he fills in events imaginatively they must be either frankly presented as such or of a kind that the reader will not even have to be told are hypothetical. They must never puzzle the reader as to their character. But unless we have read a great deal about Shelley, we do not know that he may not later have told someone the episodes that Maurois invents; unless we have read much about Goethe we are not sure that he did not positively *say* that the characters in *Werther* were founded on actuality in the way Maurois outlines. We are left uncertain what is fact and what is invented. Even if we feel confident that the drawing of the character is sound, it is irritating not to be able to tell the fictitious strokes from the historic ones. And thus biographical authoritativeness is broken.

It is only fair to say that Maurois, like nearly all really able biographical writers, relies less upon romanticized methods in his later books than in his earlier ones. *Ariel* (1923) and *Mape* (1926) are the volumes in which it runs riot. Although the author silenced most of the adverse critics who doubted his command of facts by giving his sources for every important statement made in *Ariel*, he perhaps felt himself the force of the objections outlined above, for in *Disraeli* (1927) he considerably diminished his use of the more unblushing fictional methods, and in *Byron* (1930) he supplied a full apparatus of scholarship and refrained carefully from all except minor and reasonably legitimate inventions. These volumes gain a great deal in strength as a result, without losing the valuable qualities of imaginative insight, limpid style, and colorful narration that were revealed in his earlier writings.

Nevertheless a certain unreal heightening his work always retains. In his earliest biographical effort he took the remote and almost inhuman benevolence of Shelley, with his other-worldly gentleness and his beautiful angelic anger at all cruelties, and then rendered that character in the even more highly colored and unreal though vivid medium of romance. The same impulse lies behind all the others. Existence is to be keyed to a clearer, more piercing air; life is to be higher, lower, more aromatic, more musical, more ironic, more sensational than the levels of ordinary mundane affairs. Therefore, as we have seen, Maurois chooses glamorous figures who can be portrayed with the grand gesture; lives selected adroitly for their drama and symmetry, for their ability to be handled with a certain theatrical élan and charm. Maurois has more restraint and tact than the nineteeth century romantics; he refrains from the grandiosity of a Victor Hugo or the splashing color of a Gautier, but there is for all that an *operatic* quality in his style, as if *Hernani* had been crossed with the more nostalgic appeal of *La Bohème*.

These romantic harmonies are never far removed from the 'secret need' that Maurois's theory of biography openly avows. Their appropriateness and the reasons for their choice lie in their capacity for being easily seen as a work of romantic art. Each of the careers he narrates has a natural and readily discernible symmetry of its own. Each has a certain bohemianism standing out picturesquely against the grey of a more prosaic world. Each has a semi-Quixotic attitude of defiance. But they compose so easily within this formula that we feel in it a progressive shallowness, and we pursue it with lessening conviction from Shelley to Disraeli, from Disraeli to Byron, and from Byron to Voltaire.

In *Ariel*, despite the romanticized method, there was a deep and sincere effort at penetration and fusion which is echoed in *Disraeli*; but even the more sober handling of sources in *Byron* does not convince us that the insight has not grown more superficial. Maurois has there achieved only a surface identity with his subject. The acts are the acts of Byron, but the stage-settings are the stage-settings we have seen before, the interpretations are somehow ventriloquial, and the voice is the voice of Maurois. Instead of piercing, as a great biographer must, into the characters of men profoundly different from himself, imagining himself genuinely involved in their lives and subjected to the influences that molded them, Maurois does only the far easier task of imagining himself enacting the events of their lives and their characters as his. It is the reason that his power over critical readers diminishes with each book they read.

Comparatively few British authors have gone very far in emulating the romanticized treatment of biography, but many have shown tinges of its influence. It colors with a florid and glowing tapestry of Renaissance magnificence, a flaring opulence of description, and a self-conscious brilliance of epithet, all the intricate historical investigation out of which Francis Hackett reconstructed the heavy pageantry of his *Henry VIII*. It suffuses with a deep and pure-hued romanticism the story of Lytton Strachey's *Elizabeth and Essex*, and emerges even in the concluding phrases of *Queen Victoria* where the author imagines the fading memories in the mind of the dying Queen: 'Osborne, so full of primroses . . . and Albert's face under the green lamp, . . . and Lord M. dreaming at Windsor with the rooks cawing in the elm-trees . . . and Lehzen with the globes . . . and a great old repeater-watch of her father's in its tortoise-shell-case, and a yellow rug, and some friendly flounces of sprigged muslin, and the trees and grass at Kensington.'

The Deeper Springs

The romantic method, however, becomes the inner spirit of Van Wyck Brooks's *Life of Emerson*. It hints itself in the opening sentence, 'Miss Mary Moody Emerson lived in her shroud,' and it illumines the treatment of the whole: '. . . in her passionate prayers, in her visions of the dying bed that would some day reflect lustre on her darkest fate, she apostrophized Eternity. No deceitful promises there, no fantastic illusions. No riddles concealed by the shrouds of loitering Time! None of Time's Arachnean webs, which decoy and destroy.'

We are taken within the inner consciousness of the small boy: 'He felt as if any whipper-snapper could eat him whole. What boy, what gossiping girl, could not daunt and tether him, out-state and pull him down and leave him rolling in the dust?' And then, 'What was the meaning of these gleams and premonitions, this dancing chorus of hopes and visions that hovered before him? Intimations, suggestions of what? Tantalizing, unpossessed! Yesterday he felt like a doctor; today, a dunce. Of one thing alone he was certain: He lived in a world of marvels.' The same note is sounded again and again; as here of Emerson the mature man: 'Pathetic, he felt, these graceful trees, rooted there, so patient and helpless, would-be men, creatures, by a feebler effort, of the soul that had made himself, with their long boughs and drooping leaves weeping their strait imprisonment.'

We realize gradually, through the slow sensuous melody of the narrative, with its heaped-up luxury of description, that it is not the outer life of Emerson that Mr Brooks is trying to tell us, but the essence of the man revealed in a lifelong inner monologue, a poetic rendering of the spiritual experience out of which Emerson's achievement took form. Travel-notes of the outer life, as it were, we are given, but the emphasis is all on the inner consciousness, as if a spirit voice were whispering its passionate commentary on a pageant less real than itself.

As Mr Brooks handles it, there is nothing that is wrong and much that is beautiful in such a method. No reader could imagine that Brooks was inspired with well-nigh continuous insight into the flux of Emerson's awarenesses, and therefore his aim reveals itself clearly as a heightened and poetic interpretation of a noble character. There is no deception; it is now a pastoral, now an ode or rhapsody, on Ralph Waldo Emerson, following a pattern woven by his life. But although not wrong, the method has certain dangers. The sensuous richness moves a little slowly with all its imagery; there is in the end some monotony in the inward vision. Slowness and sameness immerse the narrative in a haze where the clearness of details is swallowed and lost; everything becomes dim and dreamy.

At last the heightening that once stimulated becomes an opiate, and the intended effect is drowned in too much sweet.

The romantic method so heightened into poetry, however, is not the approach to biography by which Mr Brooks has attained the position he holds among contemporary writers. Prevailingly he has been critical and analytic; he has chosen not merely to present but to demonstrate. Attacking the problem of a man's artistic career, he has asked himself what principles and what crucial facts can explain the peculiar curve traced by this sensibility. He has tried to track down the hidden causes of individual achievement or failure. In so doing, he has been obliged to explore both the social milieu in which the artist moves and the way that milieu imposes itself on his personality. He has made himself a kind of detective of the human heart.

In his two outstanding studies—*The Ordeal of Mark Twain* and *The Pilgrimage of Henry James*—Mr Brooks's exploration presents itself almost entirely as a problem. How are we to explain what many people feel to be the progressive desiccation of Henry James's later novels, their thinning of substance beneath an ever increasing elaboration and intricately spun refinement of handling? How are we to reconcile the tremendous gusto and titanic fertility of Mark Twain's fancy with the slightness of his literary achievement? and the bitterness of his private misanthropy and pessimism with the genial and radiant sunniness of his unbounded vitality? Such are the questions Mr Brooks poses. To each he propounds an answer, and his books are the extended and brilliantly worked-out demonstrations of his thesis.

It may be worth while to examine his method in the case of Mark Twain, all the more because his results have in recent years been violently called into question. To his own contemporaries there was no doubt that Mark Twain was a great literary artist. Kipling called him 'the great and godlike Clemens,' Howells said he was 'the Lincoln of our literature,' Brander Matthews compared him with Cervantes, Bernard Shaw said that America had produced just two geniuses, Poe and Clemens, and declared that the future historian of America would find his works as indispensable 'as a French historian finds the political tracts of Voltaire.'

In our own day similar pronouncements have been made about him. To John Macy he is 'a powerful, original thinker,' to H. L.

Mencken 'a great artist' comparable to 'the great artists of the Renaissance.'

But if we try to check these ovations against his performance, what do we find? Two books that with all their faults are indeed works of genius, *Tom Sawyer* and *Huckleberry Finn*, the mordant savageness of *The Man That Corrupted Hadleyburg*, and some of *Life on the Mississippi*. And this is embedded in masses of cheap journalism, in hackwork like *A Double-Barrelled Detective Story*, in crude slapstick like *Innocents Abroad*, in sentimental chromos like *Joan of Arc*, in shoals of dreary and sophomoric humor.

How, with so little achieved and so much that was bad, did Mark Twain manage to impress himself as a figure of magnificent power? Mr Brooks's answer is that he had the power, but that it was dispersed, frustrated, and never put to its proper use. In a vague way, he claims, Mark Twain himself realized this. He had come into the world, he said, with Halley's comet; it would be a disappointment to him if he didn't go out with it. 'Why am I like the Pacific Ocean?' he asked; the answer was, 'I don't know; I was just looking for information.' The joke is significant in suggesting a sense of colossal force combined with uncertainty and doubt.

And at the same time that, even jestingly, he makes these grandiose comparisons, he is filled with self-scorn. 'Byron despised the race because he despised himself. I feel as Byron did and for the same reason.' When he read *Romola*, the only thing that hit him 'with force' was Tito's compromise with his conscience. 'Be weak, be water, be characterless, be cheaply persuadable,' was, he said, God's first command to a human being, and the only one he would never be able to disobey. Under 'a cheerful exterior I have got a spirit that is angry with me and gives me freely of its contempt.' He reached his seventieth birthday with relief; it was 'the scriptural statute of limitations—you have served your term . . . and you are mustered out.'

His profound sense of failure found comfort in the mechanistic philosophy of *What is Man?* 'You and I are but sewing-machines,' he says; and 'Man originates nothing, not even a thought.' How, if destiny had made him a sewing-machine, could he be blamed 'for not turning out Gobelins?' But deep down the despair rankled. The 'one talent it is death to hide' had been thwarted. It turned his enormous vitality into a curse, so that he fled from loneliness to immoderately protracted hours at billiards, anything, so that he might have companionship and not be alone; it poisoned his natural heartiness and cheerfulness with self-reproach; it destroyed the meaning of life and 'overspread in a gloomy vapor the mind it had never quite been able to possess.'

In order to understand how this could come to be, we must turn to Mark Twain's childhood. He was a fragile and sensitive child, 'high-strung and neurotic,' walking in his sleep at four, when one of his sisters was dying, and found, his eyes shut, 'fretting with cold in some dark corner.' Subject also to sudden ecstasies, 'venting his emotions in a series of leaps and shrieks and somersaults, and spasms of laughter as he lay rolling in the grass.'

His mother was the dominant figure in the family, 'the handsomest girl and the wittiest, as well as the best dancer in all Kentucky,' and still able to dance at eighty; energetic, strong-willed, emotional, ambitious, ruled by a stern Calvinistic conscience. Her feelings had turned away from that 'poor, taciturn, sunstruck failure,' her husband, and rooted themselves in her children. She ruled them by storm and tenderness. They must retrieve their father's failure, recover the lost gentility of the family, achieve wealth and good fame.

Over his father's dead body she impressed her demands upon the sobbing boy. He must promise 'not to break her heart.' And the little boy sobs, 'Anything!' Not to break her heart, 'he is not to quarrel heedlessly with his bread and butter, he is to keep strictly within the code, to remember the maxims of Ben Franklin, to respect all the prejudices and all the conventions . . . Hide your faces, Huck and Tom!' Mr Brooks exclaims, 'Put away childish things, Sam Clemens; go forth into the world, but remain always a child, your mother's child!'

The artist must conform to the patterns of a crude pioneer society, rapaciously acquisitive; the individualist must fit into the machine of materialism. Not to break his mother's heart he must deny or mutilate that one talent it is death to hide. The nation was bent on material conquest, the West was being opened up, it had no time for art and such-like frills. Success was making money. It took a smart man to do that, and if you were a smart man you didn't need to be much else. If you were not a smart man, and didn't make money, nothing else that was added to you availed.

The boy grew up, and for a brief interlude in his young manhood he seemed able to make the best of both worlds. He became a river pilot. It was a career that ideally combined the prestige of acknowledged success with the delights of independence, craftsmanship, glamor. The pilot alone was justified in not becoming a jack-of-all-trades, his expert skill was necessary. His life was glittering and lordly. He was an artist among pioneers. But it was not to last. 'The Civil War, with its blockade of the Mississippi, put an end forever to the glories of the old river traffic.'

Thrown out of this paradise, Mark Twain gravitated to the Nevada goldfields. But his ambition had turned sick within him. He was reckless, on a down grade, broken in pride. On the river a dandy in fancy percales and patent leathers, in the West he became even more aggressively a roughneck than any of his fellows, with rusty slouch hat and trousers slopping half in and half out of heavy cowhide boots. And as a miner he failed. He solved his dilemma by becoming a humorist. Humor enabled him to accept without hatred the slipshod environment, and humor was the only form of art a pioneer society would respect. But even when he had become a success he revolted against the fate he had chosen, and after a public reading he once groaned aloud, 'I am demeaning myself—I am allowing myself to be a mere buffoon.'

The maxims of Benjamin Franklin still held, however; he must not break his mother's heart. The golden stream of tangible approval flowed in upon the humorist, and the artist's conscience was compromised that he might not quarrel heedlessly with the prejudices and the conventions.

William Dean Howells became his mentor, and taught him decorum by a stringent censorship. After his marriage, his wife redoubled the discipline, upbraiding his low tastes and subduing his genius to the pruderies of small-town culture. When he was writing *Following the Equator* she made him delete from his manuscript such vulgar words as stench, breech-clout, and offal. She greatly preferred the romantic mediævalism of *The Prince and the Pauper* to the earthy vigor of *Huckleberry Finn.* When, in Rome, he made an irreverent joke about the old masters, 'Youth,' she said gravely, 'if you do not care for these masterpieces yourself, you might at least consider the feelings of others.' And why, Mr Brooks asks, 'did she habitually call him "Youth?" Was it not from an instinctive sense that her power lay in keeping him a child, in asserting that maternal attitude which he could never resist? He had indeed found a second mother now . . .'

Mark Twain compromised and yielded. He hated corruption and hypocrisy, he hated cruelty and oppression, he longed to destroy the 'silent, colossal National Lie that is the support and confederate of all the tyrannies and shams and inequalities and unfairnesses that afflict the peoples.' To attempt that he must be bold, he must call the ignoble thing by its name. He must risk being accused of ingratitude and bad taste. He must risk loss of the golden badge of success.

'Let us be judicious and let someone else begin,' Mark Twain said. 'We write frankly and fearlessly, but then we "modify" before we print.'

'Shades of Tolstoy and Thomas Carlyle, of Nietzsche and Ibsen and Whitman,' Mr Brooks exclaims, 'did you ever hear such words on the lips of a famous confrère? . . . Look with pity, then, out of your immortal calm, upon this poor frustrated child whom nature had destined to become your peer . . .'

He was vanquished within, but his self-scorn left him no peace. Supremely healthy of body, he became a hypochondriac of the heart. Buoyant by temperament, full of animal spirits and laughter, he lashed himself with repining and contempt. Warm and loving in disposition, he came to abhor 'the damned mangy human race.' 'Byron despised the race because he despised himself. I feel as Byron did and for the same reason.'

Such is the explanation Mr Brooks gives to Mark Twain's character. It is documented with copious quotation, developed with dramatic skill, reinforced by a penetrating application of the methods of psychoanalysis.

Is it true? Distinguished authorities have doubted or denied it, or explained it. 'Subtle and learned critics in their metropolitan isolation,' writes Ludwig Lewisohn, 'have projected upon Mark Twain their problems and aspirations. I gravely doubt whether he underwent any ordeal . . . Nor do I believe that he was frustrated by the influences in his life that he loved and honored most deeply.'

And Bernard De Voto, author of *Mark Twain's America*, denies the thesis categorically. He insists that Mark Twain 'was an artist who expressed the richness of his soul unhampered by the pruderies, repressions, and mendacities alleged to have been inflicted on him.' He affirms that both his boyhood and his creative years 'were spent in an environment that enabled him to make the most of his talent.' He claims that he needed and benefited from the censorships to which he was exposed. He is not impressed by the fullness of quotation that Mr Brooks musters in support of his thesis, for Mark Twain, he says, was not a consistent or profound thinker, but a writer whose emotions were always on the trigger; his pronouncements are so various 'that any critic may select and arrange them to suit his own prejudices.' By judicious choice, he goes on, it would be possible to assemble hundreds of quotations proving Mark Twain an art-for-art's-sake aesthete, a Left Bank expatriate, and a Marxian.

And yet, although this last objection is a powerful one, does Mr De Voto really destroy Mr Brooks's thesis? In all the protean changes of Mark Twain's sentiments is there no prevailing tone? And is that prevailing tone the tolerant skepticism of Montaigne, the earthy laughter of Rabelais, or the dreadful bitterness of Swift? Even in the harum-scarum *Huck Finn* we have the withering scorn of Colonel Sherburn taunting the mob; and with the years, in *The Man That Corrupted Hadleyburg*, in *What is Man?* in *The Mysterious Stranger*, in angry letters, that corrosive hate grows ever deeper. And if Mark Twain as an artist expressed the richness of his soul unhampered, when we survey the bulk of feeble, adolescent, and journalistic work in it we find it difficult to regard him as the titanic creative force that led people to compare him to Rabelais, to Cervantes, to Shakespeare.

That he achieved greatness is undeniable, but surely few men ever achieved greatness so fragmentary, so well-nigh buried in failure.

If he was a balanced, healthy soul vigorously fruitful and unhampered, all that dross and slag, so incommensurable with his best, is almost unexplainable. If the pioneer society of his boyhood and youth and the acquisitive society in which he spent his creative years were singularly favorable for his work, it is strange that that work was so uneven and that the same environment gave birth to no galaxy of writers glorying in the pioneer school. Strong as the objections may be to many parts of Mr Brooks's thesis, their cumulative effect is hard to overcome. *The Ordeal of Mark Twain* is a notable work of biographical interpretation, and a notable analysis of America after the Civil War.

Wit in the Archives

In Mr Brooks the biographer is sometimes overshadowed by the critic and often tinged with the social historian. Of Philip Guedalla it is hard to say whether he is a historian disguised in the dramatic garb of the biographer or a biographer wearing the toga of the historian. Are *The Hundred Days* and *The Second Empire* biographical, or are they historical narratives of the times that give them their titles, and merely oriented around the first and third Napoleons? *Palmerston*, *Gladstone and Palmerston*, *The Queen and Mr Gladstone*, and *Wellington*—these are obviously biographical, and yet they are all concerned with political figures, and often more with their public, official careers than with their personal and inward characters. *Fathers of the Revolution* is tied together by nothing more intimate than the fact that all its subjects had a hand (even if, like George III and Cornwallis, an unwilling one) in the birth of the American nation.

The uncertainty of classification is not accidental. To Mr Guedalla biography is only an annex in the great house of archives which is history, a sitting-room, as it were, in a huge public structure, where the experts can relax in front of the fire sipping their tea and enjoying a little departmental gossip, exchanging some mildly scandalous and if possible witty personalities. 'A branch of history devoted to the reconstruction of personal careers,' he has called it, and the careers he has chosen to trace are mostly ones that have marched across the European political stage. It would be carping to quarrel either with the definition or the merging of realms in themselves. But as a biographer Mr Guedalla is, unfortunately, a historian who is not enough of a historian; and as a historian he is a biographer who is not sufficiently serious about the demands of biography.

His use of history is for pageantry and display. He tries neither to reveal any of the deep essential forces animating all the seeming disorder of events nor to demonstrate how historical figures were the spokesmen or instruments of such forces. Instead we have wily —or usually, in Guedalla's rendering, not so wily—diplomats moving pieces on the chessboard of European weltpolitik with hardly any indication that this is not a game dictated solely by personal ambition or amusement. Grand old men pilot the ship of state through a narrow passage with magnificent nerve; shabby pseudo-Sphinxian adventurers fumble with their moustaches and their instruments of diplomacy and drift toward disaster. In the background a chorus of Walpoles, Creeveys, Grevilles, Crokers, and Lievens grows angry and gesticulates or sneers and titters at the scene, and brilliantly uniformed armies move across a chromo landscape from ballet into melodrama.

If Guedalla's history is mainly spectacular, doing little to give clarity or depth to his interpretations of character, these interpretations in turn are hardly any more revealing than Carlylean hero-worship in enabling us to understand how certain personalities came to play such dominating rôles in their times. Even less so, in some ways, for Carlyle does try to present his Cromwells and Fredericks as really heroic, whereas Guedalla is fond of deriding or patronizing his subjects, emphasizing their blunders and their confusion of mind.

He does not try to penetrate into the core of a man's character. Thereby he leaves a Napoleon III, for example, as vague a figure as he finds him. We do not know whether to regard him as machiavellian schemer or muddled gambler at last betrayed by destiny, as callous and cynical buccaneer or savior of society in his own fantasy. The Napoleonic legend, the Prince's belief in his star, his fatalism, his capacity for waiting and for silence, a few such things Guedalla throws out as gestures of explanation, but leaves us uncertain whether we have been following the life of a cold careerist or a man self-deceived, or some subtle mingling of the two.

With simpler, less ambiguous characters, like Palmerston, he is more successful, but even here he gives no picture of the man as an expression of his age. 'The last candle of the Eighteenth Century' is Guedalla's formula for him: but why should a man born in 1784, educated at Harrow and Cambridge, a contemporary of Peel and Grey, of Cobbett and Russell, have proved to be any more characteristically than they a product of the eighteenth century, not flickering out until 1865? The truth is that such devices as 'the last of the Eighteenth Century' represent less a principle of explanation than a trick of rhetoric; when he describes the burial of George III, in a different book, he employs it again: 'on that winter night in 1820 they were burying the Eighteenth Century.'

In spite of these manifest defects as a historian and as a psychologist, Mr Guedalla has been much read and admired. His narratives move rapidly and colorfully through scenes of dramatic action. If his interpretations of events are neither very deep nor very philosophic, his acquaintance with facts is complete and carefully documented; he presents us with a great body of clearly marshaled information. Speed, assurance, and dexterity of handling are introduced among complex circumstances, so that we add large bulks of historical events to our knowledge with a minimum of difficulty. If his portrayals of character are superficial, they are rushed along on a broad stream of steady and vigorous movement and lighted by the fireworks of a glittering wit that invites the reader to share its olympianism. In such a heady atmosphere it is very tempting for the reader also to take a seat on the heights and sneer at these silly mortals whom it is hardly worthwhile to understand.

And Mr Guedalla's wit *is* genuine. Of Palmerston's tactics in the Foreign Office, he remarks 'the *fait accompli* was his favorite argument, tending to make unwilling captives rather than loyal adherents.' When, in 1833, flights of German princes for the first time 'succumbed to sudden cravings for a sight of England,' Guedalla words it, so that Palmerston opined drily that 'Princess Victoria is hardly old enough as yet to make it worth their while,' the wit of the author reinforces that of the Foreign Secretary. And there is a flash of wicked comment in regard to Queen Victoria's dazzled admiration for the Emperor of the French: 'But then Napoleon was a gentleman, and amongst her equals the Queen had met little except royalty.'

Too often, however, this wit becomes intrusive, and instead of illumining the subject deflects attention to the author. When 'shy steam-engines' drive 'infrequent mills in sylvan Lancashire' the epithets do not focus our attention on the 'uncomfortable and remote beginnings of the modern world.' When we are told that Palmerston was 'rarely tortured by the speculations which drove his contemporaries to doubt, to test-tubes, or to Rome,' our minds are more taken by the slick art of compression involved than by the struggles of the nineteenth century conscience. The statement that at Almack's 'a stylish company leaned out from the gold bar of this social Heaven' is intended less to describe the scene than to shock us by the unexpected application of Rossetti's words.

And again and again there is an air of patronage that finally becomes insufferable. Napoleon's plan of war in 1859 was 'a perfect Empire piece': 'It ignored completely the unauthorized invention of railroads'; but, employed against an even more archaic enemy, it defeated 'with the methods of 1809 an adversary whose military thought was that of 1759.' Of the complexities of the Schleswig-Holstein question: 'Lord Palmerston, although still capable of a stirring speech upon it, had forgotten the point.' Of Palmerston's attending a course of lectures given by Guizot on the Progress of Civilization: 'We sometimes underrate the fortitude of earlier generations.' This is gratuitously patronizing; Mr Guedalla gives no *reason* for believing that it was any harder to listen to Guizot than it would be to listen to Professor Harold Laski. Finally, a witticism that is not only exhibitionistic but in poor taste: 'That autumn Mr Huskisson, always progressive, fell under a train.' Nothing in the context calls for making a joke out of a painful death.

Now, not only is a great deal of Guedalla's wit in this way designed to attract attention to the brilliance of the author, but many other features of his style have the same purpose. Again and again the choice of epithets lets us realize that he has been everywhere and seen everything. Does a minor part of his action take place in Spain, 'the heaped cupolas of Salamanca,' and 'the big, bare hills of Torres Vedras' will tell us that Guedalla knows the landscape well; and if Louis Napoleon be exiled to America the fact that New York is unguarded by 'the menacing gesture of colossal statuary' and has 'a skyline not yet serrated by the spectacular application of steel construction to architecture' will sing his familiarity with the scene of its harbor.

His Cecil de Mille technique of 'filling his panoramas with people and events contemporary with, but not related to,' his main subject has been defended as useful 'orientation' for the reader; but a brief examination of how he employs such allusions will demonstrate that they too are mainly for display rather than background. Describing the world into which Palmerston was born he writes, 'The Prince, in the first flush of that manly beauty which had so long, so golden, so positively Turneresque a sunset, was at the feet of a plump young widow from Richmond, whose religious opinions were in alarming conflict with the Act of Settlement.' If we do not already know what sort of figure George IV had in his later years, nor know that Mrs Fitzherbert, his inamorata, was a Roman Catholic, these words darken understanding instead of clarifying the scene.

Unless we are familiar with Sir Joshua Reynolds's painting of Mrs Siddons as the Tragic Muse, Guedalla's statement that she was sitting to him 'in the most becoming green and brown of the most imposing Muse that ever strayed from Helicon into the studio of a president of the Royal Academy' will serve merely to remind us that Mr Guedalla is a very cultured gentleman. Unless we not merely know that Madame de Staël was the daughter of Necker, but know as well what sort of lady she was, we will not be enlightened by the information that Gibbon 'was walking on his terrace with the accomplished, if voluble, daughter of M. Necker.'

Such flowers of rhetoric are merely ostentatious. Worse than these, Mr Guedalla often has a positive delight in allusive indirection in his narrative. A whole such series deals with the downfall of Napoleon. 'A closed carriage drove down the long road to Fréjus; a cruiser sailed for Elba . . .' After Waterloo, 'Far to the south a white face stared at Paris, stared at the flowers at Malmaison, stared at the sea . . .' 'Peace dawned . . . and the sails of a tall ship gleamed faintlier, as the *Northumberland* went down a sunlit avenue into the South Atlantic.' And, at last, 'South of the Line . . . a black island stood up out of a leaden sea.'

The same determination to impress his own brilliance upon the reader accounts for the persistence with which Mr Guedalla uses the language of irony for no justifiable purpose. 'They named the baby Henry John—Henry after his father, and John as a pure flight of fancy.' The first letter that Palmerston signed as Secretary at War 'dealt, without undue originality, with the topic of regimental accounts.' But why in Heaven's name should one's first official letter be upon an entirely original subject? 'That month the Queen succumbed to Albert's fatal beauty . . .' In Cheyne Row, in 1844, 'Mr Carlyle struggled with Cromwell, the eternal truths, and the piano practice (no less eternal) of the young lady next door.' In all these quotations Mr Guedalla suggests derogation that no possible interpretation of the facts he presents will bear out.

Even his serious handling of his themes suffers from ostentation and melodrama. The armies and generals he uses so often are always 'fumbling' for their foes or making 'slow lunges' across the countryside; it is always 'without enthusiasm' that they experience a reverse. He is too greatly addicted to a species of cryptical foreshadowing like a sorcerer making gloomy predictions. Napoleon is introduced to a gentleman named Changarnier 'whom he was to know better.' During the Kabyle war, 'somewhere in the shadow there was (the names are growing ominous) a Colonel François Bazaine.' In 'the clear dawn of the second Empire' Benedetti is a 'little Figure which was to cast so long a shadow as the evening sun went down over Ems.'

The use of the pathetic fallacy, which is hinted in the preceding quotation, becomes a consistent vice of *The Second Empire*. There is the 'clear dawn' and the 'gaslit tragedy of the Empire'; there is its high noon; and at last its autumn and sunset (the two images are used indiscriminately). 'As the shouting died away and the last flags hung limply on the autumn air in the Exhibition grounds, Napoleon was left alone again with his problems.' 'The sky was dull over Paris when the Emperor left St Cloud. There was a hint of thunder in the air, and a few early leaves had fallen.' The season was July, but we are not spared those symbolic early leaves, and the use of the thunder (a hint of it) is relentless. But whether the Emperor is being left alone with his problems, which the crowds had very chummily gathered around and helped him with until the Exhibition was over, or whether sunset is coming on with a sky that is dark and overcast, or whether the Eighteenth Century is expiring—sometimes with George III in 1820 or sometimes lingering on with Palmerston until 1865—it is clear that such use of symbolism and metaphor is no genuine recreation of scene or mood or fate, but merely a cliché.

Mr Guedalla might have been twice as good a biographer had he been only half as witty. For all his cleverness, his industry, his scholarship, his ransacking of archives, his clarity, and his vigor, he has never really written either good biography or good history, because, although he can digest enormous mountains of facts, he never finds in them anything except the man he seeks there. All his writings represent talent misapplied, and are nothing but a platform for a personal monologue. Only if he some day ceases to regard the face of history as a glass may his striking capacities no longer be wasted. As it is, they have produced a series of books the attractions of which are meretricious, and which warrant this degree of examination only because they have been the examples to a whole school of self-regarding biographies even more completely specious.

ART AND IRONY

XVIII

ART AND IRONY

Declaration of Independence

BOTH the debunkers and the romanticizers insistently directed at least part of their efforts to being interesting and exciting. However ill-judged some of their methods, this aim is an evidence of a praiseworthy if rather dim artistic purpose. The fact that we can think of their purpose as artistic in any degree explains their significance in modern biography. There have always, of course, been biographies that were works of art, and biographers who so approached them, and critics who so regarded them. But biography, in general, used to be relegated in general, even by most of its practitioners, to a position of assumed inferiority.

It was the Cinderella of letters, overawed by the grandeur of its lofty sisters drama and poetry, and even elbowed into insignificance by that glittering upstart, the novel. Like historians and philosophers, biographers were not expected to be literary artists; there was a certain surprise when a historian, like Macaulay, or a philosopher, like James or Bergson, proved supremely readable. Mostly the biographer, a mere journeyman of letters, was expected to display no more than a rather stodgy and plodding adherence to fact.

The great biographies of the past were regarded as giants. They were rare and exceptional beings having nothing to do with ordinary human stature and expectations. The occasional triumph thrown up in one's own time by a Froude or a Gosse was a lusus naturae, sometimes shocking rather than praiseworthy. Suddenly, in 1918, Lytton Strachey's *Eminent Victorians* changed all this. Almost overnight biography as a literary art became an exciting idea among readers. The brief preface which Mr Strachey wrote to his four studies became a kind of critical credo, an oriflamme and a rallying-cry for a horde of biographers who, as it were, had just had their chains struck from their limbs.

The circumstances giving special force to Strachey's pronouncements were, some of them, a little extraneous to art. But Strachey was a literary artist, and the prestige created by his wit and his lethal handling of the past gave authority to the clear and concise statement of his biographical aims. They were, first, 'through the medium of biography, to present some Victorian visions to the modern eye.' In the four lives of his *Eminent Victorians* he was trying to achieve not 'a *précis* of the truth about the Victorian age, for the shortest *précis* must fill innumerable volumes,' but at least 'certain fragments of the truth.' Part of the meaning of biography for Strachey, then, lies in its power to illustrate the spirit of an age by those 'fragments of the truth' which are embodied in the concrete lives of individuals.

Not its entire meaning, however. 'Human beings are too important to be treated as mere symptoms of the past.' They must be portrayed for their own sakes as well. And in order that they may be *portrayed*–realized, vividly and clearly and colorfully–we must eschew the example of the official biographies, with 'their lamentable lack of selection, of detachment, of design.' Instead of 'ill-digested masses of material' there must be a 'brevity which excludes everything that is redundant and nothing that is significant.' Instead of their 'tone of tedious panegyric,' the biographer must maintain 'his own freedom of spirit' and 'lay bare the facts of the case as he understands them'–'dispassionately, impartially, and without ulterior intentions.'

It was a Declaration of Independence for biographers which,

unlike Froude's defense of himself, was enthusiastically received by everyone. People were tired of reticence and respectability, and while they were thus joyfully knocking the bottom out from under their inhibitions, a sound statement of the aims of biography for the first time found a wide acceptance. Those aims have mostly been striven for since with less art than freedom, and freedom from tedious panegyric has carelessly been interpreted by many as freedom for billingsgate. Even so, the effect for true biography has been far more healthful than enforced secrecy, discretion, and hidden unmentionables.

Strachey's emphasis, above all, on art—on compression, on interpretation, on rigorous self-criticism, on style—has been germinal. More than ever before, the biographer today is aware that he is composing a work of art, arranging, ordering, emphasizing, subduing; not just flinging a mass of documentation on paper. He knows that he is interpreting, and that other interpretations are possible, but that his own must stand out clearly and justify itself. He knows that he is doing work of social importance and literary dignity. The biographer today may have, and deserve, as only a comparatively few Victorian biographers did, an artist's pride. If he fails to deserve it, the fault will be his own, not that of an environment insisting that he tell white lies and shocked if he has the courage to refuse. Despite all the qualifications with which we must regard Strachey's influence, no little of the present high status of the biographer may be laid to him.

Classic-Romantic Ironist

Offhand, it would have seemed little likely that a world moving from the hysterical relief of an ended war to emotional slump would have taken a volume of four short biographies to its bosom. And yet the post-war mood found a strange intoxication in *Eminent Victorians*. For the War had not so much been brought to a close as exhausted its victims; it was less triumph than collapse. The bitter and vindictive farce of Versailles, with its slow uncovering of secret treaties and chicanery, dulled the bright deluded ideals that had seemed to light the conflict until they were lost in a fog of disenchantment.

The leaders of civilization were either dupes or frauds, and civilization itself only a whirl of chaos. The traditional sanctities had collapsed in utter breakdown. The barbarous confusion of the present stung men to revulsion against the cultural heritage that had betrayed them into the stench of such a filthy-mantled pool as the world after the war. Aimless lassitude and despair mingled with fever, skepticism, and hatred. A Caliban in its own eyes, mankind exclaimed to the past that had made it so,

> *You taught me language, and my profit on't*
> *Is, I know how to curse.*

To this mood Strachey powerfully appealed. All the ideals—progress, liberalism, mechanical-industrial prosperity, international justice, humanitarianism—were now fouled and tarnished. It had taken a World War to bring men to the mood of Henry Adams. And the fountain-head of those ideals was the self-righteous and self-confident nineteenth century. Its solemnity, its optimism, its pomposity, its smugness: they lay there to be derided and smashed. The Victorian Age had been the womb of the present; what gave birth to monsters must be proved monstrous.

To this distorted and hysterical hatred Strachey gave a form of cerebral detachment and justice. His ironic revaluations, his icy detachment, enabled his readers to rise beyond rage and disillusion into the high white coldness of scorn at the same time that they could sate their anger by sharing that chill beauty of annihilation. He might have written, had he wished, that the aim of biography was to destroy the dead with acid, and been cheered with equal fervor.

The truth was that Strachey reacted himself with violence against Victorian culture. He chose certain of its specimens with scientific care and arranged them for exhibition, immersed in the equivocal preserving-and-destroying fluid of his irony. The age represented everything that he hated. It was parochial, muddled, pretentious, he exclaimed; and, worst of all, 'unaesthetic to its marrow bones' and 'incapable of criticism.' It was 'like one of those queer fishes that one sees behind glass at an aquarium, before whose grotesque proportions and somber, menacing agilities one hardly knows whether to laugh or shudder.'

This was precisely the right note. The idols to be destroyed—the Great Men, Gladstones, Mannings, Arnolds, Carlylean Heroes

—lost their impressiveness not by diatribe, which would have betrayed its own animus, but by a subtly annihilating laughter submerging horror. The air of scientific objectivity lent authority to the presentation, made it seem no more than an analysis of unescapable fact. The grotesquerie mingling disgust and comedy reduced the stature of the age by contemptuous patronage, but the faint air of the monstrous allowed a justifiable revulsion. Faced by the somber, menacing agilities of the creature he had called up from the vasty deep, Strachey 'both laughed and shuddered; perhaps he gave to biography a new shudder, with laughter in it, but it is a mistake to think that this laughter contains no emotion.' Impersonally judicious in manner, concealing emotion but conveying it, ironic, acid: he filled perfectly a need essential to his age.

He was enabled to do so by two strands curiously mingled in his nature. The first was a feeling for the central virtues of classicism, the clarity, the balance, the control, that expressed themselves in eighteenth century France and England. The lucidity and ease of Fontenelle and Chesterfield, the sharp strength of Swift, the malicious brilliance of Pope and Voltaire were all congenial to his mind, and he distilled something of their spirit into his writing. He moved easily in the symmetrical, well-ordered world of the eighteenth century, with its neat hard outlines and its dry sanity.

But if the eighteenth century inspired his precision and his antiseptic scorn, Renaissance England had colored with romantic dyes the other constant strand of his temperament. Its magnificence and grandeur of language glowed in his imagination, and all the chiaroscuro, the glaring contrasts, the fantastic embroidery, the stylization of that flaunting age. The tremendous excess of the Renaissance fascinated him, as eccentricity and deep-hued individuality were ever to do, whether in the periods of Sir Thomas Browne, the inspired madness of Blake, or the macabre beauty of Beddoes, whom he significantly called 'The Last Elizabethan.' Order and oddity: icy sanity and grotesque humors: these were the contrasting qualities that he held in subtle balance.

Both made themselves felt in his writing, the classic virtues of concision, lucidity, and fitness to intention perhaps more obviously than the other strain. They provide the sharpness and clarity of plan that dominates all his work. All is held firmly under control within the few simple outlines of an absolute purpose; the details and episodes follow one another with syllogistic rigor. Nothing is there that does not advance that starkly conceived aim. Each stroke is made once, and once only: the stylus bites its deep accent on the plate and moves on. This makes for the brevity and economy that everywhere limits Strachey's structure. The century of Swift and Pope, of Gibbon and Voltaire, also molded Strachey's wit; gave it the elegance and detachment, the cruel polish, that make it at times a thing of acid and ice.

Stylistically it did not invariably serve him so well. At his best, in his own field, he is matchless, using rarely a word or rhythm not calculated to express exactly what it meant. His sentences may be sturdy, swift, ponderous, simple by turns; bare and direct or intricate; but nearly always sensitively responsive to the tortuosities of the most involved ideas and twistedly complicated emotions. And then, again, his effects will become a mere parody of themselves, falling into the most commonplace of clichés. In the last paragraph of *Queen Victoria* there follow each other in rapid succession 'approaching end,' 'astonished grief,' 'monstrous reversal,' 'course of nature,' 'vast majority,' 'never known a time,' 'whole scheme of things,' 'secret chambers of consciousness,' 'fading mind,' 'shadows of the past,' 'retraced for the last time,' and 'cloud of years.' And there are many places where his rhetoric, so often brilliantly sound, becomes stale and artificial.

The romantic influence of the seventeenth century is less noticeable than the eighteenth century clarity because it is employed largely for what we are not so used to regarding as romantic effects. There is seldom either grandeur or pathos in Strachey; no lyricism, sublimity, or terror. He has no tenderness, although he is capable of sympathy tinged with irony or amusement; he can admire, but without awe; his portrayals of conflict, although dramatic, are never heroic. His emotional range, so much narrower and more restrained than we expect a romantic writer's to be, is nevertheless extremely personal and even idiosyncratic. If the study of Gibbon and Pope gave him his malicious precision of epithet, surely a no less penetrating study of Burton and Sir Thomas Browne illumined his use of the startling, the oddly colored, the fantastic.

As one reads the concluding pages of *Urn Burial*, Strachey writes, 'an extraordinary procession of persons seems to pass before one's eyes—Moses, Archimedes, Achilles, Job, Hector, and Charles the Fifth, Cardan and Alaric, Gordianus, and Pilate, and Homer, and Cambyses, and the Canaanitish woman. Among them, one visionary figure flits with a mysterious pre-eminence, flickering over every page, like a familiar and ghostly flame. It is Methuselah; and, in Browne's scheme, the remote, the almost infinite, and almost ridiculous patriarch is—who can doubt?—the only possible centre and symbol of all the rest.' In the picturesque imagery, in the use of suspense and climax, and, above all, in the unexpected adjective 'ridiculous,' has not Strachey here taken a leaf out of Browne's own book, and transposed it to his own peculiar key?

And, indeed, in this essay, he seems frequently to be describing a method which, for all the difference in emotional tone between Browne and Strachey, is essentially his own. To create his effects 'by no knock-down blow, but by a multitude of delicate, subtle, and suggestive touches, by an elaborate evocation of memories and half-hidden things'; and by 'all the resources of his art—elaboration of rhythm, brilliance of phrase, wealth and variety of suggestion,' 'to achieve those splendid strokes of stylistic *bravura*'—these phrases describe his own practice as vividly as they do Sir Thomas Browne's.

Romantic feeling dictated Strachey's attitude toward his themes as well. Not, again, either the mysticism or the sentiment that we associate with the romantic movement, but more the feeling for the fantastic and the melodramatic that we find in the last Elizabethan dramatists, like Marston, Webster, and Jonson. His melodrama, to be sure, is not so much in external action as in the abrupt revelation of grotesque contrasts between pretension and reality, or in the malicious indication of unconscious absurdity or meanness; but, though cerebral, the sudden glare is theatric. And his cynicism is like the cynicism of Marston, or like the strange, harsh, brutal honesty of Ben Jonson, although strained through a mesh of intricate subtlety.

In Strachey the old Elizabethan lion refines down to a cat, cunning, cruel, swiftly ferocious, but retaining some of the old lion-hatred of smallness, nastiness, hypocrisy, pomposity, and sentimentalism. The lion singles out the enemy to be destroyed; it is the cat, however, that plays slyly and patiently with the victim. This explains the frequency of that mingling of amusement, dislike, and superiority in Strachey's tone. It is akin to the robust laughter of Jonson in *The Alchemist* and to the strong-guts hatred of *Volpone*, but here, it is transposed to the minor key of sneer and insinuation.

Strachey's psychology, even, has a strong resemblance to Jonson's characters of humours or to the eighteenth century ruling-passion psychology. Each of his characters he conceives around a few strongly developed traits, and he uses his scenes and episodes, in all their subtle variations, to etch those traits ever deeper in the reader's consciousness. In Florence Nightingale they are inflexible will, energy, domineeringness, organizing power; in General Gordon eccentricity, religious mysticism, romance, violence, contradiction; in Thomas Arnold delectable depths of solemn absurdity and fatuousness. How like they are, even to the grotesquerie, to Jonson's Sir Epicure Mammon, or the terrible rapacity of Volpone, or the unhappy noise-tormented Morose of *The Silent Woman*!

The sharp stamp appears even in Strachey's choice of symbols for his characters: Lord Panmure as 'The Bison,' with his head made for butting, posed 'four-square and menacing, in the doorway of reform,' but gradually forced back by the Lady; Sidney Herbert, 'the stag' springing through the forest and falling into the claws of the tigress; Sir Evelyn Baring, with his temperament 'all in monochrome, touched in with cold blues and indecisive greys'; Gladstone as the labyrinth opening on the scorching pit of a volcano. Such images are, no doubt, largely rhetorical, but their unremitting use reveals Strachey's insistence on paring down a character to a sharp central conception. Development there is none, only a deepening bite in the lines.

These qualities are constantly observable in *Eminent Victorians*, always creating the characteristic flavor of that volume, often stimulating our appreciation by their brilliance, sometimes provoking antagonism by irrelevance or unfairness. In an early chapter of this book we saw how malignly Strachey pursues and lacerates the character of Cardinal Manning, without perhaps saying anything factually untrue, but with a persistent enmity that lays him open to the charge of persecution. And in none of the other biographies in *Eminent Victorians* is he free from the desire to depreciate.

His Florence Nightingale, in fact, is a valuable antidote to the sugary and sentimentalized versions of the ministering angel, the Lady with the Lamp, of previous biographers. But the cruel and unflagging determination with which Strachey shows her laboring Sidney Herbert to his death leaves her less a tyrant than a tigress, and his entire treatment of her evidences his enthusiasm for the psychological grotesque. Even more typical of the fascination exercised over him by the fantastically odd is his General Gordon, and in his hands Dr Thomas Arnold is a farce of ludicrous and ferocious dissection.

Although none of these other three displays the relentless hatred he reveals against Cardinal Manning (in *Florence Nightingale* the animus is directed against her biographers, and in *General Gordon* against Victorian statesmanship, while in *Dr Arnold* it explodes into hilarious satire), these do demonstrate even more clearly than the *Manning* a certain unscrupulousness in the handling of fact. A recent biographer of Gordon, for example, has subjected to a destructive analysis Strachey's innuendo that Gordon was a little too fond of the bottle; and it has been pointed out that there is no justification whatever for the sly intimation that underneath his flowing robes the legs of Dr Arnold were 'shorter than they should have been.' And surely, if such relatives existed, we are entitled to know who were those 'more clear-sighted' elders in Arnold's family to whom the pompousness of his schoolboy letters suggested 'the possibility that young Thomas might grow up into a prig'?

Such things lead us to Strachey's most reprehensible fault as a responsible biographer, that he does not hesitate to manipulate either facts or documents to secure a more striking effect. Consequently we never know whether we can be justified in trusting him, even when he places a thing within quotation marks. In *Portraits in Miniature* his account of Dr John North, although admittedly derived from Roger North's memoir, dramatizes his quarrel with the Fellows of Trinity in a way completely unauthorized by the source, and invents an episode of a stone whizzing into the room. In *Elizabeth and Essex* he represents the Queen's last speech to Parliament as shorter and more striking than it was, by leaving out whole passages without indication, and by omitting, transposing, adding, and altering the rhythms of what he does quote. With the words, 'And, though you have had and may have many mightier and wiser princes sitting in this seat, yet you never had nor shall have any love you better' (Elizabeth's own words were, 'any that will be more careful and loving'), Strachey represents her as making an exit to the sound of trumpets—whereas she actually spoke for another minute or so, and wound up by giving directions that the whole delegation might come forward and kiss her hand. Deviations like these are trifles in themselves, but their ultimate effect is to impair our faith in much else that the author has to say. If he will not hesitate at trifles in fact, how can we trust him in the more significant points of general fairness in handling and interpreting evidence?

These faults are almost outweighed, however, by the ingenuity and wit with which his attacks are nearly always managed. Even though unfair, how amusing is the demure postscript to the fact that Carlyle had characterized Arnold as a man of 'unhasting, unresting diligence':—'Mrs Arnold no doubt agreed,' for 'During the first eight years of their married life, she bore him six children.' And how witty is the statement that Arnold's *Roman History* 'was based partly upon the researches of Niebuhr, and partly upon an aversion to Gibbon.' Even neater is the light touch with which he flicks home the point that Queen Victoria was overwhelmed by the intellectual complexities of the government business she insisted on passing under her eye. He quotes the Queen's complaint of how busy she is kept: ' "From the hour she gets out of bed till she gets into it again there is work, work, work,—letter-boxes, questions, &c., which are dreadfully exhausting—and if she had not comparative rest and quiet in the evening she would most likely not be *alive*. Her brain is constantly overtaxed," ' he concludes the quotations; and adds, 'It was too true.'

Homage to Two Queens

Strachey's irony and his dislike of the Victorian Age are nevertheless both much mildened in his *Queen Victoria*. It is as though he had begun with the same derisive aim that animated *Eminent Victorians*, and had little by little been first touched by the youthful charm and pathos and at last subjugated by the sheer power of character and determination in his victim. Suave and caressing, he sets about weaving his subtle web; she is to be entangled in those strands of delicate ridicule—and then—he slows, falters—recovers himself in a slashing phrase, but hesitates again: something in those small teeth and that obstinate receding chin fascinates him; the little, round, solid, almost absurd figure radiates a kind of grotesque majesty, a frightening power. In the end he almost loves, almost admires her.

The opening, however, is close to pure farce. There are the seven disreputable sons of George III: the Prince Regent, 'a preposterous figure of debauched obesity'; the Duke of York, whose lady 'rarely went to bed and was perpetually surrounded by vast numbers of dogs, parrots, and monkeys'; the Duke of Clarence, with his round, rolling eyes and head like a pineapple; the Duke of Cumberland, 'hideously ugly, with a distorted eye,' and a horrible reputation—the Wicked Uncle of a fairy tale; the mildly literary Duke of Sussex; the Duke of Cambridge, who 'wore a blond wig, chattered and fidgeted a great deal'; and Victoria's high-colored martinet of a father, the Duke of Kent. There is the comedy of the Duke of Kent's sentiments about marrying to produce an heir to the throne, his brotherly feelings toward the Duke of Clarence, and his willingness to accept a marriage settlement of only £25,000 a year, without regard to the decreased value of money. 'One does not know which to admire most,' Strachey quotes Mr Creevey—'the refinement of his sentiments towards the Duke of Clarence, or his own perfect disinterestedness in pecuniary matters.' There is Victoria's answer to the King's enquiry, 'What is your favorite tune?'—'God save the King, sir,' which has been praised for its tact. 'But she was a very truthful child,' Strachey adds slily, 'and perhaps it was her genuine opinion.'

The constant insinuation that Victoria's intellectual powers were not keen receives early form again in the account of her reading Harriet Martineau's tales illustrating the truths of Political Economy: 'but it is to be feared that it was the unaccustomed pleasure of the story that filled her mind, and that she never really mastered the theory of exchanges or the nature of rent.' The delineation of the little Princess's character, however, has been going on quietly: a fixed, settled, imperturbable resolution amounting to obstinacy, a strong sense of the conventions, a tender heart, a limited, pragmatic intelligence. ('One seems to hold in one's hand a small smooth crystal pebble, without a flaw and without a scintillation, and so transparent that one can see through it at a glance.')

But the comic note does not vanish as the little girl grows up. George IV dies, leaving a wardrobe full of clothing and mementoes of ladies' hair and gloves, and is succeeded by the Duke of Clarence as William IV. 'A bursting, bubbling old gentleman, with quarter-deck gestures . . . his sudden elevation to the throne after fifty-six years of insignificance had almost sent him crazy. His natural exuberance completely got the better of him; he rushed about doing preposterous things in an extraordinary manner, spreading amusement and terror in every direction, and talking all the time.' He could not abide his sister-in-law, the Duchess of Kent, and quarreled bitterly with her over her insistence that her yacht must be received with royal salutes: 'these continual poppings,' he exploded, 'must cease.'

The eccentric old man did not live very many years; and then the nearly unknown young girl, who had never even slept away from her mother's bedroom, became Queen. The contrast of the new reign was striking. 'The nasty old men, debauched and selfish, pig-headed and ridiculous, with their perpetual burden of debts, confusions, and disreputabilities–they had vanished, like the snows of winter, and here at last, crowned and radiant, was the spring.' Strachey himself almost falls into the pellucid idyll of that opening to a reign. The long enchanted hours the Queen spent with Lord Melbourne, her Prime Minister, while he charmed and instructed her, or, bending over her hand to kiss it, found himself in tears; the intoxication of dancing through the night and then from the portico of the Palace, watching the sun rise behind St Paul's and the towers of Westminster–it was all like a dream.

But there were other qualities in Victoria than ingenuous innocence and charm. Her Uncle Leopold advised her never to let people speak to her about her own affairs without her having desired them to do so; if they did, she should 'change the conversation, and make the individual feel that he has made a mistake.' Madame de Lieven tried to talk to the Queen about foreign affairs; Victoria, beginning to speak of commonplaces, administered the reproof. The individual was made to feel that she had made a mistake. Shortly after, Leopold himself attempted to influence his niece in a matter of governmental policy. Victoria returned a long and intricate form of words, liberally interspersed with 'dear Uncles,' but signifying nothing. 'Like poor Madame de Lieven, his majesty felt that he had made a mistake.' Victoria had presented 'an absolutely unyielding front'; and 'what may be admirable in an elderly statesman is alarming in a maiden of nineteen.'

The biographer's tone is changing. Whatever qualifications there may be in his attitude, he is no longer superior; he is almost impressed. With the arrival of Albert he recovers himself. 'He was beautiful—she gasped—she knew no more.' Albert was not in love with Victoria, as she was with him. Swathed in the coils of deep infatuation, Victoria's arbitrary temper, her obstinacy, her pride, were at a disadvantage. Little by little Albert triumphed. She took her cues from him. He told her which trees were which, and, with his passion for imparting information, all about bees. She did cross-stitch while he read aloud to her Hallam's *Constitutional History of England*, or, delicious relaxation, inaugurated round games for everyone at the big round table! Albert reorganized the administration of the royal household, he planned and brought to success the Great Exhibition of 1851. His influence spread into all matters of public policy. By the close of Peel's administration, 'Albert had become, in effect, the King of England.'

From this time on, Victoria's extreme tenacity was exercised in behalf of Albert's purposes. Albert died, murmuring 'liebes Frauchen' and 'gutes Weibchen,' stroking her cheek. But even after his death the regimen he had introduced, his methodical habits, his solemnity, his principles and policies—at least so far as Victoria understood them—continued to be dominant in her transactions of official business. She ruled her children by Albert's unhumorous system of duties and schedules, although, oddly enough, the more carefully the Prince of Wales 'was guarded against excitements and frivolities, the more desirous of mere amusement he seemed to become.'

Disraeli achieved his charmed place in her affections by the reverence he displayed for the Prince Consort's memory. 'The Prince,' he said, 'is the only person whom Mr Disraeli has ever known who realized the Ideal.' 'Everyone likes flattery,' Disraeli told Matthew Arnold; 'and when you come to royalty you should lay it on with a trowel.' All the arrogance of that short, stout figure, with its folds of black velvet, dissolved for him; she became 'wreathed with smiles, and, as she tattled, glided about the room like a bird.'

Victoria grew old. She ruled her large family of children, grandchildren, great-grandchildren, with despotism; when the Prince of Wales was a man of fifty he was seen sweating with terror behind a pillar at a dinner-party to which he had been unavoidably late. She toiled through the immense and unremitting labors of state papers. She decreed that everything at Balmoral, at Osborne, at Windsor, must be irretrievably fixed in its place; photographs were taken, catalogues made, of the contents of all the rooms, every object indexed and diagramed. Time's winged chariot must be arrested. Dreadful as was her displeasure at the slightest deviation from rule, in periods of relaxation her youthful amiability returned. The little round figure brightened, the blue eyes beamed. She was dreaded and adored. 'The final years were years of apotheosis.'

But not for Strachey. Spellbound, as it were, by her tyrannic vigor during maturity, in final judgment he shakes himself free, his irony returns. The vast changes that had produced the England of 1897 had scarcely touched the Queen. 'Her conception of the universe, and of man's place in it, and of the stupendous problems of nature and philosophy remained, throughout her life, entirely unchanged.' 'From the social changes of her time Victoria was equally remote.' The emancipation of women was, she said, a 'mad, wicked folly' that 'sent the blood rushing to her head.' The political evolution that took place during her reign occurred without her comprehension and would have filled her with displeasure if she had realized its tendency: 'The complex and delicate principles of the Constitution cannot be said to have come within the compass of her mental faculties.'

Little as the Queen 'who gave her name to the Age of Mill and of Darwin' understood the currents around her, however, imperialism found in her a mystic and a potent, and an acquiescent, symbol for the prestige of the Empire. England's might, England's worth, England's destiny, were concentrated in the venerable antiquity and the imposing edifice of the throne. Morally, too, she stood for her age: its belief in morality, its belief in work, its belief in strict conventionality. 'The middle classes, firm in the triple brass of their respectability, rejoiced with a special joy over the most respectable of Queens. They almost claimed her, indeed, as one of themselves; but this would have been an exaggeration. For, although many of her characteristics were most often to be found among the middle classes, in other respects—in her manners, for instance—Victoria was decidedly aristocratic. And, in one important particular, she was neither aristocratic nor middle-class: her attitude towards herself was simply regal.'

And still, despite patronage, despite superiority, Strachey finds something irresistible about her after all. The little old lady, with her white hair and her plain mourning clothes—what was it that made her so impressive? Her imposing certitude? the surprising jet of her letters like a turned-on tap? her simplicity: it must be her peculiar sincerity, 'the vividness of her emotions and her unrestrained expression of them.' He quotes an observer, 'She talks all out; just as it is,' without concealment or reserve. 'And in truth,' he adds, 'it was an endearing trait.'

What gives *Queen Victoria* its odd and piquant flavor is the tension set up by the fact that Victoria's personality made of Strachey an unwilling and always struggling conquest against his will. It is not so much the celebrated Stracheyan irony pervading the volume as a deeper and stranger one: the irony of a divided response lending curious ambiguities to the tone. He scorned and yet admired, he patronized and almost loved; indeed, he hardly knew whether to laugh or to yield to a respectful shudder.

It was no such unwilling homage that he gave to the Age of Elizabeth. In *Books and Characters* he had written with rich insight on 'Shakespeare's Final Period': he was to return to the same age again in his essay on Sir John Harington and *Elizabeth and Essex.* All the romanticism in his nature that escaped in devious ways of mockery when he dealt with the nineteenth century could flower unpruned in the strange magnificence, the baroque profusion and splendor of the Renaissance. In dealing with the fantastic and pathetic romance between England's Virgin Queen and the chivalrous, melancholy Essex he could embroider the glowing tapestry to its richest and blazon all the pulsating melodrama. Differing from all his other work, his style is here suffused with warmth deepening to sympathy, and hardly touched by the ice of satire. Only occasionally, and then in minor figures, does the sharp edge of wit accent the painting; there is little of his usual malign caricature, with its acid pricking of a point or darkening of a shadow.

As the title suggests, *Elizabeth and Essex* is a biography of neither the one nor the other, but the dramatic story of their strange attraction, struggle, clash, and catastrophe. It gives only in retrospect the first fifty years of the Queen's life, and, passing rapidly over Essex's boyhood, brings him at eighteen to the life of the Court. The illumination of the narrative is always upon the personal relations of these two, and all the other important events in which both were necessarily involved—the defeat of the Armada, the expedition against Lisbon, the brief military alliance with Henri IV in 1591, the naval forces against Cadiz and the Azores, Tyron's Rebellion, and Essex's operations in Ireland—all these are merely sketched as background to their psychological conflict. Except that it begins with Essex's young manhood and ends with his death and then that of the Queen, it is not a full-length biography at all, but rather, like Gosse's *Father and Son,* the biography of a duel carried on in anguish and love.

The two protagonists are projected as characteristic embodiments of their age. That age—so strangely and wildly compounded of subtlety and childishness, piety and lust, the savagery of mauled dogs tearing a bear to pieces and the ethereal delights of madrigals sung to virginal and lute, the filth of London and the impassioned splendor of Tamburlaine, nerves of iron and hysterical effeminacy—was a fiery tissue of contradictions. Essex was young, handsome, and accomplished; sometimes clashing lances in the tourney, ruddy with action, and then retiring to lie in pallid melancholy for long hours with his Vergil; now hunting the deer and boar, now breathing devotion in musical syllables; sometimes entangled in lecheries with maids of honor at Court, and again meditating 'for hours the attributes of the Deity in the cold church of St Paul.'

The aging Queen was an even more bewildering figure—tall, bony, red-haired, with a steep, imperious nose and deep, fierce, almost terrifying eyes and high, raucous voice of tremendous volubility. She swore, spat, boxed people's ears in rage, roared with laughter when amused; and she was also a supreme diplomat and administrator, a cultivated lady, mistress of seven languages, a witty and elegant conversationalist, a musician, a connoisseur of painting and poetry. Constantly racked by nervous diseases, her bodily strength was nevertheless untiring. Some convulsive horror of sex gave her a fixed hatred of marriage, but she carried on affairs of state in a fandango of romantic sighs and glamorous protests.

And this same woman was subtle to extremes of prevarication and cunning, mixing vigor and sinuosity, pertinacity and vacillation. She seemed almost incapable of fixed determinations. She violently contradicted herself from day to day, shamelessly abandoning any shreds of dignity, consistency, decency, or honor in order to obtain the delays she demanded, that she must have; she floated in a sea of indecisions, tacking hectically from side to side, gaining time, in a passion of postponement. But 'the enormous apparatus of her hesitations and collapses was merely an incredibly elaborated façade'; in the end she would be swift and terrible, for 'all within was iron.'

The clash of these two, the young and reckless Essex and the old creature so virginally sentimental and so inwardly unyielding, forms the core of this 'tragic history.' From being the spoiled darling of Elizabeth's ambiguous heart, Essex rose till he became a predominant power in the state and the military hero of the people. But it was by rash and impetuous courses: the glittering serpentine wisdom of Francis Bacon pierced the glamorous carapace of romance and abandoned the dangerous man.

Elizabeth was slowly enraged by his arbitrary and contemptuous obstinacy, his blundering militarism that roused her fears, and his wasteful magnificence that horrified her parsimony. The dreadful day came when he flared into revolt against that Majesty whose 'conditions,' he had said in a moment of anger, 'were as crooked as her carcase!' but no citizens joined the abortive uprising. As he strode down Cheapside crying that his murder was plotted, 'the sweat poured down his face, which was contorted in horror; he knew it at last . . . his whole life had crashed to pieces . . . '

Convicted of high treason, he was beheaded in the courtyard of the Tower. The ax struck three times. But the body did not stir. For the Queen all became emptiness and ashes. She still discharged the duties of government, but the old spirit was gone, or glared only fitfully into action. And in but little time more, the enigmatic figure was stilled.

As a story Strachey's handling of these events is superb. That it is true to the main outlines of events may be granted; it is less so in detail, and whether it is so in spirit may sometimes be debatable. Besides such liberties in the handling of quotations as have previously been indicated, Strachey's treatment of minor characters, such as Bacon, appears occasionally to sacrifice depth of insight to cleverness and the effect of verbal imagery: he is constant in describing Bacon as the glittering serpent. The Cecils, Burleigh and his son, were not such adamantine enemies to Essex as Strachey makes them appear, but in many ways supported him and played his game; and Essex's campaign in Ireland was not all the visionary fiasco that Strachey depicts it. The five brilliantly written pages in which he describes the shattering rush of contrary impulses racing through the mind of Elizabeth after Essex's condemnation are nevertheless utterly unsubstantiated; no one knows what the Queen thought and felt during those last fateful hours. They may well have been as Strachey imagines them, but by representing them as if they had really occurred he suggests that there is some authority somewhere for them in record. The very fact that these things are so well done makes them further misleading.

Portraits in Miniature and *Characters and Commentaries* (the second of them posthumous) contain some shining individual sketches, but they do not essentially add to his stature. The first, written under the influence of Aubrey's *Brief Lives*, is really a series of miniature biographical sketches rather than biographies; the emphasis is more on characterization than on occurrences. Some of them—'The Life, Illness and Death of Dr North' (based on Roger North's memoir), 'The Président des Brosses,' detailing a squabble between Voltaire and a provincial notable of his day, and 'The Sad Story of Dr Colbatch'—are extremely amusing trifles. In others, such as 'The Abbé Morellet' and 'Madame de Sévigné's Cousin,' he conveys some of the charm of nostalgia that the seventeenth and eighteenth centuries often had for him. His 'Six English Historians' is more concerned with striking out sparks of wit than with careful evaluation, although on the congenial figure of Gibbon he has a lively and pleasant piece. *Characters and Commentaries* collects short papers and reviews written between 1903 and 1931, and contains some examples of very good as well as merely smart and clever writing. In a series of chapters on 'English Letter Writers' he defends Horace Walpole against Macaulay's violent and distorted diatribe, but does somewhat less than justice to Chesterfield and Cowper. For the rest, the volume is rounded out with a few satirical sketches and critical articles.

Sand and Gold

Strachey's critical position has fluctuated greatly in the last few years. While he was still living acclaimed as one of the greatest English biographers, with his death his prestige sharply declined. Only last year Douglas Southall Freeman described him as one of the most pernicious influences in modern biography, and there have been a number of lesser, sniping attacks. Nor is it easy to defend him wholeheartedly. His limitations in sympathy and understanding were pronounced. Although he could understand Rousseau as well as Voltaire, John Aubrey as well as Horace Walpole, he was violently unsympathetic to whole ranges of human character. Anything resembling 'enthusiasm' was almost as antipathetic to him as to the eighteenth century, and he can make only grotesques out of such personages as Lodowick Muggleton and Jeremy Collier. Sentiment repulsed him except when it was infinitely attenuated and civilized by the delicate taste of a Madame de Sévigné or a Madame du Deffand. Madame de Lieven could probably have a fairer account given of her than Strachey's; and his interpretation of Boswell is less dictated by perception than by paradox. Not only lacking in broad sympathy, his appreciation of character inclines to the eccentric rather than to the profoundly human, and he is never happier than when he has gotten hold of some oddity like Dr John North—not for purposes of piercing to the heart of the ridiculous creature, but for comedy.

In consequence, his irony instead of being profound was sometimes a cheap trick, and it is the cheapness that has been imitated by his disciples. Nearly always amusing, it is not so often justifiable, although when it is sound it has the ruthlessness of Swift and Voltaire. His rhetoric sometimes degenerates into clichés, and even some of its personal devices any perceptive reader can learn. One could make a little study of the uses of the words extraordinary and fantastic, and of the word creature, in Strachey's vocabulary. In his repetitions of an epithet, a phrase, or an image for cumulative effect he sometimes sacrificed truth to cleverness of form; and indeed the same criticism can be made of his characterizations, where the neatness, the symmetry, the formula of their construction, are perhaps a little too wrought.

But against these faults and limitations may be balanced his marked achievements. If his range is in certain ways narrow, it is in others remarkably varied. That gay spark Sir John Harington and the eternity-haunted Sir Thomas Browne, the ingenuous and muddle-headed Aubrey and the unhappy, sensitive, jealous, introspective Jean-Jacques, the mystic Blake and the skeptic Voltaire, the hilariously snickering Creevey and the exquisite refinement of Madame de Sévigné: these are a richly diversified company, and yet Strachey understood them all. That they are all tinged with the pathos of distance, that he might not have understood them so well —might not have been willing to see them so understandingly—had they lived in a later age, does not lessen the achievement of having seen them so clearly and repictured them so vividly.

Even his antipathy to the Victorian Age did not serve him entirely ill. Though he exaggerates and distorts, with a strange inverted echo of that 'lack of detachment' he deplored in it, his very partisanship has a value. It makes him a devil's advocate advancing searching reasons against the canonization of its great names. His inimical scrutiny must be shared, his strictures weighed, and weighed again, before we reject his verdicts. And, indeed, in part, it seems likely, his verdicts will never be utterly rejected. Our conception of Florence Nightingale, of Manning, of Victoria, the Prince Consort, Melbourne, Palmerston and Gladstone, Sir Evelyn Baring, and numbers of minor persons, will long and perhaps permanently be colored by his interpretations of them. To have added any permanent features to our portraits of such a group of historical figures is more than all but a few of the biographers have been able to do.

To have made so sharp and deep an impression required more than mere caricature and distortion. The two may be, indeed, vehicles of truth, and so Strachey uses them. To see a thing intensely as no one has seen it before, to portray it emphatically so that others will share your vision, requires a certain heightening of the new perceptions, a certain keying-down of the traditional or conventional aspects: pushed to its logical limit, this is caricature. It is a selective art in the same sense that classicism is selective.

That is why Strachey has sometimes been described as a classic writer and sometimes as a distortionist, depending on whether his moments of insight or his moments of prejudice have been uppermost in the describer's mind.

Even in his malice there has usually been a certain mordancy of truth, and at his best he used his method with beautiful virtuosity. The truth that he then revealed was highly selected and stylized. 'But stylization may reveal truth, though in a different way from documentary realism, and abstraction may indicate relationships as clearly or more clearly than photographic detail.' No portrayal of character can be purely objective, because our conception of a personality is the intersection between it and ourselves. Strachey's great achievement was that he forced this fact into the open. The author's point of view became explicit instead of being a muzzy, unacknowledged projection of his personality.

Such an achievement involves a high critical intelligence. This Strachey had, and applied it to the principles and the practice of his art. Far more clearly than most biographers, he knew exactly what effect he wanted to produce, why he wanted it, and, for the most part, how to achieve it. He trained himself in a rigorous and highly specialized artistry that has no exact parallel, and few equals. Cerebral, conscious, and cultivated, it understandably exercised its great influence over the biographical art in our time, quite aside from those gratuitous traits that gave it an ephemeral appeal.

Nor has that influence, despite all the animadversions upon it, been predominantly evil. For all the perversions and imitations, the flippancy, the sneer, the cheap irony, that he unleashed, he inaugurated valuable procedures as well. The hosts of obvious vulgarizers are sinking back into their natural obscurity, and those aspects in Strachey himself which are less than his best are being appraised at their true level. The fine balance of temper and perception, the clear formulation of the point of view, the selection and arrangement and concision, are permanent forces in the world of biography.

MACHINERY, STRUGGLE,
AND LIGHT

XVIII

MACHINERY, STRUGGLE, AND LIGHT

Keys to Our Times

'ANARCHY is full of lights,' Santayana tells us; and the observation becomes luminous when we survey the strange, troubled sky of our world of consciousness today. It is an anarchy of dark nebulae shot with fragmentary insights. Personal utterances shoot and glimmer across it. Autobiographies criss-cross in long gleams; memoirs of all magnitudes shine or flicker dimly; letters dazzle and die from year to year. The realm of personal revelation in our time is a night sky, mainly dark although crowded with speeding energies, a blackness so sprinkled with divergent lights as to seem a chaos void of pattern.

So many furious forces—industrialist, man of science, revolutionary, engineer, journalist, actress, millionaire—with infinitely varied orientations, all different, some alien, in character and background and outlook—statesman, too, and inventor, artist, mondaine, playwright, banker—in such confusion and even antagonism: all of these impinge on us, and all claim understanding, sympathy, agreement;

reveal their own inward vagueness or certitude. How among such a host can we choose which are significant and characteristic of our time, which can clarify the pattern of the present age? Many give oblique lights, here and there in almost all we may find a phosphorescence, some are roving comets or meteorites, glittering but errant. Only a few in this wild, modern, chaotic sky of ours are key luminaries that will enable us to chart *our* movement and isolate those tendencies that distinguish it from the past.

Some of our witnesses, despite many sparkling qualities of wit or fascination or personal drama, our purpose will exclude. These merely repeat or echo kinds of perception we have already seen in the past. There are sharp insights into personalities, amusing anecdotes, and a sometimes pleasingly malicious wit in the *Autobiography* of the Countess of Oxford and Asquith; and charming aquarelles of upper-class Victorian scholastic circles, headmasters, clerical dignitaries, and dons, in E. F. Benson's *As We Were*. A picture of the surfaces of our world these give us, but except when they enable us to see new life and forces growing within the shell of the old, they fall into a familiar pattern of the past. Horace Walpole was as malicious as Lady Asquith, and he was wittier and more vivid; Creevey and Greville give us the same peepshow into government and aristocracy in the early nineteenth century as these into Edwardian and Georgian society.

Such recollections are thus parts in a continuing tradition rather than illuminations of the present. Their impressions of a comfortable Oxford, stately and dreaming, of crises in Downing Street, of Paris, Berlin, St Petersburg, Rome, of the delights of Nice, Monte Carlo, Deauville, Carlsbad; their portraits of Darwin, Kelvin, and Faraday, of Tennyson being rude and grumpy, and the German Emperor rattling the sabre, Proust in the Faubourg St Germaine, the monk Rasputin—these represent that tradition at the point where it is least yielding to the inroads of changing conditions, at its most static and petrified. With their emphasis upon country estates and clergy, fox-hunting and privilege, art and culture as the possessions and amusements of a restricted group, polite gossip and scandal, and the hidden manipulations of politics, they seem, indeed, hardly to have moved beyond the late eighteenth century.

Of the vast body of political and diplomatic memoirs that has been piling up since the close of the War almost the same statement can be made. While ships of state careened wildly, only nominally under the command of their officers for all the directing force they seemed able to apply, cabinet members and ministers in all the governments were cannily accumulating little hoards of private papers with which to feather their nests when they were out of office. High commands and naval potentates had formed similar documentary reserves to fall back upon. But it is difficult to see in what essential way such political recollections differ from those of Lord Morley, and Morley's *Recollections* shares an identical orientation with its own author's *Life of Gladstone*. What they accomplish chiefly, by way of clearing the air, is revealing the blunders of Grey and Asquith and President Wilson, the gullibility of Colonel House and Ambassador Page, the ambiguous skill of Balfour and the trickery of Lloyd George, the ruthlessness of Clemenceau, and the contempt most of these men had for each other—and, for the most part, how well it was justified.

Not in aristocratic and governing class memoirs will we find the key to what is germinal in our time. They show us persistence and recession, but no growing shoots. Occasionally some unusually vigorous intellect like Henry Adams may present us with an analysis so penetrating as to have the value of an autopsy. And sometimes, too, a brilliantly perceptive sensibility like Mabel Dodge Luhan feels and renders the very mildew of a social order. The first volume of her *Intimate Memoirs* paints a vivid image of American society in a small upper-New-York-state city like the sleepily manorial Albany of Henry James's childhood. But its aristocracy has passed its prime, already it is in a feverish stage of semi-senescence, like a provincial version of Rome under Tiberius or Caligula, and its mortuary nightmares are taking strange forms in chartered eccentricities, luxuries, obsessive hatreds, and hidden vices. Even as a young girl Mrs Luhan sensed this gathering debility in the air, and resolved to flee from its infection. Her flight took her first to Europe and then to the New York of *Movers and Shakers*, her third volume. If the parts of these memoirs which the future has in store for us maintain the glowing colors in which she has so far painted, she may well give us such a portrayal of the present as we wish some Saint-Simon of the ancient régime had made before the rising storm.

The way of escape Mrs Luhan took, however, leads us to another of the realms of modern memoir—the worlds of literature and art.

In rebellion against the smell of death in provincial and metropolitan society, there seemed at least vitality, she thought at first, a striving for health, a responsiveness to spiritual issues, among thinkers and artists. And, indeed, there was life, of a kind; at least vividness and intensity; and we might find it too if we followed her there.

But the artist and the philosopher had historically flourished in the shadow of princes and aristocracies, they had erected complicated superstructures of interest in technique under the encouragement of enlightened patronage, and although during the eighteenth and nineteenth centuries they had broken away from that dependence and addressed themselves to growing classes, they had not really found an organic rôle in bourgeois society. In an acquisitive world the artistic and reflective temper became peripheral. The artist tended to grow esoteric, immersed in aesthetic mysteries, or a dweller in either a smart or a down-at-the-heels bohemia, or at best an antinomian. He cultivated his temperament, and as he came to seem more and more irrelevant in a society of business enterprise his temperament frequently became a psychosis.

In the letters, the recollections, the autobiographies of modern artists, then, these things are chiefly what we shall find. The artist may, like Arnold Bennett, have been writing successful potboilers for years, and give us in his *Journals* an exact calculation of the number of words he has written, how much he has been paid per word, and all the glittering restaurants in which his stammer and his white plume of hair have been noted by respectful fellow-diners. Or perhaps, like Will Rothenstein, he has been a fashionable portraitist and illustrator, part of an upper-class bohemia, intermingling with the world of fashionable people and wit. The recollections of all such artists might be indistinguishable from Rothenstein's *Men and Memories,* two brightly frothy volumes of pastels of many people—Lord Balfour, Anatole France, Fantin-Latour, Lily Langtry, Max Beerbohm, Granville Barker, Sir William Orpen, Rabindranath Tagore—all pleasant, superficial, and as evanescent as a bubble, leaving merely an impression of airy buoyancy and color, and no features whatever.

Letters like those between George Bernard Shaw and Ellen Terry reveal artists as personalities and as technicians. The two people portray themselves, and they discuss plays and the art of the actor, but seldom or never do we see these two on a stage of which the whole world is the background. They are fellow-craftsmen or they are playfully—less playfully, it may be, on her part than on his—conducting a dialogue of gallantry. We are in as narrow and specialized a world as that of Colley Cibber's *Apology*.

There is also the world of the artist as bohemian and rebel. Norman Douglas reveals it to us in *Looking Back*. This brilliant, intellectual aristocratic-bohemian ingeniously derides a society from which he stands aside. A little of an archeologist, something of a scholar, a little of a naturalist, an epicurean of foods, of arts, and of morals, he surveys the world from delicious bowers of Capri or Nepenthe and demonstrates his emancipation in mocking Socratic narratives or reflections wherein he smiles at the intellectual, moral, and artistic values of the modern world. Divorced from its currents, far above the swirl of the atoms, he looks on, ineffably Olympian, like one of the gods in Lucretius. His is the bohemian heaven.

In all his tastes, however, although he is too insouciant to be a revolutionary, Mr Douglas is in rebellion against modern society. Unlike the revolutionary, he makes no affirmations; he is simply—and individualistically—antinomian. His position implies certain values that claim his adherence, but implies them only of a solipsistic universe, and he would reverse them for a paradox. But his attitude brings him at least in the neighborhood of those artists who have felt more seriously, even painfully, their separation from the main currents of modern society.

William Butler Yeats is one of these. We can see the struggle it has meant for him in the philosophic mysticism in which he has immersed himself, as well as in those efforts to be a molding force in Irish culture of which George Moore made such gay mockery. Both the mysticism and the struggle to participate are revealed in his autobiographic writings, *Reveries Over Childhood and Youth*, *Early Memories*, and *Dramatis Personae*.

The troubling forces that led Yeats to mysticism produced the painful maladjustment of many other artists. It is these, far more than poverty, and illness, and misfortune, that make the nervous agony in *The Letters of Katherine Mansfield*. We are in a world of strange and aberrant torture, inexpressibly painful. To the practical men, the extroverts, who patronizingly like to think of the artist as inhabiting a gayly impoverished Montparnasse like Mürger's *Vie de Bohème*, it is all incomprehensible and perverse. But, even so tragically distorted, the world of Katherine Mansfield is a reflection and a product of their own.

It would be possible, then, to find in the cry of the artist an image of our time. Not, however, by regarding his personal revelation as a picture—only as a symptom. If we searched behind his distresses we might come to their causes in modern society; if we looked on him as the spirit that denies, and tried to piece together into a whole all that he was denying. For all except a few great artists have been aware only in isolated fragments of what they opposed and what values they sought to affirm. They have not seen, realized, recreated their world as a whole. The personal records of the artists could help us to chart the movement of the contemporary world, but only if we brought labor and insight to them. They would be the materials of a mosaic, a bit of glass from this, a fragment of onyx or marble or porphyry from that. No more than a few have dealt with all the crucial forces of that world, not many more have even tried to see it as a whole.

It might seem that in the sociological commentators there would be found a more practical key to our labyrinth. Mr H. G. Wells is one of these. Years ago he too was an artist, in the days of *The Time Machine* and *The Invisible Man*. Gradually, however, Wells cut himself down to no more than a nodding acquaintance with art, in order to become a compiler of information, a pamphleteer, a didactic moralizer, and a confused minor prophet. The brilliance of his creative powers still shone through all the vague philosophizing of *Tono-Bungay* and the dreary monologue of *Joan and Peter*, but lost itself almost entirely in the informational haze of *William Clissold* and a mist of opinions. And Wells himself, industriously outlining history, explaining the science of life, or making a plan of the work, wealth, and happiness of mankind, drawing every year a new up-to-the-minute blueprint of the future, became lost in a nebulous vision of clear-sighted engineers and benevolent industrialists who were to merge in an open conspiracy for the welfare of humanity, and inaugurate a radiant millennium in which everyone would be more and more like a magnified H. G. Wells.

These unfortunate tendencies mirror themselves in his *Experiment in Autobiography*. A man of many and emphatic opinions, he has no central clarity and consistence. Science has not enlightened him; it has merely given him a certain hydrogenous optimism and dogmatic bounce masquerading under a scientific-sounding vocabulary. Though he talks about the experimental attitude, Wells has for years been exuding pure Mount Sinai; and despite all his attempts to co-operate with the Fabians and other groups, his Utopian panacea of an open conspiracy has essentially neither grown nor altered since 1900. Wells has assimilated vast quantities of information, but he has never listened to anyone else's thoughts about anything. With unconscious comedy he displays an adolescent contempt for Henry James, who had admired the artist in Wells, and turns away from the unrealities of art—to the superior reality of talk, statements, argument, dogma, haranguing, repeating.

One of the most revealing passages in his autobiography is his interview with Stalin, when Stalin asked questions and Wells revealed the light. Firm in his assurance that, armed with the clues of Krupp, Mond, and Ford, mailed in chromium steel, and equipped with test-tube and crucible, he holds all the magic keys, Wells alternately scolds the world and invites it to come into his tent. And for all his constantly repeated incantation of words like scientific, facts, and control, Wells's arguments reach us in a haze that almost entirely ignores all attitudes other than his own. In the end there is something indescribably vague and muzzy about his mental processes, and they only grow blurrier as he talks about sharp scientific intelligences.

It is only hints of the modern world, therefore, that Wells supplies us with. He chants certain of its slogans, some of its catchwords, intoxicated with a kind of shining effervescence that finds in science a Merlin, a Prometheus, a wonder-worker that will solve all our problems. Behind that bubbling faith there stands perhaps the figure of the great Huxley to whom Wells gave an awed worship in his student days at South Kensington. But the promising young biological student became a journalist, and in a long magnificent blaze of imagination a creative writer, and then, hardening into immalleability, a man with a mission. Like one of the Selenites in his own earlier tale, *The First Men in the Moon*, his brain cells swelled ever larger with serried information, and grew ever more rigidly resistive to new meanings. Wells has at last become a phonograph—a phonograph with one record. It plays the Open Conspiracy, organized sometimes by Natural Aristocrats, sometimes by Samurai, New Republicans, Guilds of Aviators, but always the same.

Many scenes from the modern world are there, but only as mirages in a self-fascinated brain.

And still, Mr Wells turns our attention in a direction that holds illumination, although he hardly catches any from it himself. The world of science and industry, against which so many of the artists have rebelled—is it not the significant realm of contemporary society? In it may we not find the clue to our movement? The physicists, the chemists, the biologists, the engineers—the great industrialists and financiers—these are the people who, more than any others, have shaped the world of today. Their consciousness of their own function and of the world they are bringing into being might give us the insight we seek.

By the second half of the nineteenth century their importance was beginning to be realized. Samuel Smiles, better known for his complacent Victorian moralizing, wrote between 1862 and 1895 a whole series on *Industrial Biography; Iron Workers and Toolmakers*, *Lives of the Engineers*, and *Men of Invention and Industry*. Full of useful information, the characterization in these volumes is blurred by hero-worship, and they have no sense as a whole of the new orientation taking shape. They tell us nothing of how the world looked to these men who were changing it. And nearly all of them are silent themselves. No scientist in the nineteenth century really gives us an autobiographical account of what the universe meant to him. Charles Darwin does not do it in his brief autobiography, and Thomas H. Huxley's *Autobiography*, that disappointing fragment, leaves the question almost entirely untouched.

In recent times there is the same unfortunate dearth of evidence. There are many biographies of men of science—Cushing's *Life of Sir William Osler*, Vallery-Radot's *Life of Pasteur*, Leonard's *Loki; The Life of Charles P. Steinmetz;* and of engineers and inventors—Martin and Dyer's *Edison: His Life and Inventions* and Hamilton Schuyler's not too well handled book on *The Roeblings*. But nearly all these render their subjects as individual success stories or romances in scientific magic, not as builders of a new universe, and consequently they give no image of such a universe. And the only one of the scientists who has given a valuable literary picture of himself, Michael Pupin, in his *From Immigrant to Inventor*, has in the same way made his story a personal Odyssey, not the creation of a scientific weltanschauung.

Two opposing limitations have afflicted the biographies of the industrialists and financiers. In one group, the biographer has been blinded by admiration for these efficient freebooters. By means of the discreet arts of omission, soft-pedaling, and extenuation, he has portrayed them with gilt and a halo, arrayed in the shining luminosity of public-spirited citizens, art-lovers, and philanthropists. The brutalities of the Homestead strike all forgotten, Carnegie becomes the peace-lover, endower of libraries, and dispenser of medals to men who jump off wharves to rescue little girls from drowning. The Goulds, James J. Hill, Collis P. Huntington, the great railway pirates, all become similarly saintlified. Seen with the trusting gaze of Mrs Fremont Older, William Randolph Hearst is a Bayard crusading for the welfare of a democracy he loves.

Or else, emulating the reek raised by Ida Tarbell's *History of Standard Oil*, in the days of the muckrakers, all is damnification. *God's Gold* leaves John D. Rockefeller unsilvered of the shining dimes with which Ivy Lee exorcised the earlier taint; the Mellons, the Morgans, the DuPonts, have been portrayed simply as obscene accumulations, sources of exploitation and corruption. Matthew Josephson's *The Robber Barons* sees the new weapons of finance capitalism devoted to perpetuating a predatory feudalism; it does not show how these very exploiters were channels of the new. Their technical rôle in building up large-scale industrial units, in elaborating the economic life of modern society has been almost ignored. Wilhelm Berdrow, to be sure, partly escapes this limitation in his *Alfred Krupp* (Berlin, 1927); and Count Harry Kessler's *Walter Rathenau: His Life and Work* is characterized by Lewis Mumford as 'a biographical appendix to Veblen's theory of business enterprise showing the conflict between pecuniary and technical standards in a single personality.'

But once again we are left almost in the dark about the image these men had of their own rôles. Mond and Krupp and Rathenau did not write their autobiographies; the DuPonts and Morgans and Mellons are silent. Among the few such autobiographies, and perhaps the most important of them, is Henry Ford's *My Life and Work*. More than any other single man, Ford has recognized and brought about sweeping reorganizations in industrial methods; Wells was on the right track, at least, in recognizing his significance. But Ford has been largely a man of instinct, so that he is not altogether clear about, and only partly grasps, his own rôle. His self-explanation, furthermore, is somewhat 'vitiated by the cant that is so often associated with an American's good intentions, particularly when he must justify his arbitrary financial power.'

Dominant as the men of science, the engineers, and the industrialists have been in molding the modern world, then, they do not supply us either with the animating motives of their own activity nor with their view of world-processes. They have been too immersed in technological problems, or too involved in forging the instruments of change, to visualize its relation to the whole, or to admit its actuality without idealization. Appearing on the surface to be such objective manipulators of impersonal facts and impersonal abstractions, they are in some ways the most subjective of us all. The captains of industry have no philosophy that they can state in either intellectual or artistic terms, and when they lay claim to one it usually proves to be some naive crudity that their activities prove illusory in a hundred ways.

Our compass, our magnetic north, our Pole Star, still eludes us. Since no easy key reaches itself into our questing hands, it seems that, after all, we must turn to the artist and the reflective observer. More truly than some of our pilots the voice of rebellion and denial may have realized our direction or drift. And more than those heated with personal aims, more than the merchants or the engineers or the men of action, the philosophic observer may have apprehended the meaning of the machine and the market-place. If we look for witnesses such as these—nay-sayer and student—two voices of recent years can hardly escape us. They are those of D. H. Lawrence and Lincoln Steffens.

Student might hardly seem to many people the proper epithet for Lincoln Steffens. Journalist, muckraker, magazine-editor, Wall Street speculator, friend and enemy and unveiler of machine-politicians, intimate and adviser of presidents, wanderer on the brink of political volcanoes, sympathetic watcher of revolutions, 'red' and consorter with reds and anarchists—how, they demand, was this seventy-yeared and smiling and smart-aleck adventurer a student? Had he not been 'showing up' people and institutions for years, as if he knew it all, and asking unanswerable questions, for all the world as if he had the answers?

But Steffens knew that he did not know the answers; his career, as *The Autobiography of Lincoln Steffens* reveals, was a lifelong search for them. He was impelled from the beginning by a vast desire to understand and know, and so observing, comparing, analyzing, studying, he has found some of the answers to his questions. More than scholars in libraries and museums, or theorizers from statistics, he was a student of the modern world, living and asking his questions of life, proving his answers on his pulse. He was one of the great life-observers of our time.

And D. H. Lawrence was one of the great artists of our time, a revealer, a wrestler with stubborn and resistant truth, an illuminator of hidden things. The world that Steffens tried to analyze Lawrence rejected in a blinding flash. He repudiated modern civilization and its works from the root; both in his novels and in his *Letters*, shining autobiographic records, he underlined his rejection of the modern consciousness. More than Carlyle 'savage-prophetic,' more than Ruskin 'reddest of the red,' Lawrence rejected even the red flag of communism as insufficiently revolutionary for him; its redness was, he thought, a snare and a tragic mistake, symbolizing not the warmness of human blood and the potency of life, but an enslavement to the very inhuman principle it believed itself fighting against. For Lawrence, desperately opposing machine-tyranny, communism was simply another version of capitalism's inhuman face of steel.

He hardly looked at it closely. His supreme mission was to deny the god of the machine and shine with the dark flame with which he was filled. He was, like Spinoza, a god-intoxicated man, but the god by which he was possessed was a burning sense of human godhead being crushed by a machine-intoxicated world, a world stamping out the color and loveliness and fragrance of life to inhuman ends. And so, raising his banner against it, he burned through his life, a tragic pilgrim, living deeply, richly, intensely, now in anger and revolt, now clear with a sunny radiance. For it must not be thought, although the world mainly ignored or misunderstood his message, that Lawrence's life was all an unhappy one. He refused to work except at what he wanted to do, his stories and poems grew to their own living forms, he traveled wherever he desired to go, and told people that they were wrong and he was right. That is more happiness and success than most 'successes' achieve.

To these two witnesses, then, we shall turn. Lawrence, the artist, possessed by his daimon, pierces into the spirit of modern society.

Steffens, the enquirer, studies and analyzes its body, uncovers its workings, illuminates its physiology. Lawrence, Promethean-intuitive, mystical, often ignores, misrepresents, or distorts its operations; he scorns argument, reason, evidence, grows fantastic and perverse, listening only to his inward voice; but despite his wildest utterances he is seldom without a core of significant truth. Steffens, in his scientific curiosity, seems at first to have none of the Shelleyan enthusiasm at all, to assimilate quite imperturbably all the inefficiency, corruption, distress, and evil he reveals; but as he pursues his course we understand that he believes the only way to end an ill is to comprehend it thoroughly, that all else is heat without light. Less Promethean than Lawrence, he is also a yea-sayer; intending Jupiter's downfall, he feels almost friendly to the Olympian deities, telling them gaily how he hopes to see them shorn of their fire. From him and Lawrence, then, we shall borrow light—although Lawrence, who worded so much of his own revelation in a symbolism of darkness and dark centers and gods, might disapprove the image.

Disciple of the Dark God

Lawrence's novels are as much autobiography as his letters. For in them he dealt with his spirit's deepest needs; they are a Ulyssean search, a true pilgrim's progress, now sustained by a vision of the Delectable Mountains or of Beulah Land, again struggling through the Slough of Despond or battling the fiend Apollyon. Although so beautifully and unescapably the artist, Lawrence was never merely an art-artist. He would not carve walnuts into filigrees or make exquisitely jeweled traceries of aesthetics; not art for art's sake, he insisted, but 'art for my sake.' 'I am a passionately religious man,' he said in a letter to Edward Garnett, 'and my novels must be written from the depth of my religious experience.' And, in *Fantasia of the Unconscious*: 'The novels and poems come unwatched out of one's pen . . . [They] are pure passionate experience.'

They were so much 'one's naked self' that they were painful to release. In *The Trespasser*, he told Garnett while he was writing it, 'I give myself away so much, and write what is my most palpitant, sensitive self, that I loathe the book, because it will betray me to a parcel of fools.' But it was all beyond his control: 'It surprises me by its steady progressiveness—I hate it for its fluid, luscious quality.'

'They want me to have form: that means they want me to have *their* pernicious ossiferous skin-and-grief form, and I won't.' In no other way could his seeking be carried on. 'One sheds one's sicknesses in books,' a letter to Lady Cynthia Asquith confesses, '—repeats and presents again one's emotions, to be master of them.'

And not only in this spiritual sense were they autobiographic, in many ways they were literally so. *Sons and Lovers* was the story of Lawrence's childhood and youth, and E. T., the Miriam of that novel, has recently told her version of their attachment. In the later novels the individual circumstances are fictitious, but they are symbols of the problems with which Lawrence was wrestling, and even their scenery is literally real.

Lawrence's autobiography thus runs constantly interlinked in novels and letters. He had not one style for his letters and another for his novels, nor different sets of interests for each. He tells his correspondents the very things that are being poured into his books, with the same dionysian violence, the same bright outbursts of invective. He conveys the dark blue, the purple and emerald green, of Lake Garda, or the hotness of a Sicilian day, or the jungle-green of Ceylon, or the glowing chromatics of the New Mexican desert in his letters with word-images as gleaming as those in the novels and poems. A true life of Lawrence must therefore be woven of intermingled strands from the books and the *Letters*. They both reveal that gleaming flame of a 'brighter and intenser world' that he inhabited.

'A walk with him in the country,' writes Aldous Huxley, was a walk through a 'marvellously rich and significant landscape . . . He seemed to know, by personal experience, what it was like to be a tree or a daisy or a breaking wave . . . He could get inside the skin of an animal and tell . . . how it felt and how, dimly, inhumanly, it thought.' In his world a living current flows from earth to living beings, and from them returns into flowers, rivers, and trees. It is a liquid electricity, tingling through the universe, bathing it in a mystic vibrant animism.

He tells Cecil Gray of seeing plum trees and cherry trees in bloom with snow on the ground, and 'their lovely foamy fullness goes a sort of pinky drab,' he writes, 'and the snow looks fiendish in its cold incandescence'; so of course, that malevolent snow, he 'hated it violently.' Of a pelting rain in a pine forest, he told another friend, 'oh Lord!—the rain positively stands up on end. Sometimes one sees the deer jumping up and down to get the wet out of their jackets, and the squirrels simply hang on by their tails, like washing.'

Everywhere, intuitively, he touches life—in bachelor's buttons, 'pale gold great bubbles,' in a glacial river, 'pale, milk-green,' 'fearfully cold and swift,' in the inhuman glitter of snow-capt mountains, in anemones and shellfish and 'lizards whipping about on the rocks, like a sudden flicking of a dried grass blade.' Even scrubbing a brick floor is with him a living experience, 'my braces round my waist'; and, 'Lord,' he rejoices in the letter where he tells of it, 'to see the dark floor flushing crimson, the dawn of deep red bricks rise from this night of filth, was enough to make one burst forth into hymns and psalms.'

With emotional responses so spontaneous and rich, it must not be thought, however, as many people have done, that Lawrence was purely non-intellectual and intuitive. On the contrary, Lawrence had an acute degree of intellectual consciousness, and a penetrating intelligence. The scenes of slashing satire on highbrow artistic-bohemian circles in *Aaron's Rod* and *Lady Chatterley's Lover* were no chance shots: Lawrence had mingled with the intellectuals in London and Capri, and his derision was of the mind as well as of the feelings. In his youth he had been himself a highbrow, a great passer of examinations, and if he rejected the abstractions of philosophy and science it was not because he could not understand them: 'Indeed, he did understand them perfectly well,' Aldous Huxley remarks; 'and it was for that very reason that he rejected them.'

For the conflict in Lawrence's life grew precisely out of the fact that in him mental consciousness and instinct were both existent to an intense degree and that they were divided. His realization of this led him to an analysis of himself, then to an analysis of the causes, and then to a diagnosis of the fundamental conflicts in a civilization of which he was a typical flowering. The very root of Lawrence's struggle lay in his being an intellectual; and intellectualism, as we shall presently see, was the key to Lawrence's criticism of contemporary society.

Sons and Lovers is the first stage of this spiritual autobiography. It shows the spiritual crippling and disruption that result when a mother turns from her husband to her children for emotional fulfillment. It is Lawrence's own story, and his emotional tie to his mother is realized intensely in his poem *The Virgin Mother:*

My little love, my darling
You were a doorway to me . . .

I kiss you goodbye, my dearest,
It is finished between us here.
Oh, if I were as calm as you are,
Sweet and still on your bier!
Oh God, if I had not to leave you
Alone, my dear!

In his story, the mother 'has no satisfaction in her own life,' and selects her sons as spiritual lovers. Lawrence's own mother had been dissatisfied with her miner husband, and sought compensation in her children. She made Lawrence precociously her own little gallant lover, her knight, spurred him on to mental consciousness and too early emotional flowering, with herself as the spiritual sweetheart. Thereby she had made it a struggle, almost an impossibility, for him to escape the entangling tendrils of her love and enjoy a normal love. Paul Morel finds a girl 'who fights for his soul–fights his mother . . . The battle goes on between the mother and the girl, with the son as object. The mother gradually proves stronger,' and the son 'decides to leave his soul in his mother's hands.' When she dies, 'He is left in the end naked of everything, with the drift towards death.'

So Lawrence explains his theme in a letter to Garnett, and, thinking of his deep personal knowledge of it, 'It is a great tragedy,' Lawrence insists, '. . . the tragedy of thousands of young men in England.' It was probably Ruskin's, he thinks, dominated by the mother-will; and, as we have seen, Van Wyck Brooks believes it was Mark Twain's, always his mother's child. If these two are right, one of the tragedies of our time, linked to its drift by treacherous hidden currents.

Only painfully, with agony, did Lawrence struggle through it. In the triumph of love achieved, radiant, he could write an exultant letter: 'The world is wonderful and beautiful and good beyond one's wildest imagination. Never, never, never could one conceive what love is,' and proudly proclaim that life can be 'godlike.' But, even then, the struggle was not over, the swimmer had not overcome the currents. 'I think the real tragedy is in the inner war which is waged between people who love each other,' he says in a later letter, and cries out how a woman can make 'a man suffer by being blind to him when her anger or resentment is aroused.'

Why is there this struggle between men and women? Why do mothers turn from their husbands to their children for emotional sustenance? Why is there no peace even between those who love, but a tension of the wills? And Lawrence answers that it is because there is an unbalance in modern life between mental consciousness and intuitive knowledge, between will and feeling. When we are whole and full-balanced there is an equilibrium between the 'upper' centers of mental consciousness and the 'lower' centers of dynamic feeling, between 'light' and 'dark' forces. But all the pressure of modern education and influence tries to develop the upper centers and deny the lower.

It leads to an essentially inhuman emphasis on what Lawrence calls idealism. Idealism means making ideas—concepts, abstractions, principles—the dominant force in our lives. The purest form of idealism is science, and from science comes technology, and from technology the machine-ridden deadness of modern society. Scientists try as much as possible to rid themselves of their humanity, to transcend its limitations. They want to be pure, impersonal cerebral intelligences, reasoning machines dealing with the absolute nature of conceptual reality. They can't do it, of course, but they can stunt their emotional beings in the effort, by starving and neglect. The dinosaurs were huge monsters of bone and flesh with a spoonful of brain. The scientists make themselves into brain-monsters of mentality, living pale etiolated passional lives. They are machines rendered slightly inefficient as machines by the fact that they cannot rid themselves, as some of them wish, of their bodily needs or be entirely free of faint psychic tides.

The scientist and the industrialist combine to produce modern industrial life, reducing action more and more to machinery. In it the individual must be subordinated to the mass and become a creature of the machine, exerting only such parts of himself as minister to its needs and abandoning in himself any need the machine cannot satisfy. He is sacrificed to the 'idea' of efficiency, the idea of profits, the idea of productivity, or monopoly, or nationalism. Thus he becomes himself a machine, half-dead, and strictly monstrous. The cities created by the machine, financial centers, mining districts, mill towns, have 'the strange desolation of a ruin. Colliers hanging about in gangs and groups, or passing along the asphalt pavements heavily to work, seemed not living people but like spectres. The rigidity of the blank streets, the homogeneous amorphous sterility . . . suggested death.'

In *The Rainbow* a young girl visiting such a town asks, 'Is this place as awful as it looks?' and is told, 'It is just what it looks. It hides nothing.' Men believe that they must alter themselves to fit the pits, the factories, the sweatshops, the department stores and offices, instead of altering these places to fit them. 'Living human beings must be taken and adapted to all kinds of horrors.' Such are the Fall Rivers, the Manchesters, the Krupp and Essen works, the Pittsburghs of our day: 'Hell with the lid lifted,' Lincoln Steffens called Pittsburgh. To this mechanical world 'marriage and home is a little side-show . . . The pit matters. Round the pit there will always be the side-shows . . . the pit owns every man. The women have what is left.'

Capitalists and financiers are as much the creatures of mechanical mind as their workmen. The industrial magnate becomes, like Clifford in *Lady Chatterley's Lover*, almost 'a *creature*, with a hard, efficient shell of an exterior and a pulpy interior, one of the amazing crabs and lobsters of the modern industrial, financial world, invertebrates of the crustacean order, with shells of steel like machines, and inner bodies of soft pulp.' And 'There in the world of the mechanical greedy, greedy mechanism, and mechanized greed, sparkling with lights and gushing hot metal and roaring with traffic,' Lawrence continues in the same novel, 'there lay the vast evil thing, ready to destroy whatever did not conform.' 'It was producing a new race of mankind, over-conscious on the money and social and political side, on the spontaneous intuitive side dead . . . Half-corpses all of them, but with a terrible insistent consciousness in the other half.'

The idealism that produces this mechanical-intellectual slavery also has another form: the species of sentimental benevolence, the belief in vague Utopian aspirations and in principles that is more often called 'idealism.' It too is a subordination of life to ideas. The idealist is not a man who loves men, he only loves 'humanity'—an idea—he is a man of 'principle.'

Philanthropy is one of these forms of mechanical idealism. The philanthropist does not give others the things they would like to have; he gives them what is 'good' for them, forces his abstract benevolent will upon them. We cannot force our wills on others for their good, cries Lawrence, because nothing but what people really are can make them good, any more than we can make a judge an administrator of justice by tricking him out in robe and wig, or make a monkey a general by giving him a gold-laced uniform.

That is why Lawrence had no faith in the social reformers. They seemed to him to be as enslaved to the machinery they were fighting as their opponents; they all believed in 'ideals' and mechanical solvents. Even as early as 1910, he had 'lost touch altogether with the old "progressive" clique,' he wrote W. E. Hopkin: 'in Croydon the Socialists are so stupid, and the Fabians so flat.'

From these things spring the sterility, the emptiness, and the loss of faith that literature has echoed since the rise of industrialism. Everything knuckles down to industrialism and idealism. Talking more and more about loving their fellow-men, people squeeze the life out of them in mechanized monster-making toil, reduce them to automata outside their work with the organized mass-vulgarity of dance halls and motion pictures, and then scream with rage and hatred at anyone who doubts their loving benevolence. 'But better to die than to live mechanically a life that is a repetition of repetitions,' Lawrence exclaims passionately in *Women in Love*, '. . . There is no ignominy in death.'

And in this machine-mill of modern society, with their manhood lost among inhuman drives, naturally men made of marriage also a failure. 'Things are in the saddle,' Emerson had prophetically seen in the middle of the nineteenth century. It is the nature of man to be the craftsman, artist, poet, maker—creative—but man was surrendering his integrity for a barren triumph of intellectual power and intellectual will, and becoming enslaved to things. He had sold his birthright of creative joy for a mess of synthetic pottage. Instead of taking responsibility for creating the future, man even invented a mechanical universe to excuse his being its victim. Men were merely income-providers, machine-tenders; only women had leisure to think of art. Women became the culture-bearers, and 'pursued Culture in bands, as though it were dangerous to meet alone.' But they felt superior to their mechanized husbands, giving in so readily. How can a woman respect a man who is a mere cog in a machine, irrespective of whether he is a big cog or a little one?

To make up for the failure, the ideal of romantic love was imagined, as if it were a complete fulfillment of life. Instead of going forth from love to conquer life and create a shining future as Siegfried started to do, lovers were to swoon with palpitant ecstasy and expire like Tristan and Isolde in the drowning consummation of a love-death. It would not interfere with the dead galvanic dance of the machines, and, dead, the men could rise to go through the routine of their mechanical functions. Romantic love was simply another of the 'ideals' that were supplanting life. Men imagined ideal wives, and wives ideal husbands, and tried to make each other into these pretty doll-images. (Lawrence symbolized this in *The Captain's Doll.*) Naturally they failed.

'Love was a battle in which each part strove for the mastery of the other's soul,' he wrote in *Aaron's Rod*. 'So far man had yielded the mastery to women.' And woman 'was quite sure that the highest her man could ever know or ever reach, was to be perfectly enveloped in her all beneficent will. This was her idea of marriage.' But if the man gives in, or fails to defeat her, she despises him, and turns either to lovers or to her children, and tries to find fulfillment there. Thus a vicious circle of futility continues, the child is made into a precocious little spiritual lover to the mother, tied to a deep and ultimately wounding domination. He is taught to be intellectually conscious and never to have a single *spontaneous*, normal, whole-bodied response to anything. A worse failure than his father, in him spontaneity vanishes, and nothing remains, Lawrence cries in *Fantasia of the Unconscious*, but 'beastly benevolence, and foul good will, and stinking charity, and poisonous ideals.'

Idealism was thus for Lawrence the great perversion, obstructing the gates of life. He writes to Aldous Huxley in approval of a scheme for treating Leonardo da Vinci and Kant, Baudelaire and Proust, as 'grand perverts,' with Goethe as the worst of them all. 'I think *Wilhelm Meister* is amazing as a book of peculiar immorality, the perversity of intellectualized sex, and the utter incapacity for any *development* of contact with any other human being, which is peculiarly bourgeois and Goethian . . . He perverted himself into perfection and God-likeness.' The only remedy, Lawrence felt, was to flee idealism, to give up mental consciousness as an ideal, save for the very few. 'It is not the nature of most men to know and understand and reason very far.' Men must cease to believe in machine materialism, and making themselves into week-day adding machines and St Francis of Assisi on Sunday.

Instead they must try to be themselves, to possess themselves, and to attain their individual fullness of growth by being what they really are. They must trust the vital force of instinct. 'My great religion,' he wrote to Ernest Collings, 'is a belief in the blood, the flesh, as being wiser than the intellect. We can go wrong in our minds. But what our blood feels and believes and says, is always true. . . . I conceive a man's body as a kind of flame, like a candle flame, forever upright and yet flowing: and the intellect is just the light that is shed on to the things around.' And to another friend: ' "God enters from below," said the Egyptians, and that's right. Why can't you darken your minds, and know that the great gods pulse in the dark, and enter you as darkness through the lower gates. Not through the head.'

Only when men had learned these things could any creative step for the future be made. This was why Lawrence found 'the Socialists so stupid, and the Fabians so flat.' They all believed in ideas, instruments, machines, instead of in the flaming sword of instinct. 'It is impossible to believe in any existing body,' a letter to Mrs. S. A. Hopkin explained, 'they are all parts of the same evil game, labour, capital, aristocrat, they are the trunk, limbs, and head of one body of destructive evil.' He had no use for socialism in Mexico or communism in Russia; the Mexicans were a 'black savage mass' whom socialism reduced to 'a mush,' and the Russians were lusting after the triumphs of mechanized fleshpots. But he had no patience when business men fresh from strikebreaking declaimed against revolutionary violence: that was merely the bloodstained capitalist pot calling the communist kettle red. He sometimes felt that 'nothing but a quite bloody, merciless, almost anarchistic revolution' would be any good for the world.

It is mistaken to think that Lawrence's doctrine necessarily denies the mind or demands a Samuel Butler war on the machines. It was not mind, but intellectualism, that Lawrence was attacking: making intellectual values uppermost and denying that values draw their nourishment from the intuitive nature of man. Sometimes, in the heat of revolt, Lawrence sounds as if he demanded the annihilation of our minds, but of his clearest utterances that is not so. 'I think,' he says, again in a letter, 'unless one is so pure by instinct that one does the right thing without knowing, then one *must* know what one is after.' The mind may legitimately be used to clarify instinct, to harmonize its impulses, and aid their satisfaction; it is misused when it stifles or maims.

And there is nothing in Lawrence to indicate that, like Mr Seward Collins, he disapproves of machinery as such. There is no mysterious demon in the dynamo: the evil is in destroying human welfare for mechanical ends. As a servant the machine may be beneficent enough, but we must not make it our master. When men are sacrificed to the speed-up and to efficient routine, when we believe that by machinery we can save our souls, then not the machine, but machine-enslavement in us, becomes destructive. In this criticism of machinery Lawrence is but developing Matthew Arnold's salutary warning against a fetich that has become ever more, since Arnold's day, an obsession.

It should thus be clear that Lawrence is not, as so many have supposed him, merely the novelist of sex. Criticism has strangely often treated him as a sort of prophet of psychoanalysis and disciple of Freud (the two last things he could possibly be), and sexual joy-riders have constantly invoked his doctrines 'in defense of a behaviour, which he would have found deplorable or even revolting.' While he was writing *Lady Chatterley's Lover* he was profoundly shocked by the *Memoirs* of Casanova, and he hated the lascivious libertinism of conscious sensuality, 'sex in the head,' he bitterly called it. Nor is he a neo-primitive, following Chateaubriand into the Louisiana swamps or exalting the noble savage. Wherever he encountered primitive peoples he found them repulsive, and insisted that the human race could not 'go back.'

Lawrence's real significance is as the poet of rebellious social theory. In all the chorus of dissent with the dominant concepts and the life of our time the most radical and damaging is the voice of Lawrence. All thoughtful writers of the last hundred years have tried to plumb the essence of the deep disharmony that afflicts modern civilization, and whether in cynical comedy or tragedy that illness has been their persistent and recurring theme. More deeply and revealingly than any English artist since Blake, Lawrence deals with that subject. Compared with his interior glow the aesthetic novel becomes a kind of flimsy veneer, and the work of the propagandists and reformers such as H. G. Wells like tying a nosegay to a boiler about to explode. The canon of his writing, both in letters and novels, is a detailed analysis of the different kinds of evil our social system brings into being, and an explosive denunciation of the foul-smelling mess.

Again and again he emphasizes the delinquence of modern art reflecting the delinquences of modern European culture. Its literature is either like Ibsen a scientific analysis of disease, and 'a bit skin-erupty,' or like 'all the modern stuff since Flaubert' pervaded by 'giving in before you start.' They are all 'Writers among the Ruins,' he told Garnett; and to still another correspondent, 'I hate Bennett's resignation,' he wrote; 'Tragedy ought really to be a great kick at misery. But *Anna of the Five Towns* seems like an acceptance . . . ' And it grew worse with the years. Joyce's *Ulysses*, he wrote Aldous and Maria Huxley, was 'Nothing but old fags and cabbage-stumps of quotations from the Bible and the rest, stewed in the juice of deliberate journalistic dirty-mindedness;' and the Frenchmen published in *transition* were 'sheer rinsings of baby's napkins.'

Huxley's own work he did not like, but he read *Point Counter Point* 'with a heart sinking through my boot-soles and a rising admiration,' he told Huxley. 'I do think you've shown the truth, perhaps the last truth, about you and your generation . . .' Lucy Tantamount and Maurice Spandrell show what the cultured European has come to, able to palpitate only 'to murder, suicide, and rape'; and if this is so: '*caro*, how are we going to live through the days? Preparing still another murder, suicide, and rape? But it becomes of a phantasmal boredom and produces ultimately inertia, inertia, inertia and final atrophy of the feelings. Till, I suppose, comes a final super-war, and murder, suicide, rape sweeps away the vast bulk of mankind.'

The War, indeed, has been the ultimate defilement in all this cesspool of human defeat. It clung about Lawrence's spirit with a grey discouragement; it was a dreadful, depressing, and miasmic force. Building up the 'war-machine,' the governments were destroying the few remains of life there were in people. 'After the War,' he wrote Lady Ottoline Morrell, 'the soul of the people will be so maimed and injured that it is horrible to think of.' 'I am afraid of the ghosts of the dead,' he told her. 'They seem to come marching home in legions over the white, silent sea, breaking in on us with a roar and a white iciness.' The living soldiers, so mechanized by discipline and routine, and breaking out during their periodical releases in predictable lust, revolted him as if they were insects. 'I like men to be beasts–but insects—one insect mounted on another–oh, God! The soldiers at Worthing are like that–they remind me of lice or bugs: "to insects–sensual lust." '

It was the disintegration of Europe, a 'whirlwind of dust and grit and dirty paper'; and contemplating it almost a frenzy descended on him. 'I hate the "public" and "people," "society," so much,' one letter to J. D. Beresford shrieks, 'that a madness possesses me when I think of them. I hate democracy so much. It almost kills me. But then, I think that "aristocracy" is just as pernicious, only it is much more dead.' In this shaking despair he tried to turn his eyes away from the madness of humanity, to pretend to himself that it did not rend and torture him. 'It is the last folly to bother about the world,' he tells Katherine Mansfield hypnotically. 'One should be in love, and be happy–no more.' And, repeating the incantation, 'One must forget, only forget, turn one's eyes from the world: that is all.'

But he could not forget. His soul thirsted after a world in which he could believe. He dreamed that by stillness and detachment men might 'nourish in the darkness the unuttered buds of the new life that shall be. That is our life now: this nourishing of the germs, the unknown quicks when the new life is coming into being in us . . .' Perhaps they might, he and a few others who would feel the new impulse with him, form the nucleus of a new society. Rananim, this vision was called, and it flitted like a flame of spectral gold over the map, sometimes in Florida, then Cornwall, or Sicily, or Mexico, and he followed it over the globe in a pilgrimage that was a mingling of seeking and of flight. For the tragedy of the War had almost overwhelmed him, and his body was sick, wilting under the terrible strain. The Old World was too putrescent to be saved; he must find new unstained lands. Or perhaps–he contradicted himself–in leaving England were they 'like Jonahs running away from the place we belong'? But a gadfly drove him on, endlessly round and on.

His movements became a restless, nervous flight. The Italians have a noble dignity, 'they go by the window proudly, and they don't hurry or fret. And the women walk straight and look calm.' So he flees England to Capri. But it turns out to be 'a stewpot of semi-literary cats,' he writes Catherine Carswell; he escapes them to Taormina. He likes it better there, he writes another friend: there were fewer English there, 'and not so all-overish,' but ten days later he is telling Lady Cynthia Asquith that Taormina is 'a parterre of English weeds all cultivating their egos hard, one against the other.'

He must move on. 'We had almost booked our passage for America, when suddenly it came over me I must go to Ceylon . . . I don't believe in Buddhistic inaction and meditation. But I believe the Buddhistic peace is the point to start from—not our strident fretting and squabbling.' Alas, it was under his skin by now; he could not escape the fretting and stridency. No sooner was he in Ceylon than he knew 'The East is not for me—the sensuous spiritual voluptuousness, the curious sensitiveness of the naked people, their black bottomless, hopeless eyes—' it was like 'the world before the flood—hot dark mud and the life inherent in it,' making him feel sick. Australia, he told Catherine Carswell, was even more prehistoric: it 'was coal age, the age of great ferns and mosses.' So he came to America at last, to find only that it was as far gone as Europe in machine decay.

In the end there is something frantic about his struggles to achieve peace and a home. He falls into contradictions of his own deepest insights, incoherence, and despair. 'You ask me, if I feel things very much?' he writes Lady Ottoline Morrell, '—and I do. And that's why I too am ill. The hurts, and the bitterness sink in, however much one may reject them with one's spirit. They sink in, and there they lie, inside one, wasting one. What is the matter with us is primarily chagrin.' In his stories and essays he begins a 'pitiful backing, like a frightened horse, back to the stable, the manger, the cradle.' 'In a man and woman who are whole,' he had once declared, 'the spiritual and the sensual might be one,' balanced and whole. Now he says 'the mind . . . *hates* the dark potency of blood acts.' At one moment, in his *Studies in Classical American Literature*, he is symbolically one with Captain Ahab, hunting down, in the form of the White Whale, 'the deepest blood-being of the white race,' and the sinking of the Pequod is a fearful disaster; at another, Moby Dick, the blood nature, rightly triumphs: 'I abandon my guns,' says Lawrence. Walt Whitman is at once a great leader, spreading the gospel of the 'Open Road' and 'sympathy,' and his camp, at the end of the road, is 'the edge of a precipice,' 'a dead end.' *The Plumed Serpent* and the last stories of violation and human blood-sacrifice are the epitome of this defeat. Afterwards he is a ghost, writing stories of ghosts, and, in *The Man Who Died*, one resurrected from the grave.

'For the last two years,' writes Aldous Huxley, 'he was like a flame burning on in miraculous disregard of the fact that there was no more fuel to justify its existence. One grew, in spite of constantly renewed alarms, so well accustomed to seeing the flame blazing away, self-fed, in its broken and empty lamp, that one almost came to believe that the miracle would be prolonged, indefinitely.' But his illness grew, and at last he was hidden in a dark cloud of melancholy. 'The secret consciousness of his dissolution filled the last years of his life with an overpowering sadness.'

Even near the end he could still laugh and write with something of his old infectious vitality. The Florentine printer who, without understanding a word of English, was setting up the plates of *Lady Chatterley*, Lawrence said gaily, 'writes dind't, did'nt, dnid't, dind't, din'dt, like a Bach fugue.' But the lamp was now almost out. 'How tragically the splendid curve of the letters droops, at the end,' Huxley exclaims, 'towards the darkness!'

Lawrence was 'a symbolic man,' one of his biographers writes. 'If he was tortured . . . it was for us that he was tortured.' 'He was a prophet, a psychologist, a philosopher . . . —but more than any other single thing, the great life-adventurer of modern times.'

The Educational Dawn

The last days of Lawrence are a lamp burning out in a catacomb, now flaring up painfully in a wild radiance, sometimes burning clearly for a while with a pallid flame, and again guttering almost out. Turning then to the world of Lincoln Steffens is like coming into a clear sunshiny day. Steffens made his way through life smiling; he smiled as a child of two when he was pitched out of bed by the California earthquake of 1868; 'smiling, as always,' his mother said, 'as good as gold.' It showed, Steffens playfully interprets, that he 'could take such natural events as earthquakes all in my stride. That, I think, is why I smiled then; that is why I smile now; and that may be why my story is of a happy life—happier and happier. Looking back . . . it seems to me that each chapter of my adventure is happier than the preceding chapters, right down to this, the last one: age, which, as it comes, comes a-laughing, the best of all.'

The life of Lawrence is a dark contrast. Not only the sorrow and tragedy of his death make the difference between these two men; the very air they breathed was different. That of Lawrence was tense, his world was close around him, near, oppressive, so that he longed for horizons. Steffens's world is spacious, distance and vistas opening round, the air thin and cool. For him men and places are real in their own right, and their identities hold the answers to the whole universe of what he wants to know. For Lawrence, so possessed by his own dark inner radiation, compelled to minister to and intensify its flame, that flame alone could burn to the heart of reality. It endowed the external world with all the significance it had; useless to bring up facts, argument, evidence! 'But I don't care about evidence,' Lawrence would protest. 'Evidence doesn't mean anything to me. I don't feel it *here*,' pressing his solar plexus with his hands. Against this deep subjectivity, the world of Steffens seems almost completely objective.

It would not be true, though, to say that Steffens is unimaginative. His imagination has simply been turned outward, towards understanding men and their behavior by trying to see them as they are. The early pages of the *Autobiography* reveal that his boyhood imagination seethed with romantic color; he was never merely a California boy riding around on a horse, he was the lost heir of a lord, or a knight fighting Saracens, an explorer outwitting savages, a Napoleon of his military school. Ordinary games, marbles, tops, kites, he did not care much for. His games must be spiced with invention and make-believe, and his favorite companions, boy or adult, were those who would live in the world of romance with him.

The old bridge-tender who would be a prospector searching for gold, the cowboy who was really the son of an English peer, these were better than boys like Will Cluness, who 'could not fight Saracens that were really only Chinamen,' and who 'held it in great contempt to set traps for beavers that did not exist. There were other boys like that. They were realists, I would say now; practical men. I learned to play with such boys, too, but I preferred the fellows that were able to create a world of our own and live in it.' With them and with the bridge-tender he could people the raw gravel of the river bottom 'with Indians, Turks, beavers, and wild beasts.' The artist who painted a sunset there, burning gold in a scene of brush that was all old gold, told him that he was right. 'Your Indians are where my gold is, where all beauty is, in our heads.'

Nor is Steffens, for all his intellectual clarity and his emphasis upon growth in understanding, lacking in emotion. The emotion that is most revealed is a constant enthusiastic curiosity, a zest for living, a humming interest in all that is happening to him, a real sympathy for those around him. But the deeper emotions are there as well.

The boy who was filled with trembling pain and grief at the sale of the horse he loved, at the thought that people unknown were 'to have the power of life and death over that fine, happy, trustful, spoiled, proud creature,' is found again in the man who would not accept a card to Versailles entitling him to witness the 'victorious statesmen and generals standing over two or three of the defeated Germans, making them sign there,' who voiced his sense of pollution with the badness of the treaty by explaining that he 'had to take a bath at that very hour.'

But as the boy grew up his imagination became focused on the outer world. He wanted to understand why things were not as they seemed, not as they were supposed to be. It disillusioned him to find out, even as a boy, that horse races were not always straight, that they were 'thrown'; he shared the weeping humiliation of the negro jockey Smoke, who felt ashamed before his own horse. The bridge-tender told him things were not so bad, there was good mixed in with the crookedness. 'This railroad, for instance. It's a crook in politics, but—there's some of us keeps it going straight enough to carry freight and passengers.' It was the same with the crookedness of the State Legislature, where his friend Charlie Marple was one of the pages. It didn't work the way his father and the history books said. Charlie 'took it as it was; my father took it as it seemed to be; I couldn't take it at all . . . I remember how I suffered; I wanted, I needed, to adjust the difference between what was and what seemed to be.'

By some freak, in that military school of his, he encountered a book that 'told as a story of idiotic waste all the wars in the whole story of man,' that made war a mere stupidity. It emancipated him from respect for adults. He saw that men 'were and always had been mostly ignorant fools whom a boy, even a little fellow like me, need not look up to.' They 'did not see straight, they could not explain things to me because they did not understand them.' As he grew he became more aware of 'the unsolved problems in every science from astronomy to economics . . .'

It was hydrogenously exhilarating. 'Everything in the world remains to be done or done over. "The greatest picture is not yet painted, the greatest play isn't written (not even by Shakespeare), the greatest poem is unsung. There isn't in all the world a perfect railroad, nor a good government, nor a sound law." Physics, mathematics, and especially the most advanced and exact of the sciences are being fundamentally revised. Chemistry is just becoming a science; psychology, economics, and sociology are awaiting a Darwin, whose work in turn is awaiting an Einstein.' What a breath-taking prospect!

The realization effectively turned the boy's interests outside himself. 'No more play-acting for me. No more dreaming I was Napoleon, or a trapper, a knight, a statesman, or the younger son of a lord.' He saw that 'the world was more interesting than I was. Not much to see? No, but I have met men since, statesmen, scholars, business men, workers, and poets, who have never made that discovery. It is the scientific attitude, and some scientists have it . . .'

And, even better than the scientific attitude, Steffens began to achieve freedom from the idealism that Lawrence was later to proclaim the great evil of the modern world. Steffens could see there was a difference between the way the State Legislature was supposed to work—the ideal picture of its working—and the way it actually did work. The real thing was not like the idea of it. Political bosses were supposed to be bad men—but the boy knew Charlie Prodger, one of them, and he knew Charlie Prodger was not a bad man. Idealism in later years never prevented Steffens from mingling with the bad men, the crooked politicians, the bribers and bribe-takers, the policemen who protected criminals, the anarchists and dynamiters, the heads of railroads and electrical power companies and steel corporations who corrupted politics, and finding out what they were really like, and how things worked. He made a steady and successful fight to prevent idealism from hiding the real shape of the world from his eyes.

He entered the University of California brimful of curiosity, 'with a set of examination questions for the faculty, for the professors, to answer.' His fellow-students did not share his intellectual enquiringness. They memorized what they were told to, they accepted the system, but when he 'spoke of the implication of something we had read or heard, they looked dazed.' They were the boys the schools were made for. Still, it was possible to get an education at a university. 'It has been done; not often,' and Steffens speedily proceeded to ignore the courses he was not interested in, and work on those that did have a meaning to him.

In history he soon learned that the authorities disagreed on the facts. 'The historians did not know! History was not a science, but a field for research, a field for me, for any young man, to explore, to make discoveries in . . .' Every chapter was crying to be re-written. Two of his professors of philosophy disagreed, and went at each other, hammer and tongs; to most of the students it was only 'a fine, fair fight,' and they wanted to know what he had seen that was so much more profound. 'I said that I had seen two highly trained, well-educated Masters of Arts and Doctors of Philosophy disagreeing upon every essential point of thought and knowledge. They had all there was of the sciences; and yet they could not find any knowledge on which they could base an acceptable conclusion.' He was stunned to realize 'that it is philosophically true, in the most literal sense, that nothing is known; that it was precisely the foundation that is lacking for science; that all we call knowledge rested upon assumptions which the scientists did not all accept; and that likewise there is no scientific reason for saying, for example, that stealing is wrong. In brief: there was no scientific basis for ethics.'

He went abroad in 1889, to Berlin, then to Heidelberg, Munich, Leipzig, Paris: perhaps the European universities could teach him more. But these, 'like Berkeley, like all universities, were organized, as they still are, not for enquiry and research into the unknown but for the learning (and teaching) of the known.' The scholars did not have anything settled. 'Like the disputing professors at Berkeley, they could not agree on what was knowledge, nor upon what was good and what evil, nor why. The philosophers were all prophets, their philosophies beliefs, their logic a justification of their–religions.' In Wundt's laboratories in psychology there was an attempt at hard scientific spirit. 'We want facts, nothing but facts,' Wundt declared; and 'The laboratories where we sought the facts,' Steffens remarks, 'and measured them by machinery was a graveyard where the old idealism was a dreadful ghost and philosophical thinking was a sin.' But Wundt himself had a system, and his students felt pledged to its defense. There was no science of psychology!

'The best I had got out of all my scholastic wanderings was a belief, which was probably only a hope, that when there was a science of psychology, a science of sociology, and a science of biology, when we could know how man was born, bred, moved, and to what end, then we might lay out a program for the guidance of his conduct.' If we assumed that men were an evolving species, good might be described as all that made for development and bad as all that hindered growth, 'but to make it scientific, biology has to prove and describe evolution, psychology has to show us human possibilities, sociology has to be made a study of the effects of environment on human psychology.' Everywhere Steffens found theory, pious hopes, religion, ideals–no knowledge. 'The thing for me to do, I decided, was to leave the universities, go into business or politics, and see, not what thinkers thought, but what practical men did and why.'

So he came back to the United States, to New York, and became a reporter on the *Evening Post.* He saw brokers, superintendents of schools, Rapid Transit Commissioners, politicians, reformers. And he noticed that 'the ethics of business and the ethics of politics are such different cultures that a business man in politics will commit sins appalling to the politician, and vice versa. Morals are matters of trade or profession and form the ethics they are supposed to be formed by.' When he was assigned to Wall Street he set about forming a picture of what finance was like; he had no prejudice for it or against it, although he saw readily enough that 'the panic of '93 was a period of bad times chiefly for the innocent.' James B. Dill taught him something of legalized business piracy, and of the ways in which the New Jersey trust laws permitted plain financial crimes: 'a picture of such chicanery and fraud, of wild license and wrong-doing, that I could not, dared not, take it all down'; he couldn't even take it in. Dill laughed and laughed, laughed at his innocence, laughed at his confusion.

Transferred to reporting police news when Dr. Parkhurst began denouncing the corruption of the force, he soon discovered that the police were in partnership with the thieves, the gambling dens and saloons, the confidence men, and the houses of prostitution. 'The police were protecting from the law and from public opinion the law-breakers they were appointed and paid to protect the public from.' And when Parkhurst's vice crusade forced the closing of saloons that violated the law he was surprised to note that good citizens began to grow violent against reform. Bankers, business men, even clergymen, said Parkhurst was going 'too far,' his crusade 'hurt business.' What was the underground connection, Steffens asked himself, between business and vice?

He joined the staff of *McClure's Magazine* and began the muckraking series of exposures called *The Shame of the Cities.* From St Louis to Minneapolis, to Pittsburgh, Philadelphia, Chicago, he went, and everywhere found the picture the same. From the cities the trail reached up to the states (he remembered the California Legislature of his boyhood), and Steffens traced it in Missouri, Illinois, Wisconsin (where LaFollette was fighting the machine), Rhode Island, which was old in corruption, Ohio, Oregon, and thence to timber frauds in the Federal government itself. It was not true, he found, that 'ignorant foreign riff-raff in the big congested cities' made politics bad. They were just as bad where the population was almost pure native American. Nor was political corruption a phenomenon incident to newness or youth in the community. There was less corruption in the western states than in the East; in the New England communities it was inconceivably settled and entrenched.

From Joseph Folk, the circuit attorney of the St Louis district, he gleaned the surprising truth: 'It is good business men that are corrupting our bad politicians; it is good business that causes bad government.' Good business men were pleased when Judge Ben Lindsey tried to reform juvenile delinquents, but when he moved from the children to cleaning up the low-down wards where they were made bad it was a menace: it hurt business interests. Lindsey might 'deal with the children after they had done evil, but he must not interfere with the conditions that led them into evil. Those conditions were a part of the conditions that made business good and paid dividends.'

And Mayor Jones of Minneapolis confirmed the discovery; when reform tightened up the laws against prostitution, gambling, illegal drinking, it was the 'good citizens, property owners, whose houses were cleaned of prostitution,' who rose 'in wrath against this arrangement, which lost them their high rent.' The landlords and the bankers were able to set the clergy and the other good citizens howling with protest against reform. And the people were no better than landlords and bankers. In Rhode Island, in Connecticut, Steffens saw them, '" respectable men" who did not need the money,' selling their votes for three or five dollars. 'Wherever the farmers, wherever the common people are tempted to sell out,' Steffens concluded, 'they are found to be as corruptible as the better people, whether politicians, business men, aristocrats, or church men.'

The Federal government showed the same state of affairs. 'Just as we had observed that a railroad commission, whether State or national, established to regulate railroads, came finally to represent the railroads; as a public utility commission came to act for the companies against the consumers; and as the police, appointed to arrest crime were corrupted to license criminals—so a Federal department created to execute land, timber, and mineral laws in the public interest was organized (by political appointments) and bought by systematic bribery to take the part of the land grafters, timber thieves, and big mine-jumpers.'

Later observation in England convinced him that the older the community the more established the system is. What was still regarded as corrupt in the United States was taken for granted in England. 'There are members of Parliament who are known and expected to represent the brewers, the coal mine owners, the railroads—even certain railroads—and the banks.' The special interests we call grafts are in England simply 'privileges,' and a gentleman could defend his privileges with an absolute sense of virtue.

What did these experiences prove? 'If the graft and corruption . . . occurred everywhere, in the same form, then this universal evil must be, not an accidental consequence of the wickedness of bad men, but the impersonal effect of natural causes, which it might be possible to identify and deal with, without hating or punishing anybody.' 'It is a natural process by which a democracy is made gradually over into a plutocracy. Treason, in brief, is not a bad act; it is an inevitable, successful policy . . .' 'In a country where business is dominant, business men must and will corrupt a government which can pass laws to help or hinder business. But there must be something wrong—unsocial—at the bottom of the organization of businesses which have to control government.'

Tom Johnson, the fighting reform mayor of Cleveland, who had once been a successful business man himself, and whose imagination, honesty, and ability had sent him into politics, gave Steffens the answer. First, Johnson told him, you supposed it was bad politicians. But they turned out to be pretty good fellows. Then the blame was turned on bad business men who bribed the good fellows, until it appeared that not all business men bribed, but that the best, the biggest, the most successful, were the ones who did. So the distinction was drawn between little business men, who didn't bribe, and who were 'good,' and 'big business,' that did all the harm. 'Hell!' Tom Johnson exploded, 'Can't you see that it's privileged business that does it? Whether it's a big steam railroad that wants a franchise or a little gambling house that wants not to be raided, a temperance society that wants a law passed, a poor little prostitute, or a big merchant occupying an alley for storage—it's those who seek privileges that corrupt, it's those who possess privileges that defend our corrupt politics.'

For such a condition punishment was no remedy. 'Not big men, not bad men, not crooks, and not capitalists—not even the capitalist class!' Punishment and hatred were unscientific. 'To throw out the rascals and put into office honest men without removing that which makes good men do bad' was irrational. Society teaches the 'ideal' of success, sets up the temptations of power and riches to men and nations—and then punishes those who get caught. The only solution was to 'take down the prizes we offer to the winners.'

The accumulated cost of offering these prizes was enormous. Individual men attained wealth and power, but in order to do so they had to secure privileges, and they had to look after the big men among those who could block their road. But that was not enough, William F. Herrin, the political boss of California and the chief attorney for the Southern Pacific Railroad, told Steffens. The machine had to be oiled all the way down the line. 'We have to let these little skates get theirs; we have to sit by and see them run riot and take risks that risk our interests too.' And a single sentence stabbed home to Steffens all the effort involved in keeping the world going wrong: 'The Southern Pacific Railroad and all the companies and interests associated with us are not rich enough to pay all that politics costs.'

It was not as if all this piled-up corruption even resulted in efficiency. It didn't. 'What did you mean,' Nelson W. Aldrich, boss of the Senate, asked Steffens, 'by saying that we business men didn't understand business, even our own business?' Steffens reminded him of the long fight the consolidated trolleys had made in Providence against keeping their promise of universal transfers; what happened, he demanded, when they were finally beaten and had to give in? 'It was funny, what happened,' Aldrich said. 'Our earnings increased.' 'I knew that would happen,' Steffens told him. He had seen it happen elsewhere. And the business men didn't know that. 'You business men don't know your own business.'

That was why an A. F. of L. official, Anton Johannsen, laughed when Steffens expressed the hope that capitalists might ever act intelligently. He was present once when Steffens was explaining to a chamber of commerce that workers were also consumers and that therefore employers should pay as high wages as the productivity of labor and the management of business would allow, 'not to be kind to labor, but to improve the market.' Johannsen laughed, loud, he roared his laugh so that people turned and looked. It was no man who laughed like that, Steffens told them, 'that is no individual. That is the laugh of labor, laughing at me for thinking that capital can see and pursue its own obvious interest.' When Herbert Hoover called the White House conference of heads of industry to meet the crisis of 1929, Henry Ford alone saw what needed to be done. 'Let's meet the depression by raising wages,' he said; but no one would follow his example.

The truth was that all the ideals of that upper-middle-class bourgeoisie to which Henry Adams had glumly known that he belonged were inadequate to deal with a fully expanded industrial society. 'The ideals of America . . . are antiquated, dried up, contradictory; honesty and wealth, morality and success, individual achievement and respectability, privileges and democracy . . .' They will not work in harmony, side by side. Wealth and success inevitably compromise honesty and morality; privileges undermine democracy, and once privilege is allowed to raise its head democracy is on the decline. That is why liberalism cannot possibly deal with the problems of modern society. 'Woodrow Wilson was not only a well-grounded liberal . . . he was the strongest liberal whom we could have had in his place. He was liberalism personified, and when he failed liberalism failed.'

That was the meaning of the perhaps apocryphal story of Clemenceau and the permanent peace, as it was told to Steffens. Clemenceau had heard, he told the other peace-makers, drawing smooth his little silk gloves, and smiling sweetly, he had heard something about a permanent peace. Did they really mean that? Certainly they did, said the President and the premiers. 'Very important,' Clemenceau muttered. 'We can make this a permanent peace; we can remove all the causes of war, and set up no new causes of war.' And they were sure they proposed to seize this opportunity? They emphatically did. 'And–you have counted the cost of such a peace?'

What costs? 'Well,' said French intelligence, 'if we give up all future wars–if we are to prevent war, we must give up our empires and all hopes of empire.' The British must come out of India, France out of North Africa, America must get out of the Philippines and Porto Rico, leave Cuba and Mexico alone. No more trade routes and spheres of influence; no more tariff walls; everywhere free trade. And there were other sacrifices too. 'It is very expensive, peace.' The French were willing, but were they, the others, really? The President and the premiers protested. All that was not necessary, not all at once.

'Then,' said Clemenceau, and he sat up and hit the table once, 'then you don't mean peace. You mean war.' The French realized that it was not really peace and justice that the good men and the liberals wanted, it was security and the status quo. Security means 'the maintenance of things as they are' and 'things as they are are evil and impossible,' and therefore, the French believe, 'the only possible outcome is wars and degeneration as in the old worlds of Rome, Greece, Egypt, or–revolution. They see this with clear, logical, unlying minds' and they 'fight off—postpone—wars, revolution, and the fate of nations.'

To Steffens, by now, revolution was the only answer. Reform by propaganda and political action was impossible. 'Nothing but revolution could change the system, I thought.' He began studying revolutions. The first one handy was Mexico, then came the Russian. They taught him a number of mistakes, the mistakes people mouth about revolution over again from year to year. 'You can't change human nature.' When he saw the Mexican peons, saw how when they were given higher wages they quit work earlier each week, saw that they would work only when work was made fascinating to them by teaching the tricks of craftsmanship, he became convinced that human nature had been changed. Man was born 'an artist, and had to be made over into a profiteer.' Human nature *has* been changed in us 'and has to be changed all over the backward world to make it like us.'

And another old theory. 'When things get bad enough, the revolution is bound to occur.' After the War, in Germany, in Austria, things were so bad that the revolution could not occur. Hungry and frightened people wept and were too weak to revolt. There was a better chance of revolution, Steffens thought, 'in a country like the United States, where labor is very well off. A sudden precipitation into hard times might cause an uprising almost impossible in a state of continuous misery.'

Agitators, anarchists, communists, 'reds,'—did not make revolutions. Governments made them. The leaders of the Russian Revolution were not in Russia when the Revolution began. Steffens saw the plans that had been drawn 'to put down mobs of people who did not know they were going to rise in revolt. Government blue prints. Government preparations. It was the government that anticipated, prepared for, started, the revolution in Russia, as in Mexico.' The government knew there was unrest among the people, knew they did not hate the Germans, were discouraged by tales of bribery and mismanagement in the War. They would handle the menace by scotching it in advance; they would get the people in the streets 'and shoot the fear of God into them.' The government tried to foment bread riots by pretending there was no bread. Later it was found rotting in the cellars of the police stations. When the officers tried to incite their troops to shoot into a quiet mob, they would not. Then the people knew the soldiers were with them. There was a cry: 'The revolution is on!'

There was little looting, little fighting, save as the counter-revolution made itself felt. In the milling, stinking mob of delegates to the Soviet, Steffens found proof that 'Primitive, untaught men are good.' The first laws they passed were against capital punishment and against war and empire. 'I have been over into the future,' Steffens told Bernard Baruch on his return to America, 'and it works.'

Back in America, though, a queer idea struck him. 'The American way was not the Russian way, no;' but, '—but, yes, Bolshevik Russia and the mass machine-making United States were more alike, essentially and politically, than any other two countries that I had seen. Wasn't it this, that these two young people, the Russians and the Americans, are driving, the one consciously, the other unwittingly, toward the same end?' A vice-president of General Motors said, 'We don't think any more in business. Oh, we may have our opinions; we may think up how we can do or make something we need.' But then it went to the laboratory to be tried out, scrapped, modified, used. This was revolutionary. 'No more thinking; no more right thinking; no more believing or logical reasoning from premises to conclusions.' Experiment would blow up argument. 'No wonder my old liberal friends were sore and obstinate. A new, the new, culture was sweeping down over us, and big business, and the old root of all evil!'

America was even beginning to realize—in part—that a large share of the profits must go to the 'workers to enable them to go on buying and consuming,' 'that the producers and the consumers are one and the same people and that production and consumption must about balance; else there must be foreign markets and empire and panics.' Although business men could not bring themselves to act on it yet, they might, when they surmounted the conflict between ownership and management. 'But the United States of America, which the Russians recognize as their chief rival, is, however unconsciously, moving with mighty momentum on a course which seems not unlikely to carry our managing, investing, ruling masters of industry, politics, and art—by our blind method of trial and error—in the opposite direction around the world to the same meeting-place' as Russia, 'the land of conscious, willful hope.'

So this story, which Steffens calls 'my spiral-like story,' comes to its end. 'Some change in me, this? It is. I have not lived in vain . . . It took a war, a peace, and a couple of revolutions to do it, but it is done . . . My life was worth my living.'

It is strange to observe the way in which his story and that of Lawrence reinforce and supplement each other. Steffens too reveals, clearly, convincingly, with illustrations, how 'idealism' hides the nature of our realities from us, prevents us from seeing the obvious goings-on of the universe about us. He shows that the reformers were never able to deal with their problems realistically, and that they failed because a great deal of intensified emotion and lofty idealism impeded their ever even grasping all the detail involved. He demonstrates that the 'idealism' of good citizens made them refuse to admit it when two contradictory realities stared them in the face. They wanted both to have the cake of idealism and eat it instead of bread-and-butter. He points out that idealism—ideas, theories, systems—falsified knowledge, so that there was—and still is—no science of psychology, sociology, economics, history. Hardly any such thing as science, indeed; Lawrence did not exaggerate inexcusably in rejecting science as a pack of lies.

Steffens shows how ideas and systems deified into 'the System' sacrifice good will, honesty, intelligence, ability, and even self-respect to the machines—political machines, business machines, war and imperialism machines, until Machinery does almost seem to have become a modern Moloch. Like Lawrence, he perceives that human values, human emotions, human welfare are the real touchstones, and that by them much of our world is condemned. But unlike Lawrence, he also perceives that, despite all the perversions to which they have been misused, our machines may be made the instruments of emergent human values. We must obey the god within us, yes, he might say to Lawrence; but Steffens can also find the god in the machine.

He agrees with Lawrence in his distrust of ideas. 'No more thinking; no more right thinking; no more believing or logical reasoning from premises to conclusions.' He goes beyond Lawrence, in fact: 'no more believing.' Lawrence would have us believe—our impulses, our instincts. Steffens doubts even them. 'Human nature can't be changed?' Let's try to change it, and see! No more right thinking! No more being blindfolded and hoodwinked by pious hopes. The State Legislature is what it is, not what it is supposed to be.

And of course Steffens does not really, in the crude sense, mean 'no more thinking, no more reasoning.' All that he means is that thinking and reasoning must not be taken as *establishing* the nature of the realities in the world. We must not make a principle of having principles, we must not make a principle of a rigid method, refusing to alter it for unyielding facts. We must be like Lenin, whom Steffens admires, able to deviate from our goal, but able to admit our deviation, and head back to it; not like Wilson, the American liberal, who to justify his tacking changed his course. But Lenin had principles, had objectives, and steered his course by them. Steffens knows this, but he does not trouble to elaborate his paradox.

And we, his readers, have also been following a 'spiral-like' course, tracing in history a spiral story. For once more we find ourselves breathing the air of optimism and hope, the Shelleyan fervor for the future of mankind, just as in Lawrence we breathe something like the Byronic despair. Lawrence transposes the individualism of Byronic introspection and Blakean mysticism to the social plane, and attains by introspection and mysticism an insight into the society of modern man. And similarly, in Steffens, the intellectual atmosphere of the Shelleyan enthusiasm has changed. Steffens seizes on the experimentalism of Mill, the patient fact-collecting, the inductive method of Darwin, and with them studies the direction of modern society.

It is no longer an effervescent a priori confidence, as in Shelley, an iridescent dream. It takes that superb hope and animates it with new sources of energy and power. It believes that the course of events makes towards its own consummation—if—if only—human beings concentrate their intelligence on seeing the vital power, because the truth, in the center even of what seems evil—and direct their strength to using that knowledge. To Henry Adams the political machine was breaking down, because it was no longer operating in the way intended by the founders or congenial to his ideals. The fact that it had been seized by a new class with different aims meant only collapse and failure. Steffens sees the political machine as a going concern, doing what its engineers want it to do, and even its perversions are a scientific lesson in the practical attainment of purpose. Study of the political machine, of the economic and social organism, can direct us to the means of using them for better purposes.

That is why every pragmatic sanction really does carry with it a kind of ethical sanction too. It shows *how* success may be achieved; nothing forbids application of that knowledge to humane ends. Years ago, Dill had told Steffens that trusts were inevitable. 'You cannot stop them by force, with laws. They will sweep down like glaciers upon your police, courts, and States and wash them into flowing rivers. I am for clearing the way for them.' See what lesson could be learned from them, use them, adapt their valuable methods to human welfare. And only 'if they cannot be brought into social use, why—then—then—I would be for exploring their origin and dealing with—I mean closing up—their source.'

The rationalism of Shelley and the eighteenth century, the empiricism of Mill flowering into liberalism and liberal reform with Gladstone and Morley, dying away into skepticism and contradiction and despair in the moribund upper-class liberalism, disintegrating and chaotic, of Henry Adams! And now a new burst of belief and pride in man, Shelley's pride in the natural goodness of man, but tempered, tentative, experimental, believing not just in nebulous goodness, but in seeing how and under what conditions that goodness can be put to work, how operative and how successful! This is a spiral story indeed. Russia and America, Steffens suggests, are the two great experiments of the world. Perhaps each in its own way, or even the same way, holds the key to the future.

EPILOGUE

EPILOGUE

Pageant of the Past

As we turn our eyes backward over the way we have come, a tremendous panorama rolls there, from the immediate landscape of the present to the distant glittering pinnacles of the Renaissance. The magnificence of Wolsey, billowing in crimson damask, and Henry, virile in yellow satin luxury, reveal its wealth and pride; More discoursing to the King on the motions of the stars, Elizabeth's mastery of languages, and Essex lost in admiration of Vergil and the harmonies of Spenser, its new intellectual reach of humanistic studies and the arts. Henry's divorce was more than the sensual urge for Anne Boleyn's beauty; it was the assertion of national sovereignty against the universal Catholic empire, and it worked hand in hand with the Reformation. The fall of Wolsey and the suppression of the monasteries were the next steps, paralleled abroad by the work of Luther, and followed by Calvin and Knox. Mary's effort to turn back the tide flamed up in the red glare of Smithfield, where Protestantism cried out, 'We shall this day light such a candle, by God's grace, in England, as I trust shall never be put out.'

It lit the candle, too, that was one day to obliterate the divine right of kings. Elizabeth might rant and terrify the Commons, but she knew when she had best yield gracefully; and the pedantic, slobbering James blundered through a reign of increasing unrest, while Dr Donne wrestled in agony with sinful ambitions and worldly lusts. Charles I was 'resolved to be an absolute uncontrollable sovereign . . . or none at all': his determination united landed gentry, small burghers, and Puritans against him. The Civil War brought the Roundheads ruinously into the Duke of Newcastle's estates of Welbeck and Bolsover, smashed the glorious stained glass of Canterbury, and lost Charles his handsome head. Then, through the eyes of Colonel Hutchinson, we see Cromwell usurping the dictatorship, and the confused interlude of the Rump Parliament. Pepys and Evelyn paint the burning of rumps in bonfires and the return of the chastened Stuarts, in a monarch determined never again to set forth on his travels.

They show us also a court immersed in shameless debauchery, a navy disgracefully corrupted and ill-equipped, so that the Dutch burn the shipping up the Thames to the Medway, then vigorous naval reform and stirring victories, the hiss of melting lead in the Fire of London, and the horror of the Plague. Evelyn brings Greenwich Hospital to completion, manufacturing and commerce are swelling, the founding of the Royal Society paves the way for the intellectual triumphs of Newton. The short reign of James II, 'so strong were his prejudices, so feeble his genius,' was no more than an interlude ended by the Glorious Revolution; the Augustan Age was lighting the sky.

Sir Dudley North had carried the early principles of political economy a few degrees beyond Gresham's Law, and England's growing commerce was to carry Adam Smith farther. The wars with the Dutch, and then with France, were commercial wars; Marlborough manipulated them on the Continent and, save for the few Tory years of Harley and Bolingbroke, Walpole and the Whigs carried things before them in long fat decades of contented bribery. Pope glittered and stung at Twickenham, and in Ireland Swift grew mad with vexation and despair for humanity.

Lady Mary, the toast of the Kit-cat Club, brought back inoculation against smallpox from Turkey. In the miserable starved faces and tattered clothes of the peasant in France she had seen the dreadful hollow behind the pomp of Versailles. The Newtonian world-machine, after having been set in motion by the celestial mechanic, smoothly spun on its way; reason and the unities were in force; everything was orderly and neat. It was the England of Chesterfield and Johnson, the polished gentleman ceremoniously at his worldly ease, the old bully grubby and lovable among his friends.

But we can see new forces stirring in the scene. Rousseau's feeling for nature was bearing fruit, and when Gray crossed the Alps he exclaimed, 'None but these monstrous creatures of God know how to join so much beauty with so much horror.' The doctrines of the natural goodness of man and the noble savage flowered in a novel sympathy for native peoples and in startling political theories of the rights of man. The radical Wilkes was elected and re-elected in riotous meetings; somewhere beyond the seas deadly struggles were going on between rival colonial imperialisms. Walpole suddenly flashes them to us in Braddock's defeat, and his hot anger at the massacres and duplicities in the West Indies, his hatred of Clive, 'the heaven-born general,' looting India, the scorn with which he proclaims that he is not a *patriot* leaping to arms to defend the sacred price of sugar. The American Revolution arouses his sympathy and admiration: 'If these folk will imitate both the Romans and Cromwellians in self-denial and enthusiasm, we shall be horridly plagued with them.'

The French Revolution soon had armies lunging across Europe. Consul succeeded republic; on its libertarian ruins there reared a new and threatening throne. Napoleon dazzled the eyes of Byron and Hazlitt, but others, even liberals like Crabb Robinson, saw a worse tyranny in the place of the old. Tension deepened with the contest; and when Wellington in his short, chopping sentences pronounced a post-mortem on Waterloo, the world was made safe for reaction under the benign vigilance of Metternich and Castlereagh. Mr Creevey raved against the meanness and perfidy of the Tories in country houses where a hot pheasant and a barrel of oysters were rolled in at half past ten, and liberal publishers were put in pillory while the country embarked on an orgy of post-war speculation and extravagance.

But the hidden groundswell was still there. Its whisper can be heard in the voices of the crowd who watched the Houses of Parliament burn to the ground, and in Carlyle's denunciation of those who rode down the weavers at Peterloo: 'ye ride prosperous, very victorious–ye unspeakable!' When the uprisings of 1830 dethroned the Bourbons, even the aristocratic Greville could feel that their fate was richly deserved; an eddy of the gathering wave catches one of its opponents and cries, 'Burk Sir Walter!' at Jedburgh. Pointing for an example to the fallen heir of thirty kings, Macaulay pleaded the passage of the Reform Bill, and Creevey rejoiced over the Whig triumph.

Democracy was beginning to be audible in a sullen roar that mingled with the whirring of factory wheels and frightened Wordsworth with the danger of a class war. Orthodox political economy was enunciating the iron law of wages as Mill gradually modified his adherence to the philosophy of Bentham and Ricardo and Carlyle poured on both the acid of his scorn. Fourier and Saint-Simon phrased the first statements of economic democracy which, later in the century, Marx was to enunciate; 1848 aroused the stirring social conscience of Ruskin and stung him to a revulsion that left him in the end 'reddest of the red.' English cotton manufacturing showed Henry Adams what happens when ethical principles collide with national economic interests, but the upper middle class, growing rigid in him, was unable to modify itself, except in the direction of skepticism, to meet the new perceptions.

Skepticism was modifying other values as well. The dreadful hammers of the geologists were clinking at the end of every Bible cadence, mechanism had advanced beyond Manchester and Birmingham onto the universe of God and turned it into a 'vast, gloomy, solitary Golgotha and mill of death,' frightening Sterling with the realization that the old ecclesiastical moon and sun were only Chinese lanterns guttering in the wind of doubt. Even Mill's strong courage momentarily failed; and Darwin was soon to chill Tennyson's heart with the conception of 'Nature red in tooth and claw.' The elder Gosse fought against the change with a dying ingenuity in science, and was defeated there and in the heart of his little son.

The Greece that Byron had fought to free was a nation. Crabb Robinson saw Prussia, welding Imperial Germany into a European power, smash the hegemony of Austria in one sledge-hammer blow at Sadowa. Napoleon III helped Cavour to make a united Italy while Swinburne hymned Garibaldi and Mrs Browning hoped from *Casa Guidi Windows*. Nationalism, and then imperialism: General Gordon was one of the pawns with which predatory hands reached into India, China, South Africa, Morocco, the Belgian Congo, Egypt. Disraeli painted the empire of trade with glamor and anointed it with the sacring oils of tradition by making Empress of India the Queen under whom its spreading tentacles entangled a quarter of the globe. Henry Adams, bleakly surveying in America the same process of transforming this into a bankers' world, saw the climax of empire approaching, 'year after year, as though Sulla were a President or McKinley a Consul.' The climax was 1914.

The whole process of nineteenth century development seemed to have fallen apart. Certainly Adams felt so; 'Nine-tenths of men's political energies must henceforth be wasted on expedients . . . to patch, or, in vulgar language, to tinker—the political machine when it broke down.' The post-War waste land was filled with its hollow men who were Adams's spiritual heirs or ghosts. Ghostly liberals intermingled with desperate sophisticates pursuing distraction in artistic bohemias. In various ways the artists and writers revealed their sense of breakdown in the European tradition: some even before the War. Through all the later years of the nineteenth century Mark Twain had been bitter against 'the tyrannies and shams that afflict the peoples.' Even the flaunting aestheticism of Wilde was a protest, as was the mysticism of Yeats, the mocking detachment of Moore. Lawrence analyzed and utterly condemned the world that science, industrialism, imperialism, and idealism had made. And so we find ourselves in the present once more, facing the future which Steffens believes wears the two faces of Russia and America.

This whole unfolding drama of the modern world, with its unknown dénouement, has come to us in personal voices sounding out of the past. The great curve emerges spirally, woven out of the mingling threads of many lives, and the picture of the whole has drawn itself all the more clearly by having been composed of so many individual emotions and fates. Like a mosaic, it has been made of thousands of separate pieces, each having its own identity, its shape, hue, hardness, dullness, or clarity; and each separate identity, unique or typical, has at the same time—for the most part unwittingly–contributed its color and form to the entire design. But those individual characters and lives have never been blurred and muted in the tremendous pattern of which they were details. They, too, stand vividly before us, drawn by their own hands to their own likeness.

We can see the celebrated physician, Dr William Butler, putting a patient in the warm belly of a just-slaughtered cow, and Nokes, the comic actor, rolling his full eye in vacant amazement, in a palpable ignorance of what to do. There is the charming vision of Mrs Monfort, 'down goes her dainty diving body to the ground,' her bosom 'like a swan upon waving water'; and Gibbon, celebrating the completion of *The Decline and Fall* by 'taking several turns in a *berceau,* or covered walk of acacias,' by moonlight; and old Mr Brontë venting his fury by firing pistols out of the back door. We may watch Jane Carlyle blacking the grate at Craigenputtock while Carlyle looks on encouragingly with his pipe, and taste with Henry James the glamor of that Paris pavilion, its glassy floors and 'its redundancy of mirror and clock and ormolu vase.'

All the great interests and activities of humanity are illustrated by this company: money, ambition, religion, truth-seeking, happiness, love. There is Gibbon's philosophic assurance that he is a rich man, 'since my income is superior to my expense, and my expense is equal to my wishes,' and Scott's carelessness and monetary display; Manning's and Wolsey's grim pursuit of power, and the sense of failure that gnawed Henry Adams; Macaulay's brisk and efficient climb to success; John Keats's awe that he 'should be a Poet more than other Men–seeing how great a thing it is.' We see Donne tormented by the conflict between the good life and the world, and Bunyan wrestling with Satan; Samuel Johnson despairing before his God; George Herbert, to whom his religion was 'musick at midnight;' and Shelley defying the enskied tyrant whose willing instruments were cruel men. Raleigh's vigorous destruction of maidenheads leads us to Charles II and the fascinating Castlemaine and the hoydenish Nell Gwyn, and Pepys wantonly thrusting his hand into ladies' bosoms; we see Colonel Hutchinson pale as ashes with romantic love, and Steele courting his lovely Prue; Mill haloing the memory of his wife with shimmering glory; the misery of Dickens and the Carlyles; the ill-mated marriage of Ruskin and his Effie. Wilde drifts by with his leering Cockney youths; George Moore winks and whispers; Lawrence shows us mother-love poisoning the life of a son.

All the periods of human life are there as well. Baby Lennie Steffens tumbles out of bed smiling, as good as gold; Henry Adams awakes to the world at the age of three on a yellow kitchen floor; little blue-eyed John Ruskin sits on a low stool at his mother's skirts and dreams of blue hills; the wan pathos of Dickens wanders lonely in London and toils in the blacking factory; Bunyan plays cat and rings church bells; the child Walter Scott, scandalized by the quarrel in *As You Like It*, screams, 'A'n't they brothers?' Youth shows us Macaulay a talkative dandy in tight gloves, Herbert of Cherbury quarreling chivalrously over little girls' hair-ribbons, Victoria dancing till dawn and seeing the sun rise behind the Houses of Parliament and St. Paul's; and maturity reveals the suave diplomat Wotton, the encyclopaedic Brougham, Goethe growing portly at Weimar, Melbourne instructing his youthful Queen, Greville noting the antics of his pineapple-headed King.

As age approaches we find Congreve, prematurely diseased, with cataracts on his eyes, giving the hypochondriac Swift a pain in the great toe by mentioning the gout, and Robinson witnessing the funeral of Wellington from the windows of his club, and Ruskin eating 'Nebuchadnezzar's bitter grass' in madness and despair. At last death brings down the curtain on them all—Wolsey dying in prison of 'an excoriation of the entrails'; Pope never recovering consciousness save to say some kind thing of his friends, his humanity surviving his understanding, while Bolingbroke weeps at his bedside; Essex motionless as the axe glitters down; Lord Guilford 'with Axes and Hammers and Fireworks' in his skull, worrying about King James; Haydon, his reverend white hairs dabbled in suicide blood; and Scott to the murmur of the Tweed through the quiet autumn air.

All these men and women, and the others who have figured in this volume, and the thousands more whom we may know at our desire, intermingle to make all times a living present for us. From them we too, like the historian, may infer the great impersonal forces that operate over mankind, the factors that condition human behavior. From each of these individuals we may draw lines of reference and axes whose intersections enable us to chart events and their meanings. In time these are for us like the streets of a city we have explored, whose great avenues, green parks, architectural monuments, and plazas we know; and if someone names a place we have not seen—Coenties Slip or Abingdon Square, Wapping Old Stairs or the Serpentine—we can orient it on the map we carry in our minds. And every abstraction of history grows ten times more vital and meaningful when we can bring out concretes in its support.

Human beings do not lose their identities in this process; it is not like a cinema spectacle in which crowds of extras shrink to blobs swarming darkly over streets and squares. We are simultaneously far and near. We can watch the sweep and course and hue of societies and times, and we can see the flash of an eye and the breathing rhythm of a bosom, hear the emotion in a voice. And these are a permanent source of wealth to our understanding: to realize the richness, the variety, the excitingness, and the beauty of human personality.

The Future of Biography

Biography as an art has shown no marked advance in the four hundred years through which we have traced it. André Maurois is not superior to George Cavendish, and *Portraits in Miniature* is not a masterpiece that overshadows the *Lives of the Norths*. We should no more expect this to be so than we should expect modern tragedies to be more moving than those of Sophocles and Shakepeare, or Darwin and Planck to be greater than Aristotle. The modern scientist knows more than Aristotle; in knowledge he stands on the shoulders of Aristotle and a long line of seekers since his day, but in himself he can claim no additional eminence from this advantage. The same principle is true of biography: no factual knowledge of genetics, heredity, psychiatry, or sociology can endow a shallow biographer with insight or pour over his work like varnish the redeeming patina of art.

Tremendous changes in technique, varieties of awareness, attitudes, subjects, range, and psychological analysis there have assuredly been. They have produced many special forms of biography that have only recently come into being. Even in the eighteenth and nineteenth centuries there were the biographies whose fields impinged on the domain of history, North's *Life of Francis*

Lord Guilford, Masson's *Life of Milton*, and Morley's *Gladstone;* and these have their modern heirs in Monypenny and Buckle's *Disraeli* and the writings of Philip Guedalla.

Then we have had the industrial biographies of Samuel Smiles, the literary-critical biographies of the *English Men of Letters Series*, *The Dictionary of National Biography* and *The Dictionary of American Biography*, sociological biographies like Amabel Williams-Ellis's *The Exquisite Tragedy*, psychoanalytic ones like Joseph Wood Krutch's *Edgar Allan Poe*, and—but the list is endless. We have had biographies of a childhood and biographies of old age, biographies of two people in conflict or accord, and of groups whose fates were intertwined, biographies of character-formation and biographies of disintegration, biographies composed in scenes like a spotlight leaping on the colorful and leaving out connections, biographies confined to painting a few sharp years of crisis.

The development indicated by these new biographical emphases and forms is specialization; and it is clearly a tendency that is emergent. Biography today is responding to the impact of science. These numerous varieties of biography, from Henry James's delicate exploration of his own sensibility to Lincoln Steffens's sharpening analysis of the main currents of modern society, reveal the way in which all the sciences, from psychology to economics and sociology, have lighted up new considerations in human behavior. The case-histories of physicians and psychoanalysts, of settlement houses and welfare workers—all of them kinds of biography—also attest the scientific influence.

What do these facts suggest about how biography may be expected to move in the near future? In *The Napoleon of Notting Hill* G. K. Chesterton outlined a game which he described as one of humanity's favorites. In each generation, he said, the people listen very respectfully to all the things their wisest men have to say about the future. They gather reverentially around the sages and the philosophers and the leaders and the prophets, while all these explain how things must inevitably lead to this and that conclusion. Then, when all the predictions have been heard, they go away and do something quite different. They call it 'Cheat the Prophet.'

We may do no more than guess, then, that scientific specialization implies still more science and specialization. Biographies will lean on the discoveries and methods of Freud, Jung, and Adler; on Galton and Lombroso; on Havelock Ellis, Pavlov, Watson; and as psychology becomes more complex, really scientific, and subdivided into separate realms the biographers will follow into all of these. Sociological, political, historical, and economic biographies will become similarly specialized and intricate. Biographies will be written to reveal the effect of environment and professional activities on character; and there will be studies of the influence of internal secretions, hormones, and the endocrines on personality and behavior. Like modern science itself, constantly splitting into new subsciences, shooting up whole branches that never existed before, one tendency of biography in the future will be divergence.

The direction of science, however, is not purely centrifugal, it is also centripetal. At the same time that analysis has chopped phenomena into ever smaller categories, discrete and separate, synthesis has been endeavoring once more to bring these details into a new unification of the universe. 'Detailed research and generalizing survey are not antithetical,' Professor Preserved Smith points out, 'but complementary.' Biology and chemistry merge into physics, physics into electricity; astronomy becomes meaningless without astro-physics; the mingling of the life sciences and the mathematical ones suggests an electrical organization of all energy. Our scientists are becoming metaphysicians once more, and when Sir James Jeans begins to explain the stars or Eddington the second law of thermodynamics or Schrödinger the principle of indeterminacy the implications of these concepts lead to the ultimate nature of reality.

The same tendencies have appeared in recent years in the social sciences. Admitting that for a long time 'the specialist has reigned supreme in our schools,' Preserved Smith pleads for a return to synthesis in history. In his own *History of Modern Culture* he tries to weave together all the threads since the Renaissance—not merely the political, or the social or economic, which have had all the prestige of recent years, but the scientific, the philosophic, the pedagogical, the legal, the religious, the literary, artistic, and musical. As peoples have grown more and more obviously interdependent, with no nation or social or economic group able to live without relying upon or defending itself against others; with industrial necessities coming from all over the world—Chile, Trinidad, Persia,

Brazil, the Congo; with motion pictures spreading the same faces, costumes, surroundings, ideas, throughout the globe; as space contracts and Hong Kong becomes a neighbor of Seattle and Valparaiso of Capetown—unity, and not Henry Adams's multiplicity, appears as the dominant aspect of the modern world. To realize this modern universe we must apprehend it as 'multiplicity in unity,'—Santayana's words for the starry sphere of the sky.

This task the biographer must share. He cannot give true and significant portraits of human character and fate if he turns his eyes away from part of the testimony. Biography can select, but only for purposes of greater truth, not because some of the facts would be embarrassing or unwieldy to its hands. It must master whatever science can tell it about society and psychology. If often the future biographer may choose to play brilliant lights on various special aspects of experience, I see no reason why he, any more than the novelist, need be daunted by the complexity of his data. What the mind can discover the mind can organize. (Not every mind; but the world has never been so simple that every understanding can grasp it.) The biographer is at least as capable as any other artist of making that synthesis.

Biographies of every variety and color, then, will continue to follow the scientist into the domains of specialization. Some of them, in fact, may well be purely scientific, and have the same relationship to biography as a realm of art that parliamentary records, chronicles, and other documents have to the art of history. Others, again, like Sir Edmund Gosse's *Father and Son*, will be no less works of art because they have marked off for themselves a sharply defined field for intensive representation. And the 'pure' biography, the attempt to give in a form of art the whole career and character and meaning of an individual life, will not disappear or grow incredible because the bulk or intellectual difficulties of its data become unmanageable. The art of biography is no more endangered by the growth of science than the arts of poetry or painting or music.

Humanity passes through alternations of courage and despair; artists and poets have sometimes felt themselves disinherited by their age. But the fear that science is inimical to art is one of the groundless bugaboos of our time. It has troubled the peace of I. A. Richards and engaged the attention of Max Eastman; the arid waste land of T. S. Eliot mourning the vanished splendor of the past and the nightmare of Hart Crane gave it a certain coloring of plausibility. *The Modern Temper* took scientific disillusion away as the exclusive possession of the poets, and painted it as the orientation of modern man.

But Mr. Richards's fears for poetry are founded on a too rigidly drawn distinction between science as disinterested knowing and art as the inducing of emotional attitudes. Both art and science constantly fuse the mood of realization and the interests of action, and only so can either be valid in its own realm. And the science that portrayed man as a hapless wanderer in an alien universe is already 'a pass'd mode, an outworn theme'; for modern science, man is a part of nature, not an exile, in a world with which he is continuous, and which, although not mainly propitious, is organic. If the modern temper is indeed despair, it will have to find other extenuations than a hostile science. Younger poets have already appeared who sing in more ringing tones, facing life with new hope and light, fearing neither for science nor for man.

Wordsworth anticipated all this more than a century ago. 'The remotest discoveries of the Chemist, the Botanist, or Mineralogist,' he wrote, and he might have added all the others as well, 'will be as proper objects of the Poet's art as any upon which it can be employed,' whenever these things enter into the immediate perceptions of our lives and are 'manifestly and palpably material to us as enjoying and suffering beings.' When 'what is now called science, thus familiarized to men, shall be ready to put on, as it were, a form of flesh and blood, the Poet will lend his divine spirit to aid the transfiguration, and will welcome the Being thus produced as a dear and genuine inmate of the household of man.'

The biographer may well voice the same welcome. Neither as artist nor as truth-teller has he anything to fear from subduing every new instrument of science to his grasp. If he loses sight of his animating purpose, to be sure, and forgets that he is giving information 'not as a lawyer, a physician, a mariner, an astronomer, or a natural philosopher, but as a Man'—then he may indeed find himself in the wandering wood. But whenever science passes through the transubstantiation of art, the work of art radiates a new power. Like Antaeus strengthened by each contact with earth, art that does not lose touch with scientific fact is reinvigorated.

EPILOGUE

The biographer who brings every scientific test of precision to his task, who penetrates with its aid into every darkest cranny of his subject and clarifies its most tenuous themes, will find himself not impoverished but enriched. The biographer who makes that choice will be able to join the poets and the artists in revealing the richness of human personality. Science and art are not antithetical, but different facets of the same ultimate aim of imaginative realization of experience; when they fuse into one, their voices in unison carry the same burden: the fullness of human existence, with all its joys and pains, and the knowledge that 'There is no wealth but life.'

INDEX